24 99

BTEC National
Sport and
Exercise Science

Second Edition

BTEC National
Sport and Exercise Science

Second Edition

Jennifer Stafford-Brown
Simon Rea
John Chance

Hodder Arnold
A MEMBER OF THE HODDER HEADLINE GROUP

endorsed by
edexcel

This high quality material is endorsed by Edexcel and has been through a rigorous quality assurance programme to ensure that it is a suitable companion to the specification for both learners and teachers. This does not mean that its contents will be used verbatim when setting examinations nor is it to be read as being the official specification – a copy of which is available at www.edexcel.org.uk

Orders: please contact Bookpoint Ltd, 130 Milton Park, Abingdon, Oxon OX14 4SB. Telephone: (44) 01235 827720. Fax: (44) 01235 400454. Lines are open from 9.00 to 5.00, Monday to Saturday, with a 24-hour message answering service. You can also order through our website www.hoddereducation.co.uk

If you have any comments to make about this, or any of our other titles, please send them to educationenquiries@hodder.co.uk

British Library Cataloguing in Publication Data
A catalogue record for this title is available from the British Library
ISBN: 978 0 3410 93951 2

First Edition published 2003. This Second Edition published 2007.
Impression number   10 9 8 7 6 5 4 3 2 1
Year   2011 2010 2009 2008 2007

Cover photo by Dennis O'Clair/Photographer's Choice/Getty Images

Typeset in 11/13 Minion by Fakenham Photosetting Limited, Fakenham, Norfolk

Printed in Italy for Hodder Arnold, an imprint of Hodder Education, a member of the Hodder Headline Group, an Hachette Livre UK Company, 338 Euston Road, London NW1 3BH.

Contents

Acknowledgements

Jennifer Stafford-Brown

I would like to thank my co-authors Simon and John for all their hard work, Tamsin and Bianca from Hodder Arnold for their input, my colleagues from Edexcel and of course the contributing authors for their commitment and advice.

As always, my thanks go to my husband Matt, and our children Ellie and Alex, and also to my parents Ann and Brian Stafford for their continued support, encouragement, patience and understanding.

I would also like to thank my friends for their help and support, especially Grace Whitehead and Avril Young for their encouragement, help with childcare and never-ending supply of coffee!

Simon Rea

I would like to give special thanks to Gavin Hughes, Sue Pinson and Rebecca Woodard for their invaluable help during the writing period. Thanks also go to my fellow author, Jenny Stafford-Brown, for her patience and never-ending support, as well as to the staff and students at Oxford and Cherwell Valley College and Uxbridge College and to all my personal training clients for the inspiration and fun they have brought over the year. Thank you to my parents, Tony and Pam for their love, support and sustenance during this adventure! In loving memory of Daryl Hughes, a true sportsman and family man, who took sport and life to their very limit.

John Chance

Many people have helped along the way, for which I am grateful, however, I would especially like to thank Mum and Dad, Rachel and Anna.

Contributing authors

Chris Manley has ten years' teaching experience in FE colleges. He has been a National League Basketball Coach and Referee and is currently Divisional Leader at North West Kent College. Chris wrote both the 'Sports coaching' and 'Practical individual sports and practical team sports' chapters.

Michael Robinson has a degree in Physiotherapy and has since focused on musculoskeletal therapy. He clinically specialises in shoulder and spinal conditions, and recently attained an MSc in Practice Development. He currently manages the orthopaedic service for Bolton PCT. Michael wrote the 'Sport and exercise massage' chapter.

Julie Hancock is a Lead Verifier and trainer for a major examination board. She has been teaching for 18 years in schools, further education and, presently, in higher education at Huddersfield University as a Senior Lecturer and Course Leader within the Division of Sports & Health Studies. She is also a HSE Approved First Aid Trainer. Julie wrote the 'Sports injuries' chapter.

Every effort has been made to trace and acknowledge ownership of copyright. The publishers will be glad to make suitable arrangements with any copyright holders whom it has not been possible to contact.

The authors and publishers would like to thank the following for the permission to use the following photographs in this book:

p12 © George Tiedemann/GT Images/Corbis, **p29** ©www.purestockX.com, **p33** Jon Buckle/Empics Sports Photo Agency, **p54** Achim Scheidemann/DPA/Empics, **p55** Glyn Kirk/Actionplus, **p107** Getty Images/AFP/Ian Stewart, **p109** Matthew Ashton/Empics Sports Photo Agency, **p115** Kevin Frayer/AP Photo/Empics, **p119** Glyn Kirk/Actionplus, **p130** Dr P. Marazzi/Science Photo Library, **p131** Arthur Glauberman/Science Photo Library, **p133** (top) Martin M. Rotker/Science Photo Library, **p133** (bottom) CNRI/Science Photo Library, **p140** © iStockPhoto.com/Oleg Kozlov, **p162** Glyn Kirk/Actionplus, **p168** Shelly Gazin/The Image Works/TopFoto, **p172** Mark Baker/AP Photo/Empics, **p173** (left) Adrian Dennis/AFP/Getty Images, **p173** (right) Nigel French/Empics, **p211** (top) © Philip Wilkins/Antony Blake Picture Library, **p211** (bottom) © Comstock Select/Corbis, **p215** (top) Photolibrary.com, **p215** (bottom) © Maximilian Stock Ltd/Anthony Blake Photo Library, **p280** Glyn Kirk/Actionplus, **p293** (left) Action Images/Nick Potts, **p293** (right) © Pete Leonard/Zefa/Corbis, **p297** (left) Alex Bartel/Science Photo Library, **p297** (right) Dr M.A. Ansary/Science Photo Library, **p308** Clive Brunskill/Getty Images, **p313** © iStockphoto.com/Ana Abejon, **p319** Michelangelo Gratton/Digital Vision/Getty Images, **p325** © iStockPhoto.com/Ben Blankenburg, **p328** Neil Tingle/Actionplus, **p339** Actionplus/Steve Bardens, **p340** Rex Features/Peter Burian, **p347** SPL/Steve Allen, **p350** © Ashley Cooper/Corbis, **p352** © iStockPhoto.com/Lisa Thornberg, **p353** © iStockPhoto.com/Galina Barskaya, **p356** Action Images/Michael Regan, **p358** Jesse D. Garrabrant/NBAE via Getty Images, **p386** Siu Biomedical/Custom Medical Stock Photo/Science Photo Library, **p388** Neil Tingle/Actionplus, **p389** (left) David Boily/AFP/Getty Images, **p389** (right) Maria Zarnayova/isifa/Getty Images, **p391** (top left) © Kai Pfaffenbach/Reuters/Corbis, **p391** (bottom left) Jon Buckle/Empics Sports Photo Agency, **p391** (right) Leo Mason/Actionplus, **p392** Neil Tingle/Actionplus, **p398** Adam Davy/Empics Sports Photo Agency, **p405** ©www.purestockX.com, **p406** © Ace Stock Limited/Alamy, **p410** Donna Day/Workbook Stock/Jupiter Images, **p411** ©www.purestockX.com, **p416** © Nucleus Medical Art, Inc./Alamy, **p425** © Richard Sheppard/Alamy

Artwork by Cactus Design and Illustration Ltd from McGuinness, H. (2006) *Anatomy and Physiology*, 3rd edn, Hodder Arnold: **p9** Fig 1.15, **p10**, **p11**, **p34** Fig 2.05

Artwork by Kate Nardoni, Cactus Design and Illustration Ltd: **p3**, **p4** Fig 1.02, **p6** Fig 1.06, **p7** Fig 1.07, **p14**, **p50**, **p60**, **p111**, **p117**, **p118**, **p151**, **p152**, **p153**, **p154**, **p155**, **p160** Fig 8.09, **p179**, **p183**, **p184** Figs 9,14, **p185**, **p223**, **p242**, **p265**, **p266**, **p271**, **p272**, **p276**, **p278**, **p381**, **p410**, **p412**, **p413**, **p414**, **p415**

Artwork by David Graham from Wesson, K. *et al.* (2005) *Sport & PE*, 3rd edn, Hodder Arnold : **p6** Fig 1.05, **p8**, **p9** Figs 1.12, 1.13, **p15**, **p16**, **p17**, **p18**, **p19**, **p25** Fig 1.49, **p34** Fig 2.06, **p39** Fig 2.14, **p116**, **p166**, **p177**, **p178**, **p184** Fig 9.13

Artwork by Tony Jones, Art Construction from Stafford-Brown, J. *et al.* (2005) *BTEC First Sport*, Hodder Arnold: **p9** Fig 1.14, **p22**, **p26** Figs 1.51, 1.52, **p159**, **p160** Fig 8.08, **p162**, **p164**, **p343**, **p349**

Artwork from Stafford-Brown, J. *et al.*, (2003) *BTEC National in Sport and Exercise Science*, Hodder Arnold: **p4** Fig 1.03, **p5** Fig 1.05, **p20**, **p21**, **p130**, **p196**, **p197**, **p290**, **p294**, **p295**, **p301**, **p302**, **p379**

Study skills

The course you are studying has no externally set exams. Instead, you will be assessed in a variety of ways including practical work, presentations, case studies and other written formats.

This chapter is designed to help you with your assessments. By the end of this chapter you should:

- understand the grading criteria
- know how to use a range of research sources
- understand how to take notes
- know how to use, quote and reference your work
- know how to avoid plagiarism
- know what to do if you are absent.

Understanding the grading criteria

You will be studying a number of units and in order to pass this course you have to show that you have understood each part of each unit. The units are broken down into separate learning outcomes, each of which has different grading criteria allocated to it. The grading criteria start at pass (P), merit (M) and then distinction (D). Distinction is the highest grade you can attain. Each P, M and D criterion is split into smaller, numbered parts – P1, P2, P3, M1, M2, M3, D1, D2, etc. The number in each P, M and D varies depending on the unit. The grade that you are awarded for your work is based upon the work you present in your assessments.

An example of part of a grading grid is shown in the box below.

Once you have completed all the assessments for one unit you will be awarded a final grade for that particular unit. This grade is determined by all the grades you achieve for that unit's work. In order to pass the unit, you must meet every one of the P grading criteria. In order to attain an M you must meet every one of the P grading criteria and also all the M grading criteria. In order to attain a D you

Grading criteria

To achieve a pass grade the evidence must show that the learner is able to:	To achieve a merit grade the evidence must show that, in addition to the pass criteria, the learner is able to:	To achieve a distinction grade the evidence must show that, in addition to the pass and merit criteria, the learner is able to:
P1 describe skills, techniques and tactics required in two different team sports	**M1** explain skills, techniques and tactics required in two different team sports	**D1** analyse identified strengths and areas for improvement, and justify suggestions made in relation to personal development
P2 demonstrate appropriate skills, techniques and tactics in two different team sports	**M2** explain the application of the rules and regulations of two different team sports, in three different situations for each sport	
P3 describe the rules and regulations of two different team sports, and apply them to three different situations for each sport	**M3** explain identified strengths and areas for improvement, and make suggestions relating to personal development	

must meet all the P grading criteria, all the M grading criteria and all the D grading criteria.

You may be given a number of small assessments that cover all the unit grading criteria (usually between two and four) or you may be given one large assessment that covers all the unit grading criteria. Your assessment should include details of the grading criteria it is addressing. These may be placed in the task, on a separate grading grid or on the front sheet. If you are unsure where to find them, ask your tutor.

The grading criteria contain verbs to explain what you need to do. If you know what each of these verbs means exactly, you then know what you need to do to gain the grading criteria you are aiming for.

Pass verbs

The following verbs are found in the pass grading criteria.

Describe	Give a detailed account of something; think of it as painting a picture with words
Define	To give a brief meaning of something
Outline	A brief description of something that concentrates on the main topic or item
Illustrate	Give examples or diagrams to help show what you mean
Identify	Point out (choose the right one) or give a list of the main features or prove something as being certain
Interpret	Give the meaning of something
Plan	Write a plan of how you intend to carry out the activity
State	Give a full account
Summarise	Give the main points or essential features of an idea or a discussion; do not include unnecessary details that could confuse the main topic of concern
List	A record that includes an item-by-item record of relevant information

Merit verbs

The following verbs are often found in the merit grading criteria.

Explain	Give a detailed account to give the meaning of something with reasons; include the 'how' and 'why' of the topic of interest
Compare/contrast	Show the similarities between the two areas of interest and also the differences between the two, or the advantages and disadvantages
Discuss	Examine the advantages and disadvantages of the subject of interest and then try to complete the discussion with a conclusion
Account for	Explain the process or give a reason to explain the reason for something being the way it is
Demonstrate	Give a number of related examples or details from a variety of sources to support the argument you are making; in a practical situation, this means that you must practically carry out the activity or skill while being observed
Distinguish	Explain the differences
Examine	Inspect something closely
Interpret	Explain the meaning of something by giving examples, diagrams and/or opinions

Distinction verbs

In order to achieve a distinction, you will usually need to carry out research so that you have examined a minimum of at least two sources of information. So will need to obtain other people's views and see where they agree and disagree.

Analyse	Explore the main ideas of the subject, stating how they are related, why they are important and how each one contributes to the main area of interest
Critically analyse	Give your opinion of the subject of interest, both the advantages and disadvantages, after having considered all the evidence
Conclude	After having given evidence to support your opinion or argument give a reasoned judgement
Assess	Give your judgement on the importance of something
Criticise	Analyse a topic or issue objectively – give both the advantages and disadvantages and then make a decision based upon the evidence you present
Evaluate	Give evidence to support the good and bad points of the topic and then give your opinion based upon the evidence
Justify	Give supported reasons for your view to explain how you have arrived at these conclusions

Research sources

You will be given a great deal of information in your lectures and lessons and that, together with this textbook will give you all the information you need to pass this course. However, if you wish to attain a higher grade than a pass you will need to carry out more research to develop your understanding of the subject area.

There is a large range of resources available to you. This section will help guide you towards the appropriate resources and explain how to use them effectively.

Textbooks

Textbooks are a reliable source of information, which means that you can be certain that the information they contain is accurate. They have usually been written by subject specialists and are then reviewed by experts to ensure the work is accurate. If the textbook is endorsed by an examining board it means that its content is in line with the specifications of the course.

There is a range of textbooks available for this specific course and they may be in your library for you to look through. There are also more 'specific' textbooks available that concentrate purely on a particular topic. For example, if you are studying the anatomy unit, you may wish to refer to textbooks that are written purely about anatomy.

Internet

There is a huge array of internet sites out there, but not all are credible sources. Anybody is able to set up a website and write about whatever they want to, so you cannot be certain that the information they have written is accurate. However, sites set up by governing bodies and government information sites (e.g. British Food Foundation) are reliable and the information given should be accurate.

Journals

Journals are written by subject specialists, reviewed by subject experts and come out at regular intervals throughout the year. As they are published so frequently, the information they contain is up to date and will contain current facts and trends. Most libraries stock a range of relevant journals and you can also access some journals via the internet (some charge a subscription cost – check to see if your centre has a subscription). If you are hoping to achieve distinction grades, journals are a very good source of information to help you attain this level of understanding.

Taking notes

In order to remember all the information you are hearing or researching, it is a good idea to take notes. For some people the very act of writing something down will help them to remember that information. Note taking also means that you do not have to reread a whole chapter or section of a journal if you have forgotten it. All you will need to do is read your notes.

Taking notes in lectures and lessons

Do not attempt to write everything down that your tutor or teacher says – listen to the parts that you feel are most relevant and jot them down on paper.

You will always find it easier to take notes if you have some knowledge about the subject area. If your tutor gives you reading prior to a lecture it is a very good idea to carry out this work as you will find the lecture much more useful and learn more from it. Here is some guidance:

- you should always place the title and date at the top of your page and number each page so that your notes will make sense when you come to read them later
- make sure you can read your own writing
- read through your notes at the end of the lecture to check that you understand them.

There is a range of methods of taking notes that you can try in order to determine which one is best for you:

- shorthand – use your own shorthand, such as E = energy, F = football, MS = motor skill, and so on; the more you use this shorthand the more effective it becomes
- structured lists – these have a main heading with relevant information below; for example:

Health and Safety at Work Act 1974
Occupational factors
Environmental factors
Human factors
RIDDOR 1995

- diagrams – spider diagrams (like that in the diagram, top right), pattern notes, mind maps; with these you write the main topic in the middle of the page and then information is linked to this by lines. Underline any information that you think is very important.

Taking notes from research materials

Remember to keep to the topic in question. You can best do this by keeping the task or question close by so that you can keep checking that you are sticking to the task at hand and not researching work that is irrelevant. For example, if the task asks you to explore the aerobic energy system, research only this topic. You will not get extra marks for writing about the anaerobic energy system because the question did not ask for that. Here is some guidance:

- skim through the information to check that it is suitable for your work

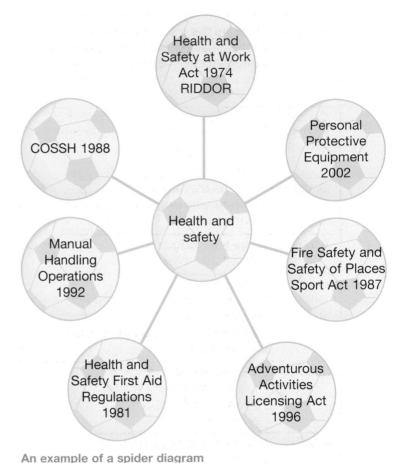

An example of a spider diagram

- make a note of the details of the book or article that you are using
- actively read the work – have a pen in your hand and start to make notes
- write down any relevant quotes that you think you may use in your work
- summarise information in your own words.

Using quotes

Once you have read through a range of resources you should try to put this information into your own words. To help justify what you say, it is a good idea to include quotes in your work. A quote is a sentence or two taken from one of your research sources, which is written word for word. To show that you are quoting the material, you must place the quote in speech marks and then state the name of the authors of the source in brackets after the quote. For example:

> **Journals are written by subject specialists, reviewed by subject experts and come out at regular intervals throughout the year.**
>
> *Stafford-Brown and Rea (2007)*

This is good practice and should be encouraged. Quotes are used to help to substantiate what you have written. For example:

People are taking much less exercise these days, more people drive to work or school and spend more time pursuing sedentary leisure activities.

> **The average adult watches over 26 hours of television each week.**
>
> *Stafford-Brown and Rea (2007)*

If you have written a summary of information that has come from more than one textbook, then you can write the summary **in your own words** with no speech marks and then quote the authors at the end of the paragraph. For example:

Aerobic fitness training has been shown to have many cardiovascular benefits. Resting heart rate decreases, stroke volume increases, hypertrophy of the left ventricle occurs, new capillaries form (capillarisation) and there is an increase in haemoglobin content of the blood due to an increase in the number of red blood cells (Stafford-Brown *et al.* (2007), Wesson *et al.* (2006)).

You will notice that when there is more than one author, it is possible to write the name of the lead author (the first one printed on the book) and then write '*et al.*', which literally means 'and the rest'. However, when you come to write your bibliography or reference page, you must list the names of every author involved in writing the book you have used.

Your quote should not really be any longer than around two sentences. It is not good practice to quote large chunks of text. That shows that you are able to copy work but does not demonstrate your understanding of that work!

Referencing your work

Any sources that you have used quotes from or have used to help you to research your assessment activity should be included in a reference section or bibliography located at the back of your work.

The types of source you have used will determine the way in which the source is referenced, below are the most conventional formats.

Book

Author. Year *Book Title (in italics)*. Edition (if not the 1st), Publisher: Publisher location, Pages used.

e.g. Stafford-Brown, J. and Rea, S. (2007) *BTEC National in Sport*, 2nd edn., Hodder Arnold: London, pp116–20.

Journal

Author. Year Article title. *Journal (in italics)*, Volume, Issue no., Pages used.

e.g. Swaine, I. (1997) Cardiopulmonary response to exercise in swimmer using a swim bench and a leg-kicking ergometer. *International Journal of Sports Medicine*, 18, pp359–62.

Website

Author. Year – look for the © at the bottom of the page *Web page title (in italics)*, Full web page address, Date you accessed the page.

McKenzie, B. (2002) *Cardiovascular tests*, www.brianmac.demon.co.uk/cvtesting.htm, accessed 22 February 2006.

Newspaper

Author. Year Article title, *Newspaper (in italics)*, Pages used.

Layer, G. (2004) Wide of mark on participation, *Times Higher Education Supplement*, p76.

How to avoid plagiarism

Plagiarism is a term given to a situation where a person has copied work from another person or another source and passed it off as their own. This is a form of cheating and any person found to have plagiarised work in their assignments will not pass that assignment and will usually face further questioning from their tutor or quality manager.

Examples of plagiarism include copying:

- work from another student
- work from a textbook
- text from the internet
- diagrams from the internet.

Any information you would like to use should be put into **your own words** or presented as a quote. If you would like to copy diagrams from the internet, again you must acknowledge that the work is not your own and give details of the website next to the diagram you have used.

Organising yourself

The very nature of your course means that you will be faced with a lot of coursework to complete. For each unit you study you will have between two and four assessments. As a result, you will probably find that there are times when you have a number of assessments set at a similar time. You must learn to organise yourself and plan your time effectively so that you are able to complete the assessment(s) to the best of your ability and still meet the deadline set for handing in the work.

Design a weekly plan that includes all of your commitments, similar to the one shown at the bottom of the page.

LEARNER ACTIVITY
- Make a list of all your weekly commitments.
- Make a list of all the leisure activities you like to do.
- Place all this information on a weekly planner and then highlight times that you could put aside for course work.

You are then able to see which days and times you can dedicate to coursework.

For each assessment, spend some time making a list of tasks that you will need to complete in order for you to finish the work. Here is an example:

- Go to library to find suitable books and journals.
- Draw and illustrate a diagram of the heart.
- Research the structure and function of blood vessels.
- Type up information on the structure and function of blood vessels.
- Find out how the cardiovascular system responds to exercise.
- Type up work on how the cardiovascular system responds to exercise.

Date Week beginning 20 Sept	Mon	Tue	Wed	Thur	Fri	Sat	Sun
Day	College 9.00–15.30	Part-time shop work 10.00–17.00	College 9.00–12.00 Football game – away 12.00–17.00	College 10.00–15.00	College 10.00–15.00	Football practice 10.00–12.00	Football game – home 12.00–16.00
Evening	Football practice 18.30–20.00			Circuit training 20.00–21.00	Cinema 19.00–23.00		

An example of a weekly plan

The list of tasks is complete once you have included everything you need to do in order to finish the assessment.

Try to estimate how long you think each task will take and then allocate a time period on your weekly day planner for each of these tasks. Days on which you have very few commitments should be your main coursework days where you aim to complete a number of tasks. Always ensure that you plan to complete the assessment with some time to spare – you may find that some tasks take longer than expected.

Speak to your tutor if you are unsure about any aspect of the task or would benefit from having certain aspects of the task explained to you again. You will find that most tutors will be happy to spend time with you in lectures or even outside of directed study times (as long as you have made an appointment and the meeting takes place in good time prior to the actual hand-in deadline) so that you are able to understand the subject and achieve a good grade.

Absence from college or school

In most centres if you are absent from lectures you are expected to catch up with the work in your own time. You should always speak to your tutor as soon as you return to your centre so that she/he can give you any handouts and/or directed reading to help you to catch up.

You may find that a 'buddy system' works well for you too, in addition to tutor support. At the start of the course, find a person that you get on with and exchange contact details such as mobile phone numbers, email, etc. If you are absent from college, your buddy will know to collect any handouts or coursework for you, give you copies of their notes, pass on details of directed reading, give you homework and also let you know if an assessment has been handed out. If you meet up with your buddy as soon as possible after the lecture you have missed, you will have more time to catch up with the work you have missed and get back on track.

You are usually expected to contact the centre to let them know that you are not able to attend and give them an idea of when you think you will be able to return. If you need to be absent for any length of time and your absence has been approved, your tutor may be able to make arrangements so that you are able to keep up to date with work while away from the centre.

Core Units

Goals

At the end of this chapter you should understand:

- the structure and function of the skeletal system
- the structure and function of the muscular system
- the structure and function of the cardiovascular system
- the structure and function of the respiratory system.

The human body is an amazing piece of machinery. We are able to take part in a huge array of activities, which is the result of many different systems and structures working together. The skeletal, muscular and nervous systems work in conjunction to produce movement and become involved in a range of activities. The cardiovascular and respiratory systems work together to provide oxygen to tissues and produce energy for the body to function.

The skeleton

The skeletal system is the central structure of the body and provides the framework for all the soft tissue to attach to, to give the body its defined shape. The skeletal system is made up of the bones, joints and cartilage, and enables us to perform simple and complex movements such as walking and running.

Axial and appendicular skeleton

The axial skeleton (Fig 1.01) is the central core of the body or its axis. It consists of the skull, the vertebrae, the sternum and the ribs. It provides the core which the limbs hang from.

The appendicular skeleton (Fig 1.02) is the parts hanging off the axial skeleton. It consists of the shoulder girdle (scapula and clavicle), the pelvic girdle, upper and lower limbs.

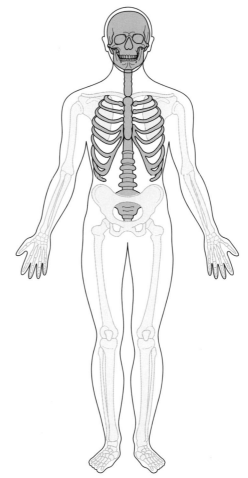

Fig 1.01 Axial skeleton

Functions of the skeleton

The different functions that the skeleton performs are as follows.

- **It provides a bony framework for the body:** the bones give the body a distinctive shape and a framework to which to attach muscles and other soft tissue. Without bones we would just be a big sac of fluids.
- **It allows movement of the body as a whole and its individual parts:** the bones act as levers and by

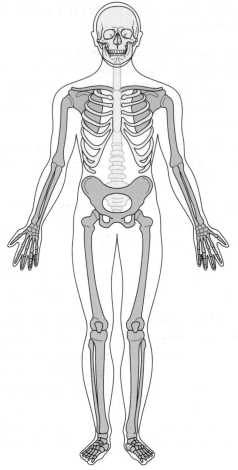

Fig 1.02 Appendicular skeleton

forming joints they allow muscles to pull on them and produce joint movements. This enables us to move in all directions and perform the functions we need on a daily basis.

- **It offers protection to the organs found within the skeleton:** the bones support and protect the vital organs they contain. For example, the skull protects the brain, the ribs offer protection to the heart and lungs, the vertebrae protect the spinal cord and the pelvis offers protection to the sensitive reproductive organs.
- **It produces blood cells:** certain bones contain red bone marrow, and the bone marrow produces red blood cells, white blood cells and platelets. The bones that contain marrow are the pelvis, sternum, vertebrae, costals, cranial bones and clavicle.
- **It stores minerals and fats:** the bones themselves are made of minerals stored within cartilage. Therefore they act as a mineral store for calcium, magnesium and phosphorous, which can be given

up if the body requires the minerals for other functions. The bones also store dietary fats (triglycerides) within the yellow bone marrow.
- **It attaches to soft tissue:** bones provide surfaces for the attachment of soft tissue such as muscles, tendons and ligaments. This is why they are often irregular shapes and have bony points and grooves to provide attachment points.

Major bones of the body

The skeleton consists of 206 bones, over half of which are in the upper and lower limbs. Babies are born with around 300 bones and over time these fuse together to reduce the number.

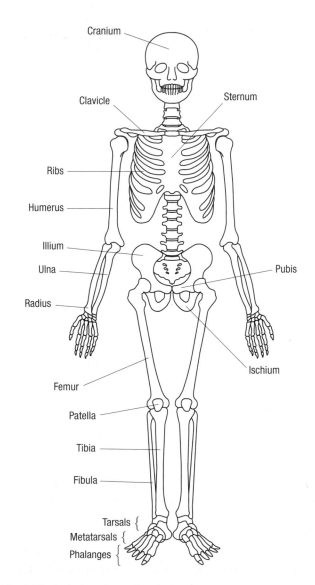

Fig 1.03 Anterior view of a skeleton

attach on to the vertebrae but are free as they have no second attachment (floating ribs).

Clavicle: this bone connects the upper arm to the trunk of the body. One end is connected to the sternum and the other to the scapula. The role of the clavicle is to keep the scapula at the correct distance from the sternum.

Scapula: this bone is situated on the back of the body. The scapula provides points of attachments for many muscles of the upper back and arms.

Arm: this consists of three bones – the humerus (upper arm), the radius and the ulna (lower arm). The ulna forms the elbow joint with the humerus and runs to the little finger. The radius is positioned beside the ulna and runs to the thumb side. When the hand moves, the radius moves across the ulna.

Hand: the hand has three areas made up of different types of bones. First, the wrist is made up of eight carpals, which are small bones arranged in two rows of four. The five long bones between the wrist and fingers are the metacarpals and the bones of the fingers are called phalanges. There are 14 phalanges all together with three in each finger and two in the thumb. There are a total of 30 bones in the upper limb.

Pelvis: the pelvis protects and supports the lower internal organs, including the bladder, the reproductive organs and also, in pregnant women, the developing fetus. The pelvis consists of three bones, the ilium, pubis and ischium, which have become fused together to form one area.

Leg: the leg consists of four bones – the femur, which is the longest bone in the body and forms the knee joint with the tibia, which is the weight-bearing bone of the lower leg. The fibula is the non-weight-bearing bone of the lower leg and helps form the ankle. The patella is the bone that floats over the knee; it lies within the patella tendon and smoothes the movement of the tendons over the knee joint.

Foot: like the hand, the foot has three areas – the seven tarsals which form the ankle, the five metatarsals which travel from the ankle to the toes and the 14 phalanges which make up the toes. There are three phalanges in each toe with only two in the big toe. The lower limb has 30 bones. It has one less tarsal but makes up for it with the patella.

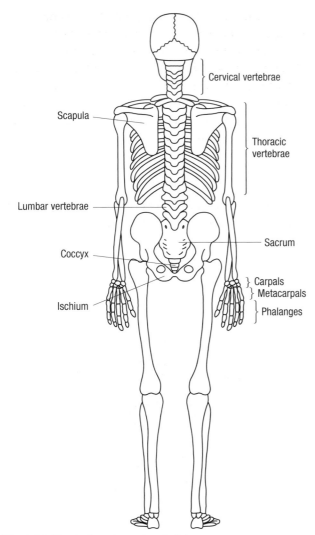

Fig 1.04 Posterior view of a skeleton

Labels: Cervical vertebrae, Scapula, Thoracic vertebrae, Lumbar vertebrae, Sacrum, Coccyx, Carpals, Metacarpals, Ischium, Phalanges

Cranium: the cranium consists of eight bones fused together which act to protect your brain. There are 14 other facial bones which form the face and jaw.

Sternum: this is the flat bone in the middle of the chest which is shaped like a dagger. It protects the heart and gives an attachment point for the ribs and the clavicles.

Ribs or costals: adults have 12 pairs of ribs, which run between the sternum and the thoracic vertebrae. The ribs are flat bones that form a protective cage around the heart and lungs. An individual has seven pairs of ribs that attach to both the sternum and vertebrae (true ribs), three that attach from the vertebrae to a cartilage attachment on the sternum and two that

Vertebrae: the spine is made up of five areas, as shown in Fig 1.05.

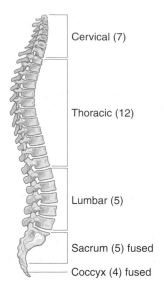

Fig 1.05 Structure of the vertebral column

The seven cervical vertebrae make up the neck and run to the shoulders. The five thoracic vertebrae make up the chest area, and the five lumbar vertebrae make up the lower back. The sacrum consists of five vertebrae which are fixed together and form joints with the pelvis. The coccyx is formed of four bones joined together, which are the remnants of when we had a tail.

Structure of a long bone

Epiphysis: this is the end of the bone.

Diaphysis: this is the long shaft of the bone.

Hyaline cartilage: this is the thin layer of bluish cartilage covering each end of the bone.

Periosteum: this is the thin outer layer of the bone. It contains nerves and blood vessels that feed the bone.

Compact bone: this is hard and resistant to bending.

Cancellous bone: this lies in layers within the compact bone. It has a honeycomb appearance and gives the bones their elastic strength.

Medullary cavity: this is the hollow space down the middle of the compact bone and contains bone marrow. There are two types of bone marrow: red marrow, which produces blood cells; and yellow marrow, which stores fat.

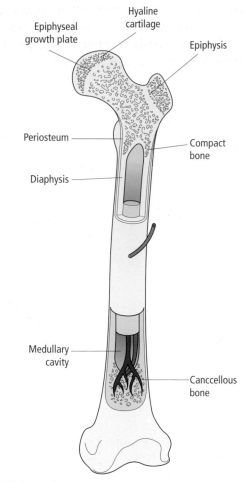

Fig 1.06 Long bone

Classification of bones

The bones of the body fall into five general categories based on their shape.

- Long bones are longer than they are wide and work as levers. The bones of the arms are of this type.
- Short bones are short, cube-shaped and found in the wrists and ankles.
- Flat bones are not totally flat, but have broad, smooth surfaces. Their function is primarily to protect organs and to attach muscles. Examples of these bones are the ribs, cranial bones and the scapulae.
- Sesamoid bones are bones located within a tendon. An example is the patella. The person who named this type of bone gave it this name because they thought it looked like a sesame seed!

- Irregular bones are all the bones that do not fall into the previous categories. They have varied shapes, sizes and surface features. This type of bone can be found in the vertebral column.

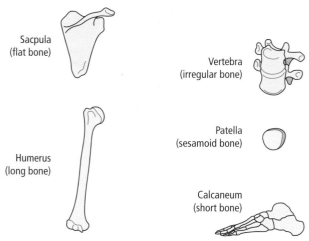

Sacpula
(flat bone)

Humerus
(long bone)

Vertebra
(irregular bone)

Patella
(sesamoid bone)

Calcaneum
(short bone)

Fig 1.07 Five types of bone

Bone growth

In a fetus most of the skeleton consists of cartilage, which is a tough flexible tissue. As the fetus develops minerals are laid down in the cartilage and the bones become harder and less flexible. This process is called ossification and it continues until we are adults. Bones keep growing until between the ages of 18 and 30, depending upon the bone and the body part. When a bone grows it occurs at the epiphyseal plate which is an area just behind the head of the bone at each epiphysis. As a bone grows, its two ends are slowly pushed away from each other.

Bones are very much alive and full of activity. We know bones are living material because they can repair if they are damaged, grow when we are young and they produce blood cells. Bones contain blood vessels and nerves. Bone is continually being broken down and replaced; this process is done by different cells:

- osteoblasts which build bone
- osteoclasts which destroy or clean away old bone.

Osteoclasts and osteoblasts replace around 10 per cent of bone every year; this means that no matter how old we are our skeleton is no older than ten years of age!

Ossification: the process of cartilage turning into bone.

Connective tissue

There are connective tissues in the body to connect tissue and stabilise joints. There are three types:

- cartilage
- ligament
- tendon.

Cartilage is a dense and tough tissue which cushions joints. It comes in three types:

- hyaline (found at the ends of bones)
- fibro (thick chunks found in the knee and between vertebrae)
- elastic (gives shape to structures such as the ear and the nose).

Ligaments have the following characteristics:

- they attach bone to bone
- they act to give stability to joints
- they are tough, white and inelastic.

Tendons have the following characteristics:

- they attach muscle to bone
- they carry the force from muscle contraction to the bone
- they are tough, greyish and inelastic.

All these types of connective tissue have a very poor blood supply, hence their whitish colour, and will take a long time to repair if they become damaged.

Key learning points

- The functions of the skeleton are shape, movement, protection, blood production and mineral storage.
- A bone is made up of a periosteum, compact bone, cancellous bone and bone marrow.
- Bones grow at their growth plates.

Joints

The place where two or more bones meet is called a joint or an articulation. A joint is held together by ligaments, which give the joints their stability.

> **Joint:** a place where two or more bones meet.

Types of joint

Joints are put into one of three categories depending upon the amount of movement available:

- fixed, also known as immovable or fibrous
- slightly movable, also known as cartilaginous
- freely movable, also known as synovial.

Fixed joints/fibrous: these joints allow no movement. These types of joints can be found between the plates in the skull.

Slightly movable/cartilaginous joints: these allow a small amount of movement and are held in place by ligaments and cushioned by cartilage. This kind of joint can be found between the vertebrae in the spine

Movable/synovial: there are six types of these joints and all allow varying degrees of movement – hinge, ball and socket, pivot, condyloid, sliding and saddle.

- **Hinge joint:** these can be found in the elbow (ulna and humerus) and knee (femur and tibia). They allow flexion and extension of a joint. Hinge joints are like the hinges on a door, and allow you to move the elbow and knee in only one direction.

- **Ball and socket joint:** these types of joint can be found at the shoulder (scapula and humerus) and hip (pelvis and femur) and allow movement in almost every direction. A ball and socket joint is made up of a round end of one bone that fits into a small cup-like area of another bone.

- **Pivot joint:** this joint can be found in the neck between the top two vertebrae (atlas and axis). It allows only rotational movement – for example, it

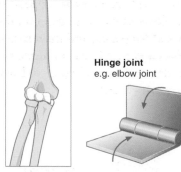

Hinge joint
e.g. elbow joint

Fig 1.08 Hinge joint

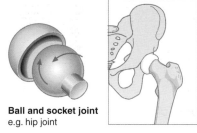

Ball and socket joint
e.g. hip joint

Fig 1.09 Ball and socket joint

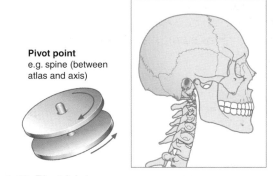

Pivot point
e.g. spine (between atlas and axis)

Fig 1.10 Pivot joint

allows you to move your head from side to side as if you were saying 'no'.

- **Condyloid joint:** this type of joint is found at the wrist. It allows movement in two planes; this is called biaxial. It allows you to bend and straighten the joint, and move it from side to side. The joints between the metacarpals and phalanges are also condyloid.

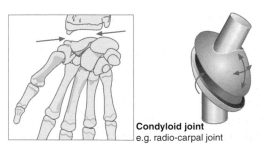

Condyloid joint
e.g. radio-carpal joint

Fig 1.11 Condyloid joint

- **Saddle joint:** this type of joint is found only in the thumbs. It allows the joint to move in three planes, backwards and forwards, and from side to side and across. This is a joint specific to humans and gives us 'manual dexterity', enabling us to hold a cup and write, among other skills.

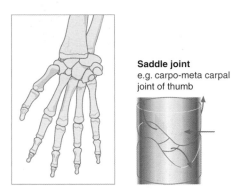

Saddle joint
e.g. carpo-meta carpal joint of thumb

Fig 1.12 Saddle joint

- **Gliding joint:** this type of joint can be found in the carpal bones of the hand. These types of joint occur between the surfaces of two flat bones. They allow very limited movement in a range of directions.

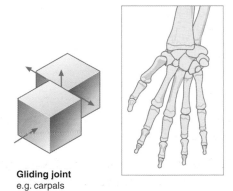

Gliding joint
e.g. carpals

Fig 1.13 Gliding joint

The structure of a synovial joint is as follows:

- synovial capsule – keeps the contents of the synovial joint in place
- synovial membrane – releases synovial fluid on to the joint
- synovial fluid – a thick oil-like solution which lubricates the joint and allows free movement
- articular cartilage – a bluish-white covering of cartilage which prevents wear and tear on the bones.

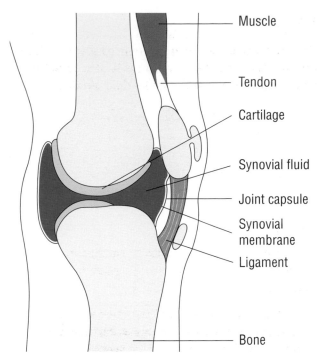

Fig 1.14 Structure of a joint

Muscle
Tendon
Cartilage
Synovial fluid
Joint capsule
Synovial membrane
Ligament
Bone

Types of joint movement

To enable us to understand sporting movements, we need to be able to describe or label joint movements. Joint movements are given specific terms.

Flexion: this occurs when the angle of a joint decreases. For example, when you bend the elbow it decreases from 180 to around 30 degrees.

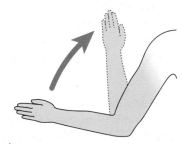

Fig 1.15 Flexion

Extension: this occurs when the angle of a joint increases. For example, when you straighten the elbow it increases from 30 to 180 degrees.

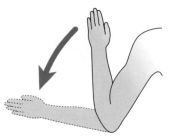

Fig 1.16 Extension

Adduction: this means movement towards the midline of the body.

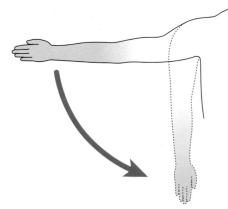

Fig 1.17 Adduction

Abduction: this means movement away from the midline of the body. This occurs at the hip during a star jump.

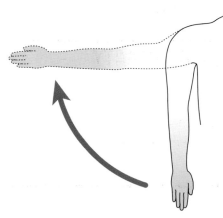

Fig 1.18 Abduction

Circumduction: this means that the limb moves in a circle. This occurs at the shoulder joint during an overarm bowl in cricket.

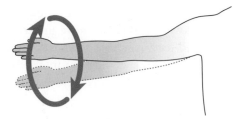

Fig 1.19 Circumduction

Rotation: this means that the limb moves in a circular movement towards the middle of the body. This occurs in the hip in golf when performing a drive shot.

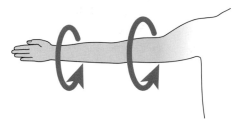

Fig 1.20 Rotation

Pronation: this applies to a specific joint. It means when the hand is facing down while the elbow is flexed. Pronation occurs as the hand moves from facing up to facing down and is the result of the movement of the pivot joint between the ulna and radius. This would happen when a spin bowler delivers the ball in cricket.

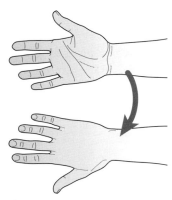

Fig 1.21 Pronation

Supination: this is a specific movement and refers to the palm of the hand when it is facing up. Supination occurs as the hand moves from facing down to facing up and is the result of the movement of the pivot joint between the ulna and radius. You can remember this by thinking that you carry a bowl of soup in a supinated position. Throwing a dart involves supination of the forearm.

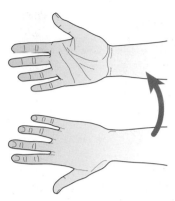

Fig 1.22 Supination

Plantarflexion: this is when the foot moves away from the shin bone and you will be pointing your toes or raising on to your tiptoes. It is specific to your ankle joint and occurs when you walk.

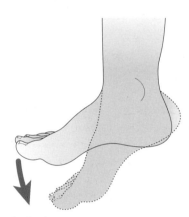

Fig 1.23 Plantarflexion

Dorsiflexion: this means that the foot moves towards the shin as if you are pulling your toes up. It is specific to the ankle joint and occurs when you walk.

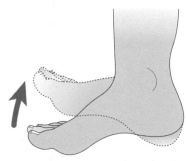

Fig 1.24 Dorsiflexion

Inversion: this means that the soles of the feet are facing each other. It occurs at the gliding joints between the tarsals rather than at the ankle joint.

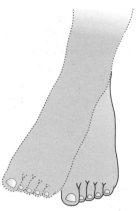

Fig 1.25 Inversion

Eversion: this means that the soles of the feet are facing away from each other. It occurs at the gliding joints between the tarsals rather than at the ankle joint.

Fig 1.26 Eversion

Hyperextension: this is the term given to an extreme or abnormal range of motion found within a joint – for example, at the knee or elbow.

LEARNER ACTIVITY
Sporting movements
Give examples of other sporting movements in which you would see the sportsperson perform each of the above types of movement.

Effects of exercise on the skeletal system

If we train for a period of around three months we will start to experience adaptations to the skeletal system:

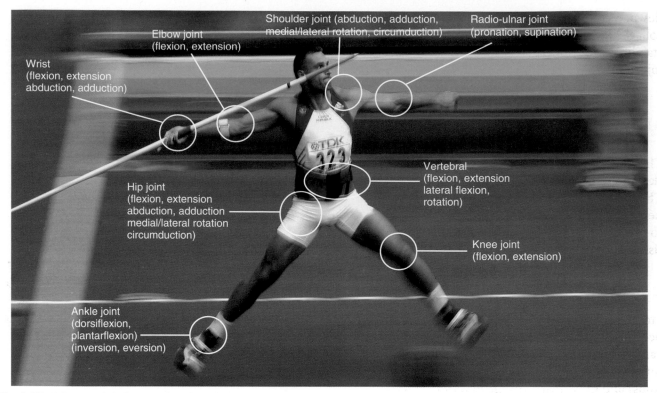

Fig 1.27 Joints and their associated movement patterns

Key learning points

- There are three types of joint: fixed, slightly movable and movable/synovial.

Type of joint	Type of movement	Examples in the body
Hinge joint	Flexion and extension	Elbow, knee
Ball and socket	Flexion and extension Abduction and adduction Circumduction and rotation	Hips and shoulders
Pivot	Rotation	Neck
Condyloid	Flexion and extension Abduction and adduction	Wrist
Saddle	Flexion and extension Abduction and adduction	Thumb
Gliding joint	Limited movement in all directions	Carpals

- increase in bone density
- stronger ligaments
- thickening of the hyaline cartilage at the ends of bones.

The bones become denser if we perform weight-bearing exercise, which is where we put a force through a bone. For example, walking and running put forces through the tibia, fibula and femur, and the body will respond by laying down more cartilage and calcium in the bones to strengthen them. Weight-bearing exercise will actually increase osteoblast activity, which means more bone is built or laid down. As the ligaments become stronger due to more collagen being laid down they also increase the stability of the joints and make them less prone to injury.

Muscular system

The muscular system works in conjunction with the skeleton to produce movement of the limbs and body. The muscular system always has to work with the nervous system because it produces a nervous impulse to initiate movement. There are three types of muscle tissue: smooth, skeletal and cardiac.

Smooth muscles

Smooth muscles are also called involuntary muscles because they are out of our conscious control. They can be found in the digestive system (large and small intestine), the circulatory system (artery and vein walls) and the urinary system. Smooth muscles contract with a peristaltic action in that the muscle fibres contract consecutively rather than at the same time and this produces a wave-like effect. For example, when food is passed through the digestive system it is slowly squeezed through the intestines.

Cardiac muscles

The heart has its own specialist muscle tissue which is cardiac muscle. It makes up the heart muscle or

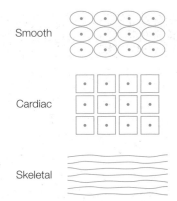

Fig 1.28 Types of muscle fibre under the microscope

myocardium and is also an involuntary muscle. The heart has its own nerve supply via the sino-atrial node and it works by sending the nervous impulse through consecutive cells. The heart will always contract fully – that is, all the fibres contract – and contracts around 60 to 80 times a minute. The function of the myocardium is to pump blood around the body.

Skeletal muscles

Skeletal muscle is the muscle that is attached to the skeleton across joints. It is under voluntary control as we decide when to contract muscles and produce movement. Skeletal muscle is arranged in rows of fibres and is also called striated or stripy due to its appearance. The coordinated contractions of skeletal muscle allow us to move smoothly and produce sports skills. There are over 700 skeletal muscles in the human body and they make up

---

LEARNER ACTIVITY Skeleton terms

Ossification	Calcium	Flexion	Leg	Bone marrow
Ribs	Abduction	Bone marrow	Immovable	Pivot

Choose a word from the list above to answer each of the following questions.

1 What is the main mineral stored in bones?
2 Where are blood cells produced?
3 Which bones protect the heart and lungs?
4 Which limb consists of four bones?
5 What is the name given to the process of cartilage turning into bone?
6 Which joint only allows this type of movement?
7 Which term describes movement away from the body?
8 This type of joint can be found in the neck.
9 This type of joint can be found in the skull.
10 This part of the bone produces new blood cells.

around 40 per cent of our body weight (slightly less for a female). Skeletal muscle is responsible for the following functions:

- producing movement
- maintaining body posture
- generating heat to keep us warm
- storage of glycogen for energy.

Fibre types of skeletal muscle

Within our muscle we actually have two types of muscle fibre which are called fast twitch and slow twitch fibres due to the speed at which they contract. If we look at the evolution of humans we were originally hunters and gatherers. This meant that we had to walk long distances to find animals to eat and then, when we saw one, we would have to chase after it as fast as we could. Therefore we adapted slow twitch muscle fibres to walk long distances and fast twitch muscle fibres to run quickly after our prey.

Slow twitch fibres (type 1)

Slow twitch fibres are red in colour as they have a good blood supply. They have a dense network of blood vessels, making them suited to endurance work and they are slow to fatigue. They also contain many mitochondria to make them more efficient at producing energy using oxygen.

> **Mitochondria:** the energy-producing organelles within cells.

Fast twitch fibres (type 2)

Fast twitch fibres will contract twice as quickly as slow twitch fibres and are thicker in size. They have a poor blood supply, are whiter in appearance and, due to the lack of oxygen, they fatigue fairly quickly. Their faster, harder contractions make them suitable for producing fast, powerful actions such as sprinting and lifting heavy weights.

Within the group of fast twitch fibres there are two types: 2A and 2B. The type which is used depends upon the intensity of the chosen activity. Type 2B work when a person is working very close to their maximum intensity, while type 2A work at slightly lower intensities but higher intensities than slow twitch fibres are capable of. For example, a 100 m

Slow twitch
(type1)   Fast twitch
(type2)

Fig 1.29 Slow twitch (type 1) Fast twitch (type 2)

runner would be using type 2B fibres while a 400 m runner would be using type 2A fibres.

Training effect on muscle fibres

The type 1 and type 2B fibres always retain their distinctive features. However, type 2A fibres can take on characteristics of the type 1 or type 2B fibres depending upon the training that is done. If you were to do endurance training, the type 2A fibres would develop more endurance, or if you were to do speed training they would develop more speed. They do not change their fibre type but they do take on different characteristics.

Every muscle in the body contains a mixture of fast and slow twitch fibres depending upon its role in the body. Postural muscles, which keep us standing upright, such as the muscles in the legs, back and abdominal areas, will be predominantly slow twitch. For example, 90 per cent of the muscles in the back are slow twitch. Postural muscles need to produce low forces over a long period of time. The arms tend to be more fast twitch as they will need to move quickly but over much shorter periods of time. The types of muscle found in the legs determine whether we are more suited to sprinting or endurance running. You will know which you have most of based on your own athletic performances. According to Bursztyn (1997), well-trained middle distance runners have around 80 per cent slow twitch fibres while well-trained sprinters may have up to 75 per cent fast twitch.

Key learning points

- Involuntary muscle   Smooth muscle and cardiac muscle
- Voluntary muscle   Skeletal muscle

Table 1.01 Summary of muscle fibre types

Slow twitch (type 1)	Feature	Fast twitch (type 2)
Red	Colour	White
Slow	Contraction speed	Fast
High	Endurance	Low
Low	Intensity used	High
Many	Blood vessels	Few
Smaller	Size	Larger
Many	Mitochondria	Few

Major muscles

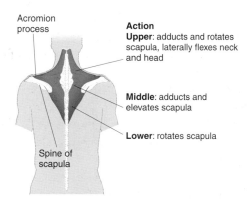

Action
Upper: adducts and rotates scapula, laterally flexes neck and head

Middle: adducts and elevates scapula

Lower: rotates scapula

Fig 1.30 Trapezius
Position: upper back **Origin:** base of skull, cervical and thoracic vertebrae **Insertion:** clavicle and scapula **Action:** elevation, retraction and depression of shoulder girdle **Exercise:** bent-over rows

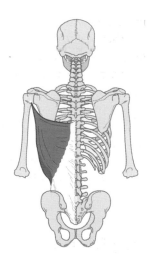

Action Adduction of humerus

Fig 1.31 Latissimus dorsi
Position: lower back **Origin:** lower 6 thoracic and all lumbar vertebrae, ilium **Insertion:** humerus **Action:** adduction and extension of shoulder **Exercise:** lateral pulldown

Anterior view

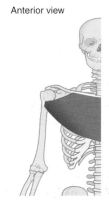

Action
Medial rotation of the humerus. Flexes the shoulder and horizontally adducts humerus

Fig 1.32 Pectoralis major
Position: chest **Origin:** clavicle and sternum **Insertion:** humerus **Action:** horizontal flexion and adduction of shoulder **Exercise:** bench press

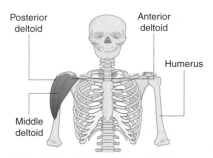

Action Anterior deltoids – flexion of shoulder
Middle deltoid – abduction of shoulder
Posterior deltoid – extension of shoulder

Fig 1.33 Deltoid
Position: shoulder **Origin:** clavicle and scapula **Insertion:** humerus **Action:** abduction, flexion and extension of shoulder **Exercise:** lateral raises

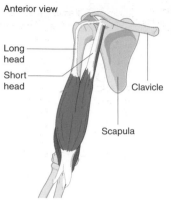

Anterior view

Long head

Short head

Clavicle

Scapula

Action
Flexes and supinates (turns palm upwards) the forearm

Fig 1.34   Biceps brachii
Position: front of upper arm **Origin:** scapula **Insertion:** radius **Action:** flexion of elbow and shoulder, supination of forearm **Exercise:** bicep curls

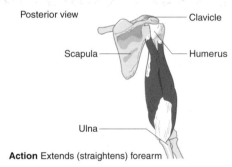

Posterior view

Clavicle

Scapula

Humerus

Ulna

Action Extends (straightens) forearm

Fig 1.35   Triceps brachii
Position: back of upper arm **Origin:** humerus and scapula **Insertion:** ulna **Action:** extension of elbow and shoulder **Exercise:** triceps extension

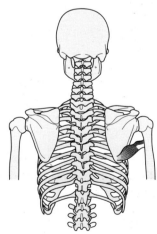

Fig 1.36   Teres major
Position: shoulder **Origin:** scapula **Insertion:** humerus **Action:** medial rotation of shoulder **Exercise:** cable shoulder rotation

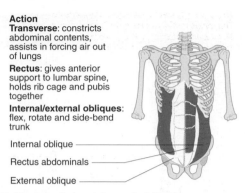

Action
Transverse: constricts abdominal contents, assists in forcing air out of lungs
Rectus: gives anterior support to lumbar spine, holds rib cage and pubis together
Internal/external obliques: flex, rotate and side-bend trunk

Internal oblique

Rectus abdominals

External oblique

Fig 1.37   Rectus abdominis and obliques
Position: front of abdomen and sides of the abdomen **Origin:** pubis and ribs, ilium **Insertion:** sternum and ilium, pubis, ribs **Action:** flexion of vertebrae and rotation of vertebrae **Exercise:** swiss ball sit-ups and side bends

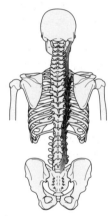

Fig 1.38   Erector spinae
Position: up and down the spine **Origin:** sacrum, ilium and vertebrae **Insertion:** ribs, vertebrae, base of skull **Action:** extension of vertebrae **Exercise:** dorsal raises

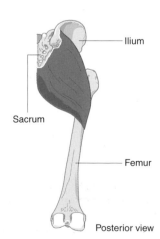

Ilium

Sacrum

Femur

Posterior view

Action   Extends hip, laterally rotates femur

Fig 1.39   Gluteus maximus
Position: bottom **Origin:** ilium **Insertion:** femur **Action:** extension of hip **Exercise:** squats

The quadriceps are made up of four muscles.
The rectus femoris acts on **both** the hip and knee joint.
The vasti muscles (medialis, intermedialis
and lateralis) act on the knee joint only.

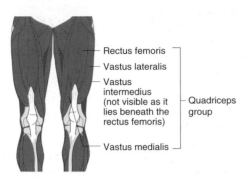

Action
Extends lower leg at the knee, flexes femur at the hip

Fig 1.40 Quadricep group
Rectus femoris **Position:** front of upper leg **Origin:** ilium,
femur **Insertion:** tibia **Action:** extension of knee **Exercise:**
leg extension
Vastus lateralis **Position:** front of upper leg **Origin:** femur
Insertion: tibia **Action:** extension of knee **Exercise:** leg
extension
Vastus medialis **Position:** front of upper leg **Origin:** femur
Insertion: tibia **Action:** extension of knee **Exercise:** leg
extension
Vastus intermedius **Position:** front of upper leg **Origin:**
femur **Insertion:** tibia **Action:** extension of knee **Exercise:**
leg extension

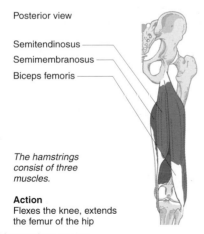

Action
Flexes the knee, extends
the femur of the hip

Fig 1.41 Hamstring group
Semimembranosus **Position:** back of upper leg **Origin:**
ischium **Insertion:** tibia, fibula **Action:** flexion of knee
Exercise: leg flexion
Semitendinosus **Position:** back of upper leg **Origin:**
ischium **Insertion:** tibia, fibula **Action:** flexion of knee
Exercise: leg flexion
Biceps femoris **Position:** back of upper leg **Origin:**
ischium, femur **Insertion:** tibia, fibula **Action:** flexion of
knee **Exercise:** leg flexion

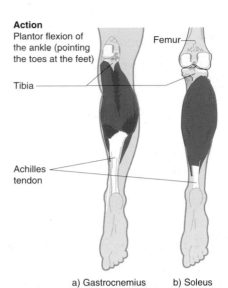

Action
Plantor flexion of
the ankle (pointing
the toes at the feet)

a) Gastrocnemius   b) Soleus

Fig 1.42 Gastrocnemius and soleus
Position: back of lower leg **Origin:** femur and tibia
Insertion: calcaneus **Action:** plantarflexion of ankle, knee
flexion and plantarflexion of ankle **Exercise:** calf raises

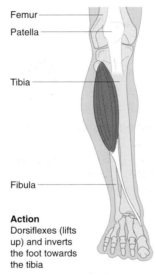

Action
Dorsiflexes (lifts
up) and inverts
the foot towards
the tibia

Fig 1.43 Tibialis anterior
Position: front of lower leg **Origin:** tibia **Insertion:** tarsals and
metatarsals **Action:** dorsiflexion of ankle **Exercise:** walking

Muscle movement

Tendons are responsible for joining skeletal muscles to
your skeleton. Skeletal muscles are held to the bones
with the help of tendons.

definition

Tendons: these join muscles to the skeleton.

Tendons are cords made of tough tissue, and they work to connect muscle to bones. When the muscle contracts, it pulls on the tendon, which in turn pulls on the bone and makes the bone move.

Group action of muscles

When muscles contract they work as a group in that the muscle contracting is dependent on other muscles to enable it to do its job. A muscle can play one of four roles, as outlined below.

- **Agonist (or prime mover):** this muscle contracts to produce the desired movement.
- **Antagonist:** this muscle relaxes to allow the agonist to contract.
- **Synergist:** this muscle assists the agonist in producing the desired movement.
- **Fixator:** these muscles fix joints and the body in position to enable the desired movement to occur.

An antagonistic muscle pair is the muscle which contracts to produce the movement and the muscle which relaxes to allow the movement to occur. For example, when you perform a bicep curl the biceps brachii will be the agonist as it contracts to produce the movement, while the triceps brachii will be the antagonist as it relaxes to allow the movement to occur.

definition

> **Antagonistic muscle pairs:** as one muscle contracts the other relaxes.

Types of movement

Muscles can contract or develop tension in three different ways:

- concentric contraction
- eccentric contraction
- isometric contraction.

Concentric contraction: this involves the muscle shortening and developing tension. The origin and insertion of the muscle move closer together and muscle becomes fatter. To produce a concentric contraction a movement must occur against gravity.

Eccentric contraction: this involves the muscle lengthening to develop tension. The origin and the insertion move further away from each other. An eccentric contraction provides the control of a movement on the downward phase and it works to resist the force of gravity.

If a person is performing a bench press (as in Fig 1.44) they will produce a concentric contraction to push the weight away from their body. However, on the downward phase they produce an eccentric contraction to control the weight on the way down. If they did not, gravity would return the weight to the ground and hurt them in the process. The agonist muscle will produce concentric and eccentric contractions while the antagonist muscle always stays relaxed to allow the movement to occur.

Concentric phase   Eccentric phase

Fig 1.44 Bench press

Isometric contraction: if a muscle produces tension but stays the same length it will be an isometric contraction. This occurs when the body is fixed in one position – for example, a gymnast on the rings in the crucifix position. When we are standing up our postural muscles produce isometric contractions.

> ## LEARNER ACTIVITY
> ### Muscle contractions
> Think of three sporting examples for each type of muscle contraction.

Muscle contraction – sliding filament theory

Muscle contraction requires energy. We get tired after exercising because our muscles run out of energy. Energy production is discussed in Chapter 2: Sport and exercise physiology.

So how does energy enable our muscles to contract? The contraction process occurs in four steps.

1 At rest, troponin and tropomyosin cover the actin and myosin filaments and prevent myosin from binding to actin. When we give the signal for our muscles to contract, calcium is released into the sarcoplasm. Calcium binds to troponin and takes it away from the myosin binding site. As it moves away, it moves the tropomyosin molecule with it. Therefore, as the troponin and tropomyosin bind to calcium, the myosin binding site is exposed.

2 The myosin heads bind to the actin filament and slide it across the myosin filament, which results in the sarcomere getting shorter.

3 Energy is used to break the attachment of the actin and myosin filaments. The myosin heads then re-attach at a site further up the actin filament, which results in further shortening of the sarcomere.

4 When the stimulus to the muscle ends, calcium ions are released from the troponin and are pumped out of the sarcoplasm. This causes the troponin and tropomyosin to bind to the myosin heads once again, which means they cannot bind to the actin molecule and contraction cannot occur.

The entire process is extremely fast and only takes a fraction of a second. The cycle then repeats itself until the muscle relaxes.

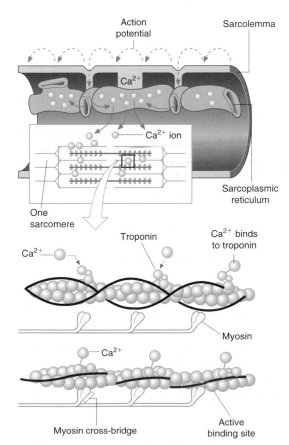

Fig 1.45 The structure of actin and myosin

The cardiovascular system

Close your hand into a fist and look at it. Your fist is approximately the same size as your heart, around 12 cm long, 9 cm wide and 6 cm thick. It is located behind the sternum and tilted to the left. The heart is made up mainly of cardiac muscle, which is also known as myocardium.

Anatomy of the heart

The heart is divided into right- and left-hand sides by the septum. The two sides are separate and have no communication with each other. Each side is further divided into two chambers. The upper chamber is called the atrium and is the smaller chamber. It acts to receive blood from the veins. The lower chamber, the ventricle, is a pump which drives blood into the arteries. The connection between the two chambers is through the atrio-ventricular valve.

The heart is made of cardiac muscle and is called the myocardium. Blood circulation is dependent upon the action of the myocardium, which varies in thickness: it is thickest in the left ventricle to produce power to pump oxygenated blood around the body, and is thinner in the right ventricle and thinnest in the atria.

The walls of the atria and ventricles are lined with a smooth, shiny membrane called the endocardium, which is a single layer of cells. The outside of the heart is covered by the two layers of the pericardium, which covers the blood vessels of the heart (coronary arteries). The inner layer of the pericardium is called the epicardium.

Valves of the heart

The heart uses valves to ensure the blood flows in the right direction. There are four main valves.

- The right atrio-ventricular valve is called the tricuspid valve and opens up to allow blood to flow from the right atrium to the right ventricle. The valve consists of cusps made of muscle and fibrous tissues that are attached to several fine, tendinous cords called chordae tendinous, which prevent the valves being forced back into the atrium.
- The left atrio-ventricular valve is called the mitral valve. It is similar to the tricuspid valve, although smaller, and acts to prevent the backflow of blood into the left atrium from the left ventricle as it contracts.
- The aortic valve opens up to allow blood to flow from the left atrium into the aorta. The coronary arteries which supply the blood to the heart muscle (myocardium) are positioned just above the aortic valve.
- The pulmonary valve allows blood to flow from the right ventricle into the pulmonary artery to take deoxygenated blood to the lungs.

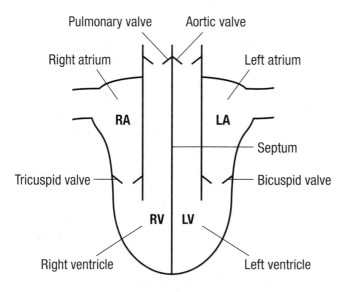

Fig 1.46 The heart

Here is a summary of structures of the heart and their functions:

- right atrium (RA) – this receives deoxygenated blood from the organs of the body
- right ventricle (RV) – this pumps deoxygenated blood to the lungs
- left atrium (LA) – this receives oxygenated blood from the lungs
- left ventricle (LV) – this pumps oxygenated blood to all organs of the body; it is larger and therefore stronger than the right ventricle as it has to pump the blood through the body
- valves – there are four one-way valves in the heart that open or close in response to pressure of blood flow
    - bicuspid valve – separates the left atrium from the left ventricle
    - tricuspid valve – separates the right atrium from the right ventricle
    - aortic valve – separates the left ventricle from the aorta
    - pulmonary valve – separates the right ventricle from the pulmonary artery.

All these valves ensure that blood flows in one direction and prevent the backflow of blood into the ventricles.

The blood vessels leading to and from the heart are as follows.

- The aorta carries oxygenated blood out of the left ventricle to the body.
- The superior vena cava returns deoxygenated blood to the right atrium from the head and upper body; the inferior vena cava returns deoxygenated blood to the right atrium from the lower body.
- The pulmonary vein carries freshly oxygenated blood from the lungs to the left atrium.
- The pulmonary artery carries deoxygenated blood from the body to the lungs.

Pulmonary circulation

The right ventricle pumps blood through the pulmonary artery to the lungs. Here, the blood 'picks up' oxygen and carbon dioxide is released into the lungs. From the lungs, the oxygenated blood is carried to the left atrium. This short loop is called the 'pulmonary circulation'.

Systemic circulation

From the left atrium the blood flows down to the left ventricle. The left ventricle pumps oxygenated blood through the aorta to all tissues of the body. Oxygen and nutrients are released from the blood to nourish cells, and carbon dioxide and other waste products are carried back to the heart via the two venae cavae. The blood enters the right atrium. Carbon dioxide is carried to the lungs and removed from the body.

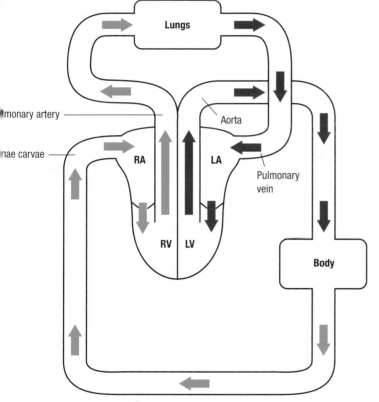

Fig 1.47 Blood flow through the heart

Nervous control of the heart

The heart muscle has its own independent nerve supply via a specialised tissue called the sino-atrial node (the pacemaker of the heart), which is situated close to the point where the vena cava enters the right atrium. When a nervous impulse is produced it will pass through both atria to the atrio-ventricular node positioned in the septum where the atria and ventricles meet. The nervous impulse pauses slightly and then enters the walls of the ventricles through the atrio-ventricular bundles (Bundle of His), one into each ventricle. These bundles break up into specialist fibres, called purkinje fibres, which carry nervous impulses to all parts of the ventricles.

The heart is controlled by the autonomic nervous system. First, the vagus nerve which slows down the heart rate and decreases the power of ventricular contraction by delivering impulses through the sino-atrial node. Second, the sympathetic nerves increase the heart rate and the force of contraction of the ventricles. This innervation of the heart is controlled through the cardiac centre of the brain, which is positioned within the medulla oblongata.

Blood vessels

Arteries are the large blood vessels which leave the heart. They have thick muscular walls which contract and relax to send blood to all parts of the body. The main artery leaving the heart is the aorta and it quickly splits up into smaller vessels which are called the arterioles. The word arterioles means 'little arteries'. Artery walls contain elastic cartilage and smooth muscle. This flexible wall allows the vessels to expand and contract, which helps to push the blood along the length of the arteries. This action is called 'peristalsis' and is how smooth muscle contracts.

Arteries do not contain any valves as they are not required and they predominantly carry oxygenated blood. The exception to this is the pulmonary artery which carries deoxygenated blood away from the heart.

- Arteries carry blood away from the heart.
- They have thick muscular walls.
- They carry predominantly oxygenated blood.
- Arterioles are the small branches off arteries.

Capillaries

Once the arteries and arterioles have divided, they eventually feed blood into the smallest blood vessels, called capillaries. These are found in all parts of the body, especially the muscles, and are so tiny that their walls are only one cell thick. The walls are very thin and there are tiny spaces in them which allow the diffusion of oxygen and other nutrients through the cell walls. The blood flows very slowly through the capillaries to allow for this process. In the capillaries the blood will also pick up the waste products of metabolism, carbon dioxide and lactic acid. There are more capillaries than any other type of blood vessel in the body.

- Tiny blood vessels one cell thick.
- Small spaces in the walls to allow for diffusion.
- Oxygen and nutrients diffuse into the cells.
- Carbon dioxide and lactic acid flow from the cells into the capillaries.

Veins and venules

The capillaries eventually feed back into larger blood vessels called venules, which are the smallest veins, and they eventually become veins. These veins are thinner and less muscular than arteries and they carry blood back to the heart. They also contain smooth muscle and contract to send the blood back to the heart. The veins are generally acting against gravity so they will contain non-return valves to prevent the blood flowing back once the smooth muscle has relaxed. These valves prevent the pooling of blood in the lower limbs. Veins will predominantly carry deoxygenated blood, the exception being the pulmonary vein which carries oxygenated blood to the heart from the lungs.

- Veins always take blood towards the heart.
- Veins have thin, muscular walls.
- They have non-return valves to prevent backflow.
- They predominantly carry deoxygenated blood.
- Venules are the smaller branches which feed into veins.

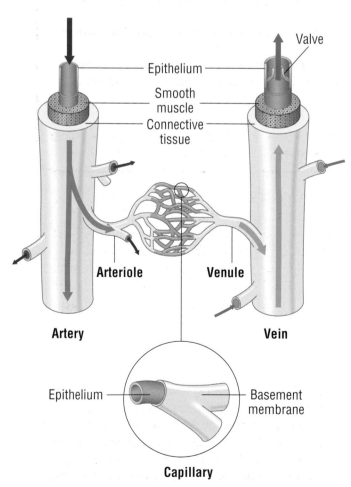

Fig 1.48 The five linked blood vessels

Blood

Blood is the medium in which all the cells are carried to transport nutrients and oxygen to the cells. Among other things, blood transports the following: oxygen, glucose, proteins, fats, vitamins, hormones, enzymes, platelets, carbon dioxide and electrolytes.

Blood is made up of four components:

- red blood cells
- white blood cells
- platelets
- plasma.

The blood can be described as a thick, gloopy substance due to the high concentration of solids it carries. The blood is made up of 55 per cent plasma and 45 per cent solids, which is a very high concentration.

Red blood cells

Of the blood cells in the blood around 99 per cent of them are red blood cells or erythrocytes. They are red in colour due to the presence of a red-coloured protein called haemoglobin. Haemoglobin has a massive attraction for oxygen and thus the main role of the red blood cells is to take on and transport oxygen to the cells. There are many millions of red blood cells in the body; for example, there are 5 million red blood cells to 1 mm^3 volume of blood.

White blood cells

White blood cells, or leucocytes, are actually colourless or transparent and are far fewer (1:700 ratio of white to red blood cells). The role of white blood cells is to fight infection and they are part of the body's immune system. They destroy bacteria and other dangerous organisms and thus remove disease from the body.

Platelets

Platelets, or thrombocytes, are not full cells but rather parts of cells. They act by stopping blood loss through clotting. They become sticky when in contact with the air to form the initial stage of repair to damaged tissue. Platelets also need a substance called factor 8 to enable them to clot. A haemophiliac is a person whose blood does not clot. This is not because they are short

LEARNER ACTIVITY Heart dissection

The aim of this practical is to examine the structure of a mammalian heart.

The equipment you need:

sheep or pig hearts	dissection boards
tweezers	scalpels
scissors	lab coats
latex gloves	disinfectant
worksheets	disposal bag/bin for hearts and used gloves

Method

Working in groups of three or four put on lab coats, goggles and latex gloves. Then complete the following activities.

1 Examine the outside of the heart and make a note of its texture and appearance.
2 Try to determine the orientation of the heart in the body.
3 The valves inside the heart should still be intact and can be shown to still work. Go to a sink and pass running water into the left and right atria; it should be possible to see the valves close.
4 Place the heart back on the dissection board, dome side up, and make an incision with the scalpel or with the scissors from the right atrium right down to the right ventricle. This should expose the whole of the inside of the right-hand side of the heart. Make a note of the appearance and texture of the inside of the heart.
5 The tendons that hold the valves in place can be seen clearly. Use the tweezers to pull on these, and make a note of their strength.
6 Dissect the left-hand side of the heart, from the left atrium down towards the left ventricle. Compare the thickness of the right- and left-hand-side ventricle walls.
7 Try to ascertain which blood vessel is which by pushing your finger down the blood vessels into the heart. Where your finger appears should give you enough of a clue to work out which blood vessel is which.

Conclusion

In your conclusion look back at the comments you have made throughout the dissection. Write down what you have found out about the heart's anatomy and explain why it has these anatomical features.

---

of platelets but rather factor 8, which enables the platelets to become active.

Plasma

Plasma is the liquid part of the blood and is straw-coloured in appearance. It is the solution in which all the solids are carried. Plasma will also carry nutrients such as fats, amino acids and glucose as well as hormones and enzymes.

The respiratory system

The respiratory system is responsible for transporting the oxygen from the air we breathe into our body. Our body then uses this oxygen in combination with the food we have eaten to produce energy. This energy is then used to keep us alive by supplying our heart with energy to keep beating and pumping blood around the body. It allows us to move and take part in sports and many more different types of activities. Each person has two lungs running the length of the ribcage; the right lung is slightly larger than the left lung. The left lung has to make space for the heart in an area called the cardiac notch.

Structure of the respiratory system

The aim of the respiratory system is to provide contact between the outside and internal environments so that oxygen can be absorbed by the blood and carbon dioxide can be given up. It is made up of a system of tubes and muscles delivering the air into two lungs. The average person takes around 26,000 breaths a day to deliver the required amount of oxygen to the cells of the body.

LEARNER ACTIVITY
Structure of the heart

Fill in the blanks in the text below.

The heart is split into _____ sides and has _____ chambers. The top two chambers are called _____ and the bottom two chambers are called _____. The heart is split into two separate sides by the _____.
There are _____ valves that allow the blood to pass through the heart in one direction.
The valve between the atrium and ventricle on the right side of the heart is called the _____ valve. The valve on the left side of the heart between the atrium and the ventricle is called the _____ valve. The valve between the pulmonary artery and right ventricle is called the _____ valve. The valve between the left ventricle and the aorta is called the _____ valve.

Composition of air

The air that is inspired is made up of a mixture of gases; the air exhaled is different in its composition of gases.

Inhaled air	Gas	Exhaled air
79.04%	Nitrogen	79%
20.93%	Oxygen	17%
0.03%	Carbon dioxide	4%

Oxygen is extracted from the air and replaced by carbon dioxide. However, most of the oxygen stays in the air and this is why mouth-to-mouth resuscitation works, because there is still 17 per cent available to the casualty.

Functions of the respiratory system

The aim of breathing is to get oxygen into the bloodstream where it can be delivered to the cells of the body. At the cells it enters the mitochondria where it combines with fats and carbohydrates to produce energy, with carbon dioxide and water produced as waste products. This energy is used to produce muscular contractions, among other things.

Fats/carbohydrates + oxygen = energy + carbon dioxide and water

It is important to say that when the body produces more energy the amount of carbon dioxide increases in the body and it becomes dissolved in water to produce a weak acid. The body does not like the acidity of the blood to increase so the respiratory centre in the brain speeds up the rate of breathing to get rid of the excess carbon dioxide. Therefore, the breathing rate increases because carbon dioxide levels rise rather than the cells demanding more oxygen.

Control of respiration

Respiration is controlled through the respiratory centre in the brain, which is located in the medulla oblongata. As levels of carbon dioxide in the blood rise, the increase in acidity is sensed by specialised cells within the arteries. Messages are sent to the brain through the nerves to the respiratory centre. Messages are then delivered to the diaphragm and intercostal muscles by the phrenic nerves to increase the rate of respiration.

Diffusion of gases

Gases will move around through a process of diffusion.

> definition
>
> **Diffusion:** the movement of a gas from an area of high concentration to an area of low concentration.

Diffusion is how gases move in the open air. For example, if a person is wearing perfume it will diffuse around a room so that everyone can smell it. This is because the person is in an area of high concentration and the gas moves to areas of low concentration.

In the lungs we have a high concentration of oxygen and in the muscles we have a high concentration of carbon dioxide. They diffuse across the semi-permeable membrane. Oxygen is attracted into the blood by the haemoglobin, a protein in the red blood cells, and it attaches to this haemoglobin.

In the muscles we have a high concentration of carbon dioxide and a low concentration of oxygen due to the process of energy production. However, in the blood we have a high concentration of oxygen and a low concentration of carbon dioxide. As a result, the oxygen diffuses into the muscles and is attracted by the myoglobin in the muscles, and the carbon dioxide diffuses into the bloodstream. It is then taken to the lungs to be breathed out.

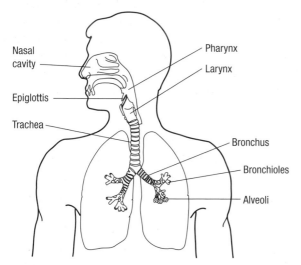

Fig 1.49 The respiratory system

Anatomy of the respiratory system

1 Air enters the body through the **mouth and nose**.
2 It passes through the **pharynx**, which is the back of the throat area.
3 It then passes through the **larynx**, which is responsible for voice production.
4 Air passes over the **epiglottis**. The epiglottis closes over the trachea when we swallow food to stop the food going down 'the wrong way' into our trachea and down into our lungs.
5 The air enters the **trachea**, which is a cartigenous tube that delivers air to the lungs.
6 The trachea divides into two **bronchi**, one into each lung.
7 The two main bronchi divide into **bronchioles**, which further subdivide 23 times and result in 8 million terminal bronchioles in each lung.
8 Around the bronchioles are the groups of air sacs called **alveoli**. There are around 600 million alveoli in each lung and it is here that the exchange of gases (oxygen and carbon dioxide) occurs. Each alveolus is in contact with a capillary where the blood is present.

The respiratory system also includes two types of muscles which work to move air into and out of the lungs:

- the diaphragm is a sheet of muscle which runs along the bottom of the lungs

- the intercostal muscles are found between the ribs (if you enjoy eating spare ribs you are actually eating the intercostal muscles).

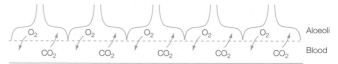

Fig 1.50 Exchange of gases in the alveoli and capillary

Mechanisms of breathing

Breathing is the term given to inhaling air into the lungs and then exhaling air out. The process works on the principal of making the thoracic cavity (chest) larger, which decreases the pressure of air within the lungs. The surrounding air is then at a higher pressure, which means that air is forced into the lungs. Then the thoracic cavity is returned to its original size, which forces air out of the lungs.

Respiratory muscles

Diaphragm: the diaphragm is a large dome-shaped muscle which covers the bottom of the ribcage. At rest it is dome-shaped but when contracted it flattens and pushes the two sides of the ribcage away from each other.

Intercostal muscles: The muscles attach between the ribs and when they contract they push the ribs up and out and increase the size of the chest cavity drawing air in. If you put your hands on your ribs and breathe in you will feel your ribs push up and out; this is the action of the intercostal muscles.

Breathing in (inhalation)

At rest the diaphragm contracts and moves downwards. This results in an increase in the size of the thoracic cavity and air is forced into the lungs.

During exercise the diaphragm and intercostal muscles contract, which makes the ribs move upwards and outwards and results in more air being taken into the lungs.

Breathing out (exhalation)

At rest the diaphragm relaxes and returns upwards to a domed position. The thoracic cavity gets smaller, which results in an increase in air pressure within the lungs so air is breathed out of the lungs.

During exercise, the intercostal muscles contract to help decrease the size of the thoracic cavity; this results in a more forcible breath out.

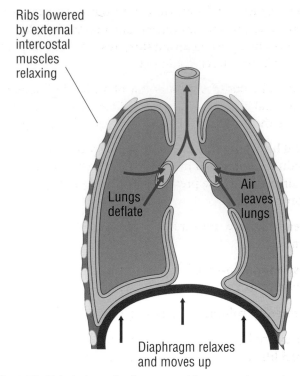

Fig 1.52 Exhalation: diaphragm and intercostal muscles

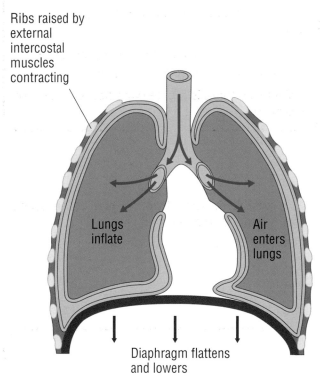

Fig 1.51 Inhalation: diaphragm and intercostal muscles

Respiratory volumes

In order to assess an individual's lung function we use a spirometer. An example of the readings given by a spirometer is shown in Fig 1.53.

An individual has a lung capacity of around five litres, which is about the amount of air in a basketball. It will be slightly lower for a female and slightly higher for a male, due to the differing sizes of the male and female ribcage.

Tidal volume is the amount of air breathed in with each breath.

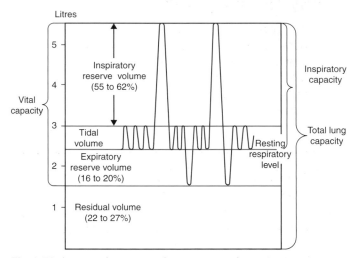

Fig 1.53 Lung volumes as shown on a spirometer trace

Inspiratory reserve volume is the amount of space that is available for air to be inhaled. If you breathe in and stop and then try to breathe in more, this extra air inhaled is the inspiratory volume.

Expiratory reserve volume is the amount of air that could be exhaled after you have breathed out. If you exhale and then stop and try to exhale more, the air that comes out is the expiratory reserve volume.

Vital capacity is the maximum amount of air that can be breathed in and out during one breath. It is the tidal volume plus the inspiratory reserve volume plus the expiratory reserve volume.

Residual volume is the amount of air left in the lungs after a full exhalation. Around 1 litre always remains or else the lungs would deflate and breathing stop.

Total lung volume is the vital capacity plus the residual volume and measures the maximum amount of air that could be present in the lungs at any moment.

Breathing rate is the number of breaths taken per minute.

Respiratory volume is the amount of air that is moving through the lungs every minute.

respiratory volume = breathing rate × tidal volume

For example, at rest a person may have a tidal volume of 0.5 litres per minute and a breathing rate of 12 breaths per minute. But during exercise both of these rise and at high intensities tidal volume may rise to 3 litres per minute and breathing rate to 35 breaths per minute.

At rest respiratory volume:
$0.5 \times 12 = 6$ litres/minute

During exercise respiratory volume:
$3 \times 35 = 105$ litres/minute

LEARNER ACTIVITY
Breathing rates

Count your breathing rate at rest for one minute.

Take part in one minute of aerobic exercise and then count your breathing rate again.

Explain why there is a difference between the two breathing rates.

Key learning points

- Air travels into the body through the mouth and nose, down the trachea and into the bronchus. It then passes into the bronchioles and down in to the alveoli. In the alveoli, gaseous exchange takes place which takes oxygen into the body and passes carbon dioxide out of the body.

- The diaphragm and intercostal muscles contract to allow you to breathe in and out.

Review questions

1 What is the function of the heart?
2 Why is the heart sometimes called a 'double pump'?
3 Which heart chamber contains the thickest myocardium? Why do you think this is?
4 Why are valves necessary inside the heart?
5 List the blood vessels leading to and from the heart through which the blood flows.
6 Give a brief account of how the structure of arteries, arterioles, capillaries, venuoles and veins is related to their function.
7 What is blood made up of?
8 Describe which structures air flows through on its way from the mouth to the alveoli.
9 Explain the mechanics of breathing in and out.
10 What happens to tidal volume during exercise? Explain why this occurs.
11 Explain how the muscles work with the skeleton in order to produce movement.
12 Give examples of how a sportsperson produces different types of muscle contraction during a game of rugby.
13 How do the respiratory system and cardiovascular system supply oxygen to the working muscles?
14 What are the different types of muscle tissue and where could you find them?
15 What happens to blood flow to the various organs during exercise and how is it controlled?

References

Beashel, P. and Taylor, J. (1996) *Advanced Studies in Physical Education and Sport*, Nelson.

Blakey, P. (2000) *The Muscle Book*, Himalayan Institute Press.

Bursztyn, P. (1997) *Physiology for Sportspeople: A Serious User's Guide to the Body*, Manchester University Press.

Kapit, W. and Elson, L. (2001) *The Anatomy Coloring Book*, Benjamin Cummings.

Kingston, B. (1998) *Understanding Muscles*, Stanley Thornes.

Kingston, B. (2000) *Understanding Joints*, Stanley Thornes.

Seeley, R. R., Stephens, T. D. and Tate, P. (2000) *Anatomy and Physiology*, McGraw-Hill.

Stafford-Brown, J., Rea, S., Janaway, L. and Manley, C. (2006) *BTEC First Sport*, Hodder Arnold.

Stone, R. J. and Stone, J. A. (1999) *Atlas of Skeletal Muscles*, McGraw-Hill.

Wesson, K., Wiggins-James, N., Thompson, G. and Hartigan, S. (2005) *Sport and PE: A Complete Guide to Advanced Level Study*, Hodder Arnold.

Sport and exercise physiology

Goals

At the end of this chapter you should understand:

- the initial responses of the body to exercise
- how the body responds to steady-state exercise
- fatigue and how the body recovers from exercise
- how the body adapts to chronic exercise.

Our body allows us to take part in a huge variety of sports and exercises. In order for us to carry out these activities the body has to undergo a series of changes that provide us with the ability and the energy to carry out these actions.

This chapter starts by exploring the responses of the cardiovascular, respiratory and energy systems to the anticipation and initial stress of exercise. There then follows a study of the response of the body after a period of around 20 minutes' exercise, when a steady state has been achieved. The mechanisms of fatigue are then explored, followed by the methods by which we recover from sports and exercise. A look at the ways in which the body adapts to repeated bouts of aerobic and anaerobic exercise completes the chapter.

Fig 2.01 A runner at the outset of exercise

The initial responses of the body

Initial response of the cardiovascular system

The cardiovascular system consists of the heart and the blood vessels through which the heart pumps blood around the body. During exercise a number of changes take place to the cardiovascular system to ensure that the muscles receive the required amounts of oxygen and nutrients. The structure of the cardiovascular system is discussed in more detail in Chapter 1: Anatomy for sport and exercise.

During exercise the heart rate needs to be increased in order to ensure that the working muscles receive adequate amounts of nutrients and oxygen, and that waste products are removed. Before you even start exercising there is an increase in your heart rate, called the 'anticipatory rise', which occurs because when you think about exercising it stimulates the sympathetic nervous system to release adrenaline.

> **Adrenaline (also known as epinephrine):** a hormone released during times of stress which gets the body ready for action – increases blood pressure, increases heart rate, etc.

One of the affects of adrenaline is to make the heart beat faster. Once exercise has started, there is an increase in carbon dioxide and lactic acid in the body, which is detected by chemoreceptors.

> **Chemoreceptor:** a group of cells that detect changes in the chemical environment round them and transmit this message to the brain so that the body can respond accordingly.

The chemoreceptors trigger the sympathetic nervous system to increase the release of adrenaline, which further increases heart rate. In a trained athlete the heart rate can increase by up to three times within one minute of starting exercise. As exercise continues, the body becomes warmer, which will also help to increase the heart rate because it increases the speed of the conduction of nerve impulses across the heart.

Cardiac output

Cardiac output is the amount of blood pumped from the heart every minute and is the product of heart rate and stroke volume.

cardiac output (litres per minute) = heart rate (bpm) × stroke volume (litres)

The shorthand for this equation is:

$$Q = HR \times SV.$$

LEARNER ACTIVITY Heart rate and exercise

The aim of this activity is to examine what happens to heart rate before and during the onset of exercise.

The equipment you need:

stopwatch or heart rate monitor	skipping rope
sports clothes	bench
pen and paper	

Method

1 If you have a heart rate monitor, place it around your chest. If not, find your pulse point either on your neck or at your wrist.
2 Sit quietly for five minutes, then take your resting heart rate. If you have a heart rate monitor, write down the heart rate that appears on the monitor. If not, feel for your pulse point, then count your heart rate for 30 seconds. Double this figure and write it down.
3 Think about what exercise you are about to perform for one minute.
4 Record your heart rate after having thought about your exercise.
5 Perform step-ups on to a bench for two minutes or skip for two minutes with a skipping rope.
6 Immediately after you have finished your exercise, record your heart rate.

Results Resting heart rate (bpm)	Pre-exercise heart rate (bpm)	Post-exercise heart rate (bpm)

Copy and complete the results table above.

Answer the following questions.

1 What happened to your heart rate immediately before you started exercising?
2 What caused this change in your heart rate and why is it necessary?
3 Explain why there is a difference between your resting heart rate and your post-exercise heart rate.

The stroke volume is around 70 to 90 millilitres. It varies depending on a variety of factors. Generally, the fitter you are, the larger your stroke volume is and males tend to have larger stroke volumes than females. At rest a person's cardiac output is approximately 5 litres per minute, while during exercise it can increase to as much as 30 litres per minute.

LEARNER ACTIVITY
Stroke volume

1 Take your resting heart rate by finding a pulse point and recording your heart rate for 30 seconds. Double this figure to give you beats per minute.

2 The average cardiac output for a person is 5 litres per minute. By rearranging the equation we can estimate a person's stroke volume (SV):

$$Q = SV \times HR$$

$$SV = \frac{Q}{HR}$$

e.g. If your heart rate was 70 bpm:

$$SV = \frac{5}{70}$$

$$SV = 0.071 \text{ litre} = 71 \text{ ml}$$

3 Note down the rest of the class's stroke volumes and then take an average.

4 Separate your class stoke volumes into males and females and then calculate an average stroke volume for the males and another for the females. Is there a difference between the two? If so, explain why.

5 What conclusions can you draw about the fitness of your class?

Blood pressure

Blood pressure is necessary in order for blood to flow around the body. The pressure is a result of the heart contracting and forcing blood into the blood vessels. Two values are given when a person has their blood pressure taken.

A typical blood pressure for the average adult male is 120/80. The two values correspond to the systolic value (when the heart is contracting) and the diastolic value (when the heart is relaxing). The higher value is the systolic value and the lower is the diastolic value. Blood pressure is measured in milligrams of mercury: mmHg.

The value for a person's blood pressure is determined by the cardiac output (Q), which is a product of stroke volume and heart rate, and the resistance the blood encounters as it flows around the body. This can be put into an equation:

$$\text{blood pressure} = Q \times R$$

where Q = cardiac output (stroke volume × heart rate) and R = resistance to flow

Resistance to blood flow is caused both by the size of the blood vessels through which it travels (the smaller the blood vessel, the greater the resistance) and by the thickness of the blood (the thicker the blood, the greater the resistance).

Changing the resistance to blood flow can alter blood pressure. This is done by involuntary smooth muscles in the arterioles relaxing or contracting in order to alter the diameter of the arterioles. As the smooth muscle contracts, the diameter of the blood vessel gets smaller, so blood pressure is increased. As the smooth muscle relaxes, the diameter of the blood vessel is increased, which decreases the pressure of the blood flowing through it. The same principle can be applied to altering the diameter of water flow through a hose. If you place your finger over part of the opening of the hose, making the diameter smaller, the water will flow out quite forcibly because it is under higher pressure. However, if the water is left to flow unhindered through the end of the hose it is under lower pressure, and will therefore not 'spurt' so far because there is less resistance.

A reduction in blood pressure is detected by baroreceptors in the aorta and the carotid artery.

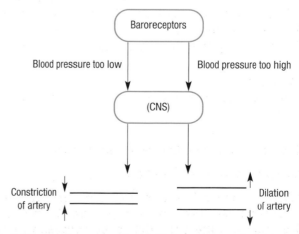

Fig 2.02 How baroreceptors initiate response to high blood pressure and low blood pressure

Baroreceptor: a collection of cells that detect a change in blood pressure. They send signals to the brain so that the body can respond appropriately.

This detection is passed to the central nervous system (CNS), which then sends a nervous impulse to the arterioles to constrict. This increases the blood pressure and also has the effect of increasing the heart rate.

When blood pressure is increased, the baroreceptors detect this and signal the CNS, which makes the arterioles dilate and reduces blood pressure.

Changes to blood pressure during the onset of exercise

Exercise has the affect of increasing heart rate, which will result in an increased cardiac output, which will have the effect of increasing blood pressure. This can be seen from the equation:

$$BP = Q \times R$$

If cardiac output is increased and the resistance to blood flow does not change then blood pressure will also automatically increase.

A typical blood pressure reading for a person at the onset of exercise would be around 120/80 mmHg.

Initial response of the respiratory system

The respiratory system is responsible for getting oxygen into the body and getting carbon dioxide out of the body. It is described in detail in Chapter 1: Anatomy for sport and exercise. The oxygen is used to help produce energy while we take part in sporting activities. The process of creating energy also produces a waste product called carbon dioxide, which needs to be removed from the body.

Pulmonary ventilation and breathing rate

The amount of air we breathe in and out per minute is called 'pulmonary ventilation' and is given the symbol V_E.

Pulmonary ventilation can be worked out using the following equation:

$$V_E = frequency \times tidal volume$$

Frequency is the number of breaths per minute.

Tidal volume is the volume of air breathed in and out during one breath.

At rest, average breathing rate is around 12 breaths per minute. The average tidal volume is 0.5 l (this will vary depending upon age, gender and size of a person).

Therefore, the average pulmonary ventilation at rest is

$$V_E = 12 \times 0.5$$
$$= 6 litres$$

LEARNER ACTIVITY
Pulmonary ventilation

1 While sitting or lying down count the number of breaths you breathe in during one minute – try to breathe as normally as possible.
2 Write this number down and then work out your pulmonary ventilation using the equation given above.
3 Compare your pulmonary ventilation with that of the rest of the class.

When you start to exercise, you need to take more oxygen into your body for it to be used to help produce energy. At the start of exercise, this increased oxygen demand occurs by breathing at a faster rate and breathing in more air and breathing out more air during each breath (i.e. tidal volume increases).

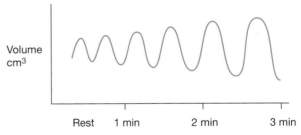

Fig 2.03 Tidal volume increasing

The intercostal muscles are used to aid breathing during exercise.

Intercostal muscles: located between the ribs, there are two kinds of intercostal muscle – internal and external. They help with inspiration and expiration during exercise.

The external intercostal muscles help with inspiration and the internal intercostal muscles help with expiration. As exercise becomes more strenuous, the abdominal muscles will also help aid expiration.

During anaerobic exercises, such as weight lifting, it is not uncommon for people to perform a Valsalva manoeuvre. This is basically the process of breathing out against a closed glottis or against a closed mouth and nose.

LEARNER ACTIVITY
Valsalva manoeuvre

Experience the Valsalva manoeuvre by performing the following exercise.

- Stand up and link both hands together in front of your chest.
- Take a deep breath in and try to pull your hands apart without letting go, pull as hard as you can.

Explain what is happening to your muscles in your chest and how your throat feels while you are carrying out this exercise.

The process of performing the Valsalva manoeuvre while lifting heavy weights helps to stabilise the shoulder girdle and torso. This helps the lifter to move the weight more efficiently. This process produces a marked increase in blood pressure and reduces blood flow to the thoracic cavity. Therefore, any person suffering with high blood pressure or heart problems should avoid this move.

> **definition**
>
> **Thoracic cavity:** the part of the body that is enclosed by the ribcage and the diaphragm and contains the heart and lungs.

Fig 2.04 Weight lifting uses the Valsalva manoeuvre

used to describe the signal travelling from the CNS to the muscle is called an 'action potential'. Nerves that signal muscles to contract are called motor neurones.

> **definition**
>
> **Central nervous system:** consists of the brain and the spinal cord.
> **Motor neurone:** a nerve that signals a muscle to contract.

Initial response of the neuromuscular system

When we want to produce muscle movement we have to get the message from our brain to our muscles. This communication between the brain and muscle is achieved through nerve impulses. A nerve impulse is an electrical current that runs from the central nervous system (CNS) through nerves and then to the muscle tissue, and results in muscle contraction. The term

The neuromuscular junction is the place at which the nerve and muscle meet. The nerve transmits its signal to make the muscle contract in the following manner.

- The pre-synaptic membrane reacts to the signal by its vesicles releasing acetylcholine.
- Acetylcholine diffuses across the gap between the nerve and the muscle (the synaptic cleft) and produces an electrical signal called the excitatory post-synaptic action potential.

- If the excitatory post-synaptic potential is big enough, it will make the muscle tissue contract.
- Once the muscle has carried out its desired movement, the enzyme cholinesterase breaks down the acetylcholine to leave the muscle ready to receive its next signal.

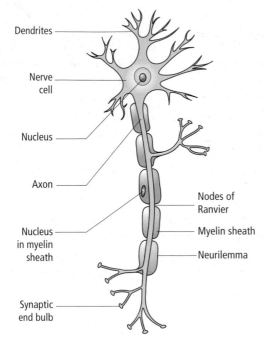

Fig 2.05 Neurone

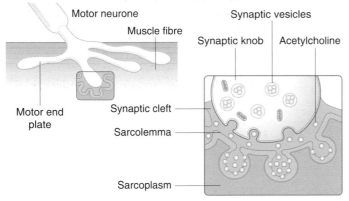

Fig 2.06 The neural transmission process

Motor units

As there are so many muscle fibres, a nerve stimulates more than just one fibre. In fact, it has a group of between 15 and 2000 muscle fibres depending on the muscle it is connected to. This group of muscle fibres is called a motor unit.

When we want to produce muscle movements, we send signals from our CNS to the motor neurones. The strength of the signal determines whether the

signal will reach the motor unit. This is called the 'all or nothing principal', which means that if the strength of the nerve signal is large enough, all of the motor unit will contract. And if the strength of the signal is not big enough, no part of the motor unit will contract. When we exercise, especially when we want to exert high levels of force, our motor units produce muscle contraction at different rates. Therefore you will find that different parts of the muscle are contracting at ever so slightly different times. This has the effect of producing smooth muscle contractions.

Muscle spindles

A muscle spindle is an organ placed within the muscle which communicates with the CNS. The purpose of the muscle spindle is to detect when the muscle is in a state of contraction. When a muscle is contracted it changes the tension on the muscle spindle. This is relayed to the CNS and the CNS can deal with this information accordingly by either increasing the contraction of the muscle or relaxing the muscle.

Initial response of the energy systems

The function of energy systems is to produce adenosine triphosphate (ATP). ATP is used to make our muscles contract and therefore allows us to take part in exercise. It is basically a protein (adenosine) with three (tri) phosphates (phosphate) attached to it.

Fig 2.07 Adenosine triphosphate (ATP)

When chemical bonds are broken, energy is released. Therefore, when a phosphate is broken off the ATP to make ADP (adenosine diphosphate – di = two) energy is released, which is used to make the muscles contract.

ATP is not stored in large amounts in skeletal muscle and therefore has to be continually made from ADP for our muscles to continue contracting. There are three energy systems that the body uses to make ATP. They differ in the rate at which they make ATP. At the onset of exercise we will want ATP supplied

Fig 2.08 Release of energy from ATP

very quickly. However, if we are on a long walk we do not need such a fast production of ATP, so the body uses a different energy system to make it.

Phosphocreatine energy system: at the onset of exercise the energy system that supplies the majority of ATP is the phosphocreatine system (also known as the creatine phosphate system). It supplies ATP much quicker than any other energy system. It produces ATP in the absence of oxygen, and is therefore an anaerobic energy system.

Phosphocreatine (PC) is made up of a phosphate and a creatine molecule. When the bond between the phosphate and the creatine is broken, energy is released which is then used to make the bond between ADP and a phosphate.

PC stores are used for rapid, high-intensity contractions, such as in sprinting or jumping. These stores only last for about ten seconds.

Lactic acid energy system: once our PC stores have run out, we then use the lactic acid system. This is also known as anaerobic glycolysis, which literally means the breakdown of glucose in the absence of oxygen. When glucose is broken down it is converted into a substance called pyruvate. When there is no oxygen present, the pyruvate is converted into lactic acid. This system produces ATP very quickly, but not as quickly as the PC system:

Glucose
↓   No oxygen
Pyruvate ——————————→ ATP + lactic acid

The lactic acid energy system is the one that is producing the majority of the ATP during high-intensity exercise lasting between 30 seconds and three minutes, such as an 800 m race.

Key learning points

- At the onset of exercise the various systems respond to try to increase oxygen delivery, energy production and carbon dioxide removal.
- Cardiovascular system: increased heart rate, increased blood pressure, increased cardiac output.
- Respiratory system: increased pulmonary ventilation, increased breathing rate, increased tidal volume.
- Neuromuscular system: increased number of nerve transmissions, skeletal muscular contraction.
- Energy system: ATP production through phosphocreatine energy system and lactic acid energy system.

Steady-state exercise

Once we have been performing continuous exercise for a period of around 20 minutes, our body reaches a 'steady state'. Continuous exercise includes all forms of exercise that have no stopping periods such as jogging, swimming or cycling. Examples of non-continuous exercise would be weight lifting, interval training and boxing.

definition

Steady state: when the body is working at a steady state it means that lactic acid removal is occurring at the same pace as lactic acid production.

Various changes will have occurred in the body to allow this steady state to occur.

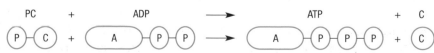

Fig 2.09 Phosphocreatine energy system

Cardiovascular

- Heart rate levels off
- Increased stroke volume
- Vasodilation of blood vessels leading to working muscles
- Blood pressure levels off
- Thermoregulation

Respiratory

- Tidal volume levels off
- Breathing rate levels off
- Oxygen is unloaded from haemoglobin much more readily

Neuromuscular

- Increased pliability of muscles
- Increased speed of neural transmissions

Energy

- Aerobic ATP production

Cardiovascular response to steady-state exercise

Heart rate peaks during the first few minutes of exercise and then levels off.

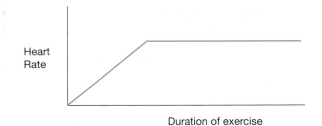

Fig 2.10 Heart rate response during continuous exercise

Stroke volume

While exercising there is an increase in venous return.

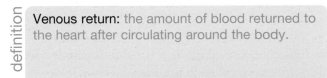

> **Venous return:** the amount of blood returned to the heart after circulating around the body.

This increased volume of blood has the effect of stretching the cardiac muscle to a greater degree than normal. This stretching has the effect of making the heart contract much more forcibly and thereby pumping out more blood during each contraction, so stroke volume is increased during exercise. This effect is known as 'Starling's Law'.

Blood flow

As stated previously, the average cardiac output is around 5 litres per minute. When this blood is circulated around the body, some organs receive more blood than others. However, during exercise, the working muscles need a greater proportion of blood in order to supply them with energy. The body is able to redirect blood flow by constricting the blood vessels leading to organs that do not require such a large blood flow, and dilating the blood vessels feeding the muscles that do. The process of blood vessels constricting is called 'vasoconstriction' and the process of blood vessels dilating is called 'vasodilation'.

> **Constriction:** becoming smaller.
> **Dilation:** becoming larger.

Changes to blood pressure during steady-state exercise

Dilation of the blood vessels feeding the working muscle acts to reduce blood pressure, but this is counteracted by the increase in blood pressure caused by increased cardiac output.

Exercise raises systolic pressure, but there is only a slight change in diastolic pressure.

Immediately after exercise there is a fall in systolic pressure as the skeletal muscular pump is no longer pumping blood from the muscles to the heart. This can lead to blood pooling in the muscles and cause the athlete to faint as not enough blood is being pumped to the brain.

Thermoregulation

Thermoregulation is the process of maintaining a constant body core temperature. In humans this temperature is 37°C. The skin temperature of the body can vary a great deal. If the core temperature is increased or decreased by 1°C or more, this will affect an athlete's physical and mental performance. When exercising we produce a great deal of excess heat. The cardiovascular system is vitally important in ensuring that we are able to lose this excess heat so that our core temperature does not increase. Excess heat is lost

LEARNER ACTIVITY Blood pressure and exercise

Work in groups of three or four.

The equipment you need:

electrical sphygmomanometer   treadmill or cycle ergometer
pen and paper   sports clothes

1 Choose a continuous exercise such as jogging on a treadmill or cycling on an ergometer.
2 Attach the sphygmomanometer to the exercising person and record their resting blood pressure.
3 Your subject should perform 20 minutes of aerobic exercise. Try to ensure that they are exercising at the same intensity throughout the duration of the exercise.
4 After about two minutes of exercise take their blood pressure (ensuring that they continue to exercise throughout).
5 After about 20 minutes of exercise take their blood pressure (ensuring that they continue to exercise throughout).
6 After a break of at least 15 minutes, record your subject's blood pressure.

Results		
Resting blood pressure	(mmHg)	
After 2 minutes of exercise	(mmHg)	
After 20 minutes of exercise	(mmHg)	
After 15 minutes of recovery	(mmHg)	

Copy and complete the table above.

1 What happened to the blood pressure after two minutes of continuous exercise?
2 What happened to the blood pressure after two minutes of continuous exercise?
3 Why did blood pressure increase during exercise?
4 Why was there a difference between the blood pressure readings at two minutes and 20 minutes?

through sweating and dilatation of peripheral blood vessels so that blood passes close to the surface of the skin. As the sweat evaporates, it cools down the skin surface. This has the effect of cooling the blood as it travels through the blood vessels that are close to the skin surface. When we are exercising at a high intensity in hot conditions, between 15 per cent and 25 per cent of the cardiac output is directed to the skin.

Respiratory responses

After having peaked in the first few minutes, if exercise remains at the same intensity, tidal volume and breathing rate level off and remain the same until exercise is terminated.

Oxygen dissociation curve

Only 1.5 per cent of oxygen is carried in the blood plasma. The majority of oxygen is transported in the blood by haemoglobin. Oxygen reacts with haemoglobin to make oxyhaemoglobin. The reaction of oxygen with haemoglobin is temporary and completely reversible. This means that oxygen can be unloaded from haemoglobin. The binding of oxygen to haemoglobin is dependent on the partial pressure of oxygen. Oxygen combines with haemoglobin in oxygen-rich situations, such as in the lungs.

Oxygen is released by haemoglobin in places where there is little oxygen, such as in exercising muscle.

The oxygen dissociation curve is an S-shaped curve that represents the ease with which haemoglobin releases oxygen when it is exposed to tissues of different concentrations of oxygen. The curve starts with a steep rise because haemoglobin has a high affinity for oxygen. This means that when there is a small rise in the partial pressure of oxygen, haemoglobin picks up and binds oxygen to it easily. Thus, in the lungs the blood is rapidly saturated with oxygen. However, only a small drop in the partial pressure of oxygen results in a large drop in the percentage saturation of haemoglobin. Thus, in exercising muscles, where there is a low partial pressure of oxygen, the haemoglobin readily unloads the oxygen for use by the tissues.

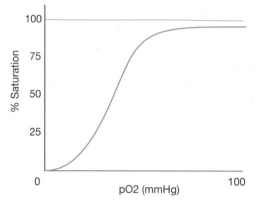

Fig 2.11 Oxygen dissociation curve

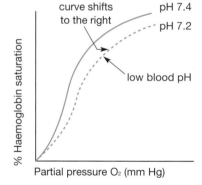

Fig 2.12 Shift in oxygen dissociation curve

Changes in blood carbon dioxide level and hydrogen ion concentration (pH) cause shifts in the oxygen dissociation curve. These shifts enhance oxygen release in tissues and increase oxygen uptake in the lungs. This is know as the Bohr effect, named after the Danish physiologist, Christian Bohr, who discovered it. During exercise, the blood becomes more acidic because of the increased production of carbon dioxide.

This increase in carbon dioxide and decrease in pH shifts the dissociation curve to the right for a given partial pressure of oxygen, releasing more oxygen to the tissues.

In the lungs there is a low partial pressure of carbon dioxide and low hydrogen ion concentration, which shifts the dissociation curve to the left for a given partial pressure of oxygen, and therefore enhances oxygen uptake.

As muscles exercise, they also increase in temperature. This has the effect of shifting the curve to the right, which means oxygen is released much

more readily. Conversely, a decreased temperature shifts the curve to the left, which increases oxygen uptake.

Neuromuscular response

As more blood is pumped through the muscles and excess heat is generated through exercising, muscle tissue warms up. The warmer the muscle tissue becomes, the more pliable it is.

definition

Pliable: able to be stretched, shaped or bent.

This means that the muscle tissue is able to stretch to greater lengths without tearing. You can apply this principle to plasticine. If you take a piece of plasticine out of its container and pull it outwards with two hands, the plasticine will quickly break in two. But if you were to warm the plasticine up by rolling it and warming it in your hands, then pull it apart, you will find it is able to stretch much further without breaking.

As the muscle tissue warms up, the rate at which nervous impulses are sent and received is increased as the heat increases the speed of transmission.

Energy systems response

The aerobic energy system provides ATP at a slower rate than the previous two energy systems discussed. It is responsible for producing the majority of our energy while our bodies are at rest or taking part in low-intensity exercise such as jogging. It uses a series of reactions, the first being aerobic glycolysis as it occurs when oxygen is available to break down glucose. As in the anaerobic energy system, glucose is broken down into pyruvate. Because oxygen is present, pyruvate is not turned into lactic acid, but continues to be broken down through a series of chemical reactions, which include:

- the Krebs Cycle – pyruvate from aerobic glycolysis combines with Coenzyme A (CoA) to form acetyl CoA; acetyl CoA enters the Krebs Cycle which combines and reacts with a number of different compounds to produce ATP, hydrogen and carbon dioxide

- the Electron Transport Chain – the hydrogen atoms produced from the Krebs Cycle enter this chain; the hydrogen atoms are passed along a chain of electron carriers and eventually combine with oxygen to form ATP and water.

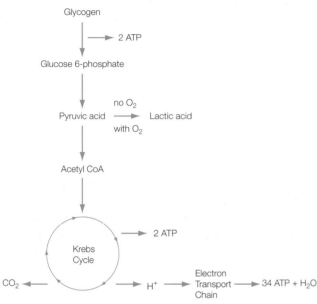

Fig 2.13 Aerobic energy system

Both the Krebs Cycle and the Electron Transport Chain take place in organelles called 'mitochondria'.

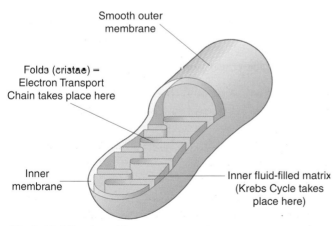

Fig 2.14 Mitochondrion

The majority of ATP is produced in these organelles, so they are very important for energy production. They are rod-shaped and have an inner and outer membrane. The inner membrane is arranged into many folds that project inwards. These folds are called 'cristae' and give a large surface area for energy production to take place.

Key learning points

- When exercising at steady state the body undergoes the following responses.
- Cardiovascular responses: HR levels off, increased stroke volume, vasodilation of blood vessels leading to working muscles, BP levels off.
- Respiratory responses: tidal volume levels off, breathing rate levels off, oxygen is unloaded from haemoglobin much more readily.
- Neuromuscular responses: increased pliability of muscles, increased speed of neural transmissions.
- Energy system responses: aerobic ATP production.

Fatigue and recovery from exercise

We cannot continue to exercise indefinitely because we will eventually fatigue.

definition

Fatigue: tiredness from physical exertion.

Fatigue occurs as a result of a number of factors, including:

- depletion of energy sources, such as reduced quantities of phosphocreatine, glucose and glycogen
- effects of waste produces, such as increased production of lactic acid and carbon dioxide
- neuromuscular fatigue, such as depletion of acetylcholine and reduced calcium ion release.

As a result, it is necessary to rest in order to recover and return the body to its pre-exercise state.

Depletion of energy sources

In order to exercise we must break down the energy stored in our body and turn it into ATP. Sources of energy include phosphocreatine, glucose and glycogen. We have only enough phosphocreatine to last us for ten seconds of maximal exercise. We then switch to glucose for energy production. We have around 15 to 20 g of glucose in our bloodstream, around 345 g of glycogen in our muscles and 90 to 110 g of glycogen stored in our liver. When our blood sugar levels are low, the liver converts either its store of glycogen into glucose or the skeletal muscles' store of glycogen into glucose. We have only enough glycogen stores to last us for around two hours. So once the body's stores of glucose and glycogen are used up we become fatigued and/or have to exercise at a lower intensity.

Effects of waste products

Lactic acid is the main by-product of anaerobic glycolysis. Blood always contains a small amount of lactic acid and during high-intensity exercise this increases greatly. The increased production of lactic acid results in the pH of the blood decreasing. A blood pH of 6.4 or lower affects muscle and neural function and eventually prevents continued exercise.

Onset of blood lactate accumulation (OBLA) is the point at which lactic acid begins to accumulate in the muscles. It is also known as the 'anaerobic threshold'. OBLA is considered to occur somewhere between 85 and 90 per cent of your maximum heart rate.

Neuromuscular fatigue

Neuromuscular fatigue means that the muscles are either not able to receive signals from the CNS that stimulate the muscle to contract or that the muscle tissue is unable to function properly.

High-intensity exercise or exercise for long periods of time can eventually interfere with calcium release, which is required for muscle contraction. If no calcium ions are available the muscle is unable to contract (see Chapter 1: Anatomy for sport and exercise, for more details on the role of calcium ions in muscle contraction).

Alternatively, transmission of nerve impulses can be affected as the availability of acetylcholine can be decreased, which prevents the nervous stimulation reaching the muscle tissue/motor unit.

LEARNER ACTIVITY
Neuromuscular fatigue

Place a heart rate monitor around your chest or take your heart rate by pressing on a pulse point and counting your pulse for one minute. Stand against a wall, then bend your knees and slide down the wall so that your knees are at right angles.

After 30 seconds or one minute count your pulse and remain in the ski squat position. Has your pulse changed significantly?

You will no doubt feel that your legs are very sore and you cannot maintain this position for very long, but your heart rate has not reached maximal values. You have had to stop this exercise because you have experienced neuromuscular fatigue in your quadriceps muscles!

Recovery process

After taking part in any type of exercise the body has to recover and return to its pre-exercise state.

Excess post-exercise oxygen consumption (EPOC) is also referred to as 'oxygen debt'. EPOC is the total oxygen consumed after exercise in excess of pre-exercise levels. It occurs when the exercise performed is totally or partially anaerobic. As a result, energy is supplied by the anaerobic energy systems, which results in lactic acid production. When the person stops exercising, breathing rate remains elevated so that extra oxygen is breathed in to:

- break down lactic acid to carbon dioxide and water
- replenish ATP, phosphocreatine and glycogen
- pay back any oxygen that has been borrowed from haemoglobin and myoglobin.

After a bout of vigorous exercise, five events must happen before the muscle can operate again:

1 ATP must be replaced
2 PC stores must be replenished
3 lactic acid must be removed
4 myoglobin must be replenished with oxygen
5 glycogen stores must be replenished.

The replacement of ATP and PC takes around three minutes and the removal of lactic acid takes around 20 minutes after stopping exercise, but the oxygen replenishment of myoglobin and refilling the glycogen stores take between 24 and 48 hours. If the exercise bout was of a very high intensity then it will take longer to recover. However, the fitter you are the faster you will recover. The faster the debt can be repaid, the sooner the performer can exercise again.

The oxygen debt consists of two separate components:

- the alactacid debt (fast component)
- the lactacid debt (slow component).

Alactacid debt

Alactacid oxygen debt is the process of recovery that does not involve lactic acid. The aerobic energy system is used to produce the ATP required to replenish the PC stores and ATP stores in the body:

$$ADP + P + oxygen \rightarrow ATP$$

$$ATP + C + P \rightarrow PC + ADP$$

Around 50 per cent of the replenishment occurs during the first 30 seconds, while full recovery occurs at about three minutes.

The alactacid oxygen debt ranges between 2 and 3.5 litres of oxygen. The fitter you are, the greater the debt because training increases the PC content within the muscle cells. However, the recovery time of a fitter person is reduced because they have enhanced methods of oxygen delivery, such as increased capilliarisation and an improved cardio-respiratory system. These increase the rate of ATP production from the aerobic energy system.

Lactacid debt

The lactacid oxygen debt takes much longer to complete and can last for minutes or hours, depending on the severity of the exercise. The process involves oxygen, which is required to break down the lactic acid produced during anaerobic glycolysis into pyruvate. Pyruvate can then enter the aerobic energy system and eventually be broken down into carbon dioxide and water.

$$lactic\ acid + oxygen = pyruvate$$

Lactic acid can also be converted in the liver to glycogen and stored either in the liver or in muscle tissue. Research has shown that an active recovery increases the rate of removal of lactic acid, so

walking or slow jogging after a bout of exercise will help to decrease the time it takes to rid the body of lactic acid. An active recovery keeps the heart rate and breathing rate up, which has the effect of increasing the rate of delivery of oxygen to the working muscles. This then helps to rid the body of the lactic acid.

Therefore, a cool-down is very important after any form of activity to maximise recovery. Failure to cool down adequately means that the levels of lactic acid will remain elevated. It is thought that this acidity level affects the pain receptors and contributes to the muscle soreness which people may feel some time after having exercised. This muscle soreness, termed 'delayed onset of muscle soreness' (DOMS), is at its most uncomfortable 36 to 48 hours after exercise has ceased.

Muscle glycogen stores must also be restored. This is attained through a high carbohydrate diet and rest. It can take several days to recover muscle glycogen stores, depending on the intensity of the exercise.

Key learning points

Fatigue occurs because of:

- a depletion of energy sources
- an accumulation of waste products
- lack of calcium ion availability
- decreased availability of acetylcholine.

Recovery after exercise involves taking in excess oxygen in order to return the body to its pre-exercise state.

Alactic phase of recovery: ATP and PC production takes place in the first few minutes of recovery

Lactic phase of recovery: lactic acid is removed and turned into pyruvate and myoglobin stores of oxygen are repleted and glycogen stores are repleted.

An active recovery increases the rate of lactic acid removal.

Adaptation to chronic exercise

Chronic exercise means that a person has been participating in regular exercise for long periods of time (a minimum of eight weeks). This regular participation affects the body in a number of ways that make it more able to cope with the stresses of the

LEARNER ACTIVITY
Recovery from exercise

The equipment you need:

- stopwatch
- running track/gym
- sports clothes

Copy the table drawn below.

Resting pulse rate
Immediately after exercise
1 minute after exercise
2 minutes after exercise
3 minutes after exercise
4 minutes after exercise
5 minutes after exercise

Take your resting pulse rate and make a note of it in the results table.

Take part in some form of intensity exercise that lasts at least five minutes.

Find your pulse, then record your pulse for a ten-second count every minute after the exercise until your heart rate returns to its original level.

Convert your heart rate into beats per minute by multiplying by 6.

Answer the following questions.

1 Explain why your heart rate was different from resting levels immediately after exercise had stopped.
2 Explain why your heart rate remained elevated after three minutes of rest?

exercise. This results in the person being able to exercise at higher intensities and/or for longer periods of time. This process is called adaptation.

Cardiovascular adaptations

The main adaptations that occur to the cardiovascular system through endurance training are concerned with increasing the delivery of oxygen to the working muscles. If you were to dissect the heart of a top endurance athlete, you would find that the size of the walls of the left ventricle are markedly thicker than those of a person who does not perform endurance exercise. This adaptation is called 'cardiac hypertrophy'.

Adaptation occurs in the same way that we increase the size of our skeletal muscles – the more we exercise our muscles, the larger or more toned they become. In the same way, the more we exercise our heart through aerobic training, the larger it will become. This will then have the effect of increasing the stroke volume, which is the amount of blood that the heart can pump out per beat. As the heart wall becomes bigger, it can pump more blood per beat as the thicker wall can contract more forcibly. As the stroke volume is increased, the heart no longer needs to beat as often to get the same amount of blood around the body. This results in a decrease in heart rate which is known as bradycardia.

An average male adult's heart rate is 70 beats per minute (bpm). Miguel Indurain, a Tour de France cyclist, had a resting heart rate of 30 bpm! As stroke volume increases, cardiac output also increases, so an endurance athlete's heart can pump more blood per minute than other people's. However, resting values of cardiac output do not change. An endurance athlete has more capillaries, allowing more blood to travel through them. This process, called capillarisation, aids in the extraction of oxygen. An increase in haemoglobin due to an increase in the number of red blood cells (which contain the haemoglobin) further aids the transport of oxygen. Though haemoglobin content rises, the increase in blood plasma is greater and consequently the blood haematocrit (ratio of red blood cell volume to total blood volume) is reduced, which lowers viscosity (thickness) and enables the blood to flow more easily.

Strength training produces very few adaptations to the cardiovascular system as this training does not stress the heart or oxygen delivery and extraction systems for sustained periods of time.

Respiratory adaptations

The respiratory system deals with taking oxygen into the body and also with helping to remove waste products associated with muscle metabolism. Training reduces the resting respiratory rate and the breathing rate during sub-maximal exercise. Endurance training can also provide a small increase in lung volumes: vital capacity increases slightly, as does tidal volume during maximal exercise. The increased strength of the respiratory muscles is partly responsible for this as it aids lung inflation.

Endurance training also increases the capillarisation around the alveoli in the lungs. This helps to increase the rate of gas exchange in the lungs and, therefore, increase the amount of oxygen entering the blood and the amount of carbon dioxide leaving the blood.

Strength training produces very few adaptations to the respiratory system as this type of training uses the anaerobic energy systems, whereas the respiratory system is only really concerned with the aerobic energy system.

Neuromuscular and energy systems adaptations

Endurance training results in an increase in the muscular stores of muscle glycogen. There is increased delivery of oxygen to the muscles through an increase in the concentration of myoglobin and increased capillary density through the muscle. The ability of skeletal muscle to consume oxygen is increased as a direct result of an increase in the number and size of the mitochondria and an increase in the activity and concentration of enzymes involved in the aerobic processes that take place in the mitochondria. As a result, there is a greater scope to use glycogen and fat as fuels. Slow twitch fibres can enlarge by up to 22 per cent, which gives greater potential for aerobic energy production. Hypertrophy of slow twitch fibres means that there is a corresponding increase in the stores of glycogen and triglycerides. This ensures a continuous supply of energy, enabling exercise to be performed for longer.

These adaptations result in an increased maximal oxygen consumption (VO_2 max) being obtained before the anaerobic threshold is reached and fatigue begins.

High-intensity training results in hypertrophy of fast twitch fibres. There are increased levels of ATP and PC in the muscle and an increased capacity to generate ATP by the PC energy system. This is partly due to the increased activity of the enzymes which break down PC. ATP production by anaerobic glycolysis is increased as a result of enhanced activity of the glycolytic enzymes. There is also an increased ability to break down glycogen in the absence of oxygen.

As lactic acid accumulates, it decreases the pH levels of the blood, making it more acidic. This increased level of hydrogen ions will eventually prevent the glycolytic enzyme functioning. However, anaerobic training increases the buffering capacity of the body and enables it to work for longer in periods of high acidity.

Energy system adaptation

Aerobic training will increase the number of mitochondria in slow twitch muscle fibres. This will allow greater production of ATP through the aerobic energy system. Greater amounts of glycogen can be stored in the liver and skeletal muscle. Aerobic training results in an increase in the number of enzymes required for body fat to be broken down, and more body fat is stored in muscle tissue, which means that more fat can be used as an energy source.

Anaerobic or strength training predominantly uses the PC and lactic acid energy system. Chronic anaerobic/strength training increases the body's tolerance levels to low pH. This means more energy can be produced by the lactic acid energy system, and the increased production of lactic acid can be tolerated for longer.

Skeletal adaptations

Weight-bearing exercise: this is where we are using our body weight as a form of resistance – walking, running, etc.

Our skeleton responds to aerobic weight-bearing exercise or resistance exercise by becoming stronger and more able to withstand impact, which means you are less likely to break a bone if you fall over. This occurs because the stimulation of exercise means the mineral content (calcium in particular) is increased, which makes bones harder and stronger. Exercise also has an affect on joints by increasing the thickness of cartilage at the ends of the bones and increasing the production of synovial fluid. This will have the affect of making joints stronger and less prone to injury. Strength training increases the strength of muscle tendons, which again makes them less prone to injury. Lastly, the ligaments which hold our bones together are able to stretch to a greater degree, which helps to prevent injuries such as joint strains.

Key learning points

Adaptations to aerobic exercise

- Cardiovascular system: cardiac hypertrophy, increased SV, decreased resting HR, increased number of capillaries, increased number of red blood cells, decreased heamatocrit.
- Respiratory system: decreased resting breathing rate, increased lung volume, increased vital capacity, increased tidal volume (in maximal exercise), increased strength of respiratory muscles, increased capillarisation around alveoli.
- Neuromuscular system: increased myoglobin content, increased number of capillaries, increased number of mitochondria, hypertrophy of slow twitch muscle fibres, increased stores of glycogen, increased stores of fat.

- Energy systems: increased number of aerobic enzymes, increased breakdown of fat.

Adaptations to anaerobic exercise

- Cardiovascular system: no significant adaptations.
- Respiratory system: no significant adaptations.
- Neuromuscular: hypertrophy of fast twitch muscle fibres, increased content of ATP, increased content of PC, increased tolerance to lactic acid.
- Energy systems: increased number of anaerobic enzymes.
- Skeletal system: increased strength of bones, increased strength of tendons, increased stretch of ligaments.

Review questions

1 What is the term given to the increase in heart rate before exercise has even started?
2 Why and how does the heart rate increase prior to exercise?
3 What happens to breathing rate during the first few minutes of exercise?
4 Explain the process whereby muscles receive nervous stimulation.
5 How does heart rate and breathing rate respond to steady-state exercise?
6 How is energy supplied to the body at (a) the onset of exercise and (b) at steady state?
7 Why are you less likely to injure yourself when you are exercising at steady state?
8 Why can we not exercise indefinitely?
9 Explain the process of recovery?
10 Explain how the body adapts to aerobic training?
11 Explain how the body adapts to anaerobic training?

References

Beashel, P. (1995) *Advanced Studies in Physical Education and Sport*, Nelson.

Clegg, C. (1995) *Exercise Physiology*, Feltham Press.

Crisfield, P. (1996) *Coaching Sessions: A Guide to Planning and Goal-Setting*, National Coaching Foundation.

Davis, R. J., Bull, C. R., Roscoe, J. V. and Roscoe, D. A. (2000) *Physical Education and the Study of Sport*, London: Mosby.

Dick, F. (1997) *Sports Training Principles*, A & C Black.

Foss, M. and Keteyian, S. (1998) *Fox's Physiological Basis for Exercise and Sport*, McGraw-Hill.

Honeybourne, J., Hill, M. and Moors, H. (2000) *Advanced Physical Education and Sport: for A-level*, Stanley Thornes.

McArdle, W., Katch, F. and Katch, V. (2001) *Exercise Physiology: Energy, Nutrition and Human Performance*, WMS & Wilkins.

Sharkey, B. (1990) *Physiology of Fitness*, Human Kinetics.

Stafford-Brown, J., Rea, S. and Chance, J. (2003) *BTEC Sport and Exercise Science*, Hodder Arnold.

Wesson, K., Wiggans, N., Thompson, G. and Hartigan, S. (2000) *Sport and PE: A Complete Guide to Advanced Level Study*, Hodder Arnold.

Goals

By the end of this chapter you should understand:

- the effect of personality on sports performance
- the relationship between stress, arousal and anxiety and sports performance
- group dynamics in sports teams
- how to plan a psychological skills training programme to enhance sporting performance.

Success in sport is derived from a series of variable factors. The athlete must be prepared physically, have the correct nutritional strategy, and ensure that they are appropriately recovered and in a positive mental state. Sport psychology deals with ensuring that the performer has this correct mental state and is able to control this state during training and training periods.

The value of sport psychology

Sport psychology: the scientific study of individuals and how they behave in sport and exercise environments, and how this knowledge can be applied in a practical and beneficial way.

Through the systematic research and study of individuals in sporting environments it has been possible to gain an insight into what makes certain performers successful. By 'modelling' these effective techniques it has been possible to improve their performance and gain an insight into excellence. Sport psychologists have developed a body of techniques to assist performers in improving their performances and developing consistency.

Sport psychology techniques can be applied to all levels of athletes:

- from giving a beginner the confidence to jump the high jump bar to helping a professional footballer score a penalty in the World Cup final
- helping coaches to produce the best performances from their athletes and stay calm as they watch
- helping fitness trainers to motivate their clients and ensure they keep performing their training routines.

Literally speaking, psychology means the study of (ology) the human mind (psyche). The work of several coaches has shown the value of psychologically preparing athletes: Bill Beswick in football, Stephen Bull with the English cricket team during the successful 2005 Ashes series, and Jos Vanstiphort with golfers Ernie Els and Retief Goosen.

The key in preparing performers mentally is understanding that we actually have control over our mind and how we think. Because we have this control we can use it either to our advantage or disadvantage. Consider the situation when we buy a new computer and it comes with a long manual about how to assemble it and work it. Some people will throw away the manual and work it out for themselves. This may or may not be successful and they will certainly never use the computer to its full capability. Other people will spend time and effort reading the manual and then applying this information to the computer. They will have a much better understanding of how it functions and its capacity. Sport psychology has been called 'a user's manual for the brain' because it helps us to understand how the brain works and what it is capable of doing. Once we gain control over our brain the possibilities are limitless.

Interesting facts about the brain

- 95 per cent of all that we know about how the brain works has been discovered in the last ten years.
- Brain cells are so tiny you can fit 10,000 of them on to a single pinhead.
- Each of your brain cells is more powerful than a standard computer.

- If we represented the size of the world's most powerful computer as a two-storey house the potential power of your brain would be represented by a building reaching to the moon and ten blocks square at the bottom.
- The human brain can generate thousands of new brain cells every day.

(Adapted from *The Ultimate Book of Mind Maps* by Tony Buzan, 2005)

Personality

The key concept that underpins all studies in sport psychology is personality. It is clear that each person has the same brain structure and that their senses will all work in the same way to provide the brain with information. However, each person appears to be different in the decisions they make and how they behave in specific situations. Personality looks at these individual differences and how they affect performance.

There is a range of definitions of personality, each with their merits and drawbacks. It has been suggested that we all have traits and behaviour that we share with other people, but we also have some particular to ourselves. However, this idea does lack depth of information. As does Cattell's (1965) attempt to define personality: 'that which tells what a man will do when placed in a given situation'.

This suggests that if we know an individual's personality we can predict behaviour. However, human beings tend to be less than predictable and can act out of character, depending upon the situation. Their behaviour may also be affected by their mood, fatigue or emotions.

Hans Eysenck (1964) sought to address the limitations of previous definitions: 'The more or less stable and enduring organisation of an individual's character, temperament, intellect and physique which determines their unique adjustment to the environment.' Eysenck's statement that personality is more or less stable allows the human element to enter the equation and explain the unpredictable. He also makes the important point that personality is 'unique'. We may have behaviour in common with other people, but ultimately every person has a set of characteristics unique to themselves.

In summary, most personality theories state the following: personality is the set of individual characteristics that make a person unique and will determine their relatively consistent patterns of behaviour.

LEARNER ACTIVITY
Personality characteristics

Choose one of the following groups of sportspeople. In pairs, discuss what personality characteristics each person has, based on your observations of their behaviour and interviews you have seen with them.

Football
Wayne Rooney
John Terry
Steven Gerrard
Rio Ferdinand
Joe Cole

Tennis
Roger Federer
Andrew Murray
Maria Sharapova
Rafael Nadal
Amelie Mauresmo

Golf
Colin Montgomery
Tiger Woods
Sergio Garcia
Phil Mickelson
Darren Clarke

Rugby Union
Matt Stevens
Paul O'Connell
Danny Grewcock
Brian O'Driscoll
Shane Williams

Athletics
Paula Radcliffe
Mark Lewis-Francis
Marlon Devonish
Ashia Hansen
Phillip Idowu

Answer the following questions.

- Are there personality characteristics they have in common?
- Are these characteristics important in their sport?
- Can these characteristics explain their success?

By giving labels to a person's character and behaviour, you have started to assess personality. By observing sportspeople we are using a behavioural approach – assessing what they are like by assessing their responses to various situations. In reality, our observations may be unreliable because we see sportspeople in only one environment, and although we see them interviewed as well, we do not know what they are truly like. A cognitive psychologist believes we need to understand an individual's thoughts and emotions as well as watching their behaviour. This we cannot do without the use of a questionnaire or an interview.

Introduction to personality theories
Matt Jarvis

Matt Jarvis (2006) identifies four factors that will determine how an individual responds in a specific situation:

- our genetic make-up – the innate aspect of our personality which we inherit from our parents
- our past experiences – these are important because if we have acted in a certain way in the past and it had a successful outcome, then it is likely we will act the same way in the future; or if we have had a negative experience in the past then the same experience in the future will be seen as being threatening or stressful
- the nature of the situation in which we find ourselves – this will cause us to adapt our behaviour in a way which suits the situation
- free will – a difficult concept in psychology and it suggests we have control over our thinking and thus our behaviour; it can be difficult to separate whether a person has chosen to behave in that way or is programmed by their genetics or past experiences.

LEARNER ACTIVITY
Your behaviour

Consider your own personality and give an example of an occasion when you felt your behaviour was the result of:

- your genetic make-up
- your past experiences
- the situation in which you found yourself
- free will.

Martens' schematic view of personality

Martens views personality as having three different depths or layers.

- Level 1 – the psychological core is the deepest component of personality and is at its centre. It

includes an individual's beliefs, attitudes, values and feelings of self-worth. It is 'the real you' and, as a result, it is relatively permanent and seen by few people.
- Level 2 – typical responses are how we usually respond to situations and adapt to our environment. It is seen as the relatively consistent way we behave. Our typical responses are good indicators of our psychological core, but they can be affected by the social environment. A person who is very outgoing and sociable with his rugby-playing friends may become more reserved at a party with people he does not know.
- Level 3 – role-related behaviour is the shallowest level of our personality, and this level shows how we change our behaviour to adapt to the situation we are in. For example, throughout the day we may play the roles of sportsperson, student, employee, friend, son/daughter, coach, etc. In order to survive we need to adapt our personalities, as it would not be appropriate to behave on the sports field in the same manner as when studying in class. We need to modify our personalities to suit the situation.

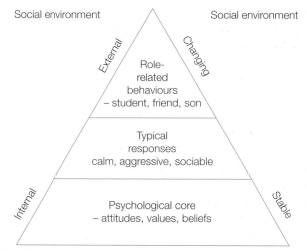

Fig 3.01 Martens' personality levels

Sheldon's constitutional theory

One of the first attempts at a theory of personality was Sheldon's constitutional or body-type theory. He tried to relate personality to somatotypes.

This theory has gathered some 'folklore' validity in that we use first impressions to make assumptions about people's personalities. We use physique, clothing, hairstyles, piercing/tattoos and other visual information to assess what a person will be like and how they will behave.

In sport we see certain body types attracted to certain sports, and to be successful in these sports they need to exhibit certain behaviour. Thus we make generalisations about the personalities of these sportspeople. For example, we have long-distance runners or cyclists who are predominantly ectomorphic, and we see them as being introverted and shy (traits needed because many hours of training are spent alone). We have rugby players and footballers who are predominantly mesomorphic and tend to be extroverted and group-centred (traits needed in order to work together with team-mates).

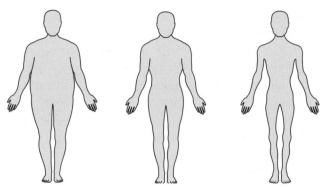

Fig 3.02 The three body types: endomorph, mesomorph, ectomorph

Physique may play a part in personality and behaviour, but people should not be stereotyped. It should not be assumed that people of certain statures will behave in certain ways, and physique cannot be used to assess success in sport. Above all, it cannot be used to assess individual differences between people, and ignores the uniqueness of each person. This theory is not so prominent today.

Trait theory

The trait approach to personality relates to the first factor of personality. Jarvis (2006) identifies that personality is based in genetics. This is called the nature approach and says we inherit personality at birth. This has some validity. For example, we can observe how different babies have different personalities from a young age. A trait is defined as 'a relatively stable way of behaving', suggesting if a person shows a trait of shyness in one situation then they will be shy across arrange of situations. Across a population the traits people have are the same, but they show them to a greater or lesser extent and this dictates their personality. This theory was very popular in the 1960s, but it is continually criticised for not considering that the situation may influence an individual's behaviour.

Social learning theory

Social learning theory, or the situational approach, takes the view that personality is determined by the environment and the experiences a person has as they grow up. Other theories (e.g. trait) take the nature or biological approach to personality in that they see it as being largely genetic or inherited. The social learning theory sees personality as the result of nurture or past experiences.

Richard Cox (1998) outlines the two mechanisms of learning: modelling and social reinforcement.

- Modelling: as we grow up we observe and imitate the behaviour of significant others in our lives. At first, this is our parents and siblings, then our friends, teachers, sports stars and anyone we regard as a role model. We often hear sportspeople, such as Michael Owen and David Beckham, being praised for being good role models to young people. This means that their conduct is good to observe and imitate.
- Social reinforcement: this means that when behaviour is rewarded positively it is more likely that it will be repeated. Conversely, behaviour negatively rewarded is less likely to be repeated. At an early age our parents teach us right and wrong by positively or negatively rewarding behaviour.

Table 3.01 Body types and personality

Body type	Description	Personality type
Endomorph	Predominantly fat or pear-shaped	Sociable, friendly, fun loving
Mesomorph	Predominantly muscular	Outgoing, confident, risk taking, adventure loving
Ectomorph	Predominantly lean or linear	Tense, shy, introverted, socially inhibited

In sport there is a system of negative reinforcement to discourage negative behaviour on the sports field. Thus, rugby players get sent to the sin bin, cricketers get fined part of their match fee and footballers get shown yellow and red cards. In particular, this theory shows why people behave differently in different situations. For example, an athlete may be confident and outgoing in a sporting setting but shy and quiet in an educational setting. The athlete may have chosen positive role models in the sporting environment and had their successful performances rewarded. In the educational setting they may have modelled less appropriate behaviour and had their behaviour negatively rewarded.

The interactional approach

The trait theory of personality is criticised for not taking into account the situation which determines behaviour. The situational approach is criticised because research shows that while situation influences some people's behaviour, other people will not be influenced in the same way. The interactional approach considers the person's psychological traits and the situation they are in as equal predictors of behaviour.

behaviour = f (personality, environment)

Thus, we can understand an individual's behaviour by assessing their personality traits and the specific situation they find themselves in. Bowers (1973) says the interaction between a person and their situation could give twice as much information as traits or the situational approach alone.

An interactional psychologist would use a trait–state approach to assess an individual's personality traits and then assess how these traits affect their behaviour in a situation (state). For example, an athlete who exhibited high anxiety levels as a personality trait would have an exaggerated response to a specific situation.

Neither personality traits nor situations alone are enough to predict an individual's behaviour. We must consider both to get a real picture.

Type A and type B personalities

A questionnaire written by Meyer Friedman and Ray Rosenman in 1959 was initially developed to identify people who were prone to stress and stress-related illnesses. However, it has some application to sport and exercise.

Type Bs will exhibit the opposite types of behaviour to type As. In sport we see both personality types being equally successful. However, with people exercising recreationally, we see higher levels of retention on their exercise programmes. Type As would benefit from exercise as it promotes type B-related behaviour. Type A behaviour is seen as causing a rise in a person's blood pressure and then increasing the risk of coronary heart disease (CHD).

Type A behaviour
- highly competitive and strong desire to succeed
- achievement orientated
- eat fast, walk fast, talk fast and have a strong sense of urgency
- aggressive, restless and impatient
- find it difficult to delegate and need to be in control
- experience high levels of stress

Type B behaviour
- less competitive
- more relaxed
- delegate work easily
- take time to complete their tasks
- calm, laid back and patient
- experience low levels of stress

Personality and sports performance

The majority of research using trait theory was done in the 1970s and 1980s. Table 3.02 overleaf summarises this research.

Motivation

If a sport psychologist were asked why athletes of similar talents achieve different levels of performance, they would consider several factors, such as personality and ability to cope with stress. However, if one subject could be said to influence everything in sport psychology it would be motivation – the reasons why we do what we do and behave and respond in the manner particular to us.

Psychologists would say that there is a reason for everything we do in life, and some of these motives are conscious and some are unconscious. As a result, it can be difficult to assess our own motivating factors, let alone anyone else's.

Table 3.02 Trait theory research

Name of researcher/s	Questionnaire used and groups studied	Research findings
Schurr, Ashley and Joy (1977)	16PF – 1500 American students	Athletes versus non-athletes. Athletes were more: • independent • objective • relaxed Athletes who played team sports were: • more outgoing and warm hearted (A) • less intelligent (B) • more group dependent (Q2) • less emotionally stable (C) Athletes who played individual sports were: • more group dependent (Q2) • less anxious (Q4) • less intelligent (B)
Francis et al. (1998)	EPQ – 133 female hockey players versus non-athlete students	Hockey players were: • more extroverted • higher in psychoticism.
Ogilvie (1968)	16PF – athletes versus non-athletes	Athletic performance is related to: • emotional stability • tough-mindedness • conscientiousness • self-discipline • self-assurance • trust • extroversion • low tension
Breivik (1996)	16PF – 38 elite Norwegian climbers	Research showed: • high levels of stability • extroversion • adventure seeking
Williams (1980)	Female athletes versus female non-athletes	Athletes were: • more independent • more aggressive and dominant • more emotionally stable

(From Weinberg and Gould, 2003)

Motivation is important to coaches and managers as they seek to get the best performances out their athletes. Jose Mourinho and Alex Ferguson are two football managers who are also seen as being great motivators of people.

Motivation can be a difficult subject to pin down and deal with because it is not steady and constant and depends on many factors. Most people will experience fluctuations in motivation. Some days they are fully prepared for the competition mentally, and on other days they just cannot seem to get themselves in the right frame of mind. This applies to all things we may do in a day, as sometimes it takes all our powers of motivation just to get out of bed!

> **definition**
>
> **Motivation:**
> 'Motive – a desire to fulfil a need' (Cox, 1998)
> 'The internal mechanisms which arouse and direct behaviour' (Sage, 1974)
> 'The direction and intensity of one's effort' (Sage, 1977)

When examining motivation five terms come up again and again.

- Fulfilling a need – all motivation arises as we seek to fulfil our needs. These may be basic biological needs such as finding food and shelter, or more sophisticated needs such as self-esteem or the need to belong and be loved.
- Internal state – a state is 'how we feel at any point in time' and this will be subject to change. As we see and feel things they will trigger an internal state which will need actions to fulfil any needs.
- Direction – the direction of effort refers to the actions we take to move towards what we feel motivated by and feel we need.
- Intensity – the intensity of effort refers to how much effort the person puts in to achieving their goal or into a certain situation.
- Energise behaviour – this shows how the power of the brain and the thoughts we have can give us the energy we need to produce the behaviour that is required to be successful in a certain situation.

Intrinsic and extrinsic motivation

To expand on Sage's definition, we can see motivation as coming from internal mechanisms or sources inside the body. We can call these intrinsic factors, or rewards coming from the activity itself. These include motives such as fun, pleasure, enjoyment, feelings of self-worth, excitement and self-mastery. They are the reasons why we do a sport and keep doing it.

> **Those who are intrinsically motivated engage in an activity for the pleasure and satisfaction they experience while learning, exploring or trying to understand something new. (Weinberg and Gould, 2003)**

The external stimuli, also called extrinsic rewards, come from sources outside the activity. This would include the recognition and praise we get from other people, such as our coach, friends and family. It could also be the approval we get from the crowd who support us. Extrinsic motivating factors would also include trophies, medals, prizes, records and any money derived from success.

> **Those who are extrinsically motivated engage in the activity because of the valued outcome rather than the interest in the activity solely for itself. (Weinberg and Gould, 2003)**

Views of motivation

Just as there are many views of personality, the same is so in examining motivation. In particular, we can examine the effect of the individual (trait) and the situation on motivation and then how the two factors interact.

The personality view

This is called the 'trait-centred view' and shows that motivation is the result of an individual's personality and how they think. For example, some sportspeople appear to be highly driven to succeed and will do anything they can to achieve their aim. Other people will be happy to let things pass them by and are unconcerned with their success or failure. These personal factors will also include the individual needs and goals a person may have as these will drive their behaviour. However, it is clear that the individual will still be affected by the support they receive and they will retain their motivation only if they have positive experiences. This can be related to the environments a person finds themselves in. For example, at school our interest in a subject was either stimulated or dampened by the quality of the teaching we received.

The situation view

Clearly, the situation we find ourselves in has a major influence on our motivation level. This can explain why a person may be highly motivated on the football field but less so in the classroom. Motivation can be influenced by the attractiveness of the environment and whether it is a comfortable place to be, or the style of the teacher or coach and the motives of the other people in the environment. It is possible, however, that the environment has no effect on a person if their own motives are so strong. You may have found a situation where you did not get on with the coach or did not like the environment, but because the outcome mattered so much to you you were successful despite this.

The interactional view

As in examining personality, we need to take a broader viewpoint when studying motivation, to consider both the personality of an individual and the situation they are operating within. The interactional viewpoint considers both these factors and says that if you want to get the most out of yourself and other people you have to put the right people in the right situations. This is important in both sport and exercise settings in getting the right fit between performers and activities. For a performer to be successful, they need the right internal motivating factors, the right environment and the right support and direction.

Aggression

Aggression in sport is a constant topic of discussion among performers and in newspapers. In most sports there is physical contact, and the line between what is acceptable and not acceptable is very thin. However, there is also scope for verbal and emotional aggression as well as physical aggression. Most famously, we saw Zinedine Zidane commit an act of physical aggression on Marco Matterazzi in the 2006 World Cup final. We could say the physical aggression used was the result of verbal aggression on the Italian's part.

Fig 3.03 Aggression in sport

Personal factors →	Interactional view	← Situational factors
Personality	Motivation	Environment
Goals		Leader support and style
Needs		Other participants

LEARNER ACTIVITY Intrinsic or extrinsic motivation

Consider each of the following statements made by athletes as to why they are motivated, and decide whether it is an intrinsic or extrinsic motivating factor.

I want to win medals.
I want to earn an England cap.
I want to reach my full potential.
I want to make money.
I want to play in a good team.
I want to play in front of large crowds.
I want to give the public enjoyment.
I want to feel good about my performance.
I want to be recognised by the public for my ability.
I want to feel mastery in my own ability.
I want to feel the joy of winning.

In reality sport and the societies it is played within have become less aggressive because the threshold of what we see as being acceptable behaviour has risen. Violent acts have decreased in football as the number of cautionable offences has increased. In rugby union players can face punishment after a match if a violent act is cited by the opposition. This theory was well illustrated in the World Cup quarter-final match between Portugal and Holland when the Russian referee, Valentine Ivanov, booked 16 players and sent off four.

In general life we refer to a range of behaviour where a person is being over-physical as being aggressive. Often these actions are mislabelled. Baron and Richardson (1994) defined aggression as 'any form of behaviour directed towards the goal of harming or injuring another living being who is motivated to avoid such treatment.'

LEARNER ACTIVITY
Your aggression

Think of two occasions when you behaved aggressively on the sports field.

- What caused you to be aggressive in this situation? Were you provoked? Was it to gain an advantage, or could you just not help it?
- What effect did it have on the outcome of the game? Did it improve your chances of victory, have no effect, or decrease your chances of victory?

If you have never behaved aggressively, think of two occasions when you witnessed aggressive acts.

Discuss your answers with a partner and then contribute them to a class discussion.

In sport psychology aggression has a specific meaning: aiming to harm or injure an opponent to gain an advantage, rather than playing in a hard manner. Gill (2000) gives us four criteria which must all be met to allow us to label an action as aggressive.

1 There must be a physical or verbal behaviour.
2 It must involve causing harm or injury, whether it is physical or psychological.
3 It must be directed towards another living thing.
4 There must be the intention to cause harm or injury.

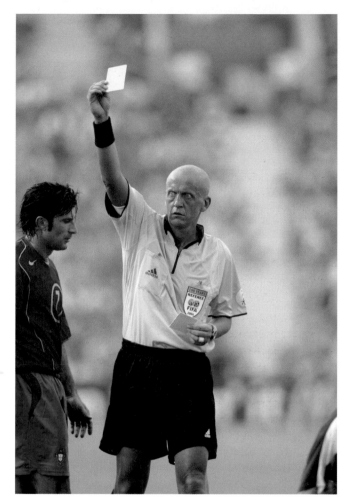

Fig 3.04 Referee cautioning a player

To summarise, aggression must actually involve a behaviour that is either physical or verbal in nature. Rather than just thinking or feeling that you want to do something, there must be an action. The result of the aggressive action can be experienced either physically or psychologically (emotionally) and it must result in harm or damage to another person. While an act of physical aggression, such as throwing a punch, has a clear outcome of harm, so can saying something hurtful or offensive to another person. It is important that the actions are carried out on another living thing because only they have feelings. So to throw your bat down when you are out is not an aggressive act, although it might be seen as unacceptable behaviour. Finally, the most difficult aspect is that the act to cause harm must be intentional. If harm is caused by accident then it is not aggressive, but if there is intent to cause harm it clearly is aggressive. The reason this is difficult is because only the individual knows what their intentions are and the officials have to make a judgement on their intention.

> **An aggressive act:** when an individual intentionally causes physical or psychological harm to another living being.

LEARNER ACTIVITY
Aggressive or not?

Look at the following examples and decide whether they are aggressive or not.

1 A footballer who has been hurt in a tackle kicks their opponent.
2 A runner elbows a competitor during an 800 m race in order to get in front of them.
3 A boxer lands a punch which knocks their opponent to the ground.
4 A rugby player tackles an opponent and lands on top of them, causing their ribs to be bruised.
5 A hockey player smashes their stick into an opponent's nose by mistake.
6 A bowler hits the batsman on the helmet with a bouncing delivery.
7 A rugby player tramples on an opponent's head in a ruck.
8 In going for a cross, two players collide causing a blood wound to each other's heads.
9 An ice hockey player swears at an opponent who makes an illegal challenge.
10 A tennis player kicks a ball away in a moment of rage.

You should be starting to realise that aggression has grey areas. We cannot tell whether an act is aggressive unless we know the motives of the person who produces the act. Plenty of sportspeople are injured, but not necessarily through acts of aggression. In order to be more specific about this area we need to split aggressive acts into three distinct categories.

- Assertive acts: when a person plays with high energy and emotion but within the rules of the game. For example, a footballer puts in hard, uncompromising tackles, or a tennis player is playing in a very tough and upbeat manner but always within the rules. This is assertive play because it is not intended to do any harm or cause any injury to their opponent, and uses force that is legitimate and within the rules.

- Instrumental aggression: when acts of aggression are used to achieve a non-aggressive goal, such as improving a team's chances of victory, they are not usually accompanied by feelings of anger. For example, if you target the opposition's star player for rough treatment by one of your team, but you are willing to accept the punishment, then you are committing instrumental aggression. This also explains the sport of boxing, where the aim is to hurt your opponent to win the fight, rather than because you do not like your opponent. Also, in a rugby scrum, ruck or maul, players use a legitimate amount of force, but this may actually harm or injure an opponent.

- Hostile aggression: an act where the primary goal is to inflict harm or injury on an opponent purely for the sake of it, usually accompanied by feelings of anger. It often occurs when an individual is continually blocked from achieving a goal and their frustration and anger build up. For example, if a player is continually fouled or verbally abused they may eventually respond aggressively as a result.

LEARNER ACTIVITY
Categories of aggression

Go back to the previous activity and, based on the above information, categorise each action as assertive, instrumental or hostile aggression.

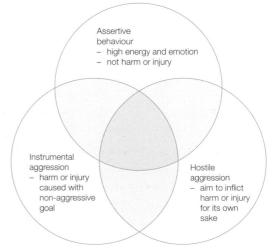

Fig 3.05 Categories of aggression

Theories of aggression

Instinct theory

This theory says that all people have an instinctive, inborn need or tendency to be aggressive. This theory is based on the work of Sigmund Freud in the early twentieth century. He defined an instinct as 'an innate tendency to behave in a certain way'. An innate response is one that we have been born with rather than one that has been learnt through experience. He said that man has two opposing instincts: the life instinct and the death instinct. He saw aggression as an innate instinct to ensure survival of human beings and part of the death instinct.

Aggressive behaviour is not always inevitable; it can be directed towards another person or it can be displaced. This release of aggression is called catharsis. People will say they play rugby or football at the weekend to get rid of the tension and aggression that builds up during the week. Other people will go swimming or running to achieve the same release of aggressive tendencies in a socially acceptable manner. This theory has also been used to explain why people fight at football matches as an outlet for their aggression, albeit in a less socially acceptable manner.

There is little research to support this theory, and it cannot explain why some people are more aggressive than others. Indeed, you may know some people who never show aggressive behaviour. It also differs across cultures and this suggests there must be external influences which make the chances of aggression more likely.

Social learning theory

This theory offers an opposing view to the instinct theory and says that aggression is learnt through modeling and imitative behaviour, rather than being an inborn instinct. Albert Bandura (1973) conducted research involving groups of children watching groups of adults playing with a doll. The children who watched the adults punching and beating up the doll produced this reaction more than the group who watched the adults playing passively with the doll. This aggressive behaviour was increased when the children were positively rewarded for their actions.

Ice hockey has attracted a lot of research due to the regularity of fighting and fouling in the sport. Smith (1988) found that the violence in the game is the result of young amateur players modelling the professionals' behaviour.

It is easy to see how a young footballer may learn to be aggressive. At a football match he sees a player making hard tackles, some of which are illegal and dangerous, and being cheered on by the crowd and his coach. The harder the player tackles, the more praise he gets and he develops a following among fans who like this type of player. The young footballer learns that this is a positive way to behave and mimics the play in his own matches. Research has shown that aggressive acts are more likely to be imitated if produced by a person of the same sex and if they are witnessed live rather than on television or in cartoon form.

Social learning theory is a very convincing theory, and we can see how the levels of aggression in sport are accompanied by rises in the level of violence in society, particularly on television and in films. However, it fails to explain how people can witness the same events and yet the majority of them will not produce an aggressive response, while a minority will mimic the behaviour. For example, a boxing match will have a cathartic effect on some supporters and will cause an aggressive response in others. It comes back to personality type and brings in the instinct theory.

Frustration–aggression theory

This theory states that aggression is the direct result of frustration that has built up due to goal blockage or failure. This theory was first proposed by Dollard *et al.* (1939), who claimed frustration would always produce aggression. However, in 1989, Berkowitz refined this theory by saying that frustration will lead to anger rather than aggression, particularly if we feel we have been unfairly treated, but we will not always produce an aggressive action. He went on to say that an aggressive action is more likely if aggressive cues are present (things related to aggression), but a person may be able to control their anger.

Table 3.03 overleaf summarises the research and findings in this area.

Stress, arousal and anxiety

Stress is usually talked about in negative terms. People complain that they have too much stress or are 'stressed out'. Sportspeople claim the stress of competition is too much for them. However, we should not see stress as an entirely negative thing because it provides us with the mental and physical energy to motivate us into doing things and doing them well.

Stressors are anything that causes us to have a stress response and these are invariably different for different people. If we did not have any stress in our lives, we might not bother to do anything all day. We need stressors to give us the energy and direction to get things done. Without any stress we would become bored and psychologically stale. This type of positive stress is called eustress (good stress). If we have too much stress is can become damaging and we call this distress (bad stress).

Eustress *good stress*
Gives us energy
  and direction
Helps us be fulfilled
  and happy

Distress *bad stress*
Causes discomfort
Can lead to illness
Can cause depression

Too much stress in our lives over a long period of time can seriously damage our health, causing coronary heart disease, high blood pressure, ulcers, impotence, substance addiction, mental health problems and suicidal tendencies.

Sport is a source of stress for some sportspeople. This is related to the experience of the performer, the importance of the competition, the quality of the opposition, the size of the crowd or previous events. The stress response will be specific to the individual.

LEARNER ACTIVITY
Your own stress
Think of a recent competition that you very much wanted to win. Try to recall how you felt before this competition started.

The feelings you had are the symptoms of stress, and they can be separated into physical (the effects on your body), mental (the effect on your brain) and behavioural (how your behaviour changed).

> **Stress:** any factor which changes the natural state of the body.

The classic definition of stress sees the body as having a natural equilibrium or balance, when the heart rate is at its resting level, the breathing rate at its resting level, and blood pressure at normal levels. Anything that changes these natural levels is a stressor. Theoretically, we could say we become stressed as soon as we get out of bed, as our heart rate, breathing rate and blood pressure all rise. Indeed, to some people the alarm going off is a real source of stress!

The stress process

McGrath (1970) sees the stress response as a process and defines stress as 'a substantial imbalance between demand (physical and psychological) and response capability, under conditions where failure to meet the demand has important consequences'.

Table 3.03 Aggression–performance relationship

Name of psychologist/s	Nature of study	Outcomes of study
Widmeyer (1984)	A range of sports	Aggression facilitates performance in sport
Gill (2000)	A range of sports	Found no correlation between aggression and success
Lefebre and Passer (1974)	Belgian football	Found losing teams received more yellow cards for fouls than winning teams
Underwood and Whitwood (1980)	English First Division	No difference in the number of fouls committed by winning and losing teams

Stress will occur when the person does not feel they have the resources to deal with the situation and that this will have bad consequences.

Causes of stress

The causes of stress are many and varied, but crucially they are specific to an individual. For example, you can have two people in the same event, each with a different stress response.

> **LEARNER ACTIVITY** Your own causes of stress
>
> Make a list of things which cause you stress. These may be related to the sports you play or other things in general life.

The sources of stress can generally be divided into four categories.

- Internal: things we think about such as past memories and experiences, current injuries, past injuries, our own feelings of self-worth, and so on.
- External: things in our surroundings and our environment, such as competition, our opponents, the crowd, the weather, spiders and snakes, transport problems.
- Personal factors: people we share our lives with such as friends, family, partners; and life factors such as money and health.
- Occupational factors: the job we do, the people we work with and our working conditions. In sport it could include our relationships with team-mates and coaches/managers.

Stress levels also depend upon personality. Those people who have a predominantly type A personality will find more situations stressful, as will people who have a high N score using Eysenck's personality inventory.

The physiology of stress

When we perceive ourselves to be in a situation which is dangerous, our stress response is activated. This has been developed as a means of ensuring our survival by making us respond to danger. For example, if we are walking home at night through dark woods and we hear noises behind us our body will instigate physiological changes, called the 'fight or flight'

Stage 1

Cause of stress

An emotional demand places physical or psychological pressure

Stage 2

Individual perception of demand

The person produces an individual view of the situation and whether it is threatening to them

Stage 3

Stress response

Production of physical and psychological changes in the individual

Stage 4

Behaviour consequences

Any positive or negative changes in performance resulting from the perceived threat

Fig 3.06 The four stages of the stress process

response, as the body is preparing to turn and fight the danger or run away as fast as it can.

The response varies depending upon how serious we perceive the threat to be. The changes take place in our involuntary nervous system which consists of two major branches:

- the sympathetic nervous system
- the parasympathetic nervous system.

The sympathetic nervous system produces the stress response and its aim is to provide the body with as much energy as it can to confront the threat or run away from it. The sympathetic nervous system works by releasing stress hormones, adrenaline and cortisol, into the bloodstream. The sympathetic nervous system produces the effects listed in Fig 3.07 overleaf.

The parasympathetic nervous system produces the relaxation response, its aim being to conserve energy. It is activated once the stressor has passed.

Involuntary nervous system

Sympathetic nervous system	Parasympathetic nervous system
increased adrenaline production	decreased adrenaline production
increase in heart rate	slowed heart rate
increase in breathing rate	slower breathing rate
increased metabolism	slower metabolism
increased heat production	lower body temperature
muscle tension	muscle relaxation
dry mouth	dry skin
dilated pupils	smaller pupils
hairs on the skin stand on end (to make us look bigger)	
digestive system slows down	digestion speeded up
diversion of blood away from internal organs to the working muscles	

Fig 3.07 The involuntary nervous system

It is not healthy for the body to be in a constant state of stress because of the activation of the sympathetic nervous system. The excess production of adrenaline is dangerous because the body requires more cholesterol to synthesise adrenaline. This excess cholesterol production raises blood cholesterol levels and is a risk factor for coronary heart disease (CHD).

Symptoms of stress

Stress has a threefold effect on the body causing cognitive (mental), somatic (physical) and behavioural responses as outlined in Table 3.04.

Arousal and anxiety

Arousal and anxiety are terms related to stress. Arousal is seen as being a positive aspect of stress and shows how motivated we are by a situation. The more aroused we become the more interested and excited we are by a situation. We can see this when we watch a football match involving a team we support. We are so aroused that we are engrossed in the action to the point where we don't hear noises around us and time seems to go very quickly. During a match that does not arouse us to the same extent we find that our attention drifts in and out as we are distracted by things happening around us.

We can look at levels of arousal on a continuum which highlights the varying degrees of arousal:

Arousal and attention span

As arousal levels increase, they can affect a performer's attention span. If a performer has a broad attention span they are able to pick up information from a wide field of vision. The more narrow the attention span becomes, the less information the performer will pick up and the more they will miss. The attention span can be too broad as the performer may try to pick up too much information.

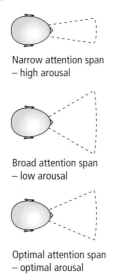

Narrow attention span
– high arousal

Broad attention span
– low arousal

Optimal attention span
– optimal arousal

Fig 3.08 Three attention spans

| Deep sleep | Mild interest | Attentive | Absorbed | Engrossed | Frenzied |

Table 3.04 Symptoms of stress

Cognitive response	Somatic response	Behavioural response
Reduced concentration	Racing heart rates	Talking, eating and walking quickly
Less interested	Faster breathing	Interrupting conversations
Unable to make decisions	Headaches	Increased smoking, drinking and eating
Sleep disturbances	Butterflies in the stomach	
Making mistakes	Chest tightness and pains	Fidgeting
Unable to relax	Dry cotton mouth	Lethargy
Quick losses of temper	Constant colds and illness	Moodiness and grudge-bearing
Loss of sense of humour	Muscular aches and pains	Accidents and clumsiness
Loss of self-esteem	Increased sweating	Poor personal presentation
Loss of enthusiasm	Skin irritations	Nervous habits

Anxiety

Anxiety can be seen as a negative aspect of stress, and it may accompany high levels of arousal. It is not pleasant to be anxious and is characterised by feelings of nervousness and worry. Again, the stress and anxiety responses are unique to each individual.

Trait and state anxiety

Trait anxiety means that a person generally experiences high levels of anxiety as part of their personality. They tend to worry and feel nervous in a range of situations and find them threatening. State anxiety is anxiety felt in response to a specific situation. It is anxiety related to a specific mood state. Usually, a person who has high trait anxiety will also experience higher levels of state anxiety. This is important for athletes because their levels of trait anxiety will determine their state anxiety in competition and as a result their performance.

Arousal and performance

Arousal levels will have an influence on performance, but it is not always clear-cut what this relationship is. The following theories help to explain the relationship.

Drive theory

Drive theory, initially the work of Hull (1943), states that as arousal levels rise, so do performance levels.

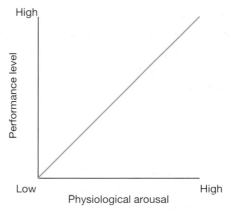

Fig 3.09 Drive theory

This happens in linear fashion and can be described as a straight line.

The actual performance also depends on the arousal level and the skill level of the performer. Arousal will exaggerate the individual's dominant response, meaning that if they have learnt the skill well their dominant response will be exaggerated positively. However, if they are a novice performer their skill level will drop to produce a worse performance.

The inverted U hypothesis

This theory is based on the Yerkes and Dodson Law (1908) and seeks to address some of the criticisms of the drive theory. This theory agrees that arousal does improve performance, but only up to a point, and once arousal goes beyond this point performance starts to decline. Fig 3.10 shows the curve looking like an upside-down U.

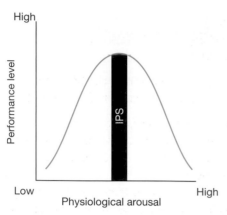

Fig 3.10 The inverted U hypothesis

This theory's main point is that there is an optimum level of arousal before performance starts to diminish. This is also called the ideal performing state (IPS) and is often referred to as 'the zone'. At this point the arousal level meets the demands of the task, and everything feels good and is going well.

Catastrophe theory

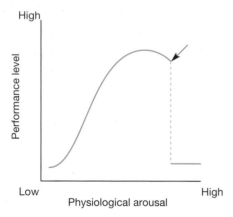

Fig 3.11 Catastrophe theory

This theory has been taken a step further by Fazey and Hardy (1988), who agree with the inverted U hypothesis, but say that once arousal level has passed, the IPS will drop off drastically rather than steadily. The point where performance drops is called the 'point of catastrophe'. The Americans refer to this phenomenon, when performance drops, as 'choking'. The history of sport is littered with examples of people or teams throwing away seemingly unassailable positions.

Individualised zones of functioning

This theory was developed by Yuri Hanin. He found that each individual athlete will have a level of state anxiety which is most comfortable for them and

produces the best performance. If a performer is outside this zone they will experience a loss in performance. The important point being that each performer is individual and needs to find their own individual zone of functioning (IZOF) to produce their best performance.

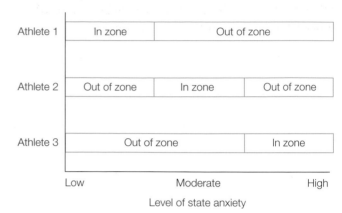

Fig 3.12 Individualised zones of functioning

Multi-dimensional anxiety theory

This theory took Hanin's IZOF theory a step further by showing that state anxiety has two components – cognitive and somatic – and that these may have a different effect on the outcome produced. Increases in state cognitive anxiety, such as self-doubt and negative self-talk, will always result in a loss of performance. However, increases in somatic state anxiety, such as increased heart rate and breathing rate, may have a positive effect on performance. This theory has received little support in research and needs further investigation.

Group dynamics

Throughout our sporting and social lives we are involved in working in groups, such as our families, school groups, friendship groups and the sports teams in which we play. Sports teams have different characteristics – an athletics team will have different teamwork demands to a rugby or cricket team. However, all groups rely on the fundamental characteristic of teamwork. In 1991 the British 4 × 400 m relay team beat the highly favoured Americans at the World Championships and Roger Black made the following comments: 'On paper we were not capable of winning the gold medal, but we had a shared belief – that the greater good of the team was more important than any individual ego. That is the secret of teamwork.'

Defining a group is not easy, but the minimum number required is two people. A group can be seen as two or more like-minded people interacting to produce an outcome they could not achieve on their own. Groups involve interaction or working with other people in order to influence the behaviour of other people and in turn be influenced by them.

Group: a group should have:
- a collective identity
- a sense of shared purpose or objectives
- structured modes of communication
- personal and/or task interdependence
- interpersonal attraction.
(Weinberg and Gould, 2003)

A group or a team?

Generally speaking, an instructor will call people who are involved in an exercise class or dance class a group, and people playing cricket or rugby a team. People involved in the group have a similar sense of purpose and may share common objectives. However, a team's members will actually be dependent on one another to achieve their shared goals and will need to support each other.

So why is the outcome of the group not always equal to the sum of its parts? For example, we can see in football that the teams with the best players do not always get the results they should. In 2006 the very talented Brazil and Argentina teams were knocked out at the quarter-final stage of the World Cup and in 2004 the European Championships were won by Greece rather than the individually talented Portugal team. In cricket the England one-day side is continually changing its players as it seeks to find a team rather than a group of individuals. We can even see the importance of a team when individual players come together in an event such as the Ryder Cup in golf. In 2004 and 2006 the British and European team beat the Americans emphatically due to the team feeling that had developed.

Stages of group development

A group of people coming together does not form a team. Becoming a team demands a process of development. Tuckman and Jensen (1977) proposed a five-stage model of group development:

- forming
- storming
- norming
- performing
- adjourning.

Each group will go through the five stages. The length of time they spend in each stage is variable.

Forming: the group comes together, with individuals meeting and familiarising themselves with the other members of the group. The structure and relationships within the group are formed and tested. If it is a team, the coach may develop strategies or games to 'break the ice' between the group members. At this point the individuals are seeing whether they fit in with this group.

Storming: a period of conflict will follow the forming stage as individuals seek their roles and status within the group. This may involve conflict between individual members, rebellion against the leader or resistance to the way the team is being developed or managed, or the tactics it is adopting. This is also a period of intense inter-group competition, as group members compete for their positions within the team.

Norming: once the hostility and fighting has been overcome, either by athletes leaving the group or accepting the common goals and values of the group, a period of norming occurs. Here, the group starts to cooperate and work together to reach common goals. The group pulls together and the roles are established and become stable.

Performing: in the final stage, the group members work together to achieve their mutual goals. The relationships within the group have become well established, as have issues of leadership and strategies for play. It is unrealistic to see the group as being stable and performing in a steady way. The relationships within the group will change and develop with time, sometimes for the good of the group and sometimes to its detriment. As new members join the group there will be a new period of storming and norming, as this person is either accepted or rejected. This re-evaluation of the group is often beneficial and stops the group becoming stale. Successful teams seem to be settled and assimilate two or three new players a year to keep them fresh. Bringing in too many new players can disrupt the group and change the nature of the group completely.

Adjourning: once the group has achieved its goals or come to the end of its useful purpose the team may break up. This may also be caused by a considerable change in the personnel involved or the management and leadership of the group.

Group effectiveness

The aim of a group is to be effective by using the strengths of each person to better the effectiveness of the group. However, the outcome is often not equal to the sum of its parts. Steiner (1972) proposed the following model of group effectiveness:

Actual productivity = Potential productivity – Process losses

Where: actual productivity = the actual performance achieved; potential productivity = the best possible performance achievable by that group based on its resources (ability, knowledge, skills); process losses = losses due to working as part of a group (coordination losses, communication problems, losses in motivation).

For example, in a tug-of-war team each member can pull 100 kg individually and as a team of four they pull 360 kg in total. Why do you think this would happen?

Social loafing

One of the problems of working in groups is that it tends to affect motivation. People do not seem to work as hard in groups compared with working on their own. Research shows that rowers in larger teams give less effort than those in smaller teams:

1 person = 100% effort
2 people = 90% effort
4 people = 80% effort
8 people = 65% effort

This phenomenon is called the Ringelman effect, or social loafing, and is defined as the tendency of individuals to lessen their effort when part of a group.

Cohesion

Cohesion is concerned with the extent to which a team is willing to stick together and work together. The forces tend to cover two areas:

- the attractiveness of the group to individual members
- the extent to which members are willing to work together to achieve group goals.

To be successful in its goals, a group has to be cohesive. The extent to which cohesion is important depends upon the sport and the level of interaction needed.

> **LEARNER ACTIVITY**
> ## Interaction and cohesion
> Place the following ten team sports in order depending upon the level of interaction and thus cohesion needed to be successful.
>
> | | |
> |---|---|
> | Rowing eights | Cricket team |
> | Tennis doubles | Volleyball team |
> | 4 × 100 m relay | Cycling team |
> | Golf team | Curling team |
> | Bobsleigh four | Synchronised swimming team |

definition

Cohesion: 'The total field of forces which act on members to remain in the group.' (Festinger *et al.*, 1950)

Types of cohesion

There seem to be two definite types of cohesion within a group:

- task cohesion – the willingness of a team to work together to achieve its goals
- social cohesion – the willingness of the team to socialise together.

It would appear that task cohesion comes first as this is why the team has formed in the first place. If the group is lucky they will find that they develop social cohesion as well, and this usually has a beneficial effect on performance. This is because if you feel good about your team-mates you are more likely to want success for each other as well as yourself.

Research says that cohesion is important in successful teams, but that task cohesion is more important than social cohesion. It does depend upon the sport being played, as groups that need high levels of interaction need higher levels of cohesion. Research also suggests that success will produce increased cohesion rather than cohesion coming before performance. Being successful helps to develop feelings of group attraction, and this will help to develop more success, and so on. This can be seen by the cycle of success, in that once a team has been successful it tends to continue being successful – success breeds success.

Tackle the 'Learner activity' (below) before reading on.

LEARNER ACTIVITY
Leadership

Before reading the section on leadership, answer the following questions.

- How would you define 'leadership'?
- Make a list of eight people you consider to be effective leaders. Choose four from sport and four from other areas.
- List eight personality qualities or traits that you think are needed to make an effective leader.
- Are the leadership qualities needed to lead in sport the same as in all leadership situations?
- Do you think an effective leader will be effective in all situations? Why?

---

definition

Leadership: 'The behavioural process of influencing individuals and groups towards goals.' (Barrow, 1977)

Leadership in sport

The choice of a manager, coach or captain is often the most important decision a club's members have to make. They see it as crucial in influencing the club's chances of success. Great leaders in sport are held in the highest regard, irrespective of their talent on the pitch. Sportspeople such as Martin Johnson, Clive Woodward, Alex Ferguson, Michael Vaughan and Linford Christie are all regarded as 'great' leaders.

Leadership behaviour covers a variety of activities, which is why it is called 'multi-dimensional'. It includes:

- decision-making processes
- motivational techniques
- giving feedback
- establishing interpersonal relationships
- confidently directing the group.

Leaders are different from managers. Managers plan, organise, budget, schedule and recruit, while leaders determine how a task is completed.

People become leaders in different ways; not all are appointed. Prescribed leaders are appointed by a person in authority – a chairman appoints a manager, a manager appoints a coach, a principal appoints a teacher. Emergent leaders emerge from a group and take over responsibility. For example, John Terry emerged to become the leader of the England football team, just as Steve McLaren emerged to become the new England manager. Emergent leaders are often more effective as they have the respect of their group members.

Theories of leadership

Sport psychologists have sought to explain leadership effectiveness for many years and they have used the following theories to help understand effective leadership behaviour.

Trait approach

In the 1920s researchers tried to show that characteristics or personality traits were stable and common to all leaders. Thus, to be a good leader you needed to have intelligence, assertiveness, independence and self-confidence. Therefore, a person who is a good leader in one situation will be a good leader in all situations.

Behavioural approach

The trait approach says that leaders are 'born', but the behavioural approach says that anyone can become a good leader by learning the behaviour of effective leaders. Thus, this approach supports the view that leadership skills can be developed through experience and training.

Interactional approach

Trait and personal approaches look at personality traits. The interactional approach looks at the interaction between the person and the situation. It stresses the following points.

- Effective leaders cannot be predicted solely on personality.
- Effective leadership fits specific situations, as some leaders function better in certain circumstances than others.
- Leadership style needs to change to match the demands of the situation. For example, relationship-orientated leaders develop

interpersonal relationships, provide good communication and ensure everyone is feeling good within the group. However, task-orientated leaders are concerned with getting the work done and meeting objectives.

The multidimensional model of sport leadership

The three models previously discussed were adapted from non-sporting examples. Although they help us understand leadership behaviour, each model has its shortcomings. In 1980, Chelladurai and Saleh presented a sport-specific model (see Fig 3.13). They proposed the view that effective leadership will vary depending on the characteristics of the athletes, the leader and the situation.

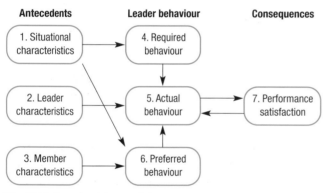

Fig 3.13 Leadership model

What does this mean?

- Situational characteristics: the characteristics of the situation the group is in, such as size, type of sport, winning or losing.
- Leader characteristics: the personal qualities of the leader. Some of the qualities needed are confidence, intelligence, assertiveness and self-motivation.
- Member characteristics: the different personality types of different groups of athletes, including age, gender, ability level and experience.
- Required behaviour: the type of behaviour required of a leader in a particular situation. For example, if a team is losing with five minutes to go, it is best for the leader to make a decision themselves rather than discuss it with their team-mates.
- Actual behaviour: the behaviour the leader actually displays.
- Preferred behaviour: the preferred leadership of the group, depending on their characteristics.

- Performance satisfaction: the extent to which the group members are satisfied with the leader's behaviour and with the outcome of the competition.

The model says that if a leader behaves appropriately for the particular situation and this behaviour matches the preferences of the group members, then they will achieve their best performance and feel satisfied.

The leadership scale for sport

The leadership scale for sport was developed by Chelladurai to assess the five main types of behaviour of coaches in their positions of leadership, and to evaluate how often they use each. They are as follows.

- Training and instruction: information is provided by the coach, aimed at improving the performance of the athlete in terms of technique and strategy.
- Democratic behaviour: the athlete is involved in reaching decisions regarding group goals and group strategy.
- Autocratic behaviour: the coach acts independently, forcing decisions on the group.
- Social support behaviour: this is aimed at improving the well-being and welfare of the athletes and developing group relationships.
- Positive feedback behaviour: this rewards individual and group actions through acknowledging athletes' efforts and performance.

Leadership in sport is a complex subject as it involves the process of influencing people towards achieving their personal goals and the goals of the group. Individuals respond to different types of leader and different types of leadership behaviour. Different leaders have different strengths and ways of leading, and may find that what was successful in one situation is not so effective in another.

Social facilitation

Social facilitation is the change in performance that occurs due to the presence of others – whether the presence is an audience or fellow competitors. There is no doubt that our performances change as the result of the presence of other people. Think about how you feel when your parents or friends come to watch you, or when you start to perform in front of an audience.

Take some time to consider the effect an audience has on you personally. How do you feel inside when performing in front of an audience? Does it improve or worsen your performance? Does it matter whether the audience is supportive or not, known or unknown to you, large or small?

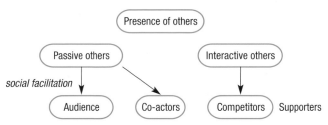

Fig 3.14 Social facilitation model

Zajonc (1965) defined the different types of people present, separating them into those people who are competing against you and those people who are merely present and not competing

> **Social facilitation:** 'The consequences upon behaviour which derive from the sheer presence of other individuals.' (Zajonc, 1965)

definition

Co-actors are people involved in the same activity, but not competing directly. Triplett (1898) did some of the earliest experiments in sport psychology. He examined co-action in the following three conditions, using cyclists:

1 unpaced
2 paced (co-actor on another bike)
3 paced competitive (co-actors pacing and competing).

His findings were that cyclists in condition 2 were 34 seconds per mile faster than cyclists in condition 1, while cyclists in condition 3 were 39 seconds per mile faster than cyclists in condition 1.

The reasons for social facilitation are not always clear. Triplett concluded that in his experiment it was due to the physical effects, such as suctioning and sheltering resulting from travelling behind another

rider, and psychological effects such as encouragement, anxiety, pressure and competitiveness which are felt as the result of cycling with someone else. Triplett concluded that it did not matter if the cyclists were competing. What was important was that 'The bodily presence of another rider is stimulus to a rider in arousing the competitive instinct.'

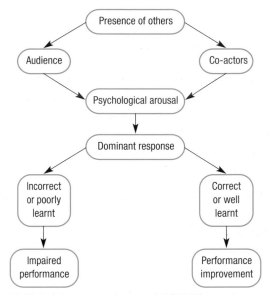

Fig 3.15 Zajonc's expanded model (1965)

Zajonc's expanded model (Fig 3.15) showed that whether the audience or co-actors have a positive or negative effect on performance depends upon how well the skill has been learnt. A poorly learnt skill will become worse, while a well-learnt skill will be improved. This links in well with the effect of stress on performance, and it can be seen that the presence of others would cause more stress.

Zajonc also looked at the relationship between the audience effect and the standard of the performer. His results are shown in Fig 3.16.

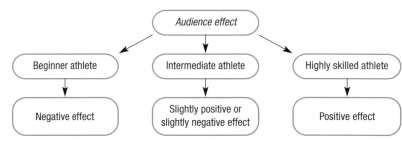

Fig 3.16 Audience effect and the standard of performer

The effect also depends upon the nature of the task – whether it is strength or skill-related. Strength tasks will usually be enhanced by the presence of others.

However, skilled tasks (especially poorly learnt skills) may suffer. Social facilitation effects tend to disappear as the individual gets used to it.

Cottrell (1968) said that it is not the mere presence of an audience which creates arousal, but that the type of audience is also very important. For example, a blindfolded audience had no facilitation effect. The following factors will affect social facilitation.

- Audience expertise: an expert audience will increase arousal level.
- Type of audience: a pro-winning audience will have more of a facilitation effect than a pro-enjoyment audience.
- Performer's evaluation of the audience: the performer decides what they think the audience wants and is aroused accordingly.
- Size: a larger audience will have more of a facilitation effect.

Home advantage

Home advantage is the view that the team playing at home has a disproportionately higher chance of winning in relation to the team playing away from home. This phenomenon was apparent in football's 2002 World Cup, where the joint hosts, South Korea and Japan, both did far better than they had ever previously done – particularly South Korea, who progressed to the semi-finals. Then, in the World Cup of 2006 which was held in Germany, all four semi-finalists were European countries.

LEARNER ACTIVITY
Home advantage

To see whether a home advantage does exist, take the sports supplement from a paper on Sunday or Monday and examine the results from three or four sports, such as football, rugby, hockey or cricket. Work out the following percentages:

- teams winning at home
- teams drawing at home
- teams losing at home.

1 Do your results support the theory of home advantage?
2 Would there be a home advantage in individual sports such as athletics, tennis or golf?
3 Why is there a home advantage?

There are many reasons why home teams are more successful. Some of these are physical and some are psychological:

- familiarity with the surroundings and the surfaces
- a supportive home crowd who give positive approval
- less intimidation from opposing supporters
- the territory is theirs and claimed by display of their playing colours
- there is less travel involved in getting to the match
- travel can cause boredom and staleness
- players do not have to stay in unfamiliar surroundings and eat unfamiliar food
- home teams are more likely to play offensively
- away teams may not be treated well by their opponents
- referees and officials may unconsciously favour the home team to seek the crowd's approval.

Home advantage may be seen as being a disadvantage to the away team rather than an advantage to the home team. It is the job of the coach and psychologist to find ways of minimising this away disadvantage.

Psychological factors in exercise environments

Many people in Britain have been persuaded to start exercising as they are aware of the benefits of exercise. People are also persuaded by impressive facilities and the atmosphere of fitness centres. Research shows that despite the best of intentions most people will fail to stick to their training programmes.

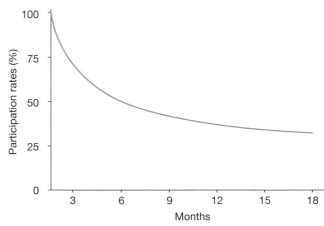

Fig 3.17 Change in participation in exercise over time

According to Weinberg and Gould (2003), the most rapid dropout occurs in the first three months, when 33 per cent of people will have stopped their exercise programme, while after six months 52 per cent of people will have dropped out. Fig 3.17 makes the important point that if a person can keep exercising for nine months they are highly likely to keep going. Why is the nine-month point so important?

Behaviour change is difficult for people because what we did yesterday is pretty much what we will do today. Everything we do we tend to do in the same way because we develop 'rituals' which work for us. For example, if you look at how you get yourself up in the morning and then ready for the day you will do it the same way every day. Therefore, adding in exercise causes us to change our rituals and at first it feels uncomfortable because it requires a lot of conscious effort. However, the more often we repeat the ritual the easier it becomes as it gets integrated into an unconscious behaviour. To make the change into an automatic behaviour takes around six to nine months by which time most people will have given up as the effort is too great.

This means that for a person to be successful the exercise has to fit into their life and it is best to set down regular times and develop a consistent routine. Also, a person has to understand the 'value' of the ritual. For example, most people clean their teeth twice a day because it has a clear health and hygiene value. Most people think they should exercise but are not always clear as to the value of exercise to them.

There are strategies to prevent dropout and promote adherence to exercise programmes, as the following sections show.

Setting goals and targets

In order to direct an individual's efforts and to give them something to work for we can set goals. This has to be done with great care so as not to negatively affect motivation. To help us do this we can use the acronym SMART:

- **S**pecific goals – related to a particular aspect of fitness (such as strength or endurance)
- **M**easurable – the goal must be quantifiable (expressed in figures)
- **A**chievable – the goal must not be set too high
- **R**ealistic – the goal must be realistically achievable
- **T**ime-constrained – there must be a time frame (set a date).

Goals can be set in the long term and the short term. A long-term goal may be achieved over the course of a year, and can be broken down into shorter-term goals, such as one-month, three-month or six-month goals. We can use outcome goals which are related to the final result and process goals which are goals we can meet to help us achieve the outcome goal. For example, if a person's outcome goal is to lose 3 per cent body fat over a three-month period, their process goal may be to exercise three times a week for the first month.

The best way to set goals is to answer three questions:

- What do I want to achieve? (desired state)
- Where am I now? (present state)
- What do I need to do to move from my present state to my desired state?

Then present this on a scale:

Present state   Desired state

   1   2   3   4   5

1 Write in your goal at point 5 and your present position at point 1.
2 Decide what would be halfway between points 1 and 5; this is your goal for point 3.
3 Then decide what would be halfway between present state and point 3. This is your short-term goal for point 2.
4 Then decide what would be halfway between point 3 and the desired state. This is the goal for point 4.
5 All these goals are outcome goals and must be set using the SMART principle.
6 Work out what needs to be done to move from point 1 to point 2. These are your process goals and must again use the SMART principle.

It is best to use a goal-setting diary to keep all goal-setting information in the same place, and to review the goals on a weekly basis.

LEARNER ACTIVITY
Your own goals

Think about your own sport and set yourself a goal which you would like to achieve in the next year. Then, using the process above, set yourself outcome goals, and then work out the process goals to get you from point 1 to point 2.

Decision balance sheet

Taking the decision to exercise can be set out on a decision balance sheet. Imagine that a person who is contemplating exercise is going through a period of behaviour change and they have two choices: taking action or not taking action. Each course of action will bring them some pleasure and some pain and this exercise helps them understand this. Hopefully the pleasure that change brings in the long term will outweigh any pain it causes in the short term. Unfortunately, some short-term pleasure has to be foregone. However, this continued behaviour would result in long-term pain (illness, dysfunction).

An example of a decision balance sheet is shown in Table 3.05.

People should become aware that their change will be done for two reasons: first, to gain the benefits of change; second, to avoid the consequences of not taking action. The following can then help them take action.

- Prompts: an individual puts up posters or reminders around the house which will keep giving them reminders to exercise. This could also be done with coloured dots on mirrors or other places where they regularly look.
- Rewards for attendance/completing goals: the individual is provided with an extrinsic reward for completing the goal or attending the gym regularly. This may be something to pamper them, such as a free massage, and should not be something that conflicts with the goal – such as a slap-up meal!
- Social support approaches: you can help people exercise regularly by developing a social support group of like-minded people with similar fitness goals, so that they can arrange to meet at the gym

at certain times. This makes it more difficult for people to miss their exercise session. Also, try to gain the backing of the people they live with to support them rather than tease or criticise them.

Barriers to exercise

We have to be realistic that people will have aspects of their life which may decrease their chances of success. A barrier is not a good word to use because it suggests it cannot be overcome; it is better to look at factors to consider and take into account.

- Lack of time: 69 per cent of inactive people give lack of time as a barrier to exercise. In reality, it may be poor time management or making exercise a low priority as they seem to find time to go to the pub or watch television. A good way of looking at this is by saying that if you don't find time now to be more healthy you will have to find time later in life to be ill!
- Lack of energy: due to the amount of time people work they can start to experience stress and mental fatigue; 59 per cent of non-exercisers said this was a barrier for them. The way around this is to explain that exercise can help to relieve stress and energise the individual. Providing breaks in the day can make an individual more productive.
- Lack of motivation: motivation is a most unstable aspect of personality and can change in line with a change of priorities, such as when work gets busy or family demands increase. The individual has to remember the benefits of their exercise and the value behind these benefits.

Other factors which may cause barriers include cost, lack of facilities, lack of support or feeling

Table 3.05 A decision balance sheet

Decision: Training three times a week in the gym

Pain of taking action	Pleasure of taking action	Pain of not taking action	Pleasure of not taking action
Loss of time	Look slimmer	Stay fat	Get to watch more television
Physically uncomfortable	Feel fitter	Feel tired and lethargic	Allowed to eat chips
Getting home later	Have more energy	Develop diabetes and heart disease	Able to go to the pub
Less available money			Can binge on chocolate

insecure. These factors need to be taken seriously and then actions put in place to overcome these factors.

Models of behaviour change

Transtheoretical model of change

When a person goes through a period of behaviour change they will go through a series of distinct stages. The best known model was developed by Prochaska and di Clemente (1983) and is called the 'transtheoretical model of change'. We will apply it to a person changing from a state of inactivity to a state of activity; it can be applied to any period of behaviour change, such as stopping smoking or dieting.

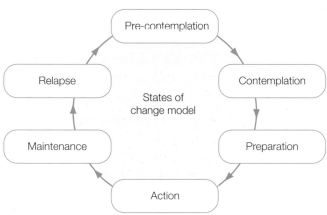

Fig 3.18 Prochaska and di Clemente's transtheoretical model of behaviour change

1 Pre-contemplation: this stage occurs when a person is inactive, happy to stay inactive and has no intention to change their behaviour.
2 Contemplation: this stage occurs when a person has the intention to start exercising in the near future.
3 Preparation: they may be preparing physically and psychologically, but they have not yet made the behaviour change.
4 Action: the period of behaviour change has started and they have started out on their exercise programme. This period lasts for as long as the change remains a conscious effort. The period is usually around six to nine months.
5 Maintenance: once the behaviour change has been integrated into the person's life and they are maintaining the change they will be in this stage.

6 Relapse: the individual has returned to their original state and has dropped the newly acquired behaviour.

LEARNER ACTIVITY
Transtheoretical model of change
Take each stage of the transtheoretical model of change and show what you could do to help the person going through a period of change. These might be psychological techniques or they may be simple things such as providing information.

The health belief model

This states that the likelihood of an individual engaging in behaviour to preserve good health depends upon the value they place on preventing disease and illness. An individual will also consider the costs and benefits of exercise or any other measures they take. This fits in with the decision balance sheet which most people use unconsciously; when they consider they are potentially at risk they will be pushed into preventative action.

Social cognitive theory

This theory, developed by Albert Bandura (1986, 1997), suggests that exercise behaviour depends upon three factors: personal, behavioural and environmental. He sees the relationship between environment and behaviour as being reciprocal as they affect each other. Our behaviour is determined by the environment and our perception of how we should behave in the environment. However, we can also influence the environment by our behaviour and thus behaviour can change an environment from being threatening to friendly, or vice versa.

Most importantly in this theory, Bandura says that self-efficacy is the key to success. Self-efficacy is our belief in our chance of success in any situation. If we believe we are going to be successful or have a good experience then it vastly improves our chances that we will be. For example, if a person believes they will score a penalty or be successful in stopping smoking then their mind will lead them to that conclusion rather than an unsuccessful one. This fits in with a quote from Henry Ford, who said, 'Whether you think you can or can't, you are probably right.' Research has shown this theory to be proven and that people who believe they will be successful stick to their programmes and have better results.

Exercise and well-being

As developing societies become more sophisticated, the resulting technology in the form of computers, mobile phones and the internet has made life more demanding and pressurised. The downside of this is that as we work harder and lives become more stressful the psychological well-being of people has been affected. This has resulted in increases in stress, anxiety, depression and other mental illnesses. These disorders can be treated by medication, but exercise has been shown to have a beneficial effect on them.

Table 3.06 shows the psychological benefits of exercise in clinical and non-clinical populations.

Why does exercise enhance psychological well-being? The research on this topic has delivered a range of reasons, some physiological and some psychological. No one theory has been agreed upon, but the physiological and psychological effects listed in Table 3.07 contribute to the enhanced well-being of the individual.

Table 3.06 The psychological benefits of exercise in clinical and non-clinical populations

Increases	Decreases
Academic performance	Absenteeism
Assertiveness	Alcohol abuse
Confidence	Anger
Emotional stability	Anxiety
Intellectual functioning	Confusion
Internal locus of control	Depression
Memory	Headaches
Perception	Hostility
Positive body image	Phobias
Self-control	Psychotic behaviour
Sexual satisfaction	Tension
Well-being	Type A behaviour
Work efficiency	Work errors

Adapted from Taylor, Sallis and Needle (1985), cited in Weinberg and Gould (2003)

Table 3.07 Physiological and psychological effects of exercise

Physiological changes	Psychological changes
Increases in blood flow to the brain	Feeling more in control
Changes in levels of hormones produced, such as serotonin, endorphins and noradrenaline	Increased feelings of competence and self-confidence
Increases in the amount of oxygen delivered to the brain and the ability of the body to consume oxygen	Positive social interactions
Reductions in muscle tension	Improved self-concept and self-esteem
Structural changes in the brain	Opportunities for fun and enjoyment

Review questions

1 What is meant by the term 'personality'?
2 Explain the three levels of personality as outlined by Martens.
3 How do trait theories and social learning theories of personality differ?
4 Discuss the two ways a social theorist says that we learn our personality.
5 Explain how stress can be a positive and negative influence on people.
6 What is meant by the terms 'arousal' and 'anxiety', and how do they influence performance?
7 What is meant by the term 'aggression'?
8 Explain the four criteria of an aggressive act.
9 Using examples, explain the difference between assertive behaviour, instrumental aggression and hostile aggression.
10 Explain the term 'motivation' and the differences between intrinsic and extrinsic motivation.
11 What is meant by the term 'group'?
12 Discuss the five stages of group development.
13 What is cohesion? Explain the two types of cohesion.
14 Discuss the multi-dimensional model of leadership and how it explains group success and failure.
15 When people start exercising why is it important to get them to the nine-month point?
16 Discuss the reasons people give for starting exercise and for giving up exercise.
17 Explain two methods of ensuring that people adhere to their exercise programmes.
18 Discuss the psychological benefits of exercise.

References

Bandura, A. (1973) *Aggression: A Social Learning Analysis*, Prentice Hall.

Bandura, A. (1977a), *Social Learning Theory*, Prentice Hall.

Bandura, A. (1977b) (Self-efficacy: toward a unifying theory of behavioural change). *Psychological Review*, 84, 191–215.

Bandura, A. (1986) *Social Foundations of Thought and Action*, Prentice Hall.

Bandura, A. (1997) *Self Efficacy: The Exercise of Control*, Freeman.

Baron, R. and Richardson, D. (1994) *Human Aggression*, Plenum.

Barrow, J. (1977) The variables of leadership: a review and conceptual framework. *Academy of Management Review*, 2, 231–251.

Beashel, P. and Taylor, J. (1996) *Advanced Studies in Physical Education and Sport*, Nelson.

Berkowitz, L. (1969) *Roots of Aggression*, Atherton Press.

Berkowitz, L. (1989) *Aggression: Its Causes and Consequences and Control*, Temple University Press.

Bowers, K. S. (1973) Situationism in psychology: an analysis and a critique, *Psychological Review*, 80, 307–36.

Buzan, T. (2005) *The Ultimate Book of Mind Maps*, Thorsons.

Cattell, R. B. (1965) *The Scientific Analysis of Personality*, Penguin.

Chelladurai, P. and Carron, A. V. (1978) *Leadership*, Sociology of Sport Monograph Series.

Chelladurai, P. and Saleh, S. D. (1980) Dimensions of leadership behaviour in sport: development of a leadership behaviour scale. *Journal of Sport Psychology*, 2, 34–45.

Cottrell, N. B. (1968) Performance in the presence of other human beings. Mere presence, audience and affiliation effects, in E. Simmell, R. Hoppe and G. Milton (eds) *Social Facilitation and Imitative Behaviour*, Allyn & Bacon.

Cox, R. (1998) *Sports Psychology: Concepts and Applications*, Wm C. Brown Communications.

Davis, R. J., Bull, C. R., Roscoe, J. V. and Roscoe, D. A. (2000) *Physical Education and the Study of Sport*, Mosby.

Dollard, J., Doob, J. Miller, N., Mowrer, O. and Sears, R. (1939) *Frustration and Aggression*, Yale University Press.

Eysenck, H. (1964) *Manual of Eysenck Personality Inventory*, University of London Press.

Fazey, J. and Hardy, L. (1988) *The inverted U hypothesis: a catastrophe for sport psychology?* British Association of Sports Sciences Monograph, no. 1. NCF.

Festinger, L. A., Schachter, S. and Back, K. (1950) *Social Pressures in Informal Groups: A Study of Human Factors in Housing*, Harper.

Gill, D. (2000) *Psychological Dynamics of Sport and Exercise*, Human Kinetics.

Hollander, E. P. (1971) *Principles and Methods of Social Psychology*, Oxford University Press.

Hull, C. L. (1943) *Principles of Behaviour*, Appleton Century Crofts.

Jarvis, M. (2000) *Sport Psychology*, Routledge.

Jarvis, M. (2006) *A Student's Handbook*, Routledge.

Latane, B., Harkins, S. G. and Williams, K. D. (1980) *Many Hands make Light Work: Social Loafing as a Social Disease*. Unpublished manuscript, Ohio State University.

McGrath, J. E. (1970) Major methodological issues, in J. E. McGrath (ed.) *Social and Psychological Factors in Stress*, Holt, Rinehart & Winston.

Oxendine, C. B. (1970) Emotional arousal and motor performance. *Quest*, 13, 23–30.

Prochaska, J. and Di Clemente, C. (1983) Stages and processes of self change of smoking. *Journal of Consulting and Clinical Psychology*, 51, 390–5.

Sage, G. (1974) *Sport and American Society*, Addison-Wesley.

Sage, G. (1977) *Introduction to Motor Behaviour: A Neuropsychological Approach*, Addison-Wesley.

Schurr, K., Ashley, M. and Joy, K. (1977) A multivariate analysis of male athlete characteristics: sport type and success. *Multivariate Experimental Clinical Research*, 3, 53–68.

Smith, M. D. (1988) Interpersonal sources of violence in hockey: the influence of parents, coaches and teammates, in F. M. Smoll, R. A. Magill and M. J. Ash (eds) *Children in Sport* (3rd edn), Human Kinetics.

Steiner, I. D. (1972) *Group Processes and Productivity*, Academic Press.

Triplett, N. (1898) The dynamogenic factors in pacemaking and competition. *American Journal of Psychology*, 9, 507–33.

Tuckman, L. and Jensen, M. (1977) *Stages of Small Group Development Revisited*, Group and Organisational Studies.

Weinberg, R. S. and Gould, D. (2003) *Foundations of Sport and Exercise Psychology*, Human Kinetics.

Wesson, K., Wiggins, N., Thompson, G. and Hartigan, S. (2000) *Sport and PE: A Complete Guide to Advanced Level Study*, Hodder Arnold.

Williams, J. M. (1980) Personality characteristics of the successful female athlete, in W. M. Straub, *Sport Psychology: An Analysis of Athlete Behavior*, Movement.

Woods, B. (1998) *Applying Psychology to Sport*, Hodder Arnold.

Yerkes, R. M. and Dodson, J. D. (1908) The relationship of strength and stimulus to rapid habit formation. *Journal of Comparative Neurology and Psychology*, 18, 459–82.

Zajonc, R. B. (1965) Social facilitation. *Science*, 149, 269–74.

Goals

At the end of this chapter you should understand:

- the key issues in research methods
- data collection techniques
- qualitative data analysis techniques
- quantitative data analysis techniques.

This chapter explains methods used in research by sport and exercise scientists. It will enable you to understand research in all disciplines of sport and exercise science. It should allow you to develop research skills, including collecting information, handling information, and mathematical and statistical skills for you to carry out your own research. Numbers and mathematical concepts put off a lot of students, but the purpose of research methods, and particularly this chapter, is to help you understand and interpret the meaning of information and to look at alternative methods of collecting data. The difference between quantitative research and qualitative research will be examined. Quantitative research is based on numerical evidence (e.g. heart rate), while qualitative research places more emphasis on what people do or say (answers given in an interview).

Key issues in research methods

Broadly speaking, information gathering or research in sport and exercise science can be divided into two types: quantitative and qualitative.

Quantitative research tends to involve numerical data (numbers). It involves measuring things and seeing how they change or what they are related to. For example, you could measure the percentage body fat of a group of people before and after a training programme. You could then investigate how body fat percentage changed. If percentage body fat went up you would deduce that the training had brought about this change or at least helped towards it.

Qualitative research has more emphasis on people's ideas, opinions and behaviour. As a coach, one of your athletes may keep getting injured while training. You could do an in-depth study into this one person (case study). Included in this study could be interviews and logs of the athlete's training; you could even observe their behaviour in training. From this information you would hope to determine any reasons for their consistent injuries.

Both quantitative and qualitative methods are useful and often it is best to use a combination of the two methods to obtain the best results.

definition

Case study: an in-depth examination of a single event.

Reliability

One of the key issues in research is reliability. This is concerned with how repeatable something is. That is, if you measured the same thing on separate occasions, would you record the same value? Let us say that you are going to take your resting heart rate every morning before you get up. You would expect the value not to change much over a number of weeks. If you recorded the same or similar values each morning, this would display reliability. You would then know that the way you were measuring heart rate was reliable.

definition

Reliability: the ability of something to perform consistently.

The two major obstacles to good reliability in sport and exercise research are:

- errors – mistakes caused by people measuring the wrong thing or not knowing how to measure something correctly
- day-to-day differences within subjects.

Good training with the equipment to be used, attention to detail and checking that the equipment is working correctly can overcome errors. Differences within subjects are a lot harder to account for. Even when measuring physiological variables using accurate equipment it is difficult to record exactly the same value. On different days people eat different amounts, sleep for different lengths of time, undertake different levels of physical activity, have differing mental states, and so on. The resting heart rate will vary from day to day due to these factors.

Researchers try and minimise these effects by standardising the test situation. In the above example you could record heart rate at the same time each morning – before breakfast and before the person has had the opportunity to be affected by what happens that day, both physiologically and psychologically. It is also good practice for researchers to make repeated observations and then report the average value; this averages out any errors or variations.

Validity

Another key issue is validity. This refers to the meaning of the information. Did you measure what you set out to measure? You may have decided, as a cricket coach, to measure the aerobic fitness of your players by getting them to perform the bleep test. Your results may be very reliable, but are they valid? Do the results of the bleep test relate to levels of fitness in your players? This is a difficult question to answer. It is often difficult, especially in a field setting, to measure exactly the variable you are looking at. A cricket coach could not practically measure the aerobic capacity (VO_2max) of his players, but he could quite easily measure their performance on the bleep test and relate it back to VO_2max values.

definition
Validity: relating to the truth or true meaning.

Choosing a valid test can be a problem in sport and exercise science research. Frequently people measure certain things and then try and make general statements about what they have found. For example, the sit and reach test is often used to measure flexibility, however it incorporates only leg and back flexibility. Even then there is debate about its usefulness in measuring this. So, to make statements about an athlete's overall flexibility based on this one test would be incorrect. It would not be valid. When making conclusions based on what you have measured, it is important to be specific about the conclusions you make unless you have taken a range of measurements. If this is the case, you can be more general in your comments.

Objectivity

Another key issue is objectivity. If two different people obtain a similar value for a measurement, it is said to be 'objective'. As a measure of the number of times your heart beats, heart rate recorded at the radial artery is an objective measure. Two different people would obtain similar values when measuring somebody's pulse. It is a simple matter of counting the number of beats in a given time, then converting this to beats per minute. Measuring blood pressure (at the brachial artery with a manual sphygmomanometer) would be less objective. The person measuring blood pressure has to decide the value of systolic pressure based on when they can hear a constant tapping sound (the Kortikoff sounds). Similarly, diastolic pressure is recorded on the absence of a rhythmic tapping sound. Both these points will be slightly subjective – that is, different people could record them differently.

definition
Objectivity: agreement between people measuring things.

Measuring systems should be designed to be objective. However, this is not always possible. Physiological measures (heart rate, respiratory rate) tend to exhibit the most objectivity. Difficult areas in which to achieve objectivity are when an opinion is required or when people are expected to judge performance. For example, scoring in gymnastics can be subjective. This is why detailed scoring systems, involving a number of judges, have been developed to try to overcome this problem.

Accuracy and precision

When you are testing and assessing athletes, you need to take special care when interpreting the results of tests. It is possible to measure things only to a certain degree of accuracy. The accuracy of a recording will depend on the precision of the equipment used. If you weighed somebody on a set of bathroom weighing scales (the ones with a marker on to indicate weight), their weight might record 84 kg. If you used a digital set of scales, the digital scales might show a recording of 84.88 kg. When weighing somebody, is 84 kg accurate enough? Is the extra precision important?

Precision alone is not enough. In the above example the scales might not be working correctly and so if they reported a value of 81.24 kg, they would be precise but wrong.

> **Precision:** the degree of agreement of a measurement.
> **Accuracy:** how close something is to its actual value.

Accuracy is a measure of how close you are to recording the actual value of something that you intend to measure. If you were measuring heart rate with a heart rate monitor and it displayed a value of 144 beats per minute (bpm), yet the real heart rate was 150 bpm, the monitor would be inaccurate.

Types of data

A group or set of numbers is referred to as data. The resting heart rates of a group of people would be a set of data. Data can include more than one type of measurement – for example, the height and weight of a number of people. With any type of measurement, the thing measured is called a variable. This is because the measurement can vary. In sport and exercise a variable is something that we measure (blood pressure, anxiety levels, flexibility). If the variable can be recorded using a number it is described as a numeric variable.

However, not all variables or sets of data have to use numbers. If you were recording the gender of a group of people, instead of numbers you could use labels (male and female). Variables with letters or words in place of numbers are called string variables.

> **Data:** a group or set of numbers.

Data can be classified according to the type of measurement. The simplest type of measurement uses what is called a 'nominal' scale. In it categories are given nominal values. Let's say gender was to be

LEARNER ACTIVITY Accuracy/precision and validity/reliability

The following is a set of body fat percentage values recorded on a group of people using body fat calipers. Body fat was measured at two different times during the day. Body fat was also recorded via under-water weighing (considered to give a truer value of % body fat).

Subject	1	2	3	4	5	6	7	8
Body fat % (calipers a.m.)	22	15	13	11	26	26	27	13
Body fat % (calipers p.m.)	21	15	14	10	24	25	27	12
Body fat % (under water)	25	17	14	12	28	29	31	16

- How could you determine the precision of the body fat calipers?
- How precise are they?
- How could you establish how accurate they are?
- How accurate are they?
- Review the results of the body fat calipers in terms of reliability and validity.
- How could reliability and validity be assessed?
- How do reliability and validity relate to accuracy and precision?

recorded in a table – males could be denoted by a 2 and females by a 1. These values would be nominal, they have no meaning, and they just identify which category each person belongs to. The values have no numerical meaning, so 2 is not twice as good as 1. They are just labels to separate each category. Nominal data is sometimes referred to as discrete data, because you can only have discrete values (male or female, yes or no).

The next type of measurement is 'ordinal'. Ordinal values also use numbers to signify categories but these numbers also give a ranking value (Liverpool = 1st, Arsenal = 2nd, Man Utd = 3rd). In the example given, each number indicates a football league position – Liverpool is first, Arsenal is second, and so on. This sort of data gives us a lot more detail than nominal data (we can now say who is the tallest, quickest or heaviest), although it does not give as much detail as we may like. In the league position example, the team in first place may be one point ahead of the team in second, while the team in second could be three points in front of the team in third. This type of data only gives a rank order (first, second, third) and not an exact value.

A more detailed type of numerical measurement is interval or ratio level data. These are two different types of data, but are often referred to as one as they are very similar.

An interval scale has equal distances between each value, hence its name. Units of measurement normally give it. An example is the Fahrenheit scale. Ratio scales are all units of measurement with set distances between values, but they also have a zero point determined by nature (time, distance, weight) or what is called an absolute zero. Therefore, a distance of 20 km is twice that of 10 km. The same cannot be said for Fahrenheit – that is, 20°F is not twice as hot as 10°F. Interval or ratio data is continuous. Continuous data can have any numeric value with any number of decimal places. The time taken to run the 100 m would be a continuous measure (a value of 11.43 secs). Interval or ratio data can be converted into ordinal or nominal scales, but this is not true the other way around. If you were to measure the exact height of some people, you could then categorise the subjects into the following groups based on their height: tall = 1, medium height = 2, short = 3. This would be converting ratio data into ordinal data.

LEARNER ACTIVITY
Data classification

Determine the levels of measurement of the following variables and give explanations for why you have chosen each particular classification.

1 blood pressure
2 compliance with an exercise programme:
 (a) followed programme = 1
 (b) dropped out = 2
3 finishing time:
 (a) < 10 secs = 1
 (b) 10–20 secs = 2
 (c) > 20 secs = 3
4 heart rate
5 distance walked

Primary and secondary data

Why do we need to take measurements in sport and exercise science? Measurement allows us to quantify things (e.g. it is possible to give a value for the number of times a heart beats in a minute). With sufficient measurement, data can be produced, so heart rate over a given time could be displayed. The production of data is important in science as it allows analysis. Hence, it would be possible to examine what happens to heart rate during a set time period or in a given situation (during exercise). Does heart rate increase, decrease or stay the same during exercise? This analysis in turn allows interpretation to infer meaning. The reason for an increased heart rate could be examined. Why did the heart rate go up? What caused it?

Data that you measure yourself is called primary data. Somebody else's data that you use would be secondary data. If you were examining the number of yellow and red cards for the teams competing in the last three football World Cups, you would need to collect the data from these World Cups. This might involve looking up information on the internet, for example. This would be secondary data, which was originally recorded by somebody other than you.

Ethical and legal issues

A lot of testing, measuring and research in sport and exercise science involves working with other people (athletes, clients of a health club). The British

Association of Sport and Exercise Sciences (BASES) has a code of conduct for its members when working with athletes.

The general principles should be followed by anybody doing research in any area of sport and exercise science. It is important to respect the rights of other people and ensure they are not negatively affected by your tests or work. This is especially true when working with children. Your subjects should be made aware of their right to withdraw from a test or programme of exercise at any time during the study. The decision to undertake a test or exercise programme is that of the individual (if they decide they do not want to continue then you must stop the test). You should explain the full procedures and programmes that any individual will be following, give them details of the group they will be in, if any, and tell them who will be testing them. This is an important part of testing as it allows you to be sure that the subject is clear what they are doing. You do not want the results to be affected by a lack of understanding on the subject's part.

As always, confidentiality is important. You should make this clear to all involved and ensure the identity of all your subjects and their information is used only for research purposes and any information will not display their names. It may be necessary to prove that the above considerations have been adhered to. For example, you may be conducting some research at a local health club, and one of the clients is injured while undergoing a fitness test. The manager of the club will want to know if it was your testing that caused the injury. In such a case, it is not only important that you have stuck to certain guidelines while testing and that you were suitably qualified, but that you can show this to be the case. You could find that the injured person decides to sue you or the club for negligence.

Informed consent

This is the reason that informed consent forms are used in research and testing situations. An informed consent form is a document that has been signed to show that your subjects have been informed of the test (told of what is going to happen) and have given their consent (agreed to undertake the test). An informed consent form should explain what risks may be involved in the study. It can also include a list of possible benefits. The form must make it clear that cooperation in the research is voluntary and that the

subject can withdraw their consent at any time. The form can also contain some detail on the testing procedure. With children, or if the test was very complicated, the procedures can be made easier to understand. The subjects should be encouraged to ask questions if they have concerns. It is a vital part of the form that the subject signs to say they have read it, understood what is in it and are happy to be part of the study.

definition

Informed consent: somebody agreeing to do something when they have been given the details of what they are to be asked to do.

The Data Protection Act

Any information on a subject, athlete or client should be kept confidential. This is in line with the Data Protection Act 1984. Records (hard copy or computerised) should be kept where only authorised personnel can access them. When reporting information to other people, personal details should be left out. For example, if you were reporting back to a group of athletics coaches regarding some research you had done on strength training, you would not include in your report or presentation the names of the subjects you had used. It would be sufficient for you to give general background information, such as age, gender, ability level, years of training, and so on.

Key learning points

- Qualitative research: research by asking questions and gathering opinions.
- Quantitative research: gathering information based on numbers.
- Quality of information: information needs to be reliable and valid.
- Data classification: data can be divided into nominal, ordinal, interval or ratio.
- BASES code of conduct: set of principles to which to adhere to when working with athletes.

Data collection techniques

Data collection is the process of obtaining information. The method used will depend upon whether you are after quantitative or qualitative information.

Qualitative techniques

Interviews

This is where the researcher will ask a series of questions to a person. Interviews tend to be used mainly with qualitative research. A good interview will rely on trust and rapport to obtain information. Interviews are good at assessing somebody's attitude towards something. They allow for probing or follow-up questions, such as 'What do you mean by ...?' This can lead to a deeper level of understanding. On the negative side, interviews are time-consuming, they can be open to biases on the part of the interviewer and can result in the interviewee giving answers that are socially acceptable.

LEARNER ACTIVITY   Interview

- Write a list of approximately 20 questions that you would like to ask a sportsperson of your choice.
- Take part in a role-play exercise where a fellow student pretends to be your chosen sportsperson. Conduct the interview using whichever method you wish to record the answers to your questions.
- Write an evaluation of the interview stating what went well and how it could have been improved.

During interviews information is usually recorded via a voice recorder or camcorder. A voice recorder is less obtrusive as some people feel nervous faced with a camera. However, the use of a camcorder can give some non-verbal information that may prove beneficial. If neither is available, you will have to record responses by hand. To become a good interviewer requires both ability and practice. If the answers obtained are to be valid, it is essential that the respondent is relaxed and at ease. It is vital that the answers given are genuine and, for this reason, it is important that you do not influence the response by the nature of your questioning or even by your presence. As with questionnaires, your research is relying on what the subject says, which may or may not be the truth. Techniques can be used to test the

validity of a person's answer (i.e. repeated or similar questions can be asked to see if the answers are the same).

Focus groups

A focus group involves a group of people (five to ten people) who focus on certain given topics. The researcher will guide the session so that the issues discussed are relevant to the research. Focus groups are very good for exploring people's ideas. As with interviews, issues can be probed in more detail. Due to the group situation people may feel less self-conscious than when being interviewed one to one. This may result in the answers being more honest. As with the interview, information can be recorded and analysed after the event.

Focus groups do have some limitations. Leading the group and facilitating discussion is a difficult skill. Often one or two people dominate the group. A lot of time can be spent discussing unnecessary information.

LEARNER ACTIVITY
Focus group

- Pick a sports-related topic that you know will generate a good debate, such as race, gender, drugs in sport, football players' wages.
- Based on this topic write down some key issues you wish to explore.
- With your fellow students organise yourself into small focus groups and lead an investigation into people's opinions on the given topic.
- Record the results of the focus group. This could be a list of five main points the group decided upon.
- Feed back these points to the rest of the class.

Observations

A further means of gaining information or data for research is to observe the subject in a given situation. Observations are common in psychology-based research – seeing what a person will do in a certain situation. This method is used because it is less obtrusive then administering a questionnaire or asking questions in an interview. Also people do not always do what they say they will do! Coaching is another area that relies on observations for obtaining information. In some sports, elaborate systems have been developed to code categories of actions or behaviour. These systems can be used by researchers to analyse coach or player behaviour, as well as being used by the coach themselves to help players improve performance. A good example of this is in football, where notational analysis systems designed to examine the amount of activity (walking, running, jumping) undertaken by players of different positions can be used to devise individualised training programmes.

There are many methods of observation:

- the observer may be external to the group, such as a coach observing their own players' performances
- the observer may be part of the group; imagine you wanted to look at football hooliganism, the best way to do this would be by becoming part of the crowd and experiencing what happens.

Observations are useful because you can see what actually happens and you are not just relying on what people say they will do. Observations are especially useful with individuals who have weak verbal skills or with people who are unwilling to talk about what they do. As with the previous methods of data collection, investigator effects may have an impact – people may react differently when they know they are being observed. It could be that the behaviour you wish to observe occurs when you are not there. All methods of data collection will have limitations.

Quantitative techniques

Quantitative techniques are mainly based on gathering numerical information. They can also give rise to qualitative information. Questionnaires would be such an example. Imagine you designed a questionnaire to measure the amount of exercise people do. Quantitative information could be in the form of the number of times a week somebody exercises, while the qualitative information might be the reasons why they exercise or how they feel when they are exercising.

Questionnaires

A very common method of collecting data in qualitative and quantitative research is to use a questionnaire. A questionnaire is a method of surveying people's opinions or habits by asking subjects to respond to questions.

The major limitation with a questionnaire is that the results consist of what people say they do or believe, and this is not always reliable. Careful planning is essential if you hope to get valid results. You can use techniques to try and identify whether people are telling the truth. One way to do it in a questionnaire is by repeating questions or asking very similar questions. If a person is telling the truth or answering each question properly (and not just skimming through the questions) you would expect the same answer to these repeated or similar questions.

You need to think about what you wish to get out of the questionnaire (i.e. what information you hope to collect). Careful consideration also needs to be given to the actual questions asked. There are two common types of question that could be asked in a questionnaire. These are closed questions and open questions.

- A **closed question** is one where you give a certain number of choices and the person has to pick one. An example would be 'How do you rate your fitness?', with the possible answers being not at all fit, slightly fit, moderately fit, very fit or extremely fit. You know the answer will be from this list.
- **Open questions** have no list. The question is open-ended such as 'How could you improve your level of fitness?' In this case the range of possible answers is almost endless.

A further concern is the order in which you put the questions. Often questionnaires collect general information first – age, gender, job, sport played, and so on. This gets people in to the habit of answering the questions. They are more likely then to complete the questionnaire. If the questions become more difficult or detailed it may be necessary to give examples.

A major problem with research involving questionnaires is people either not completing the questionnaire sufficiently or not completing it at all. To obtain the best results from a questionnaire, it should be relatively short, as you are more likely to get a response.

You also need to think about how you are going to present your results. A lot of open questions may give you lots of information, but this will be hard to summarise in a table or graph. Too many open questions are difficult to analyse and are time-consuming. Numerical data are easier to analyse, so you should try to code the possible answers (yes = 2, no = 1). There are different ways that questions can be coded. Scaled questions can be in the form of, for example, the Likert scale, which indicates a person's level of agreement with a statement or question.

Using the previous example on fitness, the following is a scaled question: How do you rate your fitness?

Not at all fit	Slightly fit	Moderately fit	Very fit	Extremely fit
1	2	3	4	5

With a scaled answer the person must pick one of the answers that they feel is most suitable. If you want more than one answer, then a ranked question would be better. An example could be 'Which sport do you enjoy participating in most?', where 1 is the most preferred and 5 is the least, and where the options are basketball, rugby, cricket, running and cycling. The respondent would then rate each sport from 1 to 5 based on their level of enjoyment of that sport.

Sometimes you may be looking for one answer, a simple yes or no:

Have you ever been skiing?   Yes   No

In this example, only two choices are needed – you have either been skiing or you have not. If necessary, further categories can be used, such as a 'Do not know' option.

When designing a questionnaire you are trying to make it as easy as possible to fill in, but also easy for you to report the results accurately and clearly.

You should try to avoid leading questions – that is, ones where you are suggesting the answer in the question. 'Do you think football players receive too much money?' could be considered a leading question, as it almost implies that footballers are paid too much money.

Also avoid unclear terms. If a question begins with 'usually' or 'mostly', how often is that? Once a day, once a week, or something different? Also try not to use jargon or technical terms. If you ask a member of the public 'How many times per week do you take part in aerobic exercise?' they may not understand the term aerobic. They may not answer the question or may answer it incorrectly.

Not only do the questions need to be made very clear, so too does how you want them answered. Will there be tick boxes or do respondents circle a number?

Once you have designed your questionnaire, try it out on a small group of people first (not the ones you aim to use it on later). Is it liable to cause offence? Check the wording that you have used. If you ask 'Which sports do you enjoy?' and then proceed to give a list, what if somebody wants to specify a sport you have not listed? You could include 'other' in the list or ask 'Which of the following sports do you enjoy?' Is the method of response easy? People tend to fill in questionnaires as quickly as they can. They do not want to spend time having to complete the answers. Are there any overlapping categories? Asking how old somebody is and then having answers of 16–20, 20–24, for example, is annoying to a 20 year old. Which category are they in?

LEARNER ACTIVITY
Questionnaire design

1 Design a questionnaire to investigate an area of sport/exercise (e.g. exercise participation).
2 Use the questionnaire to obtain data.
3 Write a report of the results of the questionnaire and provide a brief discussion of these results.
4 Prepare a presentation of the results of your investigation (this can be done individually or as a group). Things to discuss in your presentation are:
  ● an explanation of the questionnaire (why you have asked certain questions, why they are in that order)
  ● the scoring/coding system; present the data in the most effective format (tables, graphs, etc.)
  ● an analysis of your results, with constructive criticism (whether they could be improved, whether they are valid and reliable), and remember to have some implications at the end (what you have found, if you have any recommendations).

Questionnaires offer an inexpensive way of gathering large amounts of information in a relatively short time. As previously stated, the information provided can be analysed using qualitative and quantitative techniques. Normally questionnaires guarantee anonymity. This would make it difficult to have follow-up questions or to clarify if there are issues or misunderstandings. Reply rates are low with questionnaires as you get answers only from the people that are motivated enough to fill them in. This will impact on any results you obtain.

> **definition**
>
> **Anonymity:** keeping identity a secret.

Laboratory and field-based data collection

Tests are generally divided into laboratory-based tests and field based tests. Laboratory tests are performed in a closed environment.

> **definition**
>
> **Closed environment:** a situation that is tightly controlled, where things do not change.

In a closed environment things are closely controlled and maintained. The advantage of this is that there are fewer factors that will affect the results. Let's say you wanted to perform a fitness test on one of your athletes. In a laboratory-based test the room temperature would be constant, the amount of exercise can be exactly measured, and there will be no effects from spectators or fellow players. These conditions make the results reliable. That means you could reproduce the test conditions easily and be able to compare results from one test to another.

It would seem therefore that laboratory tests are very useful, and they are. But sport is not played in a lab! This is the reason for field-based tests or tests that are performed in a real-life setting. If you were a football coach and you wished to measure your players' fitness you could do this out on the football pitch, on grass, where players will play their games. You could organise the bleep test on the pitch. The results will be affected by the weather; the state of the pitch, the player's footwear, but at least the results can be related to football (i.e. running on grass).

LEARNER ACTIVITY
Quantitative data collection
- List five laboratory-based tests of performance.
- List five field-based tests of performance.
- Give the pros and cons of the ten tests you have listed.

Research design

There are a number of steps involved in designing a research project.

- First, you need a question that you are going to ask, such as how does exercise affect heart rate?
- Next you need to ask what you think will happen, based on any previous research (e.g. heart rate increases with exercise).
- Then you would need to collect the data (e.g. measure heart rate during exercise).
- Finally, you have to examine the results in line with your expectations (e.g. does heart rate go up, and by how much?).

The most common type of research design is to have two groups: one that undertakes some form of training or treatment and one that does not. You would then test both groups at the start of the research and both groups at the end of the research and see if there is a difference. This is termed a 'pre-test post-test' research design. For example, if you wanted to determine if relaxation reduced anxiety before a game, you could have two groups. The first group would receive relaxation, while the other would not. For this experiment you could make a hypothesis.

> **definition**
>
> **Hypothesis:** an idea you wish to test.

Instead of just saying relaxation has an affect on anxiety, it is normal to give three hypotheses:

- the null hypothesis
- the alternative hypothesis
- the directional hypotheses.

In the above example, the hypotheses would be as follows.

- Null hypothesis: there will be no difference in pre-game anxiety between groups one and two.
- Alternative hypothesis: there will be a difference in pre-game anxiety between the two groups.
- Directional hypothesis: group one (which undergoes relaxation) will rate their pre-game anxiety lower than will group two (the group that has no relaxation).

Not all research uses the pre-test post-test design. It may be that you are not looking at the effects of anything you do. You might wish to examine how much sport and physical education children do in schools and the effect it has on the sport they take part in outside school. In this case, the thing you are measuring is how much sport is played outside school. The thing you change would be the amount of sport and physical education done in school. But you cannot change this as the school, local education authority and the government determine it. What you can do is compare one school with another, one area with another, or even compare countries (France and England). This is termed a 'comparative study'.

Another method of research is to compare evidence or information over time, instead of comparing one region with another. You may wish to see how the amount of physical education in schools has changed over the years. This method works if you have the data or can obtain it. If there was little or no data you would have to set up a study to study things in the future. Let us imagine that you wish to see the effect of school sport and physical education on the health of children in your area. However, you have no information on the current state of health of the children. What you would have to do is monitor the sport and physical education participated in by the children, and their level of health. You would have to do this over a period of time to see if their health improved, declined or stayed the same. This type of study is called a longitudinal study. It is often used in the study of health and disease. It requires time; some longitudinal research can last for many years. Therefore, this method would not be suitable for a small research project.

Qualitative data analysis techniques

With qualitative data there tends to be lots of information (e.g. long lists of answers to questions or

descriptions of behaviour). This information needs to be reduced into a manageable amount. This process of data reduction is called coding – that is, grouping the data into meaningful segments.

definition

> **Coding:** classifying information or sorting it into groups.

Key learning points

- Qualitative data collection includes such methods as interviews, focus groups and observations.
- Quantitative data collection can involve questionnaires, laboratory-based tests or field-based tests.

LEARNER ACTIVITY
Coding qualitative data

Imagine you have interviewed a group of people as to why they like/dislike doing exercise. The answers they give are listed in the table below.

| My wife says I need more exercise |
| To get fit |
| I like the guys I play football with |
| It gets me out the house |
| I need to lose weight |
| I feel better when I have done exercise |
| All my friends play netball |
| It makes me look good |
| I enjoy running |
| I want to improve my aerobic fitness |

Segment the data into meaningful categories. You may want to divide the responses into health issues, fitness issues, psychological issues and social issues.

In qualitative analysis there are no right and wrong answers. You interpret the data as you see fit. Coding can be time-consuming, especially if the amount of data is large. To this end, computer software has been written to analyse the data. Currently the most popular qualitative data analysis packages are NUD-IST, ATLAS and Ethnograph.

Displaying data

Frequently in qualitative research, diagrams are drawn to show how something works or to clarify the relationship between various things. In the case of the previous activity looking at why people like/dislike exercise, we could have drawn the following conclusions. People do exercise for health and fitness benefits which will overlap with each other. In addition, people exercise for social or psychological benefits that again are interlinked. In diagrammatic form this may look like Fig 4.01.

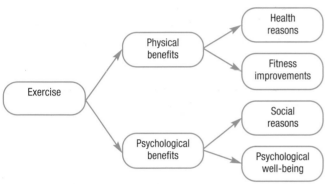

Fig 4.01 Example of a diagram that presents conclusions

LEARNER ACTIVITY
Qualitative research

- Devise a list of interview questions to look at why people drop out of doing sport or exercise.
- Interview a group of people and obtain a series of answers to our questions.
- Code the responses into meaningful areas.
- Draw a diagram to explain why people drop out of sport or exercise.

Verifying data

It is important in any form of research to verify that the data you have is accurate and the conclusions you reach are valid. In qualitative research this is done via triangulation. This is a method of cross-checking information using different sources or different methods of data collection. It is a common technique used by detectives and journalists. If two people say the same thing independently of each other, it is more likely to be true.

Triangulation: the process of checking facts from different perspectives

Key learning points

- Data reduction: breaking the data up into smaller pieces by coding.
- Displaying data: showing the results of coding in an easily understandable format.
- Verifying data: the process of checking what you have found out is true.

Quantitative data analysis techniques
Statistical tests

Numerical analysis of data is called statistics. Descriptive statistics are about describing data (i.e. the average value or the range of numbers). Inferential statistics are more detailed. They examine things like relationships or differences in data. They can be used to determine the answer to your research question or your hypothesis. Relationships look at how one thing affects another and can be analysed using correlations. Differences decide if one group is different from another.

Correlations

To measure if two things are related, a correlation can be performed. Correlation means association or relationship. For example, if the question 'Is heart rate related to environmental temperature?' is asked, it can be answered with a test of correlation. The correlation will give an exact level of the relationship between the two things. This value or number is called the 'correlation coefficient' and is normally given by the letter 'r'. If two things are in an exact relation with one another, as one goes up so does the other, they have a positive correlation. The correlation coefficient (r) to represent this is +1. If there is no relationship r is 0. However, if the relationship is the other way around, one goes up as the other goes down, this is a negative correlation. For this r would be −1. Therefore you can see that r can be between +1 and −1. A high correlation, association or relationship is just that. It does not necessarily mean that one thing causes the other.

Once you have measured r what does it mean? When a correlation is calculated a probability or significance value is also given in addition to the r value. This significance value is a number (e.g. 0.10). The value gives the likelihood of what you are testing being true. For example, if you were testing a relationship and you had a significance value of 0.10, this would mean that 10 times in 100 you would be wrong if you said there was a relationship. The good side of this is that 90 times in 100 you would be correct. In social science (sports science, psychology) the customary significance value is 0.05 (being wrong 5 times in 100). If the significance value is higher than 0.05, then there is no relationship (or at least, it is not significant). Statistically, the specific significance value of 0.05 is written as p < .05.

A Pearson product-moment correlation is one type of test that can be performed. In order to do this, a number of criteria must be met. The main assumptions are as follows.

- Data must be from related pairs – they should be collected from the same subject (e.g. height and mass from the same person).
- Data should be interval or ratio (explained previously).
- Each variable should be normally distributed (normality).

If the assumptions for a Pearson product-moment correlation are not met then a Spearman rank-order correlation is performed.

If the relationship were significant, the statistics would be reported as (r = .931, p < .05). The significance value is less than .05. This means the relationship is meaningful.

> **definition**
>
> **Normally distributed:** data that follow a particular pattern where most data points are near the average.

Difference tests

Difference tests can be divided into two types: parametric and non-parametric. Parametric statistics should be used when the data are normally distributed and interval or ratio level. Non-parametric statistics are used when the data are not normally distributed.

Difference tests are used for studying the effect of something on a group of individuals – for example, how training affects fitness levels. The outcome of difference tests is reported the same as a correlation, but, rather than a relationship, a significant difference is referred to. For example, there is a significant difference (t = 1.352, p < .05) in heart rate between a group that does exercise and a group that does not.

With parametric statistics the most frequent difference tests are t-tests. An independent t-test is used when investigating differences among groups. A dependent t-test is used when you are investigating a difference inside the group. If the data are not parametric, then t-tests cannot be performed, and alternative tests are used. The Mann-Whitney U test is a non-parametric difference test that can be used with

---

LEARNER ACTIVITY Correlation

An exercise physiologist is interested to see if there is a relationship between maximum volume of oxygen consumed (maxVO$_2$), as measured in a physiology lab, and marathon performance (best time to run a marathon). The results collected are given below.

MaxVO$_2$ (ml per kg per min)	80	75	69	56	75	63	68	64	69	76
Marathon performance (mins)	141	138	172	149	154	165	161	155	144	134

- Identify the null and alternative hypotheses for this inquiry.
- Determine which test of correlation is appropriate and run the test in Excel, SPSS or a similar spreadsheet (you may need help from your tutor to do this).
- From your results, explain the value of the correlation coefficient and what it means.
- Which hypothesis should be accepted and why?
- What might affect the results?

different groups. The Wilcoxon matched-pairs test is a non-parametric test that can be used within the same group. Another non-parametric test is the Chi square test. It looks at the frequency of occurrence of something.

Sampling

When we are conducting research we want to use the results to explain what could or would happen to anybody. However, measuring everybody is not possible so we often look at a small group of the population. This is called a 'sample'. A value (e.g. the average height) that is taken from a sample is called a 'statistic'.

The best way of selecting a sample is random sampling. Random sampling is a system where a group of subjects is selected at random from a bigger group. Anybody in the group has an equal chance of being selected for the group. With the use of random sampling, the chance of bias is reduced.

> **definition**
>
> **Bias:** the error that occurs when estimating a value from a sample of a population.

Recording and displaying data

For numbers, one method of displaying the values is to chart them as a frequency distribution. One type of frequency distribution is a scatter plot. This type of plot records a point for each time a certain value occurs. Instead of showing a series of points, vertical bars can be used. This is called a 'histogram', as shown in Fig 4.02, created using Statistical Package for Social Scientists (SPSS). SPSS is similar to Excel in that it

allows you to record and display data. It is often used due to its versatility when using statistics. The most important consideration when displaying data is the presentation. The data should be displayed in the most effective format (there is no need to include raw data). Tables of data should contain units and must have a suitable title. Graphs should also incorporate units and labels and contain a title. Any picture, photograph or diagram including graphs and histograms, but not tables, is referred to as a figure.

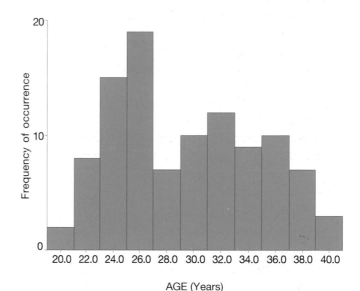

Fig 4.02 A histogram showing ages of a group of individuals

Interpreting results

With a group of numbers it is possible to use one number to represent them all. This number is the average, or as it is correctly termed, the 'central

LEARNER ACTIVITY Displaying data

This activity should enable you to enter data into tables and to produce graphs. Based on the data in the table below, create tables with the following columns (in a spreadsheet such as Excel or SPSS).

For male subjects:
Subject number | Height | Body mass | BMI |

For female subjects:
Subject number | Height | Body Mass | BMI |

- The data should be to one decimal place (e.g. 84.0).
- The last row in each table should contain an average of each column.
- The headings and averages should stand out clearly.
- Each table should be given a title to be placed above the table, e.g. Table 4.01: Anthropometric data

Gender	Height (cm)	Mass (kg)	BMI
M	186	80	23.4
M	187	74	21.2
M	190	82	22.7
M	177	72	23.0
M	188	78	22.1
M	176	97	31.3
M	185	89	26.0
M	179	66	20.6
M	192	84	22.7
M	190	85	23.5
F	165	55	20.8
F	163	75	20.2
F	165	51	19.0
F	168	51	18.7
F	156	57	23.4

tendency'. The three most commonly used measures of central tendency are as follows.

- The **mean** is the sum of all the numbers divided by the amount of numbers. This is the most common type of average. When people refer to the average they are normally talking about the mean. The mean of 8, 12, 16 and 24 would be 15.
- The **median** is a value that divides a group of numbers exactly in half. Half the numbers are higher and half are lower. If there is an odd number of values, the median is the middle one. With an even number of values, the median is the average of the two middle values. The median of 23, 47, 50, 67 and 88 is 50.
- The **mode** is the most frequently occurring value in the list of numbers. For individuals having the following ages, 17, 18, 19, 20, 20, 20, 23 and 27, the mode is 20.

definition

Central tendency: the average, a number that can be used in place of many numbers.

LEARNER ACTIVITY Averages

- Choose an easily measurable variable, such as shoe size or height, and then ask each member of your class to find out what the values are for your chosen variable.
- Then calculate the mean, mode and median for each variable.

Dispersion

Statistics can also be used to give an idea of the variation of the data. Variation in a set of numbers could be the difference in the scores (e.g. weight) across the group. The set of numbers could represent the weight of a subject measured a number of times. The terms 'between-subject variation' and 'within-subject variation' are used to describe these two issues.

The easiest measure of variation to calculate is the range or the difference between the biggest and smallest (e.g. if your oldest subject is 24 and the youngest is 18 the range is six years). The problem with measuring the range is that, to a large degree, it relates to group size: the more people you measure the bigger the range will be. A different, but more complicated measure of variation in scores is the standard deviation. The simplest explanation of this is the spread of the scores around the mean. The mean and standard deviation are sometimes shown together (e.g. average height was 1.67 m +/- 0.22 m). Interquartile range is similar to range, but it takes out the top and bottom 25 per cent of the numbers. The type of dispersion data that you report will depend on the measure of central tendency that you use. With mean, the standard deviation is used, the median uses interquartile range, and with the mode it is range.

Normal distribution

Normally distributed data peaks in the middle. In the example in Fig 4.03, if we measured IQ for a sample of the population we could say that the majority of people have an average IQ, while a small number have high and low values.

Normally distributed data is described as bell-shaped when plotted on a graph. In an exact normal distribution, the mean, median and mode are all the

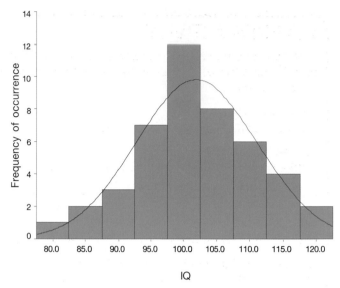

Fig 4.03 Data displaying normal distribution

same. If the distribution is asymmetrical the data are not normally distributed, which can be due to skewness (the peak is more to the left or right) or kurtosis (the curve is excessively peaked or flat).

Outliers

Outliers are unusual data measurements. They can be a result of error or they may be correct readings caused by a strange event (a subject has an abrupt change in heart rate). The trouble with outliers is that some information (like the average) can be greatly affected. If this is the case, the median could be used instead of the mean, as the outlier would not affect it. Many people try to ignore outliers. But you need to think long and hard about doing this. Was the data point a mistake or is it a genuine reading? If you have any uncertainty, you can include results both with and without outliers to see how much they differ.

LEARNER ACTIVITY Central tendency and dispersion

- For the following set of data, calculate or determine the mean, median and mode (this can be done easily in a spreadsheet).
- Comment on why the values are different. It may help to plot a frequency distribution (histogram).
- In addition, calculate or determine the standard deviation, interquartile range and range (use a spreadsheet).

Subject	1	2	3	4	5	6	7	8	9	10	11
Age	22	19	16	21	23	27	24	19	26	19	17

LEARNER ACTIVITY Displaying data

- Enter the data from the table below into a spreadsheet (e.g. Excel or SPSS), coding where appropriate.
- Produce another variable to illustrate the difference between resting heart rate and maximum heart rate.
- For each variable, look at the data and determine the level of measurement (e.g. nominal, ordinal, interval/ratio).
- For variables that are at the interval/ratio level, determine whether they are normally distributed. To do this you will need to produce a histogram. If you are using Excel you will have to make a new table from which you can create the histogram. In SPSS you can just select 'histogram'.

Age	Sport	Heart rate (rest)	Heart rate (max)
18	Badminton	80	200
19	Football	81	180
19	Hockey	88	182
18	Climbing	72	200
20	Hockey	66	189
29	Football	77	175
25	Hockey	72	200
19	Hockey	69	176
18	Football	72	190
19	Hockey	69	191
19	Hockey	79	192
19	Hockey	62	188
18	Hockey	62	193
19	Football	79	189
19	Badminton	63	193
19	Climbing	87	183
20	Climbing	68	194
19	Golf	49	183
19	Climbing	76	198
20	Badminton	57	194

Key learning points

- Parametric tests: statistical tests that can be performed on normal data.
- Non-parametric tests: tests for data that are not normally distributed.
- Distribution: the grouping of the data.
- Displaying data: showing the results of numerical analysis, commonly in tables and graphs.
- Central tendency: the average value.

Review questions

1 What is informed consent?
2 How does the data protection act relate to research?
3 Explain the following terms: reliability, validity and objectivity.
4 Describe the classification of data, giving examples.
5 What are the ethical issues involved in research in sport?
6 What are the pros and cons of questionnaires?
7 What are the important considerations when conducting an interview?
8 What are correlations?
9 How would you go about designing a questionnaire?
10 What is normally distributed data? Give examples.

References

Clegg, F. (1993) *Simple Statistics: A Course Book for the Social Sciences*, Cambridge University Press.

Silverman, D. (2005) *Doing Qualitative Research: A Practical Guide*, 2nd edn, Sage Publications.

Thomas, J. R. and Nelson, J. K. (2005) *Research Methods in Physical Activity*, 5th edn, Human Kinetics.

Research project in sport and exercise sciences | 05

Goals

At the end of this chapter you should understand:
- how to plan a research project
- how to conduct a research project
- how to produce research project
- how to evaluate a research project.

Research is about finding solutions to problems, obtaining facts and determining what is the truth. A research project allows you to bring different areas of study together. You can use your knowledge of sport and exercise science to investigate a particular topic or question you have an interest in. It could be related to a certain sport (e.g. fitness in football referees), general issues in sport and exercise (e.g. the amount of physical activity undertaken by school children), or it may arise from one of the disciplines within sport and exercise (e.g. sports injuries). Whatever topic you choose, you will have to spend a large amount of time working independently. This will include reading literature, collecting and analysing data, and writing up the whole project. The aim of this chapter is to help you achieve such a project.

Planning a research project

Often the hardest part of the plan is getting started. Thinking of a good idea takes time. It is useful to have a number of topics you hope to look at, and then if one idea proves impractical or too hard to test, you have an alternative. A good research question is something that you can answer, such as are netball players fitter than football players, or is body weight related to upper body strength. It also needs to be practical so you can test it. You need to think about the time available, what resources and equipment you have and the subjects you can use. It needs to be of importance so that your conclusions have an

implication for somebody or something. How will your research help an athlete, coach, official, teacher, administrator or manager? Finally, your research should be interesting so that others will read it and you will stay focused enough on it to complete it. It could take more than six months for you to finish the whole project.

What is to be the focus of your study? If you do not already have an idea in mind, you need to come up with one. Many people find this the hardest part of the research project. A good way to start is to think about a sport or type of exercise that you know a lot about or that takes your interest. If, for example, you are a keen cyclist, you may then wish to do a project on some aspect of cycling. Another way to narrow the area is to do it by a discipline within sport and exercise science. For example, you may decide to do a project involving biomechanics. You could even combine the two areas to arrive at a project that incorporates the biomechanics of cycling.

LEARNER ACTIVITY
- Come up with four different ideas for a project
- Discuss your ideas in groups or with the rest of the class.

Writing an introduction

Your plan will need to have an introduction, which should be the background to the research. This will include why you picked this idea, what you may already know about this topic or what you might have recently found out. Try to predict the usefulness of your research. Remember the research needs to be of some practical use. There is little point in asking a group of relatively unfit people to follow a 12-week training plan consisting of cycling, running and swimming and having your objective to see if aerobic fitness levels increase after the training programme.

You would be able to predict the results in advance with some certainty. It would be better to look at different training methods, intensities or durations and see how they compared.

Now you are becoming more specific, you can start to decide on a title. Do not worry about this too much as the title may change slightly as you find out more about your research area.

Aims and objectives

The aim or objective of the research must be clear. Along with finding a good title this is an area that people find hard to get right at first. You may have a general idea for a project (e.g. fitness in football players), but not a specific aim. Using this example what would you test? Who would you test? The topic is too general. It needs to be focused on one particular aspect of fitness in football players.

Contrast this with the following topic: the anaerobic fitness levels of college male first-team and second-team football players. This project is far clearer. What is to be measured is specific – anaerobic fitness. But you would still need to decide how to measure it and justify your chosen method. The people you are going to investigate are clearly stated. The objective is very clear. Therefore you have something that you can test. You might suggest that first-team players will have a higher level of anaerobic fitness than second-team players. This would be easy to test by measuring it in both sets of players and then comparing the values.

Having a good question to test helps make the research clear. It helps you think about how you intend to collect the data. The aim will define the scope of your project. If you are looking at fitness in young male footballers, this is what your conclusions should be about. You may like to generalise to older footballers, or females or rugby players but you would be speculating. So remember: keep the research focused on one area.

Collection of evidence

Next in your plan you should include how you aim to collect your data. This will include:

- research design
- equipment
- procedures
- methods of data collection.

The research design will depend upon what you are hoping to examine. If you aim to examine the effect of a training programme on a particular measure such as flexibility, you would need to record the value of this measurement before and after the training programme. This would allow you to see if what you were measuring had changed and to infer that your training plan had caused the change. This is referred to as a pre-test post-test research design.

The validity and reliability of the tests you are planning to form should also be taken into account.

Reliability

definition

Reliability: the measure of how repeatable a set of data is.

If you recorded the same thing on two separate occasions, would you expect the value to be the same? Imagine you were coaching a cyclist, and to monitor his training and recovery you recorded his resting heart rate each morning. Assuming your cyclist was not overtraining or suffering from an illness, you would expect the resting heart rate to remain fairly constant over a number of weeks. If you measured similar values each morning this would display good reliability. You would then be assured that your measuring technique was reliable. If the values did change, you could then be sure it was due to something other than your measuring – your athlete may be suffering from a cold, which might have elevated their resting heart rate.

Validity

definition

Validity: the meaningfulness of a set of data – does it actually measure what you intend it to measure?

Many fitness tests are available to measure different aspects of fitness. Therefore, you need to be sure that the test you are using does actually measure the component of fitness that you are interested in. For example, if you want to measure the flexibility of a person and choose the sit and reach test you are actually only really measuring the flexibility of their back and hamstrings. This may not be a true representation of their overall flexibility as they may have very flexible shoulders and hips.

Resources and equipment

The resources and equipment you are going to use will depend upon what you are going to measure. The main considerations you have are these: can you get access to the equipment you need and do you have the skills to use it? Do you need to book a room or a video camera? Do you know how to do this?

Subject considerations

The final consideration with regard to how you are going to do things concerns your subjects: what groups of people do you have access to and who are you actually planning to test? For most people after actually deciding on a topic this is one of the most difficult areas. The first thing to remember is you cannot test everybody as it would take too long. Therefore you need to pick a group. This is called a 'sample'.

When you have a potential group what are the ethical and legal issues? Does anybody need to be qualified to run any part of the test? Will the test be safe? What happens should there be an accident? Have you told the subjects what they have to do? Have they completed an informed consent form, etc.?

definition

Informed consent: telling somebody what you want them to do and asking them to sign to say they understand what is expected from them.

Recording data

Besides determining how to measure things, careful thought needs to be given to how you record the data. It could be that you have to devise a score sheet or record sheet on which to write data. You may be intending to use a computer-based system to store the results directly. Is there enough space on the system? Do you need portable storage? What about backing up the data?

Although at the planning stage you do not know what results you will get, you can outline how you intend to present them. If there are any calculations on your data, what will they be and why are they necessary? What tables and graphs do you hope to produce? How are you going to analyse your results? Which statistical tests could you use on your data?

Action plan

A good research project requires a good action plan. The plan is crucial to set out clearly what is to be done and why it is necessary. By writing the plan, a lot of the problems that you may otherwise have encountered can be avoided. You should also devise a timetable for the implementation of the project. Include deadlines for:

- researching information
- carrying out testing
- analysing results
- writing up individual sections of the research.

Table 5.01 shows an example of an action plan.

Table 5.01 Example of an action plan

Task to do	Action	Date to complete task	Actual date task completed	Follow-up activity
Determine fitness tests to use to measure aerobic fitness	Ask teacher what the centre has available	19 Oct	17 Oct	Find out if you can use the fitness tests in your planned location
Find out if you can use the fitness tests in your planned location	Ask teacher and check with site supervisor where fitness tests are planned to take place	24 Oct		

LEARNER ACTIVITY
Action plan

- Devise an action plan for a project. Make sure the plan has a clearly testable objective (something you can measure). As well as a brief introduction, you should also include the resources you will need and your research design (how you aim to test your objective). Outline how you will record and analyse data. Give a realistic timetable for your plan.
- Present the plan to your peers, justifying your research methods, and defend it from questioning.

Key learning points

- When planning a research project have clear aims. Decide what you are going to measure and how. Consider legal and ethical issues.

Conducting a research project

Sources of information

Once the topic of research has been decided, the next consideration is obtaining information about the topic. The first part of any research project will consist of reporting what is already known about the subject area. This will form the literature review. The evidence gathered will either be from a primary or secondary source. Primary data or information is that which is reported directly by the author who measured or observed it. Secondary data is reported from the original primary source by another author. If you include information from a secondary source you are trusting that the information has been recorded and analysed correctly.

Libraries

A lot of information for your project will be obtained using some form of library information system. All libraries have a method of cataloguing their information, and contain a large variety and amount of different resources from books, e-books, journals, e-journals, newspapers, videos and CD-ROMs. All

this information needs to be made available to anybody who requires it, hence the use of library catalogue or searching systems.

The system will be a database of all records of information (books, journals, newspapers) using a standard format of recording the information. The most common method of cataloguing information is by the authors who wrote it. If you know the name of an author, you can enter their name into the system and it will report all the books by that author. Most systems will have more than one way of searching. As well as being listed by author, books will be listed by title. Keyword searches are another method of looking for information (e.g. injuries). To widen the search still further the system may have a 'subject' search, which will include all works in a subject area (sports therapy, for example).

More and more people are using electronic sources of information. Many libraries subscribe to e-books and e-journals so the material can be read on the computer screen. There are also searchable databases, which have been developed in certain subject areas. 'SPORTSDiscus' is one example; it is a database of information from across the globe in the area of sport and exercise science. It can be accessed via the internet and a subscription is required.

The internet

Undoubtedly you will also want to use the internet to obtain information. The internet will have two uses. First, it can be used as a way to access information contained within libraries. It can also be used to access general information contained on the millions of web pages on the internet.

Information presented on the internet should be treated with some caution. Books, for example, are checked to make sure the information in them is correct, but this is not the case with the internet. Information can be posted on a website by anybody. It does not have to be reviewed or checked in any way. Having said that, the internet does contain some very useful websites. A good use of the internet and one that saves a lot of time is getting information that would normally have to be sent by post. You might want to obtain some information from the American College of Sport Medicine which you can find on its website. You might be after the medal table from the Athens Olympics, or maybe the mission statement of the Football Association.

Whatever the source of the information, it is important that it is reliable and valid. Reliable information is information that can be backed up. It is evidence that is reproducible. If it is valid, it is an accurate and a true account of something.

LEARNER ACTIVITY
Internet sites

Use the internet to investigate selected topics. The following internet sites are good starting points for general information:

- www.sportscoachuk.org – sports coach UK (formerly NCF)
- www.aafla.org – Amateur Athletic Federation of Los Angeles; includes publications, research reports and sports library
- www.culture.gov.uk/sport – government site including policy documents and research information on sport and media.

Resources

While you are collecting research information from the library and the internet, you also need to be thinking about actually collecting some data or doing some testing. Do you need to book a room or a gym? Is it available at the time you wish to use it? Do you need to book a video camera and can you use it? When you pick it up will the battery be charged? Will it have a spare? Why not have a dry run through everything first just to check it all works. If you encounter any problems write them down, then go away and think about what you need to change.

Ethical and legal Issues

It is essential that you keep confidential any results and information from your project. That means you should not mention people's names in your study. You could use letters or numbers to identify people if need be. This is in line with the Data Protection Act 1984. In sport and exercise research special consideration is needed because the research involves humans as subjects.

Any experiments that you design need to be ethical. For example, asking people to undertake training or a diet that could have negative effects is unethical. A great deal of thought therefore needs to go into designing the project. Even when you are happy that the research is ethical, the health and safety of your subjects is vital. The American College of Sport Medicine suggested that researchers should adhere to

the Declaration of Helsinki; this has a code of practice for measurements in humans.

If your research involves working in a school you may need to have a CRB check done to ensure that you have not committed any crimes that would prevent you from working with children.

If the testing you are planning to perform requires the participants to take part in a physical test, you should ensure that they all complete a health-screening questionnaire to ensure that they are fit and able to take part in your tests. A PAR-Q (Physical Activity Readiness Questionnaire) is a commonly used questionnaire that will help you determine if the participants you have selected are suitable to participate. An example is shown in Table 5.02 on the following page.

There is a range of questionnaires available but they all ask similar questions.

Informed consent form

Your participants should also complete an informed consent form prior to participation in any tests.

An informed consent form lets a subject know what to expect during the exercise test, and the associated risks involved. It also stresses that any participation in the tests is voluntary and that the subject has the choice to stop at any point. An example of an informed consent form is shown in Table 5.03 on page 99.

Data collection methods

Most projects will involve recruiting a group of people to test. The group you choose is called the 'sample'. If you were examining the amount of exercise undertaken by college students, it would not be practical to question all students, so you would just question a sample. The sample you use should not be biased in any way. They would not all be the same age, or all from one course, unless you specifically state '18-year-old college students'. Your sample will be made up of volunteers or those who are available at the time, such as your classmates. You should try to avoid any bias in your research as this limits any conclusions that you make.

definition

Bias: influence in an unfair way.

Table 5.02 Example of a Physical Activity Readiness Questionnaire (PAR-Q)

	Yes	No
1. Do you have a bone or joint problem which could be made worse by exercise?		
2. Has your doctor ever said that you have a heart condition?		
3. Do you experience chest pains on physical exertion?		
4. Do you experience light-headedness or dizziness on exertion?		
5. Do you experience shortness of breath on light exertion?		
6. Has your doctor ever said that you have a raised cholesterol level?		
7. Are you currently taking any prescription medication?		
8. Is there a history of coronary heart disease in your family?		
9. Do you smoke? If so, how many?		
10. Do you drink more than 21 units for a male, 14 units for a female?		
11. Do you have diabetes?		
12. Do you take physical activity fewer than three times a week?		
13. Are you pregnant?		
14. Are you asthmatic?		
15. Do you know of any other reason why you should not exercise?		

If you have answered yes to any questions please give more details

....

....

If you have answered yes to one or more questions, you will have to consult with your doctor before taking part in a programme of physical exercise.

If you have answered no to all questions, you are ready to start a suitable exercise programme.

I have read, understood and answered all questions honestly, and confirm that I am willing to engage in a programme of exercise that has been prescribed to me.

Name ....   Signature ....

Trainer name.......................................   Trainer signature..............................

Date ....

You may be a keen netball player and want to prove that netball players have higher VO_2max compared to hockey players. Your choice of subjects could bias your results in favour of this being proved correct. For example, you might choose netball players who play at a higher level than the hockey players. Or you might choose netball players who play in positions that require high levels of aerobic fitness, such as the centre and the wings, and then choose hockey players who play in positions that require low levels of

Table 5.03 Example of an informed consent form

1. Explanation of the test(s)

You will perform a test that will vary in its demands on your body. Your progress will be observed during the test and stopped if you show signs of undue fatigue. You may stop the test at any time if you feel unduly uncomfortable.

2. Risks of testing

During exercise certain changes can occur, such as the rising of blood pressure, fainting and raised heart rate, and in rare cases heart attacks or even death. Every effort is made through screening to minimise the risk of these occurring during testing. Emergency equipment and relevantly trained personnel are available to deal with any extreme situation which occurs.

3. Responsibility of the participant

You must disclose all information in your possession regarding the state of your health or previous experiences of exercise, as this will affect the safety of the tests. If you experience any discomfort or unusual sensations it is your responsibility to inform your trainer.

4. Freedom of consent

Your participation in this test is voluntary and you are free to deny consent or stop the test at any point.

I have read this form and understand what is expected of me and the tests I will perform. I give my consent to participate.

Subject signature...
Print name ....
Date ....

Tester's signature ....
Print name ....
Date ....

aerobic fitness such as the goalkeeper. This would bias your sample and probably prove your theory to be correct.

You may wish to do your test in a realistic environment. This is called a field-based test. If you use specialist facilities this is termed a 'laboratory test'. The advantages of doing laboratory tests are that they are more controlled as you do not have to worry about external factors like the weather. But remember sport is not played in a lab so field tests, although difficult, may give you a truer picture of what is actually happening.

Accuracy and precision

If you are using specialist equipment it is essential that you can use it correctly. Your major consideration will be how true is the data you collect. Data should be accurate and precise, and for this to be the case a

certain level of knowledge and skill will be required by the tester. The data can be only as precise as the measuring system. If a metre rule has only cm increments you will be able to record only to the nearest cm (i.e. 1.75 m, not 1.755 m). The accuracy of the data relates to how close your measurement is to what you actually intend to measure. Checking that equipment is calibrated correctly will help ensure accuracy.

definition

Calibration: the process of checking and adjusting equipment to ensure that it is providing accurate readings.

An example of calibrating a piece of equipment would be to pass a sample of a known percentage of oxygen through a gas analyser and check that it is giving the correct reading. If it is not, the piece of equipment should be adjusted until it is producing an accurate reading. Some pieces of equipment should be calibrated prior to every use, such as an online gas analyser, but other equipment like weighing scales rarely need calibration.

Questionnaires

Not all research involves collecting and analysing numbers. Some requires information on a person's behaviour or attitude towards something. This is common in qualitative research. Questionnaires, interviews and observations are used to gather evidence and, although the data or information is in a different format to quantitative research, the question of truthfulness or exactness is just as important. Is the information you obtain valid? If you set out to measure anxiety levels and do so using a questionnaire, are the answers you receive accurate? Does your questionnaire actually measure anxiety? Do people tell the truth? All these issues need to be addressed.

What about reliability? If you repeated your questionnaire in similar situations, would you obtain similar results?

The design of the questionnaire, the type of questions and the way they are worded can all affect the validity and reliability of your results. This will also be the case if you decide to conduct individual interviews rather than administer questionnaires.

Recording results

A clear data sheet can save both time and confusion when recording results. Imagine you have designed a questionnaire to investigate the amount of sport and exercise undertaken by college students. Once all the completed questionnaires have been returned, you need to record all the results in a clear and effective format. Putting them in one table will allow you to see all the results together and will be better for subsequent analysis.

There are many ways of recording data. For example, you could record the most common answer. This is called frequency analysis: looking at how often something occurs. You could even list things as the most frequent, the second most frequent, the third most frequent, and so on. This is called putting things

in rank order. It is important to do this sort of analysis with your data so you can start to make sense of it.

You may have used a questionnaire asking a series of questions and then coded the answers. For example, the possible answers may be strongly agree, agree, disagree or strongly disagree. By giving these answers numbers from 1 to 4 you can more easily do data analysis (i.e. what is the average reply?).

You could convert your answers to percentages and work out what percentage agrees or what percentage answered yes to a question. If you have a long list of answers or a lot of possible answers you can examine the range of responses. If you were measuring heart rates of a group during a fitness test you could use all these methods. Who has the highest heart rate (rank order), how many had heart rates between 131 and 140 beats per minute (bpm) compared with 141 and 150 bpm, or what was the average, or what percentage were below a certain figure (frequency analysis)? Even what was the difference between the highest and the lowest (range). The list of options is almost endless.

Use of media

Numbers are fairly easy to record, as are written responses. Verbal replies require a little bit more thought. You could just write down what you hear when somebody is speaking. This method is called transcribing. It is a lot more convenient and a lot more accurate to take an audio recording or a video recording. These two methods allow you to play over and over again the recording so you can ensure that you get an accurate account of what was said. Video will even lend itself to observation of the individual as well as hearing what they say. This may give you more detailed information than just the audio recording alone.

Whichever method of data collection you use, at some point the information will be converted into an electronic format, such as a spreadsheet, a database, or an audio or video file. This needs to be kept safe and it is wise to keep a duplicate copy.

Preliminary analysis

When collecting data it is good to look over it to check that it looks as it should. Do you notice any discrepancies? Are the responses to your questionnaires as expected? If all the answers are no or disagree perhaps you need to redesign your questionnaire. If you are measuring heart rate and the results are not what you might reasonably have expected, are you sure the heart rate monitors are recording correctly? A little bit of time spent early on looking at the results could save you time in the long run. You may even start to get a pattern of how the results are going, enabling you to draw some initial conclusions.

Storing information

When conducting a research project you should always keep your original data. This is the raw data. This can come in many forms – heart rate readings, heights, weights, video footage, questionnaires, data sheets and notes of an interview. If you keep this data you can then go back at any time and refer to it to clear up any questions you may have. As with any data it is worth copying the information in case the originals are lost or damaged. This is especially the case with any electronic data. Files can become wiped, corrupt or infected, computers can crash, and data can be lost so backups are essential. Remember to use different types of storage. Electronically data can be saved on your hard drive, the school or college hard drive, your flash drive, CDs, DVDs and even on the internet.

> definition
>
> **Raw data:** the original data you collect – questionnaires, video recordings and tally charts are examples.

LEARNER ACTIVITY

- Collect some data for your project (unless your tutor provides you with some data).
- Present the results of your research to the rest of the class.
- Concentrate on the results (e.g. graphs, tables, averages, percentage differences).

Key learning points

- When conducting a research project be familiar with the equipment, be clear on how you are going to collect data, and once again consider legal and ethical issues.

Producing a research project
Scientific structure of the research report

The project will be reported in writing. The general structure of a written project is given below. Obviously on the front will be the title page, followed by:

Preliminary pages
i.   Abstract
ii.   General contents
iii. Contents page for figures and tables
iv.   Contents page for appendices
v.   Acknowledgements

Introduction
Literature review
Method
Results
Discussion
Conclusion
References
Appendix

The **title page** should have on it the title of the study, the person who wrote it and the year. You may wish to include the name of your college.

The **abstract** is a summary of all sections of the report. It is a review of the entire project. The abstract must be clearly separated from the main body of the report. Normally in the region of 250 words, it will contain information on the aim, research plan, outcomes and overall conclusions. This summary of the research appears as the first page of the report, but is usually written last since you cannot summarise until the end.

The **contents** page will list the chapters or the sections of the report, together with the number of the page on which each begins. Have separate contents sections for figures and tables and appendices.

The preliminary pages will also contain the **acknowledgements**. This is the part of the project where you can write something personal, thank those people who may have helped you during the project. It should include thanks to your supervisor for support, and there might be others who you would like to mention.

The purpose of the **introduction** is to give an outline of the research area. It should address the question why you are doing the project. The introduction sets the tone of the project. What is the project all about? How did you become interested in it? It should make the objective of the project clear. It should be interesting to make the person reading want to find out more. The end of the introduction should be the aim of the research.

The **literature review** is an in-depth analysis of the research. It will be a detailed look at all areas within the project. Key terms need to be defined. You should explain why your research is needed and how athletes, coaches and physical educators will benefit. Try to evaluate what is already known about your research topic. You can use many sources of information for your literature review. Conclude the review with a statement of what it is you are going to test.

The **method** should be simple to write, as it explains what you did. It can be divided into sub-sections. In the first part explain about the subjects, how many, what groups, give details on the average age, on what sports they play or their current fitness level. This will give a good indication of the subjects that you have in your project. Next include your research design – how you collected your information. After the research design give a list of the equipment you needed to use. The final part of the method is to report the procedures you undertook. Give enough information so that anybody reading it could reproduce exactly what you did.

The **results** are the actual data collected by you. They should be presented in as clear a format as you can. They should make it easy to see what you found. You do not need to include lists of numbers or piles of questionnaires unless you are specifically asked for this. Results can be summarised using descriptive statistics. Patterns that you see in the data need to be described (e.g. heart rate increases with time). Tables and graphs are the best way of presenting lots of data but you need to write about what is in the table or graph. What was the average heart rate? What did heart rate go up to? What time did heart rate start to decrease? These are the sorts of things you need to be looking for. Besides describing results, statistics are used to analyse results to allow conclusions to be made. These are called inferential statistics. They allow you to make accurate statements about your results. Consider an investigation to see if a given training programme lowered the resting heart rate of a group of individuals. Your results might show that the average resting heart rate of the training group is 58 bpm, while that of a control group (a group of

subjects who did no training) is 61 bpm. There is a difference of 3 bpm, but is this meaningful or is the difference just due to chance? A statistical difference test (e.g. t-test) would be able to establish if the difference in the values was significant – large enough to mean something. Where calculations are performed in analysing data, a sample calculation is helpful to explain the analysis. This can be included in the main text or in an appendix.

The **discussion of results** is the most central part of your research. This is your chance to explain what has happened and why. You should analyse the results. Do not merely repeat the results that you have just described. Try to give a summary of what you found. Always refer back to the aim of your project and to what you said in the literature review. Did your idea of what was going to happen come true, and if not why not? Also explain what went wrong and why. What could you have done better or were there things beyond your control? Explain how the project could be improved. After this, discuss the implications of your findings. Ask yourself what use is the information you have found. Finally, give suggestions for future research. This is an important part of research, to give ideas as to what needs doing next.

The **conclusion** should be statements of fact. What are your main findings? These should relate back to the aim of your research. The conclusion does not need to be too long or detailed. Just list the findings and do not start new arguments or ideas here.

The **references** section will list the references used in the report. In the text you will have quotes or citations referring to other people's work and then at the end of the report you will have a detailed list. The Harvard system of referencing is commonly used in academic work. You need to report the reference in the text itself by giving the author of the work and also the year of publication. The full title of the work is given in the references section. If work is transferred into your own words, this is called paraphrasing and quotation marks are not needed. If a quote is included in the text, you should use single quotation marks.

In your report the reference would appear like this: 'Recovery for athletes is essential (Child, 2004)'. If you are referencing more than one book you can name them all, in order of date of publication: 'The stresses imposed by training can be harmful (Child, 1999; Tyzack, 2002; Watt, 2003)'. If more than one author was involved in the work you would reference them all: '(Ball, Brees, Chance and Stokes, 1989)'. You do not need to consistently list all authors. Once you have listed them once you can from then on refer to the first author followed by *et al.* This is only the case if there are more than two authors – for example, 'Ball *et al.* (1989) have shown that …'. You may come across two authors with the same surname. If this is the case use initials: 'A report (Barton, R., 2006) has indicated …'. If you need to reference more than one article by the same author in the same year add letters to the different references: 'Thomas (2000a, 2000b) showed that …'.

Sometimes it may be necessary to refer to letters, emails or conversations. These are called 'personal communications'. They would be referenced as follows: 'In a telephone conversation on 10 August 2005 Mr J. A. Gilbert pointed out that …' or 'Mr D. Goodchild's letter dated 1 May 1998 claimed that …'.

You may need to refer to work with no author's name: 'A recent report by the American College of Sports Medicine (2001) states …' or 'the *Teesside Times* (15 July 2007, p. 4) reported that …'.

There are guidelines for entries in the list of references, depending on what you are referring to. Books are referenced as follows:

Thomas, J. R. and Nelson, J. K. (2005) *Research Methods in Physical Activity*, 5th edn, Illinois: Human Kinetics.

Journals and periodicals are referenced as follows:

Morris, T. (2000) Psychological characteristics and talent identification in soccer. *Journal of Sports Sciences*, 18, pp. 715–26.

Online (electronic) material is a little different as it has not been published in the traditional way. Sometimes the date it was posted on the internet is given. Whether it is or not, the date you accessed it should be given. Therefore, an online reference would appear as follows:

Sport England (2006) Equity and Inclusion [Online]. www.sportengland.org/index/about_sport_england/ equality_standard_for_sport.htm [accessed 24 April 2006].

After the reference section is the **appendix**. Here you can include any information that does not readily fit into the rest of your report. This is where you would put your raw data (which would just fill up the results section), and data collection sheets. You can refer to any of the appendix in the main body of the report. Multiple appendices should be labelled as Appendix A, B and C, etc. If you refer to an appendix in your report you could do it like this: 'Appendix A shows that …' or 'Crowd attendances are on the increase (see Appendix A)'.

Drawing conclusions

The final part of a research project is to draw the whole process together. When discussing the results, you should attempt to cover three main areas. Initially, in conjunction with the statistical analysis, evaluate the results. What happens to the values you are measuring? Do they go up, down, stay the same or fluctuate? Are there any differences, similarities or relationships? Are your values in line with what you would expect based on previous evidence? After the analysis, be critical of your results. Are your results valid? Do they display reliability and objectivity? What errors did your investigation contain and how did this affect your results? What may limit any conclusions you aim to make? Finally, what are the implications of your results? What have you found out and what does it mean?

To recap, be analytical, be critical and draw clear conclusions.

Internal coherence

A good report will follow the format laid out above. In addition to being in the right format it should read well. The sections should link together well, so if you have talked about something in your review of literature you should refer to it in your discussion. Always keep in mind the aim of your project and constantly refer back to it. Discuss what you find in relation to what you set out to do. Make sure there is a direct link from the aim to the conclusion. If you set out to investigate whether children from one school were fitter than those from another, were they? If they were not, say so. Remember you will not always be able to prove what you had hoped to prove.

Presentation of the report

When writing up the project, it is important that it looks good and reads well. For it to look good you need to be familiar with word-processing software and spreadsheets. Using IT to record, report and present the results will go a long way to making it look professional. For it to read well you need to concentrate on sentence structure, grammar, the order in which you write things and, most importantly, you need to think about the reader.

Guidelines on report writing

- Write the report in the past tense. Say what was done (e.g. heart rate was measured), list what you found (e.g. average heart rate was 167 bpm).
- Write in the third person, do not use 'I' and 'we'. For example, 'heart rate was recorded every 30 seconds' is better than 'I recorded heart rate every 30 seconds'.
- Try and be factual rather than subjective. It should sound like a good newspaper article, one you might read in *The Times*. The wording should be clear and easy to understand, so keep it simple. If you intend to use technical terms explain them first.
- Write in paragraphs. A paragraph should be more than one sentence, but do not make them too long. The information in a paragraph should be related. Look at the report. How does it look to you? A big block of text is not appealing so try to break things up. This can be done with the use of headings.
- Headings are useful for the reader to make the text easy to follow but they can also help you, giving you a structure to follow. If you are suffering from writer's block jot down some topic headings and then try to write some information under each one.
- Make sure you write in sentences and check for spelling errors, as errors put people off what they are reading.
- Proofread the report before you hand it in as you would with any piece of work to be marked. Remember, the marker has to read it so therefore you should read it too. Ask somebody else to read it if you have time.
- Number the pages as this makes it easy for you to refer back to different sections. Normally the main text is numbered using Arabic numerals (1, 2, 3). The preliminary pages do not have to be numbered but if you want you could use lower-case Roman numerals (i, ii, iii).
- You should not assume that people will automatically understand any abbreviations that you are using. Spell them out the first time you use them, so you would refer to the British Association of Sport and Exercise Sciences (BASES) on its first appearance and thereafter just use BASES.
- If you intend to use Latin abbreviations make sure you know what they mean: i.e. means 'that is', whereas e.g. is short for 'for the sake of example'.

Oral presentation

Normally on completion of their research people are asked to give a short presentation. Your presentation might include video footage, handouts or a computer slide show. It is not possible in a short presentation to cover the whole project so pick out the main parts. Start by introducing your area of research and explain why you chose it. Give the main literature relating to your project. After this explain the method and list the main results. Graphs and tables are helpful at this point. The most important part of the presentation and the bit that will show you understand the research is where you discuss the findings. Why did certain things happen, or not happen? What went right and what went wrong? What are the implications of the study? Finish the presentation with your conclusions and remember to relate these back to your original aims.

When giving a presentation from computer try not to include too much information on any one slide. Use the slides to talk around the topic rather than just reading them out. Try to include some pictures or diagrams that people will find interesting. Maintain eye contact. Look confident – it is your research and you know what you did.

LEARNER ACTIVITY
Oral presentation

- Present some research to the rest of the class (this can be your own or somebody else's).
- Concentrate on two main areas: the reason for the research, and the results and how they were obtained.

Key learning points

- The key components of a research project are introduction, literature review, method, results and the discussion, which will include conclusions.

Evaluating the project

The evaluation of the project is both useful to you as a learning experience and to anyone that might listen to, read or hear what you have done. You could do this by performing a SWOT analysis of your project.

- **Strengths**: these will be things you have learned from the project. They could be personal things – how to collect data, how to present information – or, more generally, things like the results of your study.
- **Weaknesses**: these will be your limitations or the limitations of your research. You may have been limited in the people you could test or you may not have been able to measure what you first set out to measure. Being clear in your limitations shows you have a good understanding of your research so do not think this a negative thing.
- **Opportunities**: if you were to do the study all over again, what would you do? What could somebody else do if they were to follow up your study? How could they improve on what you did?
- **Threats**: are there any things that question the validity of your information? Are you sure the conclusions you arrived at are true? Is the information all your own?

Be specific and give examples. If you think your data presentation was one of your strong points, where is the evidence? Include an example of one of your graphs.

Recommendations

This is the reflective part of the research. Use the information from the SWOT analysis. What would you change? What did not work as expected? If you could go back several months what would you do differently? Even more importantly, what advice can you give to somebody who wants to do research in the same area? What things could they investigate that would add to what you have found? You can always improve on things, so do not be afraid to say what went wrong in your own study as it shows you have an understanding of the research that you undertook.

Key learning points

- On completion of a research project evaluate the whole process.

Review questions

1 List five possible research topics.
2 Explain why you might need a CRB check when performing your research.
3 What is informed consent?
4 List different ways to record data.
5 Outline the structure of a research report.
6 Explain the Harvard system of referencing.
7 How could you reference the internet?
8 What is a hypothesis?
9 Explain different ways you can present data.
10 What does writing in the third person mean?

Reference

Thomas, J. R. and Nelson, J. K. (2005) *Research Methods in Physical Activity*, 5th edn, Human Kinetics.

Goals

By the end of this chapter you should be able to:

- perform a notational analysis for sport
- compare a numerical model to sporting performance
- compare a technical model to sporting performance
- provide feedback on performance to an athlete or team.

Biomechanics is concerned with internal and external forces acting on the human body, and on implements used during sport (bats, balls, etc.), and the effects produced by these forces. Biomechanics is used to analyse sports technique, which allows athletes or coaches to improve performance or avoid injury. The coaching process involves observing performance, evaluating it in comparison to what should be done and then instructing the performer as to how they can improve. The observation process is more than merely looking at a performer and this chapter will focus on different methods of analysing performance.

Notational analysis for sport

Notational analysis: a simple method of recording what happens during a sporting contest.

Fig 6.01 A football manager making notes

As the name 'notational analysis' suggests, you note down what happens while observing the performers. This single recognised process makes it easier to allow for comparison between observers, players, teams and games.

Performance criteria: something that you measure to record performance.

The things that you decide to measure are called 'performance criteria'. These can be based on what an individual player does or on what the team does – or you can include both. For example, in volleyball you could record the number of times a player serves in court (equally you could record this for the whole team). You could record the number of times a team returns the ball after service. If you require more detail you could record the exact outcome of the serve – that is, does the ball hit the net (and not go over), does the ball land out of court, is the ball returned or does it land in the opponent's part of the court (an ace)? This is only one part of a volleyball match so you could also record passes (volley), hits (smash) and blocks. You would then start to gather a lot of detail on a player's or a team's performance.

Data representation

Different things can be measured in different sports. In football you could measure passes, shots, fouls, interceptions, headers, tackles, dribbling, saves. You can even measure time spent walking, jogging, running and sprinting. In basketball you might measure passes, shots (both 2 point and 3 point), free throws, fouls, assists, rebounds and dribbles. In tennis you could record serves, second serves, backhand and forehand shots. In cricket you might consider (for a batsman) scoring shots, non-scoring shots and played and missed. The number of sports and the criteria you could measure are almost endless and will depend on the detail you wish to obtain.

As you saw in the football example, not only can you measure skill but you can also measure effort. You can examine the amount of time a player is walking, running, sprinting, jumping, etc. The best way to gather any of this information is in the form of a tally chart or checklist (see the example tally chart for a volleyball game, below). This can then easily be stored on a database or in a spreadsheet. Remember, you need to think about what you are going to record.

Take football as an example. It is no good just counting the number of passes each player makes. You would be better dividing these criteria up further. You could have successful short passes (less than 5 m), unsuccessful short passes, successful long passes (over 5 m) and unsuccessful long passes. Similarly with headers, just recoding the number gives little

Team: Middlesbrough Mavericks Opponents: Stourport Swifts Date: 1 May 2006
Set No: 1

Player	Serve		Reception		Volley or dig		Smash		Block		Time on court
	+	−	+	−	+	−	+	−	+	−	**Minutes**
1	IIII	I			IIIIIIII IIII	IIIII					22
2	I	II	I		III	I	III	I	I	IIII	22
3	III		I		IIIIIIII	III					22
4	II			II	IIII	II	IIII	II	II	III	14
5	I	I	IIIII	I	IIIII			IIII	III	I	II	22
6	II	I	IIII	I	IIIII	III	III	I	II	IIIII	22
7											
8	II	I			IIII	II	I		I	II	8
9											
10											
11											
12											

information. Why not include defensive headers and attacking headers? Then, under the attacking headers, you could have on target and off target.

Data analysis

Recording the information should be fairly straightforward. If you have completed the activity above you will have realised that the two biggest problems you will encounter are the time it takes (a game of football could last for two hours including breaks) and how much you have to concentrate. For this reason you may wish to look at only part of the game. This is common when doing notational analysis. Having obtained the data, the difficult job for a coach is understanding what is going on and making the necessary changes. When you have a detailed list of what has happened during the game you need to condense this into a more manageable format. The best way to do this is to look at totals, percentages and averages. Total numbers – for example, the number of shots, number of passes or number of serves – give you an indication of player involvement. You would expect your midfield player in football to have more passes (and more successful passes) than your forward. However, you may want your forwards to have had more shots on goal. Remember, the analysis you perform is only as good as the data you collect from the game.

Statistics

> **definition**
>
> **Statistics:** the process of describing and analysing data.

The number of passes a player makes may tell you how involved they were but if you have a number of successful and unsuccessful passes you could work out pass completion percentages. Take the following example from a football match.

Player A makes 30 passes during a game and 15 are successful, while player B makes ten passes and eight are successful. What can you work out from this information?

Player A makes more passes but only has a 50 per cent success rate, player B makes fewer passes but at 80 per cent success. Does this mean player A works harder yet player B is more skilful? You would need to check other statistics to confirm this. It should at least give you some ideas as to what you should be working on in training.

Fig 6.02 Football players passing the ball

Graphical representation

The reason you are collecting all this information is to try and improve a player's or a team's performance. You will need to explain to the team or player what they are doing right or wrong. This can be more easily done using graphs rather than tables of numbers (a picture paints a thousand words).

Imagine, as a volleyball coach, you have been working on the serve in training. From your next match you could record service information. You may have successful serves for each player, which could be put into a graph and displayed in training. You could do this using a simple bar chart

Alternatively you may have a football coach who is trying to get their team to pass the ball more. You could record the number of passes for the outfield players and display this information in a pie chart. The player who has the greatest slice of the pie is the one who has passed the most. You could look at this

LEARNER ACTIVITY Notational analysis

- For the previous activity you should have a completed tally chart. Make a list of statistics you are going to measure (e.g. % passes by each player, number of points scored by each player, average number of fouls by the team).
- Record the results in a table (similar to the one shown below).

	Total passes	% Successful	Total shots	% Successful
Team				
Player 1				
Player 2				
Player 3				
Player 4				

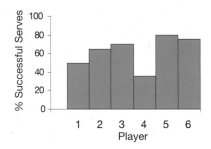

Fig 6.03 Sample bar chart

LEARNER ACTIVITY
Displaying results of notational analysis

- From the previous analysis you have done select some of the criteria (e.g. % errors, % interceptions, distance run).
- Produce a graph to display this information

over a series of games. You could then look at the average number of passes by the team in one game compared to another. You will also need to think about which type of average you use (see Chapter 4: Research methods for sport and exercise sciences). Let's say you want to look at the average number of passes per game and also the most common type of pass (e.g. less than 5 m back or square, less than 5 m forward, more than 5 m). For the average number you would take the mean (total passes divided by number of players). However, for the most common you would look at the mode (the one that occurs the most).

Key learning points

- Notational analysis – a method of recording the performance of individuals and teams.
- Performance criteria – the things that you measure (e.g. passes, catches).
- Data analysis – what you do with the data you have collected (e.g. calculate averages or percentages).

Comparing a numerical model to sporting performance

Teaching skills requires not only knowing what to teach (i.e. being aware of the correct technique), but also knowing how to eliminate errors and avoid actions that limit performance or cause injury. Developing a model of a skill allows a coach to observe, analyse and then correct the athlete's technique by comparing their performance with a standard.

The first part of developing a model of performance is to determine the aim of the skill in question. In the volleyball serve the objective is to strike the ball so the opposition either cannot return the ball or will find it difficult to do so. It is also important that the serve is legal (no foot fault, time fault, ball travels within playing area). To achieve this objective, accuracy is important, as is timing and power. If the ball is mis-hit, hit too softly or inaccurately it will be easier for the opposition to return the ball.

The next step is to devise a theoretical model of the skill. This could be done with the help of a video of an elite performer or this may have already been done and the information is available in a book or on the internet. The skill can be divided into phases and the biomechanical features of each phase identified. It is common to divide skills into three phases. It is important to identify where one phase ends and the next begins. Most striking, kicking, hitting and catching skills are divided into:

1 a preparation phase
2 a force-production phase
3 a recovery phase.

Examining the volleyball serve (see Fig 6.04), it has a preparation phase that consists of holding the ball in the non-striking hand and drawing the hitting hand back. The force-production phase involves bringing the hitting hand into contact with the ball. The recovery phase is to stop the movement of the body and be ready for the next action.

Even repetitive skills, like running, swimming or cycling, can be divided into three similar phases. Take running as an example. The preparation phase could be the foot landing on the floor (the heel strike in normal running). Driving off from the front of the foot is the force-production phase. Recovery will be bringing the foot through ready for another heel strike. If the skill is more complex, such as the triple jump, the skill can be broken into major phases that are then subdivided into further sections.

With the skill divided into parts, it is then possible to analyse each phase. For the volleyball serve, what position is the hitting hand in? What position are the hitting arm and shoulder in? What about the trunk and the legs? How is power generated? Where is the ball struck? How is topspin created or does the ball float? Look at stability and timing.

There are many ways to analyse movements. We are going to concentrate on two:

a) Preparation phase   b) Force production phase   c) Recovery phase

Fig 6.04 Skill phases

- numerical models – those involving things that can be measured in numbers (e.g. speed, distance, force)
- technical models – those involving technique aspects of a skill (e.g. foot position, hand position, centre of gravity movement).

Numerical model production

As with all methods of movement analysis, the objective is to look at what a particular athlete does in comparison to the correct model. The correct model could be based on what is in a coaching manual or determined by observing an elite performer. The important thing is to have an accurate starting point from which to make comparisons.

There are many numerical components that can be examined in sporting performance, including linear motion, angular motion and projectiles.

Linear motion

The action of objects (e.g. balls, people) can be described by measures such as distance, displacement, speed, velocity and acceleration. These quantities, which are used to describe the motion of objects, can be divided into two categories: vector and scalar. These two categories can be separated from each other by their definitions.

definition

Scalar: a simple measurement with no direction.
Vector: a measurement in a certain direction.

Distance and displacement are quantities that have similar meanings and yet the definitions are different. Distance is a scalar value that measures the length of the path a body follows during motion. Displacement is a vector quantity that refers to how far from an initial position an object has moved, or to put it more simply, its change in position. If an athlete ran 2 km north, then 2 km south, they would have run a distance of 4 km but a displacement of 0 km. Displacement being a vector quantity, the 2 km north is cancelled by the 2 km south.

Speed and velocity are related to distance and displacement. Speed is a scalar – it is a measure of how fast something is moving. If something is not moving speed is zero. Speed is determined by the equation:

Speed = distance/time

The units usually used for speed are metres per second ($m.s^{-1}$), but miles per hour or kilometres per hour/second are also used.

LEARNER ACTIVITY Distance and displacement

1 Using a piece of string measure the distance of the cycle route below.

If 1 cm represents half a mile, what is the approximate:

(a) distance
(b) displacement

of a cyclist if he completes the route?

2 A triathlon consists of swimming, cycling and running set distances. If an athlete takes part in a triathlon with the following elements:

(a) a swimming course 1600 m in length in a swimming pool
(b) a cycling course of eight laps of a 5 km road circuit, with the start and finish line in the same position
(c) a running course of one lap of a 10 km road circuit, with the start and finish separated by a 200 m straight

what would their distance and displacement be for each event?

Velocity is a vector – it measures an object's rate of change of position. Envisage a person jumping up and down yet always returning to the same position. If measured over time although they were moving up and down their change in position is zero since they would return to the floor. Similarly, an athlete completing a lap of a 400 m track would cover a distance of 400 m but a displacement of 0 as their finishing position is the same as their starting position.

The equation to work out velocity is:

Velocity = displacement/time

As with speed, the units for velocity are meters per second but direction needs also to be included, e.g. south at 30°.

Acceleration is a vector quantity that is measured by the rate at which velocity changes. Therefore, an object is accelerating if it is changing its velocity. Decelerating is the opposite of accelerating so it is slowing down. People often refer to a person accelerating if they are moving fast, but an athlete can be running very fast and still not be accelerating. Accelerating is velocity increasing; constant velocity, even if very fast, is zero acceleration.

The equation to measure acceleration is:

Acceleration = change in velocity/time taken

It can be worked out by finding:

$$\frac{(vf - vi)}{t}$$

Vf = final velocity
Vi = initial velocity
t = time interval

The units for acceleration are metres per second per second (m^2).

Angular motion

In sport, movement or motion is quite often not in a straight line, such as a golf swing or the action of the leg in running. However, the same concepts and principles used to describe linear motion can be used to explain motion in a circle. The major difference in measuring angular motion is the unit that it is measured in. With linear motion metres (m) are used to determine distance and displacement, and all following units are taken from that (e.g. $m.s^{-1}$, $m.s^{-2}$). With angular motion, changes in position are measured by angles, the units of which are degrees (°).

The position of a particular object, such as a golf club, at any moment in time is its angular position.

LEARNER ACTIVITY Speed and velocity

1 Refer back to the triathlon race mentioned in the previous activity. The time taken for the winner to complete the race was:

Distance	Time
1600 m swim	30 min
40 km cycle	90 min
10 km run	45 min

Work out the average speed and average velocity for the different components of the triathlon.

	Speed (m.s⁻¹)	Velocity (m.s⁻¹)
Swim		
Cycle		
Run		

2 Dan and Gary were competing in an 800 m race. Dan ran the first 400 m of the race in 42 seconds and the second 400 m in 58 seconds. Gary ran the first 400 m in 52 seconds and the second 400 m in 50 seconds.

Answer the following questions.

- Who won the race?
- What was the speed of each competitor?
- What was the velocity of each competitor?

This is measured with reference to something else – for example, the ground, a vertical line or another object. If angular position changes, as would be the case in a golf swing, the difference between the starting position and the final position is called the angular displacement. It is symbolised by the Greek letter theta (θ). The rate of change of angular displacement is termed angular velocity. It is calculated in the same way as linear velocity, but instead of displacement divided by time it is angular displacement divided by time.

The average angular velocity (ω) of something rotating is the angular displacement divided by the time taken to move through this displacement or angle. Hence:

Angular velocity = angular displacement/time

$$\omega = \frac{\theta}{\tau}$$

ω = average angular velocity
θ = angular displacement
t = time taken

The symbol for angular velocity is the Greek letter omega (ω) and is measured in degrees per second ($°s^{-1}$).

Angular acceleration can be calculated from angular velocity and is defined as the rate of change of angular velocity:

Angular acceleration = angular velocity/time

$$\alpha = \frac{(\omega f - \omega i)}{t}$$

α = average angular acceleration
ωf = final angular velocity
ωi = initial angular velocity
t = time taken

When examining linear motion, an object's resistance to move is called inertia and is determined by its mass. With angular motion, this resistance to movement is not only caused by the object's mass, it is also due to where this mass is located. For example, a golf club has a large proportion of its mass at the club head, while a tennis racket has its mass more evenly distributed. The golf club would have greater angular inertia. Angular inertia is more commonly called moment of inertia and is calculated as:

Moment of inertia = mass of any particle within the object $\times$ (distance from particle to axis of rotation)^2

The units for moment of inertia are kgm^2. From the equation you can see that the distance the majority of the mass is from the axis of rotation has more effect on angular inertia than the object's mass. If you increase an object's mass you increase its moment of inertia by the same level (so a heavy cricket bat is harder to swing than a light cricket bat). However, if you increase the distance between the majority of the mass and the axis of rotation (i.e. you make the object longer), the effect on inertia is the increase in distance squared (double the distance results in quadrupling the effect on inertia). Thus, swinging a driver (a long club) in golf is a lot harder than swinging an iron (a shorter club). Golf club designers are addressing this issue by designing drivers that are relatively light, using materials such as carbon fibre and titanium.

Since inertia exists (i.e. objects are reluctant to move), a force is needed to produce any movement. This will also be the case with angular motion. Imagine a tennis player putting topspin on a ball – to spin the ball they must produce a force towards the top of the ball. This force allows the ball to spin in an angular motion. In the case of the player who has just hit the topspin, if you are sitting near the umpire's chair and the tennis player hitting the topspin is on the right-hand side of the court, the direction of the force will be anti-clockwise. If the same player put a clockwise force on the ball, this would be backspin.

LEARNER ACTIVITY
Angular displacement

1 When kicking a football you record that a player's leg has moved through an angle of 105° in one-third of a second, just prior to kicking the ball.
2 From the pictures of the volleyball serve in Fig 6.04 calculate the angular displacement of the humerus (upper arm) between the starting position and finishing position. If the time it took to move from the start to the finish was 150 ms what would be the average angular velocity of the arm?

Projectiles

Projectile motion is the study of an object in flight.

Factors affecting the flight path of an object include:

● the amount of force applied to the object

- the point of force application (where the object is hit)
- the direction of force.

Take the volleyball serve as an example. The harder the ball is hit (i.e. the more force applied) the further and faster the ball will go. Where you hit the ball (i.e. point of application of force) will affect the direction it goes in. Hit it below the centre line and it will go up in the air, which is what is needed for a volleyball serve. The final thing that it is important to consider, is how the ball is struck (i.e. direction of application of force). If the ball is hit near the centre with a forward motion this will impart topspin. If the ball is hit lower down with a downward motion this will produce backspin. A spinning ball will behave more directly in the air than one that is not spinning.

> **Gravity:** the force caused by the pull of the earth's mass.

Many sports involve projectiles (balls, javelins, shuttlecocks, even humans in the long jump and high jump). A projectile is any object which has no external forces acting on it other than gravity. The flight path shape of a projectile would be symmetrical if we discount air resistance and lift. In reality, air resistance (which causes drag force) and aerodynamic factors (that cause lift) will act to affect the flight path of a projectile.

Any object moving through air, and especially water, will experience a drag force. This resists the motion of the object. The greater the speed of the moving object, the greater the drag force. For example, a cyclist experiences far greater drag forces than a runner. That is why slipstreaming plays such a vital part in cycling. A cyclist can save as much as 30 per cent of his energy by cycling close behind a competitor or team-mate.

The drag force also depends upon the size and shape of the object. A downhill skier in a tuck position wearing a racing suit will generate less drag force than a recreational skier standing more upright and wearing salopettes and a ski jacket.

The final factor that affects drag is the density of the medium of transport. Water creates more drag than air.

The flow of air around a projectile depends upon the shape of the projectile. A smooth symmetrical shape will have a symmetrical flow around it.

Fig 6.05 A downhill skier

However, in sport many objects are not symmetrical. An aerofoil is not symmetrical. Air travels faster over the top of an aerofoil than underneath it. This means that the air pressure is lower above the aerofoil than below it. The difference in pressure creates an upward force that causes the aerofoil to lift.

Various sporting objects experience lift, such as the javelin or discus. In some cases, an aerofoil is turned upside down and used to create a downward force. Spoilers on the back of racing cars force them towards the ground, making them less likely to skid off track.

Spin plays a part in the flight path of an object or projectile. A spinning or rotating object (e.g. a football kicked on one side), has more interference with the air than if it were not spinning. This causes the air to slow down on the side that is moving into the air and speed up on the side that is moving with the air. This difference in air speed causes an unequal pressure, and just as an aerofoil creates lift so the spinning ball will dip, lift or swerve depending on the direction of spin. In the case of a golf ball, which is usually hit with backspin, the ball will lift. However, it could be used for swerve (bending a football round a wall) or topspin (causing a volleyball to dip).

The surface of the object (or the balls) will have an effect on its trajectory. Examples of this are the golf and cricket ball. A golf ball is covered in dimples, which means the interaction between the surface of the ball and the surrounding air is increased. If a golf ball is hit with backspin, the dimples amplify the amount of lift force. This means the ball will travel further, which gets it closer to the hole, potentially reducing the number of shots. There is a problem though with the dimples – not only do they increase the amount of lift on a golf ball, but they also bring out any sideways movement. This is why golf balls can be hooked or sliced quite dramatically.

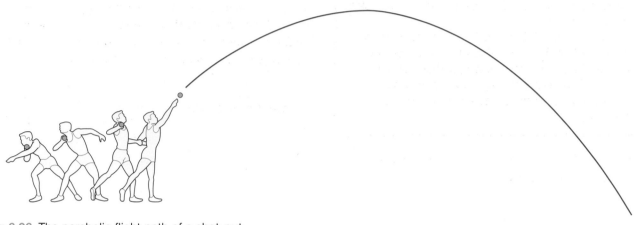

Fig 6.06 The parabolic flight path of a shot-put

Trajectory: the flight path of an object such as a ball.

In the case of a cricket ball, the seam has a key effect on its flight. The movement of air over the ball, as with any ball, interacts with the surface of the ball. But because the ball has a seam, when the air hits this it disrupts the flow of air around the ball. As with the golf ball, this causes uneven air pressure around the ball, which generates sideways movement or swing. The plan of the swing bowler in cricket is to bowl so as to cause this movement. This requires the seam to be in a certain position when the ball is released. Cricket players also polish the ball on one side to make it smooth so that when the air passes over the smooth side the change in air pressure is even greater than normal and hence the ball moves more.

A long jumper could be thought off as a projectile once they have taken off. The shape of the flight path of a projectile can be measured, including angle of release or take-off. These factors will have a big impact on how far the object will travel. If the angle of release is too high the object will go up in the air but will not go far. If the angle of release is too low the object will return to the ground before it has had much chance to go very far. Obviously the higher from the ground the object is released the longer it is in the air and so the further it can go.

> **LEARNER ACTIVITY** Projectiles
>
> Produce a series of stick figures to show the path and position of a long jumper during the flight phase of the jump. What is the angle of take-off? What affects this angle?

Measurement of movement

A more simplistic method of numerical modelling (rather than measuring velocity, etc.) is to just measure position, such as joint angles. As with the other methods of analysis, the skill is broken down into smaller phases and the position of each can be recorded. Various joint angles could be measured (e.g. ankle, hip, knee) and even the position of the centre of gravity.

concentrate on one point rather than all the body. Also if you know the position of the centre of gravity in relation to the body it will give an indication of the weight distribution or balance of the individual. Joint angles can be measured from taking a video of the skill. This is far easier than measuring joint angles during performance. If you need to measure joint angles during performance you would need to use a goniometer (this is like a big protractor).

definition

> **Centre of gravity:** a point through which all the body can be said to act – the centre point.

Detailing the movement of the centre of gravity is sometimes useful because it allows you to just

LEARNER ACTIVITY Vertical jump (continued)

Fig 6.08 Take-off phase – crouched to mid-air

Joint	Start position	End position	Muscles involved	Amount of force
Ankle				
Knee				
Hip				

Fig 6.09 Landing phase – mid-air to ground

Joint	Start position	End position	Muscles involved	Amount of force
Ankle				
Knee				
Hip				

Methodology for recording performance

Having decided on what the ideal skill is, we can now measure where our current athlete is. So far as using the numerical model is concerned, the best method of obtaining information is with the use of a video. This can easily be stored in a digital format and allows the performance to be played back at a later date to calculate numerical information.

The major limitation of using video is that you will have only two-dimensional information of a three-dimensional skill. Some skills will not be affected by this, such as running in a straight line. It is possible to record using more than one camera and combine this information.

When using a camcorder to obtain performance information there are a few things you need to remember. The image on the screen is smaller than occurs in real life. When measuring angles this has no impact. If you are examining the golf swing, the angle between the golf club and the golfer's body is the same in real life as on the screen. However, when looking at distance this is not the case. Using the same example, if you measured the distance between the golfer's feet and the golf ball it would not be the same in real life compared with on the television screen. This is referred to as perspective error.

Perspective error: objects appearing smaller than in real life when replayed on a screen.

It is therefore important that when you take a recording of a skill you have a reference object, such as a metre rule. When you play back the recording on a television you can be sure you know what distance equates to one metre. A similar thing can be done to ensure you know exactly what angle is vertical. If the metre rule is held vertically you can use this to determine exact distance and exact angles in relation to vertical.

Your second important consideration is time. If you want to measure speed (for example, club speed for a golfer or take-off speed for a long jumper) you need to be able to measure time. The easiest way to measure time is to determine how many frames per second the recording was made at. If you record

performance with a camcorder using video the recording will be played back at 25 frames per second on a television. This means that each frame lasts for 1/25 of a second. If you now want to measure club speed for a golfer driving a golf ball and you can measure on screen that the club has moved 200° in five frames, you have a simple calculation. Angular velocity (change in angle with time) is equal to angular displacement divided by the time it takes to move that displacement. In the above example we would have 200° divided by the time it takes for five frames (remember one frame is 1/25 of a second). That would give 200° divided by 5/25 second, which is equal to 1000° per second.

Fig 6.10 A golfer taking a swing

Angular displacement: the angle that something moves between from its starting position to its end position.

LEARNER ACTIVITY
Biomechanical analysis

- Obtain a recording of a sports performer undertaking a skill (use the same skill as you did for the previous activity).
- You could either record some video yourself, use some existing footage or search for a suitable clip on the internet.
- From the recording, using playback facilities, make a numerical analysis of the performance (remember it may be easier to divide the skill into phases).
- Compare what your performer does to the ideal model. (For example, is their leg velocity the same when kicking a football? Is the angle between arm and body the same when hitting the ball in a volleyball smash?)

Key learning points

- Numerical model of performance – a description of performance based on mechanical measurements (e.g. speed, displacement).
- Mechanical measurements – these can be split into linear measurements (movement in a straight line) or angular measurements (for movement about a fixed point).
- Recording performance – when recording, account for perspective error and determine the rate at which the recording is played back.

Comparing a technical model to sporting performance

As with the numerical model of analysing sports performance, for the technical model you also need to first describe the ideal: what the skill looks like performed by an elite-level performer.

The technical model uses more of a qualitative method of description. Rather than looking at the run-up speed an athletic coach would examine run-up technique (looking at knee lift, balance, arm movement). A cricket coach would look at position of hands on the bat (grip), the position of feet in relation to the body and how balanced the individual is (stance).

There is a long list of skills in different sports that can be analysed (e.g. serving, hitting, kicking, catching, throwing, jumping, running, passing, etc.). The majority of information on correct technical models will be found in coaching manuals. Good coaches remember most of the technical points related to their sport.

LEARNER ACTIVITY Technical models of elite performers

- Select a sport you are interested in.
- Produce a detailed ideal technical model of the skill. You may use coaching manuals, the internet or your own knowledge of the skill (it may be best to divide the skill into phases).

As with any method of modelling performance, the idea is to compare your performance (or your athlete's) with the correct (or ideal) model. The key to successful coaching is to be able to see where the two performances are different. You must then be able to bring about improvement. You need to highlight the areas that need improving or that contain errors.

If you are teaching the volleyball serve, one of your players may consistently serve to the left-hand side of the court. You have worked out that this is caused by them bringing their arm across their body in the recovery phase. You now need to decide how to correct the error. You might wish to break the movement down into its phases and concentrate on one phase, or you could run through the action in slow motion. A video of the correct technique could be shown. Whatever you decide, it is important that, after a period of coaching, you repeat the observation to see if your player has improved.

In group coaching sessions with beginners coaches are performing this sort of analysis all the time. They are looking at what actions the individuals are doing and then suggesting corrections based on what they see. As the performance becomes more specialist, the knowledge of the coach needs to increase accordingly. Recording the performance (via video) is useful as this allows the coach more time to observe the performance accurately.

Providing feedback on performance

Using biomechanical analysis to improve technique is based on four steps:

- describing the ideal model
- recording what your athlete is doing
- comparing the two to see what needs improving
- instructing the athlete on how to improve.

No one method of gaining information is best, as there are many ways to analyse performance. We have concentrated on two: numerical models and technical models. We could easily have looked at anatomical models of performance, ones based on examining what happens at joints (flexion, extension, etc.) and muscles (eccentric, contraction, etc.). All methods are useful and can be combined to provide a wealth of information on performance. Whichever method is used to analyse the performance, one of the main roles of the coach is instructing the athlete how to improve.

The information that the coach has may seem clear to them but remember that this may not be the case for the athlete. When giving feedback on performance (telling the athlete how they performed) and giving guidance on how to improve (telling the athlete what they need to do next) the coach should follow the guidelines given in the box below.

Coaching feedback

Clarity of information/appropriate language

Keep it simple and make it understandable. Do not use terms that the athlete would not understand. For example, telling a golfer 'The club head needs to come through faster' is easier to understand than saying 'Increase the angular velocity of the club.'

Type of feedback (verbal, written)

Use different forms of feedback. You could tell the athlete what you want them to do, but you could also show them via a demonstration. People tend to remember only about 10 per cent of what they are told, but can remember far more of what they see. You could list the main coaching points so your athlete can use them when practising alone. Written feedback can vary from a simple list of what is required to details of things like heart rate training zones.

Positive and negative feedback

Discuss strengths and weaknesses. Tell the athlete what they are good at, as people like to hear this (this is positive feedback) and it motivates them. However, do not neglect the areas for improvement – what will make a performer better. Negative feedback can also be used in the following way: every time the ball goes out the team does five push-ups. When coaching talk about good and bad aspects. Remember that if everything is good there would be no need for the coach and if everything were bad people would stop performing (many people play sport because of the enjoyment they get from it).

Evidence-based

Base things on fact. What information did your notational analysis give you, or your analysis of technical performance? Do not just coach things for the sake of coaching them. Concentrate on what you need to. If you are a volleyball coach and you have determined that serving is a problem then practise serving, give feedback on serving, aim to improve this area. You should also take into account other things that may be affecting performance. Are your athletes fit enough, motivated enough, skilful enough to perform what you are asking of them?

Confidentiality

Athletes are people. Some athletes may prefer it that you discuss their weak points confidentially. Your athletes may be lacking in self-confidence, and the way you provide feedback can have an impact on this. You may wish to start and finish on something positive and have the negative part in the middle. Remember that performance may fluctuate from day to day (e.g. due to the weather, how the person is feeling, what they have had to eat). It is worth keeping in mind that we all have bad days – even the coach!

The level and amount of feedback is related to the ability level of the athlete. As performance progresses, feedback should change from general to precise. With beginners mistakes are normally quite general and related to the whole movement, so general feedback is good. Beginners may require more motivational-type feedback. As the athlete becomes more skilful, the nature of the feedback needs to change. The feedback should be more specific concentrating on details. Often good performers can start to analyse their own performance and feedback should encourage this.

Timing of feedback is another important issue. Feedback should be given soon after the performer has done the skill. If not, there is a risk that they will not be able to relate what you are doing to the actions they performed.

Goal setting

Once you have explained to the group or individual how they are performing it is important to outline a way forward. You should give your team or athlete a clear action plan as to what they should do next. Action plans should contain targets or goals. Goals are things that your athletes can work towards and measure how well they are doing. Goals can be divided up into short-term (for next week), medium-term (for next month) and long-term (for next season). All the goals you set need to be SMART.

SMART stands for:

- **S**pecific
- **M**easurable
- **A**chievable
- **R**ealistic
- **T**ime-constrained.

Specific: the goal must be specific to what you want to achieve. This may be an aspect of performance or fitness. It is not enough to say 'I want to get fitter.' You need to say 'I want to improve strength, speed or stamina, etc.'

Measurable: goals must be stated in a way that is measurable, so they need to state figures. For example, 'I want to improve my first serve percentage' is not measurable. However, if you say 'I want to improve my first serve success by 20 per cent' it is measurable.

Achievable: it must be possible to actually achieve the goal.

Realistic: we need to be realistic in our setting of goals and look at what factors may stop us achieving them.

Time-constrained: there needs to be some sort of time frame – by the end of the season, by the end of next month.

Imagine you are a volleyball coach and your analysis of a player's serve has shown you that the particular player has a success rate of 50 per cent (from your notational analysis) and lacks a follow-through of the hitting arm (from your technical analysis), how could you set SMART goals?

Improving service technique may be a good long-term goal but in the short term you need something more specific. A good short-term goal would be to increase accuracy of service. This can easily be measured. You could measure serves in court, serves out of court (you could even be more specific and see if these change during different sets). You may set a target of 60 per cent for the next match. To know if this is achievable look at the time frame you have given. Is the player going to get enough practice between now and the next match? Is 60 per cent a realistic target to expect? What service success do your other players have? Remember to include time constraints, so you might expect 60 per cent next match but 70 per cent by the end of the season.

Future training should be based on the observations you make of your athletes. You can set goals related to both individuals and teams. The goals can be based on skills, fitness or even psychological techniques. Whichever you use, it is good to relate training back to previous performance so athletes will see the reasons for and the benefits of doing the training.

LEARNER ACTIVITY Feedback

- Based on one of the analyses of performance that you have done in the previous activities, produce some feedback that you could give to the athlete concerned.
- Using the principles discussed for giving feedback, provide a plan of how you could effectively give this feedback.

Key learning points

- Feedback – the way feedback is given is important as is the type of feedback.
- Strengths and weaknesses – both play a part in improving performance.
- Goal-setting – goals are an important focus for training and they should be SMART.

Review questions

1 List eight performance criteria that you could measure if you did a notational analysis of a team sport.
2 List eight performance criteria that you could measure if you did a notational analysis of an individual sport.
3 What information would notational analysis provide for a coach?
4 In which different ways could you display the information you obtained from notational analysis?
5 List five numerical components that you can use to analyse performance.
6 What considerations do you have when calculating numerical information from a video recording?
7 How could you measure running speed from a video recording?
8 List five things you might look at if you did a technical analysis of a sports performer.
9 What points should you consider when giving feedback to an athlete?
10 Explain why goals should be SMART.

References

Bartlett, R. (2006) *Introduction to Sports Biomechanics,* Routledge.

Carr, G. (1997) *Mechanics of Sport: A Practitioner's Guide,* Human Kinetics.

Hamilton, N. and Luttgens, K. (2002) *Kinesiology: Scientific Basis of Human Motion,* McGraw-Hill.

Hughes, M. and Franks, I. (1997) *Notational Analysis of Sport,* Routledge.

Specialist
Units

Goals

By the end of this chapter you should:

- understand the importance of lifestyle factors in the maintenance of health and well-being
- be able to assess the lifestyle of a selected individual
- be able to provide advice on lifestyle improvement
- be able to plan a health-related physical activity programme for a selected individual.

A person's lifestyle can have a huge impact on their long-term health. Lifestyle plays a key role in the prevention of a large number of diseases including coronary heart disease, cancer and obesity. This chapter will give you the knowledge and skills to assess the lifestyle of an individual, provide advice on lifestyle improvement and plan a health-related physical activity programme.

Lifestyle factors

Physical activity

definition

Physical activity: the state of being active.

Our lifestyle has become much more sedentary over the years. We now have methods of transport that require little physical exertion. Cars and buses have replaced walking and cycling. Recent studies have shown that 30 per cent of children go to school by car, and fewer than 50 per cent walk. This country has less time dedicated to PE lessons than any other country in the European Union. There are now relatively few

manual occupations, and the majority of people's careers are spent in an office-based environment. Everyday tasks such as laundry, cleaning and cooking require little effort as they are all aided by labour-saving devices. It is now even possible to go shopping by sitting in front of a computer and logging on to the internet. For entertainment, the average person spends less time participating in active leisure pursuits and prefers to sit in front of the TV. The average adult watches over 26 hours of television each week, which is a virtually totally sedentary activity.

Children also spend much less time pursing activity-based play and choose computer games, videos or the TV to occupy their free time. All these factors have led to many people taking part in very low levels of physical activity.

Physical activity can increase a person's basal metabolic rate by around 10 per cent. This elevated basal metabolic rate can last for up to 48 hours after the completion of the activity. By taking part in physical activity kilocalories will be expended. The number of kilocalories used depends on the type and intensity of the activity. The more muscles that are used in the activity and the harder you work, the more kilocalories will be used up to perform the activity. For example, swimming the front crawl uses both the arms and the legs and will therefore use more calories to perform than walking, which mainly uses the leg muscles.

The body weight of the person will also have an impact on the number of kilocalories burnt while taking part in a physical activity. The heavier the person, the more kilocalories are required to move the heavier weight. So a heavier person will burn more calories than a lighter person when performing the same activity at the same intensity.

National recommended guidelines

In order to gain the health benefits of physical activity adults should aim to participate in physical activity for 30 minutes at least five times a week. Our national recommended guidelines for children state that they should participate in moderate intensity exercise for 60 minutes per day, but the European Health Study 2006 found that they should be exercising for 90 minutes per day to gain the health benefits of physical activity.

Health benefits of physical activity

Taking part in regular exercise has consistently been shown to have many benefits to a person's physical and mental health. Many types of disease can be alleviated or prevented by taking part in regular exercise. Discussed below are the main types of ill-health that can be eased or prevented by taking part in regular exercise.

Coronary heart disease and physical activity

Coronary heart disease (CHD) is the leading cause of death in the western world. One-third of all deaths associated with CHD are due to not taking part in physical activity. Coronary heart disease is a narrowing of the coronary arteries, which are the blood vessels that pass over the surface of the heart and supply it with blood. CHD is usually a result of a build-up of fatty material and plaques within the coronary blood vessels. This is known as atherosclerosis.

definition

Atherosclerosis: build-up of fatty material in the coronary blood vessels, which makes their diameter smaller.

When a person with CHD takes part in a physically demanding task, the coronary arteries may not be able to supply the heart muscle with enough blood to keep up with the demand for oxygen. This will be felt as a pain in the chest (angina). If a coronary artery becomes completely blocked, the area of the heart muscle served by the artery will die, resulting in a heart attack.

Taking part in regular exercise appears to reduce the risk of heart disease directly and indirectly. Research has shown that exercise:

LEARNER ACTIVITY Activity diary

This activity is designed to determine how much time you spend each day taking part in physical activity and how much time is spent pursuing sedentary activities.

- Keep an activity diary for at least one full day.
- Copy and complete the table below.

Time of day	Activity	Time spent on activity

- In the middle column write an S next to the activity if it is sedentary or an A it if it requires physical activity.
- Total up the time spent on S activities and then total up the time spent on A activities.
- From your activity diary, do you think you are spending enough time pursing physically active tasks, or too long on sedentary tasks? Explain your answer.

- increases levels of HDL cholesterol
- decreases the amount of triglycerides in the bloodstream.

> **HDL cholesterol:** the 'good' cholesterol that acts to clean the artery walls, which in turn reduces atherosclerosis.

> **Triglycerides:** another type of fat; high levels in the bloodstream have been linked with increased risk of heart disease.

Hypertension and physical activity

> **Hypertension:** high blood pressure.

A person is deemed to have hypertension if their blood pressure consistently reads at 140/90 or higher. Hypertension is a very common complaint and around 15 to 25 per cent of adults in most western countries have high blood pressure. If a person with hypertension does not reduce their blood pressure they are more at risk of suffering from a stroke or a heart attack.

Diabetes and physical activity

Today more and more people are suffering from diabetes, a disease which places people at higher than average risk for heart disease. Diabetes is a disease in which the body does not produce or properly use insulin.

> **Insulin:** a hormone produced in the pancreas that controls the level of blood sugar.

The cause of diabetes is unknown, although genetics, obesity and a lack of exercise are thought to play a significant role.

There are two types of diabetes: one is insulin dependent (type 1) and the other is non-insulin dependent (type 2).

Type 1 diabetes means that the pancreas is no longer producing insulin, so it is necessary to inject insulin into the body every day to control blood sugar levels. It occurs most often in children and young adults. However, adults may become type 1 diabetic later on in life. Steve Redgrave, the British rower, became type 1 diabetic prior to taking part in the Sydney 2000 Olympics. Type 1 diabetes accounts for around 5 to 10 per cent of diabetes.

Type 2 diabetes means that a person's body is either unable to make enough insulin or it has become less sensitive to insulin. This results in elevated levels of glucose in the bloodstream. It is the most common form of the disease and accounts for 90 to 95 per cent of diabetes. Diet and exercise can often control type 2 diabetes, although insulin medication may also be necessary.

Today, type 2 diabetes is nearing epidemic proportions, due to an increase in obesity and a decrease in activity levels. It usually effects people later on in life, but because of inadequate activity and poor diet, children today are developing this disease.

There is good evidence to suggest that physical activity has a role in the prevention, and also in the treatment, of type 2 diabetes. Studies have shown that the risks of developing diabetes are lower in people who are physically active than in those who are sedentary. Exercise can also help to treat people with type 2 diabetes, as it improves a person's sensitivity to insulin.

People with uncontrolled diabetes should be referred to their doctor. They should not take part in strength training or high-impact exercises as they can strain weakened blood vessels in the eyes or injure blood vessels in the feet. People who are taking insulin should take special precautions before embarking on a workout programme because glucose levels vary dramatically during exercise. Type 1 diabetics may need to decrease insulin doses or take in more carbohydrates prior to exercise to help maintain blood glucose levels during the activity.

Obesity and physical activity

A person is classified as being obese if they are 20 per cent or more heavier than the correct weight for their height. The number of people who are obese is rising rapidly throughout the world, making obesity one of the fastest developing public health problems.

The World Health Organisation has described the problem as a 'worldwide epidemic' and has estimated

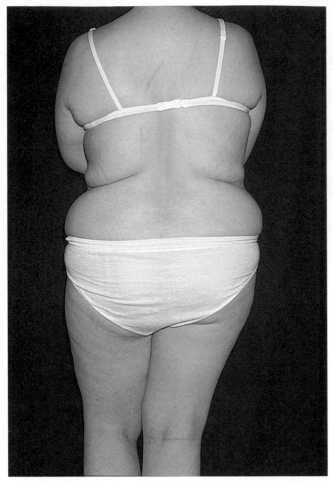

Fig 7.01 An obese person

that around 250 million people worldwide are obese, about 7 per cent of the adult population. Obesity takes years to develop and results from the amount of energy being consumed exceeding the amount of energy expended. This excess energy is then stored mainly as fat. Research to date suggests that in England over 50 per cent of the adult population are overweight and 17 per cent of men and 21 per cent of women are obese.

Obese people are at risk of developing a number of medical conditions which can cause poor health and premature death. These include:

- osteoarthritis
- rheumatoid arthritis
- some forms of cancer
- coronary heart disease (CHD)
- deep vein thrombosis (DVT)
- type 2 diabetes
- gall bladder disease
- gout

- hypertension
- stroke.

When a person takes part in exercise they burn up kilocalories, which results in the person being in a state of negative energy balance. This means that they will start to burn kilocalories from their fat stores and so lose weight.

The best forms of exercise to combat obesity are fat-burning exercises of low intensity and of long duration – walking is a very good type of exercise for obese individuals. This is because walking is a low-impact form of exercise and will therefore place less stress on the joints than a high-impact form of exercise. The person should aim to walk at a pace that increases their breathing rate and heart rate but still allows them to talk.

Arthritis and physical activity

Arthritis is a condition in which the synovial membrane of one or more joints has become inflamed. The two main forms of arthritis are:

- rheumatoid arthritis, a long-term inflammation of the synovial membrane lining the joints
- osteoarthritis, a condition in which the cartilage in the joints becomes diseased or damaged.

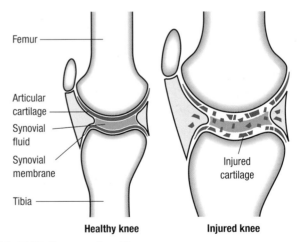

Fig 7.02 Damaged cartilage

Cartilage serves as a shock absorber, or cushion, between the bones and provides a smooth surface that allows the bones to move against each other with less friction. When this cartilage is damaged, the joint is inflamed as the cartilage becomes rougher and thinner, and the joint may swell up as there is increased production of synovial fluid. As the cartilage continues to wear away, growths of bone called bone spurs may form around the edges of the joint. Eventually, the bones that meet at the joint rub against each other, which can be extremely painful and can severely reduce movement in the joint.

Physical activity plays a key role in treating almost all forms of arthritis. Exercises that help to alleviate arthritis are mobilising exercises and exercises to strengthen muscles. Mobilising exercise helps to keep the joints moving and prevent them becoming stiff. When a person takes part in mobilising exercises, they increase the production of synovial fluid into the joint, which helps to lubricate the joint. Mobilising exercises also increase blood flow to the tissues around the joint, which helps to keep the joint healthy. Muscle strengthening exercises help to build up the muscles around the joint and so help to protect the joints. Swimming and hydrotherapy are good examples of effective ways of strengthening muscles as well as mobilising joints. A person suffering with arthritis will usually have good days when they feel less pain, and bad days when they feel more pain. It is better to exercise on good days, although taking part in exercise every day may well help to prevent joints becoming stiff and painful, and keep muscles strong.

Osteoporosis and physical activity

Osteoporosis is a disease in which the mineral density of bones is decreased, resulting in the bones becoming fragile and more likely to break. Women are four times more likely than men to develop the disease. Osteoporosis is largely preventable for most people and requires a healthy diet with the recommended daily amount of calcium and vitamin D, together with appropriate exercise.

Prevention is very important because, while there are treatments for osteoporosis, there is currently no cure. If a person has exercised regularly in childhood and adolescence, they are more likely to build strong, dense bones, which will stand them in good stead for the rest of their life. The best exercise to build bone density is weight-bearing exercise such as walking, jogging, aerobics, racket sports and hiking.

Psychological benefits of physical activity

A number of studies have attempted to explore the effects of exercise on depression and found that exercise increases self-esteem, improves mood, reduces anxiety levels, increases the ability to handle stress and generally makes people happier than those who do not exercise. It is thought that one cause of depression may be due to a decreased production of certain chemicals in the brain, specifically adrenaline, dopamine and serotonin. Exercise has been shown to increase the levels of these substances, which may have the effect of improving a person's mood after taking part in exercise. For the last decade or so, exercise has been prescribed as a method of combating depression.

Smoking

You are probably aware that smoking is bad for you. It actually kills around 14,000 people in the UK each year, and 300 people die in the UK every day as a result of smoking. These deaths occur through a range of diseases caused by smoking and include a variety of cancers, cardiovascular disease and an array of chronic lung diseases.

Fig 7.03 A normal lung (left) beside the lung of a smoker (right)

The products in a cigarette that appear to do the most damage include tar, nicotine and carbon monoxide.

Smokers are making themselves much more likely to suffer from a range of cancers; 90 per cent of people suffering with lung cancer have the disease because they smoke or have smoked. You are also four times more likely to contract mouth cancer if you are a smoker. Other forms of cancer that have been linked to smoking include cancer of the bladder, the oesophagus, the kidneys, the pancreas and cervical cancer.

Cardiovascular disease

Cardiovascular disease is the main cause of death in smokers. The excess cholesterol produced from smoking narrows the blood vessels.

When the blood vessels become narrower, blood clots are more likely to form which can then block the coronary blood vessels. A blockage in these vessels can lead to a heart attack. It is estimated that 30 per cent of these heart attacks are due to smoking.

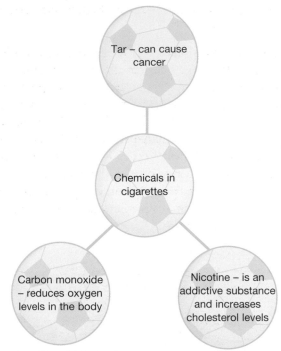

Fig 7.04 Chemicals in cigarettes

> **definition**
>
> **Coronary blood vessels:** blood vessels that supply blood to the heart.

Alternatively, the blood clot may travel to the brain, which can lead to a stroke; or it could travel to the kidneys, which could result in kidney failure; or the block may occur in the legs, which can lead to gangrene for which the main treatment is amputation.

Chronic lung disease

The following diseases are more prevalent in smokers:

- emphysema – a disease that causes breathlessness due to damaged alveoli
- bronchitis – makes the person cough excessively because of increased mucus production in the lungs.

Smoking is responsible for 80 per cent of these conditions, which basically block air flow to and from the lungs making breathing more difficult. These diseases tend to start between the ages of 35 and 45.

> **definition**
>
> **Alveoli:** air sacs in the lungs in which gaseous exchange takes place.

Other smoking-related health risks

Smoking can also damage health in a variety of other ways. A person who smokes may suffer from some of the following:

- high blood pressure
- impotence
- fertility problems
- eye problems
- discoloured teeth and gums
- mouth ulcers
- skin more prone to wrinkles.

LEARNER ACTIVITY

Government campaigns against smoking

Find out how the government is trying to make people aware of the dangers of smoking. Things that you may like to consider include:

- messages written on cigarette boxes or advertising
- adverts on the TV
- national non-smoking day (when is the next one?).

Alcohol

Alcohol is a legal drug that may be consumed by people aged 18 or over, but by the age of 16, over 80 per cent of young people in the UK have tried alcohol. In fact, in the UK people aged between 16 and 24 are the heaviest drinking group of the population. Studies reveal that one in two men and one in four women drink more than the recommended daily benchmarks, and over a quarter of males and females drink more than double the recommended daily amount.

The recommended daily benchmarks for alcohol consumption are based upon adults drinking, as there are no recommendations for children and young people as they should legally be refraining from alcohol consumption.

Recommended daily intake

The Health Education Authority recommends that women should drink no more than two units of alcohol per day and males should drink no more than three units per day. Both males and females should have at least two alcohol-free days per week.

It takes around an hour for the adult body to get rid of one unit of alcohol, and this may well be slower in young people.

25 ml of fortified wine (e.g. sherry, port)

150 ml/half an 'alcopop'

ne shot of spirit .g. gin, whisky)

One unit of alcohol

125 ml/small glass of wine

Half a pint of average-strength beer

Fig 7.05   One unit of alcohol

Effects of alcohol on the body

Alcohol affects the brain so that it compromises our judgement and suppresses our inhibitions. It decreases our physical coordination and sense of balance, and makes our vision blurred and speech slurred. Excessive drinking can lead to alcohol poisoning, which can cause unconsciousness, coma and even death. Excessive alcohol consumption can often make a person vomit, and vomiting while unconscious can lead to death by suffocation as the vomit can block the air flow to and from the lungs. The effects of alcohol have also been implicated in a large proportion of fatal road accidents, assaults and incidents of domestic violence.

Diseases associated with excess alcohol consumption

Alcohol consumption in excess of the recommended daily guidelines will often cause physical damage to the body and increase the likelihood of getting diseases such as cancer, cirrhosis, high blood pressure, strokes and depression.

Cirrhosis: excessive alcohol consumption can result in cirrhosis of the liver. The liver is the largest organ in the body. It is responsible for getting rid of poisons from the blood, helps our immune system in fighting infection, makes proteins that helps our blood to clot and produces bile, which helps with the breakdown of fats. The disease damages the liver and produces scar tissue. The scar tissue replaces the normal tissue and prevents it from working as it should. Cirrhosis is the 12th leading cause of death by disease and causes 26,000 deaths per year.

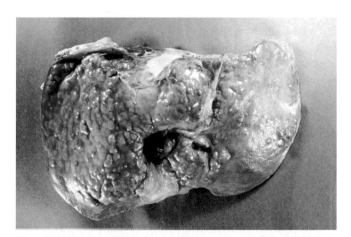

Fig 7.06   A liver affected by cirrhosis

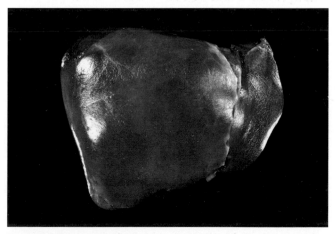

Fig 7.07   A healthy liver

Cancer: around 6 per cent of deaths from cancer in the UK are caused by alcohol (*Oxford Textbook of Medicine*, 2003). A range of cancers have been linked with excess alcohol consumption, these include:

- cancer of the mouth
- cancer of the larynx
- cancer of the oesophagus
- liver cancer
- breast cancer
- bowel cancer.

Depression: alcohol consumption has been linked with anxiety and depression; one in three young people who have committed suicide drank alcohol before they died, and more than two out of three people who attempt suicide have drunk excessively.

Stress

When we perceive ourselves to be in a situation that is dangerous, our stress response is activated. This has been developed as a means of ensuring our survival by making us respond to danger. For example, if we are walking home at night along dark streets and we hear noises behind us our body will instigate physiological changes, called the 'fight or flight' response, as the body is preparing to turn and fight the danger or run away as fast as it can.

Adrenaline is the main hormone released when we are stressed, which has the effect of:

- increasing the heart rate
- increasing the breathing rate
- decreasing the rate of digestion.

It is not healthy for the body to be in a constant state of stress because of the excess production of adrenaline. This results in excess cholesterol production that raises blood cholesterol levels and is a risk factor for coronary heart disease (CHD).

Stress and cardiovascular disease

If the excess hormones and chemicals released during stressful periods are not 'used up' through physical exertion, the increased heart rate and high blood pressure place excess strain on our blood vessels. This can lead to vascular damage. Damaged blood vessels are thicker than healthy blood vessels and have a reduced ability to stretch. This can have the effect of reducing the supply of blood and oxygen to the heart.

Stress and the immune system

Stress can decrease our body's ability to fight infection, which makes us more susceptible to suffering from illnesses. This explains why we catch more colds when we are stressed.

Stress and depression

Stress is also associated with mental health problems and, in particular, anxiety and depression. Here the relationship is fairly clear. The negative thinking that is associated with stress also contributes to these.

Diet

Our diets have changed significantly over the years. Today we have the largest range of foods available to us, but we are choosing to eat foods that are high in saturated fats and simple carbohydrates. Fast-food restaurants are flourishing because they are used so regularly by our society. Today, the nation's diet tends to be lacking in a number of important nutrients, including fibre, calcium, vitamins and iron. This is because a high proportion of the population relies on snacks and fast foods as their main source of nutritional intake. As a result, the western diet is generally high in fat and sugars, resulting in a huge increase in obesity.

Estimates in 1990 suggested that one in twenty children aged nine to eleven could be classified as clinically obese. If a person is obese they are much more likely to suffer from coronary heart disease, currently the biggest killer in Britain. As we are continuing to rely on foods that do not give us the right balance of vital nutrients, a number of people are suffering from poor nutrition. This not only impairs physical and mental functioning, but can also increase the risk of suffering from a range of diseases including anaemia, diabetes and osteoporosis. A number of nutrition experts have also linked poor nutrition to emotional and behavioural problems, such as hyperactivity and attention deficit, that are seen to occur much more frequently among children today.

A healthy diet contains lots of fruit and vegetables. It is based on starchy foods, such as wholegrain bread, pasta and rice, and is low in fat (especially saturated fat), salt and sugar. Current recommendations for a healthy diet are shown in Table 7.01.

Table 7.01 Recommendations for a healthy diet

Food	Amount we should eat	Function	Examples of food sources
Carbohydrates	50–60%	Provide energy for sports performance	
Sugars		Provide short bursts of energy	Jam, sweets, fruit, fizzy drinks, sports drinks
Starch		Provide energy for longer periods	Pasta, rice, bread, potatoes, breakfast cereals
Fat	25–30%	Provides energy for low-intensity exercise, e.g. walking	
Saturated fats		Insulates the body against the cold	Mainly animal sources: cream, lard, cheese, meat
Unsaturated fats		Helps to protect internal organs	Mainly plant sources: nuts, soya, tofu
Protein	10–15%	For growth and repair	Meat, eggs, nuts, fish, poultry

Vitamin	Food sources	Function
A	Carrots, liver, dark green vegetables, mackerel	Maintains good vision, skin and hair
B group	Cereals, liver, yeast, eggs, beef, beans	Helps to break down food to produce energy
C	Most fresh fruits and vegetables, especially citrus fruits	Fights infection, maintains healthy skin and gums, wound healing
D	Oily fish, eggs	Helps to build bones and teeth
E	Nuts, whole grains, dark green leaf vegetables	Antioxidant that prevents damage to cells
K	Leafy green vegetables, peas, milk, egg yolk	Helps to form blood clots

Mineral	Food sources	Function
Iron	Liver, lean meats, eggs, dried fruits	Blood production
Calcium	Milk, fish bones, green leafy vegetables	Helps to build strong bones and teeth, helps to form blood clots
Sodium	Salt, seafood, processed foods, celery	Maintains fluid balance in cells, helps in muscle contraction
Potassium	Bananas	Works with sodium to maintain fluid balance, aids muscle contraction, maintains blood pressure
Zinc	Meats, fish	Tissue growth and repair

Key learning points

- People are much more sedentary today and many are not meeting national recommended guidelines.
- Children should be physically active for at least 60 to 90 minutes per day.
- Adults should be physically active for at least 30 minutes five times per week.
- People who take part in physical activity are less likely to suffer from CHD, hypertension, diabetes, obesity and depression.
- Smoking has been shown to cause cancer, chronic lung disease and cardiovascular disease in some people.
- Adult males should have no more than three units of alcohol per day and adult females should have no more than two. Males and females should both have at least two alcohol-free days per week.

- Excess alcohol consumption has been shown to cause cirrhosis, cancer and depression in some people.
- Stress can cause cardiovascular disease, decrease the immune system's response to infection and cause depression in some people.
- Today, many people are eating fast food and not taking in the right quantities of macronutrients, vitamins and minerals.
- A healthy diet contains lots of fruit and vegetables, is based on starchy foods, such as wholegrain bread, pasta and rice, and is low in fat (especially saturated fat), salt and sugar.

Assessing the lifestyle of an individual

When assessing the lifestyle of an individual you will need to gather as much information as is possible on them. This can be done effectively through a comprehensive questionnaire. It will be part of an initial consultation and must cover at least the following:

- medical history
- activity history
- lifestyle factors
- nutritional status
- any other factors that will affect the person's health.

LEARNER ACTIVITY
Information gathering
Visit a local health and fitness club and find out how it gathers information on its clients' training needs and requirements. If possible, ask for the questionnaire it uses.

Key learning points

- A lifestyle questionnaire should address levels of activity, alcohol consumption, smoking, stress levels and diet. A one-to-one consultation should follow up a lifestyle questionnaire.

Lifestyle questionnaire

Section 1: Personal details

Name _____

Address _____

_____

_____

_____

Home telephone _____ Mobile telephone _____

_____

Email_____

Occupation _____

Date of birth _____

Section 2: Physical activity levels

1 Does your occupation require you to take part in physical activity? If so, what?

_____

_____

2 What are your medium-term goals over the next three months?

_____

_____

_____

_____

3 What are your short-term goals over the next four weeks?

_____

_____

_____

_____

Section 3: Current training status

1 What are your main training requirements?

✓ Muscular strength
✓ Muscular endurance
✓ Speed
✓ Flexibility
✓ Aerobic fitness
✓ Power
✓ Weight loss or gain
✓ Skill-related fitness
✓ Other (please state) _____

2 How would you describe your current fitness status?

_____

_____

3 How many times a week will you train?

_____

4 How long have you got for each training session?

_____

Section 4: Your nutritional status

1 On a scale of 1 to 10 (1 being very low quality and 10 being very high quality) how would you rate the quality of your diet?_____

2 Do you follow any particular diet?

✓ Vegetarian
✓ Vegan
✓ Vegetarian plus fish
✓ Gluten-free
✓ Dairy-free

3 How often do you eat? Note down a typical day's intake.

_____

_____

_____

_____

_____

4 Do you take any supplements? If so, which ones?

_____

_____

Section 5: Your lifestyle

1 How many units of alcohol do you drink in a typical week?_____

2 Do you smoke?_____ If yes, how many a day?_____

3 Do you experience stress on a daily basis?_____

4 If yes, what causes you stress (if you know)?

_____

_____

5 What techniques do you use to deal with your stress?

_____

Section 6: Your physical health

1 Do you experience any of the following?

✓ Back pain or injury
✓ Knee pain or injury
✓ Ankle pain or injury
✓ Swollen joints
✓ Shoulder pain or injury
✓ Hip or pelvic pain or injury
✓ Nerve damage
✓ Head injuries

2 If yes, please give details

_____

_____

_____

_____

3 Are any of these injuries made worse by exercise?_____

4 If yes, what movements in particular cause pain?

_____

_____

5 Are you currently receiving any treatment for any injuries? If so, what?

_____

Section 7: Medical history

1 Do you have, or have you had, any of the following medical conditions?

✓ Asthma
✓ Bronchitis
✓ Heart problems
✓ Chest pains
✓ Diabetes
✓ High blood pressure
✓ Epilepsy
✓ Other _____

2 Are you taking any medication? (If yes, state what, how much and why)

_____

Name:

Signature: Date:

Consultation

It is always a good idea to follow up a lifestyle questionnaire with a consultation with the individual. The person running the consultation must know when to ask questions and prompt the client, and when to listen and take notes. The main rule of thumb is that, in a consultation, the client should be doing most of the talking; the consultant's role is to ensure that questions are answered accurately and fully. The client should be made aware that their lifestyle questionnaire and the follow-up consultation is confidential, and the questionnaire stored in a secure place.

Lifestyle improvement through physical activity

When designing a physical activity programme it is important to make the programme as personal as possible. It must meet the needs of the individual it is written for or it will result in the person being unhappy or unsuccessful. The key to this is gathering as much information as possible on the individual, by asking questions such as:

- What activities do they like to take part in?
- What have they done in the past that they enjoyed?
- Do they like to exercise alone or with other people?

You should take into account the facilities in the person's area. Do they live near a gym or leisure centre? One of the biggest factors to put people off going to a gym is if it is quite some distance away and takes them a while to get there. If the gym is close to where they live or work, this makes it a much more viable option. They could go to the gym in their lunch break or on the way to or from work.

Increasing daily activity

It is actually unnecessary to join a gym or go to a swimming pool to increase physical activity levels. There are lots of ways to attain the benefits of physical activity by just adapting everyday life. If a person takes the bus or train to work, they could get off one or two stops earlier and walk the remaining distance. If a person drives to work, they could park further away from their workplace and walk the remaining distance. If cycling to work is a viable option, it is not only good for you but is also cheaper and better for the environment. Many new cycle paths are being constructed to encourage people to cycle. Choosing options such as walking up a flight of stairs instead of taking a lift or escalator also help to increase a person's activity levels.

Housework and gardening are productive ways of increasing daily activity levels. Vacuum cleaning and dusting the home, or digging the garden or mowing

Fig 7.08 Gardening can increase heart rate and help tone muscles

the lawn will increase heart rate and help tone muscles.

Reducing alcohol consumption

If a person is dependent on alcohol they must seek help to prevent the damage it does to their body and mind and to those around them.

In order to determine if a person is drinking more than the government recommended amounts of alcohol, it is a good idea to keep a 'drinking diary'. This involves noting what, how much and when that person drinks alcohol. If the person is just over the limit, simple changes could help them cut down. If they usually drink strong lager they could opt for one that contains less alcohol. Or if they usually drink wine, they could have a spritzer instead, as this will make their drink last longer and help them to drink less. If they regularly meet up with friends in pubs, they could try to find alternative venues such as a juice bar or coffee shop.

A GP can give confidential advice and support. In order to help to prevent the withdrawal symptoms of drinking, they may be prescribed anti-depressants (e.g. Valium). Two drug treatments are also available to help a person stop drinking. Once drug called Disulfiram makes the person feel very ill if they drink even a small amount of alcohol. Another drug called Acamprosate helps to reduce a person's craving for alcohol, but it does have many unpleasant side-effects. A person may attend organisations such as Alcohol Concern and Alcoholics Anonymous to help them stop drinking alcohol.

Stopping smoking

Smokers have both a physical addiction to smoking and a psychological addiction. The combination of these two factors makes cigarettes one of the most addictive drugs used today. Determining whether you are more physiologically than psychologically addicted to smoking will help to decide the best course of action in trying to stop smoking.

First of all, a person needs to think about why they smoke and identify the things they do that always make them want to light up. Once these triggers have been identified, the person can attempt to remove themselves from them. The next step is to decrease the person's dependence on nicotine. Either they can slowly decrease the amount of cigarettes they smoke over a set period or they could use a nicotine replacement therapy, such as a nicotine patch and/or nicotine gum. This process helps the person break the cigarette habit and also slowly reduces the amount of nicotine being taken into the body.

The NHS has set up a smoking helpline and runs clinics to help advise people on how to give up smoking. Each year there is a national no smoking day, which has also been effective in making people think about giving up smoking and giving them a clear target day to attempt to stop.

Reducing stress through stress-management techniques

The main methods of stress management are:

- progressive muscular relaxation
- mind-to-muscle relaxation
- meditation/centring.

Progressive muscular relaxation (PMR) involves a person tensing and relaxing the muscle groups individually and sequentially to relax their whole body and mind. It is also called 'muscle-to-mind' relaxation, as muscles are tensed and relaxed to induce complete relaxation. Each muscle is tensed and relaxed to teach the person the difference between a tense muscle and a relaxed muscle. After a muscle is tensed, the relaxation effect is deepened, which also has an effect on the involuntary muscles.

The technique is practised using a series of taped instructions, or with the psychologist giving the instructions. It usually starts at the hands by making a tight fist and then relaxing. The tensing and relaxing carries on up the arms into the shoulders, the face and neck, then down to the stomach and through the hips and legs.

These sessions last between 20 and 30 minutes, and need to be practised about five times a day to gain the maximum effect. Each time they are practised they have an increased effect and a person can relax more quickly and more deeply. The aim is that when they need to use the relaxation technique quickly they can induce relaxation using a trigger, such as tensing the hand or the shoulders.

Mind-to-muscle relaxation is also called imagery and involves the use of a mental room or a mental place. This is a place where a person can quickly picture themselves to produce feelings of relaxation when they need to relax.

Again, it involves the person using a taped script or a psychologist giving instructions. Usually the psychologist asks a person to build a mental picture of a room. This is a room where they can feel relaxed and where there is somewhere to sit or lie down. It should be decorated in a pleasing manner. Alternatively, the person may imagine a relaxing place, such as somewhere they went on their holidays or a beach or quiet place where they feel calm and relaxed. They are taught to vividly imagine this place and feel the sensations associated with being there. They do this about five times, so that eventually they can go there when they need to and are able to relax more quickly and deeply. As the person relaxes their mind, they feel the sensations transferring to their muscle groups and they can achieve overall body relaxation. It tends to work best for individuals who have good skills of imagery. Other people may feel that PMR is more effective for them.

Centring/meditation techniques involve the person focusing on one thing, such as their breathing (centring) or a mantra (meditation). By focusing their attention they become more and more relaxed. Again, these feelings of relaxation can eventually be produced when needed.

Lifestyle improvement through diet

Food preparation

The way food is prepared has a huge impact on its nutritional value. We should eat a fair amount of potatoes, but if you fry the potatoes to make chips the food then belongs in the fats and oils food group as it now has such a high concentration of fat.

You can prepare foods in certain ways to make them much healthier.

Breads and grains: pasta dishes can be prepared using lots of wholemeal pasta and a small portion of sauce. You can make sandwiches out of thick slices of wholemeal bread. You can mash sweet potatoes and regular potatoes in larger than usual quantities for a shepherd's pie topping.

Fruits and vegetables: it's healthy to eat dried fruit, fresh fruit or vegetable sticks (e.g. carrot sticks) as snacks. A selection of vegetables or salads can accompany each main meal. You can make fruit-based puddings, such as poached pears or apple and blackberry crumble. Add dried or fresh fruit to breakfast cereals. Include more vegetables in casserole dishes.

Meat, fish and vegetarian alternatives: you should use lean meat and remove skin and fat where possible.

Then grill meats wherever possible. You can include pulses in meat dishes to reduce the fat content and increase the fibre content, such as kidney beans in a chilli. Also try to eat two portions of oily fish per week.

Milk and dairy foods: choose semi-skimmed or skimmed milk and low-fat or reduced-fat cheeses. You can replace cream with fromage frais or yoghurt. Use strong-tasting cheese in cooking and then you will require smaller amounts.

Foods containing fat and foods containing sugar: do not fry these foods as it will just add more fat to them. Instead, grill or dry bake them (without oil) in the oven. Use small amounts of plant-based cooking oils (e.g. olive oil or rapeseed) when frying foods. Try making salad dressings with a balsamic vinegar base instead of oil. You can sweeten puddings with dried or fresh fruits, and drink fresh water instead of fizzy drinks.

LEARNER ACTIVITY
Your own diet
Write down the last three meals you have eaten. Try to work out how you could have made these meals healthier by using the principles shown above.

Timing of food intake

There is a saying that you should 'Eat breakfast like a king, lunch like a prince and dinner like a pauper.' This basically means that you should have your main meal at breakfast time, have a good-sized lunch and then eat your smallest meal at dinner time. The reasoning behind this saying is to have enough energy for the day and then to digest the food properly before going to bed. Heavy meals eaten before bedtime, such as a curry, take a long time to digest, which may disturb sleep. Any excess calories eaten during this meal will most probably be turned into body fat as very few people actually take any form of exercise after a late heavy meal.

Planning a health-related physical activity programme

Collecting information

When a trainer sits down to design a physical activity programme they need to consider a range of factors to ensure that the programme is appropriate and that it will benefit the person rather than harm them. They will need to consider the following factors.

- PAR-Q responses – have any contraindications to exercise been identified?
- Medical history – do they have any conditions which may affect the training programme and choice of exercises?
- Current and previous exercise history – this will give an idea about the current fitness level of the client.
- Barriers to exercise – do they have constraints such as time, cost, family responsibilities or work commitments?
- Motives and goals – what is the participant aiming to achieve and what is their time scale?
- Occupation – hours worked and whether work is manual or office-based.
- Activity levels – amount of movement they do on a daily basis.
- Leisure time activities – whether these are active or inactive.
- Diet – what, how much and when they eat.
- Stress levels – either through work or their home life and how they deal with it.
- Alcohol intake – how much they consume and how often.

- Smoking – whether they are a smoker or ex-smoker and the amount they smoke.
- Time available – the client needs to fit the training into their schedule and the trainer needs to be realistic when planning the programme.

LEARNER ACTIVITY
Lifestyle questionnaire

Find a person that you know who is wanting to change their lifestyle and incorporate more physical activity into their life. Ask them to complete a lifestyle questionnaire. Then assess whether your participant has any of the following:

- contraindications
- specific areas in their lifestyle that need addressing
- types of physical activity that would be suitable for them to participate in.

Goal setting

Short-term goals are set over a brief period of time, usually from one day to one month. A short-term goal may relate to what you want to achieve in one training session or where you want to be by the end of the month.

Long-term goals run from three months to over a period of several years. You may even set some lifetime goals which run until you retire from your sport. In sport we set long-term goals to cover a season or a sporting year. The period between one and three months would be called medium-term goals.

Usually short-term goals are set to help achieve the long-term goals. It is important to set both short- and

Key learning points

- Ways to increase physical activity – lifestyle changes, organised physical activities.
- Reducing alcohol intake – complete a drinking diary, choose drinks with reduced alcohol, seek help from GP, attend meetings designed to help people control their alcohol intake.
- Stopping smoking – identify triggers for smoking, use nicotine patches or nicotine gum, use NHS smoking helpline, seek help from GP.

- Stress-management techniques – progressive muscular relaxation, mind-to-muscle relaxation, meditation/centring.
- Diet – food preparation and timing of food intake.

long-term goals, particularly short-term goals because they will give a person more motivation to act immediately.

When goals are set you need to use the SMART principle to make them workable. SMART stands for:

- Specific
- Measurable
- Achievable
- Realistic
- Time-constrained.

Specific: the goal must be specific to what you want to achieve. It is not enough to say 'I want to get fitter', you need to say I want to improve strength, speed or stamina.

Measurable: goals must be stated in a way that is measurable, so a goal needs to state figures. For example, 'I want to cut down my alcohol intake to five units per week'.

Achievable: it must be possible to actually achieve the goal.

Realistic: we need to be realistic in our setting of goals and look at what factors may stop us achieving them.

Time-constrained: there must be a timescale or deadline on the goal. This means you can review your success. It is best to give a date by which you wish to achieve the goal.

Strategies to achieve goals

Some commonly used and effective strategies are as follows.

- **Using a decision balance sheet**: an individual writes down all the gains they will make by exercising and all the things they may lose through taking up exercise. Hopefully the gains will outweigh the losses and this list will help to motivate them at difficult times.
- **Prompts**: an individual puts up posters or reminders around the house which will keep giving them reminders to exercise. This could also be done with little coloured dots on mirrors or other places where they regularly look.
- **Rewards for attendance/completing goals**: the individual is provided with an extrinsic reward for completing the goal or attending the gym regularly. This may be something to pamper themselves, such

as a massage, and should not be something that conflicts with the goal – such as a slap-up meal!

- **Social support approaches**: you can help people exercise regularly by developing a social support group of like-minded people with similar fitness goals, so that they can arrange to meet at the gym at certain times. This makes it more difficult for people to miss their exercise session. Also, try to gain the backing of the people they live with to support them rather than tease or criticise them.

Principles of training

In order to develop a safe and effective training programme you will need to consider the principles of training. These principles are a set of guidelines to help you understand the requirements of programme design. They are:

- Frequency
- Intensity
- Time
- Type
- Overload
- Reversibility
- Specificity.

LEARNER ACTIVITY
Goal setting

With the participant chosen in the previous activity, set some short- and long-term goals.

- Ask your participant to complete a decision balance sheet.
- Devise some prompts for your participant to put up in their home and/or around their working environment.
- Determine what sort of rewards your participant would like and match these with the short-term goals you have devised.

Frequency: this means how often the person will train per week.

Intensity: this is how hard the person will work. It is usually expressed as a percentage of maximum intensity.

Time: this will indicate how long they train for in each session.

Type: this shows the type of training they will perform and needs to be individual to each person.

Overload: this shows that to make an improvement a muscle or system must work slightly harder than it is used to. This may be as simple as getting a sedentary person to walk for ten minutes or getting an athlete to squat more weight than they have previously.

Reversibility: this says that if a fitness gain is not used regularly the body will reverse it and go back to its previous fitness level. The rule is commonly known as 'use it or lose it'.

Specificity: this principle states that any fitness gain will be specific to the muscles or system to which the overload is applied. Put simply, this says that different types of training will produce different results. To make a programme specific you need to look at the needs of the person and then train them accordingly. For example, a person who was overweight would need to take part in lots of low intensity cardiovascular training in order to burn fat.

Appropriate activities

When you are devising your training programme you need to be sure that you are including activities that are appropriate to your client. If your client is obese, a training programme that includes jogging would probably not be appropriate. This kind of exercise is a high-impact exercise which places a lot of stress on the joints. If a person is obese, they will be stressing their joints to a greater degree which means they would be much more likely to injure or damage their joints. Therefore, walking or swimming would be much more appropriate as these place much less stress on the joints.

You should also try to include activities that you know your client enjoys. That way, they will be much more likely to continue their exercise programme.

LEARNER ACTIVITY
Training programme

Devise a training programme for your participant that you have used in the previous learning activities. Ensure that you take into account the training principles and your participant's preferred activities.

Exercise intensity

The intensity of exercise can be monitored by expressing it as a percentage of maximum heart rate. Your maximum heart rate is the maximum number of times your heart could beat. To find this out you would have to work to your maximum intensity, which for most people would clearly be unsafe. Therefore, we estimate the maximum heart rate by using the following formula:

Maximum heart rate = 220 − age

So, for a 17 year old their maximum heart rate would be 220 − 17 = 203 beats per minute (bpm).

To work out the heart rate training zone we take percentages of heart rate maximum. If we work between 60 and 90 per cent we would be working in the aerobic training zone, where the exercise we are performing is effective in improving aerobic fitness without being dangerous. However, it is still a wide range for a heart rate to be within, so we change the zone depending upon the fitness level of the participant.

Effective zones for different groups as % of maximum heart rate (MHR)	
Beginners	60–70% of MHR
Intermediate	70–80% of MHR
Advanced	80–90% of MHR

Rate of perceived exertion (RPE) is another measure used to monitor exercise. RPE is scale that can be used by the participant to rate how hard they feel they are working between two extremes. Rather than monitoring heart rate the participant is introduced to the scale and then asked during the aerobic session where they feel they are. Below is Borg's modified RPE scale.

1	Extremely light
2	Very light
3	Moderate
4	
5	Somewhat hard
6	
7	Hard
8	Very hard
9	Extremely hard
10	Maximal exertion

To achieve aerobic fitness gains the participant needs to be working at around 6 to 7 on the modified scale.

LEARNER ACTIVITY
Monitoring exercise intensity

Working in pairs, one person is to exercise, while the other monitors them. The exercising person should wear a heart rate monitor if available.

The exercising person should start to exercise on a treadmill or fixed cycle at a low intensity. After every five minutes of exercising at the same intensity, ask them to rate their perceived exertion on Borg's modified RPE scale and check their heart rate.

Increase the intensity and, after five minutes, repeat your measurements.

Repeat this process until the exercising person wishes to terminate the test.

Look at your data and determine if the heart rate recorded relates to the RPE. Try to explain your answer.

Key learning points

- Ensure you collect all relevant information from your client to assess their lifestyle and determine any contraindications.
- Ensure you set short- and long-term goals.
- Apply the principles of training to your training programme.
- Ensure your training programme incorporates appropriate activities.
- Ensure your client exercises at the appropriate intensity.

Review questions

1. Explain why people are less physically active today than was the case 30 years ago.
2. What are the national recommended guidelines for physical activity?
3. What are the health benefits of physical activity? Discuss in relation to common conditions.
4. What is the Health Education Authority recommended alcohol intake for males and females?
5. Explain the short-term effects of alcohol on the body.
6. What is stress and how does it affect the body?
7. Describe ways in which a person can reduce their alcohol consumption.
8. Explain the principles of training.
9. Explain different methods of measuring exercise intensity.

References

Baechle, T. and Earle, R. (2000) *Essentials of Strength Training and Conditioning*, Human Kinetics.

Dalgleish, J. and Dollery, S. (2001) *The Health and Fitness Handbook*, Longman.

Elphinstone, J. and Pook, P. (1999) *The Core Workout – A Definitive Guide to Swiss Ball Training for Athletes, Coaches and Fitness Professionals.*

Stafford-Brown, J., Rea, S. and Chance, J. (2003) *BTEC National in Sport and Exercise Science*, Hodder Arnold.

Stafford-Brown, J., Rea, S., Janaway, L. and Manley, C. (2006) *BTEC First Sport*, Hodder Arnold.

Wesson, K., Wiggins-James, N., Thompson, G. and Hartigan, S. (2005) *Sport and PE: A Complete Guide to Advanced Level Study*, Hodder Arnold.

08

Fitness testing for sport and exercise

Goals

By the end of this chapter you should:

- understand a range of laboratory- and field-based fitness tests
- understand the practice of health screening
- be able to prepare for, and conduct, appropriate fitness tests
- be able to analyse the results of fitness tests.

The ability to conduct fitness testing is a vital skill for the sport scientist to possess. All athletes and people starting exercise need to know where they are at any point in time so they can work out how close they are to where they want to be. The aims of fitness testing are to:

- ensure that the person is safe to exercise
- find out their current position in terms of fitness
- identify their strengths and weaknesses
- gain information to inform the process of writing a training programme
- be able to monitor any changes in fitness
- show a professional and caring approach.

Understanding the practice of health screening

Before you start to conduct fitness tests with an athlete or a person who wants to start exercise you will need to conduct a detailed fitness consultation. This will consist of the following:

- health screening questionnaire
- informed consent form
- identification of coronary heart disease risk factors
- identification of any causes for medical referral.

Health screening questionnaire

You will need to have prepared a detailed questionnaire to cover areas such as medical conditions, illnesses and injuries, as well as past history of exercise and lifestyle factors. A sample questionnaire is shown below.

Informed consent

An informed consent form lets a client know what to expect during the exercise test, and the associated risks involved in exercise or training. It also stresses that any participation in the tests is voluntary and you have the choice to stop at any point.

An example of an informed consent form is given in Table 8.01 on page 151.

Section 1: Personal details

Name _____

Address _____

_____

_____

Home telephone _____ Mobile telephone _____

Email_____

Occupation _____

Date of birth _____

Section 2: Sporting goals

1 What are your long-term sporting goals over the next year or season?

_____

_____

_____

2 What are your medium-term goals over the next three months?

_____

_____

_____

_____

3 What are your short-term goals over the next four weeks?

_____

_____

_____

_____

Section 3: Current training status

1 What are your main training requirements?

✓ Muscular strength
✓ Muscular endurance
✓ Speed
✓ Flexibility
✓ Aerobic fitness
✓ Power
✓ Weight loss or gain
✓ Skill-related fitness
✓ Other (please state) _____

2 How would you describe your current fitness status?

_____

_____

3 How many times a week will you train?

_____

4 How long have you got for each training session?

_____

Section 4: Your nutritional status

1 On a scale of 1 to 10 (1 being very low quality and 10 being very high quality) how would you rate the quality of your diet?_____
2 Do you follow any particular diet?

✓ Vegetarian
✓ Vegan
✓ Vegetarian and fish
✓ Gluten-free
✓ Dairy-free

3 How often do you eat? Note down a typical day's intake.

_____

_____

_____

_____

_____

4 Do you take any supplements? If so, which ones?

_____

_____

Section 4: Your lifestyle

1 How many units of alcohol do you drink in a typical week? _____
2 Do you smoke? _____ If yes, how many a day? _____
3 Do you experience stress on a daily basis? _____
4 If yes, what causes you stress (if you know)?

_____

_____

5 What techniques do you use to deal with your stress?

_____

Section 5: Your physical health

1 Do you experience any of the following?

✓ Back pain or injury
✓ Knee pain or injury
✓ Ankle pain or injury

✓ Swollen joints
✓ Shoulder pain or injury
✓ Hip or pelvic pain or injury
✓ Nerve damage
✓ Head injuries

2 If yes, please give details

_____

_____

_____

_____

3 Are any of these injuries made worse by exercise? _____
4 If yes, what movements in particular cause pain?

_____

_____

5 Are you currently receiving any treatment for any injuries? If so, what?

_____

Section 6: Medical history

1 Do you or have you had any of the following medical conditions?

✓ Asthma
✓ Bronchitis
✓ Heart problems
✓ Chest pains
✓ Diabetes
✓ High blood pressure
✓ Epilepsy
✓ Other _____

2 Are you taking any medication (If yes, state what, how much and why)

_____

Name: Signature:
Trainer's name: Trainer's signature:
Date:

Risk of coronary heart disease

Coronary heart disease (CHD) is a leading cause of death in all industrialised countries. It is caused by a narrowing of the coronary arteries, which limits the amount of blood flowing through the artery.

definition

Coronary arteries: blood vessels that brings oxygenated blood to nourish the muscle cells of the heart muscle.

Table 8.01 Example of an informed consent form

1 Explanation of the tests

You will perform a series of tests which will vary in its demands on your body. Your progress will be observed during the tests and stopped if you show signs of undue fatigue. You may stop the test at any time if you feel unduly uncomfortable.

2 Risks of exercise testing

During exercise certain changes can occur, such as raised blood pressure, fainting, raised heart rate, and in a very small number of cases heart attacks or even death. Every effort is made through screening to minimise the risk of these occurring during testing. Emergency equipment and relevantly trained personnel are available to deal with any extreme situation which occurs.

3 Responsibility of the participant

You must disclose all information in your possession regarding the state of your health or previous experiences of exercise as this will affect the safety of the tests. If you experience any discomfort or unusual sensations it is your responsibility to inform your trainer.

4 Benefits to expect

The results gained during testing will be used to identify any illnesses and the types of activities that are relevant for you.

5 Freedom of consent

Your participation in these tests is voluntary and you are free to deny consent or stop a test at any point.

I have read this form and understand what is expected of me and the tests I will perform. I give my consent to participate.

Client's signature_____

Print name_____

Date _____

Trainer's signature_____

Print name_____

Date _____

Arteries losing their elasticity is part of the ageing process. However, there are many lifestyle factors that cause damage or narrowing of the arteries. Obstructions are created as cholesterol and fatty plaques are laid down in the artery causing a narrowing of the artery space.

The coronary arteries are found only in the heart and they supply the heart with oxygen to enable it to pump. When these arteries narrow or become blocked the blood supply to the heart is reduced. As a result, carbon dioxide builds up in the heart muscle and this causes pain, which is called angina. Angina feels like a crushing pain on the chest. If this pain becomes a shooting pain into the left arm and the neck the person is having a heart attack.

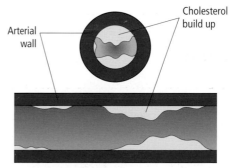

Fig 8.01 Build-up of cholesterol in an artery

The following lifestyle factors will increase an individual's chance of having CHD:

- diet high in fat (particularly deep fat fried foods)
- diet high in table salt (sodium chloride)
- obesity (particularly abdominal fat)
- smoking
- excess alcohol consumption
- older age
- male gender
- high blood pressure
- type 2 diabetes.

Fig 8.02 Smoking will increase an individual's chance of having CHD

If you consider that a person has a high risk of CHD it is best to refer them for GP clearance before you start to train them.

Medical referral

To ensure that you offer a proper 'duty of care' to your client you will need to refer them to a GP if you have any doubt regarding their safety to exercise. If your client has any of the following they must be referred to their GP:

- high blood pressure (over 160/100)
- poor lung function
- excess body fat (40%+ for a female, 30%+ for a male)
- high resting heart rate (100+ bpm)
- medication for a heart condition (e.g. beta blockers).

Or if they experience any of the following:

- muscle injuries
- chest pain or tightness
- light-headedness or dizziness
- irregular or rapid pulse

- joint pain
- headaches
- shortness of breath.

Health monitoring tests

Tests can split into two clear categories: those that measure health and those that measure fitness. Health tests are done to see if the individual is healthy enough to do the fitness tests or whether they need to receive GP clearance. Health tests will be static in nature while fitness tests will be dynamic and involve bodily movement and exertion.

Key learning points

- Before a fitness test is conducted a health screening form and informed consent form must be completed.
- A client must be screened for risk of CHD; risk factors include poor diet, obesity, smoking, excess alcohol intake, male gender and type 2 diabetes.

The health tests conducted are:

- heart rate
- blood pressure
- lung function
- waist to hip ratio
- body mass index (BMI).

When testing people it is important that the tests are safe for the client; also that the conditions the tests are performed in are consistent and stable.

The following should be taken into consideration in relation to the client.

- They should have medical clearance for any health conditions.
- They should be free of injuries.
- They should be wearing appropriate clothing.
- They should not have had a heavy meal within three hours of the test.
- They should have had a good night's sleep.
- They should not have trained on the day and should be fully recovered from previous training.
- They should have avoided stimulants such as tea, coffee or nicotine for two hours before the test.

The following should be taken into consideration regarding the environment.

- Heating in the area should be at room temperature (around 18°).
- The room should be well ventilated.
- The room should be clean and dust-free.

Validity and reliability

These two terms must be considered before a test is conducted. The two questions you must ask yourself are:

- Does this test actually test what I say it tests?
- If this test were to be repeated would I get the same results?

The first question tests its validity. For example, a speed test using a shuttle run may actually test a person's ability to turn, which is more about agility than speed.

The second question tests its reliability. The conditions of the test must always be identical so that it is most likely that the same results will be produced. However, there are many factors that may change, such as the temperature of the environment, the physical state of the athlete and the technique of the tester. All these may alter the results produced.

Test sequence

The order in which tests are conducted must be considered because it may change the accuracy of the results you produce. You may even have to do different tests on different days to produce the best results.

Our knowledge of sport science can help to decide which tests should be done first and for how long the athlete will have to rest between tests. For example, a test which requires effort over a long period of time or works to failure will require one to two hours of recovery. Also a test requiring a high level of skill or coordination needs to be done first because skill level goes down when a person is tired. The correct order to follow would be:

- sedentary tests – height, weight, body composition, flexibility
- agility tests
- maximum power and strength tests
- sprint tests
- muscular endurance test
- aerobic endurance tests.

Resting heart rate

To measure the resting heart rate you can use a heart rate monitor or do it manually. The best time to take resting heart rate is before the person gets out of bed and experiences the stresses of the day. To perform it manually complete the following steps.

1. Let your client sit down and rest for about five minutes.
2. Find their radial pulse (wrist) or brachial pulse (front of elbow).
3. Using the middle and index fingers place them over the pulse. The thumb has a pulse of its own and will produce an inaccurate reading.
4. Count the pulse for 60 seconds and record the result before repeating for another 60 seconds.
5. If there is a large variation in readings then take a third reading.

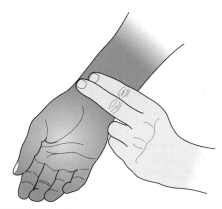

Fig 8.03 Taking a pulse rate

Here is a reference for resting heart rates for men and women:

Category	Males (bpm)	Females (bpm)
Normal	60–80	60–80
Average	70	76
Proceed with caution	90–99	90–99
GP referral	100+	100+

(Adapted from Franklin, 2000)

Blood pressure

Blood pressure is the pressure blood exerts on the artery walls and is a clear indication of general health. It is vitally important to measure blood pressure before a client exercises because it will tell you whether they are at risk of having a heart attack.

We need to split this up into the short term and long term. Short term means the blood pressure rises for a period and then falls again, while long term means that the blood pressure remains high all the time.

Factors that raise blood pressure in the short term:

- stress, anxiety and arousal
- exercise
- heavy weight training
- isometric exercises
- eating (process of digestion)
- smoking
- caffeine
- stimulant drugs.

Factors that raise blood pressure in the long term:

- inactivity
- obesity
- high-fat diet
- high salt (sodium) intake
- excessive alcohol
- smoking
- stress and anxiety
- stimulant drugs.

Blood pressure is taken by a blood pressure meter and stethoscope, or it can be done using an electronic blood pressure meter.

1   Allow the client to be relaxed for about five minutes.
2   Sit the client down with their left arm resting on a chair arm; their elbow should be at 45 degrees with the palm of the hand facing up.
3   Find the brachial pulse – it should be on the inner side of the arm just under the biceps muscle.
4   Place the cuff just clear of the elbow (about 2–3 cm above the elbow). The bladder of the cuff (the part which inflates) should be directly over the pulse.
5   Place the earpieces of the stethoscope in your ears and place the microphone over the brachial pulse.
6   Inflate the cuff up to 200 mmHg.
7   Slowly open the valve by turning it anti-clockwise and release the pressure.

8   Listen out for the first time you hear the thud of the heart beat and make a mental note of it. This is the systolic blood pressure reading.
9   Keep deflating the cuff and when the heart beat becomes muffled or disappears this is your diastolic reading.
10 Keep deflating the cuff and, if necessary, repeat after around 30 seconds.

This is a classification of blood pressure readings:

Classification	Systolic blood pressure (mmHg)	Diastolic blood pressure (mmHg)
Low	90	60
Normal	120	80
Proceed with caution	140–159	90–99
High	160+	100+

(Adapted from Franklin, 2000)

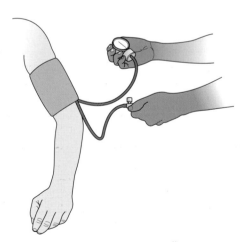

Fig 8.04 Taking a blood pressure reading

Lung function

We need to assess lung function to see whether the airways between the mouth and the alveoli are clear and conducive to good air flow. Poor lung function will limit the amount of oxygen which can be delivered to the bloodstream and the tissues.

Lung function can be measured using a microspirometer or a hand-held peak flow meter.

To use a peak flow meter proceed through the following steps.

1 Ask the client to hold the peak flow meter directly in front of their mouth.
2 Ask them to turn their head to the side and take three deep breaths.
3 On the third breath ask them to put their mouth around the end of the tube and, ensuring a good lip seal, blow as hard as they can into the tube.
4 Say that it should be a short, sharp blow as if they were using a pea shooter.
5 Repeat twice more and take the highest reading. This is called their peak expiratory flow rate (PEFR).

Fig 8.05 Peak flow meter

Factors affecting lung function:

- asthma
- bronchitis
- smoking
- environmental pollution
- gender
- age
- height
- size of ribcage.

The PEFR is a measurement of the power of the lungs. It is a hypothetical figure which tells us how much air would pass through our lungs if we breathed in and out at our maximum power for a minute. It is hypothetical because it cannot really be measured as we would faint after about 15 seconds of breathing at maximum power.

You will need to know the gender, age and height of the client to work out their acceptable score.

The PEFR for males is shown below.

The PEFR for females is shown overleaf.

If your client's score is 100 below the acceptable figure this classifies as poor lung function and they should be referred to their GP before they exercise.

PEFR for males

Age	1.55 m	1.60 m	1.65 m	1.70 m	1.75 m	1.80 m	1.85 m	1.90m
25	515	534	552	570	589	607	625	644
30	502	520	539	557	576	594	612	632
35	489	508	526	544	563	582	600	619
40	476	495	513	531	550	568	586	606
45	463	482	501	519	537	556	574	593
50	450	469	487	505	524	543	561	580
55	438	456	475	493	511	530	548	567
60	424	443	462	480	498	517	535	545
65	412	430	449	460	486	504	522	541
70	399	417	436	454	472	491	509	528

(Adapted from Franklin, 2000)

PEFR for females

Age	1.45 m	1.50 m	1.55 m	1.60 m	1.65 m	1.70 m	1.75 m	1.80m
25	365	383	400	416	433	449	466	482
30	357	374	390	407	423	440	456	473
35	348	365	381	398	414	431	447	464
40	339	356	372	389	405	422	438	455
45	330	347	363	380	397	413	429	446
50	321	338	354	371	388	404	420	437
55	312	329	345	362	379	395	411	428
60	303	320	336	353	370	386	402	419
65	294	311	327	344	361	377	393	410
70	285	302	318	335	352	368	384	401

(Adapted from Franklin, 2000)

Body mass index

Body mass index (BMI) is used to give us an idea of whether a client is obese. It then gives the extent of their obesity.

This is worked out by using the following formula:

$$\text{Body mass index (BMI)} = \frac{\text{Weight (in kg)}}{\text{Height in m} \times \text{height in m}}$$

For male who is 75 kg and 1.80 m tall:

$$\frac{75}{1.80 \times 1.80} = 23.1$$

Thus his body mass index will be 23.1 kg/m².

What does this mean? The chart below shows the classification of overweight and obesity:

	Obesity class	BMI (kg/m2)
Underweight		< 18.5
Normal		18.5–24.9
Overweight		25–29.9
Obesity	I	30–34.9
Obesity	II	35–39.9
Extreme obesity	III	> 40

> **LEARNER ACTIVITY** Your own BMI
>
> Using the formula on the left, work out your body mass index.

The body mass index has serious limitations because it does not actually measure body composition. It can be used as a quick measure to see if a person is over-fat, but it is inaccurate because it does not make a distinction between muscle and fat. Thus, someone with a lot of muscle may come out as fat!

Hip to waist ratio

Hip to waist ratio is taken as an indicator of the health risks associated with obesity and in particular the risk of coronary heart disease (CHD). Fat stored in the abdominal area is a greater risk factor for CHD because it is closer to the heart and can more easily be mobilised and taken to the heart.

Hip to waist ratio is calculated in the following way using a tape measure.

- Waist measurement is taken at the level of the navel with the stomach muscles relaxed and after a normal expiration. The tape measure is put around the waist and a horizontal reading is taken.
- Hip measurement is taken with the client standing up and is the widest measurement around the hips. It is usually taken at the level of the greater trochanter, which is at the top of the femur.

Key learning points

- Tests can be split up into two types: those which test health and are static in nature and those which test fitness and are dynamic in nature.
- Before conducting a test you must consider that both the client and the environment are in an appropriate state for the test to take place.

- A valid test is one that tests what it says it will test.
- A reliable test is one that would yield the same results if it were to be repeated.

The ratio is worked out by dividing the waist measurement by the hip measurement.

$$\frac{\text{Waist measurement}}{\text{Hip measurement}}$$

A male with a 26" waist and 30" hips would be:

$$\frac{26}{30} = 0.66$$

What do these scores mean? The chart below shows the classification for hip to waist ratio:

Classification	Males	Females
High risk	> 1.0	> 0.85
Moderate risk	0.90–0.99	0.80–0.85
Low risk	< 0.90	< 0.8

(Adapted from Franklin, 2000)

A male with a score above 0.90 and a female with a score above 0.80 will have an increased risk of developing CHD.

LEARNER ACTIVITY Hip to waist ratio

Working with a partner calculate each other's hip to waist ratio. Work out where you fall on the above table.

Preparing, conducting and analysing fitness tests

Tests are conducted to assess each different component of fitness. It is important to choose the components of fitness relative to the person you are

working with. This will depend upon their own goals and the activities they are involved in, be it sport or exercise.

Performance-related fitness

Performance in sport and exercise is dependent upon a range of components of fitness. These are shown in Fig 8.06.

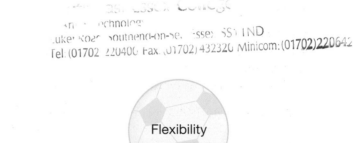

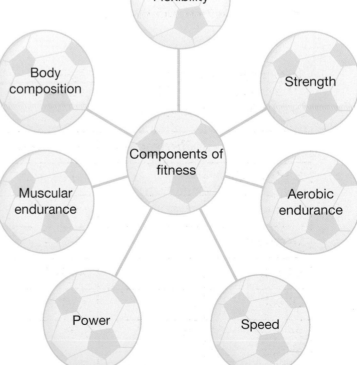

Fig 8.06 Components of fitness

LEARNER ACTIVITY Components of fitness

The following table shows a list of sports and the various components of fitness. Take each component of fitness and give it a score between 1 and 10 depending on how important it is for successful participation in that sport: 1 is not at all important and 10 and is vitally important.

Activity	Flexibility	Strength	Aerobic endurance	Speed	Power	Muscular endurance	Body composition
Rugby Union							
Basketball							
Netball							
Cricket							
100 m sprinting							
400 m sprinting							
Marathon running							
Long-distance cycling							
Tennis							
Football							
Squash							

Test protocols

The following is a list of test protocols:

- sit and reach
- 1 repetition maximum
- grip strength dynamometer
- multi-stage fitness test
- step test
- 40-yard sprint
- vertical jump
- wingate test
- one-minute press-up test
- one-minute sit-up test
- skinfold assessment
- bioelectrical impedance
- hydro densitometry.

We will now look at each of these in turn.

Flexibility

The **sit and reach test** measures the flexibility of the muscles in the lower back and hamstrings. This test is safe to perform unless the athlete has a lower back injury, particularly a slipped disc. The test is performed in the following way.

1 Warm the athlete up with five minutes' jogging or cycling.
2 Ask the athlete to take off their shoes and any clothing which will limit movement.
3 The athlete sits with their legs straight and their feet against the board. Their legs and back should be straight.
4 The client reaches as far forward as they possibly can and pushes the marker forward.
5 Record the furthest point the marker reaches.

What do these results mean? These are the categories for males and females:

Category	Males (cm)	Females (cm)
Elite	> 27	> 30
Excellent	17 to 27	21 to 30
Good	6 to 16	11 to 20
Average	0 to 5	1 to 10
Fair	–8 to –1	–7 to 0
Poor	–9 to –19	–8 to –14
Very poor	< –20	< –15

(Adapted from Franklin, 2000)

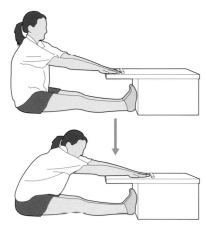

Fig 8.07 Sit and reach test

Strength

The **1 repetition maximum** (1 RM) is a measure of absolute strength and is the maximum weight that can be moved once with perfect technique.

This is clearly a dangerous test to perform unless the client is of an advanced skill level and is very well conditioned. The test will also require a thorough warm-up prior to its performance.

The test is performed in the following way.

1 Choose an exercise requiring the use of large muscle groups – e.g. a bench press or a leg press.
2 Warm up with a light weight for ten repetitions.
3 Give one minute rest.
4 Estimate a resistance that can be used for three to five repetitions.
5 Give two minutes' rest.
6 Estimate a load that can be used for two to three repetitions.
7 Give two to three minutes' rest.

8 Decide upon a load that can be used for one repetition.
9 If successful then give two to four minutes' rest.
10 Add a little more weight and complete one repetition.
11 Weight is gradually added until the client fails.
12 1 RM is the last weight that can be completed successfully.

There are no normative tables for 1 RM tests as they are used to monitor progress and strength gains. They can also be used to decide upon training loads for the individual.

The **grip strength dynamometer** is a static test to assess muscular strength in the arm muscles. Unfortunately, it will give no indication as to the strength of other muscle groups. The test involves squeezing a hand grip dynamometer as hard as possible. The test is conducted in the following way.

1 Adjust the handle to fit the size of your hand.
2 Hold the dynamometer in your strongest hand and keep the arm hanging by your side with the dynamometer by your thigh.
3 Squeeze the dynamometer as hard as you can for around five seconds.
4 Record the results and repeat after about a minute.
5 Take your best recording.

What do the results mean?

Rating	Males (kg)	Females (kg)
Excellent	> 64	> 38
Very good	56–64	34–38
Above average	52–56	30–34
Average	48–52	26–30
Below average	44–48	22–26
Poor	40–44	20–22
Very poor	<40	<20

(Adapted from Franklin, 2000)

Fig 8.08 Hand grip dynamometer

How did you score?

Category	Males (mm/O_2/kg/min−1)	Females (mm/O_2/kg/min−1)
Extremely high	70+	60+
Very high	63–69	54–59
High	57–62	49–53
Above average	52–56	44–48
Average	44–51	35–43

(Adapted from Baechle and Earle, 2000)

Aerobic endurance

The **multi-stage fitness test** was developed at the University of Loughborough and is known as the 'bleep' test because athletes have to run between timed bleeps. The test will give you an estimation of your VO$_2$max which is the measure of your aerobic fitness level. You will need the pre-recorded CD or tape and a flat area of 20 metres with a cone at either end. This test can be used with large groups as all the athletes will run together. The procedure is as follows:

1 Mark out a length of 20 metres with cones.
2 Start the tape and the athletes run when the first bleep sounds. They will run the 20 metres before the second bleep sounds.
3 When this bleep sounds they turn around and run back.
4 They continue to do this and the time between the bleeps gets shorter and shorter so they have to run faster and faster.
5 If an athlete fails to get to the other end before the bleep on three consecutive occasions then they are out.
6 Record at what point the athlete dropped out.
7 Using the tables provided you find out your predicted VO$_2$max.

The **Canadian step test** is a simple and straightforward test to perform and measures how heart rate increases with steady-state exercise.

You need a 30 cm high step, a heart rate monitor and a stopwatch. This test is carried out in the following way.

Fig 8.09 Canadian step test

1 The client steps up and down for three minutes while you monitor their heart rate.
2 You keep the client at a steady state by saying 'up, up, down, down' at a normal speech rate. The client should complete 24 steps per minute.
3 At the end of the third minute record their heart rate.
4 Compare the result to the normative data for males and females.

What does this mean?

This is the classification for males measured in bpm:

Age	18–25	26–35	36–45	46–55	56–65	65+
Excellent	< 79	< 81	< 83	< 87	< 86	< 88
Good	79–89	81–89	83–96	87–97	86–97	88–96
Above average	90–99	90–99	97–103	97–105	98–103	97–103
Average	100–105	100–107	104–112	106–116	104–112	104–113
Below average	106–116	108–117	113–119	117–122	113–120	114–120
Poor	117–128	118–128	120–130	123–132	121–129	121–130
Very poor	> 128	> 128	> 130	> 132	> 129	> 130

This is the classification for females measured in bpm:

Age	18–25	26–35	36–45	46–55	56–65	65+
Excellent	< 85	< 88	< 90	< 94	< 95	< 90
Good	85–98	88–99	90–102	94–104	95–104	90–102
Above average	99–108	100–111	103–110	105–115	105–112	103–115
Average	109–117	112–119	111–118	116–120	113–118	116–122
Below average	118–126	120–126	119–128	121–129	119–128	123–128
Poor	127–140	127–138	129–140	130–135	129–139	129–134
Very poor	> 140	> 138	> 140	> 135	> 139	> 134

(both charts adapted from Franklin, 2000)

This is a safe test to use with clients and gives us a useful means to monitor progress. It will not provide any information regarding their maximal aerobic capacity.

Speed

The **40-yard sprint** is a test for pure speed. You will need a flat running surface and a tape measure to ensure the distance is correct. You also require a stopwatch and a person who can time the run. The test is conducted in the following way.

1 The athlete warms up for several minutes.
2 They will then do the 40-yard run at a speed less than their maximum.
3 The athlete starts the test behind the line with one or two hands on the ground.
4 The starter will shout 'go' and the athlete sprints the 40 yards as quickly as possible.
5 This run should be repeated after two or three minutes and the average of the two runs taken.

What do these scores mean? Here are the categories for males and females:

Category	Males (seconds)	Females (seconds)
Elite	< 4.6	< 5.5
Excellent	4.6–4.7	5.5–5.7
Good	4.8–5.0	5.8–6.3
Average	5.1–5.5	6.4–6.7
Below average	5.6+	6.7+

(Adapted from Franklin, 2000)

What do the results mean? Here are the ratings for males and females:

Rating	Males (cm)	Females (cm)
Excellent	> 70	> 60
Very good	61–70	51–60
Above average	51–60	41–50
Average	41–50	31–40
Below average	31–40	21–30
Poor	21–30	11–20
Very poor	< 21	< 10

(Adapted from Franklin, 2000)

Fig 8.10 Vertical jump test

Power

The **vertical jump** is a test of power with the aim being to see how high the athlete can jump. It is important that you find a smooth wall with a ceiling higher than the athlete can jump. A sports hall or squash court is ideal. The test is conducted in the following way.

1 The athlete rubs chalk on their fingers.
2 They stand about 15 cm away from the wall.
3 With their feet flat on the floor they reach as high as they can and make a mark on the wall.
4 The athlete then rubs more chalk on their fingers.
5 They then bend their knees to 90 degrees and jump as high as they can up into the air.
6 At the top of their jump they make a second chalk mark with their fingertips.
7 The trainer measures the difference between their two marks; this is their standing jump score.
8 This test is best done three times so the athlete can take the best of their three jumps.

Fig 8.11 Wingate test

Anaerobic capacity

The **Wingate test** is a maximal test of anaerobic capacity and is thus suitable only for highly conditioned clients. It is used to measure peak anaerobic power and anaerobic capacity.
It is carried out in the following way.

1 The client warms up for around two to three minutes at increasing intensities until their heart rate is 180 bpm.
2 Once they are ready the client cycles as fast as they can for 30 seconds at a calculated load.

The load is calculated for use on the Monark cycle ergometer. For a person aged under 15 the load is their body weight in kg × 0.35 g. For an adult it is their body weight in kg × 0.75 g.

A 70 kg adult's workload would be worked out in the following way:

70 × 0.75 = 52.5 kg

3 The client is instructed to start and then given two seconds to achieve their maximum speed at which point the workload is added.
4 The client pedals for 30 seconds as fast as they can and the tester needs to count the number of revolutions of the flywheel every five seconds.
5 There needs to be a second tester who records the scores as they are called out for each five seconds.
6 At the end of the 30 seconds the client cools down at a light workload.

To work out the power for each five-second interval you need to use the following equation:

Power = load (kg) × revolutions of flywheel in five seconds × radius of flywheel × 12.33

This score is then divided by their body weight in kg to calculate the power per kg of body mass.

To analyse the results you need to do the following.

- Plot a graph with power in watts (y-axis) against time in seconds (x-axis).
- The peak anaerobic power is the highest power score in a five-second period.
- The minimum anaerobic power is the lowest score in a five-second period.

- The power decline can be calculated in the following way:

$$\text{power decline} = \frac{\text{peak power} - \text{minimum power}}{\text{peak power} \times 100}$$

You will need to use the table shown at the bottom of this page to record the results and then to work out the power achieved.

Muscular endurance

The **one-minute press-up test** is a test of muscular endurance in the chest and arms. You will need a mat and a stopwatch.
   It is carried out in the following way.

1 This test involves the male starting in the press-up position with their hands facing forwards and below the shoulders, back straight and pivoting on their toes. Females will perform the test from their knees with their knees, hips and shoulders all in line and their lower legs resting on the ground.
2 The subject will go down until their chest is 2 cm off the floor and push up to a straight elbow. They must maintain a straight back.
3 The number of press-ups performed in one minute without rest is recorded.
4 If a client is unable to maintain good technique or shows undue fatigue the test must be stopped.

Time	Number of revolutions of fly wheel	Power (watts)	Power per kg of body mass
0–2s			
2–7s			
7–12s			
12–17s			
17–22s			
22–27s			
27–32s			

What do these scores mean? These are the categories for males measured in the number of completed press-ups:

Age	20–29	30–39	40–49	50–59	60–69
Excellent	36	30	25	21	18
Very good	29–35	22–29	17–24	13–20	11–17
Good	22–28	17–21	13–16	10–12	8–10
Fair	17–21	15–20	8–12	7–9	5–7
Needs improvement	< 17	< 15	< 8	< 7	< 5

(Adapted from Franklin, 2000)

These are the categories for females measured in the number of completed press-ups:

Age	20–29	30–39	40–49	50–59	60–69
Excellent	30	27	24	21	17
Very good	21–29	20–26	15–23	11–20	12–16
Good	15–20	13–19	11–14	7–10	5–11
Fair	10–14	8–12	5–10	2–6	2–4
Needs improvement	< 10	< 8	< 4	1	1

(Adapted from Franklin, 2000)

The **one-minute sit-up test** is a test of muscular endurance in the abdominals. You will need a mat and a stopwatch.

The test procedure is as follows.

1 The athlete lies on the floor with their fingers on their temples and their knees bent.
2 On the command of 'go' the athlete sits up until their elbows touch their knees.
3 They will return to the start position with the back of their head touching the floor. That will be one repetition.
4 The athlete does as many as they can in one minute.

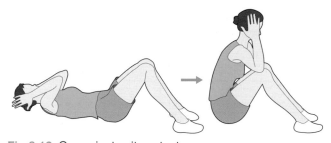

Fig 8.12 One-minute sit-up test

What do these results mean? Here are the classifications for males and females measured in the number of completed sit-ups:

Males				Females		
Age	17–19	20–29	30–39	17–19	20–29	30–39
High	49 +	44 +	39 +	42 +	36 +	30 +
Above average	44–48	39–43	34–38	32–41	27–35	22–29
Average	37–43	32–38	27–33	25–31	21–26	17–21
Below average	24–36	20–31	16–26	19–24	15–20	11–16
Low	< 24	< 20	< 16	< 19	< 15	< 11

(Adapted from Franklin, 2000)

Body composition

In very simple terms a person's body weight or mass can be split into two categories: fat mass and lean body weight (all that is not fat).

Fat mass	Lean body weight
Fat (adipose tissue)	Muscle Water Bone Organs Connective tissue

This table shows that you can lose weight by reducing any of the components of the body. However, lean body weight could be seen as healthy weight as it contributes to the performance of the body. Fat weight in excess would be unhealthy weight as it would cause a loss in performance as it requires oxygen without giving anything back to the body.

It is necessary to take a body fat measurement to show that the weight loss is fat and not muscle.

It is impossible to turn muscle into fat or fat into muscle. This is because they are completely different types of tissue in the body. A good training programme will produce a loss of fat or excess fat and a gain in muscle tissue. So while it may look like one is turning into the other this is not the case. This particularly happens when an athlete does weight training.

The **skinfold assessment** test is done using skinfold calipers. It is done using the Durnin and Wormsley sites which are as follows:

Area	Description of site
Triceps	This is taken halfway between the shoulder and elbow on the back of the arm. It is a vertical pinch.
Biceps	This is taken 1 cm above the site for the triceps on the front of the arm. It is a vertical pinch.
Subscapular	This is taken 2 cm below the lowest point of the shoulder blade. It is taken at a 45-degree angle.
Suprailiac	This is taken just above the iliac crest (hip bone), directly below the front of the shoulder.

It is carried out as follows.

1. **Triceps brachii**
   With the client's arm hanging loosely, a vertical fold is raised at the back of the arm, midway along a line connecting the acromion (shoulder) and olecranon (elbow) processes.

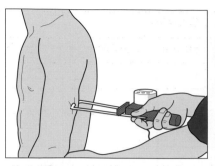

2. **Biceps brachii**
   A vertical fold is raised at the front of the arm, opposite to the triceps site. This should be directly above the centre of the cubital fossa (fold of the elbow).

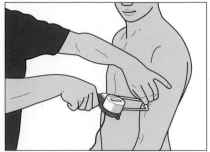

3. **Subscapular**
   A fold is raised just beneath the inferior angle of the scapula (bottom of the shoulder-blade). This fold should be at an angle of 45 degrees downwards and outwards.

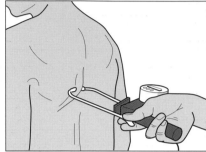

4. **Anterior suprailiac**
   A fold is raised 5–7 cm above the spinale (pelvis), at a point in line with the anterior axillary border (armpit). The fold should be in line with the natural folds downward and inwards at up to 45 degrees.

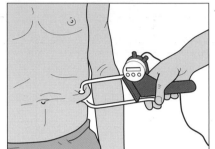

Fig 8.13 Body fat measurement

1 Take the measurements on the left-hand side of the body.
2 Mark the client up accurately.
3 Pinch the skin 1 cm above the marked site.
4 Pull the fat away from the muscle.
5 Place the calipers halfway between the top and bottom of the skinfold.
6 Allow the calipers to settle for one or two seconds.
7 Take the reading and wait 15 seconds before repeating for accuracy.
8 Add up the total of the four measurements.
9 Calculate body fat percentage using the table on the opposite page.

The **bioelectrical impedance** technique involves placing electrodes on one hand and one foot and then passing a very small electrical current through the body. The theory is that muscle will conduct the electricity while fat will resist the path of the electricity. Therefore, the more electricity that comes out of the body the more muscle a person has, and the less electricity that comes out the more fat a person has.

This technique has benefits over skinfold measurement because it is easier to do and does not mean that the client has to remove or adjust any clothing. However, it has been shown to be not such an accurate measure of body fat percentage.

Hydro densitometry or underwater weighing is a technique which is based on the Archimedes principle. It involves a person being weighed on land and then when fully submerged in water. Muscle and bone are denser than water while fat is less dense. A person with more bone and muscle will weigh more in water, have a higher body density and therefore less fat. Once the weight on land and weight in water are taken, a formula is used to work out percentage body fat.

This technique involves the use of a large pool of water and significant amounts of equipment. It is impractical for use outside a sport science laboratory.

Reasons to terminate a fitness test

There will be occasions where it becomes unsafe to continue with a test due to physiological changes within the client. The following is a list of specific situations when a test should be stopped:

- chest pains or angina-like symptoms
- excessive increase in blood pressure (250/115)
- shortness of breath and wheezing
- leg cramps or pain
- light-headedness, nausea, or pale, clammy skin
- heart rate does not rise with exercise intensity
- irregular heart beat
- client requests to stop
- signs and symptoms of severe exhaustion
- equipment fails.

Males		Females	
Sum of skinfolds	Body fat %	Sum of skinfolds	Body fat %
		14	9.4
		16	11.2
		18	12.7
20	8.1	20	14.1
22	9.2	22	15.4
24	10.2	24	16.5
26	11.2	26	17.6
28	12.1	28	18.6
30	12.9	30	19.5
35	14.7	35	21.6
40	16.3	40	23.4
45	17.7	45	25.0
50	19.0	50	26.5
55	20.2	55	27.8
60	21.2	60	29.1
65	22.2	65	30.2
70	23.2	70	31.2
75	24.0	75	32.2
80	24.8	80	33.1
85	25.6	85	34.0
90	26.3	90	34.8
95	27.0	95	35.6
100	27.6	100	36.3
110	28.8	110	37.7
120	29.9	120	39.0
130	31.0	130	40.2
140	31.9	140	41.3
150	32.8	150	42.3
160	33.6	160	43.2
170	34.4	170	44.6
180	35.2	180	45.0

(Adapted from Franklin, 2000)

Then using the following table you can categorise your body fat percentage:

Classification	Males (% body fat)	Females (% body fat)
Under-fat	< 6%	< 14%
Athletes	6–13%	14–20%
Fitness	14–17%	21–24%
Acceptable	18–25%	25–30%
Overweight	26–30%	31–40%
Obese	> 30%	> 40%

(Adapted from Franklin, 2000)

Fig 8.14 Underwater weighing

LEARNER ACTIVITY Fitness profile

Choose a sport which you are involved in and develop a fitness profile of an athlete in that sport. You will need to look at which components of fitness are important for that sport. For example, a sprinter will need to do well in the 40-yard run and vertical jump test but the multi-stage fitness test may be irrelevant.

Using a checklist, compare your own test results to the profile that would be needed for success. Analyse the results and draw up a list of your strengths and weaknesses.

Feedback on fitness testing

Once you have completed a fitness test it is important to give detailed feedback to the individual. Before you conduct a test you need to say what you are testing and explain how the test will be conducted. Feedback is given once you have conducted the test, written down the result and then worked out how the result compares to the normative tables.

Feedback should be given in the following format:

- repeat the component of fitness that has been tested
- tell them what the result of the test was
- explain what you have tested and what the score represents
- tell them how they fit in within the population norms

- tell the what the implications of the result are in terms of their health and fitness
- discuss what recommendations you would make for the future.

If you have done a blood pressure test you would give feedback in this specific way:

- 'I have just taken your blood pressure.'
- 'Your blood pressure was 120/80 mmHg.'
- 'Blood pressure is the pressure of blood in the arterial system; 120 mmHg is the pressure during the contraction phase of the heart beat and 80 mmHg is the pressure during the relaxation phase of the heart beat.'
- 'This score is within the normal healthy range.'
- 'It means you are healthy enough to take part in sport and exercise.'

The scores of all fitness tests must be recorded in writing to ensure you have the information available in the future when you come to retest.

Recommendations

Once you have completed all the tests you may write an action plan or a report on the individual; this would cover the following information:

- current situation, highlighting strengths and weaknesses
- the client's aims and objectives
- changes to be made, with options
- actions – a step-by-step guide to achieving aims
- timescale for review.

Key learning points

- Blood pressure, resting heart rate, lung function, body mass index and hip to waist ratio are all static tests which are performed to see if the client is healthy enough to perform the dynamic fitness tests.
- Performance-related fitness is made up of the following components: flexibility, strength, aerobic endurance, speed, power, muscular endurance and body composition.
- Flexibility is measured by a sit and reach test.
- Strength is measured by 1 repetition maximum and grip strength dynamometer.
- Aerobic endurance is measured by the multi-stage fitness test and the step test.
- Anaerobic capacity is measured by the Wingate test.
- Speed is measured by the 40-yard sprint test.
- Power is measured by the vertical jump test.
- Muscular endurance is measured by the one-minute press-up test and the one-minute sit-up test.
- Body composition is measured by skinfold assessment, and bioelectrical impedance and hydro densitometry tests.

Revision questions

1 Give four reasons why we might conduct fitness tests.
2 What five areas should be covered in a health screening questionnaire?
3 What is the aim of an informed consent form?
4 Briefly explain what is meant by coronary heart disease (CHD) and what factors may cause it.
5 Give five situations where you would refer a client to their GP for clearance before training.
6 The client should be in a certain state to make sure we get accurate results. What four pieces of advice would you give a client before they come for a fitness test?
7 What is meant by validity and reliability?
8 Why is the order in which you perform the tests important?
9 Why is it important to take a person's blood pressure prior to exercise?
10 What five factors will affect an individual's lung function?
11 What does hip to waist ratio give us an indication of?
12 What do the following tests measure?
   - Wingate test
   - Skinfold assessment
   - Multi-stage fitness test
   - 1 repetition max
   - Sit and reach
   - One-minute press-up test
13 Which test for body composition would you choose for your clients and why?
14 Give five situations where you would terminate a test.

References

Baechle, T. and Earle, R. (2000) *Essentials of Strength Training and Conditioning*, Human Kinetics.

Davis, R., Bull, C., Roscoe, J. and Roscoe, D. (2005) *Physical Education and the Study of Sport*, Elsevier Mosby.

Franklin, B. (2000) *American College of Sports Medicine's (ACSM) Guidelines for Exercise Testing and Prescription*, 6th edn, Lippincott, Williams and Wilkins.

Stafford-Brown, J., Rea, S., Janaway, L. and Manley, C. (2006) *BTEC First Sport*, Hodder Arnold.

Wesson K., Wiggins-James, N., Thompson, G. and Hartigan, S. (2005) *Sport and PE: A Complete Guide to Advanced Level Study*, Hodder Arnold.

Goals

By the end of this chapter you should:

- understand the fitness requirements of different sporting activities
- understand different methods of physical fitness testing
- be able to plan a fitness training programme
- be able to monitor and evaluate a fitness training programme.

Developing the correct training programme is vital to the success of the individual athlete and the team. Top-class athletes build their life around the requirements of their fitness training and have a dedicated coach for this purpose. Fitness will be important to any individual who is involved in physical activity to give them the best chances to succeed.

Components of fitness

Fitness can mean different things to different people and has been defined in different ways. When we examine fitness we need to ask 'What does this person have to be fit for?' or 'What functions does this person have to perform?' From this starting point we can build up a picture of their fitness requirements and then look at what can be done to develop their fitness.

Fitness is defined by the American College of Sports Medicine (ACSM) (1990) as:

> **a set of attributes that people have or achieve that relate to their ability to perform physical activity.**

Fitness is clearly related to performance and developing the attributes to achieve this performance.

Physical fitness

Physical fitness can be seen to be made up of the following factors.

Aerobic endurance is also called cardiovascular fitness or stamina. It is the individual's ability to take on, transport and utilise oxygen. It is a measure of how well the lungs can take in oxygen, how well the heart and blood can transport oxygen and then how well the muscles can use oxygen. When working aerobically we tend to perform repetitive activities using large muscle groups in a rhythmical manner for long periods of time.

Muscular endurance is how well the muscles can produce repeated contractions at less than maximal (submaximal) intensities. When training for muscular endurance we usually do sets of 15 to 20 repetitions. Most movements we produce in sport and everyday activities will be at submaximal intensities and all people will benefit from muscular endurance training.

Flexibility is the range of motion that a joint or group of joints can move through. Flexibility is often not given the amount of attention it should have in a training programme because people do not always see its importance. However, improving flexibility can improve performance because a greater range of motion will result in greater power development and

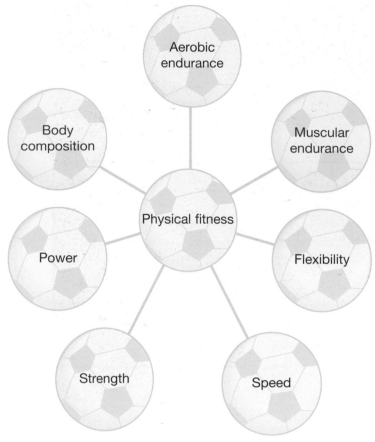

Fig 9.01 Physical fitness

will help to prevent injury and pain caused through restrictions in movement.

Speed is the rate at which the body or individual limbs can move.

Strength is the maximum force a muscle or group of muscles can produce in a single contraction. Heavy weight lifting or moving a heavy object will require strength. For example, if you have to push-start a car the success or failure of this effort will be an expression of your muscular strength. To train for strength we usually do sets of 1 to 5 repetitions.

Power is the production of strength at speed and can be seen when we throw an object or perform a sprint start. To move a heavy load quickly we need to use our power. Activities such as jumping to head a ball or a long jump will require us to express our power.

Body composition

Although not strictly a component of fitness, body composition has a direct impact on sports performance and the ability to perform certain activities.

The shape of the body is defined by three factors:

- the skeleton
- the amount of fat
- the amount of muscle.

Somatotyping is a method for describing an individual's body type or shape. 'Somatotype' describes which of these three factors are most dominant in the individual.

- **Ectomorphs** are mainly thin with low body fat and less muscle mass. They tend to have long levers and are suited to aerobic events such as long-distance running and cycling.
- **Endomorphs** are predominantly fat and may be apple or pear shaped. Some endomorphs will have a fair amount of muscle and may be found in sports such as shot-put and sumo wrestling.
- **Mesomorphs** will be predominantly muscular with low levels of body fat. They tend to have broad shoulders and narrow hips. Mesomorphs will be found in team sports such as football and rugby.

Fig 9.02 Ectomorph

Fig 9.04 Mesomorph

Fig 9.03 Endomorph

Skill-related fitness

This aspect of fitness relates to the production of skilled movement. This is the coordination between the brain, nervous system and muscles. All movement starts in the brain as it produces a nervous impulse which is transferred to the muscles through the nerves. The nervous impulse travels down the spinal cord and out through the nerves that shoot off the spinal cord. These nerves bring the nervous impulse to the muscles which then contract to produce movement.

When we learn a skill the brain sends the message to the muscles, but at the start it may not be the right message and may not produce a skilled performance. However, as we learn the skill we learn to send the right message and we develop a 'pathway' between the brain, nerves and muscles. All these skills need to have a strong pathway between the brain, nerves and muscular system.

Agility is a measure of how well you can control your body while moving through space. It is particularly important when you have to quickly change direction, such as a goalkeeper saving a deflected shot.

Balance is how well you can keep your body weight over a central base of support. It is important for us to stay on our feet during quick changes of direction.

Coordination is how well we can produce the skilled movement that is required of us.

Reaction time is how quickly you can pick up information, make a decision and then produce a reaction to it.

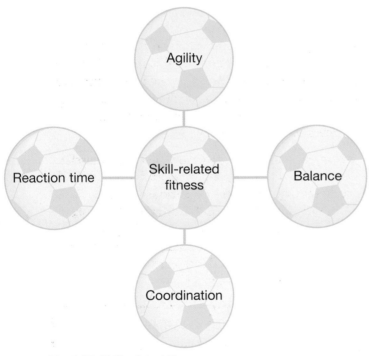

Fig 9.05 Skill-related fitness

Fitness requirements of a range of sports

In order to safely and effectively take part in sports it is necessary to have all the basic components of health-related fitness. Depending on the sport, some components need to be trained more than others. Different sports also have different skill-related component requirements, which also need to be trained for a player to excel in their sport.

Key learning points

- Aerobic endurance is a measure of how well the lungs can take in oxygen, how well the heart and blood can transport oxygen and then how well the muscles can use oxygen.
- Muscular endurance is how well the muscles can produce repeated contractions at low intensities.
- Flexibility is the range of motion that a joint or group of joints can move through.
- Speed is the how quickly the body or individual limbs can move.
- Strength is the maximum force a muscle or group of muscles can produce once.
- Power is the production of strength at speed.
- Body composition is the ratio of fat to lean body weight a person possesses.
- Agility is a measure of how well you can control your body while moving through the air.
- Balance is how well you can keep your body weight over a central base of support.
- Coordination is how well you can produce the skilled movement that is required of you.
- Reaction time is how quickly you can pick up information, make a decision and then produce a reaction to it.

There are a number of key aspects that need to be considered when planning a training programme for a sportsperson:

- the length of the activity
- the strength required
- the flexibility required
- the skills required.

If the activity lasts for a period of less than 30 minutes, aerobic fitness and muscular endurance tend not to be major components that need to be trained. Weight lifting involves short bursts of intense activity for which the sportsperson does not need high levels of aerobic fitness or muscular endurance. However, a marathon runner needs to be able to run for continuous periods of two hours and over, so aerobic fitness and muscular endurance are key areas that need to be trained.

Some sports require the athlete to have high levels of strength, speed and power so that they are able to exert high levels of force against a resistance, as in the throwing events such as the shot-put and javelin. Strength training is also necessary to build muscle mass in order to increase a person's sprinting speed.

Some flexibility is required by all sportspeople in order to avoid injury. However, some sports demand that the athlete has particularly high levels of flexibility in order to carry out the movements involved. Examples of these sports are gymnastics, martial arts and diving.

A number of sports involve a variety of the skill-related components of fitness. In order for athletes to improve in their sports they must take part in specific training practices to refine these skills. For example, a rugby player needs good hand/ball and foot/ball co-ordination, so they must take part in drills to practise these skills. Sprinters need good reaction times in order to get off to a good start in a race.

Football

Footballers need to train in a variety of the health-related and skill-related components of fitness. A player's position also influences their training programme – a goalkeeper needs quite a different training programme to that of a striker. The main components of fitness footballers need to train are as follows.

- **Anaerobic fitness**: football involves short bursts of speed and then periods of rest or walking. It is not really an aerobic activity because movement occurs at different speeds and is not steady-state or repetitive. Football and other team sports predominantly use the anaerobic system.
- **Strength, speed and power**: their training should include some resistance work in order to allow them to jump high, kick the ball hard and sprint, to reach the ball quickly, dodge and mark opponents.
- **Skill-related components**: with the agility to beat players and run after the ball as well as foot to ball coordination.

Swimming

Swimming uses all the major muscle groups of both the upper and the lower body. In this respect it is also known as a whole-body exercise. The type of fitness a swimmer needs depends on which stroke and at what distance they compete. Both sprint and distance swimmers need the following.

- **Muscular endurance**: to ensure that their muscles are able to continue to function and propel the body through the water for periods of time.
- **Flexibility**: to allow them to complete the stroke effectively. The butterfly stroke especially requires the swimmer to have a good range of movement in the shoulder joint in order to perform the stroke efficiently and effectively.

LEARNER ACTIVITY Different sports and their fitness requirements

Investigate the following sports by considering the amount of each component of fitness that is required to perform at the highest level for each one. Give each component a score of between 1 and 10 where 1 is the lowest and 10 is the highest.

	Aerobic endurance	Muscular endurance	Flexibility	Speed	Strength	Power	Agility	Balance	Coordination	Reaction time
Gymnastics										
Rowing										
Boxing										
Salsa dancing										
Archery										
Squash										
Rock climbing										

- **Aerobic endurance**: for the distance swimmer to complete long-distance swims.
- **Muscular strength**: for the sprint swimmer to increase their speed through the water.

Cycling

For long-distance cycling, such as the Tour de France, an athlete needs extremely high levels of aerobic fitness and muscular endurance. For hill work and sprint finishes they also need to train for muscular strength.

Racket sports

Tennis, squash and badminton involve bursts of intense activity for short periods. However, because these games usually last longer than 20 minutes, a player also needs to have high levels of aerobic fitness and muscular endurance. Some strength training should be carried out to hit the ball/shuttlecock with force. In tennis, some players may concentrate on improving their strength specifically to improve their serve. If the ball is hit with more strength it will travel faster, making it less likely to be reached by the opponent. There is quite a lot of skill required for these sports as the players need to have good racket/ball or racket/shuttlecock coordination. They also need to have high levels of agility in order to get to the ball/shuttlecock.

Rugby

Rugby players need a range of health-related and skill-related components of fitness, but their specific training programme will vary in accordance with their playing position. All rugby players need to train the following components of fitness.

- **Aerobic fitness and muscular endurance**: because a game of rugby lasts at least 80 minutes.
- **Strength and power**: to be able to tackle opponents, sprint and dodge opponents.
- **Good hand/ball and foot/ball coordination and high levels of agility to get to the ball**.

Methods of physical fitness training

Flexibility

Flexibility is the 'range of motion available at a joint' and is needed in sports to:

- enable the athlete to have the range of motion to perform the movements needed
- prevent the athlete from becoming injured
- maintain and improve posture
- develop maximum strength and power.

What happens to muscles when we stretch?

The stretching of muscles is under the control of the sensory nerves. There are two types of sensory nerves which are involved in allowing muscles to stretch and relax. They are muscle spindles and Golgi tendon organs (GTOs). The sensory nerves work to protect the body from becoming injured and will contract if they think a muscle is at risk of becoming damaged. This is one of our basic survival instincts because when we were hunter-gatherers injury would render us incapable of finding food and our families would starve.

The muscle spindles are sensory receptors which become activated as the muscle lengthens (due to its potential danger). When the muscle has reached a certain length they tell the nervous system to contract the muscle and prevent it being stretched any further. This protects the muscle against damage. If you perform the patella knee tap test this activates the muscle spindles. When this test is conducted, the knee extends due to the contraction of the quadriceps muscle activated by the muscle spindle. This is also called 'the myotatic stretch reflex'.

When we stretch a muscle we try to avoid this by stretching in a slow and controlled manner. The muscle spindles contract the muscle, which makes it feel uncomfortable or slightly painful. This is called the 'point of bind' where the muscle has contracted to avoid any damage.

When the point of bind is reached the stretch should be held for around ten seconds. This is because after ten seconds the muscle will relax and the pain will disappear. This relaxation is brought on by the action of the GTOs. GTOs are found in tendons and they sense how much tension there is in the muscle. Once the GTOs sense that the muscle is not in danger of damage they will override the muscle spindles and cause the muscle to relax. This is the effect that you want a stretch to have; it is called 'the inverse stretch reflex'. Once the muscle has relaxed you can either stop the stretch there or stretch the muscle a bit more until the point of bind is reached again and the process starts again.

There are various methods of stretching muscles.

Static stretching

This is when a muscle is stretched in a steady, controlled manner and then held in a static or still position. It is taken to the point where the muscle contracts and a slight pain is felt. This is called 'the point of bind'. At this point the stretch is held until the muscle relaxes and the discomfort disappears.

A static stretch can be a maintenance stretch or a developmental stretch. A maintenance stretch is held until the discomfort disappears and then the stretch is stopped. A developmental stretch is different because when the muscle relaxes and the discomfort disappears the stretch is applied further to a second point. It is taken to a point when the discomfort is felt again, it is held until the muscle relaxes and then applied again. It lasts for around 30 seconds while a maintenance stretch will last for around 10 seconds.

Proprioceptive neuromuscular facilitation

This type of stretching, known as PNF, is an advanced type of stretching in order to develop the length of the muscle. It needs two people to be involved: one person to do the stretching and one to be stretched.

It is carried out in the following way.

- The muscle is stretched to the point of bind by the trainer.
- At this point the trainer asks the athlete to contract the muscle and push against them at about 40 to 50 per cent effort.
- This contraction is held for 10 seconds.
- When the muscle is relaxed the trainer stretches the muscle further.
- Again a contraction is applied and then the muscle is re-stretched.
- This is done three times.

This is a more effective way of developing the length of the muscle as the contraction will actually cause the muscle to relax more quickly and more deeply.

Ballistic stretching

This means a 'bouncing' stretch as the muscle is forced beyond its point of stretch by a bouncing movement. Ballistic stretches are performed in a rapid, repetitive bouncing movement. It is a high-risk method of stretching due to the risk of muscular damage but it may be used in specific sports such as gymnastics. It must never be used on people training for health and fitness reasons rather than sports.

Resistance training

Resistance training means using any form of resistance to place an increased load on a muscle or muscle group. Resistance training can be used to develop muscular endurance, strength and hypertrophy (muscle bulk). Resistance can be applied through any of the following:

- free weights
- resistance machines
- cable machines
- gravity
- medicine balls
- air
- water
- resistance bands
- manually.

The following are popular methods of resistance training:

- resistance machines
- free weights
- cables
- plyometrics
- circuit training.

Concentric contraction taking place in the quadriceps muscle group

Eccentric contraction taking place in the quadriceps muscle group

Fig 9.06 A plyometric exercise

Fig 9.07 Resistance training with a machine

A range of **resistance machines** have been developed to train muscle groups in isolation. They were originally developed for body builders but their ease of use and safety factors make them a feature of every gym in the country. These machines target individual muscles and replicate the joint actions these muscles produce.

Free weights involve barbells and dumbbells and are seen to have advantages over resistance machines. Mainly, they allow a person to work in their own range of movement rather than the way a machine wants them to work. Also, when a person does free weights they have to use many more muscles to stabilise the body before the force is applied. This is particularly so if the person performs the exercise standing up. They also have more 'functional crossover' in that they can replicate movements that will be used in sports and daily life. This is seen as a huge advantage.

Cable machines are becoming increasingly popular because again they involve the use of many more muscles than resistance machines, and therefore burn up more calories. Once again, they can produce movements that are not possible on machines. For example, a golfer will need to perform rotation-type movements and can do these on cable machines.

The box at the bottom of the page shows the repetition ranges for targeting components of fitness.

Plyometrics

Plyometric training develops power, which is producing strength at speed. It usually involves moving your body weight very quickly through jumping or bounding. Any sport that involves jumping in the air or moving the body forwards at pace will need power training. Examples of plyometric training include:

- jumping on to boxes and over hurdles
- depth jumping
- vertical jumps and standing long jump
- medicine ball throws
- hopping
- bounding
- squat and jump
- press-up and clap.

It is a very strenuous type of training and an athlete must have well-developed strength before performing plyometrics. Before you take a plyometric session you must make sure the athlete is well warmed up and that you have checked the equipment and the surfaces

Objective	Muscular strength	Muscle hypertrophy	Muscular endurance	Power
Repetitions or duration	1–5	6–12	12–20	1–2 for single-effort events 3–5 for multiple-effort events
Recovery period	3–5 mins	1–2 mins	30–60 secs	2–5 mins
Sets per exercise	2–6	3–6	2–3	3–5
Frequency per week	1–2 on each muscle group	1–2 on each muscle group	2–3 on each muscle group	1–2 sessions a week

(Adapted from Baechle and Earle, 2000)

thoroughly. Ideally, you should use a sprung floor or a soft surface.

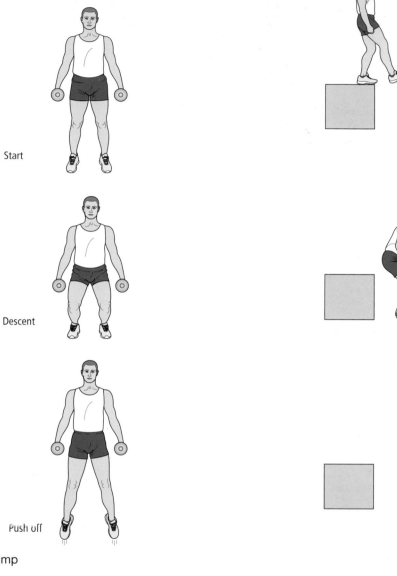

Start

Descent

Push off

Fig 9.08 Squat jump

Fig 9.09 Chest pass

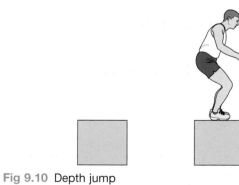

Fig 9.10 Depth jump

Aerobic fitness or pulse raisers	Shuttle runs Skipping Box step-ups Box jumps Jumping jacks Star jumps Spotty dogs Grapevines
Upper body	Press-ups Bench press with dumbbells Cable seated rows Bent-over row Shoulder press Bicep curls Tricep dips Lateral raises Dumbbell pullovers Medicine ball chest passes Medicine ball chest pass and press-up Medicine ball overhead throws
Lower body	Squats Lunges Split squats Side lunges Squat thrusts Hurdle jumps Ladder work Step-ups with dumbbells
Core exercises	Swiss ball curls Swiss ball back extension Plank Bridge Superman Rotations with medicine ball Medicine ball rotate and throw

Circuit training

Circuits have been popular in this country since the 1950s, particularly in the army! A circuit is a series of exercises arranged in a specific order and performed one after the other. There are normally eight to twelve stations set out and organised so that each muscle group is worked in rotation. Each exercise is performed for a certain number of repetitions or a set time period. Circuits can be performed for a range of fitness gains but are usually done to develop aerobic fitness or a general fitness base. They can be made specific to various sports by including exercises for the muscles used in that sport and some of the skills specific to that sport.

When planning a circuit you need to ask several questions:

- What is the objective of the session?
- How many participants will I have?
- What is their level of fitness?
- How much space have I got?
- What equipment is available?

A basic circuit session should contain exercise to improve aerobic fitness or raise the pulse rate, exercises to work the upper body, lower body and the core. When designing the circuit layout be careful not to place all the exercises for the same muscle group beside each other as this will cause undue fatigue. The circuit should follow the normal structure of a routine:

- warm-up
- main session
- cool-down
- flexibility.

The warm-up will include a pulse raiser, mobility and dynamic stretches. For example:

- walk
- walk with bicep curls and shoulder presses
- slow jog with shoulder circles
- jog
- dynamic stretches such as squat and press, step back and chest stretch
- jog with knee raises and heel flicks
- run
- jumps and hops
- sprint.

The main session should include eight to twelve exercises from the box on page 180.

The cool-down should progressively lower the pulse, but it can be combined with some stretching as well. It could follow this example:

- run (1 minute)
- jog (1 minute)
- brisk walk and stretch trapezius, pectoralis major, latissimus dorsi, triceps, deltoids
- standing stretches of adductors, calves and quads
- kneeling stretches of hip flexors and lower back
- lying stretches of hamstrings and gluteus medius and minimus.

LEARNER ACTIVITY Circuit training session

Design a circuit session of eight stations for 16 people who will work in pairs. Choose a target audience and consider the amount of space and equipment you have available. Also design a warm-up and cool-down specific to the session.

Aerobic training

Continuous training is also called 'steady-state' training and involves an individual maintaining a steady pace for a long period of time. To be effective it needs to be done for a period of over 20 minutes. It is useful for developing a strong base of aerobic fitness, but it will not develop speed or strength.

While continuous training has a role to play it can be limited in its benefits, particularly if the athlete does the same session each time they train. While initially it will have given them fitness gains there will be limited benefits after about four weeks once the body has adapted to the work. It may also produce boredom and a loss of motivation to train.

Interval training is described as having the following features: 'a structured period of work followed by a structured period of rest'. In other words, an athlete runs quickly for a period of time and then rests at a much lower intensity before speeding up again. This type of training has the benefit of improving speed as well as aerobic fitness. Interval training also allows the athlete to train at higher intensities than they are used to, and thus steadily increase their fitness level and the intensity they can work at. The theory is that you will be able to run faster in competition only if you train faster – and interval training allows this to occur. Intervals can be used to improve performance for athletes and fitness levels for people involved in exercise.

Interval training can be stressful to the systems of the body and it is important to ensure that an individual has a good aerobic base before raising the intensity of the training.

Once an athlete has reached the limit of their aerobic system they will start to gain extra energy from their anaerobic system (lactic acid system); this is demonstrated by an increased accumulation of lactic acid in the blood. The point where blood lactic acid levels start to rise is called the lactate threshold. Interval training can be designed to push an athlete beyond their lactate threshold and then reduce the exercise intensity below the lactate threshold. This has the effect of enabling the athlete to become better at tolerating the effects of lactic acid and also increasing the intensity they work at before lactic acid is produced. Well-designed interval training sessions can produce this desirable effect.

The intensity of interval training is higher than continuous work and thus there will be more energy production to sustain this high-intensity work. More energy production equals more calories burnt during training, which could lead to a faster loss of body fat (if the nutritional strategy is appropriate). As the intensity is higher more waste products are built up, resulting in a greater oxygen debt and a longer period of recovery. This longer period of recovery results in more oxygen being used post-exercise and more energy used to recover. Therefore, more energy is used during exercise and also after exercise, multiplying the potential effects of fat loss.

The main benefits of interval training are:

- improved speed
- improved strength
- improved aerobic endurance
- improved ability to tolerate the effects of lactic acid
- increased fat burning potential
- increased calorie output
- improved performance.

Interval training can be used to develop aerobic fitness as well as anaerobic fitness. When designing interval training sessions you need to consider how long the periods of work are in relation to the periods of rest. The following are recommended guidelines for training with each of the three energy systems.

- **Aerobic interval**: 1 or half a unit of rest for every unit of work.
- **Lactic acid intervals**: 2 to 3 units of rest for 1 unit of work.
- **ATP/CP intervals**: 6 units of rest for 1 unit of work.

As the intensity increases, more rest is required to guarantee the quality of each interval. If you were training for aerobic fitness you may do four minutes' work then have two minutes' rest (1:1/2). If you were training for lactic acid intervals you would have one minute's work and two or three minutes' rest.

Sample aerobic interval session

First estimate the maximum heart rate as 220 minus age and then you can work out the percentage of maximum heart rate.

For a 20 year old:

Maximum heart rate = 220 − 20 = 200 bpm
70% of max HR = 200 × 0.7 = 140 bpm
80% of max HR = 200 × 0.8 = 160 bpm
90% of max HR = 200 × 0.9 = 180 bpm

You will need to find out what workload (speed) produces each heart rate when you are running.

Basic interval

Work = 4 minutes   Rest = 2 minutes

4 sets of 4 minutes at 70% effort with 2 minutes' rest in between

Pyramid interval

Work = 3 minutes   Rest = 1.5 minutes

Warm-up

3 mins @ 80% of max HR
Rest
3 mins @ 85% of max HR
Rest
3 mins @ 90% of max HR
Rest
3 mins @ 85% of max HR
Rest
3 mins @ 80% of max HR
Cool-down

Treadmill hills pyramid

Find the speed that produces 70% of max HR and stay at this speed throughout the interval programme; then vary the gradient on the treadmill.

Work = 2 mins   Rest = 1 min

Warm-up
2 mins @ 2% gradient
Rest
2 mins @ 4% gradient
Rest
2 mins @ 6% gradient
Rest
2 mins @ 4% gradient
Rest
2 mins @ 2% gradient
Cool-down

Alternately the gradients could be set at 3%, 6%, 9%, 6% and 3%.

Sample anaerobic session
Lactic acid system

6 sets of 45 seconds (or 300 m) at 90–95% effort with 90 seconds' rest

4 sets of 75 seconds (or 500 m) at 80–85% effort with 150 seconds' rest

ATP/PC system

10 sets of 50 metres at 100% effort with 1 minute rest

Fartlek is a Swedish term; it literally means 'speed play' and it involves an athlete going out and running at a range of different speeds for a period of 20 to 30 minutes. This type of training is excellent for replicating the demands of a sport such as football, rugby or hockey where different types of running are required at different times. It can be used to develop aerobic or anaerobic fitness depending on the intensity of the running. It can also be used in cycling or rowing training. Fartlek running involves finding a base speed at around 60 to 70 per cent of maximum intensity and then fast bursts of work at 75, 80, 85 and 90 per cent mixed up into longer or shorter time periods. It can be used to challenge the different energy systems and demands of sports as well as reducing the boredom of training for long periods of time.

Core stability

If we were to take our arms and legs off our body we would be left with the body's core, which can be said to be the working foundation of the body and is responsible for providing the base to develop power. If we have a strong core we will be able to generate more force and power through the arms and legs; this is important when we kick a football or hit a tennis ball.

> **Core stability:** 'the ability of your trunk to support the effort and forces from your arms and legs, so that muscles and joints can perform in their strongest and most effective positions.'
>
> (Elphinston and Pook, 1999)

The body is made up of layers of muscles and the abdominal area is no different as it has deep, middle and outer layers which work together to provide stability.

The outer layer of muscles are the best known abdominal muscles with the rectus abdominis at the front, the erector spinae at the back and the internal and external obliques at the sides.

The middle layer is deeper muscle, which forms a cylinder or unit around the vertebrae. At the top we

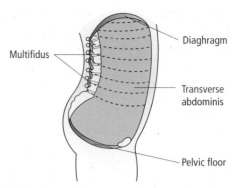

Fig 9.11 Outer layer of core muscles

have the diaphragm and at the bottom the pelvic floor muscles, while across the back we have the multifidus, and around the front and sides we have the transverse abdominis (TVA). The TVA is the key muscle here and is described as being 'the natural weight belt' because a weight belt replicates its shape and function.

The role of the inner muscles is to stabilise the vertebrae, ribs and pelvis to provide the stable working base or foundation. These muscles contract a fraction of a second before the arms or legs are moved when the body is functioning correctly. If this does not happen the chances of damaging the spine are increased.

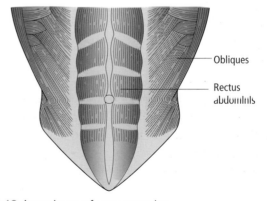

Fig 9.12 Inner layer of core muscles

The deep layer is tiny muscles which sense the position of the vertebrae and control their movement to keep them in the strongest position and prevent injury.

Activating the core muscles can be done in two ways. First, by hollowing or pulling in the abdominals or by bracing, which means contracting the muscles without them moving out or in. Different trainers will recommend different techniques depending upon their own experiences and training.

Abdominal training

The concepts of abdominal training are changing rapidly. The traditional method has been to do hundreds of sit-ups in pursuit of a perfect six-pack and then, in the late 1990s, abdominal cradles were introduced into gyms to aid people further. The 2000s have seen the introduction of Swiss balls and functional abdominal exercises into training programmes. There is still some confusion over what is the best way to train the abdominals. We need to look at a couple of misconceptions first before looking at what is the best way to train.

Fig 9.13 Swiss ball abdominal crunches

"Sit-ups will help me lose fat in the abdominal area"

No, you cannot spot-reduce fat because the muscle below the abdominal fat is separate from the fat itself and you can never be sure from where the losses in fat due to exercise will come. The way to lose abdominal fat is to increase activity level and have a correct nutritional strategy.

"Sit-ups will give me the six-pack I want"

Not necessarily, because overdoing abdominal work can cause a shortening of the abdominal muscles and pull your posture forwards, making the abdominal area shorter, squeezing the fat together and making you look fatter. In fact, if you perform back extensions it will make your posture more upright and help to keep the abdominals contracted and make them look more toned.

"Sit-ups are the best abdominal exercise"

This is debatable because sit-ups produce concentric and eccentric muscular contractions. The abdominals will contract isometrically when we train and move around in daily life. Therefore, surely we should replicate this isometric contraction when we train as it will have the best 'functional crossover' to daily life.

LEARNER ACTIVITY
Abdominal exercises

Work in pairs for this exercise.

Stand up and let your abdominals relax. Your shoulders may fall forward slightly and you may slump. Then get your partner to push you back gently from the shoulders and observe the effect this has.

Then either suck your belly button towards your vertebrae slightly or contract your abdominals and repeat the gentle push. What do you observe happens to your upper body in each case and how does the contraction of the abdominals change the way you hold yourself (your posture)?

When we train the core muscles we need to target the deeper muscles; this is done by producing isometric or static contractions.

Any exercise where you are standing up or supporting your body weight will be a core exercise. For example, a press-up is an excellent core exercise because the core muscles work to keep the back straight and the back will start to sag when these muscles become fatigued. All standing free weight and cable exercises require the core to stabilise the vertebrae while they are being performed. However, there are some specific core exercises which can be performed (see Fig 9.14).

The use of a Swiss ball to perform exercises requires an extra load on the core muscles and works them harder, as will using cables to exercise.

Fig 9.14a Plank

Fig 9.14b Side plank

Fig 9.14c Bridge

Planning physical fitness training programmes

Principles of training

To develop a safe and effective training programme you will need to consider the principles of training. These principles are a set of guidelines to help you understand the requirements of programme design. The principles of training are:

- **F**requency
- **I**ntensity
- **T**ime
- **T**ype
- **O**verload
- **R**eversibility
- **S**pecificity.

Frequency means how often the athlete will train per week, month or year. It is recommended that a beginner trains three times a week while a competitive athlete may train ten or twelve times a week.

Intensity is how hard the athlete works for each repetition. It is usually expressed as a percentage of maximum intensity. Intensity can be increased by adding more weight to be lifted, or increasing speed or gradient on the treadmill.

Time indicates how long they train for in each session. The recommended length of a training session is around 45 minutes before fatiguing waste products build up and affect training technique.

Type shows the type of training they will perform and needs to be individual to each person. A training effect can be achieved by varying the exercises an individual does – moving them from a treadmill to a rower, or a seated chest press to a free weight bench press.

Key learning points

Flexibility training is to develop the 'range of motion available at a joint'. There are various methods of stretching muscles: static stretching; ballistic stretching and PNF stretching.

Resistance training means using any form of resistance to place an increased load on a muscle or muscle group. Resistance can be applied through any of the following:

- free weights
- resistance machines
- cable machines
- gravity
- medicine balls
- air
- water
- resistance bands
- manually.

Plyometric training develops power by overcoming a resistance at speed. It can include jumping, throwing, hopping and bounding.

Circuit training is performing a series of exercises in sequence to achieve muscular and aerobic endurance, strength or speed.

Aerobic training aims to develop the efficiency of the heart, lungs and working muscles. It can be of three types: continuous training, interval training and Fartlek training.

Core stability is the strength of the muscles in the abdominal region, which act as the power base of the body. The most important muscle is the transverse abdominis.

Overload shows that to make an improvement a muscle or system must work slightly harder than it is used to. The weight that produces overload depends upon what the individual is currently used to at that moment. This may be as simple as getting a sedentary person walking for ten minutes or getting an athlete to squat more weight than they have previously. Overload can be achieved by changing the intensity, duration, time or type of an exercise.

Reversibility says that if a fitness gain is not used regularly the body will reverse it and go back to its previous fitness level. Any adaptation which occurs is not permanent. The rule is commonly known as 'use it or lose it'.

Specificity states that any fitness gain will be specific to the muscles or system to which the overload is applied. Put simply, this says that different types of training will produce different results. To make a programme specific you need to look at the needs of the athletes in that sport and then train them accordingly. For example, a footballer would need to run at different speeds and have lots of changes of direction. A golfer would need to do rotational work but sprinting speed would not be so important. A runner would need to do running predominantly, and they may get some aerobic gain from swimming or cycling but it would not achieve the best result.

There are other principles too.

Progressive overload

To ensure an athlete continues to gain fitness they need to keep overloading their muscles and systems. This continued increase in intensity (how hard they work) is called progressive overload. If you keep training at the same intensity and duration the body will reach a plateau where no further fitness gains are made. Therefore, it is important to keep manipulating all the training variables to keep gaining adaptations.

Periodisation

Periodisation means a progressive change in the type of training that is being performed to gain maximum fitness benefits. It needs to be carefully planned and would show progression from one type of training to another. For example, a sprinter will focus on developing their strength base and muscular endurance in the autumn before working on improving power and speed as they get closer to the competitive season. All training for sports performance needs to be periodised.

Macrocycle, mesocycle and microcycle are terminology specific to periodisation. The macrocycle is the largest unit of the training cycle and would cover the overall objective of the training. It will last for the length of a season or a training year. It is broken down into smaller units or mesocycles. A mesocycle is an individual phase of training and would cover a period of around a month depending upon the objective of the phase of training. A microcycle would represent each individual training session and its content. The plan would be periodised by looking at the big picture, or the macrocycle, then broken down into mesocycles, each contributing to the big picture and then the small detail of each session would be to consider how to achieve the aim of each mesocycle.

Collecting information

As an effective fitness coach it is important to be able to write an appropriate fitness training programme. There is a process that you need to go through to write an effective training session for a client.

Stage 1 – Gathering information: the first step is to gain relevant information about the person so that you can plan a personal training programme. The key is to build up a picture of the individual and what their life is like. Then you can look at what exercises you will plan for them. This is done through a questionnaire which the client will fill out on your first meeting. (See Chapter 8: Fitness testing for sport and exercise, for a sample questionnaire.)

What a person does or does not do in their life will have an effect on their health and fitness levels as well as their chances of being able to keep the training programme going. The following factors need to be taken into consideration.

- Occupation – hours worked and whether work is manual or office-based.
- Activity levels – amount of movement they do on a daily basis.
- Leisure time activities – whether these are active or inactive.
- Diet – what, how much and when they eat.
- Stress levels – either through work or their home life and how they deal with it.
- Alcohol intake – how much they consume and how often.

- Smoking – whether they are a smoker or ex-smoker and the amount they smoke.
- Time available – the client needs to fit the training into their schedule and the fitness trainer needs to be realistic when planning the programme.
- Current and previous training history – this will give an idea of the current fitness level of the client and also their skill level.

> ## LEARNER ACTIVITY
> ### Fitness questionnaire
> Prepare a questionnaire of ten questions to enable you to gather the relevant information you need to design a training programme.

Stage 2 – Establishing objectives: to ensure the success of the fitness programme it needs to be specific to the outcome a person wants. Once we have found this out we can establish goals. Their objective could be any of the following:

- cardiovascular fitness
- flexibility
- muscular strength
- muscular size
- muscle tone
- power.

Once the objectives have been established it is time to set goals to achieve these objectives.

Stage 3 – Goal setting: when setting goals it is important to ensure they follow the SMART principle – that they are specific, measurable, achievable, realistic and time-constrained. These goals should be set for the year or season, then for three months, one month and down to one week or one day. (For a full guide on how to set goals effectively see Chapter 19: Applied sport and exercise psychology.)

This goal-setting information should be kept in the training diary along with records of each training session.

Monitoring and evaluating a fitness training programme

The programme is planned out in detail and implemented with great energy and enthusiasm; likewise it must be evaluated in an organised manner. The athlete must keep a training diary for every session, whether it covered physical training, technical development or mental skills. Only then can it be accurately and systematically evaluated.

A training diary

A training diary should include the following details:

- date of each session
- detail of what was done in each session
- a record of the performances in training
- notes on how the athlete felt
- reasons as to why the athlete felt that way
- competition results
- fitness testing results
- performance reviews with their coach.

This can then be used to demonstrate progress, keep the athlete motivated and then to understand any improvements which have been made (or not).

The athlete can evaluate the success and effectiveness of their training in three ways:

- repeating their fitness tests
- evaluating performances
- reviewing their training diary.

Based on all this information the next stage of the training programme can be developed.

The diary can also be used to evaluate the reasons why the athlete did or did not achieve their goals, and any modifications or interventions can then be planned.

Key learning points

- Before designing a training programme you need to draw up a comprehensive questionnaire. It must cover the following: medical history, activity history, goals and outcomes required, lifestyle factors, nutritional status and other factors that will affect fitness.
- Frequency means how often the athlete will train per week.
- Intensity is how hard the athlete will work.
- Time is how long they will train for in each session.
- Type is the type of training they will perform; this needs to be individual to each person.
- Overload is working a muscle or system slightly harder than it is used to.
- Reversibility says that if a fitness gain is not used regularly the body will reverse it and go back to its previous fitness level.
- Specificity states that any fitness gain will be specific to the muscles or system to which the overload is applied.

Review questions

1 Define fitness and explain what it means for you in your sport.
2 Explain what is meant by aerobic endurance, muscular endurance and muscular strength.
3 Give four components of skill-related fitness.
4 Explain why you have to stretch in a slow, controlled manner.
5 Give five ways in which resistance can be applied in training.
6 What are the repetition ranges and rest periods for muscular strength, muscular endurance and muscle hypertrophy?
7 Explain the benefits that interval training has over continuous training.
8 Why may performing sit-ups not be the best method of abdominal training?
9 What is meant by the terms overload, reversibility and specificity?
10 When planning a training programme give five factors you need to consider to do with an individual's lifestyle and briefly explain why they are important.

References

Baechle, T. and Earle, R. (2000) *Essentials of Strength Training and Conditioning*, Human Kinetics.

Dalgleish, J. and Dollery, S. (2001) *The Health and Fitness Handbook*, Longman.

Elphinston, J. and Pook, P. (1999) *The Core Workout: a Definitive Guide to Swiss Ball Training for Athletes, Coaches and Fitness Professionals*, Core Workout.

Stafford-Brown, J., Rea, S., Janaway, L. and Manley, C. (2006) *BTEC First Sport*, Hodder Arnold.

Wesson K., Wiggins-James, N., Thompson, G. and Hartigan, S. (2005) *Sport and PE: A Complete Guide to Advanced Level Study*, Hodder Arnold.

10

Goals

By the end of this chapter you should:

- understand the effects and benefits of sports massage
- understand the role of sports massage professionals
- be able to identify the sports massage needs of athletes
- be able to demonstrate different sports massage techniques.

Massage can be used both to remedy problems and enhance an athlete's performance. It can also be used to treat problems arising from non-athletic, yet still physical activities such as gardening and walking. In reality most of us would benefit from massage therapy as it can promote relaxation, correct physical dysfunction and create a feeling of well-being.

The history of massage

Although there are indications that massage was used in China more than 5000 years ago, in the western hemisphere recorded history dates sports massage back to the Ancient Greeks and the original Olympic Games. Hippocrates, the Greek physician generally considered as the father of physical medicine, used massage as one of his vital therapies.

The principles behind current massage techniques were developed by Per Henrik Ling of Sweden in the nineteenth century. These techniques became known as Swedish massage and spread throughout Europe and then the world. In the 1924 Paris Olympics runner Paavo Nurmi, the 'Flying Finn', won five gold medals including two in one day with only a 30-minute break between events. Nurmi had his own personal massage therapist and he credited special massage treatments as a vital component of his

training programme. In the 1972 Munich Olympics the modern-day 'Flying Finn' Lasse Viren won two gold medals with the aid of daily massage.

As participation in sport and exercise becomes increasingly popular, greater demands are placed on today's athletes as the rewards for success increase. As they continue to improve their performances, the athletes push themselves to their physical and psychological limits. If the inevitable injuries are ignored and become chronic, they not only hinder rehabilitation but also affect performance, which makes the athlete susceptible to further injury.

> **definition**
>
> **Chronic:** long term.

Sports massage is therefore an expanding industry which aims to aid an athlete's recovery and enhance performance. It can now be seen at most major sporting events around the world.

> **definition**
>
> **Sports massage:** the systematic manipulation of the soft tissues of the body for therapeutic purposes to aid individuals participating in physical activity.
>
> **Soft tissues:** ligaments, tendons, muscles, connective tissue and skin.

The effects and benefits of sports massage

The aims of sports massage are to restore normal functional activity to the musculoskeletal system. Massage should therefore be an integral part of every athlete's pre- and post-training and competition routines, and should be viewed with similar importance to warming up and cooling down.

The general benefits of massage can be said to fall into three specific categories:

- mechanical
- physiological
- psychological.

Mechanical benefits to the athlete are:

- stimulation of soft tissues
- stretching of soft tissue to improve flexibility
- breaking down scar tissue
- correction of posture and limb alignment to improve body awareness
- reducing tension and associated pain
- reducing soreness and pain after an activity.

Physiological benefits to the athlete are:

- improved circulation via stimulation of the sympathetic nervous system to increase the supply of oxygen and nutrients to the injured tissue, thereby promoting healing
- improved circulation to remove waste products from the soft tissues via the lymphatic system
- improved circulation to reduce swelling post-injury
- sedative effect on the parasympathetic nervous system to reduce tension, induce relaxation and relieve pain
- stimulation of the nervous system to prepare the muscles for activity.

Psychological benefits to the athlete are:

- promoting relaxation
- creating a sense of well-being
- increasing confidence pre-competition.

In summary, the above effects will allow athletes to train more often, at a higher intensity and with fewer physical problems. It is therefore an essential part of an overall training programme.

The indications for sports massage

The following problems would indicate a need for sports massage based on the above benefits it can offer:

- pain post-injury or following training and competition
- swelling
- reduced flexibility
- reduced strength

- muscle tension
- pre-event nerves
- post-event fatigue or soreness
- routine part of training schedule to minimise the chance of the above situations arising
- injury prevention.

The contraindications for sports massage

Under certain circumstances, conditions may be present that sports massage may make worse and hence it should not be carried out. These conditions are collectively known as contraindications. The massage therapist needs to know what they are and how to deal with them.

- **A body temperature over 100 degrees Fahrenheit, or feeling unwell:** these symptoms suggest a period of illness, and as massage improves circulation, it may also spread toxins and potentially make the condition worse.
- **Skin diseases and disorders:** the skin may become inflamed due to allergies or medical conditions such as eczema and psoriasis. Infections can be recognised by swelling, redness, pain and heat. Massage can cause further irritation and may spread the infection through the client, on to the therapist, or even to a subsequent client.
- **Vascular diseases:** phlebitis is the inflammation of veins, and can often accompany a blood clot called a thrombosis. The clot may be disturbed by massage causing a blockage elsewhere in the blood vessels of the heart, lungs or brains, all with serious consequences. Caution should be taken if there is swelling, increased temperature and pain in the calf muscles. If a clot is suspected, urgent medical attention should be sought. Attempts to massage an area where varicose veins are present could also cause further damage and pain.

definition

Vascular: relating to the blood vessels.

- **Recently injured areas:** the site of an injury may be acutely inflamed with swelling, heat, redness, pain and probable dysfunction. Massage may act to disturb the healing process, thus making the condition worse by increasing circulation and therefore causing further swelling.

The above conditions may need a medical opinion and the client should be advised to see a doctor.

- **Pregnancy:** care should be taken if the client is experiencing nausea and vomiting. Massage of the back and abdomen must be avoided during the first 16 weeks of pregnancy as friction could promote miscarriage. In the later stages of pregnancy, massage of the lower limbs may reduce swelling and aid relaxation in areas such as the upper back and shoulders.
- **Other medical conditions:** clients presenting with a medical history of cancer, diabetes, tuberculosis, multiple sclerosis or other serious medical conditions should be advised to gain medical clearance from their doctor prior to treatment.

LEARNER ACTIVITY
Indications and contraindications

1 Which conditions would benefit from massage and which would be contraindicated.

Broken leg	Tight muscle
Anxiety	Post-training fatigue
Feeling unwell	Thrombosis
Psoriasis	Recent injury

2 List two mechanical, two physiological and two psychological benefits of massage.
3 What is phlebitis?
4 You should never perform massage on a pregnant client. True or false?

Key learning points

- The aim of sports massage is to restore normal function. Its benefits can be divided into mechanical, physiological and psychological.
- The indications for sports massage are wide-ranging and need to be known by both the therapist and client.
- Be aware of the contraindications to avoid making the client feel worse; seek medical advice if you are not certain whether to proceed.

The role of the sports massage professional

A sports massage professional has a varied job: preparing athletes for competition, helping them warm down after competition, and then dealing with any injuries or symptoms they may have. They can also treat other people who are active but not athletes.

In order to practise, the therapist ideally requires a sports therapy diploma, accredited by the Vocational Training Charitable Trust (VTCT), which can be studied at most further education colleges. It is also possible to do degrees at a limited number of universities, and private training organisations offer an excellent range of courses and career opportunities. Details of all these can be found on the internet.

To be an effective sports therapist you need a thorough base of knowledge and a range of physical and personal skills:

- **knowledge** of anatomy and physiology, exercise physiology, massage techniques and effects
- **physical** skills in massage techniques, strapping, stretching, resistance training, first aid and modalities such as heat, ice and electrotherapy
- **personal** attributes and skills – professional, honest and reliable, as well as listening and communication skills.

The therapist also needs to know their limits and when to seek advice or refer a client to a medical colleague. This is because the diagnosis of certain conditions may require more extensive training and expertise. Treatment could be provided once the all-clear was given. For this reason many therapists work alongside other specialists, such as physiotherapists, and this relationship is often of mutual benefit. Sports massage professionals may be required to perform a range of treatments in addition to the basic sports massage techniques, including strapping and electrotherapy.

The sports massage professional usually has to deal with administration and may choose to set up their own business. This business could be located anywhere, but usually they are at sports clubs, leisure centres, gyms and medical centres. Some will travel to clients' homes and others will diversify, offering additional personal training services. To this end, it is useful to have a sound knowledge of sport-specific techniques and the rigours of competition.

In summary, they have a huge role to play in the treatment of sports injuries, the conditioning of athletes and the treatment of the general public.

> ## LEARNER ACTIVITY Attributes of a therapist
>
> List three physical and three personal attributes that the sports massage therapist needs.

Key learning points

- The career is varied and rewarding, with high levels of satisfaction.
- Qualifications are necessary to become a sports therapist, as is a thorough knowledge base.
- Certain personal and physical attributes are needed if you are considering a career as a sports therapist.

Sports massage requirements
Client assessment

Once you are clear about the effects of massage and know when massage is both indicated and contraindicated, you can proceed to the assessment. This initial consultation is as important as the treatment itself, and an accurate record must be kept along with details of the subsequent physical examination.

The questioning of a client is known as the subjective assessment. It enables the therapist to build up a picture of the current issues, the client's history and what they aim to achieve from treatment.

Prior to any questioning, you should make your client aware of any health and safety issues that are specific to your facility, and the location of fire exits, fire procedures, etc.

The initial questions will establish the cause, nature and irritability of their symptoms:

- What is your presenting problem?
- If there has been an injury, how and when did it occur?
- If there has been no injury, how long have you had the problem?

- Did the problem occur immediately or gradually?
- How would you describe the symptoms, e.g. dull ache, sharp pain?
- Has there been any swelling, redness or increased temperature?
- Is the problem improving, remaining the same or getting worse?
- How is this currently affecting your function and performance?

Once you have this detailed information about the client's current status you need to build up a picture of their history:

- How is your general health?
- Have you any history of medical problems?
- Are you taking any medication?
- What physical activities are you involved in?
- At what level are you competing?
- What is your training schedule?
- What injuries, if any, have you previously suffered?
- What treatments have you previously had?

The information that you are given needs to be recorded on a record form similar to that shown on the opposite page.

At this point you may have identified a contra-indication, or may have concern beyond your level of expertise. If so, you may choose to refer your client to their doctor before progressing with treatment.

You should at this stage have a good idea of what their problem is, but you will need to verify this by examining the client. This is known as the 'objective assessment'. If appropriate, it may be necessary for the client to remove clothing, often down to their underwear, with their dignity being maintained at all times. A basic understanding of anatomy is essential for these next stages.

- You need to observe the client for limping, swelling, muscle wasting, bruising, haematomas, abrasions, redness or other abnormal signs.
- You then need to test the range of movement in the areas adjacent to their problem. First, ask the client

> definition
>
> **Haematoma:** bruising.
> **Abrasion:** grazed skin.

Confidential medical history

Name:_____   Occupation: _____

Age: _____   D.O.B.: _____

Address:_____

Tel: Day: _____   Eve: _____   Mob: _____

Sex: _____   Height: _____   Weight: _____

Sport played: _____   Frequency/intensity: _____

GP name/address: _____

Medical history: _____

Present complaint: _____

History of injury: _____

I confirm that the information I have given is accurate to the best of my knowledge and I have not withheld any details. I accept that I will receive sports massage therapy at my own risk.

Signed:_____   Date: _____

Print name: _____   Therapist signature: _____

Notes – physical assessment

to move and assess their willingness (active movement), then move the area yourself within a comfortable range (passive movement). This will assess the flexibility of the tissues in question.

- You then need to assess any muscle weakness by resisting certain movements or asking them to perform certain functional tasks.
- Finally, you need to palpate (touch) the problem area to check for muscle spasm, increased temperature, tenderness or pain.

This will complete your client assessment and provide you with all the necessary information to move on to the treatment stage. The information you are given needs to be recorded on a form which also includes the client's details. This form is an accurate record of your assessment and subsequent treatment, and needs

to be signed and dated on every entry. The information disclosed by the client is strictly confidential and should not be discussed without their authority.

Proposed treatment

The results of the assessment should be discussed with the client, along with how you intend to treat their problem and what this aims to achieve. Your plan will involve informing the client which treatments you propose to use and the number of treatments that may be required to achieve satisfactory results. This may include the client having to perform a home exercise programme such as guidance for stretches, on strengthening and posture, or how to use heat and ice.

LEARNER ACTIVITY Client assessment

- With a partner of the same gender, take the role of the client and then the therapist. Complete a subjective assessment as if it were a real situation. On completion, reflect on each other's performance and highlight both positive and negative aspects. If necessary repeat the activity.
- It can be embarrassing for a client to undress down to their underwear for treatment. With this in mind, each partner should remove clothing relevant to their injury or problem so that the assessment and treatment can be carried out. This will give you an insight into how the client may feel, making you think about another person's need for dignity.

Key learning points

- Perform a subjective examination and understand the relevance of the questions.
- Perform an objective examination based on the previous questioning, recognising the importance of maintaining client dignity.
- Understand the need to accurately document all information and to maintain confidentiality at all times.
- The assessment is essential to formulate a safe and effective treatment plan.

The client is then in a position to give you their informed consent for you to proceed. Any charges should be made clear prior to the assessment and any payments received should be accurately recorded.

Environment, appearance and equipment

You will often have to be flexible as to where you work. The environment will often be out of your control, especially if working at a sporting event. Care is essential to create an environment as near to the ideal as possible. This would involve the following:

- privacy for the client
- clean, tidy and well-ventilated room
- warmth to promote relaxation, especially if the client has to undress.

The therapist should have:

- a professional appearance, unhurried and confident
- clean hands – wash basin, soap, towels and waste disposal available
- short nails with no polish and no jewellery
- short sleeves and no wristwatch.

The following equipment should be available:

- massage couch with adjustable height and pillows
- privacy screens (for a private changing area)
- massage oils, creams or powders
- massage cologne to remove oils
- towels to cover areas not being massaged and to provide a comfortable temperature.

Client comfort is paramount, so the couch should ideally be adjustable with a face hole and a ready supply of pillows to support the head or limbs. It is also important for the therapist to be comfortable as they will adopt positions for sustained periods, day in day out, so the height of the plinth and your position requires careful attention to convey relaxation and confidence to the client.

Safe practice needs to be implemented, and an understanding of health, safety and hygiene regulations is important. You also need to note that massage is often a personal experience for both therapist and client, and although professionalism is adhered to and inappropriate behaviour does not occur, complaints may still arise. An awareness of consumer rights is therefore beneficial.

LEARNER ACTIVITY Hygiene and appearance

- Go to www.RCN.org.uk and discover how to correctly wash and dry your hands. Practise this with a partner.
- List five aspects of a therapist's appearance that would create a professional image.

Client preparation

Success depends not only on diagnosis, treatment and physical skills, but also on personal skills. It is essential that a professional rapport is developed with the client. This can be achieved by:

- relaxing the client and putting them at ease
- showing a caring attitude by listening to their concerns
- being professional at all times
- maintaining client confidentiality
- explaining the treatment course and the desired effect
- using tact and respecting their privacy and dignity.

Once the treatment has commenced, the client must be able to relax. Experience will allow you to work out whether the client wishes to talk or not.

Massage oils are used to allow smooth movement over the client's body and prevent friction. Vegetable oils such as olive and sunflower oils are commonly used as they have little fragrance and are easily absorbed by the skin. Aromatherapists use essential oils which have specific effects and should therefore only be used following appropriate training. If using oils, sports cologne should be applied post-treatment to remove any excess. The traditional lubricant for Swedish massage is talcum powder but this can cause extra friction and subsequent discomfort on dry skin. The finer powder may also be inhaled over time by the therapist, endangering their health. But as certain clients still prefer it, you should still consider using it with caution. Less frequently used are certain creams and lotions.

Massage techniques

The three main techniques used are:

- effleurage
- petrissage
- frictions.

LEARNER ACTIVITY
Clients at ease
What are the vital components needed to make your client feel at ease?

Key learning points

- The assessment results and subsequent treatment plan should be shared with the client so they can offer their informed consent to treat.
- A considerable amount of organisation is needed to prepare the environment, equipment, the therapist and the client, in order to portray a professional image and strike up an appropriate rapport.
- Awareness of health and safety legislation and customer rights are essential, and hygiene and hand washing are of particular importance.
- It is important to understand which massage medium to use – oils, powders or creams.

Effleurage

This involves a variety of stroking movements and is used at the beginning and end of a massage. It can be applied with varying degrees of pressure and is broken into light and deep stroking. Light stroking is performed with the whole hand, keeping the fingers together and with the hand relaxed. The speed and pressure will vary as the massage proceeds. The initial light stroking enables the therapist to spread the oil and identify tension in the muscle, even starting to relax the muscle. Gradually more pressure is applied, with the aim of assisting fluid flow through the tissue spaces, vessels and veins. The movement should occur up the limb towards the superficial lymph glands which can be found in the groin, back of the knee and the armpit.

Pressure should be consistent throughout a stroke, but can be increased by placing one hand on top of another or using the heel of the hand, finger pads or thumbs. The aim is to relax and sedate initially, then to stretch tissues, increase flow and drainage, reduce swelling, reduce pain by nerve stimulation, and remove waste products.

Petrissage

This is also known as kneading as the basic movement involves compressing then releasing the tissues. Direct pressure is performed in a circular motion using the palm of the hand to compress muscle tissue on to underlying structures. More localised pressure can be applied using the fingertips, thumbs and even the elbows. The next stage is similar to kneading but is

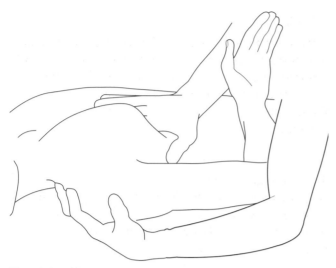

Fig 10.01 Effleurage

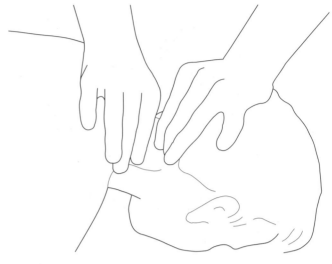

Fig 10.02 Petrissage

LEARNER ACTIVITY
Effleurage massage

Working in pairs, practise effleurage on each other's calf muscles, with strokes starting at the foot and ending at the back of the knee. Relax your partner with gentle stroking movements, warming the muscles and spreading the oils. Promote circulation, increase pressure and stimulate lymph drainage to the major superficial glands. Gradually end the massage using further gentle stroking techniques. Reflect on each other's performance and remember that practice makes perfect.

known as 'picking up' as it involves lifting the tissues up perpendicular to the underlying tissues then squeezing with the forefinger and thumb prior to release. Once the tissue is released, blood returns to it, bringing with it the essential oxygen and nutrients for healing. This technique also aims to mobilise tissues and reduce tension, promote lymph drainage and encourage relaxation.

Frictions

These are small movements over a localised area using the pads of the fingers or thumbs. Unlike other techniques they are often used where there is little soft tissue, such as the elbows, knees and ankles. Considerably more pressure is applied than during petrissage.

The action is initiated by bracing with the heels of the hands, then holding the thumbs steady and moving the fingers in a circular motion. The fingers do not move across the skin but they do move the skin across the deeper tissue. By increasing the pressure you can stimulate the deep muscle tissue and the breakdown of recently formed scar tissue by separating adhesions between repaired muscle fibres. There can be a degree of discomfort but only for a short time. The aims are to stimulate blood flow, separate adhesions, minimise the effects of scar tissue, promote flexibility and promote healing.

Although the above techniques form the basis of massage, there are other techniques in use, including tapotement, vibrations and trigger points.

LEARNER ACTIVITY
Petrissage massage

Practise this technique in a similar way to effleurage. This time decide for yourself which muscles would benefit most from this technique.

LEARNER ACTIVITY
Frictions massage

Practise this technique in the same way as the other two. Decide what injuries and which parts of your body would benefit most.

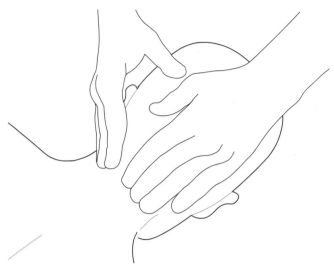

Fig 10.03 Frictions

Tapotement

This is also known as percussion and can be divided into cupping and hacking.

Cupping involves the therapist making a cup shape with their hands and, with the palms down, they strike the muscle making a dull thud, which should sound different from the slap of a flat palm. Moving the hands rapidly up and down the muscle this has the effect of improving superficial circulation and stimulating the muscle.

Hacking has a similar effect and involves using the outside of the hands with the palms facing each other to strike the muscle, usually targeting the larger muscle bulks such as the quadriceps.

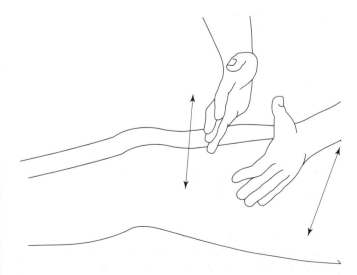

Fig 10.04 Tapotement (hacking)

Vibration

This is often used to finish off a massage. It involves the therapist supporting a muscle with one hand and vibrating the other hand from side to side as they move up and down the muscle. This aims to stimulate the muscle, and to promote blood flow and increase flexibility.

Trigger point

This massage involves the therapist applying sustained pressure in one specific place, using a finger, thumb or even an elbow. The trigger point is an area of high tension in the muscle where the fibres have failed to relax. It can cause local or referred pain where symptoms are felt at a distance away from the trigger point. Pressure is applied and the pain it creates will tend to subside after ten seconds, following which greater pressure can be applied and sustained for up to a minute. The aim is to gain relaxation and allow blood to return to the muscle.

Order of routine

Usually the techniques described above are performed in the order given, with the massage finishing with effleurage. The time you spend on each technique may vary depending on the needs of your client.

Evaluation

It is important to evaluate the effect of treatment by:

- asking for immediate feedback
- stretching and loading affected muscles
- performing specific tests
- getting client feedback once they return to sporting action.

Based on the feedback, you may prescribe more treatments or a change of technique. If symptoms persist, referral to another medical professional such as a doctor, physiotherapist, chiropractor or osteopath may be advised.

Key learning points

- There are three main massage techniques that are the basis of treatments; these need to be practised diligently in order to gain maximum benefit and to instil confidence in the client.

- Additional techniques are also available and it is important to learn when to use all the techniques and for which body parts certain techniques are most suitable.

- An evaluation after the treatment is an essential part of the overall management.

Review questions

1 What benefits does sports massage provide?
2 Give three situations when sports massage should not be used.
3 What equipment does a sports massage therapist require?
4 Describe the procedures that need to be undertaken before treatment.
5 Explain the difference between effleurage, petrissage and frictions.
6 How would you create a professional image?

References

Cash, M. (1998) *Sports and Remedial Massage*, Mosby.

Dawson, L., Dawson, K. A. and Tiidius, P. M. (2004) Evaluating the influence of massage on leg strength, swelling and pain following a half marathon. *Journal of Sports Science Medicine*, 3, 37–43.

Lewis, M. and Johnson, M. I. (2006) The clinical effectiveness of therapeutic massage for musculoskeletal pain: a systematic review. *Physiotherapy*, 92(3), 146–58.

Paine, T. (2000) *The Complete Guide to Sports Massage*, A & C Black.

Preyde, M. (2000) Effectiveness of massage therapy for sub acute low back pain: a randomised controlled trial. *Canadian Medical Association Journal*, 162, 1815–20.

Tiidius, P. M. and Shoemaker, J. K. (1995) Effleurage massage, muscle blood flow and long term post exercise strength recovery. *International Journal of Sports Medicine*, 15, 478–83.

Van der Dolder, P. A. and Roberts, D. L. (2003) A trial in to the effectiveness of soft tissue massage in the treatment of shoulder pain. *Australian Journal of Physiotherapy*, 49, 183–8.

Watt, J. (1999) *Massage for Sport*, The Crowood Press.

Analysis of sports performance

Every sportsperson is aiming to improve their performance in terms of their technical ability, physiological fitness, psychological strength and biomechanical efficiency. We tend to become even more reflective and ask more questions when things are not going well and we are losing competitions. In order to analyse our performances we need a structure or framework in which to work. This chapter provides a structure for athletes to interpret their performances and their successes and failures.

The performance profile of a sporting activity

The performance profile is a visual method of looking at performance in a broad manner. It is used by the athlete and coach to pinpoint strengths and weaknesses and this information is then used to design future actions. When a coach works with an athlete the coach can make decisions on techniques and changes, with the methods being imposed on the athlete by the coach. In this method the success or failure of the training programme is viewed by the athlete as being dependent upon the effectiveness of the coach in meeting their needs.

However, the coach only has the 'outsider' view. Butler and Hardy (1992) identified that this was a major weakness as it affected an individual's intrinsic motivation. Bull (1991) agreed that an athlete's commitment to their training schedule and the accompanying educational work would be affected if the coach who had imposed the schedules was not always present. It would seem to be a more productive relationship if the expertise of two people was utilised. The coach is the expert in terms of 'the outsider' view of the athlete's performance, while the athlete is the expert in terms of 'the insider' view of their experiences and how they are feeling.

Butler (2000) described the athlete's role as follows:

> **The athlete's assertions, discriminations and insights are not only valid but valuable. They make a significant contribution to the development of an effective training programme.**

The performance profile gives the coach and athlete a tool to provide a visual display of the areas of performance that are perceived to be important in working towards a top performance, and their assessment of the current position in relation to this.

Using a performance profile

First, you need to choose the sporting activity you want to examine and then you can look at any of the following:

- technical and tactical (shooting, passing, tackling)
- physiological fitness (strength, power, flexibility)
- psychological (motivation, arousal, confidence)
- biomechanical (speed, motion, momentum).

To construct a performance profile you would do the following.

- The athlete is asked to think about the qualities or skills which are shown by those athletes who perform at the top level of their sport in the same position, role or event as themselves.

- These qualities or skills are called the 'constructs' and they are then placed on the performance profile.
- The athlete then describes their current position in terms of their competency by giving themselves a mark out of 10. This score of 10 is in comparison to an athlete they consider to be excellent in their chosen sport.
- The coach may do the same exercise to provide the 'outsider viewpoint'.

These scores can be filled in on the performance profile and used to:

- identify their current level of competence
- identify areas of strength and weakness
- monitor progress and any changes occurring
- monitor effectiveness of training programmes
- identify any differences in the viewpoints of athlete and coach
- provide a basis for designing a training programme.

Technical analysis of a sporting activity

You can analyse a sporting activity in terms of the whole activity, an individual position or an individual aspect of the game.

Whole activity

Snooker, for example, can be broken down into the following constructs:

- stance
- cueing action
- bridging
- striking
- long potting
- short potting
- cushion shots
- snookering
- back spin
- top spin
- side spin
- deep screw
- follow through.

Positional activity

A midfielder in football would perform the following techniques:

- short passing
- long passing
- crossing
- dead ball work
- throwing in
- tackling
- blocking
- long-range shooting
- close-range shooting
- defensive heading
- attacking heading.

Individual aspect of an activity

A tennis player would perform the following backhand shots:

- smash
- volley
- half volley
- drop volley
- lob
- flat drive
- topspin drive
- slice.

	1	2	3	4	5	6	7	8	9	10
Short passing										
Long passing										
Crossing										
Dead ball work										
Throwing in										
Tackling										
Blocking										
Long-range shooting										
Close-range shooting										
Defensive heading										
Attacking heading										

Fig 11.01 Performance profile for a midfielder

LEARNER ACTIVITY
Constructs

Put together eight to ten constructs for the following sporting activities:

- 100 m sprinting
- goalkeeping
- tennis serve.

Physiological analysis of a sporting activity

This is completed in the same manner as the technical analysis except the constructs will be different (see Fig 11.02).

Psychological constructs

This is also completed in the same manner as the technical analysis, except the constructs will be different (see Fig 11.03).

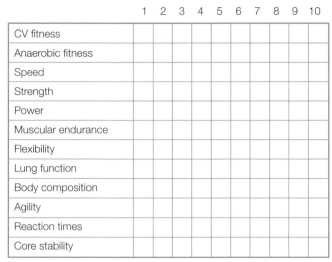

	1	2	3	4	5	6	7	8	9	10
CV fitness										
Anaerobic fitness										
Speed										
Strength										
Power										
Muscular endurance										
Flexibility										
Lung function										
Body composition										
Agility										
Reaction times										
Core stability										

Fig 11.02 Physiological constructs for a tennis player

	1	2	3	4	5	6	7	8	9	10
Intrinsic motivation										
Extrinsic motivation										
Arousal control										
Anxiety levels										
Attentional focus										
Confidence										
Controlling agression										
State management										
Concentration skills										
Relaxation skills										
Emotional well-being										
Mental rehearsal										
Imagery skills										

Fig 11.03 Psychological constructs for a boxer

	1	2	3	4	5	6	7	8	9	10
Development of velocity										
Velocity at release										
Acceleration										
Application of force										
Use of levers										

Fig 11.04 Biomechanical constructs for a javelin thrower

Biomechanical constructs

A fourth analysis can be completed of the biomechanical demands of a sporting activity (see Fig 11.04).

Benefits of performance profiling

As a technique for analysing performance, profiling works very well because it can take into account a vast amount of information for analysis by coach and athlete. It also considers the roles of coach and athlete as equally important with their different viewpoints on performance. Crucially, it takes into account the opinion of the athlete and gives them an active role in the analysis process, allowing them to take ownership of their performance and outcomes. It also allows the coach and athlete to identify any areas of mismatch where there is a differing opinion, and provides a basis for discussion. It can act as a process of education for the athlete as they become self-aware of the varying demands on them as well as their relative importance.

Performance profiles can form the basis of a review of progress on a monthly basis as the athlete and coach track their progress. They can also inform the process of goal setting to set the way forward.

Key learning points

- Performance profiling is a way of looking at performance in a broad sense.
- It involves the opinion of the athlete as well as that of the coach.
- It can be used to identify strengths and weaknesses.
- Performance profiling can be applied to technical, physiological, psychological and biomechanical components of performance.

Analysing sporting performance

The effectiveness of an individual's sporting performance comes down to a range of factors, which can be split into two categories:

- intrinsic – factors within the body
- extrinsic – factors outside the body.

Intrinsic factors would include:

- age
- health
- diet
- previous training
- motivation
- confidence
- ability level.

Extrinsic factors would include:

- group dynamics
- group cohesion
- temperature
- time of the day.

Intrinsic factors

Age

It is generally accepted that performance declines after the age of 35. Up to the age of 35 the body is building up in terms of bone and muscle strength and cardiovascular fitness. After the age of 35 these structures of the body slowly start to lose their efficiency with a resulting performance decrement, although, having said that, training will slow down this decline and maintain strength, flexibility and cardiovascular fitness. We have seen many sportspeople remain at the top level despite being over the age of 35. Martina Navratilova was winning tennis titles into her fifties. Stephen Redgrave, Steve Davis, Teddy Sheringham, Shane Warne and Gary Speed are all still able to perform at the top level in their sports despite their age.

Health

The health of an individual's organs and systems are all vital in gaining their adaptations from training and then producing top-level performances. The body functions as a whole organism made up of many systems and organs, and poor function in one area will affect the functioning of the whole organism.

Diet

There is a clear link between nutrition and health. When we eat we are ultimately feeding the cells of the body with nutrients to allow them to function and give them the basic building blocks to remain healthy. If we feed our cells with fresh, nutritious foods we will have healthy cells, contributing to our health. But if we feed our cells with poor-quality nutrients from processed or fast foods we will end up with unhealthy and ultimately diseased cells, contributing to illness.

Previous training

Our current position is the result of all the activity we have or have not done in our lives. The performance the athlete is able to produce depends upon the quality of their training programme and the fine balance between training and rest periods.

Motivation

Motivation is the amount of drive and energy that we possess at any point in time. It influences our desire to win. If we have trained hard and looked after our nutrition and rest patterns we will feel better and subsequently more motivated.

Confidence

Our confidence is the extent to which we feel we will be successful. It is affected by a range of factors. These will include our previous experiences and our perception of these experiences as either successful or otherwise. In addition, there is our perception of our opponents and our ability to deal with the environment in which we are placed. For example, we may feel more confident when we compete on our home territory and slightly intimidated when we go away. Our confidence level is closely related to our anxiety levels and if we are anxious about our performance this will start to erode our confidence levels.

Ability level

Our ability is the natural level of skills we possess and is the basis for developing further skills. Our performance is clearly the result of the ability and skills we possess.

Extrinsic factors

Group dynamics

Group dynamics refers to the sum of the processes occurring within the group that will influence its effectiveness. The most successful groups have a high level of attractiveness for the individual members, and the members will also share the same goals and work towards achieving these objectives.

Group cohesion

Group cohesion is the extent to which the individual members of the group have an attraction to the group and keep the group together. Cohesion can be task-related or socially related. Task cohesion is the extent to which you are willing to work together in the sporting environment, and social cohesion is how well you get on away from the sporting field. Task cohesion is the most important factor but it can be boosted by social cohesion.

Temperature

Extremes of temperature can have a negative effect on performance due to the effect on the physiological systems of the body. Heat can cause excess sweating, dehydration and heat exhaustion, while cold can make it difficult for the cardiovascular and muscular systems to achieve the correct temperature for optimal functioning.

Time of day

The time of day can influence performance in terms of nutritional and fatigue status. In the morning before a person has eaten they will be in a dehydrated state with low blood sugar and in a far from optimal state to perform effectively. Depending upon when they eat and drink they will fluctuate in terms of their nutritional status through the day. Other physical factors can change through the day. Mobility and flexibility will be lowest in the morning due to the inactivity of the joints and the lack of synovial fluid that has been excreted into the joint.

Performance profile analysis

The performance profile relies on the respective viewpoints of the athlete and coach. It is also useful to gather information to be used in rating the score for each construct. The opinions of the athlete and coach would be qualitative data, while the information gathered from testing would be quantitative data.

The four aspects of the performance profile could be analysed using the following quantitative data

Technical constructs:

- notational analysis
- tally charts.

Physical constructs:

- multi-stage fitness test
- 40 m sprint
- 1 rep max
- 15 rep max
- sit and reach test
- peak flow test
- skinfold calipers
- T-test.

Psychological constructs:

- questionnaires
- interviews
- observation of behaviour.

Biomechanical analysis:

- video recording
- computer packages.

Notational analysis

Notational analysis is the tracking of the actions of an individual performer through the course of a game or match to see the frequency with which they perform a particular technique. It can be done through a computer package or by hand using tally charts.

A tally chart for football is reproduced on page 204.

This information is of limited value as you also need to look at where this action occurs. This can be done by sectionalising the area of play (see Fig 11.05) and giving areas labels. This will elicit more valuable information.

This can be done with a cricket pitch, tennis or netball court. You can then track where each type of skill occurs and its outcome.

An example of tracking the passing of a footballer is also reproduced on page 205.

The uses of notational analysis are to:

- identify individual strengths and weaknesses
- analyse all the actions of a player
- build up information to rate score on performance profile
- develop an action plan to improve performance.

Tally chart: football		
Skill	**Successful completion**	**Unsuccessful completion**
Short-range pass (< 5m)		
Medium-range pass (5–15m)		
Long-range pass (> 15m)		
Dribble		
Short-range shot (< 6m)		
Medium-range shot (7–18m)		
Long-range shot (> 18m)		
Tackle		
Block		
Defensive header		
Attacking header		
Throw-in		
Free kick		
Corner		
Penalty kick		

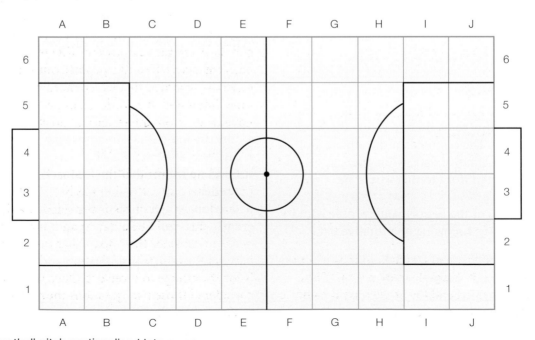

Fig 11.05 Football pitch sectionalised into areas

Passing record		
Skill	**Successful completion**	**Unsuccessful completion**
Short-range pass (< 5m)	G5–F5 D3–D2 I6–J5	F4–F3 C3–C4
Medium-range pass (5–15m)	G2–E4 C6–A6 H1–F3	D5–B4
Long-range pass (> 15m)	I4–E3 C1–B5	F6–D1 I5–D3 F1–C4

Key learning points

- The effectiveness of an individual's sporting performance is dependent upon intrinsic and extrinsic factors.
- Notational analysis involves identifying and then analysing the individual actions of each player and the outcome each achieved.
- Each component of performance is identified and each time it is performed the outcome is recorded.
- Tally charts are used to record the outcomes and frequency of each component.
- This information is used to identify strengths and weaknesses.

Providing feedback on performance

It is impossible for anyone to improve or change unless they receive feedback.

> **Feedback:** information about performance.

It has no value judgement attached to it as it is not positive or negative. It is simply information. The information is provided and the athlete has the choice of doing something about it or not.

Types of feedback

There are different categories of feedback regarding its timing and the type of feedback given. They are:

- knowledge of performance and results
- immediate and delayed
- internal and external
- concurrent and terminal.

Knowledge of performance and results

Knowledge of performance (KP) is information regarding how well skills were performed in a technical sense and will involve qualitative judgements. Knowledge of results (KR) is information regarding the outcome of the skill – whether the action produced success or failure – this is a quantitative judgement. It is possible to perform a skill well (KP) and have a negative outcome (KR) or have a poor performance (KP) and a positive outcome (KR). It is generally regarded that experienced performers are more interested in knowledge of performance, while novices are more interested in knowledge of results.

Immediate and delayed

Immediate means that the feedback is given immediately after the skill has been performed, while delayed means feedback is provided at a time after the event – this could be a day or an hour later. The coach needs to consider the impact that the feedback will have on the athlete's motivation and how important it is for the athlete to receive it. Once they have considered those two questions they can decide when to give the feedback.

Internal and external

Internal feedback is generated within the body of the athlete. As you perform a skill you will feel whether you have performed it correctly or not due to the nervous pathways you have set down to produce the movement and judge its correctness. As we hit a tennis ball we feel whether we have struck it sweetly or not. External feedback is provided by an external party who observes the performance. For example, the coach will observe the performance of the skill and offer feedback as to how it looked and how effective it was. External feedback may also be provided by using video recordings or other recording devices.

Concurrent and terminal

Concurrent means literally 'running together'. This type of feedback is provided during the performance of the skill in terms of how it feels and often the outcome as well. Concurrent feedback is usually internal in nature and clearly immediate in when it is provided. Terminal means 'at the end'. This type of feedback is provided at the end of the performance. It is usually external and is always delayed.

Delivering the feedback

Once the coach has decided on what feedback is necessary to address the individual's strengths and areas for improvement they will need to decide when, where and how to deliver it. How the feedback is received depends upon how it is delivered.

Structure

When giving feedback you should use the sandwich technique. Feedback should have this structure:

- tell them what they are doing right
- tell them what they need to improve on
- tell them something else they did right.

This means that the feedback ends on a high note and the athlete understands what needs to be improved.

Non-verbal communication

Feedback can be given visually and through gestures as well as verbally. The use of facial expressions, posture and hand gestures will convey more than the actual words used. The delivery of the message should match the message being given. This is called being 'congruent'. Also, gestures such as a pat on the back or a hand on the arm will convey information which cannot be imparted in words.

Avoiding negative approaches

Avoid any negative approaches or comments.

- Intimidation: 'If you don't improve you can find a new coach.'
- Sarcasm: 'My granny could have caught that!'
- Physical abuse: 'Unless you listen to what I say you will be doing press-ups.'
- Guilt: 'You should be ashamed of yourselves the way you played out there. It was gutless and you let your supporters down.'

Private and confidential

Ensure feedback is given in a private area as it may be sensitive and is not relevant for anyone else.

Focus on behaviour

Focus on the behaviour rather than identity. This is the difference between a coach saying 'You are an aggressive person and this is not acceptable' and 'Your aggressive actions are not acceptable.' One addresses the behaviour, which can be changed, and the other addresses the identity of the person, which is long term and relatively stable.

Using the feedback provided

Once the feedback has been received and processed by the athlete, they have to decide how to use the information. It may be used in the following ways:

- to set SMART targets combining short-, medium- and long-term goals
- to develop or change a training programme to include technical, physiological and psychological components of performance
- to inform the process of performance profiling and assessment of scoring the individual constructs.

Analysis for different levels of sporting performance

Sport England has identified four different levels of sporting performance, as follows.

Key learning points

Feedback is information about an individual's performance.

Feedback can be categorised in two ways: knowledge of performance (KP) and knowledge of results (KR). KP is information about how well the skill was performed and KR is information about the outcome of the skill.

Immediate feedback is given as soon as the skill has been performed, while delayed feedback is given at a period after the performance.

Internal feedback is derived from sources inside the body and external feedback comes from sources inside the body.

Concurrent feedback occurs as the skill is being performed and terminal feedback occurs after the completion of the skill.

When providing feedback keep in mind the following:

- using the sandwich approach of positive/negative/positive
- providing it visually as well as verbally through body language
- avoiding sarcasm, intimidation, abuse and guilt
- ensuring it is delivered in a private area
- focus on behaviour rather than identity.

Foundation level

At foundation level focus is on the participants learning and understanding basic movement skills and developing a positive attitude to physical activity. This level is concerned with giving school children positive and meaningful experiences of sport.

Beginner or participation level

At participation or beginner levels the participants will be taking part in sport for a range of reasons, such as health, fitness and social. They may also be attracted by the competitive aspects of sport. This level of participation would involve out-of-school sports teams and Saturday league players.

Performance level

At performance level the participants will be active in improving standards of performance through coaching, competition and training. This would involve the participants playing at county or national standard.

Elite or excellence level

Elite and excellence levels involve the participants reaching national standards of performance up to Olympic or world-class performances.

Purpose of analysis and resources required

Foundation level

At this level the emphasis is on fun and enjoyment, and learning the basic skills and techniques. Analysis will be limited to identifying the strengths and weaknesses of the children and giving them feedback to improve their enjoyment of the sports. The resources required are limited to support from teachers and parents.

Beginner level

At beginner level there is an emphasis on developing techniques and improving weaknesses along with developing strengths. This is a point where talent may be assessed for further development through coaching and physical training. Analysis is again done in a fairly informal manner through recommendations or even talent scouting.

Performance level

Analysis starts to become very important at this level as it is about achieving standards of performance to reach county or national level. Analysis will be conducted to:

- identify talent
- form the basis for squad selection at county and national level
- assess current level of performance
- identify strengths and weaknesses
- assess fitness level and health status
- inform the process of goal setting.

In terms of resources required there is a need to put in time and effort on behalf of personnel. This is a key stage in moving people towards becoming athletes and to ultimately developing elite potential. Equipment required will include fitness testing equipment, sport science facilities, expertise from sport scientists and time devoted to each individual.

Elite level

At elite level every aspect of an athlete's performance is analysed to the smallest degree as they seek to gain all the advantages they possibly can to improve their chances of success. At this level aspects of health, fitness and performance are analysed on a daily basis. Indeed, the athlete may be professional or training on a full-time basis. The purpose of analysis at this level is to:

● assess current health and fitness status
● identify strengths and weaknesses
● assess current level of performance
● inform the process of goal setting
● identify any future issues or problems.

As athletes at this level may have contact with their support team at facilities such as a national sports centre, they are heavily dependent on resources. These resources are human in terms of sport scientists with various expertise, and physical resources for assessing fitness levels and analysing skills and techniques.

Key learning points

● At foundation level focus is on the participant's learning and understanding basic movement skills and developing a positive attitude to physical activity. Analysis is provided at this level to help participants improve their skills.

● At participation or beginner levels the participants will be taking part in sport for a range of reasons, such as health, fitness and social and competitive reasons. Analysis is used at beginner level to improve performance and identify talent.

● At performance level the participants will be active in improving standards of performance through coaching, competition and training. Analysis is provided to assess current level of performance and how to improve it, as well as identify talent to move to a higher level.

● Elite and excellence levels involve the participants reaching national standards of performance up to Olympic or world-class performances. Analysis is done at elite level to identify any area where the athlete could improve so they can compete at the very highest level.

Revision questions

1 What is a performance profile?
2 What are the benefits of using a performance profile?
3 Why is it important to have an 'insider' view on performance as well as an 'outsider' view?
4 What is meant by technical, physiological, psychological and biomechanical analyses of performance?
5 What is meant by 'notational analysis' and what information does it provide?
6 What is the difference between an intrinsic and extrinsic factor affecting sporting performance?
7 Why is age a factor in influencing sporting performance?
8 How can diet be an influence in sporting performance?
9 What is feedback and why is it different from criticism?
10 Explain three types of feedback.
11 What is the 'sandwich technique' of providing feedback and why should it be used?
12 Explain how feedback can be given visually as well as verbally.
13 Explain briefly the four levels of participation in sport.
14 At which level is talent identified?

References

Bull, S. J. (1991) *Sport Psychology: A Self-help Guide*, Crowood.

Butler, R. J. (2000) *Sport Psychology in Performance*, Arnold.

Butler, R. J. and Hardy, L. (1992) The performance profile: theory and application. *The Sport Psychologist*, 6, 253–264.

Davis, R. J. (2003) *Physical Education and the Study of Sport*, Mosby.

Martens, R. (1997) *Successful Coaching*, Human Kinetics.

Weinberg, R. and Gould, S. (2003) *Foundations of Sport and Exercise Psychology*, Human Kinetics.

Goals

By the end of this chapter you should:

- understand the concepts of nutrition and digestion
- understand energy intake and expenditure in sports performance
- understand the relationship between hydration and sports performance
- be able to plan an appropriate diet for a selected sports activity.

As we seek to gain an extra edge in our sporting performances and to maximise the effects of our training, so the spotlight has fallen on areas other than training. Nutrition has been shown to be an area of increasing interest. We know that training brings benefits and we know that eating properly brings benefits. So if we combine the correct training with the correct nutritional strategy the gains are multiplied. Nutrition is as important for people who are seeking to improve their performance as it is for those seeking fitness gains or weight-management objectives.

Nutrients

> **Nutrients:** chemical substances obtained from food and used in the body to provide energy, as well as structural materials and regulating agents to support growth, maintenance and repair of the body's tissues.

Nutrients can be divided into two main groups: macronutrients and micronutrients. The three macronutrients are:

- carbohydrate
- protein
- fat.

Macronutrients are needed in large amounts in the diet and all provide energy for the body. They are also used to build the structures of the body and produce functions needed to sustain life.

The two micronutrients are:

- vitamins
- minerals.

They are needed in smaller amounts in the diet and contain no energy themselves. They work in conjunction with the macronutrients to produce life-sustaining functions and are needed to unlock the energy present in the macronutrients.

There are other food groups such as water and fibre. Water is not usually regarded as a nutrient because it has no nutrient value despite being highly important in sustaining life. Fibre is a type of carbohydrate so it would be part of that food group.

Carbohydrate

Almost every culture relies on carbohydrate as the major source of nutrients and calories – rice in Asia, wheat in Europe, the Middle East and North Africa, corn and potato in the Americas.

Carbohydrate should provide between 50 and 60 per cent of calorie intake and its main role is to supply energy to allow the body to function. The energy content of carbohydrate is 1 g provides 4 kcals.

There are many sources of carbohydrate, such as bread, rice, pasta, potatoes, fruit, vegetables, sweets and biscuits. They all differ in form slightly but are all broken down into glucose because that is the only way the body can use carbohydrate.

The functions of carbohydrate are to provide energy for:

- the brain to function
- the liver to perform its functions
- muscular contractions at moderate to high intensities.

When carbohydrate foods are digested they are all broken down into glucose which is then absorbed in the small intestine and enters the bloodstream. From the bloodstream it can either be used immediately as energy or stored in the liver and muscles. Glucose is stored in the form of glycogen which is bound to water (1 g of glucose needs 2.7 g of water) for storage. However, the glycogen molecule is bulky and difficult to store in large amounts. The body can store around 1600 kcals of glycogen, which would enable us to run for around two hours.

> **Glucose:** the smallest unit of a carbohydrate.
> **Glycogen:** stored glucose in the muscles and liver attached to water molecules.

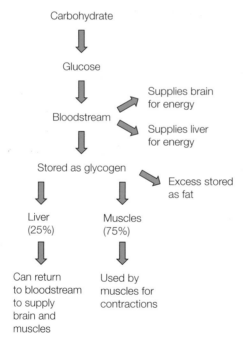

Fig 12.01 **What happens to carbohydrate when it is digested**

Forms of carbohydrate

Carbohydrates come in a variety of forms, but they are all made up of molecules of sugar. These molecules of sugar are called saccharides; they come in different forms depending upon the foods in which they are found. Eventually through the process of digestion they all become glucose. These saccharides are found as one of the following:

- monosaccharides
- disaccharides
- polysaccharides.

Monosaccharides are one saccharide molecule on its own. There are three types of monosacharride:

- glucose – occurs naturally in most carbohydrate foods
- fructose – occurs in fruit and honey
- galactose – does not occur freely but is a component of the sugars found in milk products.

Disaccharides are two saccharide molecules joined together by a bond:

- sucrose = glucose + fructose – most commonly found as table sugar
- lactose = glucose + galactose – found in milk and milk products
- maltose = glucose + glucose – found in malt products, beers and cereals.

Mono- and disaccharides are commonly known as simple carbohydrates because they are in short simple chains – existing as individual molecules.

> ## LEARNER ACTIVITY
> ### Simple carbohydrates
> The following are sources of simple carbohydrates. Put them in order of how healthy a choice you think each one would be.
>
> | | |
> |---|---|
> | biscuits | jelly babies |
> | tinned fruit | Jaffa cakes |
> | dried fruit | fruit smoothies |
> | cakes | fruit juice |
> | sweets | sports energy drinks |
> | fresh fruit | |
>
> Give three reasons why you have ranked the foods in this order.

Polysaccharides are long, complex chains of glucose molecules containing ten or more molecules. Due to their complicated structures they are called 'complex carbohydrates'.

To digest polysaccharides, the bonds need to be broken down through the process of digestion so that they can become individual glucose molecules and be absorbed into the bloodstream. If a complex carbohydrate is processed or cooked in any way these

Monosaccharides

Disaccharides

Polysaccharides

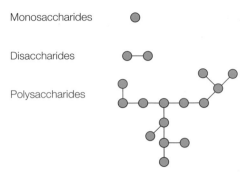

Fig 12.02 Structure of saccharides

bonds will start to be broken down before they enter the digestive system.

Polysaccharides or complex carbohydrates can come in either their natural or refined forms. Wheat and rice are naturally brown in colour due to their high levels of fibre, vitamins and minerals. Therefore, the brown varieties of bread, rice and pasta are of greater nutrient value than their white, refined varieties.

Good sources of polysaccharides:

- wholemeal, wholegrain or granary breads
- wholemeal pasta
- wholegrain rice
- potatoes
- sweet potatoes
- vegetables
- pulses.

Poorer choices of polysaccharides:

- white bread
- white pasta
- white rice
- rice cakes.

Glycaemic index

The rate at which carbohydrate foods are broken down and how quickly they raise blood glucose levels is measured via the glycaemic index. It is a ranking system which shows how quickly the carbohydrate is broken down and enters the blood as glucose in comparison to the speed glucose would enter the blood if consumed. Foods with a high glycaemic index break down quickly and rapidly increase blood glucose levels. Table sugar is a good example. Pasta would have a lower glycaemic index, breaking down into glucose more slowly. It would also have less of an immediate effect on blood glucose levels, causing a slower increase over a longer period.

Fig 12.03 Unrefined brown foods

Fig 12.04 Refined white foods

The glycaemic index is one of the most important principles in nutrition currently. We deal best with foods of a low glycaemic index which release their energy slowly and over time. Foods of a high glycaemic index cause a rapid release of glucose into the bloodstream, followed by a rapid drop in blood glucose causing hunger and fatigue. The person who eats high glycaemic index foods will experience fluctuating blood glucose levels and be tempted to overeat the wrong type of food. High glycaemic index foods, such as sweets, cakes, biscuits, fizzy drinks, white breads and sugary cereals, are linked to obesity and the development of type 2 diabetes. If a person eats low glycaemic index foods they will find that their stable blood glucose levels give them energy and enable them to concentrate throughout the day.

In the glycaemic index foods are either high, moderate or low.

High	Moderate	Low
Above 85	60–84	Below 60

The speed at which a food is broken down and enters the bloodstream is dependent on a range of factors. The following will lower the speed glucose enters the bloodstream:

- the presence of fibre in the food
- the presence of fat in the food
- the presence of protein in the food
- the type of saccharides present in the food*
- the amount of carbohydrate eaten.

* Fructose and galactose have to be converted into glucose before they can be used as energy. This process happens in the liver and takes a long time, so they enter the blood as glucose more slowly.

LEARNER ACTIVITY Glycaemic index (part 1)

Conduct an internet search using the key words 'glycaemic index' and print off a table showing the glycaemic index of a range of food types.

The following will increase the speed glucose enters the bloodstream:

- the length of the cooking process
- the amount the food has been refined or processed
- the riper the fruit has become.

LEARNER ACTIVITY Glycaemic index (part 2)

Using the table you found for part 1 look up the glycaemic index of the following foods:

- oranges
- French baguette
- baked potatoes
- muesli
- ice cream
- baked beans
- wholemeal bread
- bananas
- French fries
- wholemeal spaghetti

Using the factors which affect glycaemic index, explain why each food has the glycaemic index it does.

Fibre

Dietary fibre is the part of a plant that is resistant to the body's digestive enzymes. It is defined as 'indigestible plant material', and although it is a carbohydrate and contains calories the digestive system cannot unlock them from the plant. As a result, fibre moves through the gastrointestinal tract and ends up in the stool. The main benefit in eating fibre is that it retains water, resulting in softer and bulkier stools that prevent constipation and haemorrhoids. Research suggests that a high-fibre diet also reduces the risk of colon cancer. All fruits, vegetables and grains provide some fibre.

There are two types of fibre – soluble and insoluble – that perform slightly different functions.

Soluble fibre dissolves into a gel in water and is found in the fleshy part of fruit and vegetables, oats, barley and rice. For example, when you make porridge the oats partly dissolve into a sticky gel and this is the soluble fibre. Soluble fibre has two main roles to play:

- it slows down how quickly the stomach empties and how quickly glucose enters the bloodstream
- it binds to fat and blood cholesterol, thus decreasing the risk of heart disease.

Insoluble fibre will not dissolve in water and is found in the skin of fruit and vegetables, wheat, rye, seeds and pips of fruit. Insoluble fibre passes through the digestive system without being altered in any way. Its main roles are as follows.

- It adds bulk to faeces and speeds its passage through the large intestine.
- It helps to keep the large intestine clean and prevent bowel disease.
- It stretches the stomach and makes you feel full for longer.
- It slows down the release of glucose into the bloodstream.

It is recommended that we eat around 18 g of fibre a day. This can be done by eating foods in their natural form rather than in their processed or refined states.

Recommended daily intake of carbohydrate

A minimum recommended daily intake of at least 50 per cent of total kilocalories consumed should come from complex carbohydrate sources. The British Nutrition Foundation found that in Britain the average intake of carbohydrate is 272 g for men and 193 g for women, providing just over 43 per cent of the energy in the diet.

As with most nutrients, eating excess amounts can lead to problems. Excessive consumption of sugar (e.g. sucrose) can lead to tooth decay and is linked to a number of major diseases, such as diabetes, obesity and coronary heart disease. Excess carbohydrate in the diet will be converted to and stored as fat. Thus it is possible to gain body fat even on a low-fat diet.

Key learning points

Carbohydrate provides energy for:
- brain function
- liver function and digestion
- muscular contractions.

Carbohydrates are made up of saccharides of which there are three types:
- monosaccharides – single units of saccharides known as 'simple sugars'
- disaccharides – two units of saccharides joined by a bond called 'simple sugars'
- polysaccharides – long chains of saccharides called 'complex carbohydrates'.

Glycaemic index (GI) is the rate at which a carbohydrate food enters the bloodstream as glucose:
- high GI = above 85
- moderate GI = 60–85
- low GI = less than 60.

Fibre is 'indigestible plant material' which cannot be digested. It protects against heart disease and diseases of the colon by keeping the colon clean and the waste moving through quickly.

Protein

The word 'protein' is derived from Greek and means 'prime importance'. Proteins are of prime importance because they are the building blocks which make up the structures of the body. Muscle, skin, bones, internal organs, cartilage and ligament all have a

LEARNER ACTIVITY Carbohydrate category

Copy out the table below and place the foods listed into their correct carbohydrate category.

table sugar	sweetcorn	baked potato	strawberry jam
cola	orange	pasta	honey
apple	milkshake	bread	All-bran

Monosaccharide	Disaccharide	Polysaccharide	Fibre

protein component. We gain our protein by eating protein-rich foods such as red meat, fish, chicken, eggs and dairy products.

The diet should consist of between 10 and 20 per cent protein depending upon the specific needs of the individual. Protein also provides a source of energy: 1 g of protein provides 4 kcals.

Amino acids

The smallest unit of a protein is an amino acid. Proteins are made up of long chains of amino acids which are formed into structures. Amino acids are the smallest unit of a protein and there are 20 amino acids in total. Amino acids can be seen to be like the alphabet. In the English language we have 26 letters from which we can make up millions of words. The protein alphabet has 20 amino acids from which can be produced approximately 50,000 different proteins present in the body. Just as different words are made up of different orders of letters so different structures are made up of different orders of amino acids.

They can be split into essential and non-essential amino acids. An essential amino acid is one which must be gained through eating it in the diet, while a non-essential amino acid can be made in the liver if all essential amino acids are present. This means to produce all the structures of the body we must gain all the essential amino acids on a daily basis.

There are eight **essential amino acids** to be gained from the diet:

- isoleucine
- leucine
- lysine
- methionine
- phenylalanine
- threonine
- tryptophan
- valine.

There are 12 **non-essential amino acids** which are synthesised in the liver if all eight essential amino acids are gained from the diet:

- cystein
- tyrosine
- histidine
- glutamine
- glutamic acid
- glycine

- alanine
- serine
- proline
- aspartic acid
- asparagine
- arginine.

Foods which contain all eight essential amino acids are described as being complete, while a food which is missing one or more essential amino acid is described as being incomplete.

The following are sources of complete and incomplete proteins:

Complete protein	Incomplete protein
Chicken	Wheat
Eggs	Oats
Fish	Rice
Red meat	Pulses
Dairy products	Nuts
Soya bean	Vegetables

With the exception of the soya bean, the sources of complete protein are from animals, while incomplete proteins come from plant sources. To gain all eight essential amino acids from incomplete protein sources you need to eat a range of sources or combine protein sources. This is called 'complementary protein' and examples are:

- wheat and pulses (beans on toast)
- nuts and vegetables (nut roast)
- rice and lentils (vegetarian chilli).

All protein sources contain different amounts of amino acids. The greater the quantity of the essential amino acids in the food the higher the biological value. Eggs have the highest quality or biological value of all foods and are given a protein rating of 100. All other proteins are compared to eggs in terms of their quality and quantity of amino acids. This is shown in the box on the opposite page.

Functions of protein

When we eat protein it is digested in the digestive system and then delivered to the liver as individual

Fig 12.05 Complete protein

Fig 12.06 Incomplete protein

Food	Protein rating
Eggs	100
Fish	70
Beef	69
Cow's milk	60
Brown rice	57
White rice	56
Soya beans	47
Wheat	44
Peanuts	43
Beans	34

(Adapted from McArdle, Katch and Katch, 1999)

amino acids. The liver then rebuilds the amino acids into long chains to make up proteins. The proteins that the liver produces depend upon the needs of the body at that time. If we need to replace muscle the liver will produce the relevant proteins to replace muscle tissue.

Proteins have three specific roles in the body:

- to build structures (structural)
- to perform functions (functional)
- to provide fuel.

Protein forms a part of the following structures:

- muscle (skeletal, smooth and cardiac)
- bone
- internal organs (heart, kidneys, liver)
- connective tissue (tendons and ligaments)
- hair
- nails.

Protein forms part of the following structures which perform specific functions in the body:

- hormones (which send messages to cells – insulin and adrenaline)
- enzymes (biological catalysts which speed up reactions in cells)
- part of the immune system (white blood cells are made partly of protein)
- formation of lipoproteins (these help to transport fats around the body).

Protein is not the body's first choice of fuel but it can be used as energy. It is heavily used during endurance training and events, or at times of starvation.

Recommended intakes of protein

The average daily intake of protein in the UK is 85 g for men and 62 g for women. The recommended daily amount of protein for healthy adults is 0.8 g per kilogram of body weight, or about 15 per cent of total kilocalories. Protein needs are higher for children, infants and many athletes.

Key learning points

Proteins are long chains of amino acids. There are 20 amino acids in total: eight are essential amino acids which need to be eaten in the diet, and 12 are non-essential amino acids which can be synthesised by the liver if all eight essential amino acids are present.

Foods containing all eight essential amino acids are described as being complete protein. Foods missing one or more essential amino acid are described as being incomplete.

Protein has the following main functions:

● to build structures of the body
● to perform specific functions
● to provide fuel.

Macronutrient	Kcals per gram
Carbohydrate	4
Protein	4
Fat	9

Fats

Fats are often perceived as being bad or a part of the diet to be avoided. In fact, fats are vital to health and perform many important functions in the body. The intake of certain fats does need to be minimised and excess consumption of fats will lead to health problems.

The functions of fat are as follows:

● formation of the cell membrane
● formation of the myelin sheath which coats the nerves
● a component of the brain and nervous system
● protection of internal organs (brain, kidneys, liver)
● production of hormones (oestrogen and testosterone)
● transportation and storage of vitamins A, D, E and K
● constant source of energy
● store of energy
● heat production.

Fats and oils belong to a family called 'lipids' and they perform a variety of important roles in the body. Predominantly fats supply energy for everyday activities and movement. They are described as being 'energy-dense' because they contain a lot of energy per gram: 1 g of fat provides 9 kcals.

If we compare this figure to the 4 kcals which carbohydrates and protein provide (see box, top right) then we can see that it is significantly higher.

The difference between a fat and an oil is that a fat is solid at room temperature while an oil is liquid at room temperature.

The smallest unit of a fat is called a 'fatty acid'. There are different types of fatty acid present in the foods we ingest. In particular, a fatty acid can be saturated or unsaturated; this is important because they will be shaped differently. In chemistry shape matters because it influences the function performed. Therefore, different fatty acids perform different functions in the body.

Triglycerides

Triglycerides are dietary fats in that they are how the fats we ingest are packaged. A triglyceride is defined as 'three fatty acids attached to a glycerol backbone'. Glycerol is actually a carbohydrate which the fatty acids attach to. During digestion the fatty acids are broken off from the glycerol backbone to be used by the body as required. The glycerol is used as all carbohydrates are used, to produce energy.

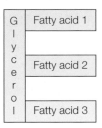

Fig 12.07 Structure of a triglyceride

Types of fatty acid

Fatty acids can be divided into:

● saturated fatty acids
● monounsaturated fatty acids
● polyunsaturated fatty acids.

A fatty acid consists of long chains of carbon atoms with an acid group (COOH) at one end and a methyl group (CH_3) at the other. The structure of the chains of fatty acids attached to the glycerol molecule determines whether the fat is classed as saturated, monounsaturated or polyunsaturated. If you think of different types of fats, such as butter, lard, sunflower oil and olive oil, you will notice that they differ in terms of their colour, texture and taste. This is because of the different types of fatty acids attached to the glycerol backbone.

A **saturated fat** is one where all the carbon atoms are attached to hydrogen molecules. The chain is said to be saturated with hydrogen.

$$CH_3 - C - C - C - C - C - C = O$$

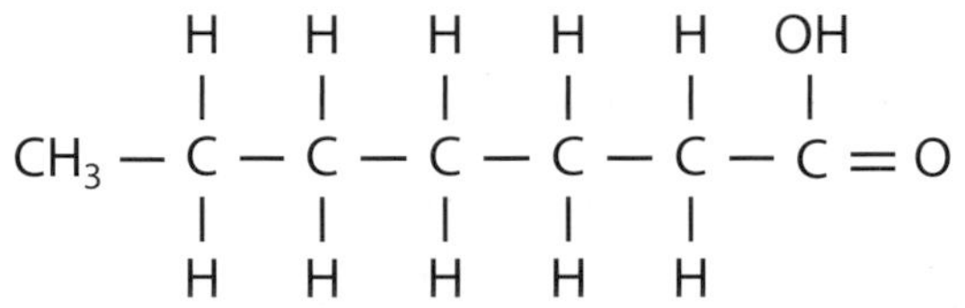

Fig 12.08 Saturated fatty acid

We can see that the carbon atoms each have single bonds between them and each carbon atom has four bonds. The hydrogen atoms possess a very slight charge and gently push away from each other. This has the effect of making the chain straight in shape. In chemistry shape matters as it affects function and it also makes the saturated fat solid at room temperature. This is because the fatty acids can pack tightly together with little space between each one. Saturated fats are also described as being stable or inert. This means that their structure will not change when they are heated. They will melt but the structure of the fatty acid chain stays the same.

The majority of saturated fats come from animal sources.

Animal sources:
- red meat
- poultry
- eggs
- dairy products.

Plant sources:
- coconut oil
- palm oil.

The Department of Health recommends a person should have a maximum of 10 per cent of daily kilocalories from saturated fat.

An **unsaturated fat** is one where there are hydrogen atoms missing from the carbon chain, causing the carbon atoms to attach to each other with double bonds. This is because carbon has to have four bonds and if there is no hydrogen present they will bond to each other. In this case the carbon chain is not saturated with hydrogen atoms and is therefore 'unsaturated'.

A monounsaturated fat is one where there is just one double bond in the carbon chain (see Fig 12.09).

Due to the slight charge the hydrogen atoms contain they push each other away. Now that there are hydrogen atoms missing it causes the chain to bend and become curved. The curved fatty acids cannot

$$CH_3 - C - C = C - C - C - C = O$$

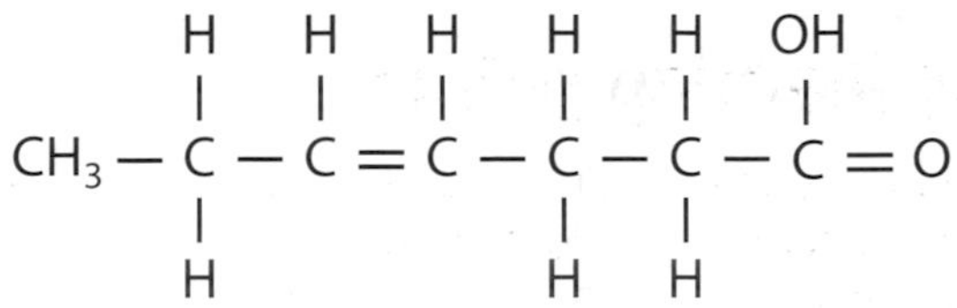

Fig 12.09 Monounsaturated fatty acid

pack so tightly together so their appearance changes and they will be in liquid or oil form. They will also be less stable or more reactive. This is because of the double bonds between the carbon atoms. Carbon attaches to itself only if there is nothing else to be attached to and it will take the opportunity to break off and attach to something else if it can. If monounsaturated fats are heated they change their structure.

Examples of monounsaturated fats are:

- olive oil
- peanut oil
- avocados
- rapeseed oil (canola oil)
- almond oil.

The Department of Health recommends a person should have a maximum of 12 per cent of daily kilocalories from monounsaturated fat.

A **polyunsaturated fat** is one where there are many double bonds in the carbon chain due to a shortage of hydrogen ions in the chain.

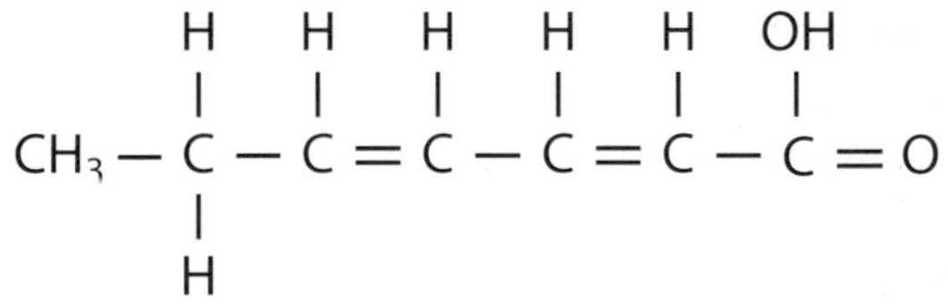

$$CH_3 - C - C = C - C = C - C = O$$

Fig 12.10 Polyunsaturated fatty acid

This has the effect of making the fatty acid even more curved and highly reactive in nature. They are also in oil or liquid form. Polyunsaturated fats are highly unstable when heated to high temperatures and will change their structure.

Examples of polyunsaturated fats are:

- sunflower oil
- safflower oil
- corn oil
- fish oils
- nuts
- seeds.

The Department of Health recommends a person should have a maximum of 10 per cent of daily kilocalories from these polyunsaturated fats.

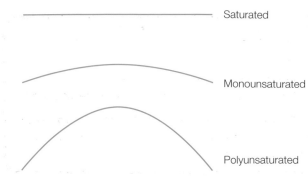

Fig 12.11 Different shapes of fatty acids

Saturated versus unsaturated fats

Saturated fats have always received bad press until recently when people realised that they have an important role in the diet. Due to their stable nature they always retain their structure. This is important because when they enter the fat cells the cells will recognise them and know what to do with them. Saturated fats are always stored as fat in the fat cells.

Naturally occurring unsaturated fats, such as olive oil, have very beneficial effects when they are stored in fat cells – they improve circulation, lower cholesterol levels and improve the health of hair, skin and nails. The problem comes when unsaturated fats are heated or processed in any way because they then change their structure and start to look like saturated fats. They become 'hydrogenated' or altered structurally and when they enter the body they are accepted into the fat cells because they look like saturated fats. Once inside the fat cells they start to cause damage to the cell and stop positive reactions occurring. The two most dangerous types of fats are:

● hydrogenated vegetable oil
● trans fats.

These have been linked to heart disease and cancer and are present in processed foods and deep-fat-fried foods.

Butter versus margarine?

In terms of fat content these two products are pretty similar. However, due to the margarine being an unsaturated fat (sunflower oil), it would appear to be beneficial to health. Sunflower oil is naturally a liquid and margarine is a solid product, which means it has been processed in some way and thus changed structurally.

The butter will not be changed structurally because it is predominantly saturated fat. For these reasons the butter is a better health choice because it is a more naturally occurring product. In particular, it is the cheap margarines which need to be avoided. If choosing a margarine check the contents for hydrogenated vegetable oil and trans fats.

LEARNER ACTIVITY Fatty acid

Look in your cupboards at home and find the fats and oils that you use to cook with. Choose three sources and look at the fatty acid content of each. Make a note of the breakdown of saturated, monounsaturated and polyunsaturated fatty acids in each source. What have you found?

Essential fatty acids

The body can make all the fatty acids it needs except for two, the essential fatty acids (EFAs), which must be supplied in the diet. These fatty acids are omega 3 and omega 6.

Sources of omega 3 and 6 are as follows.

Omega 3 fatty acids:

● oily fish (salmon, mackerel, herring)
● flax oil
● walnuts
● soya beans.

Omega 6 fatty acids:

● sunflower oil
● pumpkin seeds
● sesame seeds
● safflower oil.

Research into omega 3, and in particular fish oils, has shown that eating oily fish protects against heart disease. This is because the omega 3s may prevent the formation of blood clots on the artery walls and lower the levels of triglycerides circulating in the bloodstream.

The essential fatty acids are also thought to improve the function of the brain and promote learning as well as being beneficial for arthritics because they reduce swelling in the joints.

Cholesterol

Cholesterol can either be ingested or made in the body. It is found only in animal products and never in plants. It has some useful functions including building cell membranes and helping the function of various hormones.

There are two types of cholesterol: low-density lipoproteins (LDLs) and high-density lipoproteins (HDLs). LDLs are responsible for the deposits lining the walls of arteries and lead to an increased risk of coronary heart disease. HDLs actually reduce this risk by transporting cholesterol away to the liver and so are beneficial to health.

Recommended daily intake of fat

Fat intake should make up no more than 30 per cent of total kilocalories. Only 10 per cent of kilocalories should come from saturated fat. Dietary cholesterol should be limited to 300 mg or less per day.

There are many health problems related to eating an excess of fat, especially saturated fats. These include obesity, high blood pressure and coronary heart disease, although it is important to distinguish between the different types of fat eaten in a person's diet. Consumption of certain fatty acids (omega 3 fish oils found in tuna) is linked to a decreased risk of coronary heart disease.

As fat provides just over twice as much energy per gram as carbohydrate, a diet high in fat can make over-consumption more likely. It is thought that excess dietary fat may be more easily converted to body fat than excess carbohydrate or protein. Research suggests that more people are obese today than ever before. Obese people are more likely to suffer from a range of illnesses including coronary heart disease, adult-onset diabetes, gallstones, arthritis, high blood pressure and some types of cancer. However, most of the health problems associated with obesity are removed once the extra weight is lost.

LEARNER ACTIVITY Your own daily intake (part 1)

Using the food groups discussed, work out how many servings of each you ate yesterday.

Determine areas in you diet that you could make improvements to, suggesting alternative foods that you could eat.

Vitamins

Vitamins are organic substances that the body requires in small amounts. The body is incapable of making vitamins for its overall needs, so they must be supplied regularly by the diet.

Vitamins are not related chemically and differ in their physiological actions. As vitamins were discovered, each was identified by a letter. Many of the vitamins consist of several closely related compounds of similar physiological properties.

Vitamins may be subdivided into:

- water soluble – C and B (complex)
- fat soluble – A, D, E and K.

The water-soluble vitamins cannot be stored in the body so they must be consumed on a regular basis. If excess quantities of these vitamins are consumed, the body will excrete them in the urine. Fat-soluble vitamins are stored in the body's fat so it is not necessary to consume these on such a regular basis. It is also possible to overdose on fat-soluble vitamins, which can be detrimental to health.

LEARNER ACTIVITY Your own daily intake (part 2)

Draw a table like the one shown below on a separate piece of paper. Write down the last ten foods you ate. Now place these foods into their correct category in the table.

Simple sugars	Complex carbohydrate	Saturated fat	Unsaturated fat (mono or poly)	Protein

Key learning points

Fat performs some vital functions in the body:

- formation of the cell membrane
- formation of the myelin sheath which coats the nerves
- a component of the brain and nervous system
- protection of internal organs (brain, kidneys, liver)
- production of hormones (oestrogen and testosterone)
- transportation and storage of vitamins A, D, E and K
- constant source of energy
- store of energy
- heat production.

Saturated fats occur when all the carbon atoms are saturated with hydrogen. They are solid at room temperature, stable and unreactive. Examples of saturated fats include:

- animal fats
- fat of red meat and poultry
- dairy products
- eggs
- coconut oil
- palm oil.

Unsaturated fats occur when there is a double bond in the carbon chain due to a shortage of hydrogen. They are liquid at room temperature, unstable and reactive. There are two types of unsaturated fats:

- monounsaturated fats, which have one double bond in the chain and include olive oil and peanut oil
- polyunsaturated fats, which have more than one double bond and include sunflower oil and fish oils.

Varying amounts of each vitamin are required. The amount needed is referred to as the recommended daily allowance (RDA).

Fat-soluble vitamins

Vitamin A

- Function – to help maintain good vision, healthy skin, hair and mucous membranes, and to serve as an antioxidant; also needed for proper bone and tooth development
- Source – liver, mackerel and milk products
- RDA – 1.5 mg

Vitamin D (calciferol)

- Function – essential for calcium and phosphorus utilisation; promotes strong bones and teeth
- Source – sunlight, egg yolk, fish, fish oils and fortified cereals
- RDA – 0.01 mg

Vitamin E

- Function – antioxidant, helps prevent damage to cell membranes
- Source – wheat germ, nuts, whole grains and dark green leaf vegetables
- RDA – 15 mg

Vitamin K

- Function – used in the formation of blood clots
- Source – leafy green vegetables
- RDA – 70 mg

Water-soluble vitamins

B vitamins are not chemically related, but often occur in the same foodstuff. Their main function is to aid in metabolism of food.

Vitamin B1 (thiamine)

- Function – helps convert food to energy and aids the nervous and cardiovascular systems
- Source – rice bran, pork, beef, peas, beans, wheat germ, oatmeal and soya beans
- RDA – 1.5 mg

Vitamin B2 (riboflavin)

- Function – aids growth and reproduction, and helps to metabolise fats, carbohydrates and proteins; promotes healthy skin and nails
- Source – milk, liver, kidneys, yeast, cheese, leafy green vegetables, fish and eggs
- RDA – 1.7 mg

Vitamin B3 (niacin)

- Function – helps to keep the nervous system balanced and is also important for the synthesis of sex hormones, thyroxine, cortisone and insulin
- Source – poultry, fish, peanuts, yeast extract (e.g. Marmite), rice bran and wheat germ
- RDA – 20 mg

Vitamin B5 (pantothenic acid)

- Function – helps in cell building and maintaining normal growth and development of the central nervous system; helps form hormones and antibodies; also necessary for the conversion of fat and sugar to energy
- Source – wheat germ, green vegetables, whole grains, mushrooms, fish, peanuts and yeast extract (e.g. Marmite)
- RDA – 10 mg

Vitamin B6 (pyridoxine)

- Function – helps in the utilisation of proteins and the metabolism of fats; also needed for production of red blood cells and antibodies
- Source – chicken, beef, bananas, yeast extract (e.g. Marmite), eggs, brown rice, soya beans, oats, whole wheat, peanuts and walnuts
- RDA – 2 mg

Vitamin C (ascorbic acid)

- Function – essential for the formation of collagen; helps to strengthen tissues, acts as an antioxidant, helps in healing, production of red blood cells, fighting bacterial infections and regulating cholesterol; also helps the body to absorb iron
- Source – most fresh fruits and vegetables
- RDA – 60 mg

Folic acid (folacin)

- Function – helps the body form genetic material and red blood cells, and aids in protein metabolism; also acts as an antioxidant; research has shown that if folic acid is taken on a daily basis 30 days before conception, the fetus is less likely to suffer from birth defects such as spina bifida
- Source – green vegetables, kidney beans and orange juice
- RDA – 400 mg

Minerals

There are several minerals required to maintain a healthy body. Some are needed in moderate amounts others only in very small amounts; the latter are referred to as trace minerals.

Calcium

- Function – needed to build strong bones and teeth, helps to calm nerves and plays a role in muscle contraction, blood clotting and cell membrane upkeep; correct quantities of calcium consumption have been shown to significantly lower the risk of osteoporosis
- Source – milk and milk products, whole grains and unrefined cereals, green vegetables and fish bones
- RDA – adults 1200 mg
- Deficiency – fragile bones, osteoporosis, rickets, tooth decay, irregular heartbeat and slowed nerve impulse response; vitamin D is essential for proper calcium absorption and utilisation

Magnesium

- Function – aids the production of proteins and helps regulate body temperature; helps lower blood pressure and assists with the proper functioning of nerves and muscles
- Source – whole grain foods, wheat bran, dark green leafy vegetables, soya beans, fish, oysters, shrimp, almonds and peanuts
- RDA – 350 mg
- Deficiency – decreased blood pressure and body temperature, nervousness, interference with the transmission of nerve and muscle impulses

Phosphorus

- Function – essential for metabolism of carbohydrates, fats and proteins; aids growth and cell repair, and is necessary for proper skeletal growth, tooth development, proper kidney function and the nervous system
- Source – meat, fish, poultry, milk, yoghurt, eggs, seeds, broccoli and nuts
- RDA – 800 mg
- Deficiency – bone pain, fatigue, irregular breathing and nervous disorders

Potassium

- Function – in conjunction with sodium helps to maintain fluid and electrolyte balance within cells;

important for normal nerve and muscle function and aids proper maintenance of the blood's mineral balance; also helps to lower blood pressure

- Source – bananas, dried apricots, yoghurt, whole grains, sunflower seeds, potatoes, sweet potatoes and kidney beans
- RDA – 2500 mg
- Deficiency – decreased blood pressure, dry skin, salt retention and irregular heartbeat

Sodium

- Function – works in conjunction with potassium to maintain fluid and electrolyte balance within cells
- Source – virtually all foods contain sodium, e.g. celery, cheese, eggs, meat, milk and milk products, processed foods, salt and seafood
- RDA – 2500 mg
- Deficiency – confusion, low blood sugar, dehydration, lethargy, heart palpitations and heart attack

Trace minerals

Copper

- Function – assists in the formation of haemoglobin and helps to maintain healthy bones, blood vessels and nerves
- Source – barley, potatoes, whole grains, mushrooms, cocoa, beans, almonds and most seafoods
- RDA – 2 mg
- Deficiency – fractures and bone deformities, anaemia, general weakness, impaired respiration and skin sores

Iron

- Function – required for the production of haemoglobin
- Source – liver, lean meats, eggs, baked potatoes, soyabeans, kidney beans, whole grains and cereals, and dried fruits
- RDA – males 10 mg, females 18 mg
- Deficiency – dizziness, iron deficiency anaemia, constipation, sore or inflamed tongue

Selenium

- Function – a powerful antioxidant, aids normal body growth and fertility
- Source – seafood, offal, bran and wheat germ, broccoli, celery, cucumbers and mushrooms

- RDA – 1 mg
- Deficiency – heart disease, muscular pain and weakness

Zinc

- Function – necessary for healing and development of new cells; an antioxidant, plays an important part in helping to build a strong immune system
- Source – beef, lamb, seafood, eggs, yoghurt, yeast extract (e.g. Marmite), beans, nuts and seeds
- RDA – 15 mg
- Deficiency – decreased learning ability, delayed sexual maturity, eczema, fatigue, prolonged wound healing, retarded growth and white spots on nails

Key learning points

- Vitamins and minerals play key roles in sustaining life and the health of the body.
- Vitamins B and C are water soluble.
- Vitamins A, D, E and K are fat soluble.

Water

One of the major chemicals essential to life is water although it has no nutritional value in terms of energy. Water is used by the body to transport other chemicals. It also plays a major role in maintaining the body at a constant temperature. About 2.5 litres a day are needed to maintain normal functions in adults. This amount depends heavily on environmental conditions and on the amount of energy expenditure. In the heat a greater amount of water is needed, and exercise requires an increased intake of water due to the loss of fluid via sweating.

Only half of the body's water requirement comes in the form of liquid. The other half is supplied from food (especially fruit and vegetables) and metabolic reactions (the breakdown of food results in the formation of carbon dioxide and water).

Digestion

The digestive system is where foods are broken down into their individual nutrients, absorbed into the bloodstream and the waste excreted. It works through processes of mechanical and chemical digestion.

Mechanical digestion starts before the food enters the mouth as we cook the food and then cut it up or mash it to make it more palatable. In the mouth we chew the food to tear it apart further, then digestive juices continue this process. The chemical digestion of foods occurs through the presence of digestive enzymes which are present in the mouth and the other organs the food passes through. Enzymes are defined as biological catalysts which break down the large molecules of the nutrients into smaller molecules which can be absorbed.

The aim of the digestive system is to break the nutrients down into their smallest units:

Nutrient	Smallest unit
Carbohydrate	Glucose
Protein	Amino acid
Fats	Fatty acid

The digestion, absorption and elimination of nutrients take place in the gastrointestinal tract, which is a long tube running from the mouth to the anus. It includes the mouth, oesophagus, stomach, small intestine and large intestine.

Mouth

The technical term for the mouth is the buccal cavity and this is where the journey of the food begins. The teeth and jaw produce mechanical digestion through a process of grinding and mashing up the food. The jaw can produce forces of up to 90 kg on the food. Saliva acts to soften and moisten the food, making it easier to swallow and more like the internal environment. Saliva contains the digestive enzyme amylase, which starts the breakdown of carbohydrates. The tongue is also involved in helping to mix the food and then produce the swallowing action.

Oesophagus

When the food has been swallowed it enters the oesophagus, which delivers the food to the stomach through a process of gravity and peristalsis. Amylase continues to break down the carbohydrates.

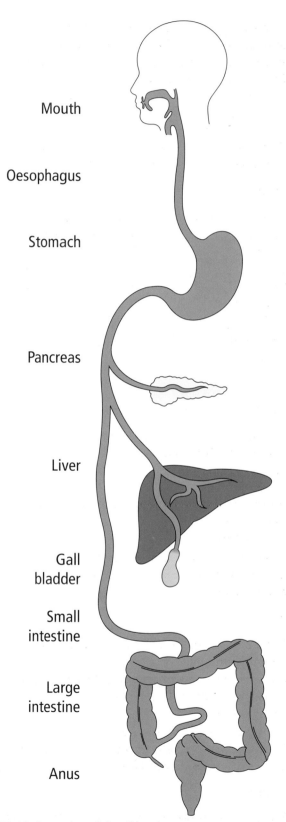

Fig 12.12 Structure of the digestive system

Stomach

The stomach is situated in the upper left of the abdominal cavity and is behind the lower ribs. The stomach continues the process of chemical digestion, but no absorption of nutrients occurs in the stomach because the pieces are still too large. The only substance absorbed in the stomach is alcohol, which can enter the bloodstream here. The stomach is made up of three layers of smooth muscle which help to mix up the food. The parietal cells that line the inside of the stomach release hydrochloric acid which helps to dissolve the food and kill off the bacteria present. These cells also release another digestive enzyme, pepsinogen, which produces protein breakdown. The stomach takes around one to four hours to empty completely, depending upon the size of the meal. Carbohydrates leave the stomach most quickly, followed by proteins and then fats.

Small intestine

Around 90 per cent of digestion occurs in the upper two-thirds of the small intestine with help from the pancreas, liver and gall bladder. The small intestine is between five and six metres long and consists of three areas:

- the duodenum, the first 25 cm
- the jejunum, the next 2 m
- the ileum, around 3 to 4 m long.

The partly digested foods (called chime) move through the small intestine partly by gravity and mainly through the peristaltic action of the smooth muscle present in the intestine walls. The peristaltic action is also aided by the action of the villi and microvilli, which push the food along. These structures line the walls of the intestine and absorption of nutrients occurs between the villi. Any waste is passed into the large intestine.

Pancreas

The pancreas is an important organ in digestion because it secretes around 1.5 litres of a juice which contains three digestive enzymes. These are amylase to digest carbohydrates, lipase to digest fats and trypsin to digest protein.

Liver

The liver is bypassed by the food but it does secrete bile, which helps to emulsify and digest fats. Bile is synthesised in the liver and is stored in the gall bladder, which sits just below the liver.

Large intestine

The large intestine, or colon, performs the following functions:

- storage of waste before elimination
- absorption of any remaining water
- production of vitamins B and K
- breakdown of any toxins that might damage the colon.

The colon contains many millions of bacteria which work to keep the colon healthy through detoxifying the waste and producing vitamins. They are intestinal micro-flora and there are as many of these present in the colon as there are cells in the body. These can be supplemented by yoghurt drinks that promote and increase the number of friendly bacteria.

Anus

The anus is the end of the gastrointestinal tract and is the opening to allow the elimination of waste products of digestion.

Energy intake and expenditure

Energy intake and expenditure can be measured in either calories or joules. One calorie is defined as the amount of energy, or heat, needed to raise the temperature of one litre of water by 1°C. A calorie should be referred to as a kilocalorie (kcal). While in Britain we use calories, the international unit for energy is a joule or, more specifically, a kilojoule. To convert a kcalorie into a kjoule you need to use the following calculation: 1 kcal = 4.2 kjoules.

Key learning points

The aim of the digestive system is to produce the mechanical and chemical breakdown of the nutrients into their smallest units.

- Carbohydrates are broken down into glucose.
- Proteins are broken down into amino acids.
- Fats are broken down into fatty acids.

The main structures of the digestive tract are:

- mouth
- oesophagus
- stomach
- small intestine (duodenum, jejunum, ileum)
- large intestine
- anus.

Other organs are vital in releasing digestive juices to aid in the chemical breakdown of foods.

- The pancreas releases amalyase to digest carbohydrates, lipase to digest fats and trypsin to digest proteins.
- The liver produces bile to digest fats.

Energy value of foods

To discover how much energy foods contain a scientist in a laboratory would use a bomb calorimeter which is used to burn foods completely and see how much energy is liberated. We know that different nutrients provide different amounts of energy:

1 g of carbohydrate = 4 kcals
1 g of protein = 4 kcals
1 g of fat = 9 kcals

Measurement of the energy produced by the body

The amount of energy produced by the body can be measured through direct and indirect calorimetry. Direct calorimetry involves having an athlete working in an airtight chamber or human calorimeter. There are coils in the ceiling which contain water circulating at a specific temperature. The athlete has a mouthpiece leading outside the chamber to enable them to breathe. As they work the circulating water heats up, dependent on the amount of heat and energy the athlete gives off during their activity.

Indirect calorimetry is done by working out how much oxygen an athlete consumes. This works because all reactions in the body which produce energy need oxygen to be present.

Basal metabolic rate

Basal metabolic rate (BMR) is the minimal caloric requirement needed to sustain life in a resting individual. This is the amount of energy your body would burn if you slept all day or rested in bed for 24 hours. A variety of factors affect your basal metabolic rate. Some speed it up so you burn more kilocalories per day just to stay alive, whereas other factors slow your metabolic rate down so that you need to eat fewer kilocalories just to stay alive.

- Age: as you get older you start to lose more muscle tissue and replace it with fat tissue. The more muscle tissue a person has, the greater their BMR, and vice versa. Hence, as you get older this increased fat mass will have the effect of slowing down your BMR.
- Body size: taller, heavier people have higher BMRs. There is more of them so they require more energy.
- Growth: children and pregnant women have higher BMRs. In both cases the body is growing and needs more energy.
- Body composition: the more muscle tissue, the higher the BMR, and the more fat tissue, the lower the BMR.
- Fever: fevers can raise the BMR. This is because when a person has a fever, their body temperature is increased, which speeds up the rate of metabolic reactions (to help fight off an infection) and results in an increased BMR.
- Stress: stress hormones can raise the BMR.
- Environmental temperature: both heat and cold raise the BMR. When a person is too hot, their body tries to cool down, which requires energy. When a person is too cold they shiver, which again is a process that requires energy.
- Fasting: when a person is fasting, as in dieting, hormones are released which act to lower the BMR.
- Thyroxin: the thyroid hormone thyroxin is a key BMR regulator – the more thyroxin produced, the higher the BMR.

Hydration and sports performance

It is possible to survive for six or seven weeks without food because the body stores energy in the form of fat, protein and a small amount of carbohydrate. However, you could survive for only two or three days without drinking water. Every day we lose roughly two litres of water through breathing, sweating and urine production. This is increased if we train or compete as water is sweated out to control the heat produced as a waste product of energy production. Therefore, we need to drink at least two litres of water a day – and more if we train or drink caffeinated or alcoholic drinks. The advice is that we should continually sip water throughout the day or take two or three mouthfuls of water every 15 minutes.

Dehydration

Dehydration is a condition which occurs when fluid loss exceeds fluid intake. The signs and symptoms of dehydration are:

- thirst
- dizziness
- headaches
- dry mouth
- poor concentration
- sticky oral mucus
- flushed red skin
- rapid heart rate.

Dehydration causes a significant loss of performance. This is because dehydration, also called hypo hydration, causes a loss of blood plasma affecting blood flow and the ability to sweat. Thus temperature starts to increase steadily. When we sweat it is predominantly blood plasma that is lost and thus cardiac output (the amount of the blood leaving the heart per minute) is reduced. Therefore, dehydration affects the circulation of the blood and the body's ability to control temperature.

Hyper hydration

Hyper hydration is when an athlete drinks extra water before exercising. This is done when they are exercising in a hot environment to prevent the negative effects of dehydration and to minimise the rise in body temperature. The advice is to increase fluid intake over the preceding 24 hours and then drink around 500 ml of water 20 minutes before the event starts. This does not replace the need to continually top up water levels during the competition.

Fluid intake

It is advised that an athlete continually take on enough fluid to cover the 'cost' of their training or competition. This may involve them consuming around 2.5 to 3 litres of water a day. It should be taken on continually and then some extra taken on 20 minutes before the event. During the event they should top up their water levels when they have a chance. Finally, they should drink water steadily for around one to two hours after their performance depending upon the demands of the event.

Choices of fluid intake

Water is a good choice, particularly bottled water served at room temperature. Chilled drinks, although refreshing, need to be warmed up in the stomach before they can leave the stomach to be absorbed in the small intestine. This slows down the speed of their absorption.

Sports drinks have a benefit over water in that they provide energy as well as fluid replacement. They are now a common sight at all sports grounds and there are three types of sport drink.

- **Isotonic:** these drinks have a similar concentration of dissolved solids as blood and as a result are absorbed very quickly. They contain 6 mg of carbohydrate per 100 ml of water and thus provide a good source of fuel as well as being good for hydration. These drinks are useful before, during and after performance, and are the most commonly used.
- **Hypotonic:** these drinks have a lower concentration of dissolved solids than blood and are absorbed even more quickly than isotonic drinks. With only 2 g of carbohydrate per 100 ml of water they are a relatively poor source of energy. They are used to hydrate after performance.
- **Hypertonic:** these drinks have a higher concentration of dissolved solids than blood and are absorbed relatively slowly. They contain 10 g of carbohydrate per 100 ml of water and are a very good source of energy but relatively poor for

hydration. They are mostly used in endurance events of over an hour and a half.

These drinks also contain the correct amounts of the electrolytes, which ensure optimum speed of absorption. On the negative side they often contain additives such as sweeteners and colourings which have a negative effect on health. They are also relatively expensive when compared with water.

An easy and cheaper alternative is to make your own sports drinks by taking 500 ml of unsweetened fruit juice, 500 ml of water and a pinch of salt to aid absorption. You will have made yourself an isotonic sports drink which is cheaper and without the additives.

LEARNER ACTIVITY
Sports drinks

Name as many different sports drinks as you can. Look through magazines, on the internet or in sports shops to help you. Note down the prices of these drinks and any claimed benefits of consuming them.

Key learning points

We need to drink at least 2 litres of water a day to keep hydrated and 2.5 to 3 litres if we are active. It is best to regularly sip water, taking two or three mouthfuls every 15 minutes.

There is a range of sports drinks available to provide fuel and rehydration.

- Isotonic drinks are of the same concentration as blood and provide good fuel and good hydration.
- Hypotonic drinks are less concentrated than blood and provide good hydration but will be a poor source of fuel.
- Hypertonic drinks are more concentrated than blood and provide a good source of fuel but will be poor for hydration.

Planning a diet for a selected sports activity

A balanced diet consists of the following quantities:

- 50–60 per cent of kcals from carbohydrates
- 10–20 per cent of kcals from proteins
- 30 per cent of kcals from fats
- a plentiful supply of vitamins and minerals from fruit and vegetables
- 2 litres of water.

When choosing foods there are some guidelines that will help you make a good choice:

- eat foods which are naturally occurring rather than processed
- eat foods that look as they occur in nature
- limit processed or take-away foods
- the best foods will not have a label containing ingredients
- avoid additives or E numbers
- eat organic foods where possible as they will contain more vitamins and minerals.

Basically what you eat will become a part of your body or affect the way your body functions so be very particular about what you choose to eat.

When deciding upon a nutritional strategy for any person you need to look at the physiological demands placed upon them and the effect these have on their body structures and fuel consumption. You may also have to make a decision about whether to use food alone or to combine food with supplements, protein shakes or multi-vitamins.

Aerobic athletes

The physiological demands on the aerobic athlete are considerable and you will have to consider the following:

- replacing the energy lost during training
- maintaining high energy levels
- repairing any damage done to the body's structures during training
- the need for vitamins and minerals to ensure correct functioning of all the body's systems
- replacement and maintenance of fluid levels.

LEARNER ACTIVITY Designing a sports drink

The aim of this practical is to make a sports drink. You need to decide which athletes you are making the drink for and when it should be consumed (i.e. if you want to make an isotonic, hypertonic or hypotonic drink).

For this experiment, if you are using equipment taken from the science lab, it must have been thoroughly sterilised. You will need:

- measuring cylinders
- beakers
- weighing scales
- glucose
- sweeteners
- flavourings – your choice
- colourings – your choice
- tasting cups
- drinking water
- salt

Method

Isotonic drink

- If you are designing an isotonic drink, you need to ensure that the carbohydrate content of your drink is between 6 and 8 per cent. To do this, for every 100 ml of water, you need to add between 6 to 8 g of glucose.
- You can then add other flavourings to your drink to make it taste better. These flavourings should not contain any carbohydrates, so use things that contain sweeteners, such as reduced-sugar squash.

Hypertonic drink

- If you are designing a hypertonic drink, it should contain at least 9 per cent carbohydrates. This means for every 100 ml of water, you need to add at least 9 g of glucose.
- You can then add other flavourings which can contain carbohydrates.

Hypotonic drink

- If you are designing a hypotonic drink, it should contain 5 per cent or less carbohydrates. To do this, to every 100 ml of water add 5 g of glucose or less.
- You can then add other flavourings, but these should not contain any carbohydrates, so you could use things that contain sweeteners.

Experiment with different flavours and quantities of flavour. Ensure that, each time, you write out exactly how much of each ingredient you use. When you have made a drink that you think tastes acceptable place it in a beaker.

Results

Go around the class and sample other people's sports drinks. Do this by pouring their drink from the beaker into your own tasting cup. Ensure that you rinse out your cup after each tasting. Draw up a table for your findings.

Conclusion

In your conclusion answer the following questions.

1 Who was your drink designed for?
2 Did your drink taste acceptable?
3 Would people buy your drink?
4 What could you have done to improve the taste of your drink?
5 Out of the class tasting session, which drinks tasted the best and why?

Anaerobic or power athletes

The physiological demands on the anaerobic athlete differ from the aerobic athlete and they will be:

- repairing the considerable damage occurring to the muscles and other structures of the body during training
- replacing the energy lost during training
- the need for vitamins and minerals to ensure correct functioning of all the body's systems
- replacement and maintenance of fluid levels.

Catabolism and anabolism

Catabolism refers to the breaking down of the structures of the body. Training, especially weight training, is catabolic in nature because it causes damage to the muscles being trained. We know this has occurred because we tend to feel sore and stiff the next day until the body has repaired itself. The process of catabolism releases energy.

Anabolism refers to the building up of the structures of the body. When the body is resting and recovering it will be in an anabolic state. Eating also promotes anabolism. While training is the stimulus to improving our fitness and strength of the body's structures it is actually when we rest that the body builds up and becomes stronger. The process of anabolism requires energy.

When looking at different athletes' diets we need to give advice on two of the nutrients specifically. They are carbohydrate to replace the energy used and protein to repair the damage which has occurred to the structures. Each performer will still require around 30 per cent of kcals to come from fats with 10 per cent from saturated fats, 10 per cent from monounsaturated and 10 per cent from polyunsaturated. They will each require at least five to nine portions of fruit and vegetables a day and enough water to replace their fluid loss.

Recommended protein intake

The amount of protein recommended is dependent upon the activity in which the individual is involved. The box top right gives estimated recommended amounts.

Therefore, if you have a sedentary person of 70 kg you would work out their requirements in the following way:

70 × 0.8 = 56 g of protein

Activity	Grams of protein per kg of body weight
Sedentary adult	0.8 g
Recreational exerciser	0.8–1.5 g
Endurance athlete	1.2–1.6 g
Speed/power athlete	1.7–1.8 g
Adult building muscle (hypertrophy)	2 g

(Adapted from Franklin, 2000)

Or a body builder at 90 kg:

90 × 2.0 = 180 g of protein

Protein is best utilised if it is taken on in amounts of 30 to 35 g at a time. If any more is taken on it is either excreted in the urine or stored as body fat. A chicken breast, tin of tuna or a small steak gives 30 g of protein. The best advice for the body builder would be to consume six portions of 30 g of protein rather than three large protein meals.

Recommended carbohydrate intake

The amount of carbohydrate recommended is based on the activity level of the individual in terms of its length and intensity.

Activity level	Recommended amount of carbohydrate in grams per kilogram of body weight
Light (less than 1 hour a day)	4–5 g
Light to moderate (1 hour a day)	5–6 g
Moderate (1–2 hours a day)	6–7 g
Moderate to heavy (2–4 hours a day)	7–8 g
Heavy (4 hours a day)	8–10 g

An endurance athlete would need 10 g a day, mainly from complex carbohydrate sources.

The continuum in Fig 12.13 shows an estimated calorie intake and clearly depends upon the size and weight of the individual.

Daily intake of carbohydrate, protein and fat

The box on the opposite page shows a summary of the studies done into male and female athletes.

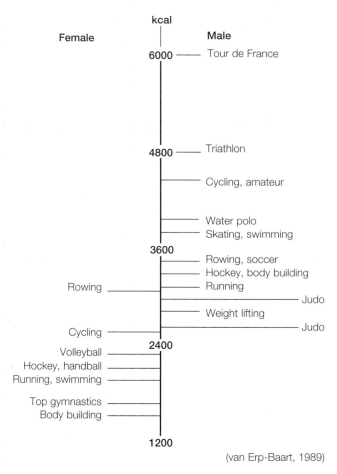

(van Erp-Baart, 1989)

Fig 12.13 Daily energy expenditure

Protein shakes

Recently there has been a boom in the use of protein shakes as a supplement to training. They are employed by athletes who want to lay down more muscle and need to gain more protein on a daily basis. Protein shakes are usually high in whey protein because it contains high levels of three essential amino acids: leucine, isoleucine and valine. These are important because they are the amino acids which are broken down most during training.

Protein shakes contain plentiful supplies of amino acids and are quick and convenient to use. However, there are several issues to consider.

- The human body has evolved to gain its protein from natural rather than processed sources (meats rather than powders).
- They often contain additives such as sweeteners, sugars and colourings.
- The process of drying the proteins into powder form damages the structure of the amino acids, making them unusable by the body.
- They are often very expensive.

Diet plans

If the amount of energy taken in (via food) equals the amount expended (physical activity and BMR) then a person will remain at the same weight. To lose weight, energy intake must be less than energy expenditure and to gain weight energy intake must exceed expenditure. Therefore, in order to lose weight a person needs to reduce intake (eat less) and increase expenditure (do more physical activity).

Athlete group	Carbohydrate %	Protein %	Fat %	Kcals per kg of body weight
Triathlete M	66.2	11.6	21.2	62.0
F	59.2	11.8	29	57.4
Cyclists M	54.3	13.5	31.7	46.2
F	56.5	14.0	29.5	59.1
Swimmers M	50.3	15.0	34.7	45.3
F	49.3	14.2	36.5	55.6
Runners M	48.0	14.0	38.0	42.2
F	49.0	14.0	36.0	42.9
Basketball M	49.0	15.0	36.0	32.0
F	45.3	16.0	34.7	45.6
Gymnasts M	49.8	15.3	34.9	37.8
F	44.0	15.0	39.0	53.3
Dancers M	50.2	15.4	34.4	34.0
F	38.4	16.5	45.1	51.7
Rowers M	54.2	13.4	23.7	
F	55.8	15.3	30.3	
Soccer M	47	14	39	
Weight lifters M	40.3	20.0	39.7	46.5
Marathon runners M	52	15	32	51

To lose one pound in body weight (approximately 0.45 kg) the energy deficit needs to be around 3500 kcals per week. If you expended 250 kcals per day and consumed 250 kcals less you would have a daily deficit of 500 kcal. In seven days you would have a deficit of 3500 kcals (500 × 7) and hence you would have lost eleven pounds in body weight.

Weight loss

We have established that in order to lose weight it is necessary to consume fewer calories than your body needs. Athletes may not be overweight, but may need to lose excess weight to compete in a lower weight category. Excess weight in the form of fat usually acts to hinder a person's performance because a heavier body requires more energy for transport. Therefore, athletes may diet to get rid of any unessential fat. The best type of diet to help the person lose weight but still have enough energy to train seems to be a low-fat diet.

Low-fat diets

A low-fat diet recommends low-fat options whenever possible, plus regular consumption of complex carbohydrates like potatoes and brown bread. Low-fat diets are usually quite filling because they involve eating large amounts of complex carbohydrates, which include fibre. Weight loss is steady at about 1.5 to 2 pounds per week. Most experts agree that faster weight loss is not sustainable as the weight lost is from the glycogen stores and not from the fat stores of the body.

Here is an example of what you might eat on a low-fat diet.

A typical breakfast:

- glass of freshly squeezed orange
- large bowl of cereal with fat-free milk
- toast with no margarine, and yeast extract (e.g. Marmite) or jam
- tea/coffee.

A typical lunch:

- large brown bread sandwich with lean meat, and large salad with low-fat dressing
- low-fat yoghurt.

A typical dinner:

- 4 oz lean chicken with potatoes (no butter) and two helpings of vegetables
- chopped fruit topped with low-fat ice cream or low-fat fromage frais.

Typical snacks:

- fruit
- low-fat yoghurts
- whole-wheat sandwiches
- cereal.

Review questions

1 Name the three macronutrients and the two micronutrients.
2 Give the energy content that can be derived from 1 g of each of the nutrients.
3 What is the smallest unit of each of the macronutrients?
4 Explain what happens to carbohydrate foods when they are digested.
5 Name the three monosaccharides and the three disaccharides.
6 Explain the difference between refined and unrefined polysaccharides in terms of their nutrient content.
7 What is the glycaemic index and why is it important in nutrition?
8 What factors will affect the glycaemic index of a food?
9 What is fibre and why is it important to have fibre in the diet?
10 What functions does protein perform in the body?
11 What is an essential amino acid?
12 Define a complete protein and an incomplete protein and give four sources of each.
13 Give five functions of fats.
14 What are the three types of fatty acids and how are they different?
15 What is a triglyceride?
16 Give three sources of saturated, monounsaturated and polyunsaturated fatty acids.
17 Name the water-soluble and fat-soluble vitamins.
18 What is the aim of the digestive system?
19 Name the main structures of the digestive tract and briefly explain what happens in each.
20 Name and summarise five factors which will affect BMR.
21 Give five symptoms of dehydration.
22 List three ways to keep well hydrated.
23 What advice would you give an aerobic and an anaerobic athlete about their diet?
24 How much protein and carbohydrate would you recommend an individual to consume on a daily basis?
25 If an athlete wanted to take a protein shake what advice would you give them?

References

Burke, L. and Deakin, V. (1994) *Clinical Sports Nutrition*, McGraw-Hill.

Clark, N. (2003) *Sports Nutrition Guidebook*, Human Kinetics.

Eisenman, P., Johnson, S. and Benson, J. (1990) *Coaches' Guide to Nutrition and Weight Control*, Leisure Press.

Franklin, B. (2000) *American College of Sport Medicine's (ACSM) Guidelines for Exercise Testing and Prescription*, 6th edn, Lippincott, Williams and Wilkins.

McArdle, W. D., Katch, F. I. and Katch, V. L. (1999) *Sports and Exercise Nutrition*, Williams & Wilkins.

McArdle, W. D., Katch, F. I. and Katch, V. L. (2001) *Exercise Physiology: Energy, Nutrition and Human Performance*, Williams & Wilkins.

van Erp-Baart, A., Saris, W., Binkhorst, R., Vos, J. and Elvers, J. (1989) Nationwide survey on nutritional habits in elite athletes. *International Journal of Sports Medicine*, 10, 53.

Goals

By the end of this chapter you should:

- understand how the development of sport has influenced how it is organised
- know about the sports industry in the UK today
- understand how contemporary issues affect sport
- understand cultural influences and barriers that affect participation in sports activities.

The state of current sport and the issues prevalent in sport today can be understood and interpreted only if we examine the society they are played in and how sports have developed. Sport in some way affects the lives of most people in our society whether it is through playing or watching sport, getting caught up in the excitement of a tournament or supporting the activities of others. Sport in Britain has developed as a result of the development of our society, and the values and features prevalent in sport are also reflected in the values and features of our society. Sport has also been used to address some of the problems in society and improve the quality of the society in which we live.

The development of modern sports

Pre-industrial sports

There are two distinct periods in Britain: sport before the Industrial Revolution and sport after it. The Industrial Revolution covers a specific period of time from 1780 to 1850. In 1800 only one in five people lived in towns, but by 1851 for the first time over 50 per cent of the population lived in urban environments. By the 1880s this had risen to 75 per cent of the population.

This was a period of major development in society because the ways people lived and worked were changing. Rather than being a country where people lived predominantly in the countryside and farmed areas of land, Britain became a society of city dwellers who worked for a wage in factories. This had a profound effect on leisure time and the form that sports took. It led to rapid changes in sports, with sports taking on the features we recognise in these activities today. Prior to the Industrial Revolution Britain was described as being an agricultural society where people lived in the countryside and farmed the land.

Mediaeval England (1066–1485)

The period from 1066 to 1485 is commonly known as the Middle Ages. At this time Britain's population mainly lived in rural areas, although there were a growing number of townspeople who worked mainly as lawyers, doctors and merchants. Society was split into three specific social groups: the nobility, the bourgeoisie (business people who were gaining wealth) and peasants. It was a period of growing prosperity because trade between merchants was booming due to the lack of conflict between lords and landowners.

Sports were played for two reasons. First, for functional reasons – to prepare men to defend their country. Archery and hunting were a way for the nobility to practise their skills. Second, as Christianity became more widespread and religious customs replaced pagan festivals as 'holy days' or holidays, more time was put aside for recreational activities. Holidays included Easter, Shrove Tuesday and Ash Wednesday, and would involve sports such as folk football, wrestling, skittles and bowls. Other entertainment was provided by musicians, dancers and acrobats.

Tudor and Stuart periods (1485–1714)

Henry Tudor's victory at the Battle of Bosworth Field is the event that signalled the end of the Middle Ages and started a period known as the Renaissance (1485–1640). Tudor rule ran from 1485 to 1617, when the Stuart's rule commenced. England during this period was still a rural, agricultural society with London as the only recognised city, with a population of 300,000. Around 10 per cent of people lived in the towns and the main source of income was farming. Society was becoming more commercial as the feudal lords who had become landlords started to see their estates as sources of income. Henry VIII (1509–47) was the best known king of this period. He reigned during a period of greater prosperity and he was able to develop cultural and sporting interests. He enjoyed literature and the theatre. He would participate in all-day hunts and had a 'real tennis' court built at Hampton Court where it can still be seen.

Sport was still used to maintain distance between social groups. The upper class had hunting on their private land, predominantly of red deer, boar and hares. Other popular sports activities were hawking and jousting. All these activities were used to prepare for war and sharpen the men's combat skills.

The peasants were involved in sport in the role of servicing the sports of the upper classes. They also had their own activities, such as mob football and baiting animals. These sports were characterised by high levels of violence which allowed the peasants an avenue to channel their energies.

When James I came to the throne in 1603 the reign of the Stuarts began and it was built on religious grounds. In 1617 he issued the 'Book of Sports', which stated that sport should be encouraged as long as it did not affect attendance at church. This era saw the development of Puritanism with influential leaders such as Oliver Cromwell, who had been made Protector of Britain. The Puritans were opposed to playing sports on a Sunday, cruelty inflicted to animals in the name of sport, and heavy drinking and its associated idleness, foul language and blasphemy.

They believed that the focus of people's lives should be on praying for the salvation of their souls and working hard rather than participating in activities that had pagan roots and diverted attention away from more worthy pursuits. However, the Puritans were only partially successful and under the rule of Charles II and the Restoration period sports started to flourish again but without ever regaining their previous popularity. Charles II enjoyed a leisurely lifestyle in which he and his courtiers were actively involved in sports and other leisurely activities.

Hanoverian period (1714–90)

This phase from 1714 to 1790 saw a change in how people earned their living. The movement from the spacious environment of the countryside to the cramped conditions of urban living was brought on by a decline in farming and a growth in the production of consumer goods. Factories were offering better wages and promising a better standard of living.

The Industrial Revolution (1780–1850)

From around the mid-eighteenth century the English economy underwent a vast transformation. It had been based on agriculture, with particularly busy periods of work for planting and harvesting. Working hours varied and there were long periods of free time available for workers to enjoy leisure activities.

The Industrial Revolution saw the development of factories producing a wide range of consumer goods. Factory owners required their workers to accept longer hours and less free time. Typically, a worker would have a six-day week, working from 7 in the morning to 7 at night. There may also have been a night shift; this was to maximise the output of factories and reduce their unit costs. Overhead costs were high and could be reduced only if machinery was being worked for as many hours as possible. The second issue was that there was a shortage of people living in the towns and cities where these factories were based, so they had to attract workers from their countryside homes. This was done by offering better wages and the lure of consumer goods to raise standards of living.

The reality was a little different from the promise because these workers traded increased wages for longer working hours and less leisure time. Also, the standards of housing were much worse than in the countryside where they enjoyed plenty of space. The perceived rise in spending and standard of living never occurred because it was more expensive to live in cities. In the cities families and workers were herded into 'slum' accommodation with little space.

Leisure activities became a problem because the violent sports could result in serious injuries, the excessive drinking led to hangovers and absenteeism, and gambling undermined the work ethic. Leisure cost the factory owners money and affected output. Factory owners supported the middle-class efforts to clean up society and impose a new form of morality. Campaigns were mounted against excessive drinking, idleness, sexual promiscuity, gambling, violent sports and the excessive holidays. The aim of the middle classes was to impose a work ethic on the population and make behaviour more polite and respectable.

The agricultural industry also underwent a parallel revolution with the scope and quantity of production increasing. This meant that the population of England became better fed, healthier and had more energy for work.

The economic forces contributed to changes in traditional sports because the employees had to bow to their employers' demands and, moreover, they had little time or energy to play aggressive contact sports. These demands were supplemented by the efforts of religious reformers, who believed violent sports led to moral corruption, and sport on the Sabbath was eventually banned. The Royal Society for the Protection of Animals (RSPCA) put pressure on the authorities to ban sports involving cruelty to animals. The Industrial Revolution led to a growth in the size of towns and cities and a reduction in the amount of space available for recreation. Folk football, which was played across vast swathes of countryside, was completely inappropriate for the urban setting. The result of all these changes was that sports slowly disappeared.

Key learning points

- The effects of the Industrial Revolution led to an increase in working hours and a decline in leisure time. Many activities were banned because they became costly in terms of working hours and productivity being lost.
- The workers had a low spending power in reality.
- The urban setting provided an inappropriate environment for playing sports.

Sports for the leisured upper classes and middle classes were still popular and carried on in pre-industrialised forms.

The 1830s and 1840s started to see an upturn in fortune for the workers, because the development of the railways led to an increased mobility. The sports of cricket and horse racing benefited from the easier access to the countryside, allowing the workers to go and watch meetings and matches. The 1840s saw a genuine improvement in real wages (meaning an increased spending power), improving diets and standard of living. There was also money available to spend on entrance fees into sports events.

The 1860s saw the development of nationally agreed rules, known as the codification of sport, and a changing attitude of the middle-class factory owners to their employees' sports activities. Two groups promoted the benefits of sport. First, the industrialists, who saw sport as promoting values which would make their workers more productive, such as teamwork and loyalty. Second, the Muscular Christians took team sports to working-class communities to teach the Bible through sport and promote the value of a healthy mind in a healthy body.

Figures from the time suggest sport was still a minority activity, but spectating was growing, as was professionalism in the sports of football, cricket and horse racing. Social change included the urban population growing from 50.2 per cent in 1851 to 77 per cent in 1900. Working-class wages rose by 70 per cent and a half-day holiday was granted on Saturdays. This meant sport could be played and watched on Saturday afternoons and is the origin of the three o'clock kick-off in football matches.

Rationalisation and regulation

'Rational recreation' is the term given to the introduction of leisure activities which were seen as being productive and moral. Up until the 1860s and 1870s the workers had relied on their public houses for amusement and entertainment, which were often socially destructive. Rational recreations were brought in by various philanthropic groups, such as the Muscular Christians and other middle-class groups who introduced new alternatives. Thus, societies such as the Mechanics Society, the Boys Brigade and the Young Men's Christian Association developed, and facilities such as libraries, public baths and sports grounds offered more purposeful activities.

This is an example of using sport and leisure as a means of social control, whereby people are persuaded to take part in positive, socially acceptable activities to prevent them from participating in otherwise socially destructive activities such as drinking, gambling and fighting. The middle-class philanthropists wanted to provide better activities for the working class to improve their standard of living, but their ulterior motive was to make sure they were healthier, fitter and more productive workers.

Twentieth-century development

Globalisation of sport

The forms of sport that were established in England in the late nineteenth century quickly spread around the world, particularly through the influence of the British Empire. Officers and soldiers brought the new codified forms of sport to the countries in which they were stationed, and the sports in turn were adopted by the natives. By the end of the nineteenth century the Olympic movement, under the influence of the French, was finding its feet and starting to involve more and more nations.

The influence of sport by the end of the twentieth century can be seen by the fact that three of the four largest international organisations were sporting organisations:

- the IAAF (International Amateur Athletic Federation) with 184 member countries
- FIFA (Fédération Internationale de Football Association) with 178 members
- the IOC (International Olympic Committee) with 171 members.

The non-sporting organisation was the United Nations, with 180 member countries.

Professionalism

The increasing playing demands of the sports of rugby, football and cricket mean that players have had to devote increasing amounts of time and energy to their sports. By the end of the nineteenth century these three sports had all embraced professionalism. As the standards of the sports rose payments had to be made to players to compensate for the wages they would otherwise have earned. Professionalism was initially looked down upon because the upper classes thought that sport should be played purely for the enjoyment derived from the activity. A class distinction arose between the upper-class amateurs and the working-class professionals, which remained until the latter part of the twentieth century. By the end of the twentieth century, professionalism was an accepted part of all sports and necessary to uphold the high standards of play demanded by the sophisticated audiences.

The development of sport as a profitable industry

As sports have increasingly embraced professionalism, their expenditure has increased. As a result they have had to increase the amount of money coming into the sport to pay these expenses. Sports and their clubs have increasingly sought sponsorship as a source of income, along with trying to make the sport more attractive and increase the number of spectators coming to matches. As sports have become more popular and widely watched, they have increasingly drawn the attention of the media. This has opened up new sources of revenue to sports and has led to increased profits.

There is also an expanding industry in sport for non-competitive participants, and this has created a variety of opportunities for private companies to invest their money and make profits. It has also resulted in a growing industry with new, exciting employment opportunities.

The development of sport in education

The key element in the expansion of sport in the education system was the 1944 Education Act, which made it policy for local authorities to provide adequate facilities for the teaching of physical education. Sport and physical education became compulsory elements of children's education and are now key features in the National Curriculum. Added to that, there are now many more opportunities to study sport at GCSE, AS and A2 level, National Diploma and degree level.

Mid-twentieth-century developments

The two world wars had a major effect on the development of sport. During World War I, in which the Allies (Britain, France, Russia, Italy and the USA) defeated the central powers (Germany, Austria, Hungary and Turkey), all sports stopped at national and international level as young people were recruited for the war and many were then killed during the fighting. The Olympic Games scheduled for 1916 had to be cancelled.

Between the wars the upper classes returned to their leisure activities, playing tennis, golf and cricket, and also indulged in overseas holidays and nights of partying. The development of the railways allowed them to visit the seaside in the summer months. The working classes returned to watching football on Saturday afternoons and the first dog racing meeting was held in 1926 at Belle Vue in Manchester.

During the 1930s Great Britain experienced a series of financial and economic problems as a result of strikes and industrial unrest. Unemployment rose to three million and the development of Nazism and Fascism led the country to feel insecure, with a negative effect on national morale

World War II again saw the cessation of sporting activities as all energy went into the war effort and training the young troops for war. The training used by the troops started to appear in schools, forming an integral part of physical education lessons.

The organisation of sport in Britain

The government in Britain still plays a key role in influencing the direction sport takes and the opportunities for participation in sport. Rather than directly being involved in sport, the government has developed agencies to influence policy for sport and this is backed up by the provision of funding. In this way the government can keep sport 'at arm's length' but still maintain some control over it. The current government's major success has been to attract the Olympic Games to London in 2012.

Central government control of sport

Sport in central government is administered through the Department of Culture, Media and Sport (DCMS) under the control of a Secretary of State for Culture, Media and Sport and a Minister for Sport. The DCMS looks after the interests of world-class sportspeople and also ensures that everyone has an opportunity to take part in sport. The roles of the DCMS in relation to sport are to:

- widen access to sport for all citizens and offer Sport for All
- promote the achievement of excellence in national and international competition
- promote physical education and sport for young people and work with the Department for Education and Skills (DfES) to promote children's play through education

- attract major sporting events to Britain, such as the successful bid for the 2012 Olympic Games
- manage schemes to support the training of athletes, such as TASS (Talented Athletes Scholarship Scheme) which supports athletes in full-time education, and funding of athletes through Lottery money.

The DCMS is not the only department representing the interests of people playing sport in Britain. Sport in schools and developing the physical education syllabus is under the control of the DfES. Sports development departments are under the control of the local authorities within the Department for Communities and Local Government.

The CCPR – Central Council for Physical Recreation – represents the interests of national governing bodies (NGBs).

NGBs – national governing bodies – all sports clubs are members of the NGB, which runs the leagues, and provides officials and disciplinary measures. For example, the Football Association (FA) is football's NGB.

ISFs – International Sports Federations – in order to be involved in international competition the NGB needs to be affiliated to a relevant ISF.

The BOA – British Olympic Association – selects, funds and manages the team to represent Great Britain and Northern Ireland at the Olympic Games.

The IOC – International Olympic Committee – organises and manages each Olympiad.

Central Council for Physical Recreation

The Central Council for Physical Recreation (CCPR) (www.ccpr.org.uk) was set up against the bleak

---

LEARNER ACTIVITY
Government representatives

Find out the current Secretary of State for:

- the Department of Culture, Media and Sport
- the Department for Education and Skills
- the Department for Transport and the Regions
- the Home Office.

Find out the current Minister for Sport.

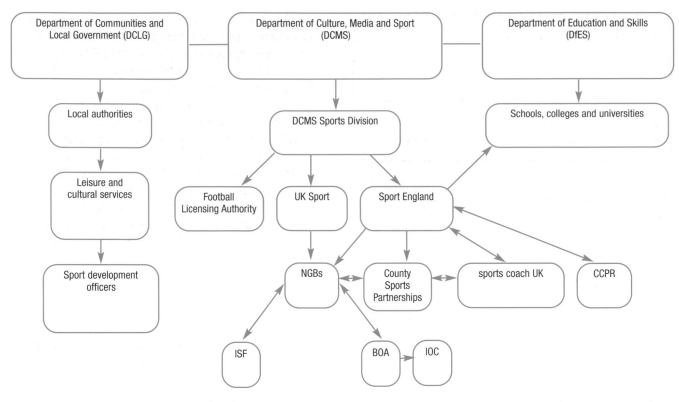

Fig 13.01 Bodies governing sport in England

backdrop of 1930s Britain, which was experiencing economic unrest and high levels of unemployment. The school leaving age was 14 and, with the exception of students in private education, this was when education stopped. There was little opportunity after school to play sport and even in state schools sport was limited.

The CCPR was the first attempt to provide government influence in sport and aimed to promote the benefits of sport. Initially the CCPR supported the work of the National Fitness Council to provide training for physical education teachers. In 1946 it was offered the use of Bisham Abbey at a low rent to be used as the national Physical Recreation Centre. Lilleshall was acquired in 1947, Plas y Brenin in 1955, and Crystal Palace was built in 1964 and Holme Pierrepoint in 1973. These national sports centres were the central facilities to provide high-quality, residential training facilities and venues for national and international competition.

The CCPR worked to gain the support of the national governing bodies and within six months of its inception 82 NGBs were signed-up members. The CCPR prepared an influential report into sport in Britain, called the Woolfenden Report, which was published in 1960. Among its main recommendations was the formation of a sports council to promote sport in Britain. The Sports Council was formed in 1965 in an advisory capacity and became an executive body in 1972 when it was decided that the CCPR should be taken over by the Sports Council and transfer all its staff and assets. This was not agreed and the CCPR still exists today representing the members of the NGBs.

UK Sport

UK Sport (www.uksport.gov.uk) was established in 1997 through a Royal Charter as the twin roles of the Sports Council were separated. The Sports Council had two remits: first, to promote excellence in sports

LEARNER ACTIVITY

Central Council for Physical Recreation

Find out the following information on the CCPR.

- How is it funded?
- What services does it provide to its members?

achievements and, second, to promote participation in sport. These were seen as being radically different and it was decided to let the Sports Council (now Sport England) continue to promote participation in sport but to give the role of developing excellence to a new body with responsibility across the UK.

The role of UK Sport is to support athletes in becoming world-class performers. In 2003 it was granted around £25 million a year, mostly from Lottery funding, to spend on its aims, which are to:

- encourage, develop and support sporting excellence in UK athletes
- identify and implement policies with a UK-wide application
- in conjunction with NGBs and appropriate home country sports councils, to provide grants for athletes
- oversee the policy on the delivery of sport science, sports medicine, coaching and drug control over the UK
- coordinate the policy for attracting major sporting events to the UK
- represent the UK internationally and to increase the influence of the UK in sporting matters.

These roles are performed through four directorates.

- Performance development: provides advice to NGBs on planning applications, allocation of grants and funding, and advises on awards from the Lottery Sports Fund.
- UK Sports Institute: a central service based in London with a network of regional centres to cater for the needs of sportspeople from Olympic sports, including disabled athletes; the support services include sport science, sports medicine and lifestyle management services to create the correct environment for the development of excellence.
- International relations and major events: the UK needs to attract major sports events to gain the social, economic and cultural benefits of sport; the

2008 Olympics being held in Beijing is seen as the completion of China being accepted as a major force in world sport, while the 2012 Olympics in London is seen as being the return of the UK as an important force in world sport.

- Ethics and anti-doping: UK Sport manages and administers a wide-reaching programme of drug testing to ensure that the ethics of fair play and honesty are maintained in British sport; this work is done under the umbrella of the World Anti-Doping Authority, established in 2000 by the International Olympic Committee (IOC). In 2005/6 there were 55 positive drug tests in the UK with power lifting having the most at eight positive tests.

Sport England

Sport England (www.sportengland.org) was formed from the old Sports Council by Royal Charter in 1997 and is responsible to the Secretary of State for the Department of Culture, Media and Sport. Sport England also operates ten regional offices across England.

It has responsibility for promoting and investing in sport and helping the government to implement its sporting objectives through the distribution of Lottery funds. The vision of Sport England is 'to make England an active and successful sporting nation'. Sport England invested around £2 bn from 1994 to 2006 to achieve its objectives. The business objectives of Sport England are to allocate its resources to get people to:

- start – to participate in sport to improve the health of the nation, particularly within disadvantaged groups
- stay – keeping people active through a network of clubs, coaches and volunteers
- succeed in sport – achieving higher levels of performance through an infrastructure capable of developing world-class performances.

Regional offices

There are nine regional offices which administer the regional policies of Sport England and deliver local initiatives (see Fig 13.02):

- North East (A)
- North West (C)
- East Midlands (E)
- London (G)

- Yorkshire (B)
- West Midlands (D)
- East (F)
- South East (H)
- South West (I).

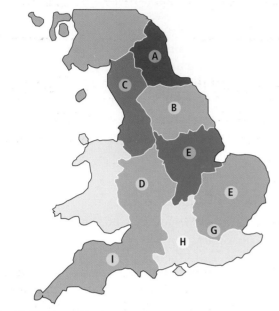

Fig 13.02 Sport England regions

There are also regional offices for the other three countries of the United Kingdom, as outlined below.

Sport Scotland

Sport Scotland (www.sportscotland.org.uk) is funded through and distributes Lottery funding to develop community links among schools and communities, and in particular to encourage participation in deprived areas and support the efforts of top athletes.
    Sport Scotland runs three national sports centres:

- Inverclyde – a residential centre for training
- Cumbrae – a water sports centre
- Glenmore Lodge – an outdoor centre.

Sport Scotland developed a strategy called Sport 21 2003–2007 to shape Scotland's sporting future, with the aim of achieving:

- a country where sport is more widely available to all
- a country where sporting talent is recognised and nurtured
- a country achieving and sustaining world-class performances in sport.

The overall target is to get 60 per cent of adult Scots to participate in sport at least once a week.

The Sports Council for Wales

The Sports Council for Wales (www.sports-council-wales.co.uk) has been in action since 1972 and has its head office at the Welsh Institute of Sport in Cardiff. Its aim is to:

- provide opportunities for everyone to participate and enjoy the benefits of sport, whatever their background or ability
- develop those individuals with potential into competitors who generate national pride through Welsh sporting achievements
- gain international recognition for Wales as a nation with a sporting culture.

In 1999 it published its strategic plan: 'A Strategy for Welsh Sport – Young People First'. The aims of this strategy are:

- the creation of sporting opportunities for children, in schools and in the community
- recruitment and development of coaches, administrators and officials, raising standards of performance and achieving excellence
- the effective distribution of SPORTLOT funds for capital and revenue purposes, addressing issues of inclusion through sport
- increasing participation by women and girls.

Sports Council for Northern Ireland

The aims of the Sports Council for Northern Ireland (www.sportni.net) are to work with partners to:

- increase and sustain committed participation, especially among young people
- raise the standards of sporting excellence and promote the good reputation and efficient administration of sport
- develop the competencies of its staff, who are dedicated to optimising the use of its resources.

National governing bodies

To be recognised as a sport there must be a governing body to control the activities of the participants involved in that sport. Governing bodies are found at a local, national and international level.

If we look at football, for example, we find the following structure.

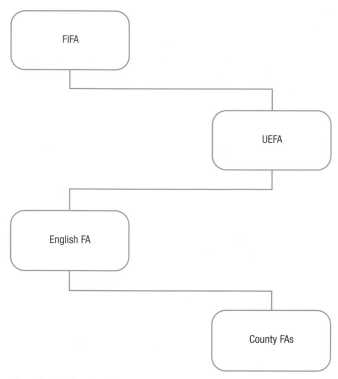

Fig 13.03 Football's governing bodies

Football has an international governing body (FIFA), a European governing body (UEFA), a national governing body (English FA) and county governing bodies (e.g. Herts FA), each of which has different responsibilities. You will find similar structures in all sports.

The roles of governing bodies are as follows:

- setting rules for the sport
- implementing the rules of the sport
- changing the rules of the sport
- finding ways of improving the sport through technology
- providing officials for matches
- organising competitions
- providing codes of conduct for players
- disciplining players who break the rules or codes of conduct
- fining or banning offending players
- providing a system of drug testing
- finding sponsorship for events and competitions
- selling the rights to show the sport on television
- raising money for the sport
- managing and developing the sport.

LEARNER ACTIVITY National governing bodies

In groups of two go to the library and find out three recent occasions when a national governing body has intervened in a sport in some way.

The Sports industry in the UK

The scale of the sports industry

In order to look at the economic importance of sport we need to examine the following factors:

- participation rates in sport
- consumer spending on sport
- employment in sport.

Participation in sport

Sport England has been looking at participation rates by area in a survey called 'The Active People Survey', published in December 2006. The results can be found on the Sport England website.

Research was done by Mori using a questionnaire. This revealed the percentage of adults participating in at least 30 minutes' moderate-intensity sport and recreation (including walking) on three or more days a week. A sample of the results is reproduced here as Table 13.01.

LEARNER ACTIVITY Active People Survey

- Go to the Sport England website and access the findings of the Active People research.
- Find out the number of people participating in sport in your region.
- Choose eight other areas from around the country and find out the participation rates in these areas.
- Compare them to the results for your area and write down three reasons why the results from your area are higher or lower than those from the other areas.

Table 13.01 Regional participation in sport

Area	% of adults participating in sport
Birmingham	20.1
Boston	11.2
City of London	19.5
Leeds	15.8
Liverpool	16
Manchester	22.2
Norwich	23.9
North Devon	21.5
Oxford	20.5
Sheffield	18.2
Southampton	18.2
Swindon	14.7
Watford	20.0

(Sports Council, 2006)

Consumer spending on sport

A key indicator of the value of an activity is its contribution to the economy. Table 13.02 shows the expenditure on sports participation and sports goods across three years.

These figures show the considerable worth of sport to the economy without looking at the value of sporting success. The figures show an increase in expenditure on sport of 31 per cent over a six-year period with a huge leap in the amount of money created by cable and satellite TV, plus the effect of the National Lottery on spending on football pools.

Employment in sport

In 2001 there were almost half a million people employed in the sports industry in Britain in the sectors listed in Tables 13.03, 13.04 and 13.05.

Table 13.02 Consumer expenditure on sport-related goods and services (£ million)

Category	1995	1998	2001
Participation sport (subs and fees)	2,060.29	2,541.93	3,663.39
Clothing sales	1,429.61	1,821.91	1,996.00
Footwear sales	898.00	1,049.00	1,059.00
Sports goods	707.45	852.95	1,287.16
TV, rental, cable and satellite subscriptions	692.37	1,212.13	1,656.21
Gambling (horse racing)	1,553.16	1,622.65	1,793.16
Gambling (pools)	469.30	166.70	74.80
Other consumer spending	2,470.32	3,150.66	3,447.26
Total	**10,278.50**	**12,417.93**	**14,979.98**

(Sports Council, 2004)

Table 13.03 Private-sector employment in sport

	Employment in '000s
Spectator clubs	41.94
Participation clubs	15.33
Retailers	80.84
Manufacturing	11.84
TV and radio	12.65
Subtotal	*162.59*
Voluntary sport	60.47
Commercial non-sport	157.92
Subtotal	*218.39*

(Sports Council, 2004)

Table 13.04 Public sector (central government)

	Employment in '000s
Transport	0.03
Administration	1.62
Subtotal	*1.65*

(Sports Council, 2004)

Table 13.05 Public sector (local government)

	Employment in '000s
Sports facilities	35.76
Education	25.16
Transport/police	6.13
Subtotal	*67.04*
Total for all sectors	*449.658*

(Sports Council, 2004)

Structure of the sports industry

When we look at provision for sport we look at three things:

- who provides the money to fund the sports
- why they provide this money
- what sports they provide for.

Sports provision is provided by three very different sectors (see Fig 13.04).

What do these mean?

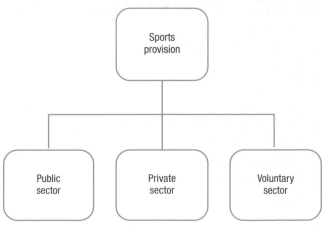

Fig 13.04 Sports provision

- Public sector: this is money spent by the government on sport. Public means the money is raised by charging the general public tax and then this money is invested in sport.
- Private sector: this means that money is invested by private individuals to provide sports facilities. These individuals invest their own money with the hope of making a profit for themselves.
- Voluntary sector: this means that sport is run and funded by volunteers to provide sporting opportunities for other people with the same interests. They do not want to make profit – they just want to play sport.

Public sector

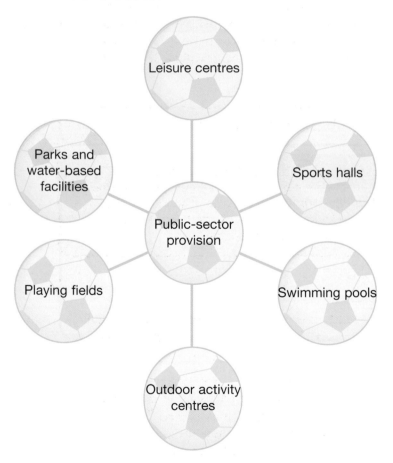

Fig 13.05 Public-sector provision

You can identify public-sector facilities by the following.

- They are funded by money from the local authority.
- They are large in size.

- They are usually named after the town, city or area.
- They are priced to be available to everyone rather than to exclude people.
- They offer facilities for team and individual sports.
- Their facilities offer sports opportunities rather than comfort or luxury.
- The people who work there are employed by the local authority.
- They often receive grants from Sport England or the national governing bodies of sport.

Public-sector facilities are provided by local authorities with the aim of offering people a positive activity to do in their leisure time. These facilities often lose money as they do not charge enough money for entrance or membership to make a profit. This is not important because their priority is to improve the quality of people's lives and offer them the benefits of taking part in sport.

Private sector

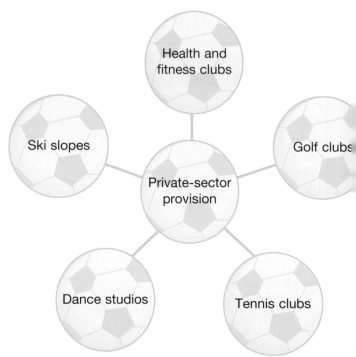

Fig 13.06 Private-sector provision

You can recognise private-sector facilities by the following.

- They are usually named after a person or given an attractive name.
- They mainly provide for individual sports.

- They offer exclusive memberships which are paid monthly or yearly.
- They are often expensive to join.
- They tend to be plush and luxurious.
- They are aimed at certain groups of people rather than the general public.

There are several large chains of health and fitness clubs in Britain which meet all these criteria. David Lloyd Leisure, Cannons, Next Generation, Esporta and Virgin Active clubs would all fit. These companies are interested in providing for sports and physical recreation with the aim of making money for the individuals or shareholders who have invested their money. As a result their membership fees are high to attract the more wealthy people. Their facilities are also more luxurious to attract these types of people and aim to keep them as members.

Voluntary sector

The voluntary sector includes sports clubs, which offer opportunities to play competitive sport.

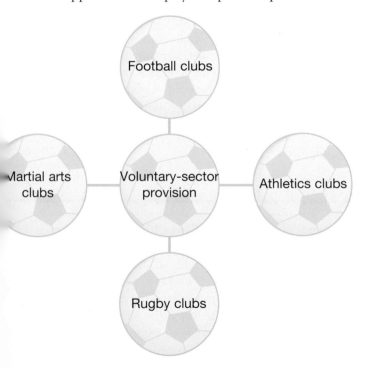

Fig 13.07 Voluntary-sector provision

You can identify voluntary-sector clubs by the following.

- They provide for competitive sports.
- They offer opportunities for only one sport.

- They are funded by members on a yearly membership basis and charge fees for individual matches as well.
- They rarely own their own facilities and hire facilities from the public sector.
- They may receive sponsorship from local businesses.
- They are managed by a committee voted for by the members.
- They are usually named after their town or city.
- They are not trying to make a profit.
- They have to be affiliated through the national governing body.

In summary, voluntary-sector clubs are funded and run by members for the benefit of all the members, with the aim of providing opportunities to be involved in sport on a competitive level. If you look at the sports you are involved in outside school or college it is very likely that it will be through the voluntary sector.

LEARNER ACTIVITY Local sports facilities

In groups of four or five complete a brainstorming session of all the sports facilities you have in your local area. Then, using the criteria set out above, divide them into public, private or voluntary sector.

Provision levels of sport

To have an organised and meaningful approach to sports provision we can see provision as addressing two areas:

- **sports development** – giving people the opportunity to learn the basics of sports and sports skills, and the opportunity to teach sports.
- **sports equity** – to examine the inequalities in sport and develop strategies to give people equal opportunity to participate in sport regardless of race, age, gender or ability.

Sport England has developed a sports development continuum, as follows.

- **Foundation:** learning and understanding basic movement skills and developing a positive attitude to physical activity.

- **Participation**: taking part in sport for a range of reasons – health, fitness and social.
- **Performance**: improving standards of performance through coaching, competition and training.
- **Excellence**: reaching national standards of performance.

How contemporary issues affect sport

The world of sport is an ever changing one. Every week there are new sets of results and every week it seems there are new issues that emerge. Take a look at the back (and front!) pages of any newspaper and you will find the latest scandal being dissected before an ever information-hungry public. When an athlete takes a banned substance or a football manager takes a bung, sport suffers and the authorities have to act if they want to maintain their credibility. To understand how contemporary issues affect sport we need to look at each one in turn and discuss the negative and positive aspects that arise.

Media

'The media' refers to the means of communication that reach large numbers of people. The happenings in sport are reported through a variety of media:

- newspapers
- television
- radio
- internet
- films
- books
- magazines
- teletext services.
- mobile phones.

Local and national press

Each area in the UK has its own local newspaper. The local newspaper has a small circulation compared with the national newspaper and its aim is to provide local information only. It will therefore print only local sports stories. It will give reports on the best local teams and will cover national news only if there is a local angle, such as 'Local girl wins national judo championships'. In the same way, national

newspapers report world events primarily if there is a UK angle, such as 'England win 2006 Women's World Team Squash Championship'.

It is the editors who make decisions about what news we receive. They decide which news is most important and which news is most relevant. An editor will always have one eye on whether people will be interested in a particular story and if they can relate to it.

Television

Television is the most important aspect of the media in sport. Since the first televised World Cup in football in 1970 to the Sky and Setanta deal with the Premiership to pay £1.7 billion for three years from 2007/8 it has often been about money. TV companies are prepared to pay high prices for the rights to show the best sporting events. The largest events are the FIFA World Cup, the Olympics and the Superbowl. Some 800 million people worldwide watch the Superbowl each year. And the Superbowl viewing figures occupy nine out of the ten most watched sporting events on television in the USA. Only the women's figure skating from the 1994 Winter Olympics can make it into the list, at number 10! With these types of viewing figures the TV networks are able to hike up their advertising rates and, at their peak in 2000, 30 seconds of airtime during the Superbowl could cost US$2.5 million!

In the UK, 20.4 million viewers tuned in to watch Italy win the 2006 World Cup final. During the match this figure dropped to as low as 13.6 million. But for the penalty shootout it rose back to the peak with 17 million watching BBC and 3.4 million watching ITV. In contrast, the Wimbledon men's tennis final which was shown earlier had an audience of 7.1 million on BBC watching Roger Federer take the title. The average Premiership football game shown on Sky TV in 2006 attracted audiences of 1.25 million. Pay-per-view games in 2006 attracted audiences of 215,000. The average crowd at a Premiership football match in 2006 was 34,000. In 2001 the Office for National Statistics reported that UK children aged between six and sixteen watch three hours of TV per day compared with two hours elsewhere in Europe.

Table 13.06 shows the viewing figures for one week in September 2006. It shows how terrestrial channels (BBC1 and 2, ITV, Channel 4 and five) still dominate overall viewing figures, but that channels like Sky Sports 1 have a relatively large share of viewers considering they show only sports programmes.

What is the effect of the media on sport? Table 13.07 lists some of the positive and negative effects.

Sport is presented on television in a 'mediated' form, meaning that television professionals have made decisions about how the sport is presented. It is usually done to make the sports event more attractive to the floating viewer. They know that the devoted sports fans will watch anyway, so they are seeking to attract the attention of viewers who are less committed to the sport, but may enjoy the sense of occasion. As a result, television changes sport to maximise its attractiveness and its number of viewers.

Table 13.06 Hours of viewing, share of audience and reach – multi-channel homes: including timeshift (week ending 24 September 2006)

Channel	Average daily reach		Weekly reach		Average weekly viewing	Share
	'000s	%	'000s	%	Hrs:mins per person	%
ALL/ANY TV	32,101	72.9	40,913	92.9	23:37	100.0
BBC1 (incl. Breakfast News)	20,232	46.0	35,294	80.2	4:33	19.2
BBC2	10,338	23.5	26,967	61.2	1:31	6.4
TOTAL BBC1/BBC2	22,567	51.3	36,815	83.6	6:04	25.7
ITV (incl. GMTV)	17,131	38.9	32,695	74.3	4:21	18.4
CHANNEL 4/S4C	11,037	25.1	28,137	63.9	1:39	7.0
five	7,502	17.0	22,632	51.4	1:05	4.6
TOTAL/ANY COMM. TERR. TV	22,534	51.2	37,056	84.2	7:05	30.0
Total terrestrial	27,764	63.1	39,195	89.0	13:09	55.7
Sky One	2,757	6.3	9,935	22.6	0:22	1.6
Sky Two	1,239	2.8	5,721	13.0	0:08	0.6
Sky Three	1,391	3.2	6,367	14.5	0:07	0.5
Sky News	1,367	3.1	4,591	10.4	0:07	0.5
Sky Sports 1	2,033	4.6	6,109	13.9	0:34	2.4
Sky Sports 2	1,752	4.0	5,795	13.2	0:18	1.3
Sky Sports 3	598	1.4	2,375	5.4	0:05	0.3
Sky Sports News	1,832	4.2	5,902	13.4	0:09	0.6
Sky Premiership Plus	82	0.2	523	1.2	0:01	0.1
Sky Sports Extra	264	0.6	1,329	3.0	0:02	0.1
All Sky Sports	4,284	9.7	10,625	24.1	1:08	4.0

(Broadcasters' Audience Research Board Ltd, 2006)

Table 13.07 Positive and negative effects of the media on sport

Positive	Negative
● More participation may result from the desire to emulate the superstars	● Less participation as people become couch potatoes, watching too much TV
● Increased amount of money in the sport which can go to help grassroots	● The majority of the money goes to players/clubs – very little goes to grassroots
● Allows the players to be full-time professionals and so raises standards	● Only certain sports get enough TV money to allow them to be professional
● Clubs can provide better facilities/equipment/players	● The popular/successful clubs get richer and the poor clubs remain poor
● Positive role models can promote good behaviour	● Negative role models can promote poor behaviour
● Can bring different ethnic groups together – e.g. the multi-ethnic French World Cup squads in 1998 and 2006	● Increased media hype may lead to nationalism and 'anti' feelings towards others

The effects of increasing television coverage of sport are as follows.

● **Money**: increased sums of money come into the sport from television companies who pay for the rights to broadcast the sports. Also, sponsors become more willing to spend more money on sponsoring sport as they know it will receive national attention. Hence, sports' finances receive a boost on two fronts, and this enables them to spend more money on players, players' wages and stadiums. The development of football in the 1990s was based on increased income from television companies and firms offering sponsorship. This extra income enabled the owners of the clubs to spend money on players from overseas, who were superstars of the sport. In turn this makes the sport more attractive to the viewers, who are willing to pay more to watch sport on television and at the grounds. For world events the risks can be great as evidenced by some Olympics which did not turn a profit, but the earnings can also be huge. The 2006 World Cup made profits of £741 million, with the cost of staging the event outstripped by sales of tickets, merchandising, sponsorship and media rights.

● **Changes in the rules of the game**: in order to make sports more attractive, the rules can be amended to make the action faster or to penalise negative play. In Rugby Union the points for a try rose from four to five, bonus points are given to teams scoring four or more tries and losing by fewer than five

points. One-day cricket has punished bowlers delivering no balls by offering batsmen a free hit on the next delivery from which they cannot be out. In hockey the offside rule was changed and in netball players no longer have to wait for the umpire's whistle to restart play.

● **Changes in the presentation of the sport**: as an example, cricket authorities addressed the problem of low attendances by introducing day–night cricket matches, which start at around 4.00 p.m. and run until around 10.30 p.m. This caters for people who are at work during the day, but are keen to watch a match in the evening. The matches themselves have been organised as part of family entertainment, where the players are introduced by music, and there is additional entertainment such as firework displays, bouncy castles and barbecues on offer. To make the game look more spectacular, the players wear coloured clothing and use a white ball with black stumps. More recently the introduction of 20/20 games has proved most popular, with cricket gaining some of its largest attendances for this fast-paced game, although its detractors argue that it bears no resemblance to the normal game of cricket and shouldn't be taken seriously.

● **Changes in starting times**: the start times of matches are regularly changed to suit the needs of the television audience. Football games may kick off any time between 11.00 a.m. and 10.00 p.m., depending on where the game is played and when the audience is available. This is great for the television viewers, but comes at a high cost to the spectators at the game, who become very inconvenienced. Televised games on a Sunday are shown at 4.00 p.m. and not 3.00 p.m. after an enforced change one week attracted a much larger audience. The Monday-night games are an attempt to generate the sort of audience loyalty seen in the USA where Monday-night football is watched religiously.

- **Sponsorship**: in the world of corporate sponsorship, how a brand performs off the pitch is just as important as how the players perform on the pitch. FIFA uses Sponsorship Intelligence, a company that researches the impact of events such as the 2006 World Cup. At this event it claims that Coca-Cola 'won the World Cup' in terms of successful promotion. Its research showed that out of the 15 World Cup sponsors the best remembered was Coca-Cola, something it says might be attributed to that company's support of the World Cup since Mexico 1970.

Other forms of media coverage

Radio is an increasingly popular medium and due to the wealth of radio stations on air, it is possible to devote stations entirely to sports coverage. BBC Radio Five Live is a current affairs and sports station that offers a viable alternative to television through its in-depth coverage.

Books are increasingly becoming an important source of media coverage, and they have the advantage of interpreting events we may not have fully understood at the time. Recently, Wayne Rooney signed a £5 million deal plus royalties to write five books over the next 12 years: a good example of how a player can make money off the field.

Visit any large newsagents and you will see the wide array of **sports magazines** available. The internet has also become a rich source of information for people following sports, and there is a vast number of websites dedicated to sport in general and to individual sports. The problem has been that much information has appeared in an unedited, unmediated format and often reflects the views of a minority.

Deviance

Deviance is a form of behaviour which is considered to violate society's norms and therefore to be

unacceptable. In sport this manifests itself in a number of ways such as drugs, gamesmanship and violence. A sportsperson can exhibit positive and negative deviance.

Positive deviance equals over-commitment. For example, over-training or playing on through injury and pain and much of the 'no pain no gain' philosophy supports this behaviour. In many sports we applaud the images of athletes covered in blood but carrying on for their country.

Negative deviance equals either a desperate or calculated breaking of the rules or norms. This is the more recognisable side of deviance – e.g. using banned substances to win a race.

Drugs in sport

The most notorious drug cheat was probably Canadian sprinter Ben Johnson, who tested positive at the 1988 Seoul Olympics for an anabolic steroid called stanozolol. Johnson had been beaten by his nearest rival, Carl Lewis, about a month before in an emphatic manner. When the Olympic 100 m final came around, Johnson led from gun to finish and won easily in a new world record time of 9.79 seconds. Two days later he tested positive for drugs and was stripped of his medal and world record. It was common knowledge that Johnson had been using illicit drugs for years, but he maintains that the drug he was using was not stanozolol and that he had been set up.

But the problem hasn't gone away. Statistically speaking, Athens 2004 was twice as bad as the previous worst Olympic Games for doping offences. By the time the flame was extinguished in the Olympic Stadium, 24 doping violations had been uncovered. That is double the previous highest number of 12 at Los Angeles in 1984.

More recently we have seen sprinter Justin Gatlin, 100 m world record holder, testing positive for elevated levels of testosterone. And in the UK Dwain Chambers, the 25-year old European 100 m champion and record holder, was the first athlete in the world to be punished for taking tetrahydrogestrinone (THG), a previously undetectable steroid. Chambers' positive test caused his 4 × 100 m team to be stripped of their European gold in 2002 and silver in the World Championships in 2003. When he had served his ban and was reinstated in the 4 × 100 m team for the European Championships in 2006 and the team won gold again, Darren Campbell, who had lost both

LEARNER ACTIVITY Classification of drugs

To understand more about drugs, research the effects of drugs by completing the following table.

Name of drug	What they do	Sports associated	Side effects
Anabolic steroids			
Stimulants			
Narcotic analgesics			
Peptide hormones			
Blood doping			
Beta blockers			
Diuretics			

previous medals because of Dwain Chambers, refused to take part in the lap of honour. Under British Olympic Association rules Dwain Chambers can never compete at the Olympics for Team GB as it has imposed its own life ban for anyone who fails a drug test.

The World Anti-Doping Agency

The World Anti-Doping Agency (WADA) (www.wada-ama.org) has the following mission statement:

WADA is the international independent organization created in 1999 to promote, coordinate, and monitor the fight against doping in sport in all its forms. Composed and funded equally by the sports movement and governments of the world, WADA coordinated the development and implementation of the World Anti-Doping Code (Code), the document harmonizing anti-doping policies in all sports and all countries.

LEARNER ACTIVITY Drug use in sport

Think about the following statements and then decide whether you agree or disagree with each one.

		Agree	Disagree
1	Drug use in sport gives users an unfair advantage.	☐	☐
2	Sports are natural and drug use is unnatural.	☐	☐
3	Morally the issue of drug use in sport is clear-cut – the use of drugs is always wrong.	☐	☐
4	Sport is a healthy activity and should not be polluted by products that will potentially damage health.	☐	☐
5	There are no good reasons why athletes should use drugs.	☐	☐
6	Drugs are taken by choice and users should be severely punished.	☐	☐
7	If athletes relied more on the advice of doctors there would be less drug taking in sport.	☐	☐
8	Sporting bodies like the IOC, Sports Council and national governing bodies are doing everything they can to eliminate drug use in sport.	☐	☐

Gamesmanship

We often talk about sports performers playing fairly, but find it hard to define what playing fairly is. Is a player who appeals for every decision playing fairly or trying to influence the referee? Some definitions may help:

Gamesmanship: not playing within the unwritten rules of the game and destroying the ethics, spirit, goodwill, fairness, etc.
Letter of the game: written rules of play.
Spirit of the game: playing fairly and abiding by unwritten rules, and expressing the correct attitudes and ethics of the game.
Sportsmanship: playing within both the written and unwritten rules.

LEARNER ACTIVITY

Look at the examples below and think about how each behaviour fits into the definitions above:

- kicking the ball off the pitch when the opposition has an injury
- not 'walking' in cricket
- shaking hands with the opposition at the end of the game
- deliberately punching an opponent in a scrum
- pretending something has distracted you when your opponent is about to serve
- clapping someone who makes a century in cricket
- arguing with the referee after a decision has been made
- faking an injury to get another player booked
- taking a dive
- lending your opponents a practice ball to warm up with
- taking a banned substance.

As sport has become increasingly pressured with a 'win at all costs' approach taking over from the old ideals of athleticism (playing fairly as an amateur), so we have seen a rise in gamesmanship. Much sport is professional and the rewards for winning are great. There is pressure from fans, managers and, in world competitions, the nation, all desperate for a win. It is becoming less and less likely to find role models who will not compromise their ethical stance.

Sports initiatives

Sport has often been used as a power for good. It has been argued that sport is good for society and has a positive influence. For example, those who believe it is functional claim it can increase participation, reduce crime and anti-social behaviour, and improve the nation's health. The government certainly subscribes to this view. It spends millions each year to provide sport and leisure opportunities for all and is particularly interested in deprived areas or those with high incidences of crime. There are a number of anti-crime initiatives the government has introduced which use sport as a vehicle for providing an alternative to committing crime. Sport England (which receives money from government funds) has a representative within the Home Office who has been working closely with the Community Cohesion Unit to show how sport can unite communities, especially in deprived areas.

Social exclusion

To understand social exclusion it helps to look at occupations and income. Type of employment and income can be considered together as one is dependent on the other. This is addressed further in the next section.

Health

Sport England also believes it can make an important contribution to improving health and reducing the estimated £8.2 billion cost of inactivity to the NHS. The 'Everyday Sport' physical activity campaign encourages even the most inactive people to incorporate a little more activity into their daily lives, taking small steps that can make a big difference – from taking the stairs instead of the lift or getting off the bus a stop early, to joining a sports club. Other initiatives include 'Sporting Champions', a scheme that takes sports stars into schools and communities to inspire young people about sport.

Racism

If we look at Britain as a whole, we can see that some sports are more popular in some areas and less popular in others. One of the major factors influencing the sports we play is where we are brought up. For example, rugby league is more prevalent in the north of England and rugby union in the south of England and Wales. Scotland has its own sports, such as skiing, curling and its Highland Games, and Ireland has sports such as hurling and Gaelic football.

Britain has developed into a multi-racial society. Many members of the population are from African-Caribbean or various Asian and European backgrounds. Many were initially drawn to Britain by the need for jobs during the 1950s.

Some ethnic groups choose to retain separate cultural identities within British society, but black sportspeople participate successfully in most sports in Britain. However, racism does still occur in British sport, although it is not usually the overt racism that black footballers suffered in the 1980s and early 1990s.

> **definition**
>
> **Race:** the physical characteristics of a person.
> **Ethnicity:** the cultural adherence of a person or group, characterised by their customs and habits (religious beliefs, diet, clothing, leisure activities and lifestyle).

Racism describes the oppression of a person or group by another person or group on the grounds of physical differences. Racism in British sport occurs in two ways, through racial stereotyping and stacking.

- **Stereotyping:** historically, racial discrimination has excluded black people from achieving in the workplace, so many black people entered sport as an arena where they could improve their life chances. Thus, many young black people spent more time improving their sporting ability at the cost of their academic abilities. This produced two stereotypes:
  - black people are naturally good at sport
  - black people are not intelligent.
- **Stacking:** black people tend to be guided into certain sports and certain positions within teams. They tend to predominate in sports such as track and field athletics, football, basketball and boxing. These sports tend to be inexpensive, requiring little specialist equipment, and can be practised relatively cheaply. Within these sports black people tend to dominate in certain positions or events, usually those requiring physical rather than intellectual or decision-making qualities, such as wingers in rugby rather than positions of centrality.

This stacking comes from a stereotype that black people have a natural, genetic ability to be quick and powerful, but lack high intellectual abilities. This stereotype has in the past been perpetuated by teachers and coaches of sports who, when choosing teams, place black people in a position or an event because they believe all black people are fast and powerful.

More recently black and Asian players have broken down these stereotypes. In football in the 1980s and 1990s the majority of black players were forwards. That stereotype no longer exists with players like Rio Ferdinand and Ashley Cole dominating in their defensive positions. However, an Asian football star is yet to emerge in the England football team.

> **LEARNER ACTIVITY** Stacking and stereotyping
>
> How does racism through stacking and stereotyping occur in the following sports in Britain?
>
> | cricket | athletics |
> | tennis | swimming |
> | golf | rugby |

Racism has been tackled on the football terraces under the Football Offences Act 1991, which makes it illegal to take part in racist chanting. An arrest can be made only if there are one or more people chanting and if the chants are causing distress to the person they are aimed at.

The 'Kick it Out' campaign to combat racism in British football has been fairly successful and it is now less of an issue. However, there are constant allegations of racism against black players in British teams when they are involved in international competitions.

This is a very difficult area of sport to debate (see the 'Learner activity' on the opposite page). Many arguments can be made on each side. However, it is important to remember that social influences are as strong as other factors. Peer pressure, role models, historical success and society's norms all exert big pressures on young people looking for a sport and an identity. Concepts such as 'white flight' – the avoidance of seemingly black-dominated sports such as sprinting, may occur. In the same way financial implications may simply be at the root of it all. There is no one answer and looking for a simple 'yes' or 'no' is not the way to answer this question. You might like

LEARNER ACTIVITY Black athletes debate

Debate the following issue in a group: Are black athletes superior in sport?

Here are some points to help you discuss the question. Do some research and see if you can find some more.

For:

● the black population in Britain is approximately 5 per cent and yet 40 per cent of English Premiership players are black
● nearly every world record in athletics track events is held by an athlete of African origin, and in the Athens 2004 Olympics in the 100 m final there was not a single white competitor
● the vast majority of heavyweight boxing champions have been black.

Against:

● there is no scientific research that has been able to prove any genetic superiority
● many sprint events (such as swimming 50 m freestyle) are dominated by white athletes
● many sports, like tennis, are dominated by white players in the UK.

to look at the question in the activity again and think about how difficult it is to generalise about an entire population of people.

Sexism

Before starting a discussion of the relationship between sex and sports participation it is useful to examine the definitions of the terms we will use.

> **definition**
>
> **Sex:** the biological and therefore genetic differences between males and females.
> **Gender:** the learned social and cultural differences between males and females, in terms of their habits, personality and behaviour.

Here is a comparison of men's and women's sport (General Household Survey figures, 1996):

● 71 per cent of men participate in sport, compared with 57 per cent of women
● 42 per cent of men participate in outdoor sports, compared with 24 per cent of women
● twice as many men as women watch sport
● there are very few female professionals as compared with men
● the men's singles prize money at Wimbledon 2006 was £655,000 and the women's £625,000
● there are few women in administrative positions in sport; IOC members for GBR are HRH The Princess Royal, Craig Reedie, Matthew Pinsent and Phil Craven

● the history and growth of sport is documented mainly in terms of the development of male sport
● sport in the media is dominated by male sport.

> **definition**
>
> **Sexism:** sexism means different things to different people. The following definition gives us a framework to work within:
> 'Sexism is a practice based on the ideology that men are superior to women. The ideology is expressed through a system of prejudice and discrimination that seeks to control and dominate women. It is systematically embodied in the structures and organisations of that society.' (Hargreaves, 1994)

Here are some possible reasons why women's participation rates are lower than men's.

● Historically, women in partnerships with men have taken on domestic responsibilities and thus any sport is fitted in between responsibilities of childcare, cooking, working, cleaning, washing, and so on. Sport can be time-consuming and costly, especially if childcare is needed.
● Class inequalities accentuate gender inequalities. Middle-class women have much higher participation rates than working-class women, as they typically have more money and access to private transport. The fitness boom has mostly benefited middle-class women.
● The major biological difference between men and women is that women can bear children and this has psychological and social repercussions. Women

are allocated to reproductive, mothering and childcare roles, which limit the time and opportunity they have for sports activities. However, women are waiting longer now before having a family and this has improved their situation. Also, gender equality has meant that childcare and nurturing roles are more commonly shared between partners.

- Every society has a set of beliefs and values that dictate what is acceptable behaviour for women (and men) in all spheres of their lives, and sport is included in these values. Many people consider that some sporting activities can induce masculine traits in women, especially in competitive sports. Strong opinions are held as to what sports are acceptable or unacceptable for girls or women. Even strong peer pressure may prevent women from considering certain sports.

The conventional image of sport is based on chauvinistic values and male identity formation. Sport is the arena for the celebration of masculinity. To be successful at sport you need to show skill, power, muscularity, competitiveness, aggression, assertiveness and courage. To be successful at sport is to be successful as a man, and to be uninterested or not talented is to be less of a man.

However, more recently body image has changed to accept a fitter, stronger female. Successful sportswomen have broken the old stereotypes and fashion has changed to support the image of a toned body as opposed to a flabby unfit one. Of course, there is also the argument that successful female athletes are a threat to the male-dominated world of sport. The reticence of males towards female sport could be simply viewed as a threat to male hegemony.

What other reason could the British Board of Boxing Control (BBBC) have for not sanctioning women's professional boxing for so long? Its arguments at the time were based on possible breast cancer in female boxers and a weakened state during a woman's period – none of the potential brain damage arguments that all boxers face. It was not until 1998 when the Equal Opportunities Commission backed Jane Couch (world champion at the time) that the BBBC was forced to allow her to fight professionally. Then there was the landmark case of Theresa Bennett, an 11 year old who won her county court case to play alongside boys in her local football team, only to have the FA go against the wishes of her club and have the decision overturned at the Court of Appeal.

LEARNER ACTIVITY
Female participation

Discuss the following questions with a partner.

- Which sports are regarded as socially acceptable for females?
- Which sports are not so socially acceptable for women, and may conflict with the behaviour expected of them?

It could be argued that to be successful at sport a woman must show masculine traits that contrast with the so-called feminine traits of agility, balance, flexibility, coordination and gentleness. Successful sportswomen not only have to be exceptional athletes, they also have to retain their femininity.

Commercialisation of sport

Commercialisation refers to the practice of applying business principles to sport. The advantages and disadvantages of commercialisation are outlined in Table 13.08.

Advertising

This is the way a company makes itself known to the public. In sport this can be through using advertising boards around stadiums, placing an advert in the programme, TV commercials using sport stars, etc. Sponsorship, merchandising and endorsement all act as types of advertising.

Sponsorship

An agreement between a company and a team/governing body/stadium/competition. The company agrees to pay a certain amount to have its logo appear on kit or merchandising.

Merchandising

The sale of goods that are linked to the club, player or competition. Usually this is replica kits, flags, scarves, stickers, etc.

Table 13.08 The advantages and disadvantages of commercialisation

Advantages	Disadvantages
Sponsorship can help an event that would otherwise not happen without the money provided	The event becomes reliant on the sponsors and would not happen if they pulled out
Endorsements can help boost a performer's wages and sales of a product	The product may be unethical; the performer may not actually wish to use the product; the company may drop a performer who behaves badly or underperforms
Merchandising can help a club provide better facilities and buy better players	The fans could feel like they are being cheated, especially when shirts constantly change and prices are too high
Advertising can be a way for a performer to make extra income or back a worthy cause such as a charity	It can appear the performer has 'sold out', or may seem like they are not taking their sport seriously enough

Endorsement

When a player promotes the use of a product. Companies pay well for a sports star to say their product is worth buying.

LEARNER ACTIVITY
Commercialisation of sport

List as many examples of commercialisation of sport as you can think of.

Commercialised sports do not work in all societies. They are predominantly found in developed societies where people have enough free time to be involved in watching sport, disposable income to spend on sport and means of private transport to travel to the venues.

Education and sport in schools

Sport in schools has often been controversial. When working-class schools first started in the 1870s children were drilled in military fashion so that they could be prepared for war. More recent controversy in the 1980s saw teacher strikes over pay lead to a withdrawal of teacher support for after-school sports fixtures when their pay demands were not met. When the National Curriculum started in the early 1990s the suggestion was that all school children should receive two hours of PE per week, but in reality many schools provided less. Alongside this in the 1990s was the scandal of many schools selling off their playing fields for redevelopment.

The government response in the mid-1990s was a report called 'Raising the Game', which promised funding and increased status for schools that could persuade their teachers to provide more after-school activities and raise money for new facilities. The result was Sportsmark status for many schools and new specialist sports colleges with PE teachers taking on new roles such as school sports coordinators. The future for schools PE in the UK will no doubt centre on the 2012 London Olympics. The first response to this has been the proposal for school 'Olympics' to be held across the country each year in the run-up to 2012.

Other issues centre on how we do things in the UK. For example, countries like Australia have talent identification programmes in schools, which test students and assess their suitability for different sports. In this way they have encouraged a number of school children to take up events they would previously not have thought of, such as rowing. In the UK we have been accused of having a laissez-faire approach to identifying talent. Although some might argue that this allows us to value all equally.

Child protection

Following a number of high-profile child abuse cases involving sports coaches, new legislation has been put in place. All people working with children must be police-checked for any convictions involving children, and child protection training is now mandatory on most coaching courses.

LEARNER ACTIVITY
Contemporary issues

- Write a report that provides an in-depth understanding of the effects of four contemporary issues in sport.
- Try to look at both sides of the argument for each issue.
- Provide further examples to back up your arguments.

Evaluation of contemporary issues

- Extend your report by evaluating the importance of the arguments you have formulated in your report.
- Make suggestions on the potential impact of each issue.
- Draw conclusions on the outcomes of each issue, both actual and perceived.

Cultural influences and barriers that affect participation

While we can see that sport benefits people and fulfils needs in their lives it is important to point out that not all people have an equal access to sporting opportunities.

LEARNER ACTIVITY Barriers to sport participation

Ask yourself the following questions and then in groups discuss your answers and why that is the case.

- Is sport played by men and women in the same numbers?
- How many black British golfers do you see?
- Why are there lots of Asian cricketers but very few Asian rugby players?
- Why do British tennis players tend to be from wealthy families?

These may be issues you take for granted, but in reality these differences exist because of the way our society is organised and how it has developed. A range of factors affect participation in sport, including:

- gender
- ethnic origin
- age
- socio-economic classification.

Gender

Statistics prepared by Sport England clearly show that women have lower participation rates than men (see Table 13.09).

With the odd exception, we can clearly see that men are more active than women. The figures show that as a group 65 per cent of men and 53 per cent of women had participated in at least one sporting activity in the four weeks before the interview. The only discrepancies were in sports such as keep fit and yoga, which traditionally attract more females.

Ethnic origin

Recent statistics have shown a direct relationship between ethnic origin and participation in sport (see Table 13.10).

This and other research shows that:

- white ethnic groups have the highest participation rates
- people of Pakistani origin have the lowest participation rates
- women of Pakistani origin have particularly low rates of participation
- certain ethnic groups are well represented in some sports but very poorly represented in others.

Britain is now regarded as a multiracial society and we must work to meet the needs of all groups. Sports development officers are working hard to offer opportunities to people from all ethnic groups and meet their specific needs – e.g. offering women-only swimming sessions for Muslim women.

Age

Age and also an individual's stage in the life cycle are key factors in influencing the level of participation and also the choice of sports. Younger people tend to

Table 13.09 Percentage of men and women aged 16+ participating in sport in the four weeks before interview

Sport	Men	Women
Walking	34.6	33.7
Swimming	12.3	15.2
Keep fit/yoga	7.1	16.5
Weight training	8.6	3.5
Running	7.1	3.1
Golf	8.3	1.3
Soccer	9.8	0.5
Tennis	2.2	1.6
Badminton	2.2	1.5
Fishing	3.1	0.2

(Sport England, 2002)

choose more physical contact sports such as football and rugby, while older age groups will still be active but in more individual sports with less physical contact (see Table 13.11).

The relationship between participation and age is not always clear-cut, as swimming and keep fit have fairly stable levels of participation across the age groups. Fishing and golf increase slightly with age before falling off again, and soccer and running decline is related to age.

Socio-economic classification

Socio-economic classification is a system of classifying people based on their occupation and thus potential income (see Table 13.12).

Barriers to sports participation

The relationship between gender, ethnicity, age and socio-economic group and sports participation has

Table 13.10 Percentage of adults aged 16+ participating in the four weeks before interview, by ethnic origin

Ethnic group	Participation excluding walking	Participation including walking
White	44.1	59.4
Any minority ethnic group	34.6	45.5
Indian	30.4	46.3
Pakistani/Bangladeshi	21.7	25.9
Black (Caribbean, African, other)	33.2	43.7
Other (Chinese, none of the above)	45.1	56.5

(Sport England, 2002)

Table 13.11 Percentage of adults aged 16+ participating in the four weeks before interview, by age

Sport	16–19	20–24	25–29	30–44	45–59	60–69	70+
Walking	40.7	41.1	42.3	50.5	52.0	46.1	26.8
Swimming	46.2	46.3	47.6	48.2	33.3	19.8	8.1
Keep fit/yoga	29.8	33.2	33.3	27.9	19.8	10.7	6.2
Snooker	42.5	41.3	30.3	19.4	10.7	6.2	3.5
Weight training	18.6	19.8	20.4	12.3	5.6	1.4	0.5
Running	19.7	18.1	18.0	13.9	4.6	1.0	0.2
Golf	14.6	17.4	17.1	14.5	10.9	8.1	4.0
Soccer	33.5	26.1	20.2	10.9	2.1	0.3	0.1
Tennis	24.0	14.7	10.1	8.7	4.8	2.1	0.5
Fishing	8.1	5.2	5.2	6.1	6.3	4.9	1.6
At least one activity	90.1	88.3	88.3	85.1	77.2	64.4	39.4

(Sport England, 2002)

been clearly shown and these could be perceived as barriers to participation. All these under-represented groups have something in common: they all have special requirements. Sport is predominantly marketed at young, white males and this group is well represented in sport. So arrangements have to be made to ensure that sports activities are accessible to all.

There are other barriers which may have to be overcome:

- time
- resources
- fitness levels
- ability
- lifestyle
- medical conditions.

Time

Time is a major reason cited by people as a barrier. There are 24 hours in a day and we have to choose

Table 13.12 Participation in sport, by socio-economic classification

Sport	Large employers/ higher managerial	Higher professional	Lower managerial and professional	Intermediate	Small employers	Lower supervisory and technical	Semi-routine	Routine	Long-term unemployed
Walking	47.1	46.2	41.7	32.7	30.0	29.4	28.5	23.5	19.5
Swimming	24.0	19.9	17.7	13.7	11.9	11.2	8.8	7.8	7.4
Snooker	9.9	9.2	9.6	10.2	9.4	9.1	8.5	7.0	5.5
Keep fit/yoga	20.8	18.3	15.3	14.8	11.1	9.4	7.1	6.3	4.6
Weight training	11.4	8.5	7.3	6.9	5.1	4.0	4.0	2.5	2.0
Running	10.1	8.1	6.6	5.2	3.3	3.4	2.2	2.3	3.2
Golf	9.5	8.4	6.1	4.2	4.8	4.7	3.3	3.8	4.2
Soccer	6.1	5.4	5.5	4.2	4.9	3.6	1.8	1.7	0.0
Tennis	3.1	4.0	2.7	1.8	1.7	0.5	0.8	0.5	1.0
Fishing	1.1	1.1	1.2	1.5	2.5	2.3	1.6	1.5	0.8

(Sport England, 2002)

how to spend them. The management of time involves allocating time for work requirements, family responsibilities, activities for survival, such as eating and washing, sleep and time for relaxation. People need to find activities which fit in with their weekly schedule and put these times into their diary. They can then make arrangements for work and time to fit these activities in.

Resources

Resources include facilities, equipment and clothing. There is an uneven spread of facilities across the UK. Provision is dependent upon location (city or countryside), natural resources (such as water or mountains), the policy of the local authority on spending for sport and the demand from consumers. Equipment and clothing requirements can seriously deter people from sports – for example, the expense of going skiing or playing golf.

Fitness

It is perceived that people who play sport or take exercise are fit and will look down on those who are not. This perception puts people off because they see their current situation as being miles away from where most people are or want to be. It needs to be explained to these people that there are many activities which can be performed at their own pace and as they get fitter they can increase the intensity they work at. Walking would provide adequate exercise for an unfit person and they can then move on to brisk walking, jogging or even running in their own time.

Ability

Not having the required skills and ability is a concern for some people as they do not want to look foolish or show themselves up. It is important that relevant coaching is provided to enable people to acquire the skills needed and develop their ability. This is done through local sports development initiatives and government-sponsored schemes.

Lifestyle

Lifestyle issues, such as stress, smoking, alcohol and drug consumption, place barriers in front of people. All these activities will detract from attempts to do sport because smoking, alcohol and drug use all negatively affect health and make a person feel less likely to want to exercise. Stress and stressful situations mean a

person is focusing on other issues and cannot contemplate playing a sport or taking exercise. These lifestyle issues need to be dealt with before a person can consider playing sport regularly and being successful.

Medical conditions

These are a serious consideration in a person playing sport, as if a person exercises inappropriately with a medical condition it can make the condition worse; in the case of heart disease it may lead to their death. Having said that, there is virtually no medical condition which does not benefit or improve through regular exercise. Before a person plays sport or exercises they will be screened by a qualified person and then appropriate interventions need to be put in place to ensure the person takes part in the activity safely.

Strategies and initiatives

Sport England and local authorities are well aware of the problems faced by people from different cultures and the barriers faced by the general population. Since its inception in 1972 the Sports Council (now Sport England) has run a series of campaigns which started with 'Sport for All' and included 'Ever thought of sport?' and '50+ and all to play for'. These campaigns were aimed at specific groups with low participation rates, such as women and older people.

Recent strategies have included:

- Game Plan
- Every Child Matters
- Sporting Equals
- TASS
- Plan for Sport 2001
- Active Sports
- Sportsmark.

Game Plan

Game Plan was published in December 2002 to present the government's vision for sport up to 2020 and the strategy to deliver this vision. It includes strategies for developing excellence in performance and promoting mass participation.

Every Child Matters

Every Child Matters is a national policy which is to be achieved through local initiatives. The aim is for school provision to improve the children's attainment and life chances involving the actions of pupils, parents, teachers and governors. Sport and leisure activities are a part of this scheme by using school facilities to deliver courses.

Sporting Equals

Sporting Equals is a strategy to promote racial equality in sport with the specific aims of developing a society where:

- people from minority ethnic groups can influence and participate equally in sport at all levels, as players, officials, coaches, administrators, volunteers and decision-makers, working with partners to develop awareness and understanding of racial equality issues that impact on sport
- governors and providers of sport recognise and value a fully integrated and inclusive society
- a sporting environment is established where cultural diversity is recognised and celebrated.

Talented Athlete Support Scheme

The Talented Athlete Support Scheme (TASS) aims to provide funds for talented athletes at schools, colleges and universities to gain access to support for the development of their excellence. Money is provided for equipment, travel costs and sport science support, such as nutritional advice, sport psychology and physiological testing, and medical support such as physiotherapy and sports massage.

Plan for Sport 2001

This document was published in 2001 under the title 'A sporting future for all' and was an action plan setting out the vision and how it will be delivered. The action plan covers initiatives to develop sport in education and the community, and the modernisation of sporting organisations.

Active Sports

Active Sports is delivered on a local county basis and outlines the steps local authorities are taking to develop partnerships to deliver increased opportunities to participate in sport. For example, in Oxfordshire there is a network of partners working together to achieve the following aims:

- to increase participation in sport and active recreation
- to improve the levels of performance in sport
- to widen access to sport and active recreation
- to improve health and well-being.

Sportsmark

Sportsmark was introduced in 2004 as a partnership between the Departments for Education and Skills and for Culture, Media and Sport. It is an accreditation scheme for secondary schools to reward their commitment to developing out-of-hours sport provision as well as a well-designed PE curriculum. There are two levels of award: Sportsmark and Sportsmark Gold, at which a school can achieve a distinction award.

LEARNER ACTIVITY
National strategies
In groups of threes or fours research one of these initiatives further and present your findings to the rest of the group. Each group will have five minutes to present their topic.

Review questions

1 Why is it important to study sport in the context of the societies in which it is played?
2 When did sports start to appear in the forms we recognise today?
3 Why did sports have to change? Give three reasons.
4 Explain what happened to society during the Industrial Revolution.
5 What is meant by the term 'rational recreation'?
6 Discuss the four main themes in the development of sport in the twentieth century.
7 What is the government department responsible for sport?
8 What are the respective roles of Sport England and UK Sport?
9 How can we assess the economic importance of sport?
10 Explain the differing aims of the three sectors of provision for sport in Britain.
11 What is meant by the term 'media'?
12 How do the media affect sports events?
13 How is sport changed through its presentation on television?
14 Explain the positive and negative effects of the increasing amount of sport shown on television.
15 Name four types of drugs athletes may use and explain what effects each has.
16 What are the relationships between gender, ethnicity, age and socio-economic classification and sport?
17 Name three barriers to sports participation and explain why they are barriers.
18 What is TASS and how does it help athletes?
19 Explain the aim of the strategy 'Every Child Matters'.

References

Beashel, P. and Taylor, J. (1996) *Advanced Studies in Physical Education and Sport*, Nelson.

Beashel, P., Sibson, A. and Taylor, J. (2001) *The World of Sport Examined*, Nelson Thornes.

Cashmore, E. (2000) *Making Sense of Sport*, Routledge.

Clarke, J. and Critcher, C. (1985) *The Devil makes Work*, Macmillan.

Davis, R. J., Bull, C. R., Roscoe, J. V., Roscoe, D. A. (2000) *Physical Education and the Study of Sport*, Mosby.

Dunning, E. (1996) *Figurational Sociology and the Sociology of Sport*, University of Leicester, MSc in the Sociology of Sport, Module 5, Unit 8.

Dunning, E. (1996) *Notes on the Early Development of Soccer*, University of Leicester, CRSS.

Dunning, E. (1996) *The Civilizing Process*, University of Leicester, CRSS.

Dunning, E. and Sheard, K. (1979) *Barbarians, Gentlemen and Players*, Martin Robertson.

Haralambos, M. and Holborn, M. (1995) *Sociology: Themes and Perspectives*, Collins Educational.

Hargreaves, J. (1994) *Sporting Females – Critical Issues in the History of Women's Sport*, Routledge.

Haywood, L., Bramham, P., Capernhurst, J., Henry, I., Kew, F. and Spink, J. (1995) *Understanding Leisure*, Stanley Thornes.

Hodgson, D. (1996) *Anyone For Cocktails: Drugs, Sport and Morality*, University of Leicester, CRSS.

Polley, M. (1998) *Moving the Goalposts – A History of Sport and Society Since 1945*, Routledge.

Sport England (2001) *A Review of the Economic Importance of Sport*.

Stafford-Brown, J., Rea, S., Janaway, L. and Manley, C. (2006) *BTEC First Sport*, Hodder Arnold.

Torkildsen, G. (1999) *Leisure and Recreation Management*, E&FN Spon.

Vamplew, W. (1996) *Industrialisation and Popular Sport in the Nineteenth Century*, University of Leicester, CRSS.

Walvin, J. (1994) *The People's Game (the History of Football Revisited)*, Mainstream Publishing.

Wesson, K., Wiggins, N., Thompson, G. and Hartigan, S. (2005) *Sport and PE: A Complete Guide to Advanced Level Study*, Hodder Arnold.

Websites

www.ausport.gov.au – Australian Sports Commission

www.bbc.co.uk/sport – BBC Sport

www.ccpr.org.uk – Central Council of Physical Recreation

www.culture.gov.uk – Department for Culture, Media and Sport

www.olympics.org – Olympic Movement

www.oxonactivesports.co.uk – Oxfordshire Active Sports

www.skysports.com – Sky Sports

www.sportdevelopment.org.uk – Resources for Students

www.sportengland.org – Sport England

www.sportingequals.com – Sporting Equals

www.sports-drugs.com – Sports Drugs

www.tass.gov.uk – Talented Athlete Scholarship Scheme

Instructing physical activity and exercise

The fitness industry continues to expand in a rapid manner and so does the demand for fitness trainers and instructors. The increasing competition has meant that customers are also looking for quality instructors who are knowledgeable and professional in their approach. This chapter looks at the knowledge and technical skills which are required to become an effective instructor of physical activity and exercise.

Principles of safe and effective exercise sessions

Components of fitness

Fitness is a wide-reaching concept and the instructor needs to be able answer the following question: 'What does this client need to be fit for? or 'What daily functions do they need to able to perform?'

Any of the following answers may apply:

- lose a bit of weight to look and feel better
- improve my endurance so I can play with my children
- put on some muscle so I can do more tasks
- improve my golf
- stop feeling this back pain
- be more effective at work

- have more energy on a daily basis
- be able to run a marathon.

Fig 14.01 Playing with children

Each of these activities will involve a range of the components of fitness, which are the different aspects of fitness.

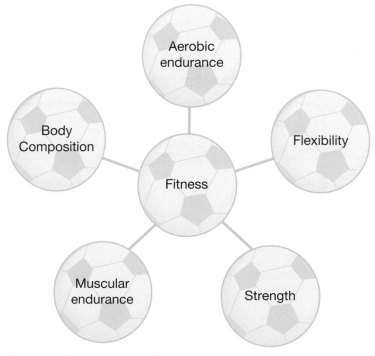

Fig 14.02 Components of fitness

Aerobic endurance

Also called cardiovascular fitness, this is the ability of the body to take in, transport and use oxygen. It depends upon the efficiency of the lungs in taking on oxygen, the heart in transporting oxygen and the working muscles in using oxygen. Examples of activities needing aerobic endurance fitness include long-distance running, swimming and cycling.

Flexibility

This is the range of movement available at a joint or group of joints. Examples of activities needing flexibility include dancing, gymnastics, running and most everyday functions.

Strength

This is the maximum force that a muscle or group of muscles can produce. Examples of activities needing strength include weight lifting and scrummaging in rugby.

Muscular endurance

This is the ability of a muscles or group of muscles to produce low-intensity forces repeatedly for long periods of time. Examples of activities needing muscular endurance include running, aerobics and carrying bags of shopping.

Body composition

This is the make-up of the body in terms of how much of the body weight is fat and how much is not fat, which we call lean body weight (LBW). Many people would like to lose excess body fat and/or gain

muscle bulk as they feel that this will make them look better.

Fig 14.03 Running

Adaptations to training

Our participant will start training because they are unhappy with their current position and they want to change something. They will be looking for 'training adaptations' or for their body's systems to adapt to the stimulus of training. Cardiovascular and resistance training will cause slightly different changes to occur.

Adaptations to aerobic endurance training

Lungs

- Respiratory muscles become stronger
- Lungs become more efficient
- Lungs are able to extract more oxygen from the air

LEARNER ACTIVITY Components of fitness

Using the following table decide, by giving a score from 1 to 10, the extent to which each component of fitness is required by the performer.

Component	Rugby union	Sprinting	Gymnastics
Aerobic endurance			
Flexibility			
Strength			
Muscular endurance			
Body composition			

Heart

- Heart muscle becomes larger
- Increase in the amount of blood pumped in each beat (stroke volume)
- Increase in amount of blood pumped per minute (cardiac output)
- Fall in resting heart rate

Blood and blood vessels

- Increase in number of capillaries (capillarisation)
- Increase in size of blood vessels
- Decrease blood pressure
- Increase in blood volume and red blood cell count

Muscles

- Increase in number and size of mitochondria (energy-producing parts of cells)
- Increases tolerance to lactic acid
- Increased aerobic enzyme production (muscles will become better at producing energy using oxygen)
- Muscular endurance increases

Bones

- Bone density increases (if activity is weight bearing, like running)

Adaptations to resistance training

- Increase in muscle size (hypertrophy)
- Increase in strength of ligaments and tendons
- Increase in bone density
- Improved nervous system function
- Decreased body fat
- Improved body composition (ratio of muscle to fat)
- Increased resting metabolic rate
- Improved posture
- Less risk of injury

Principles of training

When designing an effective training programme you must take into account a range of factors to make sure that the programme is effective. These are called the 'principles of training'. When designing a training programme these principles of training must always be applied.

Frequency: this means how often the participant will train. This may be three times a week.

Intensity: this means how hard the participant will be training. Intensity is usually stated in terms of what percentage of their maximum heart rate they will work at or by using the rate of perceived exertion.

Time: this means the length of each training session.

Type: this refers to the type of training they will be performing. For example, cardiovascular or resistance training.

Overload: this means applying intensity to the participant's training which is slightly higher than they are used to. The exact intensity of overload depends upon the individual's level of fitness and it can be produced by changing time, intensity or type.

Reversibility: this means that any adaptation which can be gained can also be lost if the training stops. It is commonly known as the 'use it or lose it' principle because if you don't use the fitness gain you will quickly lose it.

Specificity: this means that any adaptations that occur will be specific to the training that has been performed. When designing a training programme every exercise must be specific to the needs of the individual, whether they are a golfer, a runner or want to lose some fat. If a programme is not specific the individual will not get the gains they require.

The principles of training spell the acronym FITTORS:

- Frequency
- Intensity
- Time
- Type
- Overload
- Reversibility
- Specificity.

Health and safety for exercise sessions

The health and safety of the individuals we are instructing in exercise environments is of paramount importance to a gym instructor. This is to ensure that they work within the law of the country and ensure the safety of participants, themselves, colleagues, employers and employees. We are living in an

LEARNER ACTIVITY Principles of training

Match the definitions to the terms.

Term	Definition
Frequency	How long the session lasts
Intensity	Working a system harder than it is used to
Time	How many times a week they will train
Type	Fitness gains can be lost as well as achieved
Overload	Fitness gains will depend upon the type of training done
Reversibility	How hard a person works
Specificity	Description of the training performed

increasingly litigious society where there is always blame to be apportioned.

Health and Safety at Work Act 1974

This Act is the basis of the British health and safety legislation and it clearly sets out the duties of employers and employees in implementing safety for themselves and the public. The Act says that employers must do everything that is 'reasonably practical' to ensure safety. This includes:

- providing a safe working environment
- the safe use, storage and handling of dangerous substances
- production of a written health and safety policy
- maintaining a safe working environment, and appropriate health and safety equipment and facilities.

The Act also covers employees in the following ways:

- to take reasonable care of their own health and safety, and use the safety equipment provided
- to inform the employer of any potential risks to health
- to report any accidents and incidents.

Therefore we need to minimise this risk by doing several things before training our participant.

- Fill out a detailed medical questionnaire and lifestyle form. This is called a PAR-Q or

participation questionnaire and identifies any medical conditions and injuries a person may have; it helps us in our programme design.

- Fill out an informed consent form where the client is made to understand the risks of exercise and sign that they are willing to accept these risks.
- Check the training environment before every session to ensure all equipment is working properly and that there are no injury risks.
- Ensure the trainer is appropriately qualified and insured against personal injury.
- Check the client before every session to ensure they have no injuries and are dressed properly.
- Conduct a full warm-up and cool-down with the client.

Physical activity readiness questionnaire (PAR-Q)

There are a range of questionnaires available but they all ask similar questions. An example is shown on the opposite page.

The Exercise and Fitness Code of Ethics

The Exercise and Fitness Code of Ethics is a document produced by an organisation called the Register of Exercise Professionals (REPs). The code ensures that we deal with our clients in an appropriate manner and that we make their safety our priority. The code of ethics covers four main areas.

Physical activity readiness questionnaire (PAR-Q)

	Yes	No
1. Do you have a bone or joint problem which could be made worse by exercise?		
2. Has your doctor ever said that you have a heart condition?		
3. Do you experience chest pains on physical exertion?		
4. Do you experience light-headedness or dizziness on exertion?		
5. Do you experience shortness of breath on light exertion?		
6. Has your doctor ever said that you have a raised cholesterol level?		
7. Are you currently taking any prescription medication?		
8. Is there a history of coronary heart disease in your family?		
9. Do you smoke, and if so, how many?		
10. Do you drink more than 21 units of alcohol for a male, and 14 units for a female?		
11. Are you diabetic?		
12. Do you take physical activity less than three times a week?		
13. Are you pregnant?		
14. Are you asthmatic?		
15. Do you know of any other reason why you should not exercise?		

If you have answered yes to any questions please give more details_____

_____

_____

If you have answered yes to one or more questions you will have to consult with your doctor before taking part in a programme of physical exercise.

If you have answered no to all questions you are ready to start a suitable exercise programme.

I have read, understood and answered all questions honestly and confirm that I am willing to engage in a programme of exercise that has been prescribed to me.

Name _____   Signature _____

Trainer's name _____   Trainer's signature _____

Date _____

Principle 1 – Rights

- Promote the rights of every individual to participate in exercise, and recognise that people should be treated as individuals.
- Not condone or allow to go unchallenged any form of discrimination, nor to publicly criticise in demeaning descriptions of others.

Principle 2 – Relationships

- Develop a relationship with customers based on openness, honesty, mutual trust and respect.
- Ensure that physical contact is appropriate and necessary and is carried out with within the recommended guidelines and with the participant's full consent and approval.

Principle 3 – Personal responsibilities

- Demonstrate proper personal behaviour and conduct at all times.
- Project an image of health, cleanliness and functional efficiency, and display high standards in use of language, manner, punctuality, preparation and presentation.

Principle 4 – Professional standards

- Work towards attaining a high level of competence through qualifications and a commitment to ongoing training that ensures safe and correct practice, which will maximise benefits and minimise risks to the participant.
- Promote the execution of safe and effective practice and plan all sessions so that they meet the needs of participants and are progressive and appropriate.

(Adapted from *The Code of Ethical Practice* (2005), produced by the Register of Exercise Professionals)

Contraindications

A contraindication is any factor which will prevent a person from exercising or make an exercise unsafe. The aim of the PAR-Q and the initial consultation is to identify any potential contraindications and then decide what needs to be done about them to minimise their chances of being a risk.

Common contraindications to exercise are:

- blood pressure higher than 160/100
- body fat higher than 30 per cent for a male and 40 per cent for a female

- diabetes mellitus
- resting heart rate higher than 100
- lung disorders
- blood pressure medications and blood thinners
- coronary heart disease
- angina pectoris
- joint conditions.

There are many more contraindications and the rule to follow is that if you are in doubt then refer the participant to a doctor prior to training.

Warm-up

A warm-up is performed to make sure that the heart, lungs, muscles and joints are prepared for the activities which will follow. The warm-up also helps to activate the nervous system. A warm-up can be specific to the training session which is being performed or it can be more general.

A warm-up involves general body movements of the large muscle groups in a rhythmical, continuous manner. For example, you may use running or cycling to warm up the muscles for a weight training session. The limitation of this is that it does not prepare for the movements which are to follow and the neuromuscular pathways have not been activated. This would be particularly dangerous for an athlete.

A specific warm-up involves the rehearsal of the exercises which are to follow. This may be through replicating the movement with dynamic stretches or using low-intensity resistance training exercises to prepare for the heavier weights to follow.

A warm-up can be summarised as having three main objectives:

- to raise the heart rate
- to increase the temperature of the body
- to mobilise the major joints of the body.

By gradually raising the temperature it will give the heart time to increase stroke volume and thus cardiac output. As the warm-up continues we start to experience a widening of the blood vessels within the muscles (vasodilation). The capillary beds within the muscles will open up and allow more oxygen and nutrients to flow through the muscles. Also, the warm-up should involve some of the movements that the person will perform in their main session. This gives the warm-up 'specificity' and acts as a rehearsal for the exercises to come.

A typical warm-up will involve the following components:

- a pulse raiser
- joint mobility
- dynamic stretching for muscles.

The **pulse raiser** involves rhythmical movements of the large muscle groups in a continuous manner. This would involve CV-type activity such as running, rowing or cycling. The pulse raiser should gradually increase in intensity as time goes on. A pulse raiser would typically last for around five minutes but may go on for ten minutes. At the end of the warm-up the heart rate should be just below the rate that will be achieved during the main session. A person who is fitter is able to warm up more quickly as their body is used to it, while an unfit person will take longer and needs to warm up more gradually.

A warm-up for a run may involve one minute walking, one minute brisk walking, one minute jogging, one minute running and then one minute fast running. An advanced performer could progress to running very quickly.

Joint mobility is used to enable the joints to become lubricated by releasing more synovial fluid on to the joints and then warming it up so it becomes more efficient. This means moving joints through their full range of movement. The movements will start off through a small range and slowly move through a larger range until the full range of movement is achieved. The joints that need to be mobilised are shoulders, elbows, spine, hips, knees and ankles. If a trainer is clever they can use the pulse-raising movements to also mobilise the joints. For example, rowing will have the effect of raising the pulse and mobilising all the joints.

Dynamic stretching is a relatively recent introduction but is very important for the specific preparation of the muscles for the movements which are due to follow.

definition

Dynamic stretching: stretching the muscles through their full range of movement in a controlled manner.

Static stretching, where a muscle is stretched and held, has been proved to be of limited value in a warm-up. The reasons being that static stretching causes a fall in heart rate and tends to relax the muscles. It can also act to desensitise the muscle spindles which protect the muscle against injury. Static stretching has a role to play in a warm-up because a short, tight muscle may prevent the participant from performing some of the exercises in their main session with perfect technique. For example, tight hamstrings make squatting and bent-over rows very difficult to perform well.

The benefits of dynamic stretching are that it:

- keeps the heart rate raised
- stretches muscles specifically through the range of movements they will be doing
- activates the nervous system and improves synchronisation between the nerves and muscles.

To perform dynamic stretching you need to copy the movements in the session you will perform. These movements are repeated in a steady and controlled fashion. In performing a set of ten repetitions you slowly speed up the movement as the set progresses. Figures 14.04, 14.05 and 14.06 show dynamic stretches.

Fig 14.04 Squat and press

Fig 14.05 Rear lunge with arm swing

Fig 14.06 Chest stretch

Main component

Content

The content of the main component can vary and is specific to the needs of the client. It may involve some of the following:

- CV training
- resistance training
- aerobics
- mixture of CV training and resistance training.

The main component will last around 40 minutes dependent on the length of the warm-up and main session (a training session generally will last an hour).

Resistance training

The participant should aim for around eight to ten exercises covering all muscle groups at least once. The larger muscle groups may be worked more than once. The design of a resistance training programme is covered later in this chapter.

Aerobic training

An aerobic session may last between 20 and 60 minutes, although it is agreed that 35 minutes is a good target to aim for. Designing aerobic training programmes is also covered later in this chapter.

Methods of monitoring exertion

When you are training aerobically it is important that the intensity worked at is closely monitored. This can be done by a number of methods:

- heart rate training zones
- rate of perceived exertion
- Karvonen formula.

Heart rate training zones: the intensity of exercise can be monitored by expressing it as a percentage of maximum heart rate. Your maximum heart rate is the maximum number of times your heart could beat. To find this out you would have to work to your maximum intensity which for most people would clearly be unsafe. Therefore, we estimate the maximum heart rate by using the following formula:

Maximum heart rate = 220 − age

For a 20 year old their maximum heart rate would be 220 − 20 = 200 bpm.

This is clearly a theoretical maximum heart rate because it is unlikely that every 20 year old in the country would have the same maximum heart rate. In reality there will be a massive variation but it can be useful as a guideline.

To work out the heart rate training zone we take percentages of heart rate maximum. If we work between 60 and 90 per cent we would be working in the aerobic training zone, where the exercise we are performing is effective in improving aerobic fitness without being dangerous. It is still a wide range for a heart rate to be within, so we change the zone depending upon the fitness level of the participant.

Rate of perceived exertion (RPE): this was developed by Gunnar Borg and is a scale which can be used by the participant to rate how hard they feel they are working between two extremes. Rather than monitoring heart rate the participant is introduced to

Effective zones for different groups as % of maximum heart rate (MHR)

Beginners	60–70% of MHR
Intermediate	70–80% of MHR
Advanced	80–90% of MHR

the scale and then asked during the aerobic session where they feel they are on the scale of 1–15 (see Table 14.01).

Table 14.01 Borg's 15-point scale

1	Rest
2	Extremely light
3	
4	Very light
5	
6	Light
7	
8	Somewhat hard
9	
10	Hard
11	
12	Very hard
13	
14	Very, very hard
15	Exhaustion

Table 14.02 Borg's modified RPE scale

1	Extremely light
2	Very light
3	Moderate
4	
5	Somewhat hard
6	
7	Hard
8	Very hard
9	Extremely hard
10	Maximal exertion

Borg's scale has been modified to a ten-point scale (see Table 14.02) because some participant's have found working between 1 and 15 difficult.

To achieve aerobic fitness gains the participant needs to be working around 12 to 15 on the 15-point scale and around 6 to 7 on the modified scale.

Karvonen formula: this is a more advanced way of working out a heart rate training zone. To find out the participant's heart rate training zone you need to know the following information first:

- age
- resting heart rate
- required exercise intensity (percentage of maximum intensity).

Age predicted maximum heart rate (APMHR) = 220 – age

Heart rate reserve (HRR) = APMHR – resting heart rate (RHR)
Target heart rate (THR) = HRR × exercise intensity + RHR

A participant, 20 years old, has a resting heart rate of 60 and wants to work at 70 to 80 per cent of their maximum intensity. They would have the following heart rate training zone:

APMHR = 220 – 20 = 200 bpm

HRR = 200 – 60 = 140

Target heart rate reserve = 140 × 0.70 + 60 = 158 bpm
Target heart rate reserve = 140 × 0.80 + 60 = 172 bpm

We get a training zone of between 158 and 172 bpm for this participant.

Cool-down

A cool-down is performed to return the body to its pre-exercise state. If you consider that once you have finished training your heart rate is still high and the blood is still being pumped to your working muscles you will need to slowly bring the heart rate back to normal.

The cool-down has four main objectives:

- to return the heart to normal
- to get rid of any waste products built up during exercise
- to return muscles to their original pre-exercise length
- to prevent venous pooling.

The aim of the cool-down is opposite to the aim of the warm-up in that the pulse will lower slowly and waste products such as carbon dioxide and lactic acid are washed out of the muscles. Also, as the muscles work during the main session they continually shorten to produce force and they end up in a shortened position. Therefore, they need to be stretched out so they do not remain shortened. Also, as the heart pumps blood around the body, circulation is assisted by the action of skeletal muscles. The skeletal muscles act as a 'muscle pump' to help return the blood to the heart against gravity. If the participant stops suddenly the heart will keep pumping blood to the legs, but because the muscle pump has stopped the blood will pool in the legs. This causes the participant to become light-headed and they may pass out.

The cool-down consists of the following activities:

- lower the heart rate
- maintenance stretching on muscles worked
- developmental stretching on short muscles.

Lowering the heart rate

To lower the heart rate you need to do the reverse of the pulse raiser. First, choose a CV-type exercise involving rhythmical movements and the large muscle groups. This time the intensity starts high and slowly drops to cause a drop in heart rate. This part should last around five minutes and an exercise bike is a good choice because it enables the client to sit down and relax as well. The gradual lowering of the intensity allows the muscle pump to work and avoid venous pooling. You want to ensure the pulse rate is around 100 to 110 bpm at the end of the pulse lowerer.

Stretching

Two types of stretching can be used in the cool-down: maintenance and developmental. A maintenance stretch is used to return the muscles worked to their pre-exercise state. During training they will be continuously shortened and they need to be stretched out to prevent shortening. Stretching will also help eliminate waste products from the muscles and also prevent soreness the next day. A maintenance stretch is one where the muscle is stretched to the point of discomfort and then is held for around ten seconds or until the muscle relaxes and the stretch goes off. All

muscles worked in the main session will need at least a maintenance stretch.

Developmental stretching is used on muscles which have become short and tight. They may be short because they have been overtrained or due to the positions adopted on a daily basis. If a person is sat down all day, either in front of a computer or driving, they may develop shortened pectorals, hamstrings, hip flexors and adductors.

Developmental stretching involves stretching a muscle and then holding it for around ten seconds until it relaxes. Once it has relaxed the stretch is increased and held for ten seconds; this is repeated three times.

LEARNER ACTIVITY
Possible questions

In your own words write down what you would say to a participant who asked the following questions.

- Why do I need to warm up?
- Can I just cool down when I have a shower?
- Does it matter how hard I work during my training session?
- How can I tell if I am working hard enough?

Designing and planning an exercise programme

To ensure that participants are happy with their progress and will keep training it is important that the trainer is able to design exercise programmes and session plans which are relevant to the specific needs of the participant. This section looks at the process you need to go through in order to write an effective training session for the participant.

Stage 1 – Gathering information

To enable the trainer to design a specific exercise programme you need to carry out a comprehensive initial consultation. This will involve the participant filling out a questionnaire about their health, medical conditions, goals and lifestyle. This is followed up by a face-to-face discussion to find out more information about the participant. The trainer will be building up

Key learning points

Cardiovascular fitness (CV) is the ability of the body to take in, transport and use oxygen.

Flexibility is the range of movement available at a joint or group of joints.

Speed is the rate at which we can move our limbs or our body.

Strength is the maximum force that a muscle or group of muscles can produce.

Muscular endurance is the ability of a muscle or group of muscles to produce low-intensity forces repeatedly for long periods of time.

Power is the production of strength at speed.

Frequency is how often the participant will train. This may be three times a week.

Intensity means how hard the participant will be training.

Time is the length of each training session.

Type refers to the type of training they will be performing.

Overload means applying intensity to the participant's training which is slightly higher than they are used to.

Reversibility means that any adaptation that can be gained can also be lost if the training stops.

Specificity means that any adaptations that occur will be specific to the training that has been performed.

A typical warm-up will involve the following components:

- a pulse raiser
- joint mobility
- dynamic stretching for muscles.

The cool-down consists of the following activities:

- lowering the heart rate
- maintenance stretching on muscles worked
- developmental stretching on short muscles.

---

a detailed picture of this participant and their life so that the exercises they choose and the programme they design will have the best chance of succeeding.

Factors to consider

When the trainer sits down to design the programme they need to consider a range of factors to ensure that the programme is appropriate and that it will benefit the participant rather than harm them. The trainer will need to consider the following.

- PAR-Q responses – have any contraindications to exercise been identified?
- Medical history – do they have any conditions which may affect the training programme and choice of exercises?
- Current and previous exercise history – this will give an idea about the current fitness level of the client.
- Barriers to exercise – do they have constraints such as time, cost, family responsibilities or work commitments?
- Motives and goals – what is the participant aiming to achieve and what is their timescale?
- Occupation – hours worked and whether work is manual or office-based.
- Activity levels – amount of movement they do on a daily basis.

- Leisure time activities – whether these are active or inactive.
- Diet – what, how much and when they eat.
- Stress levels – either through work or their home life, and how they deal with it.
- Alcohol intake – how much they consume and how often.
- Smoking – whether they are a smoker or ex-smoker and the amount they smoke.
- Time available – the client needs to fit the training into their schedule and the trainer needs to be realistic when planning the programme.

LEARNER ACTIVITY
PAR-Q questionnaire

- In pairs using a PAR-Q run a consultation with a partner. First, ask the questions on the PAR-Q and then prepare a series of other topics that you may want to find information about.
- Identify five actions you will recommend to the participant.

Client groups

Clients are the central focus of the fitness industry and it is essential that we understand the individual needs and goals of each one. Each person needs to be treated as an individual to ensure they remain on their training programme. Clients will come from a range of backgrounds, ages, fitness levels, shapes and sizes. You may see the following groups of people as clients:

- varied ability levels – beginners, intermediates, advanced
- varied fitness levels – low, moderate or high
- elderly
- juniors
- athletes
- people with specific goals, such as running a marathon or weight loss
- pregnant women
- people with medical conditions such as asthma or diabetes.

When you meet a new client it is important that you consider what this person is feeling and thinking. You need to place yourself in their shoes to consider what it is they need. We call this 'walking a mile in their shoes'.

Fig 14.07 A young gymnast

Activity selection

When we have gathered information about the participant we select an appropriate intervention in terms of the exercises we choose. You need to consider the following factors.

- Likes and dislikes – What is the participant comfortable doing? Why do they not like certain exercises?
- Accessibility – Where can they get to for their training? This may be physical or limited by cost.
- Culture – Are they limited by their culture in terms of expected roles and responsibilities, and also dress codes?
- Equipment available – Are activities limited by the venue and what it has to offer? You may be training in a gym or maybe at the client's home or in a park.

> ## LEARNER ACTIVITY
> ### Training activities
> Prepare a list of activities that you could perform if you were training your participant in the park or at their home.

Stage 2 – Establishing objectives

To ensure the success of the programme it needs to be specific to the outcome a client wants. Therefore, it is important to find out exactly what this is. If you ask them what they want to achieve they will say that they want to get fit. You need to question them further and find out what this means to them. You may need to make suggestions as they may not know themselves. Their objectives could be any of the following:

- CV fitness
- flexibility
- weight loss
- improved health
- muscular strength
- muscular size
- muscle tone
- power.

Once you have established the objectives it is time to plan the programme.

Stage 3 – Planning the programme

Programme design is an area of controversy, and different trainers have different ideas about what is right and wrong. Usually the programme will use the structure shown in the box below and in Table 14.03.

The training programme will usually last for one hour. The length of each component will depend upon the objectives of the client and the importance they place on each.

Programme design rules

When designing the programme you need to follow rules and then check that you have done so.

Rule 1: Work muscles in pairs to keep them balanced. All muscles work in pairs and if they are not worked as pairs the body can become unbalanced. This means that joints will move out of their correct place, causing a change in posture and possibly pain. It also increases the chances of injury. The body works as a complete unit and it must be trained in this way too. Many gym programmes focus on a few muscle groups – usually the chest, arms and abdominals – as these are seen to make a person more attractive.

The main pairs of muscles are:

- pectorals and trapezius
- latissimus dorsi and deltoids
- biceps and triceps
- abdominals and erector spinae
- quadriceps and hamstrings.

A check must be made to ensure that all muscle pairs have been worked equally.

Rule 2: Large muscle groups should be trained first. If you are training several muscles in one session it is

---

Programme structure

Warm-up	Raise pulse Mobilise joints Dynamic stretches	5–10 minutes
Resistance component	6–10 free weight or resistance machine exercises	30–45 minutes
CV component	Walking, running, cycling or rowing	20–60 minutes
Abdominal training	Abdominals and lower back	5 minutes
Cool-down	Lower the pulse Developmental stretches Maintenance stretches	5–15 minutes

---

Table 14.03 Meeting the objectives

Objective	Strength	Muscle size	Endurance	CV
Repetitions or duration	1–5	6–12	12–20	20 mins+
Recovery period	3–5 mins	1–2 mins	30–60 secs	N/A
Sets per exercise	2–6	3–6	2–3	1
Frequency per week	1–2 on each muscle group	1–2 on each muscle group	2–3 on each muscle group	3 session a week

(Adapted from Baechle and Earle, 2000)

important that the large muscle groups are trained first. The large muscles are the gluteus maximus, quadriceps and hamstrings, pectorals, latissimus dorsi and trapezius.

These muscles need to be worked first because they require the most effort to work and are best exercised when the client is feeling fresh. Second, if the smaller muscles become tired early on in the session it will be difficult to work the large muscles as hard.

Rule 3: Do the difficult exercises first. Each exercise will have a difficulty rating and this depends upon two main issues: how many joints are moving and how much balance is needed. An exercise where only one joint moves can be seen as simple, while an exercise with two or more joints moving will be complex. Also, the more balance that is needed the more difficult an exercise becomes. The most difficult exercises need the most skill and should be done early on in the exercise session.

Rule 4: Work the abdominals and lower back at the end of the session. The abdominals and lower back are called the core muscles and these keep the body's posture correct. If they are tired out early on it increases the risk of the spine becoming injured. They should be exercised after the resistance and CV work have been done.

Following these rules will make sure that the programme is performed in a safe and effective way.

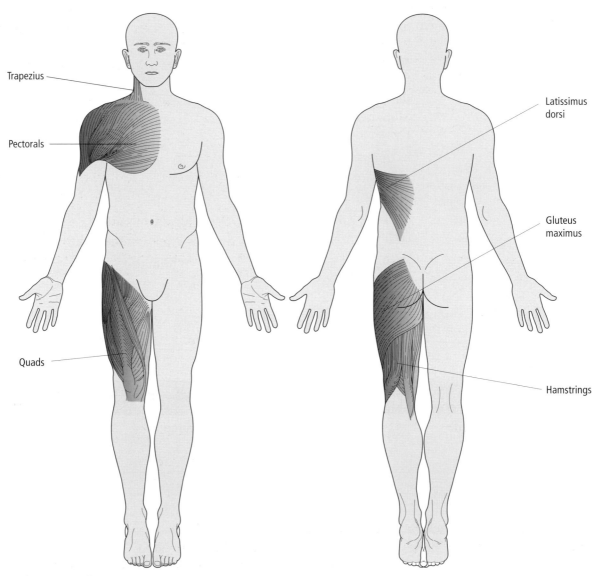

Fig 14.08 Large muscle groups

Considerations for aerobic training

It is important to consider that not everyone will want to go to a gym to improve their fitness. You will need to be flexible in finding ways to make them more active in their daily lives. The Health Education Authority (HEA) has offered guidelines concerning health and fitness.

To improve cardiovascular fitness you need to train three times a week for between 20 and 60 minutes at 60 to 90 per cent of your maximum heart rate – jogging, running, swimming, cycling or rowing.

To improve health you need to be involved in an activity which makes you slightly warmer and slightly out of breath for 30 minutes between five and seven times a week.

This can involve activities such as brisk walking, gardening, mowing the lawn or recreational swimming. Also you can look at extra ways to increase activity levels, such as walking rather than taking the car, taking the stairs instead of the lift, getting off the bus at an earlier stop or parking the car in the furthest away parking spot!

Leading an exercise session

Preparation of the session

When you take a participant through their exercise programme you need to follow a clear structure to ensure the training session is safe and that good customer care is applied.

Before the session starts you need to check the equipment and the environment:

- availability of equipment
- equipment is in working order
- all cables are strong
- floor is clear of equipment and cables
- temperature
- ventilation.

Questions and explanations

The session will start when you meet the participant. At this point you need to explain some safety issues and procedures. The following questions are appropriate to screen the participant prior to the session.

Key learning points

There are a range of factors which will need to be considered when designing an exercise programme, including: medical history, exercise history, barriers, motives and goals, occupation, activity levels, leisure time activities, diet, stress levels, alcohol intake, smoking, time available, current and previous training history.

An exercise programme should have the following components:

- warm-up
- resistance component
- CV component
- abdominal training
- cool-down.

When designing an exercise programme you need to follow four rules.

Rule 1: Work muscles in pairs to keep muscles balanced.

Rule 2: Large muscle groups should be trained first.

Rule 3: Do the difficult exercises first.

Rule 4: Work the abdominals and lower back at the end of the session.

According to the HEA recommendations, to improve cardiovascular fitness you need to train three times a week for between 20 and 60 minutes at 60 to 90 per cent of your maximum heart rate. To improve health you need to be involved in an activity which makes you slightly warmer and slightly out of breath for 30 minutes between five and seven times a week.

- Have you any illnesses or injuries I need to be aware of?
- Have you eaten today?
- Is your clothing appropriate and have you taken off your jewellery?

Then you need to explain some procedures:

- fire exits and fire drill
- first-aid kit, first aider and nearest telephone
- position of water.

Finally explain:

- the training programme and its demands
- the aims and objectives of the session
- the process of instruction.

Delivery of the session

The aim of the exercise session is to get the participant working for as much time as possible in a safe and effective manner. It is important that the participant is supported and pushed to work as hard as they can within their limits.

The instructor will perform the following roles.

Communicate effectively

It is important that the client is able to understand you and respond in the way you would like them to. We communicate mainly through the words we use and also how we deliver these words and the body language we use. It is good practice to listen to your client and assess their level of knowledge before deciding how you will deliver your instructions. If a person is new to the gym you should keep things simple and use less technical language. The more experienced client will be able to communicate using more technical language.

Give instructions

An instruction is providing information on how to perform a technique. When providing instructions you must say what you want the client to do rather than what not to do. If you use the word 'don't' as in 'don't lock your knees', it increases the chances that they will actually do it!

Demonstrate

The instructor needs to give demonstrations to show the participant how to perform the technique. Once a demonstration has been give the instructor can explain the technique to the client and then let them practise to get the feel of the movement.

Provide motivation

The reason most people do not achieve the results they want is because their motivation is too low. They give up when the going gets tough. You will motivate them with what you say, how you say it and by using positive body language. This will push them to work as hard as they can within the limits of their fitness.

Fig 14.10 Trainer and participant

Observe and correct techniques

The instructor needs to observe the client's technique from a variety of positions by moving around the client. Once they have observed for a short period, feedback needs to be given about what they are doing right and then what parts need to be corrected.

Modify exercises

If an exercise is too easy or too hard it can be modified in a variety of ways: changing the length of the lever used, getting them to stand up and resist the force of gravity, change the range of movement or the speed of movement (tempo).

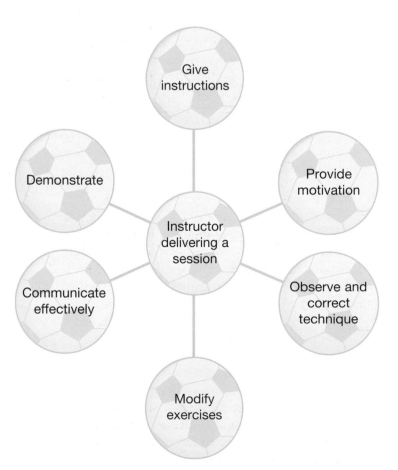

Fig 14.09 Instructor delivering a session

End of session

Once the session is finished you have two roles to perform.

- **Gain feedback:** it is important to ask the participant how they felt the session went and what they liked or did not like. Also, ask about the intensity of the session – whether it was too easy or too hard. This is vital when you reflect on your work and assess whether there are any changes that need to be made for next time to make your session even more effective.
- **Put equipment away and check for damage:** it is important to tidy up your equipment and leave the environment in a safe and acceptable state for the next person. Also, if any damage has occurred, it must be reported so that repairs can be made.

Reviewing an exercise session

The purpose of reviewing sessions

To improve as a trainer and a person it is vital to regularly review your performance and identify any changes that need to be made. We can receive feedback from a range of sources and it is all useful.

Feedback is information about performance. It is neither good nor bad, it is just information. It allows us to improve our performance in the following ways.

- **Track progression:** we can assess whether our training is having the desired effect on the participant. This can be done through fitness testing or from their own perspective.
- **Adapt sessions:** if we are not achieving our aim or an exercise has had a negative response we can adapt the programme to achieve a different response.
- **Improve own performance:** we need to identify any weaknesses we may have as then we can improve how we work with our participants. Our strengths will always work for us but we will only improve if we address our weaknesses.

Codes of practice

We must always be sure that what we do is ethical. Reflecting on how we act, talk and work with our clients will ensure we stay within accepted codes of behaviour.

Continued professional development

For a trainer to continue to improve their skills they need to be continually attending conferences and taking courses. This development should work on improving our weaknesses. It is also a requirement of the Register of Exercise Professionals (REPs) that each trainer who is a member of the Register must achieve 24 points for training per year.

Conducting a review

The ideal time to conduct a review is as soon as you can after a session while the issues are still fresh in your own mind and your participant's. You may even be able to ask the participant some questions during the cool-down period, as the work is less intense and they will be starting to relax. You need to ask them specific questions regarding the session and its outcomes.

You could use a form like the one shown overleaf and cover the following detail.

Self-evaluation

The client may not pick up things you see or feel yourself so you must ask yourself the same questions and answer them in an honest manner. Particularly, you must assess yourself in terms of the safety of the session and then whether it was effective. Did it really meet the aims that you have set for your session?

The benefits of self-evaluation are as follows.

- You can plan future sessions to ensure they are enjoyable and effective.
- Good evaluation is likely to increase the chances of the client sticking to their training programme.
- The client will stay interested and motivated.
- The client will keep progressing.
- You are able to identify any training needs you may have.
- You can set yourself goals for personal development and any training needs you may have.

Peer evaluation

As part of your support group you may work with a colleague and observe each other's training sessions. This may give a third perspective on the training and highlight issues you would not have considered yourself.

Modifying an exercise programme

There are many ways to change a participant's training programme to ensure they continue to achieve overload and keep interested and motivated:

- change a training principle
- frequency – increase the number of times they train a week
- intensity – make the programme harder by increasing speeds or resistance
- time – make each session longer

- type – change the training they do from aerobic to resistance training.

The body is expert at adapting and will only gain benefit from an exercise for a limited period. Therefore, if we change an exercise we gain a new stimulus for the body to adapt to. So change from resistance machines to free weights or cable exercises and a change will occur.

You can also give the participant a new target each week to continue to push them – cycle 5 km in under ten minutes or run 5 km in 25 minutes.

SMART targets

Regular evaluation can lead to improvements in performance. If you set yourself specific goals then you can monitor your actual performance. Achieving goals relies on effective goal setting using the SMART principle. This stands for:

- **S**pecific
- **M**easurable
- **A**chievable
- **R**ealistic
- **T**ime-constrained.

As you continue to evaluate yourself and improve your training skills, communication skills and motivation skills, you will see yourself become a more professional and effective trainer.

Review form

1. Did you think the programme was effective in meeting your aims?

2. What did you enjoy and not enjoy about the training session?

3. To what extent did you feel safe?

4. Could the session be improved in any way?

Review questions

1 Define five components of fitness and give an example of an activity for each one.
2 Give three adaptations for each of the following systems of the body: respiratory (lungs), cardiovascular (heart and blood vessels) and muscular.
3 Give four adaptations to regular resistance training.
4 What is the Health and Safety at Work Act and what general areas does it cover?
5 What is a contraindication and list five of them.
6 What are the three objectives of a warm-up?
7 Describe the differences between static and dynamic stretches.
8 Give three methods of monitoring intensity and briefly describe each one.
9 What activities should be performed in a cool-down?
10 How can the following factors impact upon the design of a training programme: medical history, current exercise level, occupation and stress levels?
11 Explain the four main rules of programme design.
12 Explain five roles an instructor will perform during a training session.
13 Why is it vital to review your performance after every training session?
14 Give two ways you could modify a participant's training session.

References

Baechle, T. and Earle, R. (2000) *Essentials of Strength Training and Conditioning*, Human Kinetics.

Dalgleish, J. and Dollery, S. (2001) *The Health and Fitness Handbook*, Longman.

Stafford-Brown J., Rea, S., Janaway, L. and Manley, C. (2006) *BTEC First Sport*, Hodder Arnold.

Goals

By the end of this chapter you should:

- understand how common sports injuries can be prevented by the correct identification of risk factors
- know about a range of sports injuries and their symptoms
- know how to apply methods of treating sports injuries
- be able to plan and construct treatment and rehabilitation programmes for two common sports injuries.

While participation in sport and physical activity has a lot of positive aspects, such as improving fitness levels and being involved in a social group who share common interests, it also has a negative aspect in the form of incurring physical injury. This chapter will identify different types of sports injuries and how they can occur. It will consider both physiological and psychological responses to injury and then suggest some methods to prevent and treat sports injuries. Finally, the chapter will outline a range of rehabilitation procedures that can be considered, together with important information on tracking and documenting injuries and their treatment.

Risk factors and prevention of sports injuries

Taking part in sport can result in injury to any part of the body. These injuries can be caused by a variety of factors which can be grouped into two categories:

- extrinsic risk factors
- intrinsic risk factors.

Extrinsic risk factors

An extrinsic risk factor is something external to the body that can cause an injury. These include:

- inappropriate coaching or instruction
- incorrect technique
- environmental conditions
- other sports players
- equipment, clothing and footwear issues.

Inappropriate coaching or instruction

Inappropriate instruction given by a coach or a trainer is an obvious way in which sports participants can easily become injured. It is vital that all instruction is given by someone who has an up-to-date depth of knowledge about the sport and is also able to communicate this appropriately and effectively. It is essential that the rules and regulations for the sport, as laid down by the specific governing body, have been correctly interpreted and are appropriately enforced. Likewise, during training activities, it is important that the information given by the coach/trainer is reliable. For this reason, many governing bodies have coaching schemes that are constantly reviewed so that coaching qualifications can be maintained at the highest and safest of standards.

Incorrect technique

The technique of performing an action or specific sport skill is usually dictated by the guidance that the sports participant has received from the PE teacher, coach, trainer or instructor. This being the case, the above is particularly relevant. But it is very easy for individuals to start to slip from these standards if they are not reinforced at the right time. If correction does not occur the participant can soon start to adopt bad habits in terms of skill level and performance. This incorrect performance of skill can in turn lead to injury problems. An obvious example is weight lifting, where back injuries particularly occur due to incorrect and bad or poor technique.

Environmental conditions

The environment in which we perform sports can also have a big impact on the likelihood of sustaining an injury. The environment encompasses the area in which a sport is played, so if you were playing basketball the environment would consist of the sports hall, and include the playing surface, the lighting and the temperature. If the lighting was poor, a player may be more likely to misjudge attacking or defensive moves and injure themselves or another player. If the surface was wet, a player would be more likely to slip over because the surface becomes much more dangerous when it is wet.

Other sports players

Some sports are obviously more susceptible to incurring sports injuries as the rules of the sport allow for tackles, scrums, etc. These are called contact sports. For instance, after a rugby game players will often come away with at least a few bruises from tackling or being tackled by other players. In non-contact games, players can also sustain sports injuries from other players from foul tackles or accidental collisions.

Equipment, clothing and footwear issues

It is important to remember to always use the equipment needed to play a particular sport correctly or this too can increase the chances of injury to either the player themselves or to other players. For example, if a javelin, shot-put or a discus are not held and thrown correctly any improper use could cause serious damage to an individual.

The use of appropriate clothing can also be an issue. Certain sports require, as stipulated by the respective governing body of the sport, certain pieces of protective clothing, such as shin pads for football, pads, gloves and helmets for cricket and hockey.

Other sports, by their very nature, need to have clothing which is very flexible and allows a full range of movement. For example, gymnasts wear clothing which allows them to perform complex movements on the floor and on specialised equipment. If restrictive clothing was worn this could greatly reduce the range of movement allowed and therefore cause injury.

Correct footwear for the correct surface that the sport is to be played on is a must. There is a phenomenal array of specialised footwear for all sports including running, basketball, tennis/squash, gymnastics, football and rugby. All these specialised pieces of footwear are made to be supportive to the player and totally suitable for the surface required for the sport. Football has grass, artificial turf and sports hall floors as its main playing areas and there are specialised shoes and boots for each surface. However, although a sportsperson may be wearing the correct footwear, certain types of footwear make a person more susceptible to injury. For instance, the studs on a footballer's or rugby player's boot can make the wearer more susceptible to leg injuries because the studs plant the foot in the ground, so if the person is turning on a planted foot they are more likely to twist their knee.

Incorrect footwear can also be a factor in causing a person to injure themselves while playing sport. For example, a marathon runner needs a lot of cushioning in their trainers to absorb the repeated impact of running. If they were to wear trainers with little padding they would be much more likely to sustain an overuse sport injury.

Intrinsic risk factors

An intrinsic risk factor is a physical aspect of the athlete's body that can cause an injury.

These include:

- inadequate warm-up
- muscle imbalance
- poor preparation
- postural defects
- poor technique
- overuse
- age.

Inadequate warm-up

This is a very common cause of sports injury. The warm-up prepares both the body and the mind for the exercise that is to come by gradually taking the body from its non-active state to being ready for the exercise. How long it takes to warm up will vary from person to person, and will depend on their level of fitness. The environment will also affect the length of the warm-up. In cold surroundings it will be necessary to carry out a longer warm-up than in hot surroundings.

A warm-up should consist of three components:

- a pulse raiser to get the blood flowing more quickly around the body and so help to warm up the muscle tissues and make them more pliable

- a mobiliser, in which the joints are taken through their range of movement, such as arm circles, to mobilise the shoulder joint
- the main muscles that are going to be used in the sport should be stretched.

LEARNER ACTIVITY Warm-up

Devise a warm up for a sport of your choice that consists of the following components:

- a pulse raiser
- a mobiliser
- a stretch.

Muscle imbalance

A muscle imbalance means that one muscle in an antagonistic pair is stronger than the other. This is often seen in footballers who have strong quadriceps muscles from extending their knee to kick the ball, but their hamstring muscles are not as strong. This can result in knee injuries because the hamstring muscles are not strong enough to put a brake on the kicking action of the knee. As a result, when a striker goes to score a goal they can over-kick, so that their knee hyperextends and gets injured.

Poor preparation

This includes a player's fitness levels specific to the sport they are going to take part in. If a person is not fit to take part in a sport they are more likely to injure themselves because they are so tired that they develop a poor sports technique. A sportsperson must also acclimatise to the environment in which they are going to play. For example, if a marathon runner living in England takes part in a race in Australia in the summer time, they have to train in hot conditions to get their body used to the heat.

Postural defects

Most people are born with a slight postural defect, such as having one leg slightly longer than the other. If there is a large difference between the two legs, this can affect the person's running technique, which may then place more strain on one side of the body, which would make the person more likely to sustain injuries after long periods of exercising.

Poor technique

If a person is not using the correct methods for exercising, they are more likely to sustain a sports injury. For example, if a swimmer continues to perform the front crawl stroke incorrectly with their arms, they may be prone to shoulder or elbow injuries. Note how this differs from the description of incorrect technique in the extrinsic factors section. Poor technique is related to the individual's performance without the use of equipment as opposed to incorrect techniques related to the misuse of equipment to perform a movement.

Overuse

An overuse injury is caused because a sportsperson does not take time to recover after exercise. Every time we exercise we place our body under strain, which means the body has to repair itself afterwards. If a person does not allow their body to repair itself it will become weaker until eventually parts of the body become injured. Also, if we continue to use specific parts of the body over a long period of time the repair is sometimes difficult to manage. A runner puts a lot of pressure and strain through their body and particularly through the knees. Injuries to the knee joint can start to be a problem if a runner has trained or competed for a long period of time, even allowing for rest periods within training.

Age

The type of injury that is most common varies with the age of the subject and also the level of competition. In young children most injuries are due to falling. In older children injuries that result from collisions and violence are more common. In older age groups and in top-level sportsmen and women there are less acute injuries and more overuse injuries and those that are due to intrinsic factors.

Preventative measures

Besides maintaining fitness and doing a warm-up, an important way to prevent sports injuries is to wear protective clothing. As already noted, some sports require their use by the governing body in order to minimise injury. Some sports do not have these but an individual can still consider protecting themselves with the use of certain items such as a gum shield or knee pads.

Suitable clothing minimises the risk of sustaining an injury in any sport. At the very least, people should wear loose-fitting or stretchy clothing and appropriate footwear. Jewellery should always be removed.

Supervision by a suitably qualified coach will also help to prevent injuries. Supervision should ensure that the sports performer is using the correct techniques for their sport. They will also be able to design training programmes that can adapt with the performer's needs. For example, if the sports performer is not training to the best of their ability, the coach may include more rest during one week of the training programme to ensure the person has recovered suitably from their training. A coach will also ensure that the equipment and environment is appropriate for training and, if not, they would ensure that either protective clothing or equipment is used or an alternative safe training session is carried out.

Sports injuries and their symptoms

The repair of injured soft tissue, such as muscle, actually commences within the first 24 hours following injury. One of the first signs that soft tissue is injured is the appearance of swelling. When the injured area starts to swell it will feel painful. This is due to the swelling creating pressure on the nerves surrounding the damaged tissue. The swelling occurs because the surrounding blood vessels are ruptured, allowing blood to bleed into the area and tissue fluid to gather around the injury site. The injured area will usually look red because the blood vessels surrounding the site dilate, which also has the effect of making the injured area feel hot. The injured area

---

LEARNER ACTIVITY

Identify the pieces of protective equipment that sportspeople wear during competition in order to minimise the risk of incurring an injury for the following sports:

- football
- cricket
- fencing
- hockey
- rock climbing
- weight lifting
- rugby
- boxing
- canoeing
- gymnastics.

LEARNER ACTIVITY

In the following sports injuries an extrinsic or intrinsic factor has been identified that might be the cause. Suggest what preventative measures you would take to avoid the injury.

Injury	Extrinsic factor	Preventative measure	Intrinsic factor	Preventative measure
Dislocated finger	Ball hitting finger			
Hamstring pull			Muscle imbalance	
Concussion	Tripped and slipped on wet sports hall floor			
Ankle strain			Poor/inappropriate warm-up/training/ overuse injury	

will show a reduced function or a total inability to function because of the pain and swelling.

The level of the above signs and symptoms will be directly related to the degree of the injury – the greater the degree of damage, the greater the effects of inflammation.

It is over a period of between 48 and 72 hours and up to 21 days that the repair is carried out with vigour by the body. The body's clotting mechanism seals the end of the torn blood vessels so that further blood plasma cannot escape into the surrounding tissues.

As the immediate effects of injury subside the healing/repair process begins. This consists of:

- absorption of swelling
- removal of debris and blood clot
- growth of new blood capillaries
- development of initial fibrous scar tissue.

After 12 hours, and for the first four days, the cells soon become active and new capillary blood vessel buds form and gradually grow to establish a new circulation in the area. With the new blood supply the debris of dead cell tissues and the initial blood clot that was formed is cleared.

Scar tissue

The damaged tissue is repaired by scar tissue. It is important to remember that scar tissue has 'plastic' properties.

> **Plastic properties:** it can be stretched and 'moulded'.

definition

Scar tissue is not elastic like muscle. It will form in a haphazard pattern of 'kinks and curls' and will contract or shorten if not carefully stretched daily for many months after the injury.

There is a great need for the new scar tissue to form in parallel 'lines' to give it strength. Correct 'stretching'

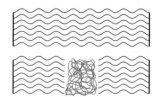

Fig 15.01 Scar tissue (bottom)

causes the scar tissue to line up along the line of stress of the injured structure. Therefore injured muscles or ligaments should be carefully mobilised and stretched daily (beginning five days after the initial injury).

The stretching will ensure that the scar is moulded to the desired length and improve the strength of the healed area (scar), and thus reduce a recurrence of damage to the scarred area and injured structure.

Muscular system

For a detailed discussion of skeletal muscular structure and function read Chapter 1: Anatomy for sport and exercise.

Ligaments and tendons

Other tissues that are frequently damaged during sport are ligaments and tendons. These are also soft tissue and are primarily made out of collagen. Ligaments connect bone to bone and tendons connect muscles to bone. Ligaments and tendons can adapt to changes in their mechanical environment due to injury, disease or exercise. A ligament or tendon is made up of fascicles.

Each fascicle contains the basic fibril of the ligament or tendon and the fibroblasts, the cells that make the ligament or tendon.

Unlike normal ligaments, healed ligaments are partly made up of a different type of collagen, which has fibrils with a smaller diameter, and are therefore a mechanically inferior structure. As a result, the healed ligament often fails to provide adequate joint stability which can then lead to re-injury or a chronically lax (permanently slightly unstable) joint.

For additional information on ligaments and tendons see Chapter 1: Anatomy for sport and exercise.

Classification of injuries

There are many ways in which we can classify the severity of an injury. One example is that there are three general stages of injury which can be applied to most sports injuries:

1. acute stage (0 to 72 hours after injury)
2. sub-acute stage (72 hours to 21 days after injury)
3. chronic continuum (21 days after injury).

Note that the severity of the injury will dictate stages 2 and 3 of the above model – less severe will reach stage 3 sometime before day 21, more severe may take longer than 21 days.

The following are examples of specific injuries and how they can be classified.

Haematomas

A haematoma is bleeding either into or around a muscle. If the bleeding is within the muscle it is called an 'intramuscular' haematoma. This type of haematoma will lead to a pressure build-up within the muscle tissue as the blood is trapped within the muscle sheath. This will result in a marked decrease in strength of the injured muscle, a significant decrease in muscle stretch and a long recovery period.

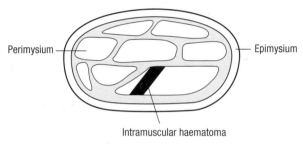

Fig 15.02 An intramuscular haematoma

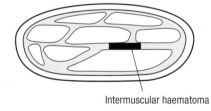

Fig 15.03 An intermuscular haematoma

Bleeding around the muscle tissue is called an intermuscular haematoma. This type of haematoma is much less severe than an intramuscular haematoma because the blood can escape from the damaged muscle and into the surrounding tissues, so there is less pressure in the area and the injury recovers much more quickly.

Sprained ankle

Injuries to the ligaments of the ankle are usually graded into three categories.

- A first-degree sprain is the least severe. It is the result of some minor stretching of the ligaments, and is accompanied by mild pain, some swelling and joint stiffness. There is usually very little loss of joint stability.

- A second-degree sprain is the result of both stretching and some tearing of the ligaments. There is increased swelling and pain and a moderate loss of stability at the ankle joint.

- A third-degree sprain is the most severe of the three. It is the result of a complete tear or rupture of one or more of the ligaments that make up the ankle joint. A third-degree sprain will result in massive swelling, severe pain and gross instability. With a third-degree sprain, shortly after the injury most of the localised pain will disappear. This is a result of the nerve endings being severed, which causes a lack of feeling at the injury site.

From the explanations above, you can see that pain and swelling are the two most common symptoms associated with an ankle sprain. You can also expect some bruising to occur at the injury site. The associated swelling and bruising are the result of ruptured blood vessels and this in turn will produce heat or inflammation.

Psychological responses to injury

The response to injury varies from individual to individual. It may vary within an individual alone dependent on when the injury occurs – at the start of a training session, middle of a season, during a major competition.

The reaction initially is negative in the main but positive attitudes can be formed. For example, it may give an individual more personal time to spend with family and friends, or time to develop new skills such as coaching, or to work on other aspects of their performance. Generally, though, the reaction is negative.

In reality, while some individuals struggle with the negative feelings that they experience, most cope without great difficulty, particularly if the injury is not so severe.

Various theoretical models have been proposed to explain the response to injury. These all include as early reactions:

- shock
- disbelief
- denial.

These are followed by possible further responses:

- anger
- depression

- tension
- helplessness
- acceptance
- adaptation
- reorganisation.

After the initial shock is over, many athletes tend to play down the significance of the injury. However, as the injury becomes more apparent, shock is often replaced by anger directed towards themselves or towards other people. The responses can vary in intensity depending on situational and personal factors but can be especially strong in individuals whose self-concept and personal identity are based on being 'an athlete/a player/a competitor'. The loss of this identity due to the inability to perform can cause much distress.

Following anger, the injured athlete might try bargaining or rationalising to avoid the reality of the situation. A runner may promise to train extra hard on return to training. By confronting reality, and realising and understanding the consequences of the injury, an individual can become depressed at the uncertainty of the future. An injured individual who belongs to a team may start to feel isolated from the 'group' and this in turn can lead to depression. It must be noted, however, that depression is not inevitable and has not always been observed during the grief reaction in research studies.

Tension and helplessness are then generated as the individual becomes frustrated at not being able to continue as normal with training or playing. Again, the isolation that injury causes, from a normal routine or from being with 'the team' can be difficult for some people to accept.

Finally, the individual starts to move towards an acceptance of the injury and adaptation of lifestyle while injured. The focus is then turned to rehabilitation and a return to sports activity. This stage tends to mark the transition from an emotional stage to a problem-coping stage as the individual realises what needs to be done to aid recovery. The timescale for progression through these stages can vary considerably depending on the individual and the severity of the injury, and setbacks during rehabilitation can lead to further emotional disturbance. In cases of very serious injury and ones in which the emotional reactions are prolonged, the skills of a clinical psychologist might be required.

It must be stressed that this process may not be a linear one for all individuals who experience some of these feelings.

Motivations and goal-setting strategies have been shown to help some people. It is possible as a coach, trainer or parent to help an injured individual recover sensibly, effectively and more positively by encouraging them to follow professional advice relating to physical rehabilitation. You can also reassure them that the feelings they are experiencing are not uncommon.

The channelling of a positive attitude can ease the rehabilitation for not just the injured player but also those around them!

Key learning points

- Physiological responses to injury – how the body reacts to an injury immediately after its occurrence and how it adapts over a period of time.
- Physical signs of injury may include swelling, blood, damaged tissue, discoloration, abnormal alignment of a limb or joint.
- Non-physical signs may include pain and heat (inflammation).
- Adaptation over time will include:

  absorption of swelling

  removal of debris and blood clots

  growth of new blood capillaries

  development of initial fibrous scar tissue.

Psychological responses to injury – how the sports person mentally reacts and copes with the physical injury. This response can vary from individual to individual; be determined by the severity of the injury; be different dependent on when the injury occurs, e.g. start of the playing season; and can change within an individual during the course of rehabilitation.

Injuries can be categorised into soft tissue and hard tissue injuries. Soft tissue refers to the muscles, tendons, ligaments and skin, whereas hard tissue refers to the skeleton, including joints, bones and cartilage.

Soft tissue injuries

Strains

A strain is a twist, pull and/or tear to a muscle or tendon, and is often caused by overuse, force or over-stretching. If a tear in the muscle occurs, surgical repair may be necessary. Muscle strains can also be classified into three categories.

First-degree strains commonly exhibit the following symptoms:

- few muscle fibres are torn
- mild pain
- little swelling
- some muscle stiffness.

Second-degree strains commonly exhibit the following symptoms:

- minimal to moderate tearing of the muscle fibres
- moderate to severe pain
- swelling and stiffness.

Third-degree strains commonly exhibit the following symptoms:

- total rupture of the muscle
- severe pain
- severe swelling.

Sprains

A sprain is a stretch and/or tear to a ligament and is often caused by a trauma that knocks a joint out of position, and over-stretches or ruptures the supporting ligaments. Sprains often affect the ankles, knees or wrists.

Muscle contusions or haematomas occur due to direct trauma, commonly a blow to the outer part of the thigh or back of the calf; this injury is commonly referred to as a 'dead leg' – it is a bruising of muscle tissue caused by the muscle being squashed between the object causing the impact and the underlying bone. The muscle fibres are squashed and associated capillaries are torn. This results in bleeding into the area with resultant haematoma formation. Usually the haematoma formed is fairly small. But in some circumstances the bleeding may be extensive and can cause a 'pressure problem'.

Oedema is swelling in the tissue due to trauma. The swelling may be a combination of tissue fluid and blood. The blood comes from local damage to capillaries at the injury site.

LEARNER ACTIVITY

In small groups discuss the types of injuries you and your colleagues have sustained while playing different sports.

Fill in the table below with your answers to highlight both the main physiological condition (fractured tibia) and the psychological response to that injury (upset, angry).

Sport	Injury sustained	Cause	Preventative measure	Psychological response

Having completed the table, compare the following categories:

- the severity of the injury (i.e. how severe or not the injury sustained was) and the type of psychological response
- the cause of injury (i.e. extrinsic or intrinsic) and the psychological response.

Are there any similarities or differences dependent on the nature of the injury?

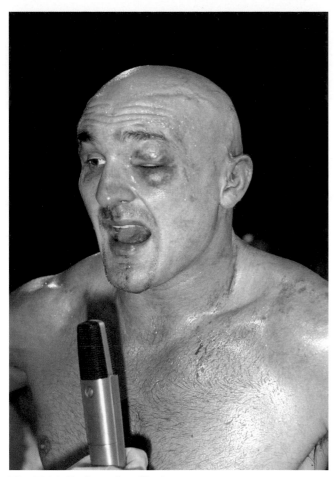

Fig 15.04 Oedema (swelling)

An **abrasion** is when the surface of the skin is grazed so that the top layer is scraped off, leaving a raw, tender area. This type of injury often occurs as a result of a sliding fall.

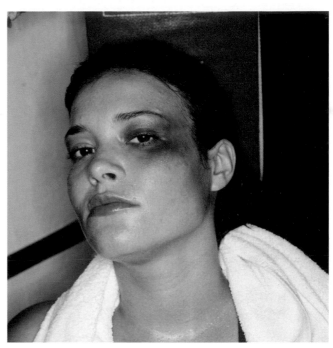

Fig 15.05 Contusion (bruising)

Bursitis is inflammation or irritation of a bursa. Bursae are small sacs of fluid that are located between bone and other moving structures such as muscles, skin or tendons. The bursa allows smooth gliding between these structures. If the bursa becomes inflamed it will feel painful and restrict movement within that area. Bursitis is an injury that usually results from overuse.

Tendonitis is inflammation or irritation of a tendon. It causes pain and stiffness around the inflamed tendon, which is made worse by movement. Almost any tendon can be affected with tendonitis, but those located around a joint tend to be more prone to inflammation. Tendonitis usually results from overuse.

A **contusion** is the technical term for a bruise. Contusions are often produced by a blunt force such as a kick, fall or blow. The result will be pain, swelling and discoloration.

Hard tissue injuries
Dislocation

Dislocation is the displacement of a joint from its normal location. It occurs when a joint is over-stressed, which makes the bones that meet at that joint disconnect. This usually causes the joint capsule to tear, together with the ligaments holding the joint in place. Most dislocations are caused by a blow or a fall. If a person has dislocated a joint then it will usually look out of place, discoloured and/or misshapen. Movement is limited, and there is usually swelling and intense pain.

Subluxation

A subluxation is when one or more of the bones of the spine moves out of position and creates pressure on, or irritates, the spinal nerves. This interferes with the signals travelling along these spinal nerves, which means some parts of the body will not be working properly.

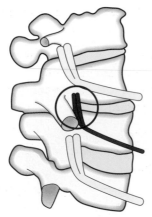

Fig 15.06 A subluxation

Cartilage damage

Normal synovial joint function requires a smooth-gliding cartilage surface on the ends of the bones. This cartilage also acts to distribute force during repetitive pounding movements, such as running or jumping. Cartilage injury can result in locking, localised pain and swelling around the affected area. It appears as a hole in the cartilage surface. As cartilage has minimal ability to repair itself, it needs treatment in order to minimise the deterioration to the joint surface.

Haemarthrosis

Haemarthrosis is where there is bleeding into the joint. It is a serious injury, and swelling of the injury site occurs very rapidly. The swelling works to protect the joint structures by limiting or preventing movement of the injured joint.

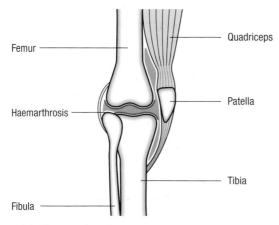

Fig 15.07 Haemarthrosis

Fractures

A fracture is the technical term for a broken bone. They result whenever a bone is hit with enough force to make it break, creating either a small crack or, in a serious fracture, a complete break. There are five main types of fracture.

- **Transverse fractures** are usually the result of a direct blow or force being applied at a sideways angle to the bone. The resultant shape of the bone ends helps transverse fractures stay in alignment more easily than those of other fractures, where the resultant ends do not line up so readily.

Fig 15.08 A transverse fracture

- **Spiral fractures** are also known as **oblique fractures**. They usually occur as a result of a twisting movement being applied about the long axis of the bone, for example, the foot being held trapped by football boot studs while the leg twists around it.

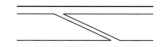

Fig 15.09 A spiral fracture

- A **comminuted fracture** is where there is splintering of the bone so that the bone is broken into a number of pieces. This type of fracture can take longer than others to heal, and is usually caused by direct trauma.

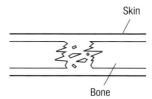

Fig 15.10 A comminuted fracture

- A **stress fracture** is an overuse injury. It occurs when muscles become fatigued and are unable to absorb added shock. Eventually, the fatigued muscle transfers the overload of stress to the bone, causing a tiny crack called a stress fracture. Stress fractures usually occur because of a rapid increase in the amount or intensity of training. The impact of an unfamiliar surface or incorrect trainers can also cause stress fractures.

Fig 15.11 A stress fracture

- An **open fracture** is also called a **compound fracture**. It is generally a more serious type of injury because the bone breaks through the skin. The break causes considerable damage to surrounding tissue and can cause serious bleeding if a large artery is ruptured. It also exposes the broken bone to the possibility of infection, which can interfere with healing.

Fig 15.12 An open fracture

First aid

First aid is the immediate treatment given to an injured person. When a suitably qualified person arrives on the scene they then take over the care of the person. Anyone with some knowledge of first aid can have a huge impact on the health of an injured person, so it is always useful to know some basics. By completing a recognised first-aid qualification you will gain a very good basic knowledge of what to do in an emergency situation. It is not in the scope of this book to cover all aspects of first aid because practical work is required to complement the theoretical principles of first aid. Therefore this section will cover only some very basic aspects of first aid.

Immediate treatments

It is necessary to establish what is wrong with the person. If they are lying on the ground you should follow the guidelines below.

1 Assess the situation – identify any risks to yourself and to the casualty.
2 Make the area safe, such as turning off an electric switch.
3 Assess the casualty and give first aid if appropriate. Establish if the person is conscious and then check

their ABC. This would be thoroughly covered in a first-aid course:

- **Airway** – they have an open airway
- **Breathing** – they are breathing
- **Circulation** – check their circulation by assessing if they have a pulse.

4 Try to get help as soon as possible.
5 Deal with the aftermath – complete an accident or incident report.

If you follow a first-aid course you will be taught how to:

- check the ABC
- open a person's airway
- deal with them if they are not breathing by performing artificial resuscitation
- check if a person has a pulse and how to administer cardiac compressions if they do not.

Calling for an ambulance

If a person is injured and you believe the injury requires professional attention, you must ensure that someone calls for an ambulance. If you are dealing with a casualty by yourself, minimise the risk to them by taking any vital action first (check their airway, breathing and circulation), then make a short but accurate call.

- Dial 999 and ask for an ambulance.
- Give your exact location.
- Give clear details of the accident and the severity of the injuries your casualty has sustained.
- Give the telephone number you are calling from and the sex and approximate age of the casualty.

If you get someone else to make the call, always ask them to report back to you to confirm that the call has been made.

When the paramedics arrive, tell them as much as possible about how the casualty has behaved, such as if they are unconscious, if they needed artificial resuscitation, and so on.

Contents of a first-aid box

A first-aid box should contain a number of items in order for a person to effectively administer first aid. The contents of a first-aid box for a workplace or leisure centre must conform to legal requirements and must also be clearly marked and readily accessible. Below is a list of materials that *most* first-aid kits contain:

- sterile adhesive dressings (plasters) – there should be a range of sizes for dressing minor wounds
- sterile eye pads – a sterile pad with a bandage attached to it to cover the eye following eye injuries
- triangular bandages – these can be used as a pad to stop bleeding, or to make slings, or used as a sterile covering for large injuries such as burns
- large and medium wound dressings – a sterile, non-medicated dressing pad with a bandage attached to it
- disposable gloves – these should be worn at all times when dealing with blood or body fluids
- face shield for resuscitation – this may be used to prevent contamination by the casualty's vomit, blood or other body fluids.

Bleeding

A person may suffer from external bleeding, which is usually obvious to the first aider as blood flows out from the site of injury. Internal bleeding, however, is not so obvious – it is not visible as the blood is flowing out of the injury site into the body. The first aider should ensure they are adequately protected when dealing with a casualty who is bleeding to ensure that they do not expose themselves to any blood-borne viruses such as HIV.

External bleeding should be treated in the following manner.

- Lay casualty down.
- Apply direct pressure with a gloved hand or finger to the site of bleeding. As soon as possible, place a clean dressing over the wound.
- Elevate and rest the injured part when possible.
- Seek medical assistance.

Internal bleeding is difficult to diagnose, but some of the potential signs and symptoms are:

- coughing up red frothy blood
- vomiting blood
- faintness or dizziness
- weak, rapid pulse
- cold, clammy skin
- rapid, gasping breathing.

The treatment for a person you suspect has internal bleeding is as follows.

- Lay the casualty down.
- Raise the legs or bend the knees.
- Loosen tight clothing.
- Urgently seek medical assistance.
- Give nothing by mouth.
- Reassure the casualty.

Shock

When a person is suffering from shock, there is not enough blood going to the major organs of the body. Shock can be caused by number of things, including burns, electric shock, allergic shock or severe injuries. A person suffering from shock will usually have cool, moist skin, a weak, rapid pulse and shallow breathing. Other symptoms may include nausea, vomiting or trembling. The treatment for a conscious casualty suffering from shock is to reassure them, then try to find and treat the cause of shock, such as control any bleeding. Keep the casualty lying down and check for neck, spine, head or abdomen injuries. If none of these injuries is apparent then the casualty's feet should be raised so that they are higher than their head.

Unconscious adult casualty

If you see a person lying on the ground, talk to them first to see if they respond – they may just be asleep! If they do not respond, speak to them with a louder voice, asking them if they are all right. If you still receive no response, gently shake them. If the person is not injured but is unconscious, they should be placed in the recovery position, see Figure 15.13. This position helps a semi-conscious or unconscious person breathe and allows fluids to drain from the nose and throat so that they do not choke. The casualty should not be moved into the recovery position if you suspect that they have a major injury, such as a back or neck injury.

Fractures

There are five different types of fracture. All the closed fractures can be treated in a similar manner, but an open fracture needs special attention. A person can be diagnosed as having a fracture if the injured area looks deformed or is tender, if there is swelling in the area, if the casualty cannot move the injured part, or

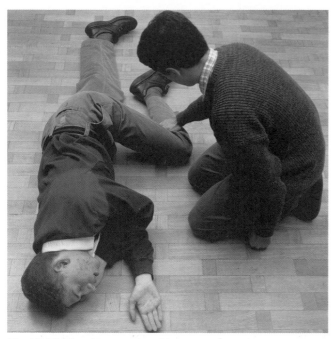

Fig 15.13 The recovery position

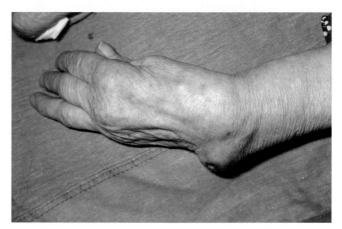

Fig 15.14 A fracture

if there is a protruding bone, bleeding or discoloured skin at the injury site. A sharp pain when the individual attempts to move the injured body part is also a sign of a fracture. The casualty should be told firmly not to move the injured part, since such movement could cause further damage to surrounding tissues and make the casualty go into shock.

A fracture should be immobilised in order to prevent the sharp edges of the bone from moving and cutting tissue, muscle, blood vessels and nerves. The injured body part can be immobilised using splints or slings. If a casualty has an open fracture, the first aider should never attempt to push the bones back under the skin. A dressing should be applied to the injury site to protect the area and pressure should be applied in order to try to limit the external bleeding. A splint can be applied, but should not be placed over the protruding bone.

SALTAPS

The sooner an injury is treated, the greater the chances of a complete recovery and the faster the rehabilitation. The immediate treatment can be summarised by the acronym SALTAPS:

- **S**ee the injury occur and the mechanism of injury
- **A**sk the casualty what is wrong and where they have pain

- **L**ook for signs of bleeding, deformity of limbs, inflammation, swelling and redness
- **T**ouch the injury or close to the injury for signs of heat, tenderness, loss or change of sensation and pain
- **A**ctive movement – ask the casualty to move the injured area; if they are able to, ask them to move it through its full range of movements
- **P**assive movement – try to move the injured site only if a good range of movement is available
- **S**trength – if the casualty has been taken through the steps above with no pain, use resisted movements to assess loss of function; for example, with an injured ankle you would assist the casualty to their feet, then ask them to stand unaided, then progress the test to walking and running.

This process will determine the extent and severity of the injury, although it may be obvious. Treatment at this stage should consist of protect, rest, ice, compression and elevation (PRICE), which is described below.

In minor injuries all stages of SALTAPS can usually be completed. But if a person sustains a serious sports injury, such as a fracture or dislocation, the assessment should not be completed because further injury may occur.

PRICE

If a person has suffered from a soft tissue injury such as a strain or a sprain, ensuring that they follow the **PRICE** regime will help to limit the severity of their injury:

- **P**rotect the injured body part from further injury
- **R**est – as soon as a person has injured themselves they should be told to discontinue their activity;

further activity could cause further injury, delay healing, increase pain and stimulate bleeding

- **Ice** – an ice pack or cold compress should be applied to the injured area; this will help to reduce the swelling and pain of the injury
- **Compression** – gentle pressure should be applied to the injury site by surrounding the area with padding, a compressive bandage or a cloth; compressing the injured area will reduce blood flowing to the injury site and also help to control swelling by decreasing fluid seeping into the injured area from adjacent tissue; after applying a compression bandage, the casualty's circulation should be checked by squeezing the nail beds of the injured limb; if blood is seen to return to the nail bed on release, the compression bandage is not too tight; the compression bandage should be reapplied after 24 hours in order to maintain compression over the injury site
- **Elevation** – the injured area should be supported in a raised position above the level of the heart in order to reduce the blood flow to the injury, which will further help to minimise swelling and bruising at the injury site.

Cold application

Cooling an injured body part to minimise the swelling and bruising of an injured area and to reduce pain is essential. When a person sustains a soft tissue injury, blood vessels are torn and blood cells and fluid escape into the spaces among the muscle fibres. By cooling the injury site, the local blood vessels are constricted, so blood flow to the area is reduced. The application of something that is cold to the injured area not only has the effect of decreasing the flow of this fluid into the tissues but also helps to slow the release of chemicals that cause pain and inflammation. Cold also decreases the feeling of pain by reducing the ability of the nerve endings to conduct impulses.

Because cold reduces bleeding and swelling within injured tissue, it is best used immediately after injury has occurred, and for up to 48 to 72 hours after an injury.

Ice bags (plastic bags with ice cubes in, a bag of frozen vegetables or chemical cold packs) can be used. Never apply ice directly on to the skin. The injured area should be covered with a cloth towel in order to prevent direct contact of the ice with the skin, which

could cause a blister or 'ice burn'. The cold application should be applied to the injured area for no more than ten minutes. During this time the person's skin will pass through four stages of sensation:

1 cold
2 burning
3 aching
4 numbness – as soon as the skin feels numb the cold therapy should be stopped.

The cooling procedure should be repeated every two waking hours. There are a number of methods of cold treatments (cryotherapy) on the market, including ice and gel packs, ice bath immersion and cans of spray.

Heat treatments

The application of heat to an injury site will act to dilate the local blood vessels, thus increasing the blood flow to the area. This type of treatment should only be given in the sub-acute stage in order to aid in the healing process. The increased blood supply will have the effect of absorbing the swelling and removing the dead cells from the injury site. It will also help to increase the growth of new blood vessels in the area and help scar tissue to form. The application of heat to muscles allows them to relax and aids in pain relief. Heat treatment would not be suitable during the early stages of injury, on an open wound or where tissues are very sensitive, such as the genital region.

Contrast bathing

Contrast bathing is the process by which alternating treatments of both hot and cold therapy are applied to the injury site and should be used during the sub-acute phase. The application of a hot treatment will increase the blood flow to the area and, when this is followed by a cold treatment, the blood flow to the area will decrease and take with it the debris from the injury site. The injured site should be immersed in alternating hot and cold water for periods ranging from one to four minutes, with increased time initially in the cold water.

Support mechanisms

In order to help protect and support some injuries it is possible to use a variety of products that are readily available at chemists, sports retailers and via the internet including tubigrip, tape and neoprene support.

Bandaging and taping can be carried out in order to prevent injury, or to treat or rehabilitate an injured joint. Both are performed in order to increase the stability of a joint when there has been an injury to the ligaments that normally support it. They limit unwanted joint movement, support the injury site during strengthening exercises and protect the injury site from further damage.

Taping involves the use of adhesive tape (e.g. zinc oxide tape), whereas bandaging uses strips of cotton and/or specialised pressure bandages. Their purpose is to restrict the joint movement to within safe limits. Taping should not be carried out if the joint is swollen or painful, or if there are any lesions around the taping area. The person who applies the taping/bandaging should be careful to ensure that they do not bind the injury site too tightly so that circulation is affected.

It should also be noted that some individuals have an allergic reaction to some types of tape, such as zinc oxide. Ideally, they should be asked about this possibility before application of the tape. If there is any uncertainty, an underwrap can be applied to provide a protective barrier between the skin and the tape. Unfortunately this can impair the tape's performance as tape also provides a proprioceptive response mechanism by having its contact directly with the skin. It reminds the individual that it is there to protect and maintain a joint within a range of movement.

The use of tape may well provide support and comfort for a sportsperson, but the benefits of use over approximately 20 minutes are diminished due to the material properties. This said, it is often used for time periods well beyond the 20-minute mark and its proprioceptive response declines after this amount of time. The psychological value of tape is valuable for a lot of players at all levels of competition, to the extent that it may even be applied to an injury that has fully recovered but the player still feels 'comforted' by the application of the tape!

Bandaging can be used to create pressure around the injury site in order to restrict swelling.

Key learning points

- Soft tissue injury – injury to muscles, tendons, ligaments and skin.
- Hard tissue injury – injury to the skeleton, i.e. bones, joints and cartilage.
- First aid – the immediate treatment given to an injured person, preferably by a qualified first aider.
- SALTAPS – See, Ask, Look, Touch, Active movement, Passive movement, Strength.
- PRICE – Protect, Rest, Ice, Compression, Elevation.

LEARNER ACTIVITY
Assessing an injury

- Imagine you are a player for a successful local sport club (you can contextualise this scenario to your sport), and you are also a qualified first aider. One of the players in your team sustains an injury (again of your choice) during a training session.
- Run through the series of steps you would follow in order to assess where the injury had occurred and the extent of the damage.
- Remember to stop the process of SALTAPS in the appropriate section if your player has a serious injury.

Rehabilitation considerations

Rehabilitation is the restoration of the ability to function in a normal or near-normal manner following an injury. It usually involves reducing pain and swelling, restoring range of motion and increasing strength with the use of manual therapy (massage and manipulation), therapeutic methods such as ultrasound and an exercise programme.

If a sportsperson does not rehabilitate their injury effectively, they are much more likely to sustain another injury to the same area.

It should be taken into consideration that as well as the physical rehabilitation of the player, the psychological rehabilitation may also need to be considered. The trauma of the injury itself and the resulting exclusion from training/coaching sessions, competitions, matches and after-competition social events can be very difficult for some individuals to come to terms with. In some cases this alone can force injured players to try to start playing again much too soon.

Physical rehabilitation process

For rehabilitation to occur, an accurate and immediate diagnosis is needed to help establish effective treatment and rehabilitation management of an injury. Therefore it is essential that an appropriately qualified person diagnoses the injury as early as possible. This may include a sports therapist, a physiotherapist, a doctor or some other suitably qualified person.

The diagnosis relies on accurate information given by either the injured person or someone who saw the injury happen. The smallest of details can make a difference to how accurate a diagnosis can be. So all information, including information regarding the environment, previous injury history, as well as the actual injury event is very important to communicate.

Post-injury treatment and rehabilitation

There are numerous ways in which to classify injury and its management. The following is a commonly accepted role model. This is called the 'stepladder approach' to rehabilitation.

Phase 1: The aim of treatment at this stage is to:

- prevent as much of the initial swelling as is possible (e.g. if sprained ankle injury do not remove footwear at this stage – it will help with compression)
- protect the injured part from any further damage (e.g. remove from field of play)

Phase 1	Immediate post-injury phase (0–20 mins post-injury)
Phase 2	Acute phase (up to 48–72 hrs post-injury)
Phase 3	Sub-acute phase (3–10 days)
Phase 4	Active rehabilitation stage Mobilising exercises for joint range Strengthening exercises
Phase 5	Functional rehabilitation/training stage

(Football Association)

- control any bleeding (apply cover and add pressure)
- help to relieve the pain (help support or position the injured part in a comfortable position – non-weight-bearing).

So the use of cold compression, elevation and rest are vital.

Phase 2: The aim of treatment at this stage is to:

- control any bleeding and swelling (maintain sterile cover and cold compress, elevate)
- relieve pain (cold compress and elevation)
- protect from further damage (advise to refrain from using as much as possible)
- give advice for home treatment (do not wear compression bandages throughout the night, correct use of ice, PRICE etc.).

Phase 3: During this stage the injury should be in the early stages of recovery:

- absorption of swelling
- removal of debris/dead cells from the area
- growth of new blood vessels
- development of scar tissue.

The use of treatments such as contrast bathing, elevation and massage, and passive exercises, such as non-weight bearing exercises, will help to disperse the products of inflammation. The joint should be moved through its pain-free range in order to increase the range of movement, help to strengthen and lengthen the muscles around the injury, and also to help the scar tissue to form in alignment. Throughout these exercises the person should feel no pain.

Contrast bathing as well as the use of heat packs may also aid the healing process. It may be necessary to use walking aids to protect from further injury or bandages for added support. The use of strengthening exercises specific to the injured area will help the tone of muscle and encourage stability around a joint. Attention to scar tissue development is essential during this stage

Phase 4: Before starting active rehabilitation it is important to make sure that the following applies to the injured part.

- There is no significant inflammation.
- There is no significant swelling.
- While there may be some joint stiffness, there is some range of movement free from pain.

- There is the ability to undertake some weight-bearing.

Initially the range of movement needs to be improved as there may have been some weakening of muscles through injury. For every week of immobilisation, a person may lose up to 20 per cent of their muscle strength. Therefore it is important to start to encourage movement first through non-weight-bearing exercises and then to progress to weight-bearing activities.

The use of supports may still be necessary in the early part of this stage. Prolonged immobilisation will lead to stiffness of the joints in the injury area and a decrease in ligament strength. However, if the injured area is mobilised early on in the rehabilitation process, regrowth of the damaged tissues is encouraged and sports ability and skills are maintained.

A selection of exercises used for the injured part should be encouraged on a regular basis as well as continuing to exercise the rest of the body without undue pressure on the injury. Care should be taken to avoid over-exercising, which may result in more damage and therefore a delay in rehabilitation.

The two main types of exercises that should be used throughout this stage are:

- mobilisation activities to improve the range of movement and reduce joint stiffness
- strengthening activities that will help stability of joints and strengthen the weakened muscles.

Phase 5: The aim of treatment at this stage is to:

- improve balance and movement coordination
- restore specific skills and movement patterns to pre-injury level
- provide psychological reassurance of function.

Progression to a functional phase is dependent on the ability to repeatedly perform a task at the level below.

Here are some examples of exercises in the stepladder approach.

Phase 1: play/exercise should cease as soon as injury occurs. 'Playing on through the pain' is not the best advice. Immediate treatment should be given as specified earlier.

Phase 2: very little exercise should be performed during this stage as the aim of the treatment is to control the bleeding and swelling, and protect the injured body part from further damage. PRICE is recommended at this stage for up to 72 hours.

Phase 3: contrast bathing and massage are used during this phase along with stretching. Stretching the injured body part is very important in order to help ensure that the new tissue is laid down in the correct orientation. If there are any signs that the injured body part is not ready to commence this stage, such as heat or swelling around the injury, then stretching should not be started. When stretching, the person should have their injured body part made as warm as possible. This can be done through the use of a thermal heat pack or soaking in a hot bath. Stretches should be held (static stretches) to the onset of discomfort for 15 to 20 seconds. However, a person should never stretch to the extent that they are in pain. Stretching should be performed for short periods of time and frequently throughout the day.

Phase 4: the strengthening exercises that can be used start with isometric exercises. This is where the muscle contracts but no joint movement occurs. Once these have been carried out and no pain has been felt, concentric muscle contractions can be introduced. This is where the muscle shortens – for example, the biceps shortening in a biceps curl.

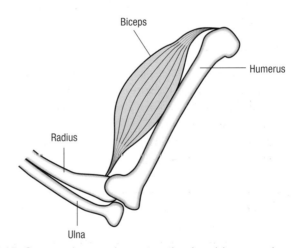

Fig 15.15 Concentric muscle contraction in a biceps curl

Once this type of muscle contraction can be carried out with no pain, eccentric muscle contractions can be performed. This involves the muscle lengthening under tension. An example of this is the quadriceps muscle lengthening as the knee flexes into the sitting position.

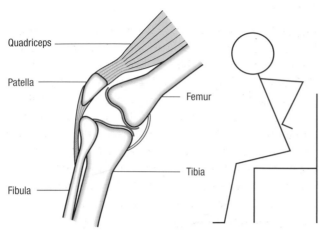

Quadriceps

Patella

Femur

Fibula

Tibia

Fig 15.16 The quadriceps muscle demonstrates an eccentric muscle contraction when getting into a sitting position

If the person has injured their leg(s), initially all the strength-training exercises should be carried out in a non-weight-bearing position, so the injured body part should not take the weight of the body. Instead, the person should be sitting down, lying down or standing on their good leg. The next stage is partial weight-bearing, where the arms are used to help support the body weight. Lastly, the exercises can be carried out with the full body weight on the injured body part.

Phase 5: initially this stage should involve the very basic elements of the sportsperson's usual sport. For example, a footballer would start with running on the spot or in a straight line. Then they would progress to running up and down hills, then on a diagonal and changing direction. This would then progress to skill training. Once they are able to complete these exercises with no problems, they can commence full training and eventually be ready for competitive play.

Psychological rehabilitation

Throughout the injured player's physical rehabilitation programme alongside it must run a psychological rehabilitation programme to deal with the feelings and emotions of the individual during the altering stages and phases of recovery to full fitness.

Frequently athletes react to injuries with a wide range of emotions including denial, anger and even depression. An injury often seems unfair to anyone who has been physically active and otherwise healthy. Although these feelings are real, it is important to move beyond the negative and find more positive

strategies to cope with this setback. In many cases dealing positively with an injury will make for a more focused, flexible and resilient athlete/player.

The following are some suggestions that can help form a psychological coping strategy alongside the physical rehabilitation of an injury.

Learn about the injury

The individual should learn as much as possible about the cause, treatment and prevention of their injury. Not fully understanding an injury can cause fear or anxiety. The professional treating the individual should be aware of this, but if the nature of the injury is not explained there is some uncertainty about the recovery as far as the injured player is concerned. Identification of the facts is a good starting point in the psychological rehabilitation process.

At the start of the physical rehabilitation process, diagnosis is key. If the individual knows *and* understands the answers to some of the following questions a lot of uncertainty can be removed before the related feelings have time to develop.

- What is the diagnosis (what type of injury is it)?
- How long will recovery take?
- What type of treatment is available?
- What is the purpose of the treatment?
- What should be expected during rehabilitation?
- Can alternative exercise help?
- What are the warning signs that rehabilitation is not progressing?

By understanding the injury and knowing what to expect during the rehabilitation process, an individual will feel less anxious and may also feel that they have a greater sense of control over their recovery.

Responsibility for the injury

This does not mean that the individual should blame themselves or anyone else for the injury that they have sustained. What it means is that they accept that they *have* an injury and that they can be in control of their own recovery. By taking on responsibility for the recovery process individuals tend to find a greater sense of control and some go through the process quickly, rather than dwelling on the past or blaming the injury on an outside factor.

Monitor attitude

Just as the person dealing with the physical rehabilitation will keep records on the progress of the individual, it is also important that the psychological aspects are considered and recorded. If an individual has accepted their injury and is positive at the start of rehabilitation, it does not mean that they will stay like this, feeling exactly the same over a period of time. Particularly if the recovery does not go as planned it can be very easy for an individual to become disillusioned.

Using support

A common response after an injury is to feel isolated and to withdraw from being around team-mates, coaches and friends. It is important to maintain contact with others during recover from an injury. Team-mates, friends and coaches need to be good at listening when there is emotion to vent, or able to offer advice or encouragement. Simply realising that others around the injured player care and are willing to help so that the injury does not have to be faced alone can also be a tremendous comfort. So, it might be that the injured player is encouraged to go along to training, to matches, remain around the gym and the weight room, or be visible and included by being an active member of the group – for example, scoring or compiling data, such as the number of tackles, etc.

Set goals

When not injured most sports people set themselves targets and goals to achieve, perhaps in training, or in a match, or by the end of a season. Injury does not mean that this should stop. Planning or setting goals can be a very positive focus. Rather than viewing the injury as a crisis, it can be made another training challenge. The goal is now focused on recovery rather than performance. This will help keep the individual motivated. By monitoring these goals it becomes easier to notice small improvements in the rehabilitation of the injury. This in turn encourages confidence in the recovery process. It is important that realistic goals and targets are set so this should always be done in conjunction with the person in charge of the physical rehabilitation process. Most athletes have a tendency to try to speed up their recovery by doing too much too soon. It is important that the injury is accepted and that the individual takes professional advice and knows their own limits.

Training to stay fit

Depending upon the type of injury incurred, it may be possible to continue training to some extent and maintain cardiovascular conditioning or strength. This is vitally important to how quickly someone can go back to playing after the injury. If their overall fitness has dropped during the rehabilitation phase while the injury has been dealt with, the individual is not at an appropriate level of fitness to return to playing. A good alternative training programme should be devised between the coach/trainer, the therapist and the injured player to ensure appropriateness throughout.

With the right knowledge, support and patience, an injury can be overcome without it being a totally negative experience. By taking things slowly, setting realistic goals and maintaining a positive, focused approach most athletes can overcome minor injuries quickly and major injuries in time.

Recording data

With any accident or incident resulting in a person being injured it is important to keep accurate and up-to-date records to help prevent, where possible, the injury happening again.

This information will normally be maintained by a coach, a teacher or a sports centre, or wherever the injury took place. This information is necessary to protect individuals from being sued for malpractice but also helps to highlight issues which may prevent other similar injuries.

It may help to make sports environments safer, and more importantly, for the coach/trainer, it can help to log the process of injury–treatment–rehabilitation. This can become an accurate record to be used as a template for similar injuries on other players or to identify the recurrence in the same player which may lead to taking into account why the injury is happening regularly. This could be down to inappropriate training regimes, inappropriate fitness levels and/or insufficient time to rehabilitate through the differing phases.

LEARNER ACTIVITY Rehabilitation process

- For the sportspeople below, identify an injury and the types of exercise you would recommend for stage 5 – the functional rehabilitation stage in their injury rehabilitation programme:
  - a football player
  - a swimmer
  - a gymnast.
- For each of the following identified injuries what would you suggest the sportsperson, therapist, coach or trainer uses in terms of psychological support alongside an appropriately advised and managed physiological rehabilitation programme:
  - a football player with a severe knee ligament injury who is experiencing 'depressed' mood states due to being excluded from the team
  - a basketball player who has an extensive strain to ankle ligaments due to slipping on a wet sports hall floor and is angry at the sports hall management for not making sure the floor was clean and clear
  - a gymnast who has dislocated a shoulder after a fall from a piece of apparatus and is very upset at being unable to train, and feels that they are never going to be fit in time for the next major competition.
- Give an example of a sportsperson who has sustained a sports injury. Explain what you would have done if you were their sports therapist. Include in your analysis:
  - SALTAPS
  - PRICE
  - methods of rehabilitation, both physiological and psychological.

Review questions

1. What is an extrinsic risk factor?
2. Why is a warm-up necessary in order to help avoid sustaining a sports injury?
3. What is an intrinsic risk factor? Give three examples.
4. What are the main methods of preventing sports injuries?
5. Identify and explain three possible reasons why a sportsperson may sustain a soft tissue sports injury.
6. Identify and explain three possible reasons why a sportsperson may sustain a hard tissue sports injury.
7. Identify various psychological responses to an injury and suggest why these may be different depending on:
   - the severity of the injury
   - the cause of the injury
   - the individual who has sustained the injury.
8. Why are sportspeople more likely to injure an area that has previously been injured?
9. What is the purpose of scar tissue?
10. Explain why it is difficult to identify an exact timescale for each stage of injury.
11. Explain what SALTAPS is and when you would use it.
12. What does PRICE stand for and when would you use it?
13. What is the purpose of first aid?
14. What does ABC stand for in relation to first aid?
15. Name six things that a first-aid box should contain.
16. What is cryotherapy?
17. What is contrast bathing and what is its purpose?
18. Why would you use taping on a sports injury?
19. What are the five stages of injury treatment and rehabilitation in the stepladder approach?
20. What psychological issues are faced by some sportspeople after sustaining a sports injury?
21. How might the psychological factors associated with the time of injury be managed alongside the physiological issues facing a sportsperson's rehabilitation?

References

Crossman, J. (2001) *Coping with Sports Injuries: Psychological Strategies for Rehabilitation*, OUP.

Flegal, M. J. (2004) *Sport First Aid* (3rd edn), Human Kinetics.

Heil, J. (1995) *Psychology of Sport Injury*, Human Kinetics.

O'Connor, B., Budgett, R., Wells, C. L. and Lewis, J. (2001) *Sports Injuries and Illnesses: Their Prevention & Treatment*, Crowood Press Ltd.

Peterson, L. and Renstrom, P. (2000) *Sports Injuries: Their Prevention & Treatment*, 3rd edn, Taylor and Francis.

Rubin, A. (2003) *Sports Injuries and Emergencies: A Quick Response*, McGraw-Hill Education.

Shamus, E. and Shamus, J. (2001) *Sports Injury – Prevention & Rehabilitation*, McGraw-Hill Education.

Sneyd, S. (technical adviser for Sports Coach UK) (2003) *How To Coach Sports Safely*, Coachwise Solutions.

sports coach UK (1999) *Sports Injury: Prevention and First Aid Management*, Coachwise Solutions.

sports coach UK (2000) *Emergency First Aid For Sport*, Coachwise Solutions.

Taylor, J. and Taylor, S. (1997) *Psychological Approaches to Sports Injury Rehabilitation*, Lippincott Williams & Wilkins.

Goals

By the end of this chapter you should:

- understand the role, responsibilities and skills of a coach
- understand the techniques used by coaches to improve the performance of athletes
- be able to plan a coaching session
- be able to deliver a coaching session.

Sports coaches are vital to the success of a number of programmes across a range of sports. They are at the heart of participation and performer development. Whether the coach of an after-school club or a top international coach with support staff, coaches are at the very centre of the development of sport.

This chapter will assist those starting on the coaching ladder to learn the rules and responsibilities, the qualities and characteristics of sports coaches. It will provide an understanding of the role of the coach in promoting a positive coaching experience.

The role of the coach

Effective coaches tend to find new ways of improving existing practices or theories. Some adapt the way in which they practise, others deal with how to play specific strategies in differing situations. Other coaches integrate new developments or technologies to improve performance. Consider the trampoline coach who adapts a harness that supports a performer for use while learning somersaults, allowing them the freedom to twist at the same time and add to the range of skill and techniques achievable. Performers who work with innovative coaches speak about how they are never bored and always trying something new.

Trainer, educator and instructor

The difference between a teacher, educator and instructor is hard to discern. Teaching implies a transfer of learning through demonstration, modelling or instruction. Coaches can also teach emotional and social skills. Young performers in particular can be encouraged to increase their social awareness, learn to cope with losing and winning, and develop self-confidence. Good coaches will be aware that people learn in different ways. They then adapt and use a range of techniques to ensure that learning takes place.

In some cultures trainers and coaches are taken to mean the same thing. Since all sport requires some kind of physical exertion, it is important that these physical demands are recognised and that allowance for these demands is incorporated into coaching programmes.

A sound knowledge of anatomy, physiology and fitness theory is essential for coaches. In the role of trainer, you might expect to design and implement training programmes for your performers.

LEARNER ACTIVITY
Training programme

You are assisting an experienced coach in your sport. The coach asks you to put together a typical six-week pre-season training programme for your athletes specific to your sport. Using a recognised training plan format, plan a typical pre-season session plan for a sport of your choice.

Motivator

Motivation can come merely by providing a stable environment in which to learn, in a positive and safe atmosphere. Performers who constantly find negativity are certain at some point to become despondent and suffer a reduction in self-confidence and improvement.

Evidence suggests that performers who receive praise and positive feedback are likely to get more from their performances. When providing feedback to performers you would employ the following technique: KISS, KICK, KISS.

This technique would be applied in providing feedback such as in skill learning. When communicating with performers, the emphasis with this technique would be to start your feedback with a positive comment. There is nearly always something that is positive in any performance. Second, a corrective comment can be presented in as positive a manner as possible. Finally, leave the interaction with a positive comment and possibly an action plan. Consider a tennis player struggling to make a particular shot:

KISS – 'Good positioning prior to the shot and you watched the ball well.'
KICK – 'You should consider how you back lift the racket, you could prepare your grip earlier.'
KISS – 'If you practise these changes you will almost certainly improve.'

Role model

In almost every coaching situation players will look mostly, if not entirely, to the coach as their source of inspiration and knowledge, never more so than when working with children. Children often imitate the behaviour and manner of their coach. For this reason it is vital that coaching is safe and responsible, and that behaviour is considered good practice.

The coach can influence player development in a number of ways.

- Social – sport offers a code of acceptable social behaviour, teamwork, citizenship, cooperation and fair play.
- Personal – players can be encouraged to learn life skills, promote their own self-esteem, manage personal matters like careers or socialising, and develop a value system including good manners, politeness and self-discipline.
- Psychological – coaches can create environments that help performers control emotions and develop their own identities. Confidence, mental toughness, visualisation and a positive outlook on life can be developed or improved.

- Health – in taking care to design coaching or training sessions to include sufficient physical exercise, good health and healthy habits can be established and maintained.

Fig 16.01 A tennis coach and player

The responsibilities of a coach

Many expectations are put upon a coach. Some of these responsibilities are clear-cut, others less so. Coaching and playing sport should always be enjoyable, and to that end coaches should not be overburdened by expectation. Common sense and a good knowledge of safety and ethics will provide the basis of a responsible coach.

As coaching is now considered a profession, so coaches will increasingly be measured and assessed, whether paid or voluntary, and increasingly expected to work to a code of practice.

A coaching code of practice

So that performers achieve their potential, coaches should:

- remain within the bounds of adopted codes of practice
- maintain safe and secure coaching environments
- make best use of all facilities and resources
- establish good working relationships with all involved
- control the behaviour of participants where possible.

Many sports governing bodies and sports coach UK have established a code of conduct for sports coaches, which includes the following sections.

- Rights – coaches must respect and champion the right of every individual to participate in sport. Coaches should ensure that everyone has the opportunity to participate regardless of age, gender, race, ability, faith or sexual orientation.

For example, you would organise sessions in a place that has childcare arrangements, and you would be sensitive to religious festivals of all denominations and make allowances for the absences of performers on notable religious dates.

Coaches also have a responsibility to ensure that no discriminating behaviour occurs during their working sessions. Every member of the coaching group should have the right to feel part of the group, free from prejudice.

- Relationships – coaches need to establish relationships with performers that are based on openness, trust and mutual respect. This is not just about effective communication. Good coaches understand how their performers think and what is best for them. Performers will also learn better in an atmosphere of trust and respect for their coach. Involving performers in the decision-making process is an excellent way of establishing an effective relationship with a performer. When deciding what is best for a performer or group of performers, an example could be a situation where the coach presents the performers with information about their performance, such as a particular phase of play in a tennis competition.

Having supplied that information and perhaps offering their opinion, the coach could present the performer with a range of options that relate to the best course of action – how to improve on the last period of play. The performer who has an input into the decision in this process will come to appreciate the knowledge and analytical skills of the coach and over time their relationship will develop based on trust and respect.

Coaches should also anticipate and deal with potential relationship problems such as:

- dealing with parents
- dropping players from squads
- assuming control as a carer.

Personal standards

Coaches should demonstrate model behaviour at all times. Their influence should always be positive and would usually mean working to a code.

LEARNER ACTIVITY
Club policy or code

Write a policy or code for coaches at your sports club regarding the following issues:

- abusive language
- equal interest in participants
- professionalism
- respect for officials and opponents
- accepting defeat.

Your club wants you to make the points clear for all of the club's new and existing coaches.

Professional standards

It is not enough to achieve a coaching qualification. Coaches should have a commitment to continual and ongoing learning or professional development. This could include:

- attaining higher-grade qualifications
- attending workshops and seminars
- being aware of changes to their sport.

Skills of sports coaches

The essential skills required of a sports coach are illustrated in Fig 16.01.

Fig 16.02 Skills of sports coaches

Management

The key ways to demonstrate good leadership in coaching are:

- checking that participants are well prepared and organised

- checking that participants and appropriate others are well deployed
- safe management and coordination of equipment and facilities
- safe and well-delivered sessions
- maintaining support and guidance to participants
- establishing and maintaining effective communication with appropriate others within the coaching environment.

It is important that coaches motivate participants by ensuring that they remain interested and challenged. Coaches will get the best from their sport if they are self-motivated and working in an atmosphere that allows them to:

- enjoy their coaching sessions
- share their experiences with others and socialise with peers and friends
- compete in a safe and non-threatening environment
- achieve negotiated goals
- remain fit and healthy
- achieve success or reward
- please others and receive praise
- create a positive self-image.

Organisation

Planning and organisation are critical to the success of coaching. When planning a session there is much to consider, but the main points are to:

- have identified a set of goals for the session
- have an awareness of the resources available
- have enough information about the participants
- have developed a plan that allows participants to achieve.

During a session coaches need to be constantly making judgements about the following.

- Is the practice working?
- What could be adapted and how?
- Are the facilities being used to full advantage?

Many coaches now keep records, usually in the form of logbooks. Many coaching qualifications require candidates to complete logbooks as part of the formal assessment process. Few coaches have the privilege of just turning up, coaching and going home. Often coaches are also involved in booking facilities, arranging equipment or contacting participants, which involves a great deal of organisation. Some coaches delegate these responsibilities as in the example for a senior women's volleyball team shown at the top of the opposite page.

In some clubs such as this, some or all of these responsibilities and others are undertaken by appropriate others, usually with the coach in control of exactly who is capable and most responsible for the task.

Communication

Perhaps the single most valuable skill is the ability to convey your thoughts and ideas in such a way as to be easily understood. It is not enough to just present your opinions: you must be able to send effective messages – these are mostly non-verbal signals. Consider the body language of a coach in a variety of scenarios. The main feedback a performer receives in almost every sport is non-verbal body language from their coaches.

Talking too much can lead to confusion. The pace, tone and volume of the spoken word will all have a marked effect on participants. The coach who spends most of their time shouting abuse will quickly lose the respect of their participants and will be less likely to be successful.

You must also be able to receive incoming messages. This particular skill is concerned with understanding and interpreting the signs and signals of others, player, officials, etc. You must also listen to opinions from players regarding tactical decisions, drills in practice or perhaps even concerning opponents.

You must also be able to check message reception. Good coaches will question their players and check their understanding. If an instruction is not understood, this is either the fault of the performer lacking concentration or the coach in the quality of the message. One way of ensuring understanding is to ask players to explain a concept in their own words.

Role/responsibilities

Coach: team selection
Assistant coach: warm-up, cool-down and general preparation
Player 1: telephone players to arrange meeting place for away fixtures
Player 2: washing and looking after kit
Player 3: contacting officials prior to games
Player 4: maintaining website and making travel arrangements
Player 5: all communication with league
Player 6: introducing new players and schools liaison
Player 7: seeking sponsorship

LEARNER ACTIVITY
Non-verbal communication

Read the following scenarios.

- An angry basketball coach infuriated because players have failed to understand their instruction.
- The badminton coach who appears confused at the tactic that one of their players has employed.
- The trampoline coach who is pleased with the performer's execution of a difficult routine.

In each case describe gestures, facial expressions and body language that would be typical. Then suggest what effect this would have on the participants in each case.

Devise a list of gestures, facial expressions and body language that you would employ as a coach and, where possible, state in what situations you would use them in your own sport.

Teaching

One of the key processes of teaching is an understanding of how people learn. Drills and practices need to be designed in a way that allows participants to progress at an appropriate pace. As a rule of good practice, the following model is useful when teaching skills:

- introduce and explain the technique
- demonstrate the technique
- practise (allow performers to experience the technique)
- observe and analyse the participants
- identify and correct errors.

It is vital that learning is achieved in simple, short and logical steps. The most valuable knowledge that a coach can gain is through learned experience, judging for themselves and from their performers what is effective and what is not.

Coaching is a continuous process which lends itself to self-reflection and evaluation. Since the knowledge and skills required to be a successful coach are constantly changing and developing with the sport, it is unlikely that coaches will ever reach the point where they will know all that there is to know!

Techniques to improve performance

Coaches in all sports have a number of techniques at their disposal that they can use to improve the performance of their athletes.

Coaching diaries/logbooks

Diaries come in different sizes, paper or electronic. They can be used to record personal thoughts, make appointments or log training sessions. Diaries can be useful in aiding self-reflection, planning and evaluation of coaching sessions.

Guidelines for getting the most from your diary are as follows.

- Complete the diary soon after the coaching session.
- Write down what happened in order.
- Focus on what went well first.
- Describe what needs improvement.
- Action plan to develop what needs to be improved.

The benefits of diaries are that they can show progress over a period of time and are usually honest and describe how you felt about a situation at that time.

Performance profiles

If a trampolinist is not performing a somersault correctly or is not coping with the physical demands of the sport, the coach or trainer can design a suitable exercise or coaching programme. But, what if the trampolinist has trouble with their nerves before the start of the competition or they have some kind of mental block that stops them from executing a skill?

Although not always obvious, the following psychological factors can affect sporting performance.

- Confidence: belief in yourself and your abilities.
- Concentration: the ability to attend to relevant cues, not being distracted.
- Control: the extent to which you feel able to influence events.
- Commitment: the level to which you apply yourself.

Key learning points

The roles of a sports coach are many and varied, and include teacher, trainer, motivator and instructor.

Coaches can have a direct influence on the lives of their performers in terms of their social, psychological, personal and health development.

Most coaches in the UK work to a code of conduct or practice that is established to set the parameters of acceptable behaviour and effective coaching.

The essential skills toolkit of a successful sports coach includes:

- management
- communication
- teaching
- organisation.

- Re-focusing after errors: the ability to adjust to negative outcomes in a positive way.
- Enjoyment: the amount of fun that you can have.

To use a performance profile you would talk with the performer and ask them to tell you how they feel about their sport. Do they ever feel anxious, and if so when? Do they understand the terms above and, if so, how do they rate them?

In the box below a performer has been asked to rate out of ten the importance of each of the factors and then rate their own proficiency in that factor.

Performance factors	Importance to performer	Self-assessment
Confidence	9	9
Commitment	10	10
Concentration	9	6
Control	9	8
Re-focusing after error	10	6
Enjoyment	7	9

Fig 16.03 Coaching the team

It seems that the performer's main emphasis for any intervention should be focused on the areas that they identify as a weakness, in this case re-focusing after errors and concentration.

In the same way, coaches can adapt this approach and apply it to their own coaching (as in the example overleaf).

Observation and analysis

It is possible to be observed and analysed by your team or club mates, your coach and by yourself, particularly if you have access to a video of your performance.

Interviews

It is possible to get a great deal of information from an interview. You could ask a performer about what they consider to be their strengths and weaknesses, or you could ask them about what tactics they might use against a particular opponents.

SWOT analysis

This is a subjective analysis of a performance or a performer's ability. Table 16.01 overleaf shows an example of a SWOT analysis carried out on a golfer.

Simulation or conditioned practice

This is about artificially creating a competition-like situation in a practice session, or a particular condition that may be likely to happen in a competitive situation. A basketball coach might consider the merits of initially removing defenders, or outnumbering them in a practice situation that is aimed at improving a particular attacking focus. Defenders can be added when the techniques are well practised. Or, conversely, extra defenders could be added so that the attacking technique could be practised under greater pressure. Similarly, defenders in these practices could be asked to take one of three roles according to the conditions required by the coach:

- passive, offering little resistance other than presence
- active, playing under normal conditions, tempo, intensity
- pressure, playing with extra intensity.

Conditioned games are used when a coach wants to create a situation that is likely to happen in a game, such as practising defending free kicks in football. Or simply adding a condition that emphasises a teaching point, such as choosing a target area on a tennis court with a chalk circle or hoop where the player is expected to return the balls in a practice drill.

Coaching factors	Importance to coach	Self-assessment
Planning and preparation	9	9
Needs of participants considered	10	10
Technical progression and sequencing	9	6
Health and safety observed	9	8
Goals defined at start of session	10	6
Technically accurate instructions/ demonstrations	7	9
Appropriate content and structure		
Variety of drills		
Monitored progress		
Skills related to game situation		
Errors identified and corrected		
Control and behaviour of group		
Time management		
Debrief and feedback to participants		
Checked player understanding		
Stopped and brought group together		
Evaluated against objectives set		
Made provisions for future planning		

Table 16.01 SWOT analysis of a golfer

Strengths	Weaknesses
A good relaxed swing	Not accurate with driving clubs
Excellent body positioning in relation to the ball	Putting is inconsistent
A low-risk safety-first approach	Poor technique in short iron game (head up too early)

Opportunities	Threats
Opponent has no knowledge of the course	Environment – windy day
Short game practice has been improved in recent weeks	Opponent is a better player
Has learnt how to mentally rehearse	Can be prone to getting annoyed easily and letting it spoil their game

LEARNER ACTIVITY SWOT analysis

Interview a performer using the SWOT analysis form below and progressing through the following steps.

- Ask your performer what they consider to be their own personal strengths and weaknesses.
- Watch them in competitive situations and see if you can add to their strengths and weaknesses. It would help to research what the perfect model for their position/sport is, or simply imagine who you would consider to be the best in the world in their position.
- Identify any potential opportunities that they may have in their performance, such as extra training time or access to a scouting report on their opponent.
- Identify any threats to their performance, such as a stronger opponent, difficulty concentrating, a slippery surface or poor equipment.
- Draw up a brief action plan that shows what they might practise or change before their next performance.

Strengths	Weaknesses
Opportunities	Threats

Video analysis

Video gives the person who watches it an objective record of a performance. The greatest benefit of video is the playback feature, including slow motion, which can be used to demonstrate skill execution, tactical efficiency or a more general generic performance evaluation.

Here are some guidelines on the use of video analysis in sport.

- Do not try to film your performers and coach them at the same time. Ask someone reliable to do the filming and brief them on what you want – follow the player or the ball, try and capture tactics or specific techniques, etc.
- Try to pick up all of the sound as it can provide useful feedback.
- Start the recording before the action and end it well after, judging players' body language before and after performance.
- Label and date the film immediately, to keep a record.

Notation

Notation is a way of collecting data and can be done by hand or with a computer. Hand notation is a system of recording detailed analysis of a sport and literally noting the data on a sheet of paper using a pre-defined set of symbols. Systems like this exist for many sports, such as tennis, archery and football.

The advantage of these systems is that they are inexpensive and, if completed by a skilful recorder, will produce quick information in real time, so that the coach or performer can have instant access to detailed information. The main disadvantages of this system are that it is open to human error, can be difficult to interpret and can be difficult in certain conditions such as bad weather.

On the next page there is an example of a match analysis sheet for a team sport. This could be filled in by the performer, a peer or a neutral observer, scoring 1 to 10 for both achieved and target scores.

Team sport match analysis			
Date:	Opponent:		Result:
Analysis area		**Mark**	**Target**
Positional play			
Tactical awareness/decision-making			
Fitness levels			
Skills/techniques			
Cooperation/teamwork			
Concentration/psychological factors			
Diet/nutrition			

LEARNER ACTIVITY Conditioned practice

For each scenario below suggest a condition that a coach might use in a practice session. Note how they might organise the practice, and what the condition/s would be.

- You are a tennis coach and the junior players that you coach are playing in their first tournament at the weekend. Most of them are very nervous, to the extent that you think their performance may suffer. There will be spectators, including their parents.
- You are a rugby coach responsible for a team that is not very good at tackling or covering break-away plays. In your next fixture you play a team that handles the ball well, switches the ball well in either direction and is particularly strong at exploiting gaps in defensive lines. Think of practices that encourage communication and decision-making.
- You are a kayak instructor responsible for a group who are reasonably experienced paddlers. They are about to embark on their first overnight expedition, much of which requires them to be in remote areas with no means of external contact. You need to satisfy yourself that all the participants are aware of their role in a variety of emergency situations.

Key learning points

- Coaches can make good use of reflective diaries in order to improve their coaching performance.
- Performance profiles can be used for performers and coaches alike.
- Coaches are expected to make interventions to improve performance having identified areas for development.
- Coaches can condition games to facilitate the teaching of a specific skill or tactic.

Plan a coaching session

Planning can be separated into the following stages:

- collecting and reviewing relevant information
- identifying participant needs
- goal setting
- identifying appropriate resources
- identifying appropriate activities to enable goals to be achieved
- planning coaching sessions and/or programmes.

Before you coach any session you need to answer the following questions.

- What is the starting point, what are their skill levels, who are they?
- Where do they want to be and what do they want from you?
- How will you achieve this?
- What will you need to do this – facilities, equipment, etc.?
- How will you/they know if they have improved?

To plan an effective coaching session or programme of sessions, the coach needs to establish:

- the number of participants, as this will affect the kinds of practices that the coach can employ
- the age of participants, as this will affect the kinds of practices that the coach can use, and even how they might approach coaching that group
- the level of experience and ability of the participants

- whether the participants have any special requirements relating to diet, health, culture or language.

An example of a session planner is reproduced in the box below.

Setting SMART goals

It is a good idea to use the SMART principle when planning your sessions or season.

Specific: this means that the session meets what you want it to meet, and is specific to the sport. For example, you could focus a cricket batting session on dealing with short-pitched, fast deliveries, thus being explicit and specific.

Measurable: this is the way in which you measure your results. If you have identified that you want to improve a basketball player's jump shooting, then you might measure this by counting how many shots are successful in a training or game situation and then measure again after the training programme.

Session Planner	
Date:	Venue:
Time:	Duration:
Group:	No. of participants:
Equipment required:	Aims of session:
Safety checks required:	
TIME	CONTENT
	Warm-up:
	Fitness work:
	Main technical skills work:
	Game play/tactical work:
	Cool-down:
Injuries/issues arising:	
Evaluation of session:	

Achievable: what you set out to improve must be possible. It would not be fair to ask a beginner in trampolining to complete a complicated routine with multiple somersaults.

Realistic: it must be possible and realistic to achieve what you intend to achieve.

Time-constrained: there should be a reasonable amount of time to achieve the learning goal. Some goals will be short term in nature and established to be achieved in the next session, others more long term and established for the entire season.

Health and safety

The health and safety of all involved in sport should be the most important of considerations of the coach. In most cases it is necessary to ensure that facilities and equipment are safe and well maintained, and that performers are adequately aware of key health and safety issues, particularly relating to their own safety and the safety of others.

Coaches should consider the following as a checklist, though it is by no means exhaustive.

- The context in which the sport will take place – the facilities and equipment. Does the provider have a normal operating procedure and emergency action plan? This should cover number of players allowed, coach:learner ratio, conduct and supervision, hazardous behaviours, fire and evacuation procedures.
- The nature of the sport, for playing and training:
  - what to do when rules are not observed
  - what to do with injured players
  - not teaching activities beyond the capabilities of the performers
  - in competitive situations matching performers where appropriate by size, maturity or age.
- The players:
  - Are you aware of any special individual medical needs, and the types of injuries common to the sport?
  - Safety education – informing players of inherent risks and establishing a code of behaviour.
  - Team-mates and opponents to be aware of their responsibilities to each other.
  - Players should be discouraged from participating with an existing injury.
- The coach:

- safe practices
- safe numbers for the area
- arranging appropriate insurance
- dealing with and reporting accidents
- being aware of emergency actions.

Risk assessments

Risk assessments are not just forms to fill out. A risk assessment is a skill that helps prevent accidents or serious events. You need to consider what could go wrong and how likely it is.

Risk assessments should be kept and logged, and stored in a safe place. Examples of risk assessments for sporting activities are wide ranging and will depend upon who they are prepared for, the nature of the sport and the competence of the person making the assessment.

LEARNER ACTIVITY
Session plan

As part of your job, you have been asked to coach some sessions in your own sport with a group of beginner adults at the local leisure centre. Design a sample session plan and complete six session plans indicating:

- participant details
- your objectives for all six sessions
- a risk assessment for your activity.

Contingency planning

Nothing ever goes completely to plan and for that reason it is good practice to plan for the unexpected so that everyone remains safe and continues to learn. Consider the following as examples of what can happen and what you could plan for.

- Weather threatens your outside session.
- You fall ill and are no longer able to continue as coach.
- There are not enough participants for the session.
- The facility is double-booked when you arrive for the session.
- The group are not responding to your style of coaching or the practices that you have chosen.

The components of a session

While the demands of the structure of sessions for different sports are quite different, the general rules for the layout of sessions are common to all sports.

Warm-up: to physically and mentally prepare and focus the performers.

Skill learning phase: the objectives of the session are established and employed through a series of drills or practices, perhaps with a competition, followed by an evaluation.

Cool-down: the final and often ignored phase that is concerned with restoring normality to body functions and that has a role to play in injury prevention and emotional control.

Fig 16.04 A coach working with skiers

Key learning points

- Planning is the first stage of coaching and requires the gathering of information relating to performers, facilities and resources.
- Effective coaches use session planners to show what they have planned for a session and to maintain a record.
- Health and safety is the most important consideration in the planning and delivery of coaching sessions.
- Contingency plans are back-up plans that can be used in the event of an unforeseen circumstance that threatens the safety or quality of the coaching session.

Deliver a coaching session

This is concerned with the actual 'doing' part of coaching, and will help with the principles of coaching sessions.

Like the planning of a session, delivering a session follows a logical path.

- Ensure the session plan fits all.
- Identify any risks to the delivery of the session.
- Introduce and start planned activities.
- Manage the behaviour of all involved.
- Monitor and adapt the session as it progresses.
- Summarise and conclude the coaching session.

Once the session is under way, the coach should work to maintain what is going well, and the role of the coach changes to become more of a manager/supervisor.

Skills should be introduced, followed by an explanation which could help performers understand their relevance and when they could be used in a competitive situation.

A competent demonstration should follow, which could be from the coach or with the aid of a video model. This must be a technically correct example and should be thorough, without too much explanation. There should be a balance between verbal instruction and visual demonstration. There will also need to be a balance between activity, instruction and discussion depending on the age, experience and maturity of performers. It is essential for the coach to note the differing rates of learning of individuals.

Performers will then need time to practise the skill or technique. Coaches can use questions to check understanding. The role of the coach changes again to become one of observer/analyst, and it is here that the coach will be looking to assist learners and correct any faults.

To improve performance the coach must have highly developed awareness relating to how to identify errors, compare to a perfect model example and, most importantly, knowledge of how to bridge the gap using feedback, observation and application of a range of suitable techniques.

There is no substitute for practice at this stage. A session that is continually interrupted by a coach for whatever reason is less likely to be successful. It is also important that a coach does not attempt too much in one session.

Most coaches enjoy this part of the coaching process the most, but it is too easy to forget what the aims of the session are and how to keep track of achievement.

LEARNER ACTIVITY
Skill introduction

Using the following as a process, describe how you would choose to introduce a skill or technique from a sport of your choice:

- explain
- demonstrate
- practise
- observe
- analyse.

Explain your reasoning where appropriate.

Reviewing a session

It is important to consider that coaching does not end at the end of a session when everyone has cooled down or even gone home. Coaching is a continuous process, and the best coaches reflect on what happened and, more importantly, how to improve. A well-considered evaluation should aid the improvement of subsequent sessions.

The process is as follows.

- Collect, analyse and review – information about the session from feedback, self-reflection and from others.
- Session effectiveness – identify the effectiveness of the session in achieving objectives.
- Review key aspects – drills or practices.
- Identify development needs and take steps to action them.

When evaluating a session a coach should consider the following.

- **Performance against pre-set goals**: effective coaches will be familiar with the goals for the season, both long and short term. There should be an opportunity to decide to what extent, if at all, the session objectives were met and to what extent this matched the other goals.
- **Participants' progress**: the review will enable coaches to monitor the performer's progress over a period of time, and help plan for future sessions. Typical review questions could be:

- How well did the performers learn the skills or techniques introduced to them?
- What performance developments were evident for each participant?
- Are the performers ready to progress to the next session?
- **Coaching ability:** this is the part where the coach can review their own performance:
  - What went well?
  - What went less well?
  - How did the performers respond?
  - Were the performers bored or restless?
  - Did the coach behave acceptably?
- **Future targets:** this is all about planning for future goals and objectives based on achievements and progress made by participants.

Tools for the review process

There are a number of tools that coaches can use.

- Videos – an excellent way of improving your coaching effectiveness. Videos can be used to judge coaching actions, interaction with your performers, facial expressions and gestures, as well as what you say.
- Critical analysis and self-reflection – self-reflection allows you to explore your perceptions, decisions and subsequent actions to work out ways in which performers can improve technical, tactical or physical ability.
- A mentor – a mentor coach can help provide you with a role-model figure who can offer you practical solutions, work as a sounding board and generally provide you with a range of support.
- Coaching diaries – these can act as a permanent source of information to record your own thoughts and feelings, and serve as a true account of what happened and when. Diaries or logs can certainly help with self-reflection and form the basis of action plans for improvement.

Formative and summative reviews

A formative review occurs during the process of coaching and changes can be made immediately. A summative review is done at the end of the coaching session as you reflect on the process overall.

Key learning points

- Delivery of a coaching session starts with an effective warm-up related to that activity or sport, and finishes with a cool-down and evaluation.
- Coaches could structure the skill-learning phase to include an introduction, explanation, demonstration, practice and review.
- At the end of a session the coach should take time to reflect on the quality of the session and plan for future improvements.

Review questions

1 Describe the role of motivator for a coach.
2 In what ways can a coach influence the development of individuals?
3 Provide examples of what a code of practice for coaches should include.
4 What are the advantages of a coaching diary or log?
5 What is a coaching intervention and describe one?
6 What is a conditioned game?
7 What kind of information would be essential to a coach prior to starting a first session with a group of beginners?
8 Describe the process of teaching a particular skill from any sport, e.g. basketball lay-up shot, assuming that you do not need to consider warm-up and cool-down.
9 When evaluating a coaching session, what do you need to focus on?
10 Describe the role of a mentor in the coaching process.

References

Crisfield, P. (2001) *Analysing your Coaching*, Coachwise.

Miles, A. (2004) *Coaching Practice*, Coachwise.
Stafford-Brown, J., Rea, S., Janaway, L. and Manley, C. (2006) *BTEC First Sport*, Hodder Arnold.

Goals

By the end of this chapter you should:

- be able to use a range of skills, techniques and tactics in selected team and/or individual sports
- understand the rules and regulations of selected team and/or individual sports
- be able to assess your own performance in selected team and/or individual sports
- be able to assess the performance of a team in two selected team sports or other individuals in selected individual sports
- be able to use a range of skills, techniques and tactics in selected team and individual sports.

Sport and sports participation are on the increase in the UK. Sport has many purposes: to improve health, for enjoyment and the natural human urge to compete among others. There are many different types of sports, and this chapter includes details of how to improve your performance in sport and your knowledge of the rules and regulations, as well as the ways in which you can measure and assess performance.

Team and individual sports

Team sports are those in which two or more players compete together with a single aim. They include sports such as football, rugby, netball and lacrosse.

Individual sports are those in which the competitor usually competes on their own and is solely responsible for their own actions. It includes sports such as gymnastics, judo, trampolining and golf.

Sports can be further classified as follows.

- **Invasion sports**: these are games such as football, netball, basketball and rugby where the object of the sport is to invade the opponent's territory.

- **Court sports**: these are non-contact sports because opponents are normally on opposite sides of a net, such as badminton, volleyball and tennis.
- **Target sports**: these involve the use of marksmanship and include golf and archery.
- **Striking/fielding**: these games have a batting and a fielding team, and include cricket, baseball and rounders.
- **Martial arts**: these come from different ancient fighting methods, many of which originated in the Far East, such as judo, tae kwon do and karate.
- **Water sports**: these are activities undertaken on or in water, including swimming, sailing and water polo.
- **Field sports**: hunting sports associated with the outdoors, such as shooting and fishing.

Skills and techniques in team and individual sports

Technique is a way of undertaking a particular skill. If a basketball player is able to perform a jump shot well, it is said that they have a good technique in playing the shot.

There are many shared skills in different team sports, and having the awareness and ability to undertake them will be an advantage to your team. These include:

- passing – moving the ball around your team-mates
- receiving – being able to receive a pass from a team-mate
- shooting – aiming at a specific target such as a goal or a basket
- dribbling – moving around with the ball
- throwing – there are many ways of throwing an object, normally specific to the sport being played
- intercepting – this is where a player stops the ball from reaching its intended place; this could be through a block or a tackle
- creating space – this means moving away from opponents so that you are in a position in which you can receive a pass or create a shooting opportunity.

In addition to the skills and techniques required of a sport, players may also be judged on other criteria such as their performance over the duration of a game. Below are two case studies: one for a team sport and the other for an individual sport.

All sports are made up of a range of specific skills. In tennis there are a number of different shots that you can play at different times during a game. Playing these effectively will allow you to win points. These include:

- forehand drive with spin variation
- forehand volley
- the service
- the lob
- the smash
- return of service.

Case study

Skills and techniques in football	
Outfield	**Goalkeeper**
Ball control with both feet	Dealing with crosses
Running with the ball	Shot stopping
Passing	Narrowing angles
Heading in attack and defence	One on one
Turning with the ball	Organising a defence
Shooting with preferred foot	Defending free kicks
Crossing from wide positions	Distribution – throwing
Tackling	Distribution – kicking
Jockeying	Dealing with back passes

All these skills can be compared with technical models and can be assessed with regard to:

- preparation – body position/alertness
- execution – technique/timing
- result – consistency/recovery.

Case study

Skills and techniques in snow boarding:

- front side sliding
- back side sliding
- toe carving
- heel carving
- swing to the hill from steep traverse
- carved turns
- controlled descent of a slalom course.

Fig 17.01 Snowboarding

LEARNER ACTIVITY Skills and techniques

- Using the examples of football or snow boarding, apply the same principle to another team or individual sport. Note the skills that you would consider the most important in those sports.
- Identify a personal set of strengths and weaknesses based on the skills that you have identified as being important.

Tactics

Tactics: these are plans and actions to achieve a goal.

Tactics in sport are usually focused directly or indirectly on winning. Tactics can depend upon the opposition, players of the other team or opponents, the importance of the competition and maybe the weather. Tactics can be:

- pre-event tactics – a particular plan before the event
- in-event tactics – a plan implemented during the game such as switching from man-to-man to zone defence in basketball.

Tactics can fail if the opposition work them out too easily, if the tactic is employed too late or if the player or players are simply not able to understand or execute the necessary tactic(s).

Consider the range of options that a tennis player has at their disposal. First, where should they stand while waiting for their opponent's return? If the ball is likely to come over the net in the middle and low, then the player might consider standing close to the net to make a volley. In this way the player has selected a tactical position and shot selection. The same player might also consider serving the ball to the forehand or backhand of their opponent, some with spin, some without and some faster than others. This is known as variation.

If the conditions of the match are that the player is losing, that player might start to play defensive shots in an attempt to prevent them from falling further behind.

Tactics can include playing precise formations against specific opponents. Football teams may play more defensively away from home and opt to play with more defending players rather than strikers. In certain sports opposing players may be marked to stop them having a positive effect for their team.

Other tactics may include working on specific set plays such as line-outs in rugby, and corners and free kicks in football.

In order to improve your performance, it is a good idea to actually watch yourself perform the skill. Have a friend or a coach video you while you perform a set skill. You can then analyse your performance and see what you are doing. You may be surprised and realise your body is not doing what you thought it was doing! You will then need to amend the skill, practise it and video yourself again to check that you are now performing the skill properly.

Rules and regulations

The rules and regulations of any sport are normally set and amended by its national governing body (NGBs) and international sports federations (ISFs). These are set to ensure that the sport is played fairly and that the opponents are aware of how to win.

LEARNER ACTIVITY Tactics

- For the following tactics give a description and when they might be applied. An example would be full-court pressure defence in basketball – defenders of a team pressurise their opponents across the whole of the court. It could be applied to force the opposition to make mistakes and to score points quickly from steals.

Team sports	Individual sports
Man marking in football	Slowing down between points in tennis
Setting an attacking field in cricket	Three shots to the green on a par 5 hole
Kicking for touch in rugby	Repeated drop shots in badminton

- For one of the tactics above, or another from a sport of your choice, explain the tactical significance of these strategies, detailing in what conditions they may be employed.
- Describe two other tactics from the same sport, again detailing the conditions in which they can be applied.

Key learning points

- Sports can be divided into invasion, court, target, striking and fielding, martial arts, water and field sports.
- Tactics are plans and actions to achieve a goal. Tactics in sport are usually focused directly or indirectly on winning.
- Team and individual sports are different not just in terms of numbers, but also in terms of the skills and techniques to be developed and assessed.

International sports federations and national governing bodies may change the rules and regulations periodically as they look to improve the sport. For example, FIBA, the international governing body for basketball meets every four years at a world congress with a view to changing or clarifying rules to the benefit of the sport.

Time

Many team sports have time constraints and are split into periods of play.

- Ice hockey has three periods of 20 minutes.
- Basketball has four periods of 10 minutes.
- Rugby union has two halves of 40 minutes.

Usually the team with the most points or goals is declared the winner, and if the scores are tied the game is normally declared a draw. For sports like rugby and football the timing is described as real time since the start and finish times are exact (except for added time), whereas basketball and ice hockey are played in artificial time because the game clock is stopped on a regular basis for a variety of reasons, meaning that the whole of the running game time is spent on the court/field of play.

In some sports a winner can be declared before the allocated time has elapsed. Often in test match cricket, a team will have bowled out a team twice and scored the required number of runs before the five days are completed.

Few individual sports are constrained by time, the outcome of the event usually being determined by the success of the competition, and usually by accruing points to a critical point.

Scoring

Each sport has a different scoring system, with the team or individual with the most points usually being declared the winner. An exception to this is golf where the player who has taken the fewest strokes is the winner. Scoring may include putting the ball into a goal in football and handball.

LEARNER ACTIVITY National governing bodies

Name as many of the governing bodies for sport as you can in the table below, both national and international. Two examples are given.

Team sports

Sport	NGB	ISF
Cricket	England and Wales Cricket Board (ECB)	International Cricket Council (ICC)
Rugby union		
Hockey		
Netball		
Rugby league		
Volleyball		
Ice hockey		

Individual sports

Sport	NGB	ISF
Tennis	Lawn Tennis Association (LTA)	International Tennis Federation (ITF)
Trampolining		
Badminton		
Table tennis		
Swimming		
Squash		
Fencing		

Facilities and equipment

Specific sports require certain facilities to enable play to take place. Different surfaces can be used for different sports, and often sports are played on a range of surfaces. Tennis is a good example as it can be played on grass, clay and hard surfaces, and can be played inside or outdoors. Occasionally rules may be adapted for sports played on different surfaces.

Many sports require the participants to wear or use specialist equipment. In football the laws of the game insist that all players must wear shin guards to protect their lower legs. In sports such as hockey, rugby and cricket, players may wear specific equipment to reduce the risk of injury. This could include arm guards, helmets and padding.

You can find the rules and regulations of each sport via its national governing body. The NGB looks after many aspects of a sport, including organising major competitions, running coaching schemes and dealing with the development of the sport at all levels.

Fig 17.02 A cricket umpire indicating a leg bye

Unwritten rules and etiquette

Unwritten rules cover those situations in sports where the normal rules of the sport are unclear or require the discretion or cooperation of the competitors. Examples include the following.

- **Football:** when a player appears to be injured the opposition often put the ball out of play, and in an act of fair play the other team returns the ball to its generous opponents.
- **Fencing:** points in fencing are scored when an opponent strikes another. In a fast-moving sport the electronic scoring apparatus can misinterpret an inaccurate contact, such as the blade contacting the floor. Sporting opponents often either concede the point or suggest that the contact was not eligible for scoring.
- **Cricket:** a batsman can choose to 'walk' on appeal. In other words, if a fielder appeals for a dismissal decision, the batsman can choose to walk from the field of play, effectively admitting that they were out.
- **Golf:** players can 'give' competitors shots, usually when their opponent's ball is very close to the hole. In doing so, they allow them to score that shot without actually playing it.

Officials

Officials in sport have wide-ranging roles and duties, from football fourth officials, trampoline judges, athletics markers, cycle marshals and netball umpires to cricket third umpires. The role of these officials varies in terms of their physical nature, their proximity to the event and the support that they receive from their co-officials.

Playing surfaces

The amount and type of surface played on in sports is many and varied. While some surfaces can be used for

LEARNER ACTIVITY Surfaces

Complete the grid below, suggesting the kinds of surfaces that each sport is usually competed on.

Basketball	
Hockey	
Ice hockey	
Rugby union	
Cricket	
Golf	
Badminton	
Tennis	
Squash	
Gymnastics (floor routine)	

a variety of sports, others are more specialised. The level of competition can also have a bearing. Artificial surfaces also come in many varieties – with rubber crumbs or sand drainage.

Situations

Rules and regulations are often used to describe what should be done in certain situations, such as what to do if a player handles the ball in football, or when a ball is out of bounds in golf. Where rules are broken, officials have a predetermined course of action and a penalty may follow.

LEARNER ACTIVITY Situations

State what action the appropriate official should take in the following situations. You may need to speak with an expert from that sport or look on the governing body website for that sport.

Sport	Situation	Outcome/action
Football	Player tackles another from behind and makes no contact with the ball	
Basketball	With the ball at their disposal from out of bounds at the halfway line, the player passes the ball to a team-mate in their back court	
Baseball	Pitcher hits the batter with a stray pitch	
Rugby union	Ball is accidentally fumbled forwards while being passed between team-mates	
Cricket	Batter hits ball, which then hits a fielder's helmet left behind the stumps in the correct place	
Golf	Player swings a club while attempting to play the ball; no contact is made with the ball, and the player records their card counting only the shots where the ball was hit	
Badminton	Player stretches to reach a shot, cannot reach, so throws their racket to the shuttlecock, which causes the shuttle to cross the net successfully	
Tennis	Player running wide of the court plays a shot that does not go over the net but lands on the opponent's side	
Squash	Player accidentally gets in the way of another, causing him to lose the point	
Swimming	Relay team having completed their four legs celebrate by jumping into the pool before the last team completes	

Football rules

Football rules are known as the 'laws of the game'. There are 17 laws, which have changed marginally over the years. The international sports federation, FIFA, adapts them as it considers necessary. Recent examples of this include changing the offside law to encourage more attacking football.

The following is a summary of the 17 laws.

- **The field of play:** this law looks at the surface, dimensions, layout and markings of the football pitch.
- **The ball:** the shape and dimensions of the football are covered, as well as replacing the ball should it burst during a match.
- **The number of players:** there should be 11 players at the start of a match, including a designated goalkeeper; the use of substitutions is also looked at.
- **The players' equipment:** the health and safety considerations of what players wear is mentioned. No jewellery should be worn and all players must wear shin guards. The goalkeeper must also wear a top that distinguishes him from the other players.
- **The referee:** this law looks at the responsibilities of the referee, which include enforcing the laws, taking responsibility for the safety of the players, acting as a timekeeper, punishing serious offences and providing a match report to the relevant authority.
- **The assistant referees:** assistant referees assist the referee to control the game, signalling when the ball goes out of play and any offences that the referee may miss.
- **Duration of the match:** a football match is played over two equal periods of 45 minutes. This time may be reduced for youth football. Time can be added for substitutions, injuries and time wasting, at the referee's discretion.
- **The start and restart of play:** the team that wins the toss of a coin can choose which goal they want to attack; the game starts with a kick-off, where all players must be in their own half of the pitch; this method is also used after a goal has been scored.
- **The ball in and out of play:** the ball is out of play when the whole ball crosses one of the perimeter lines or when the referee blows his whistle to stop play.
- **The method of scoring:** the rule states that a goal is scored when the ball crosses the line between the posts and under the crossbar. The team with the most goals wins.

- **Offside:** a player is offside if 'he is nearer to his opponent's goal line than both the ball and the second last opponent' and receives a pass from one of his team-mates. The player also needs to be in his opponent's half and interfering with the game. However, you cannot be offside if you receive the pass from a goal kick or throw-in.
- **Fouls and misconduct:** fouls and misconduct are penalised by either a direct or indirect free kick. There are ten offences that result in a direct free kick, including kicking, tripping or pushing an opponent. Indirect free kicks are given for infringements such as a goalkeeper picking up a back pass or throw-in, or for impeding an opponent. Direct free kicks are given for offences that are committed by a player in their own penalty box and are awarded as a penalty kick.
- **Free kicks:** following a foul, a free kick is awarded, which will be either direct or indirect. Opponents must be a minimum of ten yards away from the ball. A direct free kick shot directly into the opponent's goal will be awarded a goal, while a goal can be scored from an indirect free kick only if it has touched another player before going into the goal. A referee will signal an indirect free kick by raising one arm into the air above their head.
- **The penalty kick:** awarded when an offence is committed by a player in their own penalty area. The goalkeeper must remain on their line until the ball has been kicked. A penalty taker cannot touch the ball until it has touched another player if they miss.
- **The throw-in:** the ball is thrown back on to the pitch when the ball goes out of play on either side of the pitch. A throw-in is taken with two hands on the ball and the ball must be released from behind the player's head.
- **The goal kick:** the ball is kicked back into play from within the goal area when the ball crosses the goal line and was last touched by an attacking player. The ball must leave the penalty area before it can be played again.
- **The corner kick:** a corner is awarded when the ball crosses the goal line and was last touched by a defending player. The kick is taken from within the corner arc. A goal can be scored direct from a corner kick.

The FA has set a number of regulations to help the running of football in England. Regulations are rules controlled by the organising bodies.

Key learning points

- Rules are established and controlled by national governing bodies (NGBs), such as the Rugby Football Union (RFU).
- Sports can be played in real time, like one-day cricket, or in artificial time, like basketball.
- Unwritten rules are situations that can occur when players and officials can choose to demonstrate fair play.
- Governing bodies are responsible for any necessary changes to rules or changes to interpretations of rules.

The FA has included regulations on:

- the control of youth football
- the doping control programme
- disciplinary procedures.

Assessing the performance of a team or individual

Performance assessment

Performances can all be assessed. Assessment should always be done with a mind to improve future performances.

Some assessors try to correct errors in performance by simply shouting instructions like 'You are not trying hard enough' or 'Get more aim on your shot' in basketball. These instructions give the sportsperson an idea of what they should be doing but not how to achieve this. To analyse techniques from a coach's viewpoint it is important to:

- sort the effective technique from the less effective
- break down complete movements into simple parts
- concentrate on the techniques that need the most improvement, in the right order.

There are many different factors to consider when evaluating a team's or individual's performance.

- How well do they perform specific skills?
- Are they using the correct techniques?
- Are they using appropriate tactics?
- Are they successful at employing these tactics?

There are several ways in which to assess performance:

- Assessment can be completed by the individual, known as self-assessment.

- Peer assessment is the assessment of an individual or a group of individuals on performance.
- Other observers could be teachers, coaches or judges.

Here are some key terms in assessing performance.

- **Observation** – involves watching sporting performances.
- **Analysis** – deciding what has happened.
- **Evaluation** – the end-product of observation and analysis. It is the final process where decisions are made and feedback is given to the performer.
- **Qualitative analysis** – largely subjective, meaning that it is open to personal interpretation and is therefore subject to bias or error. The more knowledge the observer has the more valid the observations.
- **Quantitative analysis** – more involved and scientific, and involves the direct measurement of a performance or technique. Match statistics recorded while the game is in progress are called 'real-time', while match statistics recorded after the events are called 'lapsed-time' analysis.

There are a number of methods of assessment that can be used to assess performance.

Video analysis

Video gives the person who watches it an objective record of a performance. The greatest benefit of video is the playback feature, including slow motion, which can be used to demonstrate skill execution, tactical efficiency or a more general generic performance evaluation.

Here are some guidelines on the use of video analysis.

- Do not try to film your performers and coach them at the same time. Ask someone reliable to do the filming, and brief them on what you want – follow the player or the ball, try to capture tactics or specific techniques, etc.

- Try to pick up all the sound, as it can provide useful feedback.
- Start the recording before the action and end it well after, judging players' body language before and after performance.

- Label and date the film immediately to keep a record.

Here is an example of a match analysis sheet for a team sport. This could be filled in by the performer, a peer or a neutral observer, scoring 1 to 10 for both achieved and target scores.

Date	Opponent	Result	
		Mark	Target
Analysis area			
Positional play			
Tactical awareness/decision-making			
Fitness levels			
Skills/techniques			
Cooperation/teamwork			
Concentration/psychological factors			
Diet/nutrition			

Here is an example of a match analysis sheet for an individual sport. Again, this could be filled in by the performer, a peer or a neutral observer, scoring 1 to 10 for both achieved and target scores.

Date	Opponent	Result	
		Mark	Target
Analysis area			
Positional play			
Tactical awareness/decision-making			
Fitness levels			
Skills/techniques			
Self-discipline			
Concentration/psychological factors			
Diet/nutrition			

Notation

Notation is a way of collecting data and can be done by hand or with a computer.

Hand notation is a system of recording detailed analysis of a sport and literally noting the data on a sheet of paper using a pre-defined set of symbols. Systems like this exist for many sports, such as tennis, archery and football.

The advantage of these systems is that they are inexpensive and, if completed by a skilful recorder, produce quick information in real-time, so that the coach or performer can have instant access to detailed information. The main disadvantages of this system are that it is open to human error, can be difficult to interpret and can be difficult in certain conditions, such as bad weather.

Here is an example of a profile of a hockey player's skills and techniques. The darker column is the assessment of the level of performance by the performer and the lighter column is the assessment of the level of performance as identified by the coach.

If you look at the results, it is clear that there are differences in opinion as to level of performance. It is important that, if there are differences, the coach and performer discuss the issues and decide on what needs development in practice and game situations and how that can be achieved.

LEARNER ACTIVITY
Peer assessment

Arrange a session in a team or individual sport of your choice. Ask a fellow competitor or team-mate to complete an evaluation of your performance using an analysis sheet.

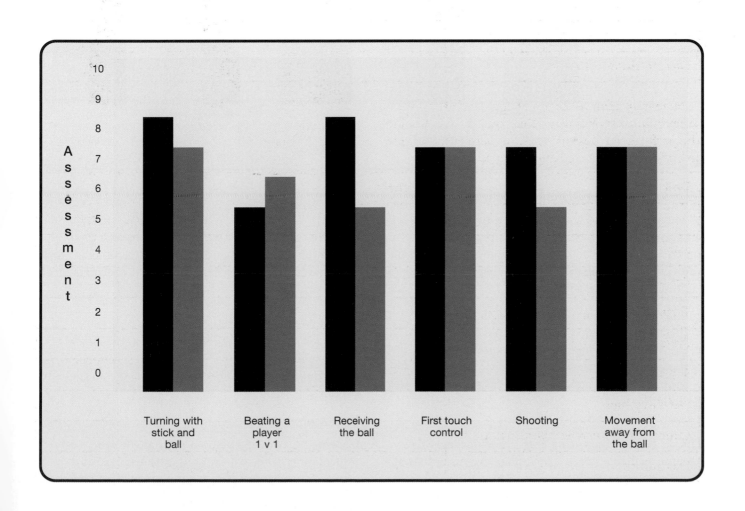

Here is an example of a profile of a basketball player's tactical awareness. The darker column is the assessment of the level of tactical awareness identified by the performer and the lighter column is the assessment by the coach.

Looking at the profile produced, it would seem that there is a difference in how the coach perceives the player is able to recognise the opponent's tactics. A discussion could follow where the coach and performer discuss their differences of opinion openly, providing examples that will help improve the understanding between coach and performer.

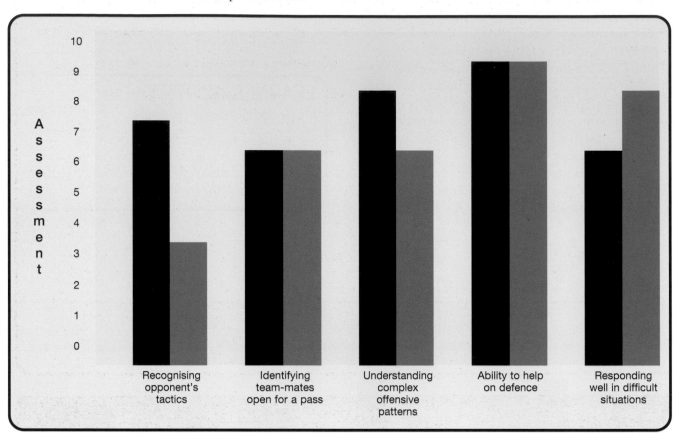

Technology in performance analysis

As video and sound technology improve, new software packages have been developed that can analyse all physical activities. Packages such as Kandle and Dartfish are capable of producing a range of exciting analysis tools including:

- video delay systems
- distance and angle measurement
- overlays and comparators that compare other performances
- multi-frame sequencing that breaks down complex skills
- drawing and annotation tools.

Thanks to ever decreasing costs these packages have become available in schools and colleges as well as at professional sports clubs.

Critical analysis and self-reflection

Self-reflection allows a performer to explore their perceptions, decisions and subsequent actions to work out ways in which they can improve technical, tactical or physical ability.

A mentor

A mentor should be someone who is a role-model figure, who can help provide practical solutions, work as a sounding board and generally provide a range of support.

Coaching diaries

Coaching diaries can act as a permanent source of information to record thoughts and feelings, and serve as a true account of what happened and when.

LEARNER ACTIVITY SWOT analysis

Interview a performer using the SWOT analysis form below and progressing through the following steps.

- Ask your performer what they consider to be their own personal strengths and weaknesses.
- Watch them in competitive situations and see if you can add to their strengths and weaknesses. It would help to research what the perfect model for their position/sport is, or simply imagine who you would consider to be the best in the world in their position.
- Identify any potential opportunities that they may have in their performance, such as extra training time or access to a scouting report on their opponent.
- Identify any threats to their performance, such as a stronger opponent, difficulty concentrating, a slippery surface or poor equipment.
- Draw up a brief action plan that shows what they might practise or change before their next performance.

Strengths	Weaknesses
Opportunities	**Threats**

Table 17.01 SWOT analysis of a golfer

Strengths	Weaknesses
A good relaxed swing	Not accurate with driving clubs
Excellent body positioning in relation to the ball	Putting is inconsistent
A low-risk safety-first approach	Poor technique in short iron game (head up too early)

Opportunities	Threats
Opponent has no knowledge of the course	Environment – windy day
Short game practice has been improved in recent weeks	Opponent is a better player
Has learnt how to mentally rehearse	Can be prone to getting annoyed easily and letting it spoil their game

Diaries or logs can certainly help with self-reflection and form the basis of action plans for improvement.

SWOT analysis

An example of a SWOT analysis carried out on a golfer is shown in Table 17.01.

Performance profiling

Performance profiling is a method that can be used by a performer or, more typically, applied by a coach or observer. Put simply, it is an inventory of attributes, skills and techniques that form the basis of an assessment grading model.

Performance profiling can be used to analyse and record technical or tactical factors as well as psychological attributes.

Scouting

This is a process where an expert observer can identify either a talented individual or produce a report about an opponent. In the first case it could result in bringing a new player to a team to strengthen the existing squad. The second aspect, gaining knowledge of how your opponent performs, is an underused approach in this country. A simple observation and a few notes can be very useful in deciding how to prepare for the next match. If a tennis player knows that their opponent has a fast, hard service but is poor on their backhand, then their preparation should have a greater emphasis on service returns under pressure and returning the ball to their opponent's weaker side.

Development

The last stage is what to do once performance has been assessed. In other words, what to do about what you have discovered, be they strengths or points for improvement.

Aims and objectives

Following analysis it is important to collate the information relating to the performance improvement. Having done this, there needs to be an established set of priorities that will form the basis of the plan of action. These aims or objectives need to be the foundation of the targets to be set.

It is a good idea to use the SMART principle in designing an action plan. SMART stands for:

- **S**pecific
- **M**easurable
- **A**chievable
- **R**ealistic
- **T**ime-constrained.

Specific: this means that the action plan meets what you want it to meet. For example, instead of saying that attacking play is a technical weakness in football, you could say that running off the ball, pass completion and beating a defender are weaknesses.

Measurable: this is the way in which you measure your results. If you have identified that you want to improve a basketball player's jump shooting, then you might measure this by counting how many shots are successful in a training or game situation, and then measure again after additional training sessions.

Achievable: what you set out to improve must be possible. It would not be fair to ask a beginner in trampolining to complete a complicated routine with multiple somersaults.

Realistic: it must be possible and realistic to achieve what we intend to achieve.

Time-constrained: there should be a reasonable amount of time to complete an action plan or achieve a goal.

Key learning points

- Performances can be analysed by the performer themselves, their peers, and observers such as coaches.
- Video capture and analysis is a very effective performance assessment tool, especially features like slow motion, freeze frame and video playback.
- SMART goals should be used to establish action for the improvement of performance.

Review questions

1 What is an invasion sport? Give three examples.
2 In team sports creating space is essential. Explain with the aid of three examples how this is achieved in these sports.
3 Describe a range of skills that could be assessed in an individual sport of your choice.
4 Identify how you could go about becoming an official in your sport. Find out how much the course costs, how long it takes and how you are assessed.
5 What is the difference between qualitative and quantitative analysis?
6 Describe four capabilities of advanced technological packages such as Kandle or Dartfish.
7 What is a mentor?
8 What is a performance profile and how does it work in performance analysis?

References

Crisfield, P. (2001) *Analysing your Coaching*, Coachwise.

Galligan, F., Crawford, D. and Maskery, C. (2002) *Advanced PE for Edexcel, Teacher's Resource File*, Heinemann.

Miles, A. (2004) *Coaching Practice*, Coachwise.

Stafford-Brown, J., Rea, S., Janaway, L. and Manley, C. (2006) *BTEC First Sport*, Hodder Arnold.

18

Outdoor and adventurous activities

Goals

By the end of this chapter you should:

- know about the organisation and provision of outdoor and adventurous activities
- understand the safety and environmental considerations associated with outdoor and adventurous activities
- be able to participate in outdoor and adventurous activities
- be able to review your own performance in outdoor and adventurous activities.

Outdoor and adventurous activities are very popular these days. Many of these activities require people to work as a team, which helps them to learn social skills and leadership skills.

The aim of this chapter is to introduce outdoor and adventurous activities and to help give tips in developing skills and techniques in these activities. The chapter explores the organisations and range of provision for outdoor activities including governing bodies and the places in which these sports can take place. As most outdoor and adventurous activities do involve an element of risk, safety considerations are also covered. The effect of these activities on the environment is also explored so that outdoor pursuits participants can be made aware of how to protect the environment and still enjoy their activities.

Provision of outdoor and adventurous activities

Outdoor and adventurous activities normally take place in an outdoor rural environment and often contain an element of danger or risk. These activities can be placed into two main categories: land based and water based.

Land-based activities

As the name suggests, these types of outdoor and adventurous activities take place on land. Examples include the following.

- **Rock climbing:** this involves using a range of methods to climb vertical rock faces. Climbers use harnesses, ropes and safety equipment to help them climb.
- **Mountain walking:** this is basically the practice of hiking and navigating mountains. In Britain the classification of a mountain is that it has to be 2000 ft above sea level.
- **Caving:** caving involves exploring caves. It may involve some potholing whereby the person has to manoeuvre their body through small passage ways.
- **Orienteering:** this sport uses a map and compass to determine the correct travel route. It is often performed competitively whereby people have to navigate across challenging terrain from point to point aiming to arrive at the finish first.
- **Mountain biking:** this is basically off-road cycling which uses specially designed mountain bikes. It can be performed recreationally or competitively.

Fig 18.01 Mountain biking

Water-based activities

These sports are carried out in or on water. Types of water include the sea, rivers, canals, lakes, etc. Activities include the following.

- **Canoeing:** people often mistake kayaking for canoeing. A canoe is an open-top boat and is usually paddled by kneeling up and using a single paddle.
- **Kayaking:** a kayak is similar to a canoe, except the paddler is fully enclosed, and uses a double-bladed paddle from a sitting position.
- **Wind surfing:** this is more correctly known as sail boarding. Windsurfing uses a small board and is powered by wind acting on a single sail, which is connected to the board via a flexible joint.
- **Sailing:** this is done in a wind-propelled boat. A rudder helps to steer the boat and a sail is used to harness the wind and propel the boat across the water.

Fig 18.02 Kayaking

LEARNER ACTIVITY Outdoor activities of interest

Make a list of all the outdoor activities you would like to try and explain what it is about them that interests you.

National governing bodies

National governing body: the people or committee who make up a team for the purpose of administering and running the operations of their chosen sporting activity.

There are many providers of outdoor and adventurous activities in the UK. Most activities have their own governing bodies that are responsible for the activity in Great Britain.

The governing bodies promote their activity, liaise with other agencies to try to improve the access and availability of their activity and also offer personal development and coaching qualifications. Many governing bodies provide job opportunities either through coaching and educating or in administration.

The British Orienteering Federation

The British Orienteering Federation (BOF) is the official governing body for orienteering in the UK. Its responsibilities include overseeing development and coordinating a range of orienteering events.

The BOF has a national badge scheme, which awards badges on the basis of performance over a series of events. It also runs five coaching awards, which specialise in teaching orienteering in a range of different environments, and caters for beginners through to experts.

The British Canoe Union

Canoeing is the most popular watersport in the UK. The British Canoe Union (BCU) is the governing body for canoeing and kayaking in the UK, with a membership of 60,000. Its prime aim is to encourage and provide opportunities for people to be able to participate in canoeing. The BCU is currently working on improving access to more rivers in England and Wales.

The BCU operates a widespread range of coaching and education courses. These courses are designed to ensure that coaches and participants are sufficiently prepared to take part in the sport and that the coaches have the relevant qualifications to instruct participants in all aspects of technique, skills and safety.

The Royal Yachting Association

The Royal Yachting Association (RYA) is Britain's national association for all forms of recreational and competitive boating. This includes sailing, motor cruising, sports boats, sail boarding, inland boating, powerboat racing and personal watercraft.

It helps to organise competitions and offers a range of training schemes. Around 185,000 people per year complete RYA training courses in 20 different countries. Other aims of the RYA include:

- to increase boating participation
- to promote safety while afloat
- to protect boaters' rights to enjoy their activity in a responsible way
- to achieve international competitive success.

Mountain Leader Training UK (MLTUK)

Mountain Leader Training UK (MLTUK) is the coordinating body responsible for improving the nation's education and training in the skills required for leadership and instruction for safe rural walking, hill and mountain walking, rock and ice climbing, and other associated activities that take place in cliff and mountainous environments.

Where appropriate, MLTUK works in conjunction with other bodies to help their cause. MLTUK is the coordinating body for all mountain training schemes in Great Britain. It oversees the training and assessment of approximately 6000 leaders, instructors and guides, and is the awarding body of the Mountaineering Instructor Award (summer), Mountaineering Instructor Certificate and European Mountain Leader Awards. MLTUK also has direct links with the mountaineering councils (the British Mountaineering Council, Mountaineering Council of Ireland and Mountaineering Council of Scotland), enabling the training schemes to support the needs of the sport as a whole.

The British Caving Association

The British Caving Association (BCA) is the governing body for underground exploration in the UK. It represents people with either a sporting interest or a scientific interest in caves. Some of its aims are to:

- maintain and seek to improve access to caves and sites of special interest
- seek to achieve a better public understanding of all matters to do with caves and caving
- promote and advise on training, equipment, science and safety
- promote and administer caver training
- provide necessary services and information on behalf of cavers in general
- organise and/or support meeting and events, including training, conservation, science and education.

Statutory bodies

There are many organisations that have an effect on the running of outdoor and adventurous activities. Examples of these include the Countryside Agency, which is responsible for looking after the British countryside and running England's national parks.

National parks

There are currently 12 national parks in England and Wales:

- the New Forest
- the Norfolk Broads
- Snowdonia
- the Pembrokeshire Coast
- the Brecon Beacons
- Dartmoor
- Exmoor
- Northumberland
- the Peak District
- the Lake District
- the North York Moors
- the Yorkshire Dales.

They all provide excellent opportunities to participate in a range of outdoor and adventurous activities.

National sports centres, managed by Sport England, also exist to provide top-level participants with the opportunity to train and prepare for competition. Holme Pierrepont in Nottingham is the National Water Sports Centre, and has a regatta lake and slalom course amongst its facilities. Plas y Brenin is the National Mountain Centre and is located near Snowdonia in North Wales. Its location means that it can it offer some of the best places to participate in mountaineering, climbing and canoeing. It also has a climbing practice wall, ski slope and indoor canoe pool.

Voluntary bodies

The Ramblers' Association is Britain's biggest charity working to promote walking and improve conditions for all walkers. It has 143,000 members in the UK and has been in place for 70 years. Its aims are to:

- safeguard Britain's network of public paths
- provide information to help plan walks and enjoy them in safety and comfort
- increase access for walkers – its work helps to establish statutory rights of access to the outdoors

- protect the countryside and green spaces from unsightly and polluting developments
- educate the public about their rights and responsibilities, and the health and environmental benefits of walking.

Urban outdoor pursuit centres

Due to the increase in the number of people living in more urban areas (built-up towns and cities) there has been an increase in the number of facilities offering alternative opportunities to participate. Somebody who participates in rock climbing and lives in London will find it difficult to get to natural rocks regularly to practise.

As technology has advanced, there have been many manmade facilities created that replicate natural resources. Indoor climbing walls and manmade lakes have meant that more people gain the opportunity to participate in a wider range of activities. An example of modern technology is seeing artificial ski slopes being replaced by real snow indoor skiing facilities. Xscape, in Milton Keynes and Castleford, near Leeds, is a company that has built indoor skiing arenas, with slopes containing real snow.

Therefore the construction of manmade facilities has increased participation in many activities, which otherwise would not be easily accessible to some people.

LEARNER ACTIVITY Provision for outdoor activities

Select four outdoor activities of your choice.

Research places where you may participate in these activities that are:

- close to you
- some distance away from you
- based in an urban environment.

Safety considerations

The Adventure Activities Licensing Authority is a non-departmental public body (NDPB) currently sponsored by the Department for Education and Skills (although, in 2007, this is due to be transferred to the Department for Work and Pensions).

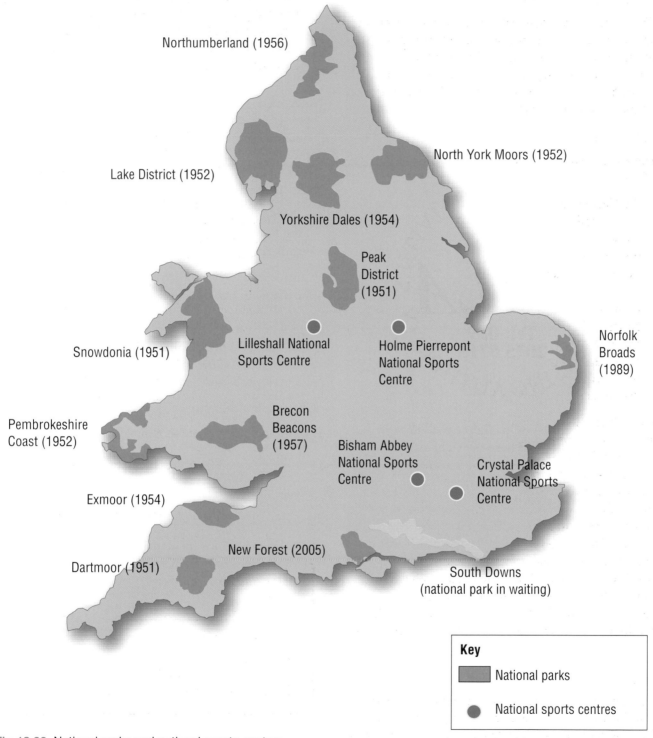

Northumberland (1956)

North York Moors (1952)

Lake District (1952)

Yorkshire Dales (1954)

Peak District (1951)

Lilleshall National Sports Centre

Holme Pierrepont National Sports Centre

Norfolk Broads (1989)

Snowdonia (1951)

Brecon Beacons (1957)

Pembrokeshire Coast (1952)

Bisham Abbey National Sports Centre

Crystal Palace National Sports Centre

Exmoor (1954)

New Forest (2005)

Dartmoor (1951)

South Downs (national park in waiting)

Key

National parks

National sports centres

Fig 18.03 National parks and national sports centres

If it is satisfied that the provider meets nationally accepted standards of good practice, it will issue a licence. This helps provide the public with assurances that the activities are not exposing the participants to unnecessary danger or risks of injury. (Details of when, what and how can be found on its website, at www.aala.org.uk.)

Taking part in outdoor activities can be immensely beneficial, as well as great fun. You can often find yourself miles away from the roads, shops and other

Key learning points

- Each outdoor activity has a governing body which administers and runs the operations of its chosen sporting activity.
- National parks and national sports centres provide opportunities for outdoor activity participation.
- Urban outdoor pursuit centres allow outdoor activities to take place in urban environments.

people. But this isolation could prove to be very dangerous if you do not have the right safety awareness if you or a member of your team get into difficulty. You should follow safety precautions to help keep yourself and your party safe.

Risk assessments

A risk assessment is a procedure used to help prevent any potential accidents and injuries. This process is usually performed by the manager or instructors working in the outdoor pursuit centre. The assessment allows people to take time to consider what could go wrong when taking part in their activity. The risk assessment examines the possible hazards that may occur, the risks involved, the likelihood of them happening and how the hazards are being prevented. Risk assessments should be logged, kept and reviewed regularly to see if they are up to date and none of the details has changed.

An example of a hazards would be:

- a strong current in the sea, used for windsurfing
- ice on a footpath.

A risk is linked to the chance of somebody being harmed by the potential hazard. Risks are often

definition

Hazard: a potential source of danger which has the potential to affect someone's safety or cause an injury.
Risk: the possibility of something bad happening.

categorised into how likely they are to happen, and how serious they are likely to be if they do happen. Something that is a low risk means that the likelihood of it happening is low, whereas something that is high risk means that it is likely to happen. Examples of risks include:

- slipping on ice and twisting your ankle
- the boom hitting your head while sailing
- capsizing while kayaking.

Control measures are the measures taken to control (i.e. manage) the risks (see below).

Undertaking a risk assessment

Once you have highlighted a hazard the easiest way to assess it is to use the following formula to assess any potential problems that may arise:

Likelihood × severity

Likelihood – is it likely to happen?

1 Unlikely
2 Quite likely
3 Very likely

Severity – how badly someone could be injured.

1 No injury/minor incident
2 Injury requiring medical assistance
3 Major injury or fatality

Here is an example: Capsizing in a kayak

Likelihood of happening	Severity
2. Quite likely	1. No injury

By multiplying the likelihood against the severity you will be able to draw up a chart that looks at the potential problems and make a decision on whether you want to take the risk or whether it is too much of a hazard. The example above would be 2 × 1 = 2

Likelihood × severity	Is the risk worth taking?
1	Yes with caution
2	Yes possibly with caution
3	Yes possibly with extreme caution
4	Yes possibly with extreme caution
6	No
9	No

Control measures

Control measures reduce the likelihood of an accident happening. This could include specialist protective equipment to help minimise the risk of injury.

- Mountain bikers wear helmets in case they fall off their bike.
- Safety ropes are used in climbing to minimise the risk of falling.
- Hiking boots are worn when mountain walking to minimise the risk of slipping and twisting an ankle.
- Life jackets or buoyancy aids are worn for most water sports to minimise the risk of drowning.

LEARNER ACTIVITY Hazards and risks

Make a list of three outdoor activities. determine at least five hazards and five risks you may encounter while taking part in each of these activities, and five corresponding control measures.

LEARNER ACTIVITY Safety equipment

Choose three of your favourite outdoor activities. Make a list of all the safety equipment you need in order to reduce the risk of injury.

An example of a risk assessment form is given on the next page.

LEARNER ACTIVITY Risk assessment

Copy and complete the risk assessment form on page 346 for an outdoor activity of your choice.

Contingency plans

A contingency plan is about expecting the unexpected. It is planning for any event that might happen. In this way it is possible to imagine and then calculate what you would do in any given situation. You or your instructor should have devised a contingency plan for every activity so that they know what to do should such a situation arise.

When planning an activity you could ask yourself a series of 'What would I do if . . .' questions:

- What would I do if someone become seriously injured?
- What would I do if the minibus breaks down?
- What would I do if the weather becomes really bad?
- What would I do if a participant gets lost?
- What would I do if we run out of food and drink?
- What would I do if the leader is unable to continue?

Emergency procedures

When an emergency occurs it is important that you remain calm. If there are casualties it is important to

Key learning points

- A hazard is something that has the potential to cause injury or compromise safety.
- A risk is the likelihood of something happening.
- A risk assessment is a list of possible hazards that states the likelihood of them happening, and ways of controlling them.
- The level of risk is worked out by multiplying likelihood or risk by severity. A risk level of 6 or more means that either more safety precautions should be introduced or the activity should not take place.

Risk assessment

Location of risk assessment: _____

Risk assessor's name: _____

Date:_____

Hazard	People at risk	Likelihood	Severity	Level of risk	Control measures

Casualty: a person injured or killed as a result of an incident.
Emergency: a serious incident that happens suddenly or unexpectedly and is likely to require different forms of assistance.

summon assistance as soon as possible. Use either a mobile or public phone to dial 999 and ask for an ambulance (and possibly the mountain rescue team, depending on where you are located). You will need to give them the following details:

- the name and age of the casualty, and a description of their injuries
- the exact location of the injured person – grid references and the map sheet number
- the time and nature of the accident
- the weather conditions.

You should then stay on the phone until you are met by the emergency services.

If the injury is life-threatening a rescue helicopter may have to be brought in. If this is the case, there are a few precautions that you will need to follow before and during its arrival.

- Secure all loose equipment; this can be done with stones or rucksacks.
- Raise your arms in a V shape as the helicopter approaches; this will signal to the helicopter that you are the casualty group. Do not wave to the helicopter as this is the signal for everything is OK.
- Shelter the injured person from the rotor downdraught.
- Do not approach the helicopter unless directed.

If you do not have a mobile phone or there is no signal, you would have to send a distress signal. If you have a whistle with you, give a series of six loud blasts followed by one minute's silence. Continue this process until you receive a response. If you are in an area where it may be difficult for other people to hear this sound, you should use a visual signal. Smoke from a fire gives a good visual signal. If you hear or see an aircraft, you should try to attract its attention with a mirror, glass or any other shiny object. You should also try to spread out any bright clothing you have on the floor which will help draw attention to yourselves.

At night you should use a torch to signal the code SOS. This is done by giving three short flashes, three long flashes followed by another three short flashes.

LEARNER ACTIVITY
Emergency procedures role play

In groups of four imagine one of you has injured themselves on a mountain. Two people carry out a role play to determine how they will get help. The fourth person should observe and give feedback to the group on what they thought they did well and how they could improve.

Safety equipment

You should always carry a basic first aid kit with you on any outdoor activities. If you are taking part in water-based activities, make sure the following pieces of safety equipment are kept in a sealed watertight container:

- ten plasters in various sizes
- two large sterile dressings for management of severe bleeding
- a medium sterile dressing for care of larger wounds
- four triangular bandages to support suspected broken bones, dislocations or sprains
- an eye pad in case of a cut to the eye
- four safety pins to secure dressings
- disposable gloves.

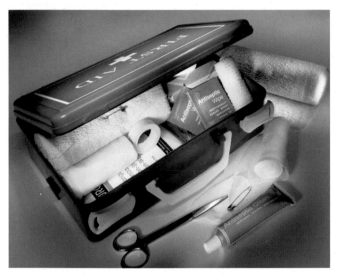

Fig 18.04 A first-aid kit

You should also carry the following:

- a survival bag – a large heavy-duty bag that you can climb into to keep you insulated against the cold
- a torch and spare batteries in your rucksack so that you can see where you are going and give distress signals if required
- a whistle in your pocket or on a string around your neck so that you can give distress signals
- enough food for your journey as well as emergency rations (energy-dense foods such as Kendal mint cake or a Mars bar) just in case you find yourself trapped or having to spend longer out on the activity than you intended.

Environmental considerations

When enjoying walking in the outdoors it is essential that you respect the environment to preserve its beauty. Some of the areas you choose to explore may be subject to special protection, such as Areas of Outstanding Natural Beauty (AONBs). An area of natural beauty is an area with a greatly valued landscape that should be preserved. There are 41 in England and Wales, and they include coastlines, meadows and moors.

There are also National Nature Reserves (NNRs), which are places designated to putting wildlife first. They help to protect, preserve and study wildlife and their habitat. Nearly every rural county has an NNR. The majority of NNRs have access for visitors.

The Countryside Rights of Way Act 2000 (known as CRoW) was put in place in order to increase the public's ability to enjoy the countryside. It allows the public access to open country and registered common land whereas before some people were restricting access. It aims to modernise the rights of way system, provide better management for AONBs and strengthen wildlife enforcement legislation. Wherever you walk in the countryside you should always adhere to the Countryside Code:

- Always close and secure gates after yourself.
- Leave property as you find it.
- Protect plants and animals – do not damage or move plants, trees or rocks from their natural habitat.
- Do not leave litter of any type, take it home with you and dispose of it properly.
- Keep dogs under close control.
- Consider other people – do not make too much noise and do not block entrances and driveways with your vehicle.

Key learning points

- Distress signals: six loud blasts on the whistle followed by one minute of silence, to be repeated until help arrives.
- Torchlight flashes: three short flashes, three long flashes, three short flashes, break and repeat.
- Enjoy, but always respect, the environment in which you participate in your outdoor activity. Always follow the Countryside Code.

Participate in outdoor and adventurous activities

There is a host of skills and techniques required for each outdoor activity you choose to take part in. As there is not enough room in this book to detail every skill and technique required for each activity we will explore only map reading, navigation and route planning, as these skills are required for a number of outdoor and adventurous activities.

Maps

Maps give an accurate representation of the ground as seen from above. They are then scaled down to different sizes. Most maps you will use are Ordnance Survey (OS) maps, with a scale of 1:25,000. This means one unit of length represents 25,000 units on the ground. So, if one unit was 1 cm, 1 cm would cover 250 m on the ground. Maps contain different symbols to show different landmarks on the ground. They also contain the following useful information:

● map title – the area of ground that the map covers
● key to the symbols
● the year the map was made
● the sheet number – the whole of the UK is covered by 203 sheets
● adjoining sheet numbers
● grid numbers
● a scale line to measure distances.

Measuring distance

There are a two main methods you can use to measure the distance of your route. The cheapest method uses only a piece of string. Take a piece of string and place it along the exact route on the map. Place the string on the scale line and count the distance it covers. This should give you an idea of the route you are planning. You could also use a commercially made map measurer which you run along your route and it will tell you the distance covered.

Navigation

Navigation: the process of plotting and following a route from one place to another.

There are a number of different methods you can use to navigate your journey. The best one to use will be determined by the lay of the land, the weather and the time of day or night. No matter what type of navigation you use, you will always need a map.

Across an OS map you will see a series of lines going up and across the map, dividing it into 1 km block squares. These lines are blue; the ones that run across the map are known as Eastings and those that run up and down the map are Northings. The lines are numbered and allow you to pinpoint your exact location on a map. When giving a grid reference you should always give the Eastings first. A good way to remember this is to think 'Go along the corridor and then up the stairs.'

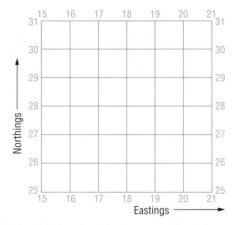

Fig 18.05 A grid showing Eastings and Northings

LEARNER ACTIVITY
Route planning

● Look at an OS map and plan a route from an area that contains water or forest to another area that contains a building of some sort. Work out the distance using a piece of string and the scale line on your map.
● If you have one available, carry out the same exercise using a map measurer.
● Compare the distances you get and try to explain why there may be any differences.

LEARNER ACTIVITY
Grid references

Look at a map and choose three features. Give the grid references of these three different features.

Contour: lines on a map that show you the height of the land.

Most areas that you plan to walk through will not be totally flat. Therefore, contour lines are drawn on to maps to show the height of the land above sea level. The height between contour lines on OS maps is 10 m. The height is written into some of these lines. The numbers are written with the top of the number facing uphill.

Fig 18.06 Contour lines

Contour lines also give you a good impression of the shape of the land. Areas of the map that contain lots of closely packed contour lines show that the land has a steep slope. Valleys and ridges can also be shown by these lines.

Fig 18.07 Contour lines showing valleys and ridges

LEARNER ACTIVITY Contours

Look at a map and choose an area with contours. Now try to draw the formation of the land in relation to the contours.

Setting the map

Setting the map is a method of placing the map in a position so that all the features are lined up and your location is at the central point. So, if you were to look to your left, you would see the same features on the ground as you would on the map, and the same would be true for looking ahead or to your right. You may find the writing on the map is upside down when you have set it.

This process can be carried out without any problems if there is good visibility. Look for a prominent feature on the map such as a church, a hill or a village then turn the map so that the features on the ground are in line with you at the central point. If visibility is poor – fog or night-time – you will have to use your compass to set the map. The compass will show you where magnetic north is. Then you will need to line up north on the map with north on the compass. While you are walking, ensure that you keep the map set (i.e. change its position) as you change direction so, if you turn right, turn the map in the same direction so that it remains set.

Using a compass

You need to carry your compass in such a way that it is accessible at all times and you are able to move it in any direction. You must also be able to let it go without losing it. The best method of carrying a compass is to attach a long cord to it and carry it over one shoulder.

Fig 18.08 A compass

definition

Bearing: a direction of travel, between 0 and 360 degrees from north in a clockwise direction.

Taking a bearing

When you are walking in poor visibility you will need to take bearings from your map and walk on a bearing. Place the compass on the map so that the arrow is pointing in the direction you wish to travel. Then line up the baseplate with where you want to travel to. Then turn the compass housing so that the north arrow is pointing to the north on the map. Ensure the lines within the compass housing are running parallel to the grid lines running northwards.

Now you need to convert the bearing to a magnetic bearing by adding magnetic variation, which is 5 degrees. Hold the compass horizontally in front of you. Change your direction until the red end of the compass needle is over the orienteering arrow and parallel to the lines in the bottom of the housing. Look in the direction of the travel arrow to see if you can see a feature on the landscape that it lines up with. You can then walk towards this feature. When you have reached the feature, stop and repeat the process until you have reached your desired location. If you do not see a feature to walk towards, hold the compass in front of you and keep walking in the direction of the travel arrow.

Measuring distance travelled

There are two methods of estimating the distance you have covered: timing and pacing.

Timing

This process works on the principal of estimating your walking speed and knowing how long you have been walking for. The speed that you walk at will vary depending on whether you are walking uphill or on flat terrain. Most fit people walk at a speed of about 5 km per hour on flat ground. You then need to add ten minutes for every 100 m of height gained or one minute for every 10 m gained (Naismith's rule). Walking down steep hills will take longer than walking on the flat, so you should add 1 minute for every 30 m descent.

Pacing

This process uses the principle of counting the number of steps you have taken and estimating the distance covered from these steps. It takes an average-sized male about 60 double steps to cover 100 m. From this you can then work out how far you have

travelled. You need to be aware that the size of your pace will vary depending on whether you are travelling uphill or downhill.

Fig 18.09 Taking a bearing

> ### LEARNER ACTIVITY Pacing your distance
>
> Work out your own paces by counting how many double steps you take when walking along a 100 m athletics track.

Planning your route

This process should be thought through carefully and planned properly. If you do not give it full attention you may find yourself walking up some very steep mountains or having to walk through boggy ground when you really just wanted to have a fairly easy walk. Think about what you want to accomplish on your expedition and the features you would like to see, such as lakes or forests. Think about how far you would like to walk and the time it will take you, or if you are in a group, how long it would take your slowest walker.

You will also need to factor in meal breaks. You may wish to aim to eat lunch at a certain place by a river or in a cafe. If you are planning an overnight expedition, make sure you have given yourself enough time to reach your campsite or have chosen an appropriate place to pitch your tent for the night. You should then prepare a route card and make sure you leave a copy of it with someone, preferably a police officer at the nearest police station to your route or a person at the nearest mountain centre. This is very important as it will not only aid your navigation, but if you get into difficulty, this route card can be used to locate and rescue you.

An example of a route card is shown below.

Use of equipment

The equipment used for taking part in outdoor activities is often very specialised and specific to the activity. There are, however, some generic items that are worn for both water-based and land-based activities.

Water-based activities

For most water-based activities you will usually need to wear either a wetsuit or a drysuit and a buoyancy aid.

Wetsuits are used to try to protect your body from the cold water and are used during the warmer seasons – late spring, summer and early autumn. They use your own body heat to keep you warm by trapping air, and then the neoprene of the wetsuit helps to keep you warm by acting as an insulator for your body heat. When you fall in the water or capsize, you will feel cold for a short while as your body heat warms up the layer of water trapped in the wetsuit. For a wetsuit to work effectively, it is essential that it fits the wearer snugly.

An alternative to wetsuits are drysuits. These are worn during the colder seasons such as late autumn, winter and early spring. They are designed to keep the wearer dry, even when the person is totally submerged in water. Underneath the drysuit, a person usually wears thermal clothing to keep them warm. A drysuit does not need to fit as snugly as a wetsuit because it is airtight so it sucks the suit closer to your body.

A buoyancy aid is different from a life jacket. A buoyancy aid will help to keep you afloat if you fall into the water, whereas a life jacket will not only help to keep you afloat, but is designed to help keep your head up and out of the water should you fall unconscious during your time submerged. Buoyancy aids are usually worn for windsurfing, kayaking and small dinghy sailing because they allow greater mobility than life jackets. Life jackets are usually worn on larger sailing boats as these tend to be used for sailing further out into the water and further away from help and rescue.

Team leader: R. Ambler Date: 26.10.06			Starting point: GR 328800 Finishing point: GR 337621				ETD: 0800 ETA: 1800	
Leg	From	From	To	To	Bearing	Bearing	Distance	Remarks, hazards, etc.
	Location	GR	Location	GR	Grid	Mag		
1	River	327645	Stile	337644	342	347	500m	Cairns
2	Stile	337644	Xroads	341044	54	59	1700m	Steep slope

Fig 18.10 A life jacket

Key learning points

Ensure you can demonstrate an understanding of the following:

- know how to read and set a map
- ensure you are able to read and give grid references
- know how to use a compass
- know how to take and follow bearings
- know how to write a route card.

The equipment you use for your outdoor activity is necessary to ensure your safety and enjoyment. Always find out exactly what you need to wear and take with you. Research the different types of equipment available and then determine what is best for you, based on the time of year and the location of your activity.

Land-based activities

For most land-based activities, one of the most important pieces of equipment you will buy is your footwear. If you choose the wrong type or if they do not fit you properly it could mean your activity has to be ended prematurely due to blisters or injury. Both hiking boots and shoes are available. Boots give ankle support which helps prevent twisting ankles on uneven ground. The top of the boot or shoe should be waterproof or water repellent. The soles should be able to give good grip on all walking surfaces you may face. The soles should also provide some cushioning from the impact of walking.

Review performance in outdoor and adventurous activities

Having completed an activity, it is important to gain some feedback on how to improve performance. Feedback can come from a number of sources.

Fig 18.11 A buoyancy aid

- From yourself: a log book, how the activity felt, did you complete the skill effectively, etc.
- From your peers: verbal feedback, comparison of ability, how well you work as a team, etc.
- An assessor: did you achieve the set target?
- An instructor: verbal feedback, video footage.

Strengths and areas for development

Information about strengths and weaknesses provides us with a template for improvement. You should be able to learn something new about your abilities after every activity session. Examples of development feedback could be:

- poor or ineffective stroke (canoeing or kayaking)
- ineffective/unsafe knots used (climbing)
- ineffective communication with the group
- inaccurate pacing technique (hiking).

All of the above can be improved. You should develop your own self-assessment techniques, paying particular attention to what needs to be improved and in what order.

Target setting

Once a decision has been made about your areas of development, it is an appropriate time to think about setting targets. Remember that you may not be able to achieve your desired skill levels immediately and while these remain your long-term goal it is important to set realistic short-term targets to lay the pathway to achieving your skills. When you have identified areas for development, it is good practice to apply the SMART principle. This stands for the following:

- **S**pecific
- **M**easurable
- **A**chievable
- **R**ealistic
- **T**ime-constrained.

Specific: the target must be specific to what you want to achieve. For example, you may need to improve your paddle position in order to complete an Eskimo roll.

Measurable: targets must be stated in a way that is measurable, so they need to include figures. For example, I want to be able to hike 15 km in eight hours.

Achievable: it must be possible to actually achieve the target.

Realistic: we need to be realistic in our setting and look at what factors may stop us achieving the target.

Time-constrained: there must be a timescale or deadline on the target. This means you can review your success. It is best to state a date by which you wish to achieve the goal.

From this information you can then determine your aims and objectives. Do you want to be able to complete certain awards for your chosen outdoor activity? If this is the case, you will have to investigate whether there are any clubs in your area that run the activity or perhaps you could go on a residential course at an outdoor pursuits centre. From this information you will be able to continue developing your skills and techniques in your chosen outdoor activities and possibly eventually take on instructing qualifications and pursue a career in these sports.

LEARNER ACTIVITY Finding out about clubs

Select two outdoor activities that you have taken part in. Find out:

- the nearest clubs that cater for these activities
- the award scheme for each activity
- what you need to be able to do to achieve your first or next qualification in this activity.

Review questions

1 Select four outdoor activities of your choice; for each, name the governing body and the main objectives of that body.
2 Explain the purpose of a risk assessment.
3 Explain how you would get help should an emergency situation arise while taking part in an outdoor activity.
4 What does SMART mean in relation to setting targets?
5 What is the purpose of planning an escape route?
6 Explain the purpose of the Countryside Code and give examples of what it includes.
7 Describe how you would set a map.

References

Cox, D. (2002) *The Sailing Handbook*, New Holland Publishers.

Hanson, J. and Hanson, R. (1997) *Ragged Mountain Press Guide to Outdoor Sports*, McGraw-Hill.

Lockren, I. (1998) *Outdoor Pursuits*, Nelson Thornes.

Long, S. (2003, revised 2004) *Hill Walking*. Mountain Leader Training UK.

Rowe, R. (1989) *Canoeing Handbook, Official Handbook of the British Canoe Union*, Chameleon Press.

Websites

www.bcu.org.uk – British Canoe Union
www.thebmc.co.uk – British Mountaineering Council
www.ramblers.org.uk – Ramblers Association
www.rya.org – Royal Yachting Association

19

Applied sport and exercise psychology

Goals

By the end of this chapter you should:

- know about the role of sport and exercise psychologists
- be able to implement techniques to influence motivation
- be able to use imagery in sports performance
- be able to apply techniques to control arousal
- be able to plan a psychological skills training programme.

Sport psychologists need to have a detailed understanding of theory so that they have a framework in which to understand the behaviour of athletes. They also need to have a range of techniques to diagnose the strengths and weaknesses of an athlete. Once the weaknesses have been diagnosed, techniques can be applied to improve the performance of the athlete. This work with the individual athlete is where a sport psychologist will prove their value to the athlete or team.

The role of the sport psychologist

The traditional route to become a sport psychologist is to train at university in sport science, psychology or a similar degree and then to study sport psychology at masters or PhD (doctoral) level. There are now specific degrees in sport psychology as well. To work with sports teams you will need to be registered with the British Association of Sport and Exercise Science (BASES).

All of us apply psychological techniques in our daily lives and to our sporting performance to help improve our chances or performance. Most people do it in an unconscious, amateur manner, and so learning how to do it in a formal, trained way can change how they function on a daily basis. For example, when our alarm clock goes off in the morning we have a study in motivation. Are you sufficiently motivated to jump out of bed and get on with the day or are you motivated to reset the alarm and miss college? If we have clear goals for the day we will greet the alarm going off and feel driven to get out of bed.

The sport psychologist seeks to understand the individual and how they function on the sports field. They will ask themselves some simple questions:

- What is this person experiencing?
- How are they feeling?
- What thoughts are they having?
- What pictures have they got in their head?
- What are they saying to themselves?

We must remember that everyone is different and experiences the world and events in an entirely unique way. Our experience is unique and no one else will experience things in this way. The sport psychologist needs to find out the experience of the athlete they are working with and then experience the situation in the same way as best as they can. This is called 'calibration' and is essential to the success of the psychologist/athlete relationship.

Sport psychologists may have more than one role. The three roles they may assume are:

- the practical consultancy role
- the research role
- the teaching role.

The practical consultancy role

An important role for the sport psychologist is in working with athletes and teams to give them skills and techniques to improve and enhance their performance. Psychological skills training can also help to improve the enjoyment of competition and the satisfaction of the competitors.

This may be on a full-time basis as we can see happening with the England cricket, football and rugby teams, or on a part-time basis as and when needed. The sport psychologist will not replace anyone on the coaching team. Rather they will be used to complement the work of the team members. Some sport psychologists will work in the fitness industry to help people with their motivation to stick to their training programmes and achieve the results they want.

Fig 19.01 Sport psychologist coaching an athlete

The research role

In any area of science it is the responsibility of people working within that field to build upon the body of information that has been gained. As a sport psychologist works they will have experiences and gain information which they can use themselves and pass on to other practitioners. Many sport psychologists are involved in formal research, which involves setting up research experiments, recording results and then writing and presenting papers at conferences. Research can involve the use of questionnaires to elicit information, equipment to gain data or the observation of behaviour patterns in specific situations.

The teaching role

Many sport psychologists are based in universities or other educational establishments. They will teach general programmes in sport psychology, applied sport psychology or in specialist areas such as sports teams or psychology for tennis.

The sport psychologist will be involved in all or some of these areas. This chapter focuses on the practical consultancy role. Within this role there are five main areas where the sport psychologist can add value to the athlete's performance. These are covered in the following section.

Practical support from a sport psychologist
Training to enhance performance

The sport psychologist provides the performer with a range of techniques to help improve their performance. This includes skills to:

● help the athlete prepare for the performance
● help them during their performance
● employ when certain events occur during the competition.

In order to work with an athlete we need to adopt a set of beliefs; an important one is 'Everyone is in control of their brain and the thoughts that they have.'

It is important to believe this because if we have no control over our thoughts then we can do nothing about it. But if we are in control we can change how we are feeling at any point in time. If I ask you to think of a happy memory from your childhood you will notice that it changes the way you feel and makes you act in a different way.

When working with athletes a good place to start is the performance equation developed by W. Timothy Gallwey in his book *The Inner Game of Golf*:

Performance = Potential − Psychological interference

Performance is what actually happened. It is the outcome or result.

Potential is as good as they can possibly be and is the sum of an individual's ability, skills, knowledge and education.

Psychological interference is the mental processes which prevent an individual achieving their full potential at any point in time. It will include factors such as lack of motivation, effects of stress and anxiety, past experiences and memories, lack of self-esteem or confidence, limiting self-beliefs, poor concentration and negative attitude. This can be seen as the unconscious ways our own brains will sabotage our efforts to become the best we can possibly become.

Clearly, the role of the sport psychologist is to eliminate or minimise any psychological interference so that performance comes closer to matching potential. In effect, we want the processes of our own brains to work for us rather than against us.

LEARNER ACTIVITY
Performance, potential and psychological interference

Consider your most recent performance and ask yourself the following questions.

- How close was my performance to my actual potential or best possible performance?
- What psychological interference was I experiencing?
- What thoughts did I have before and during performance which may have affected my performance negatively?
- What do I need to work on to eliminate psychological interference in the future?

Team building and social development

The function of groups or teams is the sum of the individual components of the group. The sport psychologist needs to analyse how the group is working and the positive or negative effects of these actions. The aim of working with teams is to develop 'team spirit' which is about how attracted the individuals are to the group. Key to the functioning of a group is how and by whom the group is led.

The success of the England rugby team in winning the 2003 World Cup is attributed in part to the influence of the captain, Martin Johnson, in inspiring people to follow his lead and uniting the team. The failure of the England football team at the 2006 World Cup was attributed in part to the weak leadership of Sven Goran Eriksson and David Beckham. Before the Ashes series of 2006/7 there was great debate over whether Andrew Flintoff or Andrew Strauss should captain England and the effect this would have on team dynamics and performance.

Lifestyle management

The outcome the athlete achieves depends not only upon what they do on the day but what they do with every minute of every day. Actions can be seen to add to or take away from their chances of success. Their ability to organise their life with the demands of work, training, travelling, eating, sleeping, relaxing, developing relationships and socialising is key to their chances of success.

The events in their non-competitive life can add to their stress, affect their mental state and drain their resources. The sport psychologist can offer advice on how to manage their time and energy most effectively.

Dealing with injury

Periods of injury can be devastating for the athlete because their identity as an athlete is formed by their ability to perform and the performances they achieve. To have this taken away affects self-confidence and identity. Their motivation will be to get back to competition as quickly as possible and this may include taking risks with their health.

The sport psychologist may need to offer counselling to the athlete to address their issues of confidence and ensure that they are dealing with feelings of anxiety or depression they may be experiencing. Also, they may need to look at motivation and realistically set goals to ensure that they will return to competition only when they are truly ready.

Coach education

Just as a sport psychologist will work with an athlete or team, so they will also work to educate coaches in how to deal with their athletes and teams. This is usually done through the coaches' training programmes which are set up by the governing body. Coaches need to have psychological skills to deal with their athletes in terms of knowing how different people are motivated and how what they say may affect the team or individual.

The case may arise where the coach needs the sport psychologist. Watching athletes and teams perform can be deeply frustrating and stressful. We need only watch football managers to see the emotions they are experiencing and the effect this can have on them.

Fig 19.02 The stress of being a manager

Key learning points

The sport psychologist has three main roles:

- the practical consultancy role
- the research role
- the teaching role.

Sport psychologists can assist athletes, teams and coaches in five main ways:

- training to enhance performance
- team building and social development
- lifestyle management
- dealing with injury
- coach education.

Techniques to influence motivation in sport and exercise

Goal setting

The main way that a sport psychologist develops motivation is through the use of goal setting.

> **Goal:** what an individual is aiming to achieve. It is the outcome they desire from their actions.

In reality, goals are the dreams we have for ourselves, but goal setting gives these dreams legs and starts moving us towards them. A goal usually represents a situation we want to be in, which involves us moving away from the situation we are currently in.

Why does goal setting work?

Goal setting works because it gives our wants and desires a specific outcome and gives us the steps we need to move towards this outcome. It gives our daily actions a meaning or framework to work within and gives us direction in life. Goals will work to direct our energy and efforts.

' **What you focus on you will move towards** '

How do I know what I want? This is not always so easy but what is important in actually getting somewhere is knowing where you want to go. Ask yourself the following questions.

- What are the things that are most important to me?
- What specifically do I want or if I could have anything in the world what would it be?
- What will I see, hear and feel when I have it?
- How will I know I have achieved what I want?

Particularly ask yourself the following question: 'If I have this goal what will it bring me?'

This will help you to understand the 'value' behind the goal. The goal itself will bring you something important or of worth to you.

Short-, medium- and long-term goals

Short-term goals are set over a brief period of time, usually from one day to one month. A short-term goal may relate to what you want to achieve in one training session or where you want to be by the end of the month.

Medium-term goals will bridge the gap between short- and long-term goals and are set from one to three months.

Long-term goals will run from three months to over several years. You may even set some lifetime goals which run until you retire from your sport. In sport we may set long-term goals to cover a season or a sporting year.

Usually short-term goals are set to help achieve the long-term goals. It is important to set both short-term and long-term goals – particularly short-term goals because they will give a person more motivation to act now. If you have to give in a piece of coursework tomorrow it will make you work hard tonight but if you have to submit it in one month then you are unlikely to stay in tonight and complete the work! Short-term goals will have the most powerful effect because they influence what we are doing now, in this moment.

Outcome and process goals

An outcome goal focuses on the outcome of an event or performance, such as winning a race or beating an opponent. A process goal focuses on the process or actions that an individual must produce to perform well – for example, train three times a week or gain eight hours sleep a night.

Both types of goal are important and we find that short-term goals are normally process goals while long-term goals are outcome goals.

The process goals will be the small steps we take towards the big outcome or goal. A marathon race is the result of millions of small steps and it is each individual step which is most important at that time.

SMART goals

When goals are set you need to use the SMART principle to make them workable. SMART stands for:

- Specific
- Measurable
- Achievable
- Realistic
- Time-constrained.

Specific: the goal must be specific to what you want to achieve. This may be an aspect of performance or fitness. It is not enough to say 'I want to get fitter.' You

need to say 'I want to improve strength, speed or stamina', etc.

Measurable: goals must be stated in a way that is measurable, so they need to state figures. For example, I want to improve my first serve percentage is not measurable. However, if you say I want to improve my first serve success by 20 per cent it is measurable.

Achievable: it must be possible to actually achieve the goal.

Realistic: we need to be realistic in our goal setting and look at what factors may stop us achieving the goal.

Time-constrained: there must be a timescale or deadline on the goal. This means you can review your success. It is best to state a date by which you wish to achieve the goal.

How to set goals

The best way to do this is to answer three questions:

- What do I want to achieve? (desired state)
- Where am I now? (present state)
- What do I need to do to move from my present state to my desired state?

Then present this on a scale:

Present state   Desired state

|—————|—————|—————|—————|—————|

1   2   3   4   5

- Write in your goal at point 5 and your present position at point 1.
- Decide what would be halfway between points 1 and 5. This is your goal for point 3.
- Then decide what would be halfway between present state and point 3. This is your short-term goal for point 2.
- Then decide what would be halfway between point 3 and the desired state; this is the goal for point 4.
- All these goals are outcome goals and must be set using the SMART principle.
- Work out what needs to be done to move from point 1 to point 2. These are your process goals and must again use the SMART principle.

It is best to use a goal-setting diary to keep all goal-setting information in the same place, and to review the goals on a weekly basis.

Process goals
(1 → 2)
1. Run three times a week
2. Run 20 k in total
3. Join a running club
4. Have a nutritional consultation
5. Get 8 hours sleep a night

Fig 19.03 Example of goal setting using a continuum

LEARNER ACTIVITY
Goal setting

Think about your own sport and set yourself a goal which you would like to achieve in the next year. Then, using the process above, set yourself outcome goals and work out the process goals to get you from point 1 to point 2.

Additional techniques and factors

Use imagery: if we can imagine ourselves when we have achieved our goal or are achieving our goal, it can increase to the power of the goal and really implant the image on our nervous system.

To use imagery you need to do the following.

- Sit down and close your eyes.
- Bring up a picture of yourself when you have achieved your goal.
- Make this picture really big – as big as a cinema screen.
- Make the picture very colourful and make it bright.
- Make the picture highly focused.
- Run the picture through as a film rather than a photograph.
- Feel the feelings associated with achieving the goal.
- Focus on the picture and how good it feels to have achieved your goal.
- As you breathe deeply, lock in the pictures and feelings.
- Practise this regularly to increase its worth and make it really compelling.

Be positive: always state the goals in a positive way to show what you are moving towards rather than

moving away from. Rather than say 'I will avoid defeat' you should say 'I will win.' And rather than say 'I will hit the ball out of play less' you may say 'I will keep the ball in play.'

Resources: be aware of what resources you may need. What do you need to achieve your goal in terms of physical resources such as equipment and facilities, other people for support or as role models, and your own qualities such as determination and commitment?

Count the cost of achieving this goal: everything in life has a cost and you can have what you like as long as you are willing to pay the price. The cost may be financial or personal, as it may affect how much time or money you have. It may affect the relationships you have and there will be losses as well as gains. Be realistic and ask yourself 'Is the cost worth it?' or 'What are the wider implications of gaining this goal?' Every action will have consequences you intend and some that you did not intend, and you need to foresee these.

Performance profiling

Performance profiling is a way of getting the athlete to analyse their own strengths and weaknesses. It can be a way of monitoring improvements in psychological skills, as well as being used to motivate and energise athletes.

The benefits of performance profiling are as follows.

- It considers what the individual feels is important.
- The individual is actively involved and will feel some ownership over their performances.
- It is used to motivate and monitor improvements.
- It is specific to each athlete.
- The visual display helps to give it more power.
- It enables the athlete and coach to identify areas of weakness.

Process of performance profiling

Performance profiling is completed in the following way.

Introduce the idea of performance profiling: this may be a new concept for the athlete and a period of explaining the process will be valuable. You will need to cover the following information:

- how it works
- the benefits and how the results can be applied

- the fact that there are no wrong or right answers and what is important is the individual's view
- examples of completed performance profiles (anonymous).

Elicit the constructs: the sport psychologist will need to ask the athlete to come up with ten psychological factors which are vital to their performance. You may ask a question such as 'What psychological factors do you consider to be most important in helping you to achieve your best performance?'

The sport psychologist may assist the process by making relevant suggestions if the athlete is struggling to come up with good responses. The ten factors they come up with are called 'constructs'.

Assessment of constructs: the athlete is asked to complete the following tasks.

- Rate themselves on a scale of 1 to 10 to show their current level of competence at each construct. A rating of 10 would represent their idea of perfection.
- Rate how far they would like to progress towards their idea of perfection. They may feel that a score of 10 is not necessary and they would be happy to get to 7.

Plotting the performance profile

Once the above tasks have been completed you can present the information on a grid such as the one below. The dark bars show current levels of competence and the lighter bars show desired levels.

You can then use this information in different ways:

- to assess their strengths and weaknesses
- to see what they feel is important in their sport.

As their coach you may have different ideas about what is important and their level of skill. This exercise will highlight any differences in your points of view.

You can identify the following information from the profile:

- areas of perceived strength – where they score 5 or more (aggression control)
- areas of perceived weakness – where they score less than 5 (arousal control)
- areas resistant to change – where there is little difference between their current rating and the rating they would like to achieve (attitude).

Other applications of performance profiling

Performance profiling was borrowed from industry, where it has been used by employers to get their workers to evaluate their current performance in their job. It can

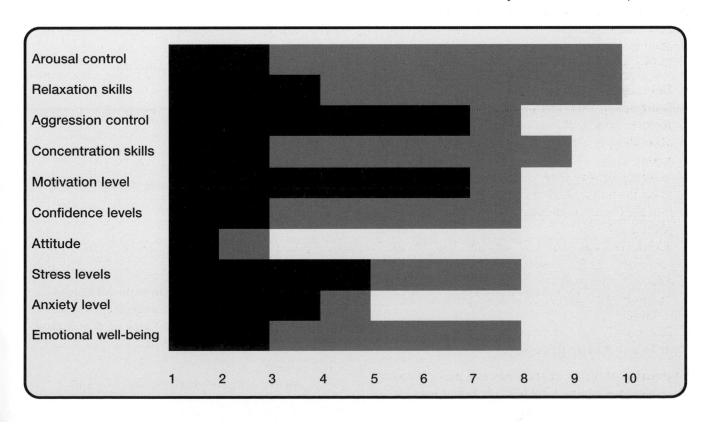

be used to identify performance in any aspect of the athlete's life. It could be used in the following situations:

- to improve physical fitness levels
- to improve technical performance or skill level
- to improve the management of their lifestyle.

The only difference is that the constructs they come up with relate to the other aspects of their life. A footballer may use the profile to examine their technical skills such as:

- long passing
- short passing
- long-range shooting
- close-range shooting
- crossing
- dribbling
- heading
- tackling
- taking corners
- taking throw-ins
- positioning.

Performance profiling is a relatively new technique to sport psychology. It has some clear benefits over goal setting and, importantly, considers a wide range of aspects of performance rather than focusing on one or two. Most importantly, it considers what the individual feels is important and focuses the process on their responses.

Decision balance sheet

The decision balance sheet is a technique used to help the individual to weigh up the gains and losses of going through a period of change in behaviour. They may wish to adopt a new behaviour and move away from old habits. It works very well in the exercise environment to help convince an individual of the need to start taking exercise. The technique works in the following way.

- Ask the client to consider what will be the pain of taking action and what will be the pleasure of taking action?
- Ask the client what will be the pleasure of not taking action and what will be the pain of not taking action?

Fig 19.04 gives an example of a decision balance sheet for a client who wants to start exercising because they are overweight.

Analysing the results

People will take action to achieve their goals because of the serious consequences of not taking action. In this case the consequences of maintaining their current behaviour are ill health and feeling tired continually. However, they have also considered the consequences of changing their behaviour in terms of losing money, avoiding bad foods and spending less time drinking in the pub. It is important to see that the losses they incur are all in the short term and the gains they make are in the long term. This can sometimes be a difficult sacrifice to make. When put in black and white in front of them they will be continually reminded and this will have more power.

Motivation and time

Motivation is an unstable and variable concept and is affected on a daily basis by people's moods and experiences. It is the aim of the sport psychologist to understand the individual and how they are experiencing the current moment and then adjust themselves to their behaviour. The techniques are useful to keep motivation going over a period of time, but unless goals are reviewed on a regular basis (weekly at least) they can become forgotten and lose their power. Also, the effectiveness of techniques will wear off after time and 'they will work for as long as they work'. Therefore you need to keep changing the techniques of motivation you use.

Decision:			
Take action		Not take action	
Pain	Pleasure	Pain	Pleasure
Physically uncomfortable	Feel slim	Will get fatter	Keep eating chocolate
Less money	Be fitter	Keep feeling tired	Keep eating takeaways
Loss of time	Be stronger	Will get ill	Going to the pub
Getting up early	Have more energy	Will feel unattractive	Watching televison
	Will fit into my clothes	Feel like a blob	
	Have more compliments	Everything will feel like an effort	

Fig 19.04 The decision balance sheet

Key learning points

Techniques to develop motivation include:

- goal setting
- performance profiling
- decision balance sheet.

Goals can be short term (one session to one month), medium term (one month to three months) or long term (six months to a lifetime).

Goals must follow the SMART principle:

- Specific
- Measurable
- Achievable
- Realistic
- Time-constrained.

Performance profiling is a method of getting the individual to analyse what is important to them and then looking at their level of satisfaction with their current position and their desired position.

A decision balance sheet makes an individual aware of the consequences of taking their chosen course of action.

Imagery and mental rehearsal in sport and exercise

Imagery is one of the most important techniques in sport psychology because the pictures and thoughts that we have in our head will influence how we feel and then how we behave. If we can have positive thoughts and images it is going to be beneficial to our performance.

What is imagery? Imagery is the creation or re-creation of an image or experience in your mind rather than physically practising the skill. It will involve the employment of all senses in actually recreating the experience. Imagery is used extensively by many athletes, particularly golfers and track and field athletes. Jack Nicklaus, one of the most successful golfers of all time, explains how he uses visualisation:

> **Before every shot I go to the movies in my head. Here is what I see. First I see the ball where I want it to finish, nice and white, sitting up high on the bright green grass. Then I see the ball going there – its path and trajectory and even its behaviour on landing. The next scene shows me making the kind of swing that will turn the previous image into reality. These home images are the key to my concentration and to my positive approach to every shot.**

Imagery is a skill and some people will be better at it than others. If you find developing images difficult then you will need to use the practices later to help you with this skill.

Why does imagery work?

Imagery works because when you imagine yourself performing a skill the brain is unable to differentiate between a real experience and an imagined experience. As a result, the brain sends impulses to the muscles via the nervous system. These impulses are not strong enough to produce a muscular contraction, although you may see twitches. As the impulses are passed down the nervous system so the pattern becomes imprinted on the nervous system and is there for whenever you physically perform the skill. It is as if you have been there without actually going there.

Imagery can be used for the following skills:

- management of mental state
- mental rehearsal
- relaxation techniques
- developing confidence
- concentration skills.

Management of mental state

Control your emotions or they will control you.

This is an important skill which has been developed through a set of techniques called neuro-linguistic programming (NLP). It is increasingly being applied in sport. To practise NLP you have to accept a set of assumptions called presuppositions. Three of these are as follows.

- You are in charge of your mind and therefore your results.
- People have all the resources they need to succeed and achieve their desired outcomes.
- There are no unresourceful people, only unresourceful states.

If we are in charge and we are feeling bad then it is our responsibility to do something about it and no one else's. The key word here is state. This is the mood you are in at any given moment. Our state is dependent upon our perception of a situation or event and describes how we are feeling. A state is either productive or unproductive in that it will benefit or hinder us. It is that clear-cut and in NLP is called a resourceful or unresourceful state. A resourceful state would be one of confidence, determination or calmness, while an unresourceful state may be anger, fear or depression.

The model works in the following way.

- The event is what is happening at any point in time and is delivered to the individual through the senses of sight, sound, touch, taste and smell.

- The event is filtered by our brains because otherwise too much information will be delivered to the brain and it would be unable to process the information. The filter will delete significant portions of what happened. This is why two people can witness the same event but have a different interpretation of what happened because they delete different portions of the event. We distort what happened depending upon our values and memories, and finally we generalise the event to other events which we think are similar. We say, 'It was a bit like this or that.'
- Once filtered, the working space of the brain is delivered with information in the form of pictures, sounds and feelings. This is called the internal representation or how we are thinking and seeing the situation. This will directly affect our state. The term 'representation' is important because it suggests it is a representation of reality rather than reality itself. It is the way you see the world or your own map of reality.
- State is how we are feeling at any point in time.
- Our state is reflected in our body language as our posture, facial expressions and breathing are changed by our feelings. If someone is depressed or sad, they tend to slouch forward and look troubled or pained. Someone happy will hold themselves more upright, be smiling and seem relaxed.
- The resourceful or unresourceful state we are experiencing and its resulting body language will affect how we behave. Unresourceful states act as blockages to prevent us achieving a good outcome. Resourceful states put us in a state of flow where things come easily.
- Our behaviour will directly influence the outcome we achieve.

When we are playing sport we need to be in control of our emotions and adopt a positive state to be in a position to achieve positive outcomes. The

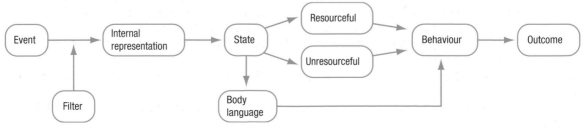

Fig 19.05 State management model

Olympic silver medallist in the javelin, Steve Backley, used a state management technique called 'My best day' (see the case study, below).

Case study

My best day

'If you are in control of your mental state then you are a dangerous animal in competition. Here's a great little trick to use when you are preparing for a big game or event: It's called 'My best day'. Go back in your mind and remember a day when you were great at what you do. Re-live it. Remember how you walked, how you talked, your breathing – everything about what it felt to be you on that day and emulate it. It's an insight into your own excellence.'

(Steve Backley, the *Guardian*, 2005)

This is also called 'recreating the winning feeling' as you re-experience how it felt when you were performing at your best.

Mental rehearsal

Mental rehearsal is taking time to sit down and think about your sport. It is seeing, feeling and hearing yourself playing your sport. It can be used in different ways:

- developing and practising skills
- reducing anxiety about an event
- practising 'what if' scenarios
- developing confidence before an event
- to replay and review performance.

Rather than just physical practice, mental rehearsal can complement your skill development. You need to have well-developed imagery skills to be able to perform mental rehearsal effectively.

Mental rehearsal can be used before, during and after competitions to ensure the best performance. Roger Black, who won the 400 m silver medal in the 1996 Olympics, talks about the power of mental rehearsal:

> **For the Olympic Games I walked around the stadium four months prior and I kept that picture in my mind every day. I ran it from every lane. I could close my eyes now and run the 400 m race and I would feel how I would feel.**

LEARNER ACTIVITY Practising state management

- Consider how you feel when you perform at the best of your ability. You may come up with states such as self-confident, powerful, in control, in flow, energetic, strong, motivated, calm, tranquil or relaxed.
- Choose three of these states and write them down on a piece of paper by deciding which three would be best when you are performing your sport.
- Under each state write down three past occasions when you have strongly been in that state and give each one a name. These may have been in your sport or they could come from your work, school or social life. For example, you may have felt highly motivated or confident during a particular exam.
- For each of the past three occasions you have felt this state, you are going to recreate exactly what you experienced and then implant it on your nervous system. Use the following steps.
  - Remember a time when you felt totally (state).
  - As you go back to that time see what you saw, feel what you felt and hear what you heard.
  - When you have recreated the experience fully then make a tight fist with your left hand.
  - Then go on to the next mental state, and do the exercise for all three states.
- When you need to change your mental state you will make a tight fist with your left hand and the feelings will come rushing back.
- Practise this technique because the more often you practise it the quicker and more powerfully the state will come to you.
- Practise this technique during your training and sporting performances and see what effect it has on the outcomes you achieve.

LEARNER ACTIVITY Improve imagery skills

This exercise can be done by a teacher or friend reading out the instructions, or recording the instructions and doing it yourself. This session should be preceded by a short relaxation session as the brain works best when it is relaxed. Then imagine the following:

Your favourite sportsperson . . . . . . a beach you visited on holiday . . . . . . snow covering the field . . . . . . the face of one of your parents . . . . . . your front door at home . . . . . . a piece of equipment you use for your sport . . . . . . your old school building . . . . . . your dream car . . . . . . a sports stadium . . . . . . the sky at night . . . . . . a sunset . . . . . . your first bicycle

The sound of . . . . . . falling rain on a roof . . . . . . the cheering of a crowd . . . . . . training shoes as you run . . . . . . hitting a ball with a racket . . . . . . your favourite song . . . . . . a dog barking . . . . . . a sports car . . . . . . your friend's voice . . . . . . the sea washing on to a beach

The feeling of . . . . . . a ball in your hand . . . . . . wearing training shoes . . . . . . sunbathing . . . . . . having a warm shower . . . . . . having finished a training session . . . . . . kicking a ball . . . . . . holding a tennis racket . . . . . . winning a race

The smell of . . . . . . freshly cooked chips . . . . . . warm bread . . . . . . freshly cut grass . . . . . . the garden just after it has rained . . . . . . the sea . . . . . . walking past a coffee shop . . . . . . a bunch of flowers . . . . . . food cooking on a barbecue . . . . . . perfume

The taste of . . . . . . sweet and sour sauce . . . . . . sweat as you train . . . . . . cold cold water . . . . . . eating chocolate . . . . . . toothpaste . . . . . . a cup of coffee

Once you have completed this write down which of the senses you were able to visualise best with and which was the most difficult. We will all have senses which are stronger than the others and it is our weaker senses that we really need to work on. Your strongest sense is also the one which you use best to learn through. Some people will learn through seeing pictures and images, others through hearing explanations and others through experiencing how it feels.

Here are some guidelines for mental rehearsal.

- Precede the session with a short relaxation session.
- Bring up the picture and make sure it is big, colourful, sharply focused and bright as a film.
- Employ all your senses by hearing the sounds associated and also the feelings of performing.
- Visualise at the correct speed (same speed as the action).
- Always visualise yourself successfully executing the skills.
- Visualise from inside your head looking out.
- Practise in intervals of five to ten minutes a day.

LEARNER ACTIVITY
Mental rehearsal

Choose five skills from your sport and spend one minute rehearsing each in your mind.

'What if . . .' scenarios are used to prepare in case you find yourself in certain situations during a competition. They were heavily used by Sally Gunnell, who won the 400 m hurdles in the 1992 Olympic Games:

> **It felt comfortable; it felt familiar. If something happened – if I hit a hurdle or came off the eighth hurdle and wasn't in the lead – it felt familiar and I knew I should get back in the race. The race that I won – the Olympic final – I had visualised so many times. I included every situation and different athletes, whether they were inside or the outside of me.**

A footballer may practise the following scenarios:

- going 1–0 down
- going 2–0 up
- having one of your players sent off
- taking a free kick in the last minute of the game to win it
- being booked early in a match.

Once the performance has been completed, you can run through it in your mind. This will help to identify the good and poor parts and correct any mistakes you have made. Understanding your mistakes will help to protect and develop self-confidence for the future. This can be done at a specific time and is best done as soon after the event as is possible.

Self-confidence is the extent to which you expect to be successful. You can use imagery to recall times when you were sure about being successful. Or you can use the following exercise to help you experience what it would be like to be completely self-confident.

LEARNER ACTIVITY
Self-confidence

Use a role model to develop confidence through the following steps.

1 Think of a sportsperson who is totally self-confident.
2 Observe their posture, their facial expressions and their behaviour.
3 Now go over to your role model and float into their body. Experience their posture, what they see and hear, and what they feel.
4 Then take yourself back into your body and keep the feeling of self-confidence.
5 See yourself acting and feeling confident in specific situations.
6 Keep repeating this activity until the feelings are locked in.

Arousal levels

According to the inverted U hypothesis our performance is related to our arousal level. If we are overaroused then we need to reduce arousal by using relaxation techniques. Conversely, if we find ourselves underaroused then we need to use energising techniques to raise our arousal level.

There are a range of tools which can be used to assess levels of arousal, the most common being:

- competitive state anxiety inventory-2 (CSAI-2)
- sport competitive anxiety test (SCAT).

While CSAI-2 measures state anxiety, which is constantly changing, SCAT measures trait anxiety, which is a stable aspect of our personality.

An example of a CSA1–2 inventory is shown on the next page, and an example of a SCAT on page 369.

LEARNER ACTIVITY
CSAI-2 test

Complete the CSAI-2 for yourself (see page 368) and analyse the results. You will need to look at your scores for cognitive anxiety, somatic anxiety and self-confidence.

LEARNER ACTIVITY SCAT test

Complete the SCAT test (see page 369) and then work out your score for trait anxiety.

Relaxation techniques

There are a range of relaxation techniques which address different aspects of the effects of stress and anxiety:

- progressive muscular relaxation (PMR)
- mind to muscle techniques (imagery)
- biofeedback
- breathing control.

Certainly relaxation techniques control arousal before and during performance; they can also be used for other purposes:

- to lower levels of trait and state anxiety
- to help the athlete fall into a deep sleep before or after a competition
- to keep the athlete calm and reduce energy lost through nervous worry before a competition
- to relax and recover during breaks in play or between races or matches
- to help recovery from illness and injury
- to help them enjoy their life in general.

When performing relaxation techniques it is important to follow these instructions:

1 Find a place where you will not be disturbed.
2 Sit or lie down in a comfortable place.
3 Close your eyes and turn down the lighting.
4 Put on some relaxing music.
5 Enjoy the experience.

Competitive state anxiety inventory-2 (CSAI-2)

Below are several statements that athletes have used to describe their feelings before a competition. Without spending too long on any one statement, circle the appropriate number to the right of the statement, to indicate how you feel at this moment. There is no right or wrong answer.

	Not at all	Somewhat	Moderately so	Very much so
1. I am concerned about this competition	1	2	3	4
2. I feel nervous	1	2	3	4
3. I feel at ease	1	2	3	4
4. I have self-doubts	1	2	3	4
5. I feel jittery	1	2	3	4
6. I feel comfortable	1	2	3	4
7. I am concerned that I may not do as well in this competition as I could	1	2	3	4
8. My body feels tense	1	2	3	4
9. I feel self-confident	1	2	3	4
10. I am concerned about losing	1	2	3	4
11. I feel tense in my stomach	1	2	3	4
12. I feel secure	1	2	3	4
13. I am concerned about choking under pressure	1	2	3	4
14. My body feels relaxed	1	2	3	4
15. I am confident I can meet the challenge	1	2	3	4
16. I am concerned about performing badly	1	2	3	4
17. My heart is racing	1	2	3	4
18. I am confident about performing well	1	2	3	4
19. I am worried about reaching my goal	1	2	3	4
20. I feel my stomach sinking	1	2	3	4
21. I feel mentally relaxed	1	2	3	4
22. I am concerned others will be disappointed by my performance	1	2	3	4
23. My hands are clammy	1	2	3	4
24. I am confident because I can mentally picture myself reaching my goal	1	2	3	4
25. I am concerned I won't be able to concentrate	1	2	3	4
26. My body feels tight	1	2	3	4
27. I am confident about coming through under pressure	1	2	3	4

Scoring

Add up your scores in the following question-number groups to get three totals:
(a) 1, 4, 7, 10, 13, 16, 19, 22, 25 =
(b) 2, 5, 8, 11, 14, 17, 20, 23, 26 =
(c) 3, 6, 9, 12, 15, 18, 21, 24, 27 =

Interpretation of results

Score for (a) is cognitive or mental anxiety and should be a low score (9–18).
Score for (b) is somatic or physical anxiety and should be moderate (19–26).
Score for (c) is self-confidence and should be high (27–36).

Any deviation from these scores means there is an anxiety issue and a psychological intervention needs to be made.

Sport competitive anxiety test (SCAT)

Read the following statements and decide whether this is how you usually feel when you compete in sport. Answer each question quickly and go with your instinct.

	Hardly ever	Sometimes	Often
1. Competing against others is socially enjoyable	☐	☐	☐
2. Before I compete, I feel uneasy	☐	☐	☐
3. Before I compete I worry about not performing well	☐	☐	☐
4. I am a good sportsperson when I compete	☐	☐	☐
5. When I compete, I worry about making mistakes	☐	☐	☐
6. Before I compete I am calm	☐	☐	☐
7. Setting a goal is important when competing	☐	☐	☐
8. Before I compete I get a queasy feeling in my stomach	☐	☐	☐
9. Just before competing, I notice that my heart beats faster than usual	☐	☐	☐
10. I like to compete in games that demand considerable physical energy	☐	☐	☐
11. Before I compete I feel relaxed	☐	☐	☐
12. Before I compete I am nervous	☐	☐	☐
13. Team sports are more exciting than individual sports	☐	☐	☐
14. I get nervous wanting to start the game	☐	☐	☐
15. Before I compete I usually get uptight	☐	☐	☐

Scoring

Questions 2, 3, 5, 8, 9, 12, 14 and 15 will receive: Hardly ever = 1, Sometimes = 2, Often = 3.
Questions 6 and 11 will receive: Hardly ever = 3, Sometimes = 2, Often = 1
Questions 1, 4, 7, 10 and 13 should be ignored as they are used to disguise the purpose of the test.

Add up your total and you will score between 10 and 30.

Interpretation of results

10–16 = low trait anxiety
17–23 = medium trait anxiety
24+ = high trait anxiety

Progressive muscular relaxation (PMR)

This technique is excellent for people who are experiencing the symptoms of somatic anxiety such as tension in muscles and butterflies in the stomach. This can be assessed through the use of CSAI-2. It also works well for people who have poor imagery skills.

LEARNER ACTIVITY Experiencing PMR

This can be done as a group with the lecturer reading out the following instructions for the group to follow.

Find a comfortable position, either sitting or lying down.
Begin by making a tight fist with your left hand, really tighten the fist and feel the tension in your hand and up your arm.
And now relax and let the fingers be loose and notice the difference.
Once more make a really tight fist and notice the tension.
Now relax.
Repeat this with your right hand.
Make a tight fist and feel the tension while the rest of your body stays relaxed.
Feel the tension in the hand and arm and relax.
Notice how much more comfortable it is to be relaxed.
Now make tight fists with both hands.
Analyse how the tension feels and do the opposite of contraction and relax.
Let the fingers be loose and feel the relaxation.
Observe the difference between tensing the muscle and then relaxing it.
Continue to relax your hand in this way (20 seconds).
Now contract your biceps by bending your elbows.
Notice the tension in the upper arm . . . and relax.
Let the whole arm relax and notice the difference.
Now straighten the arms so that you feel tension in the back of the upper arm.
Feel the tension and relax.
Now return to a comfortable position and feel the relaxation spread throughout your arms.
Concentrate on the relaxation of the arms without any tension and notice how heavy your arms become when relaxed . . . relaxed and heavy . . . relaxed and heavy.
Now focus on the face.
Wrinkle up your forehead by raising your eyebrows . . . wrinkle tightly . . . and now relax.
Pull your eyebrows together and as you frown notice the tension . . . now relax and feel the tension being replaced by relaxation.
Now squeeze your eyes tightly shut and feel the tension . . . . now relax without opening your eyes.
Notice how relaxed the forehead and eyes have become.
Tighten your jaw by clenching your teeth and feel the tension . . . . now relax.
Press your tongue hard against the roof of your mouth . . . . and relax by dropping your tongue to the back of the mouth.
Now pucker your lips and form an O . . . . and relax and notice the difference when tensing and relaxing.
Now feel relaxation spreading through your entire face, your forehead, eyes and jaw and let the relaxation become deeper and deeper.
Now push your head into the floor and feel your neck tense.
Roll your head to the right and feel the change in tension . . . . now to the left and back to the middle . . . . relax and feel the muscles relax and relaxation become deeper.
Now pull up your shoulders to your ears without tensing your arms.
Feel the tension . . . . relax . . . . and repeat now moving the shoulders around in a circle . . . up . . . forwards and backwards and feel the tension in the shoulders . . . . now let the shoulders relax and notice the contrast in tension and relaxation.
Now arch your back and feel the tension along the spine and let go to a comfortable position.
Once more arch your back and feel where there is tension . . . . and relax.
Rest and feel the relaxation spread through the back and how the back becomes heavy . . . . relaxed and heavy.

LEARNER ACTIVITY Experiencing PMR (continued)

Now tense the buttocks and thighs by pressing your heels into the floor . . . . Relax and feel the difference.

Repeat tensing the thighs and buttocks . . . . tense and relax and notice the difference.

Stretch your feet and toes away from your face and tense your calves.

Focus on the tension and relax the feet and calves.

Now pull your feet up towards your face and feel the tension in the shins.

Now relax and start to feel your legs become heavy . . . . relaxed and heavy . . . . and the feeling of warmth spreading through the body.

Now focus on your breathing and take a deep breath and hold the breath.

Now let the breath go and feel the air leaving your lungs.

As you exhale the relaxation deepens . . . . and notice the comfortable feeling.

Repeat breathing. . . . breathe in . . . hold for five seconds and let the breath go and the tension is replaced by relaxation.

Each time you breathe out you should become more and more relaxed . . . . . . breathe slowly and calmly.

Now relax on your own for a while and focus on how the music makes you feel more and more relaxed.

(Wait for two to three minutes.)

Now listen to me once more.

Each time you practise this program you will experience an increased effect with the relaxation becoming deeper and you will achieve a relaxed state quicker each time.

You will start to understand the difference between tensed and relaxed muscles and understand and feel the meaning of deep relaxation.

You will also feel calmer each time you do the programme and the calmness will bring a feeling of certainty, tranquillity and restfulness.

Now wake up slowly by bending and stretching your arms and shaking your legs and take a couple of deep breaths.

Open your eyes and keep the feeling of relaxation. Feel certain about yourself and good in every way.

Mind to muscle techniques (imagery)

These techniques will work with a person who is experiencing cognitive anxiety as identified through CSAI-2. They rely upon a person having well-developed imagery skills.

LEARNER ACTIVITY Relaxation techniques

Write a report on the two relaxation techniques you have experienced and, for each, highlight:

- what you found worked well
- what you found did not work well
- which technique you preferred
- explain why this worked best for you.

Biofeedback

This method relies on us becoming aware of what happens to our body as we become aroused and anxious. We need to be aware of the signs and symptoms of arousal and anxiety. We experience changes in our heart rate, blood pressure and skin temperature. These are monitored by devices such as heart rate monitors and blood pressure meters.

Biofeedback uses a device which makes a noise when we become warmer and our heart rate rises, and it make less noise as we relax. Another popular method is to use a biodot, which changes colour as we become warmer and more stressed. As we relax, the skin temperature falls and the biodot changes colour. This method teaches the athlete what it feels like to be relaxed and they can reproduce these feelings when they need to be in a relaxed state.

LEARNER ACTIVITY Mind to muscle techniques

This can be done as a group with the lecturer reading out the following instructions for the group to follow.

Sit or lie down in a comfortable position. Let your body become relaxed and heavy. Slowly let the relaxation spread through your body. Let your chest fall and rise as you breathe slowly and steadily. Now let yourself become consciously aware of your toes and let them relax completely. Now focus on your lower legs and think relaxation into your calf muscles. Move your focus to your upper legs and allow them to relax completely. Feel your legs become warm, relaxed and heavy as they sink into a comfortable state.

Pause.

Now focus on the muscles of the lower back and let them relax and feel how the tension drains away from those muscles. Now the feeling of relaxation spreads into the upper back as it starts to feel warm and free of tension. Now think about your fingers and let them become loose and warm. Let them relax completely. Then relax your forearms, upper arms and shoulders. Feel how heavy they become as they are drained of tension and feel how they sink into the floor. Relax your neck and then feel the muscles around your jaw become relaxed as your jaw falls slightly forward. Feel the muscles at the side of your eyes loosen and become relaxed. Feel how your head has become totally relaxed and has found a comfortable position.

Spend a moment scanning your body for areas of tension and, when you find tension, think relaxation into the area. Your body starts to feel warm and heavy. Enjoy how great it feels to be relaxed in this way.

As you lie there start to focus on your breathing and the gentle rise and fall of your chest. Breathe in and out five times and each time you breathe out notice how you become more and more relaxed.

While you are relaxing there think back to a really relaxing time that you had when you were on holiday. Think about a hot day that you spent on a beach. Imagine yourself standing in the foyer of the hotel. You are wearing a T-shirt and shorts and have a sun hat on. You are carrying a beach bag with what you need for the day. Leave the hotel and, as you do, notice how bright the sun is and the feeling of entering the heat of the day. You walk towards the beach and notice the sound your sandals make as they flap back onto your feet.

Quickly you reach the beach and you look out to the sea and see the golden sand stretching as far as you can see. When you get on the sand you take your sandals off and immediately feel the heat of the sand permeating the skin on your feet and the warmth spreads up your legs. You can also feel the sand between your toes. You find yourself a sun lounger and take out your brightly coloured towel to spread on the lounger. You lie yourself down and put on some sun cream. As you lie down you become aware of the gentle sound of the sea lapping on the shore and the soft caw sound the seagulls make. You also feel the gentle breeze as it moves across your skin and slowly you feel the heat from the sun. The heat works through your skin to your muscles and you can almost feel it warming your very bones. As you lie there you become more and more relaxed and wrapped up by a sense of well-being and happiness. You feel calm and confident and in control of your life at this point in time.

Pause for two or three minutes.

This can always be your special place where you can go when you need some space to relax and recover or reduce your anxiety level.

As you lie there you have a peaceful, tranquil feeling through your entire body and mind. You feel very relaxed and good in every way.

LEARNER ACTIVITY Script and music

In your classroom the lecturer can read out the following script. It could be complemented by using some high-energy music.

Stand up and close your eyes. As you stand there become aware of the energy buzzing around your body. You feel the energy in your legs and how energy comes up through your feet from the floor. Now focus on the energy in you arms and again become aware of the activity in your muscles as nerve impulses are fired. Now focus on your chest and stomach area and become aware that your body has a centre of energy in the middle of your body. This is called the solar plexus and is at the base of your sternum. You can feel how it pulses energy into your chest and stomach and how it replaces any feelings of fatigue.

Now in your head imagine that you are walking up a set of stairs. When you come to the top of the stairs walk across the landing to a yellow door and wait outside for a moment. I want you to imagine that beyond this door is an energy room. The room is very bright and has white walls. At the front of the room is a huge glass window and through the window the only thing you can see is the sun. You can also feel the heat of the sun. The only thing in the room is an energy machine. You can imagine this machine in any way you like but it must have two handles to hold on to.

Enter the room and, as you do, feel how the energy in the room fills your body and you start to feel highly energised. You can feel the energy from the sun entering your body, giving you strength and power. You walk over to the energy machine and you hold on to the handles. The energy machine transfers its energy to you and you feel the energy enter your arms, upper body and then into your legs. You start to feel highly invigorated as energy fills up every cell of your body. Let the energy enter your body for as long as you need.

This energy can be stored in your solar plexus at the base of your sternum. Stand away from the machine facing the sun and feel how your body is full of energy and that you have enough power and spirit to achieve what you have to achieve.

Now as you stand there, feel the energy leave your solar plexus and travel through your stomach into your legs and all the way to your toes. Through your chest, into your face and arms, all the way down to your fingers. As you stand there you feel that you could run through the walls and overcome any obstacle put in your way.

(Play music to accompany this part.)

Each time you practise this programme you will experience an increased effect and find you access the energy more quickly. Remember that you have everything you need to succeed inside you and you can access it whenever you need it. If you experience a time during training or performance when you need energy use this technique to provide it.

Breathing control

Breathing control is a method often used by athletes to reduce muscle tension and to lower anxiety levels. When we become stressed and anxious we experience short and shallow breathing, and when we are relaxed our breathing deepens.

To aid relaxation we can teach the athlete to breathe deeply and slowly from the diaphragm to produce mental and physical relaxation. If they are focusing on their breathing it will shift their attention from whatever is causing them stress. It can be done in a standing or sitting position. Get the individual to place their hands on their stomach and see how the hands move out and fall back as they breathe in and out.

Once they have learnt how to breathe properly they can use it at the appropriate time during a competition.

Energising techniques

If the athlete is not feeling aroused there are ways of raising the arousal level. Many coaches use music to psych their athletes up and raise their energy levels. This can be a personal choice or a team may develop a theme tune which they play before performing to lift them. You can also use the state management technique and imagine times in the past when you felt energised, and recreate that feeling. Also scripts similar in style to relaxation scripts can be employed to raise arousal and energy levels. The script used in the 'Script and music' activity above relies heavily on imagery skills.

Key learning points

Imagery is the recreation of pictures and movies in our mind. It can be used for the following skills:

- management of mental state
- mental rehearsal
- relaxation techniques
- developing confidence
- concentration skills.

Imagery works because it develops a nervous pathway between the brain, nervous system and the muscles. This pathway becomes imprinted on the nervous system and thus strengthens the movement pattern of any given skill.

CSAI-2 and SCAT are methods of analysing levels of arousal, which can then be managed through relaxation or energising techniques.

Relaxation techniques include:

- progressive muscular relaxation
- mind to muscle techniques
- breathing control
- biofeedback.

Energising techniques include using imagery to recreate an energetic environment.

Planning a psychological skills training programme

Assessing mental skills

An assessment of an individual's mental strengths and weaknesses can be made in different ways.

It can be done with a questionnaire like the one below.

Once you have identified any weaknesses in the programme you can then plan a training programme for the individual. This programme must have clear objectives that the individual is aiming to achieve. To demonstrate how this can be done look at the case study on page 376.

For Sarah, in the Case Study, the aims of psychological skills training are:

- to address her high levels of anxiety
- to address her self-confidence
- to develop skills to help her control her moods.

Action plan

- Goal setting to address motivation and develop positive goals.
- Relaxation training to address the high levels of arousal and anxiety she experiences.
- Self-talk and imagery training to address any confidence problems which may also be causing under-performance.
- State management techniques to help her control her moods.

Example questionnaire

Name:
Sport played:

1. Explain any past experience you have of psychological skills training.

2. Explain your involvement in sport and any important competitions or events coming up.

3. What do you consider to be your psychological strengths and weaknesses?

Example questionnaire (continued)

Below is a list of statements, circle the answer appropriate to your experience.

4. I always feel motivated to succeed, whatever activity I am doing.

| Don't know | Never | Sometimes | Usually | Always |

5. I always work towards clear goals.

| Don't know | Never | Sometimes | Usually | Always |

6. I set myself goals on a weekly basis.

| Don't know | Never | Sometimes | Usually | Always |

7. I always make full use of my skills and abilities.

| Don't know | Never | Sometimes | Usually | Always |

8. When I am involved in my physical activity, I often find my attention wavering.

| Don't know | Never | Sometimes | Usually | Always |

9. I am easily distracted during whatever activity I am involved in.

| Don't know | Never | Sometimes | Usually | Always |

10. I perform much better when I am under a lot of pressure.

| Don't know | Never | Sometimes | Usually | Always |

11. I become very anxious when I am under pressure.

| Don't know | Never | Sometimes | Usually | Always |

12. If I start to become tense, I can quickly relax myself and calm down.

| Don't know | Never | Sometimes | Usually | Always |

13. I find it easy to control my emotions whatever the situation.

| Don't know | Never | Sometimes | Usually | Always |

14. I am always able to remain upbeat and positive, whatever the situation.

| Don't know | Never | Sometimes | Usually | Always |

15. If I am criticised by a coach or trainer I tend to take it very badly.

| Don't know | Never | Sometimes | Usually | Always |

Example questionnaire (continued)

16. I am easily able to deal with unforeseen situations.

Don't know   *Never*   *Sometimes*   *Usually*   *Always*

17. I have my own set of strategies for dealing with difficult situations.

Don't know   *Never*   *Sometimes*   *Usually*   *Always*

Analysing the results
Questions 1–4 relate to motivation and the solution is goal setting.
Questions 5–6 relate to concentration and the solution is concentration training.
Questions 7–10 relate to arousal and anxiety and the solution is relaxation techniques.
Questions 11–14 relate to self-confidence and the solution is self-talk.

There is no scoring system as such, but the questions are designed for you to establish areas of strength and weakness.

Case study

Sarah is an 18-year-old national standard tennis player. As much as she enjoys her sport and competing she finds that she gets very nervous in the two days leading up to competition. This affects her self-confidence and she finds she goes on court almost expecting to lose, and her motivation becomes to avoid losing. As a result, when she wins she feels relief about winning rather than joy about winning. She also finds her mood can change quickly depending upon the state of the game.

Training plan

Week 1: Goal setting
Establish the basis of psychological skills training and ensure motivation for physical and mental training.

Week 2: Imagery training
Develop skills of imagery and practise mind to muscle relaxation techniques to employ the use of imagery.

Week 3: Relaxation
Practise progressive muscular relaxation five times.

Week 4: State management
Exercises to practise state management and build up the strength of the feelings.

Week 5: Imagery
Using imagery to develop self-image and increase levels of confidence.

Week 6: Mental rehearsal and sitting relaxation
Learn to relax sitting up, to make mental rehearsal for competition more practical. Mental rehearsal will bring all the skills of the training programme together.

LEARNER ACTIVITY
Action planning
Consider the case study below and develop an action plan to help address the issues.

Case study

James is a very talented 16-year-old cricketer who has been selected to play for his county. He is a fast bowler who can scare batsmen when he is playing well. However, he never feels sure he is going to compete well and often his bowling is erratic as he loses his line. As a result, some days he is successful and sometimes he concedes many runs. When James bats he says to himself to keep calm and take his time, but as soon as he faces the bowling he tries to hit every ball to the boundary and is often out early in his innings.

Backing up the training programme

While the outcomes of the training programme are clear it is important to back the training programme up with certain measures to ensure it is successful. This can be done with the following measures.

- Set clear goals using the SMART principle, as discussed earlier.
- Use a psychological skills diary or logbook to record progress in each session and then in actual performances.
- Ensure that the programme is evaluated against its objectives for its success regularly.

Evaluating the training programme

In order to assess the success of the training programme you need to gather evidence about its value. Sources for evaluation could include:

- results and outcomes
- questionnaires
- interviews
- observation of behaviour
- psychological skills training diary.

Here are some questions you can ask.

- Which skills and techniques did you employ during competition and training?
- How have these techniques affected your performance?
- Have you been feeling different during your sport this season?
- What issues do you feel are still affecting you?
- What training do you need to improve your performance further?

These questions will form the basis for a more in-depth interview to discuss how the professional psychological training relationship will continue and develop. Once the evaluation has been completed the outcomes can be stated in the form of an action plan covering:

- current situation highlighting strengths and weaknesses
- their future aims and objectives
- areas to work on
- actions – a step-by-step guide to achieving their aims
- timescale for actions and review.

Review questions

1 Explain the three roles of a sport psychologist.
2 Discuss five main areas with which a sport psychologist can help athletes, coaches and teams.
3 Discuss the three parts of Gallwey's performance equation and how it can be applied to sports performance.
4 Why is goal setting of interest to a sport psychologist and their athletes?
5 Explain the use of the acronym SMART in goal setting.
6 When using imagery to assist in making goal setting more powerful, how would you help a person to develop the image in their mind?
7 Briefly explain how you would implement the technique of performance profiling.
8 Explain how imagery can be used to improve sporting performance and why it works.
9 Explain two techniques that can be used to reduce arousal levels.
10 What five psychological areas may you develop through a psychological skills training programme?

References

Gallwey, T. (1986) *The Inner Game of Golf*, Pan Macmillan.

Gould, D. and Weinberg, R. (2000) *Foundations of Sport and Exercise Psychology*, Human Kinetics.

Grout, J. and Perrin, S. (2004) *Mind Games*, Capstone.

McKenna, P. (2004) *Change Your Life in Seven Days*, Bantam Press.

O'Connor, J. (2001) *NLP and Sports*, Thorsons.

Orlick, T. (2000) *In Pursuit of Excellence*, Human Kinetics.

sports coach UK (2002) *Imagery Training*, sports coach UK.

Weinberg, R. and Gould, D. (2003) *Foundations of Sport and Exercise Psychology*, Human Kinetics.

20

Applied sport and exercise physiology

Goals

By the end of this chapter you should:

- understand how temperature and altitude affect exercise and sporting performance
- know about the physical differences between people of different genders and races, and their effect on exercise and sporting performance
- understand the impacts that the physiological effects of ageing have on exercise and sporting performance
- know about the advantages and disadvantages of ergogenic aids for exercise and sports performance.

This chapter explores the stress heat and cold place on an athlete's body and how the body is able to maintain a constant core temperature. The effects of altitude are also studied. This chapter will also examine how an athlete's gender, race and age impact upon their sporting ability and therefore dictate the requirements of their training programme. It is widely known that today many athletes try to enhance their performance by using ergogenic aids. Many different types of ergogenic aid are available, some are acceptable means of improving performance, others are banned and any athlete found to be taking these aids will be disqualified from competing. The pros and cons of taking some of these aids will be examined in this chapter.

Temperature and exercise and sporting performance

Thermoregulation: the process of maintaining a constant body core temperature. In humans this temperature is 37°C.

The core of the body consists of the head, chest and abdomen.

Fig 20.01 The body core

The skin temperature of the body can vary a great deal. If the core temperature is increased or decreased by 1°C or more, this will affect an athlete's physical and mental performance. Larger changes in core temperature lead to hypothermia or hyperthermia, both of which can be fatal.

Hypothermia: lower than normal core temperature.
Hyperthermia: higher than normal core temperature.

To assess the core temperature of a person, there are a number of places a specialised thermometer can be placed: the mouth, the ear, the rectum or under the arm. For sports scientists the ear is the most common site for measuring core temperature. Or if the exercise allows, the rectal thermometer is used as this gives the most accurate reading of the true body core temperature.

LEARNER ACTIVITY Core and skin temperature

The aim of this activity is to determine what the core temperature and the skin temperature of a person are.

You will need the following equipment:

- oral thermometer
- skin thermometer
- sterilising fluid
- pen and paper

Method

1 Place a sterile thermometer under your tongue and leave it there for a few minutes.
2 Take the thermometer out of your mouth and record the temperature reading.
3 Place a skin thermometer on your hand and record the temperature reading.
4 Place the skin thermometer on your neck and record the temperature reading.
5 If you have time, take external readings from other parts of your body.
6 Disinfect/sterilise all thermometers before allowing another person to use them.

Record your results in the table below:

Core temperature (°C)	
Hand temperature (°C)	
Neck temperature (°C)	

Then answer the following questions.

- Is your core temperature the same as that of the person sitting next to you? If not, why do you think this is?
- Why is your skin a different temperature to your core temperature?
- Is there a difference between skin temperature readings taken from different sites on your body? Try to explain why this is.

Heat transfer

There are four different methods of heat transfer, some of which can be used to rid the body of excess heat and some to gain heat.

- **Conduction:** place your hand on the desk in front of you. How does it feel? If it feels cold you are losing heat to it via conduction. If it feels hot you are gaining heat by conduction. Conduction involves the direct transfer of heat from one object to another. Normally this method of heat loss is not significant unless a person is exercising in cold water. This is because water conducts heat away from the body approximately 25 times more quickly than air. At the same temperature, a person in water will lose heat from the body two to four times faster than in air.

- **Convection:** blow air over your hand. How does your hand feel? Your hand will probably have felt cooler after having air blown over it. This blowing

of air molecules across your hand is the basis of convection. As air molecules are moved across the body, heat will be lost because convective air currents carry the heat away. Wind will increase the flow of air over the skin, thus increasing the amount of heat lost through convection. This is why a breeze feels good on a hot day, and why we use fans to help keep us cool.

- **Radiation:** at rest, radiation is the main method of heat loss. It is the process by which heat is lost (via electromagnetic waves) to cooler objects in the environment, such as the floor, walls, trees, etc. How much heat a person loses through radiation is determined by their size, mass and body composition. People with a high body fat percentage will lose less heat through radiation than a person with a low body fat percentage, because body fat acts as an insulator to radiative heat loss. In contrast, a tall slim person will lose more heat through radiation than a short stocky

Fig 20.02 Cooling of the body by convection

person. In warm climates, the sun radiates heat to the body, which increases its temperature. This makes getting rid of excess heat during exercise more difficult, because the sun's heat must also be dissipated.

Fig 20.03 Cooling of the body by radiation

● **Evaporation of sweat:** in humans, evaporation of sweat from the body is the major method of heat dissipation, particularly during exercise. Heat is transferred continually to the environment as sweat evaporates from the skin surfaces and produces a cooling effect. If the environment is humid, evaporative heat loss is reduced. Heat is only lost when sweat evaporates, which it will not do in humid conditions. Therefore, on a hot, humid day,

an athlete can be dripping with sweat, but because the sweat is not evaporating this does not cool them down.

Fig 20.04 Cooling of the body by sweating

definition

Humid: high percentage of water molecules in the air.

Responses of the body to high temperature

Exercise increases metabolic rate by 20 to 25 times, and could increase core temperature by 1°C every six minutes if heat loss did not take place. This would result in death from hyperthermia if exercise continued. Therefore, with the added stress of a hot environment, an exercising athlete has to maximise heat loss in order to perform optimally and to avoid hyperthermia.

The hypothalamus acts as a thermostat and initiates the responses that protect the body from overheating. It receives information about the temperature of the body via two sources:

● indirectly from the thermal receptors in the skin
● directly by changes in blood temperature.

Methods of heat loss in a hot environment

Heat loss through radiation is not possible if the environment is hotter than the person exercising.

LEARNER ACTIVITY Dilatation and constriction

The aim of this activity is to see how blood vessel dilatation and constriction affect the colour of the skin. (The outcomes of this activity will apply only to Caucasian learners.)

You will need the following equipment:

- large beakers
- thermometer
- hot water
- paper towels
- ice cubes
- skin thermometers (if available)

Method

1 Working in small groups, fill a large beaker with warm/hot water. Ensure the water is not too hot for you to place your hand in! Take the temperature of the water and write it down.
2 Look at your hand and make a note of its colour.
3 Place your hand in the water for about three minutes.
4 Remove your hand from the water, towel it dry, then record the skin temperature. Note down the colour of your hand.
5 Fill a large beaker with cold water and add a few ice cubes. After two minutes, take the temperature of the water and note it down. Ensure the water is not too cold for you to bear.
6 Place your hand in the water for about three minutes.
7 Remove your hand from the water, towel it dry, then record the skin temperature. Note down the colour of your hand.

Results

Record your results in the table below.

Temperature of water (°C)	Colour of hand
Hot	
Cold	

Then answer the following questions.

- Why did your hand turn the colour it did after having been placed in hot water?
- Why did your hand turn the colour it did after having been placed in cold water?
- By what process was your hand trying to lose heat when it was placed in the hot water?

Therefore, there are only three forms of heat loss available to a person exercising in a hot environment.

- **Conductive heat loss** occurs by the peripheral blood vessels dilating and bringing blood close to the skin's surface. This results in the rosy-coloured skin associated with Caucasian hot athletes. The heat from the blood warms the air molecules around the person and any cooler surfaces that come into contact with the skin. Conductive heat loss works in conjunction with convective heat loss.
- **Convective heat loss** occurs much more rapidly if there is increased air flow around the body – if it is windy or a fan is being used. If there is little air movement, the air next to the skin is warmed and

acts as a layer of insulation that minimises further convective heat loss. If the warmed air surrounding the body is frequently changed due to increased air currents, heat loss through convection will continue to remove excess body heat.

- **Evaporative heat loss** provides the main source of heat dissipation. As the sweat evaporates, it cools down the skin surface. This has the effect of cooling the blood as it travels through the blood vessels that are close to the skin surface. For evaporative heat loss to occur maximally, the person must be hydrated and have normal levels of salt and electrolytes in their body.

LEARNER ACTIVITY Heat loss

Name the main method(s) of heat loss in the following conditions and explain your answers:

- swimming in cold water
- running on a cloudy, windy day
- cycling on a hot sunny day.

The circulatory system is vitally important in ensuring that these three methods of heat loss can occur. Not only does the blood have to supply the muscles with oxygen and nutrients, it also plays a major part in thermoregulation. The blood is redirected to the periphery by dilatation of peripheral blood vessels. In extreme conditions, 15 to 25 per cent of the cardiac output is directed to the skin. As a result of these two cardiovascular demands, the heart rate is higher when exercising in the heat than in normal conditions.

Heart rate is also elevated because of the slight to severe dehydration that often occurs while exercising in the heat. If the person is dehydrated, the plasma volume is decreased. A decreased plasma volume will lead to a decreased stroke volume. Therefore, as we know:

cardiac output = heart rate × stroke volume
Q (l per min) = HR (bpm) × SV (ml)

In order for cardiac output to remain the same, heart rate has to increase to make up for the decreased stroke volume:

$$Q = \uparrow HR \times \downarrow SV$$

LEARNER ACTIVITY Cardiovascular system and hot conditions

The aim of this activity is to see how the effect of exercising in hot conditions affects the cardiovascular system. Ensure that this activity is supervised by a qualified tutor and a risk assessment has been carried out prior to participation.

You will need the following equipment:

- bleep test
- tape recorder
- heart rate monitors
- results table
- sports kit (shorts and T-shirt for test 1 and tracksuit bottoms, sweatshirt, woolly hat and gloves for test 2)
- weighing scales
- sports hall

Method

Test 1: normal conditions

1 Each person is weighed wearing shorts and T-shirt.
2 Working in pairs, place a heart rate monitor on the first person taking the test.
3 The first person takes part in the bleep test. At the end of each stage, the exercising person calls out their heart rate while their partner records this number and the appearance of the exercising person.
4 Once the exercising person has exercised to voluntary exhaustion, they towel down, put on a clean T-shirt and record their body weight.
5 The process is repeated for the second person.

Test 2: hot conditions

This test should be carried out at least 72 hours after test 1. Ensure each person taking part is fully hydrated before taking part in this test.

1 Each person is weighed wearing shorts and T-shirt.
2 Working in pairs, place a heart rate monitor on the first person taking the test.
3 The person taking the test then puts on tracksuit bottoms, a sweatshirt, woolly hat and gloves.
4 The first person takes part in the bleep test. At the end of each stage, the exercising person calls out their heart rate while their partner records this number and the appearance of the exercising person.

LEARNER ACTIVITY Cardiovascular system and hot conditions (continued)

5 Once the exercising person has exercised to voluntary exhaustion they remove their tracksuit bottoms, sweatshirt, hat and gloves, towel down and put on a fresh T-shirt and shorts. The person is then weighed.

Results

Record the results in the table below.

Stage	Heart rate		Appearance	
	Test 1	Test 2	Test 1	Test 2
1				
2				
3				
4				
5				
6				
7				
8				
9				
10				

Plot the heart rates for the normal and hot conditions on a line graph.

Test 1
Weight before:
Weight after:
Weight difference:

Test 2
Weight before:
Weight after:
Weight difference:

Then answer the following questions.

● Was there a difference in the heart rates at each stage in the two tests?
● Was there a difference in the person's appearance in the two tests at each stage of the bleep test? Was there any difference between the weight loss in test 1 and test 2?
● Did the person manage to reach the same stage in the bleep test in both tests? Explain your results.

Effects of high temperature

If the body is unable to lose the excess heat generated from exercising and/or from the environment the person will suffer from hyperthermia. There are three major forms of hyperthermia:

- heat cramps
- heat exhaustion
- heat stroke.

Heat cramps are muscle spasms caused by heavy sweating. Although heat cramps can be quite painful, they do not usually result in permanent damage.

Heat exhaustion is more serious than heat cramps. It occurs primarily because of dehydration and loss of important minerals. To lose body heat, the surface blood vessels and capillaries dilate to cool the blood. When the body is dehydrated during heat exhaustion, the blood volume is reduced so there is not enough blood to supply both the muscles and the skin with their required blood supply. This results in the peripheral dilated blood vessels constricting, which significantly reduces heat loss. This can be observed in Caucasian athletes. If you look at the face of a Caucasian athlete suffering from heat exhaustion, it will suddenly change from a red rosy appearance to a much paler colour or white.

If a person ignores the symptoms of heat exhaustion and continues to exercise, they will suffer from heat stroke, which is a life-threatening condition and has a high death rate. It occurs because the body has depleted its supply of water and salt, and results in the person's body temperature rising to dangerous levels. If the core temperature of the body reaches 43°C or more, the proteins start to break down and change their structure permanently. Imagine cooking an egg. The egg white is mainly made up of protein. When the egg white reaches a certain temperature (around 43°C) its structure changes from a runny, viscous medium to a solid. The same principle applies to the body's proteins such as the enzymes and hormones. Once heated to a certain temperature, the structure of the body's proteins permanently changes and is no longer able to function. Therefore, it is vitally important that the core temperature is not elevated to this degree.

Responses of the body to low temperature

When humans are exposed to a cold environment at rest, the body attempts to prevent heat loss as well as increase heat production. It does this via three main physiological mechanisms:

- constriction of the peripheral blood circulation
- non-shivering thermogenesis
- shivering.

First of all, the body decreases the blood supply to the peripheral circulation by constriction of the peripheral blood vessels (vasoconstriction). The purpose of this is to keep the blood close to the body core and redirect it away from the body's extremities and skin surface, where it would be cooled down by the environment. In humans, vasoconstriction can reduce heat loss by up to a third. The presence of subcutaneous fat also aids in maintaining the heat of the blood as fat is a very good insulator.

definition

> **Subcutaneous:** under the skin.

Second, a person will experience an increase in their metabolic rate, which is brought about by an increased release of the hormones thyroxin and adrenaline. An increased metabolic rate will generate body heat. This process is called non-shivering thermogenesis.

Lastly, a person will experience a rapid involuntary cycle of contraction and relaxation of skeletal muscles, which is called shivering. The process of shivering can actually increase the metabolic rate to four to five times above resting levels.

A person can also conserve heat by adding clothing, which is a behavioural mechanism for minimising heat loss.

Effects of cold temperatures

The effect of a cold environment on exercise performance depends largely on the severity of the cold and the type of exercise performed. Exposure to a moderately cold environment may actually have a positive effect on performance, as the cardiovascular system no longer has to divert blood to the periphery for heat loss in addition to supplying the exercising muscles with blood. This results in less stress being placed on the heart than when exercising in the heat.

Therefore, it is not surprising that record performances during long-distance running and cycling are usually achieved in cool climatic conditions.

Exposure to a very cold environment may cause frostbite or hypothermia. Frostbite usually occurs in a person's fingers or toes. It happens when a part of the body becomes extremely cold, significantly reducing blood supply to the area, which results in the body tissue freezing. The ice crystals that form rupture and destroy the body's cells. The region involved turns a deep purple or red colour and has blisters usually filled with blood. This tissue will then have to be amputated to prevent infection from spreading to other parts of the body.

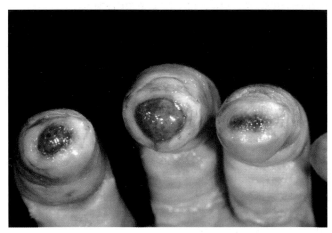

Fig 20.05 Frostbite

Hypothermia is defined as a drop in the body's normal core temperature to 35°C or below. The condition usually comes on gradually and its severity varies in relation to how low the body core temperature drops. If it drops to 30°C or below this can lead to cardiac and respiratory failure, which is soon followed by death.

High altitude and exercise and sporting performance

Anywhere more than 1500 m above sea level (5000 ft) is considered to be at high altitude. The further above sea level you travel the lower the barometric pressure becomes. This means that the higher up you go, the 'thinner' the air becomes as there are fewer air molecules in the atmosphere.

Therefore, although the percentage of oxygen, carbon dioxide and nitrogen within the air remains the same (20.93 per cent, 0.03 per cent and 79.04 per cent respectively), every breath of air you take contains fewer and fewer molecules of oxygen (and carbon dioxide and nitrogen). As a result, a person must work harder to obtain the same quantities of oxygen compared with when they are at low altitudes. This means that an athlete who exercises or competes at high altitude will have to breathe much faster to take in enough oxygen for their energy systems to work normally than when they exercise at lower altitude.

In 1968 the Olympic Games were held in Mexico City, which stands at an elevation of 2300 m and is therefore classed as being at high altitude. In order to try to overcome the effects of the thinner air, the athletes went through a period of acclimatisation, during which they trained at high altitude for a number of weeks. The body responds physiologically by adapting to cope with the decreased levels of oxygen in the air.

Responses of the body to high altitude

The body undergoes a number of changes to increase oxygen delivery to cells and improve the efficiency of oxygen use. This response usually begins immediately and continues for several weeks.

The body's initial responses to being at high altitude are:

- an increase in respiratory rate (hyperventilation)
- an increase in heart rate (tachycardia).

When a person arrives at high altitude their respiratory rate and depth increase. The increased breathing rate has the effect of causing more carbon dioxide to be expired and more oxygen to be delivered to the alveoli. The respiratory rate peaks after about one week of living at high altitude, and then slowly decreases over the next few months, although it tends to remain higher than its normal rate at sea level.

Heart rate also increases because the body's cells require a constant supply of oxygen. As there is less oxygen available in the blood, the heart beats more quickly to meet the cells' demands. Heart rate will also start to decrease as more time is spent at high altitude.

Effects of high altitude

After a person has spent a number of weeks at high altitude, their body adapts by making cardiovascular and metabolic changes. The cardiovascular adaptations are:

- decreased maximum cardiac output
- decreased maximum heart rate
- increase in the number of red blood cells
- increased haemoglobin concentration
- increased haematocrit
- increased capillarisation.

The bone marrow contributes to acclimatisation by increasing red blood cell production and, therefore, the blood's haemoglobin concentration. This increase is triggered by the kidneys' increased production of erythropoietin (EPO). New red blood cells become available in the blood within four to five days, and have the effect of increasing the blood's oxygen-carrying capacity. An acclimatised person may have 30 to 50 per cent more red blood cells than a counterpart at sea level.

The cardiovascular system also develops more capillaries in response to altitude. This has the effect of improving the rate of diffusion of oxygen from the blood and into the muscles by shortening the distance between the cells and the capillary.

All these adaptations in the weeks following exposure are aimed at increasing oxygen transport to the body cells. This results in a reduction in the cardiac output required for oxygen delivery during rest and exercise compared with pre-acclimatisation.

The metabolic adaptations are:

- increased excretion of bicarbonate via the kidneys
- an increase in 2,3-diphosphoglycerate (DPG) within the red blood cells
- an increase in the number of mitochondria and oxidative enzymes
- increased levels of lactic acid leading to reduced levels of lactic acid production.

The increased breathing rate means that more carbon dioxide than normal is breathed out, resulting in the body becoming more alkaline. To compensate for the body's increasing alkalinity, the kidneys excrete bicarbonate (an alkaline substance) in the urine. This adaptation occurs within 24 to 48 hours.

Within the blood cells DPG increases. This is an organic phosphate that helps oxygen to dissociate (unload) from the haemoglobin to the body's cells much more easily. The increase in DPG helps to compensate for the blood's reduced oxygen level.

The increased number of mitochondria and oxidative enzymes appears to be due to the switch in the body's preferred fuel for energy production. At low altitude, carbohydrate is the usual energy source, but at altitude fat is the preferred fuel. This change is not well understood, but may be due to the fact that a reduced oxygen supply causes a higher lactic acid level in the muscles and bloodstream. Carbohydrate metabolism also leads to increased production of lactic acid, but fat metabolism does not produce lactic acid as a by-product. Therefore, the change of the main metabolic fuel from carbohydrate to fat results in a reduced level of lactic acid production.

The body's adaptation to high altitude helps significantly, but does not fully compensate for the lack of oxygen in the air. There is a drop in VO_2max by 2 per cent for every 300 m elevation above 1500 m, even after full acclimatisation.

Methods of adaptation to high altitude

Athletes can acclimatise prior to competition at high altitude in a number of ways. The most common approach is for the athlete to spend a period of no less than two weeks training and living at the competition altitude prior to the event.

Some problems do arise in this approach. Primarily, the athlete is not able to train to such a high intensity as when they are at sea level because of the reduction in oxygen molecules in the air. Therefore, their VO_2max is reduced. They may also suffer from slight insomnia that would have an impact on their recovery from training.

Some athletes acclimatise by training at a low altitude and then sleeping at a high altitude or in a high-altitude chamber (see Fig 20.06). The reasoning behind this is that the athlete can train at maximal levels if they are at low altitude, and then are exposed to hypoxic stress while sleeping, thus increasing the production of red blood cells and other physiological adaptations.

Fig 20.06 High-altitude chamber

definition

Hypoxic stress: lower than normal oxygen levels.

Gender and exercise and sporting performance

Males and females rarely compete against each other in the sporting arena. Aside from the obvious differences between genders, there are a range of physiological differences that mean one gender would have an unfair advantage over the other. Hence the need for single-sex competitions.

Body composition

One of the main differences between the genders that affects athletic performance is the difference in body composition. Males tend to have greater muscle mass and lower fat mass compared with females.

A high percentage of body fat is not always a hindrance in sport. As females have a greater percentage of fat than males, they are more buoyant (body fat weighs much less than muscle mass), so they use up less energy than males staying afloat. Therefore, using the same amount of energy, females will be able to swim faster than males. This, together with their increased insulation from the cold, makes females more suited to open-water swimming, such as swimming the Channel.

Maximal oxygen consumption

An untrained male will have an average absolute VO_2max of 3.5 litres per minute. An untrained female will have an average absolute VO_2max of 2 litres per minute, which is 43 per cent lower than the male's. The main reasons for this difference are that males are usually bigger than females and the difference in body composition between the genders. Females have

Table 20.01 Differences in body composition between the sexes

Body tissue	Composition (%)	
	Male	Female
Muscle	45	36
Bone	15	12
Essential fat	3	12
Storage fat	12	15
Other tissue	25	25
Total	100	100

approximately 10 per cent more body fat than males, which will reduce their VO$_2$max because fat mass hinders performance.

Females also have a lower blood haemoglobin content than males. This means that their blood has a lower oxygen-carrying capacity than a male's, affecting aerobic energy production. Research has shown that the female heart is slightly smaller relative to body size than the male heart. A relatively smaller heart would mean that a female's stroke volume is relatively lower than a male's. As cardiac output is the product of heart rate multiplied by stroke volume, for a female to maintain a certain cardiac output, her heart must beat faster than a male's:

$$Q = HR \times SV$$

Therefore, body size and fat percentage, the difference in oxygen-carrying capacity of the blood, plus differences in the size of the heart might explain the gender differences in VO$_2$max.

Thermoregulation

If you study males' and females' sweat rate per kilogram of body weight, women usually have lower sweat rates than men. Therefore, on average, males are able to lose more heat through evaporative heat loss than females. However, as females have a higher body surface-area-to-volume ratio than males, they are able to lose more heat through radiation. Research has shown that these variations in heat loss between the sexes evens out, so that there is no real difference in the ability to dissipate heat.

Flexibility

Females are usually much more flexible than males, especially in the hip, shoulder and elbow joints. This could be due to the fact that females usually have less muscle tissue than males which means that there is less resistance provided for stretching.

Muscle strength and power

If you were to extract exactly the same amount of healthy muscle from a male and from a female, then test the muscle tissue for the amount of force it could produce, there would be no difference between the two. Therefore, there is no difference in the strength of the muscle tissue between the sexes.

Fig 20.07 Male and female body builders

However, on average, males are stronger than females because of the difference in body composition. The average female has less muscle mass than the average male. The reason for this difference is largely due to the hormone testosterone. Testosterone acts on the body in a number of ways, including increasing muscle growth. Studies have shown that females who took testosterone injections for a period of time increased their muscle mass and decreased their body fat percentage. The females undergoing this study also began to develop secondary male characteristics, such as growth of facial hair, deepened voices and increased aggression.

Studies have also shown that the number of slow-twitch and fast-twitch fibres is no different in the male and female populations. Therefore, it is not the muscle quality that differs between the sexes, but the muscle quantity.

Training differences between males and females

Research suggests that males and females should not take on the same volume of training. It would appear that elite female athletes perform optimally at a training volume that is around 10 to 15 per cent lower than that observed in elite male athletes. If the volume of training is increased for a female it often does not improve performance and can lead to overtraining. This is again due to the hormone testosterone. Testosterone is responsible for aiding muscle growth and is also critical for tissue repair. As training results in the breakdown of tissues, males are able to recover much more quickly from training than females because of this hormone.

It is important to note that all these differences are based on average results taken from males and females. In reality, there are many individual women with significantly higher VO_2max values, strength, endurance and training ability than individual men.

Race and exercise and sporting performance

Take a look at the 2004 Olympic 100 m sprint semi-final (Fig 20.08). What do you notice about the line-up? Now carry out research to find out who won the endurance races in the 2004 Olympics. Where were the winners from? What about the swimming competition (Fig 20.09)? What do you notice about the race of the swimmers?

LEARNER ACTIVITY Male and female strength

The aim of this activity is to determine if there is a difference in strength between the males and females in your class. Differences in upper body and lower body are also compared.

You will need the following equipment:

- multigym or free weights
- pen and paper
- weighing scales

Method

1 The whole class should warm up thoroughly before taking part in any strength tests.
2 Working in pairs, go around the multigym or use the free weights. Lift an amount you feel comfortable with, then continue adding weights until you have reached your 1 rep max. Ensure that you have short breaks between lifts. Write this weight down.
3 Record your body weight.
4 Work out what weight you lifted (kg) in relation to your body weight (kg). This can be calculated by:

$$\frac{\text{weight lifted (kg)}}{\text{body weight (kg)}} \times 100$$

5 Complete a table that takes into account the whole class's results. Then work out the average weight lifted in each exercise for males and for females. Repeat this, but use weight lifted in relation to body weight.

Results
Complete a table like the one below.

Exercise	Weight lifted (kg)	Percentage of body weight

Then answer the following questions.

- Was there a difference in the average weight lifted by each sex? Can you explain why there is this difference?
- Which exercise produced the greatest difference between the sexes? Why do you think this is?
- Why is body weight sometimes taken into account when comparing the amount of weight a person can lift?

Fig 20.08 The 2004 Olympic 100 m sprint semi-final

Fig 20.09 A 2004 Olympics swimming final

It seems clear that athletes of certain races are better suited to certain sports. At present, the top athletes for both short- and long-distance running events tend to come from Africa.

West African athletes

At present, every men's world record from 100 m to 1 mile belongs to a runner of African descent. In sprinting, the last time a white athlete held the world record for the 100 m was in 1960. The 10-second time barrier for sprinting 100 m has been broken 200 times, but always by black athletes. This would lead us to believe that athletes of African origin have a natural athletic advantage for this discipline over competitors whose ethnic origin lies elsewhere.

Research suggests that this theory does hold true, and that the physique of athletes from this region is better suited to sprinting. These athletes generally have lower body fat, longer legs in comparison with the rest of their bodies and narrow hips. They also tend to have greater muscle mass, higher bone mineral density, higher levels of testosterone, a higher percentage of fast-twitch muscle fibres and more anaerobic enzymes.

Research strongly suggests that no amount of training can break through the percentage of genetically inherited fast-twitch muscle fibres. The greater the number of fast-twitch fibres an athlete has, generally the better they will be suited to speed events. Therefore, if an athlete does not have a certain proportion of fast-twitch muscles, they cannot hope to be a champion sprinter or jumper. This would suggest that sprinters are born and cannot be made.

Fig 20.10 Carl Lewis

East African (Kenyan) athletes

With regard to the middle- to long-distance running events, the East Africans, particularly the Kenyans, are dominant. The top 60 times for the 3000 m steeplechase are all held by Kenyan athletes. Kenyan athletes also hold more than half the top times for the 5000 and 10,000 metres.

The vast majority of top Kenyan runners come from one area of the country, the Kalenjin region. Athletes from this part of Kenya have won more than 70 per cent of Kenya's Olympic medals in world running. The fact that the Kalenjin region is at high altitude has made many scientists believe that their adaptation to living there has given them an increased athletic prowess at endurance events. These athletes have been shown to have a greater number of red blood cells, a larger lung capacity, a high proportion of slow-twitch muscle fibres and more energy-producing enzymes in their muscles, which are better able to utilise oxygen than those of athletes living at normal altitudes. These adaptations would increase the athlete's oxygen-carrying capacity and would certainly aid the athlete in endurance running events.

Caucasian athletes

White people (Caucasians) tend to have more natural upper-body strength, and to have evolved with a mesomorphic body type and relatively short arms and legs. As a result they dominate weight lifting and wrestling. They also excel at the field events and hold 46 out of the top 50 throws for shot-put and hammer.

Fig 20.11 Oleksiy Kolokoltsev

Caucasian people also tend to dominate the swimming events – very few African athletes reach any swimming final. This could be due to the fact that African athletes tend to have heavier skeletons and smaller chest cavities, which would leave them at a disadvantage when competing in water.

Indian athletes

Athletes of Indian origin excel in a number of sports – in particular, cricket. This is probably due to social and cultural influences rather than a physiological predisposition to the sport.

Research clearly shows that genetic evolution has strongly influenced the physiological make-up of people living in different environments, which may well determine if a person has the chance to be an elite athlete. However, dedication, commitment and good fortune are also factors that play a major role in determining if the athlete will win or lose.

As well as the physiological traits of athletes coming from different ethnic origins, it is also necessary to take into account the social, cultural and economic factors of the country the person grew up in, as these have a huge effect on determining whether a person will take up certain sports. This may help to explain why some races excel in some sports but not in others.

LEARNER ACTIVITY
World records

Research the world records for the following events:

- men's marathon
- men's 100 m sprint
- women's 5000 m
- men's shot-put
- women's 200 m
- men's 100 m freestyle swim
- women's 4 × 100 m freestyle swim.

Find out the ethnic origin of each world record holder and try to explain why this person may be more physiologically suited to this event.

Ageing and exercise and sporting performance

Any person who plans to work in the sports industry may deal with people of differing ages. People of different ages have differing needs in terms of their training requirements and sporting and exercising abilities. Most people are aware of how a typical adult responds to exercise and training programmes, but few know how children and older adults (50-plus) respond.

The younger person

Contrary to popular belief, children are not mini-adults. They grow and mature at their own rates and their chronological age may differ greatly from their biological age. For girls, puberty may take place between the ages of 8 and 13, and for boys from 9 to 15 years. Understanding of how children respond to exercise is limited because measurement techniques and equipment developed for use with adults are often not appropriate for use with young people. However, it is clear that children should take part in exercise on a regular basis. The National Association for Sports and Physical Education recommends that school-age children should take part in 60 minutes or more of physical activity every day. It is better for the child if the activity is broken down into bouts of around 15 minutes.

Any person supervising exercising children should be suitably qualified. Coaching qualifications for specific sports, combined with first aid and an awareness of children's exercising needs, are usually adequate. Anyone wishing to supervise children who are exercising in a gym using weights or taking exercise classes should have specialist knowledge and qualifications to demonstrate a sound understanding of children's physiology as a very minimum.

Strength training for children

A child's strength-training programme should not be a scaled-down version of an adult's weight-training programme. The reason behind this is that children are still growing. An inappropriate strength-training programme could damage their growth plates at the end of their bones, which could result in growth problems. A suitably qualified person should design a programme for the child. One of the most important aspects of this programme is to ensure that the child has the correct lifting techniques. Children should aim to lift lighter weights with a high number of repetitions. A strength-training programme for children should not attempt to increase muscle bulk until the child has passed through puberty.

Thermoregulation and children

Children are much more prone to overheating than adults. This is partly because they do not have a fully developed sweating mechanism, and also because they have a much higher surface area to volume ratio. This means that they will gain (or lose) heat much more quickly than adults. Therefore, if you are supervising children who are playing or exercising on a hot day be sure to have lots of rest periods, lots of drinks, sun hats, sun cream and try to stay out of the sun wherever possible.

The older person

People today are living on average much longer than they did than before. At the beginning of the twentieth century only 4 per cent of the population were aged 65 or older; by 1996 this number had increased to 16 per cent and it is predicted that, by 2026, 41 per cent of the population will be over 65. This is partly due to better nutrition, medicine and sanitation.

The quality of a person's life as they get older can be greatly improved through exercise participation. When a person gets older they face a variety of anatomical and physiological changes which can be reversed or slowed down through regular physical activity.

Skeletal changes

Once you reach the age of 30, your skeleton should be at its strongest. From there on, there is a gradual loss of bone mass which means that the skeleton becomes weaker and more prone to fractures. Women are particularly vulnerable to weaker skeletons after the menopause as they no longer produce the same levels of oestrogen, which helps make the skeleton strong. There is also a reduction in a person's flexibility as they get older. This reduced range of movement is due to the ligaments becoming thicker with less elastic connective tissue. It has been estimated that around 80 per cent of older adults suffer from arthritis, which is not only uncomfortable but can also significantly impair a person's mobility.

definition

Arthritis: inflammation of a joint, or joints, causing pain, swelling and stiffness.

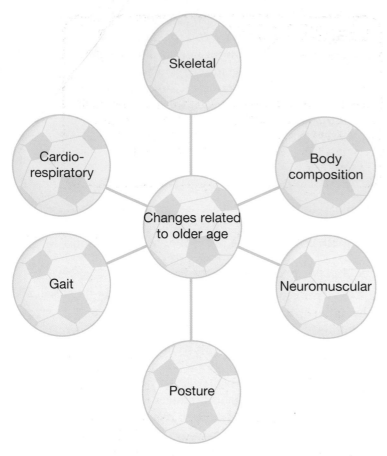

Fig 20.12 Changes related to older age

definition

VO$_2$max: the ability to take up and use oxygen.

Neuromuscular changes

A person is at their strongest and most powerful when they are in their thirties, and this remains relatively constant until they reach their fifties. After this, around 10 oz of muscle mass is lost every year. By the age of 70, both males and females will have a 40 per cent reduction in their muscle mass. This reduction in muscle mass is partly due to a reduced production of the hormone testosterone. Not only does muscle mass decline with age, but also the number of functioning fast-twitch muscle fibres decreases. Research has found that there is a link between a loss of muscle strength and an increased risk of falling.

Connective tissue also becomes less elastic resulting in increased stiffness which is also a common complaint in people as they get older.

Cardiorespiratory changes

Cardiorespiratory function declines after the age of around 25. If person does not remain physically active their VO$_2$max will drop by 1 per cent every year after the age of 25.

This decline is due to a reduction in maximal heart rate. As maximal heart rate = 200 – age, it is clear to see that the older you become the lower your maximal heart rate will be. A person's arteries and arterioles are also affected by ageing. They become less elastic and can become thickened. This has the effect of increasing a person's blood pressure. The oxygen-carrying capacity of the blood is reduced as haemoglobin levels drop.

A person's lungs become less effective as they become older. They become less elastic, there is an increase in residual volume and a reduction in the number of alveoli in which gaseous exchange takes place.

Body composition

As a person gets older, they lose muscle mass and gain body fat. Muscle mass is lost because of a reduction in testosterone production. As muscle uses up more calories than fat tissue, when a person starts to lose muscle tissue their basal metabolic rate slows down.

Unless a person reduces the amount of calories they take in, they will gain body weight in the form of fat. As people get older, few actually do consume fewer calories than when they were younger which results in weight gain in the form of body fat.

Body posture

A person's body posture is important to help maintain balance and for efficient mobility. As the skeleton becomes weaker, a person's body posture changes. The shoulders become rounder and the head comes further forwards, known as 'kyphosis'. This, together with a decline in eyesight, leaves older people more susceptible to falls.

Gait

Gait is the term used to describe how a person walks. As a person gets older, their gait pattern will alter. Speed of walking and stride length decrease, with an increase in pelvic tilt, more time in double leg support (i.e. stationary, with two feet on the ground) and decreased movement at the ankle.

Physical activity and the older person

Physical activity will have a positive impact on all the aforementioned anatomical and physiological effects of ageing. Regular participation in a range of different types of exercise will help to delay the impacts of ageing.

Skeleton

Regular weight-bearing activity and/or resistance exercises such as walking, jogging or weight training will help to maintain the strength of the bones of the skeleton, which will make them less likely to break.

Neuromuscular

Decreased muscle strength has been linked to an increased incidence of falling. Older adults that regularly take part in resistance exercises find that they increase or preserve muscle strength.

Cardiorespiratory

Physical activity of moderate intensity has been shown to prevent or reduce the effects of ageing on the cardiorespiratory system.

Body composition

Regular moderate aerobic and resistance physical activity has been shown to effectively increase or maintain the muscle mass of an older person. This helps to decrease the amount of body fat gained as a person gets older.

Body posture

Regular physical activity helps a person to maintain a good body posture as they get older. Weight-bearing exercise or resistance exercises help to keep the skeleton and muscular systems strong. This helps to keep a person's back in the correct position, and thereby helps to maintain a good body posture.

Gait

Regular physical exercise will help an older person maintain their walking pattern. Resistance training will help to strengthen the abdominals, which helps to reduce pelvic tilt. Regular mobility exercises will help to maintain a good range of movement in the ankle. Moderate aerobic exercises will help to maintain stride length and frequency.

LEARNER ACTIVITY
Exercise programme for an older person

Design an exercise programme for an older adult. Include activities that you think they will enjoy. Evaluate the health benefits this person will receive if they take part in your exercise programme.

Ergogenic aids for exercise and sports performance

definition

Ergogenic aid: something that is taken to improve sporting performance.

Instances of athletes using performance-enhancing substances date back over 2000 years. As far back as 668 BC, the winner of the 200 m sprint in the Olympic Games prepared for the event with a special diet of dried figs. In sport today, virtually all athletes take substances to improve their performance. This is because they face enormous pressure to excel in competition. Winning a race not only gives them a gold medal, they can also earn a lot of money and a lot of fame from a win. The competition life of an athlete is relatively brief, which means that they have only a short time to do their best work. Although athletes must know that training is the best path to victory, they are also aware that some drugs can boost their efforts and give them a greater chance of victory even at the expense of their health and their athletic careers.

Some of the substances athletes take are illegal, as defined by the International Olympic Committee (IOC), whereas others are perfectly legitimate ways of naturally improving one's performance, such as consuming a sports drink during a game, or eating large amounts of pasta the night before an endurance race.

The practice of using banned substances to enhance athletic performance is called doping. The first drug tests on athletes were conducted at the 1968

Olympic Games in Mexico. Since then, drug testing has become a major part of sporting competition and new methods of detecting drugs are always being sought.

Banned ergogenic aids

The majority of banned ergogenic aids used by athletes today were initially designed by the medical profession in order to treat patients with various illnesses or disorders. Many types of drugs are available to the athlete, and what they take is determined by the sport in which they compete. The main effects of the different groups of drugs are to:

- build muscle mass
- increase the delivery of oxygen to exercising tissues
- provide pain relief
- stimulate the body
- relax
- reduce weight.

Building muscle mass

Athletes competing in sports that require a high muscle mass, such as weight lifting, throwing events, sprinting or boxing, may take muscle-building drugs. There are a variety of drugs available that increase the muscle mass of an athlete, including anabolic steroids, human growth hormone (hGH) and insulin.

Anabolic steroids: anabolic steroids are manmade substances. They were developed in the late 1930s primarily to treat hypogonadism, which is a condition in which the testes do not produce enough testosterone. This reduction in testosterone production resulted in impaired growth, development and sexual functioning. It was later discovered that anabolic steroids could not only treat males with hypogonadism, but could also increase the growth of skeletal muscle in humans.

Athletes and others abuse anabolic steroids to enhance performance and improve physical appearance. Just taking anabolic steroids will not increase muscle bulk. The athlete must still train hard to achieve an increase in muscle mass. The main advantage in taking these drugs is that the muscles recover more quickly from training. This allows the athlete to train at a higher level and for longer than if they were not taking these drugs.

The main disadvantages of taking anabolic steroids are:

- liver and kidney tumours
- jaundice
- high blood pressure
- severe acne
- trembling.

There are also some sex-specific side-effects. For males these are:

- shrinking of the testicles
- reduced sperm count
- infertility, baldness
- development of breasts
- increased risk for prostate cancer.

And for females these are:

- growth of facial hair
- male-pattern baldness
- changes in or cessation of the menstrual cycle
- enlargement of the clitoris
- deepened voice.

Scientific research also shows that aggression and other psychiatric side effects may result from abuse of anabolic steroids. Depression can be experienced when the person stops taking the drugs and may contribute to them becoming dependent on anabolic steroids.

Human growth hormone: human growth hormone (also know as human chorionic gonadotropin, hCG) is a naturally occurring hormone produced by the pituitary gland. It is important for normal human growth and development, especially in children and teenagers. Low hGH levels in children and teenagers result in dwarfism. Growth hormone stimulates the development of natural male and female sex hormones.

Growth hormone is not banned for female athletes because it would not lead to muscle development and might naturally occur in high levels if the athlete is pregnant.

In males growth hormone acts to increase testosterone levels and results in increased muscle development, as with anabolic steroids. Excessive growth hormone levels increase muscle mass by stimulating protein synthesis, strengthen bones by stimulating bone growth and reduce body fat by stimulating the breakdown of fat cells.

When the effects of growth hormone were first learnt, the hormone could not be produced artificially. This meant that athletes could only obtain growth hormone in its natural form, either from dead bodies or dead animals. Research suggests that athletes or athletes' coaches would rob graves for the sole purpose of extracting growth hormone from the brains of people who had recently died. Clearly, this was a highly unethical and illegal process, so athletes would also extract growth hormone from dead animals. But if the athletes took the hormone from dead animals they ran the risk of contracting animal diseases such as Creutzfeldt-Jakob disease (CJD). Nowadays, growth hormone can be produced in laboratories and is widely available. The use of hGH has become increasingly popular because it is difficult to detect.

The side effects of growth hormone in males are the same as those for anabolic steroids together with enlarged internal organs. The athlete taking the drug may also develop acromegaly, which results in the person's hands, feet and lower jaw growing much larger than normal. If a person's lower jaw grows faster than the rest of the bones of the face, their teeth will become misaligned and they will often need to wear a brace.

Insulin: insulin is produced naturally in the body by the pancreas. Its main function is to help control the concentration of sugar within the bloodstream. If there is too much sugar, insulin acts to remove this sugar by stimulating the synthesis of glycogen or fat.

Athletes may take insulin in combination with anabolic steroids or growth hormone as it also helps to increase muscle mass by stimulating protein synthesis.

The main side-effects of abusing insulin are hypoglycaemic responses such as shaking, nausea and weakness. If too much insulin is taken this may lead to severe hypoglycaemia, which could lead to coma and death.

> **Hypoglycaemia:** low blood sugar levels.

definition

Increasing oxygen in tissues

Athletes competing in endurance sports may abuse drugs that increase the oxygen supply to their muscle tissues. There are two main methods of increasing the oxygen supply to the tissue: erythropoietin (rhEPO) and blood doping.

Erythropoietin: EPO is a naturally occurring protein hormone that is secreted by the kidneys. After being released into the bloodstream it acts on the bone marrow, where it stimulates the production of red blood cells (erythrocytes). Medically, EPO is used to treat certain forms of anaemia.

Since EPO increases a person's red blood cell count, it will result in increased blood haemoglobin concentrations. Therefore, after taking EPO, a person's blood will have an increased oxygen-carrying capacity, which potentially has the effect of increasing performance. Endurance athletes, such as those who compete in marathons, the Tour de France and cross-country skiing, have used EPO to increase their oxygen supply by as much as 10 per cent.

EPO is difficult to detect because it is identical to the naturally occurring form produced by the body. As there is no established normal concentration range of EPO it is very difficult to determine if an athlete has been using it.

The main side effect of taking EPO is an increase in the 'thickness' of the blood. This thickened blood will not flow through the blood vessels very well because it has a greater resistance. As a result, the heart must work harder to pump blood around the body, which will increase the chances of the athlete suffering from a heart attack.

Blood doping: blood doping is the practice of artificially increasing the amount of red blood cells in the body to increase oxygen delivery to the tissues in an attempt to improve athletic performance. Records show that blood doping research was initially conducted in the Second World War to try to increase the endurance of pilots. As the pilots who were dropping bombs had to avoid anti-aircraft guns, they needed to fly higher. But flying at higher altitudes disturbed the normal functioning of the central nervous system, which resulted in errors being made. In 1944–45 the US Navy infused 1300 ml of blood into two subjects and tested their physiological reactions at simulated high altitude. They found that these subjects were able to tolerate lower oxygen levels and had normal functioning of the central nervous system. Research also showed that the subjects exhibited a lower heart rate response during exercise following the transfusion.

Once the effects of blood doping were realised by the sporting world, blood doping became an illegal method of increasing the athlete's oxygen-carrying capacity of blood. There are two main methods of blood doping. First, athletes may undergo a homologous transfusion, in which they receive blood from an individual of the same blood type. The red blood cell count is then increased by the amount that is transferred. The second method is via autologous transfusion. This means the athlete's own blood is used. An amount of blood is removed from the athlete and frozen for six to eight weeks. Over this period, the athlete's body makes new red blood cells to replace those that have been removed. The removed blood is then transfused back into the athlete which results in the athlete having an increased number of red blood cells compared with pre-transfusion.

The side effects of blood doping are the same as for taking EPO, but there is also the increased risk of contracting diseases such as HIV or of receiving the wrong blood type if the athlete undergoes homologous transfusion. Reports have also been made in the past of athletes receiving blood from a person who was taking performance-enhancing drugs. Once the blood was transfused, the receiver would have traces of the drug in their bloodstream and would test positive for these drugs.

Pain relief

At some point in their career, most athletes will probably suffer from a sport injury. If this injury occurs during competition, athletes may try to mask their injury pain with drugs, such as narcotics, cortisone and local anaesthetics.

Narcotics are taken in order to reduce the amount of pain felt from injury, or can be used as recreational drugs. The main narcotics used are morphine, methadone and heroin. They act to give the person a 'high', which helps to mask the pain of the injury.

Narcotics affect a person's mental abilities, such as balance and coordination. This may have a detrimental effect on performance. In addition, athletes who continue to compete with a sport injury run the risk of further damage or complications to the injured area.

Stimulants

The main stimulants used by athletes are amphetamines. Stimulants act to mimic the action of the sympathetic nervous system.

Stimulants have the effect of constricting the blood vessels supplying blood to skin, dilating the blood vessels supplying the heart and skeletal muscles,

dilating the bronchioles to increase ventilation and increasing the release of glucose from the liver. They have the effect of increasing a person's mental alertness and also help to conceal feelings of exhaustion. As a result, athletes competing in endurance events, contact sports or those demanding fast reactions may take stimulants to enhance their performance.

As stimulants hide feelings of fatigue, it is possible for athletes to over-exert themselves to the point where they can suffer heat stroke and cardiac failure. Other side-effects include increased blood pressure and body temperature, increased and irregular heartbeat, aggression, anxiety and loss of appetite. If an athlete requires medication to treat asthma or other common respiratory disorders they are at risk of inadvertently taking stimulants as these commonly prescribed substances often contain powerful stimulants.

Beta blockers

Beta blockers are used medically to treat heart disease, lower heart rate and blood pressure, and reduce anxiety. These drugs act to interfere with actions of the sympathetic nervous system, which controls involuntary muscle movement.

Beta blockers slow the heart rate, relax muscle in blood vessel walls and decrease the force of heart contractions. Athletes may use these drugs in sport in order to reduce anxiety levels and to prevent their body from shaking. As a result, athletes who take part in sports that require steady nerves and hands (snooker, archery, shooting and darts) may abuse this type of drug.

Fig 20.13 An archer

The side-effects of taking this drug include lowered blood pressure, slow heart rate and tiredness. In extreme cases, the heart may actually stop because it has been slowed down too much.

Diuretics

Diuretics help increase the excretion of fluids from body tissues and reduce high blood pressure.

The main reason diuretics are misused by competitors in sport is to reduce their body weight quickly in sports where weight categories are involved. Hence, boxers, weight lifters or judo competitors may take them to remain in their weight category. If their body weight is only slightly above the category lower limit, they will be competing against athletes who are larger than them and, therefore, also presumably have a greater muscle mass, which would leave the athlete at a disadvantage. Athletes may also take diuretics to reduce the concentration of other banned substances by diluting the urine, or to attempt to eliminate the banned substance from their body to escape detection of the drug through testing.

Possible side-effects of taking diuretics include dehydration, which could then lead to dizziness and fainting, vomiting and muscle cramps. If the athlete becomes severely dehydrated through taking the diuretics, the effect on the kidneys and the heart could lead to death.

Review questions

1 What climatic stresses will the England football team face when playing in the 2010 World Cup in South Africa, and how could they try to prepare for these?
2 If you were coaching a group of male and female athletes to perform at high altitude, how would you train them and would you give them exactly the same training regime? Explain your answer.
3 Research the 1968 Olympic Games held in Mexico City. Name three events in which world records were broken and three events where the results were not as good as had been expected. Try to explain these findings.
4 Explain why you think Kenyan athletes are dominating long-distance running events.
5 Research an athlete of your choice who has been banned from taking part in sports because they have been found to have taken a pharmacological aid. Name:
   - the aid
   - how it may have enhanced their performance
   - possible side effects from taking this aid.

Goals

By the end of this chapter you should:

- know about the provision of exercise for specific groups
- understand the benefits of exercise for different specific groups
- know about exercise referral schemes
- be able to plan and deliver an exercise session for a specific group.

In today's society people are living longer and experiencing an increase in the prevalence of medical diseases and disorders. It is generally understood that there is no medical condition that cannot benefit from some form of physical exercise or activity. The government is well aware of this link and is assigning money to the management of medical conditions through the establishment of exercise referral schemes and schemes through the National Health Service.

For fitness trainers, it is becoming increasingly rare to find people who are completely free of all medical conditions or injuries. Thus, it is important to have an appreciation of these medical conditions, enabling you to discuss the condition and then deal with the person in a safe and effective manner.

The provision of exercise for specific groups

When we discuss specific groups we need to have something to compare them with to make them specific. We have two clear types of specific group:

- those who are in a specific stage in life
- those who have medical conditions.

The special groups examined are:

- older people
- children
- pre- and post-natal women
- disabled people
- obese people
- heart disease such as high blood pressure and coronary heart disease
- pulmonary disorders such as asthma
- diabetics
- arthritis
- osteoporosis.

Provision for sport in Britain is a joint effort between sectors of provision:

- private – individuals investing their own money in sport to make a profit
- public – government or local authority investment in sport to provide a low-cost service
- voluntary – like-minded individuals working together to create opportunities for each other.

With regard to special groups, as listed above, the majority of the provision comes from the public sector. This is due to the motives of each provider. The private sector is mainly motivated by investing money to make a return as profit. The voluntary sector involves volunteers giving their time to create opportunities to play competitive sport.

The public sector invests its money to improve the quality of life of its taxpayers and to benefit society in general. This includes promoting the health and well-being of each person. Thus, the aims of the public sector fit in with the aims of the schemes provided. That is not to say that the private sector will not be involved, rather that it will be less involved. All sports facilities are covered by the law of the land, which stipulates that all buildings must be adapted to the needs of disabled people and be sensitive to their requirements.

Meeting the needs of people is done through a range of measures:

- appropriate facilities
- provision of classes and activities for different groups

- appropriate equipment or adaptations to equipment for specific groups.

LEARNER ACTIVITY Meeting user needs

In groups of three or four visit a sports or leisure centre and find out the following information.

- Which sector of provision does it fall into?
- What activities has it targeted at each specific group (get hold of a programme of classes and activities)?
- How have the facilities been modified to cater for the needs of each group (you can do this by looking around the facilities and questioning)?

When you look at the programme of classes and activities look out for activities with special names as they are rarely as simple as 'Exercise class for 50+'. The class list may have a guide which describes what each class entails and who the target market may be. If in doubt ask a member of staff.

Exercise referral schemes

The aim of an exercise referral scheme is to provide an alternative to treating a patient by giving them a prescription for medication. The belief is that exercise has a role to play in managing medical conditions and improving health. Therefore, rather than being given a prescription for medicine the doctor will give them a prescription for exercise in the form of a referral to a sports centre. The patient will take the prescription along and be dealt with by the fitness trainer who is qualified to work with such individuals.

All schemes will have variations but follow the same basic format. A scheme lasts for ten to twelve weeks and takes place either in groups or on an individual basis. Each patient has to have written referral from their GP and will have to pay a nominal fee. The fee is usually around £1 a week or £12 for the full course. This is to make the programme available to all members of society and promote equality. The nominal fee also help to keep the person on the exercise programme as they have made a financial commitment. The programme starts with an initial assessment by the qualified trainer, who will then design a specific training programme for the patient. There will be follow-up reassessments at the mid- and end-points. Once the programme is complete the patient may be prescribed another 12

weeks of training on the programme or encouraged to keep themselves active and join the gym. This is at the discretion of all the health professionals involved.

There can be regional variations in the exercise referral schemes provided, due to the staffing and facilities available. However, they will all be working towards achieving the same outcomes. A set of guidelines has been developed to ensure that the schemes maintain some common features in their operation. In 2001 the government developed guidelines called the National Quality Assurance Framework (NQAF) to allow local authorities to base their schemes on common criteria.

All exercise referral schemes are based on a development model which has five distinct stages.

1 Selection of the patient by the GP
2 Physical assessment of the patient and appropriate intervention applied
3 Long-term support to help the patient stay physically active
4 Evaluation of the patient experience and health outcome
5 Return into the community.

Stage 1: Selection of the patient by the GP – there are seven guidelines which are given to the individual GP and nurses to consider when they are making their decision to refer a patient. The seven guidelines are as follows:

- The scheme should cater for adults (over the age of 16) except in exceptional situations. The scheme also needs to address issues of equality and social inclusion. This means it needs to be cheap enough to be affordable by all groups in society.
- The scheme should be aimed at people who are sedentary. This means they are doing less than 30 minutes of moderate-intensity activity per week. Moderate intensity is activity which makes you slightly out of breath and slightly sweaty.
- Serious medical conditions, such as coronary heart disease (CHD) and mental health problems, should have clear measures for them to be identified.
- The scheme needs to develop strategies to promote the uptake of provision by all groups – for example, laying on transport for the elderly and isolated groups, and reduced costs for the unemployed and old age pensioners.
- The scheme must ensure that the needs of high-risk patients are catered for by staff with the appropriate qualifications and experience.

- The scheme must employ a model of behaviour change to take a person through the stages of change. When a person starts exercising they may move through five distinct stages. The stages are contemplation (thinking about exercise), preparation (putting in place preparations to become active), and action (actually made the change to become active), maintenance (keeping up their current activity) and relapse (they have stopped exercising).
- The exercise referral scheme should reflect the values of the health improvement programme of the care trust in that area.

Stage 2: Assessment of the patient and intervention applied – all schemes should consider the following.

- For each patient there must be a written activity plan which clearly outlines the aim of the referral, details of the medical condition and how it is being managed (medication) and the effect these will have on the patient's training and daily activity.
- The patient must give written consent to the trainer that they agree to undertake an assessment and a programme of exercise.
- The physical assessment must be specific to the needs of that patient and the tests selected appropriately.
- A copy of the exercise plan devised by the trainer should be sent to the GP to be placed in the patient's file.
- The trainer must inform the patient how the scheme operates and what is expected of them.
- The trainer must make sure that a copy of the GP referral form, the patient's consent form and their programme of activity are filed in a secure and confidential place. They also must be available for inspection by the health trust.
- The content of the exercise programme must be specific to the individual needs of the patient.
- The trainer must ensure that the patient is involved in the decision-making process to help them develop a healthy lifestyle.
- The trainer needs to closely monitor the attendance of the patient and investigate the situation if they do not train for two weeks. If a patient does not train for three weeks a letter needs to be sent to the GP, and likewise if the patient drops out of the exercise referral scheme. This is because the patient's medication and care may have changed when they are exercising and they may be in danger if it is not adjusted.
- An assessment needs to be conducted at the mid-point of the scheme to monitor the patient's progress.

- An assessment needs to be done at the end of the scheme to assess the outcomes.
- Once the programme is complete, the GP and the exercise professional will consult to decide upon the next step. The choices are to prescribe another programme of exercise or to return the patient to the community.

Stage 3: Long term support to help the patient stay physically active

- The patient is encouraged to keep a record of their progress through the use of a diary or by setting goals.

Stage 4: Evaluation of the patient by the GP

- Once the 12-week programme is complete the patient will take part in an evaluation to assess the outcomes of the programme.

Stage 5: Return into the community

- The patient can either continue on the scheme or they can return to finding a way to exercise in the wider community.

LEARNER ACTIVITY Exercise referral scheme

In groups of two prepare a list of benefits and drawbacks for the trainer of working within an exercise referral scheme. Think beyond any financial gains or losses.

Legal considerations

When dealing with specific groups we are faced with people who are at greater risk than the general public. Their conditions may be unstable and their symptoms may set in quickly. Therefore, we have to be clear about who is responsible for the well-being of the patient while they are training.

All people involved in the network of care for the patient have a legal responsibility. When we train any client we owe them 'a duty of care', which means we must do everything reasonably possible to keep them safe. The same applies for a patient with a specific need and there will be more people involved in the network who owe a duty of care. This will include the GP who referred them and other people supporting them. When they are training with the trainer it is the trainer's full responsibility that they are kept safe. This is why it is imperative to keep detailed records of everything that is done with each patient in case something does happen. You may need to show that you were not negligent in any of your dealings with the patient to prevent yourself being sued.

Benefits of exercise and appropriate forms of exercise

You will look at each specific group in the following manner:

- a brief summary of the condition and the factors you will need to consider
- any associated risks with the group
- the benefits of exercise for the group
- recommendations of exercise for the group.

Prior to exercise, factors such as screening participants, completion of informed consent forms and planning of the exercise sessions should be considered. During the delivery of each session, you should ensure the participant is appropriately warmed up, appropriate motivation and feedback is given during the session, and that the session ends with an appropriate cool-down.

You should aim to carry out a review process at the end of each session so that you can determine your strengths and areas for improvement. This is covered in Chapter 14: Instructing physical activity and exercise. If you are not going to or have not already studied this chapter, ensure that you read the sections on designing, planning and reviewing an exercise programme.

> **LEARNER ACTIVITY** Working with special groups
>
> In groups of four consider the following questions.
>
> - What do you think are the benefits of working with special groups?
> - What problems may you face when working with special groups?
> - What do you think you need before you would be ready to work with special groups?

Older adults

Up to the age of 35 the structures of our body such as muscle and bone are building up. After this age we start to lose muscle and bone, and the tendons and ligaments become weaker. The loss of bone is called osteopenia and the loss of muscle is called sarcopenia. In particular the ageing adult will lose their type 2 muscle fibres and as a result strength will be decreased.

The amount of muscle we have affects the speed of our metabolism. Metabolism is the number of calories we use on a daily basis and if it is lowered we are more likely to lay down fat. Unless we keep active we will lose around 1 lb of muscle a year and lay down around 2 lbs of fat a year. This results in a creeping fat gain over time. The main effects of ageing are:

- loss of muscle mass
- loss of bone density
- gain in body fat
- loss of muscular strength
- loss of muscular endurance
- decline in cardiovascular fitness
- lower ability to maintain balance
- changes in posture.

All these effects of ageing can be reversed through a programme of resistance training with some cardiovascular work. In particular, resistance training is very important.

> **Both aerobic and resistance exercise are beneficial for older adults, but only resistance training can increase muscle strength and muscle mass.**
>
> **(Baechle and Earle, 2000)**

Here are some safety guidelines for training older adults.

- Always have a thorough consultation with the person and ensure you use a medical questionnaire (PAR-Q) to identify any medical conditions.
- If there are any medical conditions present or concerns, always refer to their GP before training using a written letter.
- Older adults take longer to warm up – at least five to ten minutes is recommended.
- When using resistance training the intensity should be relevant to their level of strength; overload should be applied progressively.
- Allow periods of between 48 and 72 hours between training sessions to allow for recovery.
- All exercises should be pain free; if there is pain then change the range of movement or change the exercise.

Fig 21.01 Older people exercising

The benefits of exercise for older adults are:

- increases in muscle strength and endurance
- less risk of falling due to improved balance
- improved body composition
- improved cardiovascular function
- increased bone density
- reduced symptoms of medical diseases
- greater ability to perform daily activities and functions.

Exercise recommendations

Cardiovascular fitness

Frequency	3–5 times a week
Intensity	Resting heart rate + 20 bpm up to 40–70 of max heart rate
Time	20–30 minutes
Type	Walking, swimming or cycling (depending on structural health status)

The equipment should be chosen to avoid excess stress on bones and joints. Walking is a good choice for most older adults. Exercise in water is a good option for those who need to avoid weight-bearing exercise, and stationary cycling would have the same effect. Group training makes the session more sociable and may improve retention over time. When increasing the training load increase duration before intensity.

Resistance training

Frequency	2– 3 times a week
Intensity	10–15 repetitions until loss of good technique
Time	8–10 exercises, at least one set of each for 20–30 minutes in total

Type	Machines and free weights depending upon individual ability and mobility

Initially use low resistance to allow the older person to adapt. Perform large movements involving more than one joint. Ensure normal breathing patterns are maintained and that breath holding is avoided. Always ensure good technique and that exercises are performed in a controlled manner.

Flexibility training

Frequency	2–3 times a week
Intensity	Take to the point of discomfort
Time	10–15 seconds per stretch
Type	All major muscles and those which are shorter than their functional length

Keep stretching pain free. Slowly stretch the muscle into position and avoid any bouncing or jerky movements.

(All these guidelines are adapted from the American College of Sports Medicine's guidelines for exercise prescription (2006).)

Young people

When considering how to train a young person you will need to consider both their chronological age and their biological age. Chronological age is their age in years and months and biological age looks at their stage of development and maturity. Clearly, biological age is much more important to us as there can be large variations in the maturity levels between two 11-year-old children. Biological age will consider their muscular strength and development of their skeleton.

The main considerations in training young people are their bone and muscle development. When a long bone develops the growth occurs at each diaphysis in the growth cartilage which is present predominantly at the epiphyseal plate. Once the epiphyseal plate has completely hardened (ossification) then the bone will stop growing. If this growth cartilage becomes damaged bone growth may be impaired.

> **A particular concern in children is the vulnerability of the growth cartilage to trauma and overuse.**
>
> **(Baechle and Earle, 2000)**

The concern is that trauma to the bone can affect the supply of blood to the bone. The blood will deliver a steady supply of oxygen and nutrients to the bone, and without this supply the bone will not develop.

As the child grows their muscle mass will steadily increase. At birth muscle mass accounts for around 25 per cent of the baby's body weight and once they have reached adulthood it makes up around 40 per cent. As muscle mass increases strength will also increase. Strength will peak soon after their peak height has been reached.

Fig 21.02 Children enjoying exercise

The benefits of training for young age groups are:

- increased muscular strength and endurance
- reduced risk of injury
- improved motor skills
- improved sporting performance
- reduction of body fat
- decreased mental stress
- less chance of developing future adult diseases.

The risks of training young people are:

- overuse injuries to underdeveloped joints
- lower tolerance of anaerobic exercise
- less developed systems for dissipating heat (less able to sweat)
- less able to deal with cold environments
- faster to fatigue during aerobic exercise.

Exercise recommendations

'Young people' covers a wide variation within stages of development and this must be considered before applying the guidelines.

Cardiovascular fitness

Frequency	5–7 times a week
Intensity	Moderate
Time	Up to 60 minutes a day in periods of 15 minutes
Type	Age-appropriate activities promoting fun and enjoyment

Resistance training

Frequency	2–3 times a week (with rest days in between)
Intensity	Light loads initially (increasing by 5–10 per cent as strength increases)
Time	20–30 minutes per session
Type	Exercises focusing on movements involving several joints (6–15 repetitions)

Flexibility training

Frequency	2–3 times a week
Intensity	Until slight discomfort is felt
Time	Hold for 8–10 seconds
Type	Maintenance stretching only; all major muscle groups

LEARNER ACTIVITY Working with young people

In groups of four complete the following tasks.

- What activities could you do which would be suitable for a group of eight to nine year olds?
- Design a circuit training session for a mixed group of 12 to 13 year olds.

Pre-natal women

Pregnancy is a time of rapid physiological change for the female. As a trainer it is vital to understand the physiology behind what is happening to the female's body. More and more women have become wise to the benefits of exercising when pregnant, for themselves and their babies. However, the medical profession has always had a conservative approach to training when pregnant due to the instability of the situation and the changes occurring. The view is generally not to put yourself at risk unnecessarily. As a trainer it is vital to understand the following:

- the physiological changes occurring
- the risks of exercise
- the benefits of exercise
- how to prescribe exercise.

The period of a pregnancy is divided into three trimesters:

- the first is 0 to 3 months
- the second is 4 to 6 months
- the third is 7 to 9 months.

During the first trimester we refer to the developing baby as an embryo and during the second and third trimesters we refer to it as a fetus. It only becomes a baby when it has been born. The fetus/embryo is attached to the wall of the uterus via the placenta, which is a large structure full of blood vessels providing oxygen, nutrients and a means to exchange waste. It also provides a protective barrier against disease and produces hormones to maintain the pregnancy. The fetus/embryo develops in a fluid-filled sac, which contains amniotic fluid to keep the fetus at a stable temperature, provide for some shock absorbency and offer protection.

Clearly, a trainer will have some concerns about training a pregnant woman, most of which come from a lack of understanding or knowledge. The following is a list of concerns a trainer may have:

- risk of miscarriage
- physical damage to the fetus/embryo
- morning sickness and nausea
- joint problems, back pain and ligament damage
- changes in posture
- overheating of the mother and fetus
- loss of oxygen to the fetus.

To limit these risks the American College of Gynaecologists (ACOG) has produced a series of guidelines for trainers to work within:

- Choose regular, moderate-intensity exercise.
- Stationary cycling, swimming, walking and stretching are recommended.
- Avoid exercises which have jerky, bouncy movements and involve jumping or sudden changes in direction.
- Don't exercise lying on your back after the fourth month.
- Use longer periods of warming up and cooling down.
- Stop exercise when fatigued and consult a doctor if any unusual symptoms occur.
- Increase intake of calories to cover the energy cost of exercise.
- Keep well hydrated by taking on fluid before, during and after exercise.
- Avoid hot and humid environments.

(Adapted from ACOG, 1994)

Training considerations

During the first trimester the hormone progesterone will cause blood vessels to dilate (expand) and this will cause the following effects:

- lower blood pressure
- increased heart rate
- feelings of sickness, fatigue and dizziness.

This loss of blood pressure is called 'vascular underfill' and means that the pregnant woman has the same amount of blood in a larger blood vessel and thus there is underfill in the blood vessel. This causes the symptoms of light-headedness and fatigue.

During the second trimester the blood volume starts to increase, although it is mainly plasma. The red blood cell count will start to rise towards the end of the second trimester, causing the following effects:

- blood pressure returns to normal
- heart rate returns to normal
- mother starts to feel less nauseous and fatigued.

The mother will also experience a change in their centre of gravity due to the developing bump at the front. Also, after about the fourth month of the pregnancy the hormone relaxin is released which has the effect of making the joints more mobile. Its role is to allow the pelvis greater movement for when the head of the baby passes through it. It will also affect every other joint in the body and cause the mother to become less stable.

During the third trimester the mother becomes much larger in weight and size and this becomes a problem. She will experience the following effects:

- rise in blood pressure
- lowered heart rate
- difficulty raising heart rate.

The mother will become even less stable and have difficulty balancing. She may also be fairly breathless and have back pain. She will experience difficulty getting up from and down to the floor.

The pelvic floor muscles are a group of muscles which run across the pelvis and hold up the contents of the abdomen. When a woman becomes pregnant the contents of the abdomen become heavier due to the increased size of the uterus. There is increased pressure placed on the pelvic floor muscles and they become stretched and weak. If this happens the mother can become incontinent (leaking urine) because these muscles control the action of the bladder. There are specific sets of exercises which can be performed to work these muscles. They involve lifting the pelvic floor muscles – stopping yourself going to the toilet and then holding them there for ten seconds.

The mother needs to be realistic that the aim of pre-natal exercise is to make the pregnancy and the delivery of the baby easier. It is not a time to worry about increasing their level of fitness or minimising weight gain. They can expect a whole host of benefits through training:

- improved circulation
- less fluid accumulation in the lower limbs
- fewer leg cramps
- strengthening of weaker muscles
- reduced risk of incontinence
- reduced feelings of sickness
- less chance of constipation
- improved self-image
- easier and less complicated labour.

Exercise recommendations

When deciding upon what exercises to perform you must consider the following issues.

- What stage of pregnancy is the mother in?
- What size is she?

- What is her current level of fitness?
- Has she any contraindications to exercise?
- What is the potential for injury of the chosen exercise?
- Can she still lie on her back (up to four months)?
- Will the exercise place extra stress on the pelvic floor?

Cardiovascular fitness

Frequency	3–5 sessions a week
Intensity	40–70 per cent of maximum intensity
Time	20–30 minutes per session
Type	Low-impact, rhythmical activity, such as swimming, cycling or walking

Resistance training

Frequency	2–3 sessions a week
Intensity	15–20 repetitions to form failure
Time	8–10 exercises with one or two sets
Type	Exercises to cover all major muscle groups

Flexibility training

Frequency	2–3 sessions a week
Intensity	To the point where mild discomfort is felt
Time	Hold for 8–10 seconds
Type	Maintenance stretches on all major muscle groups

General recommendations are to keep well hydrated. Ensure an extra 250–300 calories a day to cover the energy cost of exercise. All sessions should include pelvic floor exercises.

Post-natal women

After the birth of the baby the mother may be keen to return to exercise as she feels that her body has changed due to the pregnancy. Having said that, we need to consider that there is now a baby to be looked after and the mother may feel overwhelmed by the experience. Also, the woman's body has experienced a major trauma and there is damage to many structures.

The benefits of exercise are:

- promote weight loss
- improve self-image
- return tone to abdominal muscles

- return strength to stretched muscles
- return flexibility to shortened muscles
- improve posture.

Due to the massive stress that the body has undergone, it is recommended by ACOG that the mother lifts nothing heavier than the baby for the first two weeks. Then at six weeks the mother will have a GP check-up, after which she can start to resume normal daily activities, including training. The only exception to this is if she has delivered the baby through Caesarean section in which case she should not exercise for eight to ten weeks.

Post-natal concerns are as follows.

- **Joint instability and injury**: there will be relaxin present in the body for three to twelve months and thus the joints are still unstable and prone to injury.
- **Injury due to weak abdominal muscles**: the abdominal muscles may either be stretched or even split and thus weaken the core of the body.
- **Damage to pelvic muscles**: as the baby's head passes through the pelvis it will stretch and tear the surrounding tissue, the result being that it can make it sore for the mother to sit, or change the position of the pelvic bones.

Exercise recommendations are:

- choose low-impact aerobic exercise
- use only maintenance stretching
- start off with very gentle stomach exercises, such as stomach tightening
- ensure good posture and work to loss of form on resistance exercises
- include pelvic floor exercises in every session.

Obesity

One of the most popular subjects is obesity and growth of obesity levels in children.

definition

Obesity: 'Excess body fat frequently resulting in a significant impairment of health.' (Wallace, in Durstine and Moore, 2003)

Only recently has obesity been recognised as a disease in its own right. The problem has always been that obesity brings on other medical conditions due to the stress it causes to the organs and structures of the body. In the National Health Survey 2003 of adults in England, the figures showed that 22.2 per cent of men and 23 per cent of women were classified as clinically obese. Childhood obesity stood at 16 per cent with 32 per cent of children being overweight. It is a burgeoning problem in our society.

Obesity can bring on the medical conditions depicted in Fig 21.03.

This is important because when we come to design a training programme for an obese person we may also have to consider that they have other medical conditions to further complicate the issue.

The concerns of training obese people are:

- very low levels of fitness
- poor cardiovascular fitness
- low body strength in relation to weight
- stress on weight-bearing joints of the hip, knee and ankle

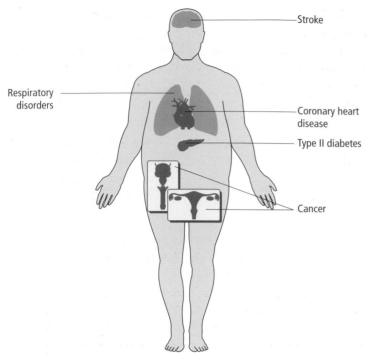

Fig 21.03 Medical conditions brought on by obesity

- less mobility and awareness of their lower limbs
- difficulty getting up from and down to the floor
- certain machines may not be suitable due to their design
- poorer sense of balance.

Any intervention applied must be combined with nutritional advice. The best way to lose weight in a sustainable way is to reduce calorie intake by around 250 kcals a day and increase activity level by 30 minutes a day. This should result in a loss of around 1 lb of body fat a week.

The benefits of exercise are:

- loss of body fat
- increase in muscle
- improvements in body composition
- raised metabolic rate
- improvements in medical conditions
- more energy
- better able to perform daily functions
- improved self-esteem and body image.

Exercise recommendations

Cardiovascular exercise

Frequency	5–7 times a week
Intensity	60–70 per cent of maximum
Time	20–60 minutes

Type	Non-weight bearing, low impact such as rowing, cycling or walking

Resistance training

Frequency	2–3 times a week
Intensity	10–15 reps to form failure
Time	8–10 exercises, one or two sets
Type	Large muscle groups, limit weight bearing on the lower limb

Flexibility training

Frequency	5–7 times a week
Intensity	To point of mild discomfort
Time	6–8 stretches on all major muscle groups
Type	Use standing stretches if they have trouble with mobility

(Adapted from ACSM, 2006)

Water activity or aerobics can be a good choice as water creates a non-weight-bearing environment and provides considerable resistance to work against.

Fig 21.04 Exercising in water

Heart disease and hypertension

Heart disease is a catch-all term which refers to disorders of the heart muscle and blood vessels of the heart, and problems with the valves and the nerve supply (sino-atrial node). The treatment of these is conducted by medical professionals, although there is a role for fitness professionals in cardiac rehabilitation. The most common disorder that is dealt with is high blood pressure (hypertension).

Blood pressure: the pressure blood exerts on the artery walls.

As the blood leaves the left ventricle it is pumped under great pressure into the aorta to give it the power to be distributed around the body. A wave of pressure passes through the arterial system each time the heart beats. This pressure falls when the heart relaxes. This is called blood pressure and there are two readings:

- systolic blood pressure – the pressure of blood in the arteries during the contraction of the heart
- diastolic blood pressure – the pressure of blood in the arteries during the relaxation phase of the heart.

Normal blood pressure would be expressed as 120/80 meaning a systolic reading of 120 mmHg and a diastolic reading of 80 mmHg:

Category	Systolic reading	Diastolic reading
Normal	120	80
High blood pressure	160	100
Mild hypertension	140	90
Low blood pressure	90	60

High blood pressure has no obvious symptoms and people can live without realising they have it. As a result, it is called 'the silent killer' and needs to be detected using a sphygmomanometer and stethoscope. High blood pressure causes structural changes to the arteries that supply blood to the organs of the body. As a result, it can affect blood supply to organs such as the brain, liver, kidneys and the heart itself.

Any person who is diagnosed with high blood pressure needs to receive clearance from their GP before being allowed to start training. This is because exercise will raise blood pressure even further and could lead to a heart attack.

Low blood pressure is less dangerous as it will not place such stress on the organs of the body. It needs to be managed because it can cause spells of dizziness and fainting.

The benefits of training hypertensives are:

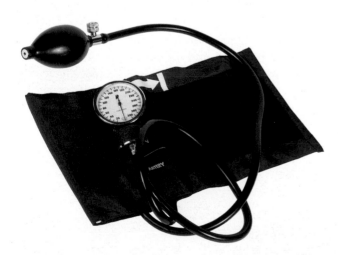

Fig 21.05 A sphygmomanometer (blood pressure meter)

- lowering of systolic and diastolic blood pressure
- loss of weight
- decrease in medication needed to control hypertension.

Exercise recommendations

The following exercise precautions need to be taken.

- Hypertensives need longer periods of warming up and cooling down because their circulation may be poor.
- Ensure they breathe regularly as breath-holding raises blood pressure.
- Avoid any isometric muscle contractions or heavy power work.
- If blood pressure is taken as over 200/115 on that day do not train.

Cardiovascular training

Frequency	3–5 times a week
Intensity	50–70 of max HR
Time	20–60 minutes
Type	Walking, jogging, cycling, rowing and swimming

Resistance training

Frequency	2–3 times a week
Intensity	15–20 reps to form failure
Time	8–10 exercises, one or two sets
Type	All major muscle groups

Flexibility training

Frequency	2–3 times a week
Intensity	Hold stretch at point of discomfort
Time	10–15 seconds per stretch
Type	All major muscles

Other considerations are:

- reduce the weight when working above the shoulders
- work to loss of form rather than failure
- modify lifestyle to reduce smoking and drinking alcohol, and reduce weight.

Asthma sufferers

Asthma is a disorder affecting the respiratory system where the airways become obstructed and resist the flow of air. This obstruction may be due to inflammation, mucus production or contraction of the smooth muscle in the airways. An asthma attack is characterised by an inability to breathe out. The asthmatic may be able to breathe in but not out. An asthma attack is defined as 'a period of difficult breathing'. Asthma affects around 3 million people in Britain.

There are three characteristics of an asthma attack.

- Contraction of the smooth muscle, causing a narrowing of the airway. The bronchioles are lined with smooth muscle which assists the passage of the air through the airways. During an asthma attack these go into spasm, which means they do not relax after a contraction and make breathing out difficult.
- Inflammation – the bronchioles are lined with structures called mucus membranes which produce mucus to keep the air clean. They can become irritated and inflamed, causing the airway to narrow.
- Increased mucus production – as the mucus membranes become inflamed they start to produce more mucus, which causes congestion in the airways.

During an asthma attack the asthmatic experiences a tightening of the chest, shortness of breath, wheezing when they breathe, coughing and coughing up mucus. They may also experience anxiety and panic.

Asthma is managed through the use of inhalers of which there are two types:

- relievers – these tend to be blue in colour and are used when the asthmatic becomes short of breath; they will relax the contraction of the smooth muscle.
- preventers – these tend to be brown in colour and are used morning and night to reduce the inflammation of the mucus membranes.

Fig 21.06 Asthma reliever

Fig 21.07 Asthma preventer

The benefits of exercise are:

- increased strength of the respiratory muscles
- improved lung function
- less occurrence of smooth muscle contraction
- greater tolerance to exercise
- less medication needed.

Exercise recommendations

Cardiovascular training

Frequency	3–7 times a week
Intensity	Light to moderate activity (60–70 per cent of max)
Time	30 minutes per session
Type	Walking, jogging, cycling or rowing

Resistance training

Frequency	2–3 times a week
Intensity	15–20 reps to form failure
Time	6–8 exercises, one or two sets
Type	All major muscle groups

Flexibility training

Frequency	2–3 times a week
Intensity	Hold stretch at point of discomfort
Time	10–15 seconds per stretch
Type	All major muscle groups

Other considerations are:

- training should be conducted in a warm, dust-free environment
- medication should be taken around ten minutes before training
- keep well hydrated as this reduces mucus production
- stop immediately if symptoms of breathlessness occur.

Diabetes

Diabetes mellitus is a metabolic disorder where the person is no longer able to deal with carbohydrate-based foods such as bread, pasta and rice. Carbohydrates are always broken down into their smallest unit which is glucose and then glucose is used as energy immediately or stored in the muscles and liver. A diabetic experiences high levels of glucose in their bloodstream because they cannot store the glucose in their muscles and liver. This is due to the action or inaction of the hormone insulin.

Insulin is a hormone which is produced in the pancreas (a gland just under the stomach). As soon as we eat carbohydrate foods the pancreas releases insulin into the bloodstream. Insulin acts to open the cells of the muscles and liver to allow glucose to flow into them and be stored. It acts like the key to the door of the cells. If there is no insulin or less insulin produced the glucose will remain in the bloodstream and this is what happens to a diabetic. Unfortunately, high levels of glucose will cause damage to many structures of the body.

There are two main types of diabetes, as follows.

- **Type 1 diabetes:** this occurs when the pancreas does not produce any insulin. It is the result of the insulin-producing cells of the pancreas being destroyed and is described as being an auto-immune disorder. This means that the body's immune or defence system has become overactive and has destroyed these cells by mistake. It usually occurs in childhood after the body has been dealing with a childhood illness such as chicken pox or mumps. This type of diabetic has to inject insulin and is called an IDDM: insulin-dependent diabetes mellitus.
- **Type 2 diabetes:** this occurs when the pancreas produces less insulin or poorer-quality insulin so that the cells of the muscles and liver no longer recognise the insulin and do not act upon it. In effect, the cells become resistant to the effects of insulin and this is called 'insulin resistance'. It is common in obese people when the effect of obesity is to place stress on the body's systems and cause the cells to become insulin-resistant. This type of diabetic may take a diabetic pill or control their condition through their diet and is called a NIDDM: non-insulin-dependent diabetes mellitus.

In the short term diabetes is characterised by either very high levels of blood glucose (hyperglycaemia) or very low levels of blood glucose (hypoglycaemia).

- Hyperglycaemia is caused by missing an insulin injection or eating the wrong types of food –

something high in sugar. The high levels of sugar damage the structures of the body and can lead to a person entering a coma.
- Hypoglycaemia is caused by low levels of glucose as the result of missing a meal, taking too much exercise or injecting too much insulin. As blood glucose levels fall the diabetic may feel dizzy and start to shake, feel hungry and thirsty, find it difficult to concentrate and have severe mood swings.

In the long term poorly controlled hyperglycaemia in diabetics can cause the following problems.

- **Eye problems:** the glucose in the blood can block the small capillaries in the retina at the back of the eye, causing blurred vision and even blindness.
- **Circulatory disorders:** the glucose can stick to the artery walls making them more attractive for fats to become attached. This causes a narrowing and even blockage of the artery resulting in high blood pressure and heart disease.
- **Nerve damage:** the glucose can damage the myelin sheath surrounding the nerves, causing a loss of sensation, particularly in the hands and feet.
- **Kidney damage:** the excess urine has to be excreted out and this puts strain on the kidneys.

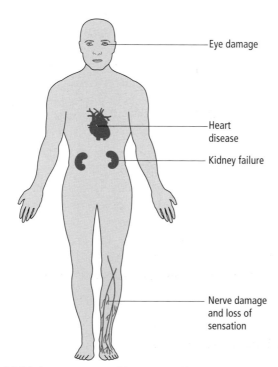

Fig 21.08 Long-term problems associated with poorly controlled diabetes

The benefits of exercise are as follows.

- It will burn off any excess glucose.
- It has an insulin-like effect and means the sufferer needs to inject less insulin.
- It will help to control weight which contributes to insulin resistance.
- It will help to prevent the long-term damage which occurs.

Exercise recommendations

Cardiovascular training

Frequency	3–5 times a week
Intensity	40–70 per cent of max
Time	20–40 minutes
Type	Low-impact, non-weight-bearing rhythmical exercise, such as cycling or rowing

Resistance training

Frequency	2–3 times a week
Intensity	15–20 reps to form failure
Time	6–8 exercises, one or two sets
Type	All major muscle groups

Flexibility training

Frequency	2–3 times a week
Intensity	Hold at a position of mild discomfort
Time	10–15 seconds per stretch
Type	All major muscle groups

The advice to diabetics about training is:

- always wear med alert identification
- train at the same time each day
- set up a routine of injecting, eating and training
- wear comfortable shoes to prevent foot damage.

LEARNER ACTIVITY Working with people with diabetes

In groups of two prepare a brief talk to educate your partner on the following.

- Learner 1 will explain what diabetes is and the two different types of diabetics.
- Learner 2 will explain the short- and long-term risks of diabetes, why the diabetic needs to exercise and what they should do.

Arthritis

Arthritis is a general term meaning inflammation of joints. There are many types of arthritis, the two main ones being osteoarthritis and rheumatoid arthritis.

Osteoarthritis is a condition which occurs mainly in the weight-bearing joints of the hip, knee and ankle. It can occur in a joint where there has been a previous injury, or when a person is obese or is older. It is a result of 'wear and tear' in a joint. As a joint becomes worn the cartilage will start to wear down and it becomes replaced by bone. This is especially the case if ligaments are stretched because they are less effective at holding the joint in place. This movement of bone on bone can cause friction and pain, and result in swelling of the joint as more synovial fluid is released on to it. The bone formation can also be irregular and create small, bony spurs. The joint can become misshapen and look red and swollen. It will cause pain and a loss of function.

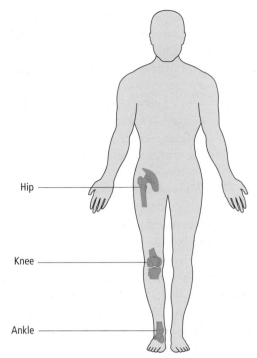

Fig 21.09 Joints affected by osteoarthritis

Rheumatoid arthritis is an autoimmune disease (like type 1 diabetes) where the body's immune system breaks down cartilage and replaces it with bone. The process can start at any age but is most common between the ages of 30 and 50. It starts with the small peripheral joints such as the fingers and wrist or toes and feet, and moves up to the larger joints of the elbow, shoulder, knee and hip. It can also spread into the joints of the back and neck and even the jaw.

Rheumatoid arthritis causes a swelling and deformation of the joints, creating redness and pain. The bone-on-bone action causes changes in the synovial capsule and more synovial fluid is released, causing the swelling. It can go through periods where the symptoms disappear to periods where the pain is intense.

The benefits of exercise are:

- strengthening the surrounding muscles can take the pressure and pain out of the joint
- it maintains the mobility and flexibility of the joint and muscles
- it relieves symptoms and pain.

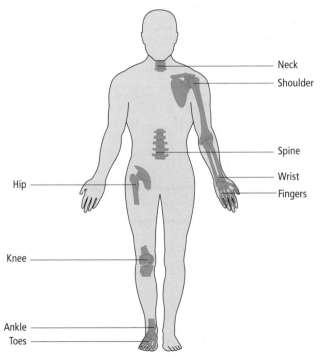

Fig 21.10 Joints affected by rheumatoid arthritis

Exercise recommendations

Cardiovascular training

Frequency	3–5 times a week
Intensity	40–60 per cent of max

Time   Start at 5 minutes and work up to 30 minutes

Type   Low-impact activity such as walking, cycling or swimming

Resistance training

Frequency   2–3 times a week
Intensity   Build up to 10–12 reps
Time   6–8 exercise; hold end position for up to 6 seconds
Type   Use isometric movements for affected joints (static contractions) and normal concentric contractions for unaffected joints

Flexibility training

Frequency   1–2 times a day
Intensity   Hold at a position of mild discomfort
Time   10–15 seconds per stretch
Type   All major muscle groups

Other considerations for arthritics are:

- ensure they have good-quality footwear to lessen impact
- do not train when joints are inflamed or painful
- train later in the day when joints are warmed up.

> **LEARNER ACTIVITY** Working with people with arthritis
>
> In groups of four prepare a poster which educates people on the two types of arthritis, the cause of arthritis and what type of training should be done by an arthritic.

Osteoporosis

Osteoporosis is a disease which affects the bones (osteo). The bones lose mass and become porous (porosis) or thinner. The effect of this is that they are more susceptible to fractures. The joints particularly affected are the hip, wrist and spine. It is predominantly, although not exclusively, a disorder that affects women. One in three women will experience an osteoporotic fracture compared with one in twelve men.

Osteoporosis occurs when more bone is destroyed than laid down. This is due to the action of osteoblasts and osteoclasts:

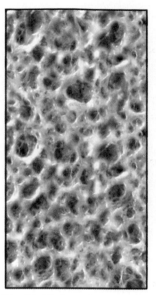
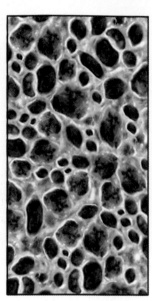

Fig 21.11 Solid bone matrix (left) and weakened bone matrix (right)

- osteoblasts build or lay down bone
- osteoclasts destroy or clean out old bone.

Up to the age of 35 the number of osteoblasts will be greater than the number of osteoclasts and thus we lay down more bone than we lose. However, after the age of 35 the number of osteoblasts falls and the number of osteoclasts increases, which causes a steady loss of bone and bone density.

This loss of bone is accelerated by various factors:

- family history
- female gender
- post-menopause in women
- low body weight
- lack of activity
- smoking
- excess alcohol intake
- poor diet (especially low in calcium and vitamin D).

Exercise is undertaken to protect against the possibility of osteoporosis occurring rather than when osteoporosis has been diagnosed. If a person has a number of the risk factors it is advised they train to offset the effects of bone loss from their mid-thirties. The benefits are:

- development of bone through weight-bearing exercise

- strengthening of muscles around potential fracture sites
- improved balance and coordination prevents falls leading to fractures
- improved posture.

Exercise recommendations

Cardiovascular training

Frequency	3–5 times a week
Intensity	40–70 per cent of max
Time	20–30 minutes per session
Type	Weight-bearing activity such as walking, jogging or step aerobics

Resistance training

Frequency	2–3 times a week
Intensity	8–10 reps, two or three sets of exercises putting forces through bones (squats, lunges, bench press, shoulder press)
Time	6–8 exercises
Type	All major muscles, weight bearing and around potential fracture sights

Flexibility training

Frequency	2–3 times a week
Intensity	To the point of mild discomfort
Time	10–15 seconds per stretch
Type	All major muscle groups

Other considerations are as follows.

- The potential osteoporotic may also consider hormone replacement therapy to replace the oestrogen lost after their menopause. Oestrogen promotes the activity of the osteoblasts.
- Nutritional advice should be given to ensure the person receives enough protein, calcium, vitamin D, phosphorous and magnesium to ensure the ingredients for bone-building are present.

Conclusion

Specific groups are a new and developing area in the health and fitness industry and may offer considerable challenges to the trainer. Before dealing with any of these groups you need to be appropriately qualified to REPs Level 3. You also need to have the confidence and knowledge to show the client that they are safe in your hands and to reassure them.

The trainer must realise that when we talk about special groups we are talking in fairly general terms and no two clients will be identical. Therefore, it is important to look at each client individually and look at what we call the 'presenting factors', meaning 'How does this medical condition affect this person?' and 'What symptoms do they actually have and what can we do about it?'

It is most important to follow the relevant protocols and if in doubt to refer the client to a GP or other professional, rather than just trying something. In these terms it is important to have a network of people around you to help and reassure you. That said, working with specific groups can be a very interesting and rewarding experience.

Review questions

1. Explain why the public sector is most likely to be involved in exercise referral schemes.
2. List and briefly explain the five stages of an exercise referral scheme development model.
3. Give four criteria used to select patients for exercise referral schemes.
4. Explain five effects of the ageing process.
5. Why is training young people of particular concern to the trainer?
6. Explain three risks of training pregnant women.
7. Explain what happens to blood pressure, blood volume and heart rate in the three trimesters of pregnancy.
8. What are the benefits of a mother training during the post-natal period?
9. Define obesity and explain the effect it has on the body.
10. What issues may obese people face when training?
11. What are the categories for normal, high, mild hypertension and low blood pressure?
12. What are the three characteristics of an asthma attack?
13. Explain the two different types of diabetes.
14. Give the four long-term complications of uncontrolled diabetes.
15. Differentiate between osteo and rheumatoid arthritis.
16. What type of training should a potential osteoporotic perform?

References

American College of Obstetricians and Gynaecologists (ACOG) (1994) Exercise during pregnancy and the post partum period, *Technical Bulletin* 189, ACOG.

American College of Sports Medicine (ACSM) (2006) *Guidelines for Exercise Testing and Prescription*, Lippincott, Williams and Wilkins.

Baechle, T. and Earle, R. (2000) *Essentials of Strength Training and Conditioning*, Human Kinetics.

Durstine, J. and Moore, G. (2003) *Exercise Management for Persons with Chronic Diseases and Disabilities*, Human Kinetics.

Goals

At the end of this chapter you should:

- know about the opportunities for work-based experience in sport
- be able to prepare for a work-based experience in sport
- be able to undertake a work-based experience in sport
- be able to evaluate a work-based experience in sport.

There is a huge variety of jobs in this sector so it is vital for learners to be aware of the range of occupations available and to gain first-hand experience of what the job entails. Not only will this give you a better picture of what is expected of you in your career of choice, it will also demonstrate your commitment to future employers.

This chapter gives information that will allow you to plan and carry out a practical work-based experience within the sports industry. It explores the different types of sports industry organisations, sources to locate jobs, how to apply for jobs, interview skills and how to evaluate your experience.

Opportunities for work-based experience in sport

The various sectors that provide opportunities for work-based experience in sport include:

- health and fitness – gyms, health clubs and leisure centres
- sport and recreation – football, hockey and swimming clubs
- outdoor education – outdoor pursuit centres, water sports centres and indoor ski slopes.

The provision of sports facilities and opportunities in Britain is the result of the interaction between the public, private and voluntary sectors.

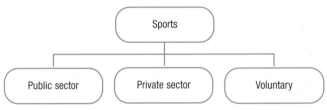

Fig 22.01 Sports provision

Public-sector provision

definition

The public sector: institutions funded by money collected from the public in the form of direct and indirect taxes.

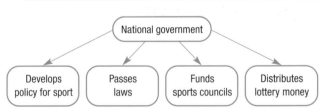

Fig 22.02 National government's responsibilities in sports provision

The public sector collects money through income tax, community charges, business taxes, valued added taxes on spending and national insurance. It then makes decisions on how to spend this money. These decisions are based on priorities and are seen as political decisions. The government may see the National Health Service and education system as priorities for spending and this position would be the basis for its decisions on spending. If the government does not see sport as being important it allocates only a relatively small amount of its budget to sports facilities, organisations and performers.

The public sector is made up of national government and local government (or local authorities), each of which has different responsibilities in sports provision.

National government is funded by taxes (income tax, VAT, business taxes) and receives money from the National Lottery (Lotto). Its role in sport is indirect, as it does not fund buildings or the running of facilities, but provides money to other organisations to spend on sport. It has a role as an 'enabler' and the main recipient is Sport England. National government provides grants and loans to local authorities, as well as offering technical assistance. Sport is the responsibility of the Department of Culture, Media and Sport (DCMS). It has the following roles in sport:

- represents interests of sport, arts, tourism and heritage
- promotes sporting success at the highest levels
- helps develop government sporting strategy
- funds the Sports Councils in Britain and Northern Ireland
- funds other agencies involved in sports provision
- distributes money raised by the National Lottery.

Sport England is responsible for the development of sport in England, while the Sports Councils for Scotland, Northern Ireland and Wales are responsible for the development of sport in their respective countries. Their main purpose is to:

- get more people involved in sport
- provide more places to play sport
- win more medals through higher standards of performance.

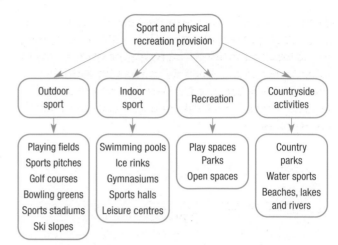

Fig 22.03 Local government's responsibilities in sports provision

Local government

Local government or local authorities are responsible for providing facilities for sport and physical recreation. Provision is usually divided into the areas shown in Fig 22.03.

Facilities in the public sector are usually named after the town or city they are in – e.g. Colchester Leisure Centre, Watford Baths, Wimbledon Recreation Centre.

LEARNER ACTIVITY
Government role in sport

Find out the following information.

- Who is the Secretary of State for the Department of Culture, Media and Sport?
- Who is the Minister for Sport?
- Where is your local office of Sport England or Sports Council for Scotland, Northern Ireland or Wales?
- What is the address of your local office?

LEARNER ACTIVITY Sport and society

The government (national and local) spends around £1000 million a year on sport. There are many courses to study sport in Britain and there is a huge amount of media coverage of sport. Thus, we can assume that sport is significant in British society. But why? What are the benefits of playing, watching and talking about sport?

Answer the following questions.

- List the ways you can think of that sport contributes to the British economy.
- What benefits does sport have for participants and spectators? Consider why you participate in or watch sport.
- What are the social benefits of sports participation and watching sport? How does it improve the world we live in?
- What are the international benefits of sports participation?
- What are the educational benefits of sports participation?

The majority of funding comes from the council tax and will go to the county council, with the rest going to the local authority and some to the county police force. Other sources include receipts from trading, such as leisure centre entry fees, rents from council housing, loans from banks and grants from national government.

Private-sector provision

Private sector: sport is provided by individuals or groups of individuals who invest their own money in the facilities with the main aim of making a profit.

Private-sector sport is provided by individuals or groups of individuals (companies) who invest their own money in facilities. As a result, these facilities are usually named after people, such as David Lloyd clubs, although some have a brand name, such as Virgin Active or Cannons.

The private sector provides sports facilities for two main reasons:

- to make a return on their investment for themselves and their shareholders
- to make a profit out of sport.

Claims are sometimes made that it is for other altruistic reasons, such as improving the standards of a sport or improving the community the facilities are in. However, they would not exist unless they could make a profit.

The private sector provides for sports increasing in demand. It is able to respond quickly to new trends or to instigate new trends. It provides facilities where it can attract large numbers of customers, or more exclusive facilities where it can attract fewer customers but charge more. It is involved in the following areas:

- active sports – tennis, golf, health and fitness suites, snooker and pool, water sports and ten-pin bowling
- spectator sport – stadiums for football, rugby, cricket, tennis, golf (football is by far the most popular spectator sport)
- sponsorship – this has risen dramatically over the last 15 years.

The role of the private sector can be well summarised by this quote from George Torkildsen (1991):

> **The major difference between the commercial operator and the public or voluntary operator is the raison d'être of the business, the primary objective of the commercial operator being that of financial profit or adequate return on investment.**

The voluntary sector

The voluntary sector: clubs that operate as non-profit-making organisations and which are essentially managed by and for amateur sportsmen and women.

Most amateur clubs are run on a voluntary basis. Some voluntary clubs own facilities, but the majority hire facilities, usually provided by the public sector. Most clubs, such as football and athletics clubs, that people join to enable them to participate in competitive sport are in the voluntary sector. Voluntary-sector clubs often work in partnership with the private or public sector. They might use public-sector facilities or gain sponsorship from the private sector. In the evening you may find the swimming pool at your leisure centre being used for swimming club or kayaking club training.

Funding of voluntary clubs

The voluntary sector is funded primarily by its members in the form of subscriptions. Every club will have an annual subscription fee and match fees. This is to cover the costs of playing, travel and equipment. The club may try to raise some money in the form of sponsorship. This is often by a local company or by one of the players. Some clubs have local benefactors who put money into a club as a gesture of goodwill. Clubs also run fundraising events such as discos, race nights or jumble sales, particularly if they are trying to raise money for a tour or special event.

Clubs can apply for other sources of funding:

- National Lottery grants
- grants from national governing bodies
- grants from government
- grants from the local authority.

These types of grants are usually to enable clubs to build or improve their facilities.

LEARNER ACTIVITY
Voluntary clubs

Go to your college library and find out the names of voluntary clubs in your area for the following sports:

- athletics
- ice skating
- rugby union
- rugby league
- hockey.

Partnerships

Partnerships occur when two or more of the sectors come together to provide opportunities for sport. We have already seen how the public sector rents out its facilities to the voluntary sector to give them an opportunity to play sports. Sponsorship, which is primarily provided by the private sector, is given to the public and voluntary sectors.

Sports facilities are also built as partnerships. The new English National Stadium at Wembley is a private-sector initiative by Wembley plc, but it has received a National Lottery grant from the public sector. It will also go into partnership with other private-sector organisations to raise finance and gain sponsorship.

Compulsory competitive tendering (CCT), introduced to the leisure industry in 1990, was aimed at developing partnerships between the public and private sectors. The aim was to hand the management of sports centres to private-sector organisations while the ownership of the centres remained with the public sector (local authorities). The theory behind this arrangement was that the private-sector companies would aim to run the centers for profit and thus they would be run more efficiently. Today we can still see the benefits of this arrangement in our local sports facilities.

LEARNER ACTIVITY
Partnerships in sport

Visit your local sports centre and find examples of partnerships between the three sectors.

Types of occupation

There is a huge range of jobs available in the sports industry, from sports massage therapist to mountain leader. In order to gain the skills and qualifications you require, you may need to continue your studies to a higher level or complete a part-time course. The following list gives a range of different jobs available in the sports industry but is by no means exhaustive:

- fitness instructor
- leisure attendant
- sports centre manager
- kayak instructor
- sports coach
- sports development officer
- sports/PE teacher or lecturer
- mountain leader
- professional sports performer
- sports massage therapist
- sport and exercise scientist
- sports nutritionist
- sport psychologist
- sports groundsman
- sports retailer.

Fitness instructor

This involves assessing people's fitness levels, designing their exercise programmes and instructing these programmes in the gym. Fitness instructors may also teach aerobics classes and circuit classes, and supervise people in the gym.

Instructors need sound anatomy and physiology knowledge gained from a sport science course, and also a recognised fitness instructor's award from a training organisation such as Premier Training International, YMCA or Focus. To teach specific skills, such as aerobics, circuits or stability ball work, extra qualifications are required. First aid and CPR qualifications are also essential. Instructors must have good communication skills, be friendly and able to remain calm under pressure.

Leisure attendant

Leisure attendants are responsible for preparing and supervising the sports hall, swimming pool and changing rooms in a leisure facility. Most leisure attendants are also involved in coaching or supervising sports sessions in their sports hall.

A sports qualification is desirable but not essential. The National Pool Lifeguard Qualification is compulsory in order to work in a swimming pool. To coach sports, leisure attendants need specific national governing body coaching awards.

Leisure attendants need to be outgoing and people-orientated. Communication skills are important as you may have to deal with a range of people.

Sports centre manager

Managing a sports centre involves some of the following activities:

- managing and motivating staff
- programming facilities and organising activities
- establishing systems and procedures
- preparing and managing budgets
- monitoring sales and usage
- marketing and promoting the centre
- dealing with members and any complaints or incidents.

Managers may have been promoted into this position having qualified with a BTEC First or National Diploma or GNVQ. Most managers will hold higher-level qualifications such as a degree or HND in leisure management or business studies.

To be an effective manager you need the following personal qualities: confidence, enthusiasm, assertiveness, communication skills, self-motivation, presence and professionalism.

Kayak instructor

A kayak instructor is usually qualified in a range of outdoor pursuits and works at an outdoor pursuits centre. The role involves checking equipment, ensuring weather conditions are appropriate and then teaching a range of skills to kayak safely and effectively.

You will have to have a high level of personal proficiency (three-star minimum) and then attend an instructor training course. You also need to be qualified in rescue skills and first aid. You must have good communication skills, be able to withstand cold and wet working conditions, and also have very good safety awareness.

Sports coach

Sports coaches are usually former or current competitors in their sport. They are responsible for developing the physical fitness and skills of their athletes. They need to be able to evaluate their athletes' performances and offer feedback to improve these. As a result, they require knowledge of many aspects of sport science, such as anatomy and physiology, biomechanics, nutrition, psychology and sports injury.

Every sport has its own system for awarding coaching qualifications, and coaches must hold the relevant award. Many coaches also hold qualifications in sport or sport science.

Coaches need to be able to motivate athletes and have their trust. They need to be good communicators and listeners, and able to show patience and empathy towards their athletes.

Sports development officer

A sports development officer works to increase participation rates in sport and provide opportunities for people to play sport in a local area. They work for local authorities and may have responsibility for specific groups of people, such as ethnic minorities, women or disabled people.

Most sports development officers have at least a BTEC National in sport or sports science, and usually also hold a degree or HND in sport, sport science or leisure management, along with a range of coaching qualifications. You need an interest and knowledge in a range of sports and the needs of a community. You have to be able to communicate with people from different backgrounds and be sensitive to their needs. Good leadership, motivational skills and an organised approach to work are also necessary.

Sports/PE teacher or lecturer

You can teach PE in schools to children from the age of four to eighteen years. If you choose the younger-aged children you also usually have to teach a range of other subjects from the National Curriculum. If you teach PE in a secondary school this is usually the only subject you will be required to teach. A lecturer teaches in a college or university and usually specialises in a few subject areas, such as physiology or psychology.

A teacher needs to be educated to degree level and to be qualified as a teacher. There are two ways to do this:

- take a four-year teaching degree such as a Bachelor of Education (BEd) or a Batchelor of Arts with Qualified Teaching Status (BA (QTS))
- take a three-year degree in sport science or sport studies and then complete a one-year Postgraduate Certificate in Education (PGCE).

To study to become a teacher you must have passed GCSE English and maths (at grade C or above and a science if you wish to teach primary or key stages 2/3), and at least two A levels.

Teaching is a very demanding profession and you need to be patient and able to deal with young people and their various needs. Teachers need to be organised, and able to maintain discipline and adapt their communication skills to the group they are teaching. You should also have a good level of personal fitness and enjoy working with young people.

Mountain leader

A mountain leader may work in an outdoor pursuits centre and lead mountain walks or they may be involved in leading a venture scouting group and instruct the group on how to carry out an expedition.

A mountain leader must have gained a great deal of personal experience walking and navigating in the outdoors. They must then attend a mountain leader instructor course, which involves mountain walks, night walks and camping overnight. They must keep a logbook and then complete a mountain leader assessment to ensure they are proficient in all the skills required for mountain leading. They can then carry out a mountain leader course for winter conditions and undergo another assessment. A mountain leader must be able to withstand cold and wet conditions, have excellent navigational skills, a first aid qualification, good communication skills, and excellent health and safety knowledge.

Professional sports performer

Ultimately the goal of every sports performer would be to play their sport fulltime at a professional level. However, it is only the most talented who get this opportunity and there are only a limited number of sports where you can play professionally. Football,

cricket, rugby league, rugby union and golf have the largest number professional players. However, most professional players have a second job to ensure their income.

No formal qualifications are needed, although you need to investigate the best route into a sport as every sport will be slightly different in how it recruits young players.

Technical efficiency at the chosen sport, along with physical fitness, are the most important assets, as well as self-motivation, commitment and determination.

Sports massage therapist

A sports massage therapist has a varied job, using their massage skills to prepare athletes for competition, helping them to warm down after competition and then dealing with any injuries or soreness they may suffer. They can also treat the public who have injured themselves during non-sporting activities such as gardening.

A sports massage therapist needs to hold a sports therapy diploma. These courses are accredited by the Vocational Training and Charitable Trust (VTCT) and can be studied at most colleges of further education. Private training organisations, such as Premier Training International, also offer these courses in an intensive 12-week format. It is possible to do a degree in sports therapy or sports rehabilitation at a limited number of universities.

A sports massage therapist always needs to adopt a professional approach, as their job involves physical contact with people. They should be patient, caring and sensitive to an individual's needs. A high standard of personal hygiene and good communication skills will be important to be successful.

Sport and exercise scientist

The aim of the sport and exercise scientist is to maximise the performance of an individual in their care. This will involve applying their knowledge and skills in the subjects of physiology, biomechanics and psychology to give the performers any possible advantage. Physiology will involve fitness testing and monitoring physical condition; biomechanics will involve examining the performer's technique and equipment to analyse where improvements can be made; psychology will be applied to ensure the performer is correctly prepared mentally.

A sport scientist will hold a degree in sport science and possibly a master's degree or a PhD in their chosen field of expertise.

Sports nutritionist

A sports nutritionist gives an athlete advice about how to organise their diet to ensure they maximise the effects of their training and reach competition in the best possible shape. They may also provide advice on the use of supplements.

A sports nutritionist needs to be qualified as a dietician first. This will involve completing a three-year degree to become recognised as a state registered dietician. To specialise in sports nutrition you need at least one year's experience before completing a sports dietetics course run by the Sports Nutrition Foundation.

Sport psychologist

A sport psychologist is involved in mentally preparing athletes for competition. It is a varied job which will differ depending on the individual needs of performers. A psychologist is involved in helping teams and individuals set goals for the short and long term, learn strategies to control arousal levels and stay relaxed in stressful situations. They are also often involved in lecturing and conducting research, as well as actually practising their skills.

A sport psychologist would usually be a graduate or sport scientist who had then completed postgraduate training. This would involve a master's degree or a PhD in sport psychology.

Psychologists need to have good listening and interviewing skills in order to assess the needs of their athletes and to develop strategies to help them. A psychologist should be able to build up a relationship of trust and be seen as someone who the athlete can talk to confidentially.

Sports groundsman

A groundsman is responsible for preparing and maintaining the condition of outdoor facilities, such as golf courses, cricket pitches, football pitches and tennis courts.

Entrance qualifications are not essential. You can study for an NVQ in turf management, or go on to HND or degree level. These courses need to be recognised by the Institute of Groundsmanship (IOG).

Sports retailer

Sports retail involves working in a sports shop selling sports goods. This can involve using your knowledge of sport and matching a client's needs to specific products. Different types of runners require different types of running shoes and you need to be able to identify which shoes they need.

A knowledge of sport is needed, but many people working in retail need business skills and customer care skills. A qualification in business studies or leisure studies would be appropriate. If you have aspirations to run a sports shop, it may be necessary to hold an HND or degree in a management-based subject.

An ability to deal with members of the public and a willingness to meet their needs is necessary. You must be good at communicating and be able to stay calm under pressure.

Fig 22.04 Sports groundsman

LEARNER ACTIVITY Skills and qualifications
- Think about the career you would like to pursue.
- Make a list of all the skills and qualifications you have to date and what you will need in the future.
- Make a list of all the advantages and disadvantages of this career.

Work placement considerations

Before choosing your work placement, you will need to bear in mind a number of factors to ensure the location and the actual placement are suitable for you.

Location

While deciding where you would like to carry out your project you should also include in your decision-making the locality of the placement. If the sports facility is not within walking distance how are you going to get there? You will need to investigate methods of public transport and look at the cost and travel times. If the facility is too far away from home for you to travel in to every day you will have to see if the facility provides staff accommodation and if it would be available to you. Alternatively, you may have family living near to your chosen facility and be able to stay with them for the duration of the placement.

Placement requirements

You need to speak to your supervisor prior to the placement in order to see if you need to provide your own clothing and, if so, what is required. Most leisure centres provide their staff with a uniform but outdoor pursuit centres staff usually provide their own clothing. This could be quite expensive if you do not have any of your own already, so it may be worth asking your supervisor if they have any kit you could borrow for the duration of the placement.

Any equipment you require will usually be provided, such as a whistle for a lifeguard. Again, it is worth asking your supervisor if you need to buy anything and check that you can afford it prior to your placement.

Occupation information

The purpose of a work placement is to help you determine if the job you have chosen to undertake or observe is suitable for you. Therefore, once you have thought of a job you would like to perform you will need to find out if you have or are going to have the right qualifications to be accepted on this job.

If you would like to work in outdoor pursuits, you will need to have a good level of personal proficiency and/or be working towards water-based or land-based outdoor pursuits qualifications – mountain leader, kayak instructor, etc.

On top of the qualifications required, every job has a different set of roles and responsibilities that you must examine and check to see you are capable of carrying them out. Working in the sports industry often entails working unsociable hours. If you want to work only in the daytime you may have to consider a different job.

Regulations

There are a number of regulations in place to help protect employees, employers and customers whilst at work:

- Health and Safety at Work Act 1974
- Control of Substances Hazardous to Health Regulations (COSHH) 1994
- Health and Safety (First Aid) 1981
- Safety at Sports Ground Act 1975
- Fire Safety & Safety of Places of Sport Act 1987
- Children Act 1989.

Skills

While on your work placement you will probably realise that you already have a number of skills that are appropriate. You may realise that you have good interpersonal skills and find it easy to deal with customer's questions and/or complaints. But you will no doubt also find that there are some skills that need to be developed. You may find it difficult to meet deadlines or that you are always rushing to get to work on time. You would need to improve your time-management skills.

You will be taught a number of new practical skills such as putting up and taking down equipment. You will no doubt have some knowledge of this from practical units you have covered and find that you just need to adapt these skills to meet the requirements of the new apparatus.

Preparation for a work-based experience

Aims and objectives

You need to consider what your aims and objectives are prior to your work-based experience in sport.

> **Aim:** the broad long-term target of your experience.
> **Objectives:** a number of targets that, combined, will allow you to reach your aim.

Personal skills

A work placement is an opportunity to try out a job and start to understand what knowledge and skills are needed for that position. Answering the questions below will start to give you an idea of what your next step should be. You can discuss this audit with your tutor or work placement officer when you have a meeting with them to arrange your industrial placement. This will help you to gain a placement which is fulfilling, worthwhile and develops your skills and personal qualities.

Ask yourself the following questions.

- What skills have I at present? Look at practical skills of coaching and teaching, key skills such as written and verbal communication, problem-solving and application of number, IT and skills gained from previous work experiences such as clerical and administrative skills.
- What skills would I like to acquire? This is difficult because there may be skills you have not gained because you haven't been in a situation to gain them. As a result, you may not be aware that you need them. However, try to be realistic and think what skills you may need in a job, such as communicating with the general public.
- What qualifications have I gained? This is just a list of all the qualifications you currently hold. Also list here any qualifications you are hoping to gain.
- What personal qualities have I got? Think about personal qualities in the following areas.
  - **Working with other people:** are there particular people you would not like to work with? Do you prefer to work in large or small groups? How do you feel about working as part of a team? Are you happy dealing with the public?
  - **Leadership:** how good are you at leading groups? Do you prefer to lead large or small groups? How do you feel about selling to people?
  - **Responsibility:** how do you feel about responsibility in the following areas – cash, equipment, other people's work, meeting deadlines, other people's safety and welfare.
- What do you want from a job? Split this up into what you would want and what you would not want. Consider the following areas.
  - **Pay:** do you want enough to get by on or is getting a high wage important to you? Would you like to be paid by results? Would you like to be paid extra for extra work you have done?
  - **Hours:** do you want to work fixed hours (9 to 5), or do you not mind doing shift work? How do you feel about overtime?
  - **Prospects:** how important are the opportunities for promotion and the presence of a career structure?
  - **Location:** do you have a fixed idea of where you want to work, or are you willing to relocate to find the right job? How important is an easy journey to work to you?
  - **Working with others:** is it important for you to work as a part of a group, or would you rather work alone? How do you feel about managers and supervisors, and are you looking for a certain style of leadership?
  - **What the job entails:** are you looking for job satisfaction or a job that pays well? Are you keen to utilise certain skills and abilities? Do you want to help other people?

Targets

Once a decision has been made about your future career it is an appropriate time to think about setting targets. Remember, you may not be able to walk into your dream job immediately and while this remains your long-term goal it is important to set realistic short-term targets to lay the pathway to achieving your dream job.

When targets are set you need to use the SMART principle to make them workable. SMART stands for:

- **S**pecific
- **M**easurable
- **A**chievable
- **R**ealistic
- **T**ime-constrained.

Specific: the target must be specific to what you want to achieve. You may need to improve your lifesaving leg kick in order to pass your pool lifeguard award.

Measurable: targets must be stated in a way that is measurable, so they need to state figures. For example, I want to be able to tow a person 25 m in one minute.

Achievable: it must be possible to actually achieve the target.

Realistic: we need to be realistic in our setting and look at what factors may stop us achieving the target.

Time-constrained: there must be a timescale or deadline on the target. This means you can review your success. It is best to state a date by which you wish to achieve the goal.

Application process

After having read a job specification you can then decide if you would like to apply for the role. To apply for work you need to use a suitable method to approach a prospective employer. Most job advertisements will specify which method you should use. There are three main methods that you may be asked for.

- **Curriculum vitae (CV)** – a concise written document that summarises your skills, qualifications and experience to date for a prospective employer. It needs to be accompanied by a covering letter.
- **Application form** – some jobs will not accept a CV and will ask you to complete a pre-designed application form asking you to show why you are suitable for the job. This also needs to be accompanied by a covering letter.
- **Letter of application** – some jobs will require you to apply in writing. The information will be similar to that of a CV, but presented in a different format.

Curriculum vitae

A CV is used for a range of reasons:

- to demonstrate your value to the employer
- as a marketing tool to get an interview
- to sell yourself to the employer.

There are three main styles of CV.

- **Chronological** – this is the most common format and involves you presenting your experiences of education and work in date order.
- **Functional** – this type highlights your skills and is directed towards a certain career. You may be qualified in more than one subject, but you would highlight only the skills that are relevant for the type of work you are trying to gain.
- **Targeted** – this type of CV emphasises skills and abilities relevant to a specific job or company. It is tailor-made for one job. You would examine the job specification and then adapt your CV to show how you meet the it.

Preparing a CV

A CV needs to be prepared meticulously and you should spend time deciding what your main selling features are. If you are still a student, you may not have been involved in full-time work, but you will still have important features to highlight. You must include any work experiences, part-time and voluntary work you have undertaken. You will need to start by compiling a biography of your life with dates and events. You will also need to consider what skills you have at present, and which ones are transferable to the type of work you are seeking.

A CV should include the following information.

- **Personal details** – full name and address, home telephone number and mobile number, email address and date of birth.
- **Current position and employment** – if you are employed, your position and your main responsibilities.
- **Key personal skills** – highlight your main personal skills, attributes and abilities.
- **Education and qualifications** – the names and dates of all academic qualifications received, with the most recent first.
- **Training or work-related courses** – any additional vocational or on-the-job training you have received.
- **Previous employment** – all the past employment you have had with the following information: name of employer, job title and a brief summary of responsibilities. Also include any periods of work placement.
- **Leisure interests** – the interests you have outside the academic environment; the sports you play and at what level (it may be appropriate to list

some of your achievements in sport), and other hobbies and activities in which you are involved. It is particularly good to state any positions of responsibility you have held, such as club captain, scout leader or cadet force rank.

- **Other relevant information** – anything else you feel may be of value to the employer, such as an ability to drive.
- **References** – the name, addresses and phone numbers of two people (referees) who can vouch

for you. If you have a current employer, they should be the first; if not, a past employer or someone else in a position of responsibility, such as a teacher, would be appropriate. It is important that you ask them before using them as a reference in case they are not willing to write you a reference.

Sample CV

An example CV is shown below.

Curriculum vitae

Name:	Rebecca Sewell
Date of birth:	17 October 1982
Address:	125 Mill Crescent, Reading, Berks RG6 3JS
Nationality:	British
Tel:	01345 245131 (home); 01345 684877 (work); 07754 759868 (mob)
Email:	racsewell@aol.com

Current employment

Fitness instructor at the Premier Gym in Reading (2004–6)

A graduate in Sport Science (BSc Hons) with specialist skills in fitness instruction, teaching circuits and aerobics and core conditioning training.

Main responsibilities:
- teaching aerobics and circuits
- conducting fitness assessments, designing exercise programmes and instructing workouts
- selling memberships and sports clothing.

Key skills include:
- fitness testing, programme design and instructional skills
- ability to teach exercise to music
- good communication skills
- good motivator of people
- financial management skills of budgeting and monitoring budgets
- computer and internet literate
- first aid and CPR competent
- selling and marketing skills.

Education and qualifications

2000–3	Thames University. BSc (Hons) Sport and Exercise Science (2:1 gained)
1998–2000	Reading College of Sport. BTEC ND Sport Science: 8 distinctions, 8 merits, 2 passes
1995–9	Campbell School, Reading. 10 GCSEs: PE (A), English Lang (A), English Lit (A), French (A), Biology (B), Maths (B), Chemistry (B), German (B), Geography (B), Physics (D)

Work-related courses

Fitness Trainers Award (2003)
NVQ RSA Exercise to Music (2002)
NPLQ (2004)

Curriculum vitae (continued)

First aid at work (2005)
Stability ball training (2006)

Previous employment
2003–4   Leisure attendant at Springfield Baths.
Main duties included pool supervision and lifeguarding, laying out equipment in the sports hall, coaching and teaching children's sport at weekends and during holidays.

Previous work experience
1999   Three-week placement at Hills Spa Health and Fitness Centre.
This involved shadowing the fitness trainers and duty manager, serving the members and advising them in the gym.

Hobbies and interests
I am involved in local athletics and am captain of the ladies' team. I run the 800 m and 1500 m and am currently the Berkshire county champion at 800 m.
I enjoy travelling overseas, particularly to Australia and New Zealand.
My hobbies are reading and going to the cinema.

Other relevant information
Full driving licence and own car.

Referees

Mr W. Samways	Miss J. Gatehouse
Fitness Manager	Head of Sport Science
Premier Gym	Thames University
Garfield Road	Stratton Way
Reading	Easthampton
Berks RG16 4LP	Bucks BK34 7BJ
01345 874098	0152 854339

LEARNER ACTIVITY
Prepare a CV

Using the example provided, prepare a CV for yourself which you could send to a prospective employer.

Completing an application form

Many employers will produce their own application form, which you need to fill in when applying for a position. They will use this form to select the candidates they wish to interview. It is important to give yourself plenty of time to complete the form. Forms that are completed incorrectly or untidily will probably be discarded without being read. If you complete the form properly, you will already have an advantage over your rivals. Remember, you get only one chance to make a first impression. Here are some useful tips on completing the form.

- Photocopy the form first and use the copy to practise on. Check over what you have written and, when you are satisfied, copy it on to the original.
- Read the instructions on the form carefully and follow them exactly. For example, it may ask you to use black ink or block capitals. This is important because the form may need to be photocopied and will copy well only in black ink.
- Even if some of the information on the form is given in the covering letter, you must still include it on the form. Never write 'refer to CV', as the reader may not bother.
- Think about answers very carefully and plan your responses. For example, questions such as 'Why do

you want to work for this company?' need to be researched and responded to appropriately.

- Check that your referees are willing to provide a reference for you before you put in their details.
- Take a photocopy of your form so that you can remind yourself what you wrote before an interview.
- Make sure you do not miss the closing date, and post the form well in advance.
- Include a covering letter with your application form.

Letter of application

A letter of application relates your experience to a specific company or job vacancy. It should always be sent with a CV and perhaps an application form. It should be businesslike and complement the information in your CV. If you are writing in response to an advertisement, make reference to the job title and where you saw the vacancy advertised, and ensure the letter is addressed to the correct person. Indicate why you are attracted to the position advertised, and highlight why you think you are suitable and what key personal skills and experiences you have that are relevant to the vacancy. Finish the letter by stating that you look forward to hearing from them soon and would be delighted to attend an interview at their convenience.

> **LEARNER ACTIVITY** Write a letter of application
>
> Use the template on the next page to draft a letter of application.

Preparation for interview

One of the most important parts of the interview is the preparation that takes place beforehand. Learn all you can about the company and the job role. This can be done via the internet or it would be even better if you actually went to visit the workplace. During the visit not only will you have worked out how to get there you will also be able to see how people dress, exactly what facilities are available and even ask some of the staff questions.

Questions

You should think about which questions you are likely to be asked. For example: Why are you interested in this job? What are your strengths? What are your weaknesses? What do you think this job entails? Why do you think you will be good at this job?

Once you have worked out suitable answers, practise answering them out loud either with a friend or in front of a mirror. You may wish to record yourself with a camcorder or tape recorder and then see or hear yourself 'in action' and make improvements where necessary. You should also study your body language, which includes your facial expressions, mannerisms and gestures. If you smile and look enthusiastic this will portray the right image. You may find that you slouch or have a blank facial expression without even being aware of it while answering questions.

Be prepared to discuss anything you have written on your CV or letter of application. You may be asked why you decided to study a BTEC qualification or to explain your choice of work placement, etc.

You should also prepare questions to ask the interviewers as this will show them that you are interested and want to know more about the company or job role. Be sure not to ask questions that have already been answered within the job role specifications or during the course of the interview.

Dress

You will need to decide what you are going to wear well in advance of the interview. If you are not sure what to wear, it is best to choose smart, dark-coloured clothes such as a suit or smart trousers or skirt and a shirt/blouse. Clothing that is too tight or revealing is rarely acceptable attire for an interview. Ensure that your clothes are clean and ironed and also comfortable. Ensure that your hair is clean and you have a suitable haircut or style for the interview. If you have lots of visible body piercings, you may wish to take some out in order to portray the image you think the company is looking for.

Location

If possible, go and visit the place you are going to for interview beforehand. Travel at the same time of day you will be leaving for your interview time so that you

(Your name) _____

(Your address) _____

(Name of person applying to) _____

(Address of company writing to) _____

Date _____

Dear _____ (person's name)

(First paragraph to explain why you are writing, i.e. for which job and where you saw the vacancy)

(Next paragraph to explain what you are currently doing, i.e. employment or education)

(Next paragraph to discuss why you are applying for the job and what you like about it)

(Next paragraph to justify why you are suitable for the position – relevant experience or skills)

(End your letter by saying that you can attend an interview and hope to hear from them soon)

Yours sincerely*

_____ (Sign your name)

_____ (Type your name)

* If you do not have a person's name and addressed the letter to 'Dear Sir or Madam', you should end with 'Yours faithfully'.

Fig 22.05 How to write a letter of application

can see if there are any issues with rush hour traffic, etc. You should always plan to arrive at your interview location at least ten minutes in advance to allow time to compose yourself.

Interview skills

Body language

Body language can say an awful lot about how we feel, how confident we are and how enthusiastic we are. People will often make a first impression about someone based upon their body language alone. Therefore, it is important to convey the right message by using appropriate body language.

- Greet your interviewer with a firm handshake.

- Maintain eye contact as this shows that you are interested in what the person has to say. You should not overdo the eye contact, though, as this can sometimes look threatening.
- When answering questions, emphasise key points by leaning forward and using expressive gestures.
- Speak with an expressive voice to convey your enthusiasm and interest rather than a monotone voice which suggests a lack of interest and boredom.
- You should sit with your back up straight as this communicates self-assurance and eagerness. Do not slouch as this gives the impression that you are not interested or are lacking in confidence.
- Do not fidget or twiddle your fingers while the interviewer is talking as this shows you are not paying attention.

- When the interviewer is talking, nod your head and smile in relevant places to demonstrate your interest in what they are saying.

Answering questions

You will have rehearsed many of the answers that you give during the interview and therefore know what you need to say and how to say it. However, you will undoubtedly be faced with a few questions that you have not prepared for. Give yourself a few seconds to sit and think about your answer and then respond honestly and as positively as possible. If you do not understand the question, ask the interviewer to repeat it. If you still do not understand the question you can respond in a variety of ways.

- Ask 'Do you mean …?', which shows that you understand some of what they said but need clarity.
- Ask them to explain their question in more detail.

> **LEARNER ACTIVITY** Role play an interview
>
> Imagine you are having an interview for a job of your choice. With a partner carry out a role play interview. The interviewer must have a copy of your CV and ask appropriate questions relating to your CV and the job role.
>
> The interviewer should then give feedback as to what they thought was good and which areas need to be improved.

Undertake a work-based experience

While undertaking your work-based experience there are a number of situations and considerations you will need to think about prior to and during the experience.

Planned activities

While on your work-based experience you will probably participate in planned activities. These may include testing chlorine levels in the swimming pool, staff meetings, cleaning duties, setting up and checking equipment, etc. Ensure you know the timing of these events, have been shown exactly what needs to be done and have a supervisor where necessary to ensure you are carrying out these planned activities safely and effectively.

Wherever you work you are part of a team that is responsible for running a safe and secure environment. Most working environments have a manual that covers details on how every part of the facility should operate under normal conditions and what to do in an emergency situation. These are usually referred to as Normal Operating Procedures (NOP) and Emergency Operating Procedures (EOP).

The NOP gives instructions on how to deal with everyday situations, whereas the EOP gives instructions on how to deal with minor and major emergency situations such as disorderly behaviour from customers or dealing with a drowning incident.

Working in the sports industry usually means you deal with customers on a regular basis. You therefore need skills in dealing with the public. These skills are very important so that you can be sure you are giving the customers the treatment they deserve to ensure they keep coming back to your leisure facility. You will need to learn what the customers' needs are and how you can meet these requirements or even exceed them.

> **definition**
>
> **Customer care:** the level of assistance and courtesy given to those who use the facility.

Equal opportunities

Every person should ensure that they deal with the people that they meet in an unbiased and equal way whether it is at work, home or school. This means that you should not discriminate for reasons of race or ethnic origin, gender, culture, disability, sexual orientation or social differences.

Different age groups

In the leisure industry you can expect to deal with people of all ages, from babies and toddlers right through to the over-sixties. Therefore, you should be able to have an understanding of their needs – be aware of where the baby changing facilities are, ensure you know about reduced prices for the over-sixties, be aware of special swimming sessions for different groups, etc.

Different cultural backgrounds

You need to be aware of different cultural needs and be able to cater for them accordingly. Some cultures will not allow males to see females in their swimsuits. Therefore, you must be able to give these females details of when there are female-only swimming sessions. These sessions would also have to have only female lifeguards on duty too. You should be aware of people who use the facility who do not have English as their first language and ensure there are signs and promotional materials that they can understand.

Special needs

A good leisure facility is able to cater for every person in its local area, including people who have specific needs. An example of a person with a special need is someone with restricted mobility. These people may require the use of a walking stick or wheelchair. In these cases the facility should have appropriate access so that they may enter the building unaided. If the building is on two storeys there must be a lift or ramps to allow the person to move up to the next floor. If the facility has a swimming pool there must be some form of access available for people with disabilities, such as a chair hoist.

Record-keeping

You will need to record your activities while on placement so that you are able to assess exactly what you have done and how well you have performed these activities.

The best method of recording this information is to keep a daily diary of activities. Information that you may wish to include in your diary is as follows.

- Interview a member of staff and find out what the roles and responsibilities of their job are, and how they have come to be in their position. Also find out what qualifications they have and what skills they need to do their job effectively.
- Find out the organisation's operating procedures for a range of tasks. An operating procedure is how a company completes certain tasks. This will depend upon the type of organisation you work for, but try to find out how it deals with new customers, how it manages the work it does in the gym, how it deals with cash and cashing up, how it manages the pool, and so on.
- It is of utmost importance that you are inducted in health and safety procedures on your first day. Take a note of the following: what the evacuation procedure is, where the fire exits are, where the

assembly point is, where the first-aid kit is, who is a trained first aider, where the phone for emergencies is, where the fire extinguishers are, what safety equipment is available and when you need to use it.
- Make a record of what you did each day in the workplace and any new skills you gained.
- Every day ensure you record the objectives you have met or are close to meeting, and check them off against the SMART targets you have set for yourself prior to starting the work-based experience. You may find that you need to review the timescales or other factors in your SMART targets as you may be achieving some of your targets faster or slower than expected.

Evaluate a work-based experience

So that you and your tutor(s) are able to assess how well you have performed on your work-based experience, you should carry out a full review of your placement and present your evaluation to these people.

Monitor and review

In order to be able to assess your work placement project you should review your work periodically to ensure it is all going to plan. Try to evaluate your strengths – are you working well with the team? Then assess which areas you need to improve. For example, do your customer service skills need attention?

Always be vigilant to see if any opportunities arise that may improve your experience. This could be something as simple as asking to sit in on a staff meeting which may give you additional information for your job role.

Make a note of the skills you have acquired and developed while on the placement. You may wish to record this evidence on your CV as they will probably be transferable skills and therefore relevant for future employment.

From your time on the work placement you should have a good idea of what you need to do to develop your career in the sports industry. You may find that some organisations will pay for you to carry out any further training needs you require, while others will expect you to fund the training yourself.

You should also try to gain feedback from a variety of sources, including your supervisor, colleagues and possibly a customer or two that you have had regular contact with. Through interviews or questionnaires try to gauge their assessment of your performance. You can then use this information to determine the areas in which you excel and the areas in which you need to improve.

Presentation

Try to work out the best way of presenting your evaluation. Here are a few ideas:

- poster presentation
- oral presentation
- diary/logbook
- written assignment
- video presentation.

You may wish to use one form of presentation or a combination. This will depend on a variety of factors, including who you are delivering the presentation to and the facilities you have to use.

Review questions

1   Explain the three different sectors that provide for sport.
2   Which sector has the main aim of making money?
3   Describe the skills and qualifications required for three sports jobs of your choice.
4   Name five different places where you could look for jobs in the sports industry.
5   What is the purpose of a CV?
6   Explain how body language should be used effectively in an interview.
7   Explain how you can prepare yourself for an interview.
8   On a separate sheet of paper write a letter of application for a sports career of your choice.

References

Torkildsen, G. (1991) *Leisure and Recreation Management*, Spon Press.

Websites
www.bases.org.uk – British Association of Sport and Exercise Scientists
www.exercisecareers.com – Exercise Careers
www.jobswithballs.com – Jobs with Balls
www.leisureopportunities.co.uk – Leisure Opportunities
www.sportengland.org – Sport England

Index